Lecture Notes in Computer Science   11163

Commenced Publication in 1973
Founding and Former Series Editors:
Gerhard Goos, Juris Hartmanis, and Jan van Leeuwen

More information about this series at http://www.springer.com/series/7408

El Hassan Abdelwahed · Ladjel Bellatreche
Mattéo Golfarelli · Dominique Méry
Carlos Ordonez (Eds.)

Model and Data Engineering

8th International Conference, MEDI 2018
Marrakesh, Morocco, October 24–26, 2018
Proceedings

 Springer

Editors
El Hassan Abdelwahed
Cadi Ayyad University
Marrakesh, Morocco

Ladjel Bellatreche ⓘ
LIAS/ISAE-ENSMA
Futuroscope Chasseneuil Cedex
France

Mattéo Golfarelli ⓘ
University of Bologna
Cesena, Italy

Dominique Méry ⓘ
University of Lorraine
Vandœuvre-lès-Nancy, France

Carlos Ordonez
University of Houston
Houston, TX, USA

ISSN 0302-9743   ISSN 1611-3349 (electronic)
Lecture Notes in Computer Science
ISBN 978-3-030-00855-0   ISBN 978-3-030-00856-7 (eBook)
https://doi.org/10.1007/978-3-030-00856-7

Library of Congress Control Number: 2018954770

LNCS Sublibrary: SL2 – Programming and Software Engineering

This Springer imprint is published by the registered company Springer Nature Switzerland AG
The registered company address is: Gewerbestrasse 11, 6330 Cham, Switzerland

Preface

The International Conference on Model and Data Engineering (MEDI) is an international forum for the dissemination of research accomplishments on database modeling and data management. Specifically, MEDI provides a stimulating environment for the presentation of research on database models, database theory, data processing, database systems technology, and advanced database-oriented applications. This international scientific event, initiated by researchers from Euro-Mediterranean countries, also aims to promote the creation of North-South scientific networks, projects, as well as faculty/student exchanges. This year, 2018, marks the 8th edition of MEDI, making it a well-established conference. Our 8th edition, was held on Marrakesh (Morocco), followed the success of the Óbidos (Portugal, 2011), Poitiers (France, 2012), Armantea (Italy, 2013), Larnaca (Cyprus 2014), Island of Rhodes (Greece 2015), Almería (Spain, 2016), and Barcelona (Spain, 2017).

MEDI 2018 received 86 submissions from 36 countries around the world. The selection process was rigorous, where each paper received at least 4 reviews. The Program Committee, after careful discussions, decided to accept 23 full papers and 4 short papers, yielding an acceptance rate of 27% for full papers and 32% overall. Accepted papers covered broad research areas on both theoretical systems and practical aspects. Some trends found in accepted papers include requirement engineering, reverse engineering, advanced modeling for Cloud Systems, IOT applications, query processing in emerging hardware, parallel processing, Semantic Web, graph databases, sentiment analysis, cyber physical systems, formal methods, and NoSQL databases.

We are honored to have two distinguished guests as keynote speakers: Georg Gottlob, Professor of Informatics at Oxford University, UK, and a Fellow of St John's College, giving a talk entitled "Data Science with Vadalog: Bridging Machine Learning and Reasoning," and Mohamed Mosbah, Professor of Computer Science at LABRI, University of Bordeaux, France, whose talk is entitled: "Modeling Distributed Algorithms by Local Computations with Applications."

The EasyChair conference management system was set up for MEDI 2018, supporting submission, review, and volume edition processes. We acknowledge that it is an outstanding tool for the academic community.

We would like to thank all the authors who submitted their work to MEDI 2018. We are grateful to the Program Committee members and external reviewers for their high-quality reviews and discussions. Finally, we wish to thank the Organizing Committee members for their continuous support.

Finally, MEDI 2018 has received financial support of several sponsors, among them. Cadi Ayyad University (UCA), Mohammed VI Polytechnic University (UM6P), Faculty of Sciences Semlalia Marrakech (FSSM), and Laboratoire d'Ingénierie des Systèmes Informatiques (LISI). Many thanks for their contribution.

For conference attendants, we hope they enjoyed the technical program, informal meetings, and interaction with colleagues from all over the world; and of course, we are confident they enjoyed the exciting city of Marrakesh, Morocco. For readers of these proceedings, we hope these papers are interesting and they give you ideas for future research.

July 2018

El Hassan Abdelwahed
Ladjel Bellatreche
Matteo Golfarelli
Dominique Méry
Carlos Ordonez

Organization

General Co-chairs

El-Hassan Abdelwahed   Cadi Ayyad University, Morocco
Ladjel Bellatreche   LIAS/ENSMA, France

Program Committee Co-chairs

Matteo Golfarelli   University of Bologna, Italy
Dominique Méry   LORIA - Université de Lorraine, France
Carlos Ordonez   University of Houston, USA

Organizing Committee Members

My Ahmed El Kiram   Cadi Ayyad University, Morocco
Souad Chraibi   Cadi Ayyad University, Morocco
Essaid El Bachari   Cadi Ayyad University, Morocco
Zahir Jihad   Cadi Ayyad University, Morocco
Sana Nouzri   Cadi Ayyad University, Morocco
Tarik Agouti   Cadi Ayyad University, Morocco
Issam Qaffou   Cadi Ayyad University, Morocco
My El Mehdi Bouhamidi   Cadi Ayyad University, Morocco

Program Committee

El-Hassan Abdelwahed   Cadi Ayyad University, Morocco
Alberto Abello   Universitat Politècnica de Catalunya, Spain
Yamine Ait Ameur   IRIT/INPT-ENSEEIHT, France
Idir Ait Sadoune   LRI - CentraleSupélec, France
Sabeur Aridhi   LORIA - Université de Lorraine, France
Kamel Barkaoui   Cnam, France
Ladjel Bellatreche   LIAS/ENSMA, France
Orlando Belo   University of Minho, Portugal
Sidi Mohamed Benslimane   University of Sidi Bel Abbes, Algeria
Jorge Bernardino   ISEC - Polytechnic Institute of Coimbra, Portugal
Alexander Borusan   TU Berlin/Fraunhofer FOKUS, Germany
Drazen Brdjanin   University of Banja Luka, Bosnia and Herzegovina
Francesco Buccafurri   UNIRC, Italy
Wellington Cabrera   University of Houston, USA
Antonio Corral   University of Almeria, Spain
Alain Crolotte   Teradata Corporation, USA
Florian Daniel   Politecnico di Milano, Italy

Timos Sellis	Swinburne University of Technology, Australia
Giovanni Simonini	Università di Modena e Reggio Emilia, Italy
Neeraj Singh	INPT-ENSEEIHT/IRIT, University of Toulouse, France
Riccardo Torlone	Roma Tre University, Italy
Ismail Toroslu	Middle East Technical University, Turkey
Predrag Tosic	University of Idaho, USA
Goce Trajcevski	Northwestern University, USA
Javier Tuya	University of Oviedo, Spain
Theodoros Tzouramanis	University of the Aegean, Greece
Michael Vassilakopoulos	University of Thessaly, Greece
Panos Vassiliadis	University of Ioannina, Greece
Robert Wrembel	Poznan University of Technology, Poland
Yiqun Zhang	University of Houston, USA

Additional Reviewers

Berkani, Nabila
Boden, Christoph
Bonfanti, Silvia
Bouchez-Tichadou, Florent
El-Hokayem, Antoine
Galicia Auyon, Jorge
Gounaris, Anastasios
Haq, Anam

Hewasinghage, Moditha
Ivančević, Vladimir
Jaber, Mohamad
Jovanovic, Petar
Kiefer, Martin
Kunft, Andreas
Liao, Kewen
Mammar, Amel
Meiners, Jens

Morshed, Ahsan
Pekergin, Nihal
Rafailidis, Dimitrios
Ristic, Sonja
Sarker, Bishnu
Sellami, Akrem
Varga, Jovan
Velentzas, Chronis
Yavari, Ali

Invited Papers

Data Science with Vadalog: Bridging Machine Learning and Reasoning

Luigi Bellomarini[1,2], Ruslan R. Fayzrakhmanov[1], Georg Gottlob[1,3],
Andrey Kravchenko[1], Eleonora Laurenza[2], Yavor Nenov[1],
Stéphane Reissfelder[1], Emanuel Sallinger[1], Evgeny Sherkhonov[1],
and Lianlong Wu[1]

[1] University of Oxford, Oxford, UK
ggottlob@gmail.com
[2] Banca d'Italia, Rome, Italy
[3] TU Wien, Vienna, Austria

Abstract. Following the recent successful examples of large technology companies, many modern enterprises seek to build knowledge graphs to provide a unified view of corporate knowledge and to draw deep insights using machine learning and logical reasoning. There is currently a perceived disconnect between the traditional approaches for data science, typically based on machine learning and statistical modelling, and systems for reasoning with domain knowledge. In this paper we present a state-of-the-art Knowledge Graph Management System, Vadalog, which delivers highly expressive and efficient logical reasoning and provides seamless integration with modern data science toolkits, such as the Jupyter platform. We demonstrate how to use Vadalog to perform traditional data wrangling tasks, as well as complex logical and probabilistic reasoning. We argue that this is a significant step forward towards combining machine learning and reasoning in data science.

Modeling Distributed Algorithms by Local Computations with Applications

Mohamed Mosbah

LaBRI, Bordeaux INP, Univ. Bordeaux,
CNRS, F33405 Talence, France
mosbah@u-bordeaux.fr

Abstract. We present a model based on local interactions for modeling, proving and implementing distributed algorithms. Many examples of distributed algorithms illustrate this approach, together with an integrated software environment.

Keywords: Local computations · Distributed algorithms · Formal proofs

Problems related to distributed systems are a major concern of research in computer science. We can particularly mention the design and the development of distributed architectures or distributed programming environments, the specification and the verification of distributed algorithms, as well as the study of (wired or wireless) communication networks. All these paradigms are essential for the safety and the security of distributed systems. However, the development of distributed systems is yet not well understood. In particular, distributed algorithms are difficult to design and to study, and even to represent, mainly when nodes communicating only with their neighbours must participate to achieve a global goal.

The design, validation, verification and debugging remain a hard task for most programmers and computer scientists. This is due to the intrinsic complexity of distributed algorithms and programs compared to serial ones. Programmers must coordinate and synchronize communication between processes. This problem becomes crucial for critical environments for which safety and security must be guaranteed. For the success of all those undertakings it is crucial to master the mechanisms and local phenomena at the foundations of such systems. This requires the investigation into different models of distributed computation, the fundamental understanding of local interactions and the ability to solve global problems only by local actions. This talk will focus on different models that are used to represent these systems.

We detail local computations model that allows a high level encoding of distributed algorithms by graph relabeling systems making it easy the integration of mathematical proofs into distributed computations. In this formalism, a distributed system is represented by a labeled graph; the nodes represent the processors and the edges represent the links between them. The labels are used to encode the internal states of processors and/or channels. A rule in such a calculus is defined by a small context graph (used as an 'anchor' for application in the host graph) together with two labeling configurations to this context, one to describe the local state before rule application, and the other to specify the local state after rule application. The transformation is strictly local; there are no long-distance side-effects.

A general proof schema for proving distributed computation, together with a unified framework ranging from the early design until the implementation, will be presented. In fact, he high level encoding of distributed algorithms by graph relabeling systems makes it easy the integration of mathematical proofs into distributed algorithms. On the other hand, it is possible to formalize the semantics of local computations with proof assistants, such as Event-B or Coq. Many examples will be discussed, such as leader election, spanning tree computation, coloring. An integrated software environment, including the design, the proof and the visualization of distributed algorithms will be presented.

References

1. Abdou, W., Abdallah, N., Mosbah, M.: Visidia: a java framework for designing, simulating, and visualizing distributed algorithms. In: Proceedings - IEEE International Symposium on Distributed Simulation and Real-Time Applications, DS-RT, pp. 43–46 (2014)
2. Boussabbeh, M., Tounsi, M., Kacem, A.H., Mosbah, M.: Towards a general framework for ensuring and reusing proofs of termination detection in distributed computing. In: Proceedings - 24th Euromicro International Conference on Parallel, Distributed, and Network-Based Processing, PDP 2016, pp. 504–511 (2016)
3. Boussabbeh, M., Tounsi, M., Mosbah, M., Kacem, A.H.: Formal proofs of termination detection for local computations by refinement-based compositions. In: Butler, M., Schewe, K.D., Mashkoor, A., Biro, M. (eds.) ABZ 2016, vol. 9675, pp. 198–212. Springer, Cham (2016)
4. DAMPAS Homepage. http://visidia.labri.fr/
5. Ktari, M., Haddar, M., Mosbah, M., Kacem, A.H.: Maintenance of a spanning tree for dynamic graphs by mobile agents and local computations. RAIRO Theor. Inf. Appl. **51**(2), 51–70 (2017)
6. Méry, D., Mosbah, M., Tounsi, M.: Refinement-based verification of local synchronization algorithms. In: Butler, M., Schulte, W. (eds.) FM 2011. LNCS, vol. 6664, pp. 338–352. Springer, Heidelberg (2011)

Contents

Communication and Information Technologies

Safety and Security

Algorithmics and Text Processing

Specification, Verification and Validation

Invited Paper

Data Science with Vadalog: Bridging Machine Learning and Reasoning

Luigi Bellomarini[1,2], Ruslan R. Fayzrakhmanov[1], Georg Gottlob[1,3(✉)],
Andrey Kravchenko[1], Eleonora Laurenza[2], Yavor Nenov[1],
Stéphane Reissfelder[1], Emanuel Sallinger[1], Evgeny Sherkhonov[1],
and Lianlong Wu[1]

[1] University of Oxford, Oxford, UK
ggottlob@gmail.com
[2] Banca d'Italia, Rome, Italy
[3] TU Wien, Vienna, Austria

Abstract. Following the recent successful examples of large technology companies, many modern enterprises seek to build knowledge graphs to provide a unified view of corporate knowledge and to draw deep insights using machine learning and logical reasoning. There is currently a perceived disconnect between the traditional approaches for data science, typically based on machine learning and statistical modelling, and systems for reasoning with domain knowledge. In this paper we present a state-of-the-art Knowledge Graph Management System, Vadalog, which delivers highly expressive and efficient logical reasoning and provides seamless integration with modern data science toolkits, such as the Jupyter platform. We demonstrate how to use Vadalog to perform traditional data wrangling tasks, as well as complex logical and probabilistic reasoning. We argue that this is a significant step forward towards combining machine learning and reasoning in data science.

Keywords: Knowledge graphs · Data science · Machine learning
Reasoning · Probabilistic reasoning

1 Introduction

Enterprises increasingly depend on intelligent information systems that operationalise corporate knowledge as a unified source across system boundaries. Such systems crucially rely on insights produced by data scientists, who use advanced data and graph analytics together with machine learning and statistical models to create predictive actionable knowledge from suitably preprocessed corporate data by means of data wrangling. To maintain their competitive edge, companies need to incorporate multiple heterogeneous sources of information, including streams of structured or unstructured data from internal systems (e.g., Enterprise Resource Planning, Workflow Management, and Supply Chain Management), external streams of unstructured data (e.g., news and social media

E. H. Abdelwahed et al. (Eds.): MEDI 2018, LNCS 11163, pp. 3–21, 2018.
https://doi.org/10.1007/978-3-030-00856-7_1

feeds, and Common Crawl[1]), publicly available and proprietary sources of semi-structured data (e.g., DBpedia [11], Wikidata [46], UniProt [19], data.gov.uk), structured data extracted from web pages using web data extraction techniques [24], as well as internal and external knowledge bases/ontologies (e.g., Research-Cyc[2], DBpedia [11], Wikidata [46], FIBO[3]). The integration of such diverse information is a non-trivial task that presents data scientists with a number of challenges including: the extraction and handling of big data with frequently changing content and structure; dealing with uncertainty of the extracted data; and finding ways of unifying the information from different sources.

Following the trend of large technological companies such as Google, Amazon, Facebook, and, LinkedIn, it is becoming common for enterprises to integrate their internal and external sources of information into a unified *knowledge graph*. A knowledge graph typically consists of graph-structured data to allow for smooth accommodation of changes in the structure of the data, and knowledge layers, which encode business logic used for the validation and enrichment of data and the uncovering of critical insights from it. Graph-structured data may stem from data directly exposed as graphs (e.g., RDF[4] used by triple stores such as GraphDB[5], Property Graphs used by graph databases like neo4j[6], and JanusGraph[7]) or relational or semi-structured data that exhibits graph structure. The consolidated and enriched knowledge graph is then processed using the standard data science toolkit for graph analytics (including languages such as Cypher[8], SPARQL[9], and Gremlin[10]), statistical analysis (using the R statistical framework), and machine learning (using toolkits such as Weka[11], scikit-learn[12], and TensorFlow[13]).

The creation of a coherent knowledge graph from multiple sources of unstructured, semi-structured, and structured data is a challenging task that requires techniques from multiple disciplines. *Entity resolution* [18] is used to combine multiple sources of (semi-)structured data that do not share common identifiers. The goal is to identify pairs of entities that refer to the same real-world object and merge them into a single entity. The matching is performed using noisy, semi-identifying information (e.g., names, addresses) and relationships, and employs specialised similarity functions for strings, numbers, and dates, to determine the

---

[1] http://commoncrawl.org/.
[2] http://www.cyc.com/researchcyc/.
[3] https://spec.edmcouncil.org/static/ontology/.
[4] https://www.w3.org/RDF/.
[5] http://graphdb.ontotext.com/.
[6] https://neo4j.com/.
[7] http://janusgraph.org/.
[8] https://neo4j.com/developer/cypher-query-language/.
[9] https://www.w3.org/TR/rdf-sparql-query/.
[10] https://tinkerpop.apache.org/gremlin.html.
[11] https://www.cs.waikato.ac.nz/ml/weka/.
[12] http://scikit-learn.org/.
[13] https://www.tensorflow.org/.

overall similarity of two entities. *Information extraction* [43] is used for automatically extracting structured data from unstructured sources (i.e., news and social media feeds). Thus, for example, the news feed "PayPal buys Hyperwallet for $400M" could result into the structured statement "acquire(PayPal, Hyperwallet)". Information extraction is typically combined with entity resolution to correctly incorporate the extracted information within an existing knowledge graph.

Publicly available datasets are often equipped with ontologies which describe relationships between entities. In such cases *ontological reasoning* needs to be applied to validate whether the results of entity resolution and information extraction violate any of the constraints imposed by the ontology as well as to enrich the data with new information stemming from the newly produced facts. Further note that, unsurprisingly, the use of *machine learning* is pervasive throughout the stages of the data scientist's workflow: from semantically annotating web page elements during web data extraction, through deciding whether entities should be matched during entity resolution, to predicting numerical trends during data analytics over the knowledge graph. Finally, observe that although *uncertainty* is intrinsic to many of the tasks in the data scientist's workflow, it is typically resolved by the means of a threshold. For example, during entity resolution, the similarity of the attributes of two entities is typically converted to a probability for the two entities to be the same, and they are matched if the probability exceeds a certain threshold. Similarly, the information extraction stage typically associates output facts with level of uncertainty stemming from the extraction process, but likewise to the case of entity resolution, the uncertainty is converted into a probability for a fact to hold, and a hard decision is made on whether it should be included or not. Interestingly, one can do better than that. One may want to impose levels of uncertainty using business rules to better inform the decision of whether and how the knowledge graph should be updated. One such rule, for example, could be that public companies are much more likely to acquire private companies than vice-versa (the so called *reverse takeover*). Such rules can be produced by a domain expert or learned from the data using rule learning [7]. Furthermore, instead of ignoring the uncertainty, after it is being used to determine whether to accept a fact or a match, for example, one could alternatively incorporate this uncertainty into the knowledge graph and propagate them into the further stages of data wrangling and data analytics workflow.

To carry out the different stages of the described workflow data scientists need to use and coordinate a number of tools, languages, and technologies: for data access they require tools for web data extraction, various data-base management systems, triple stores and graph databases; during knowledge graph construction they require tools for entity resolution, information extraction, ontological reasoning, and uncertainty management; and during the analysis stage they require tools for graph analytic, machine learning and statistical modelling. The coordination of all these tools can be very challenging.

In this paper we present the Vadalog engine: a state-of-the-art Knowledge Graph Management System (KGMS) that provides a unified framework for integrating the various tools and technologies used by data scientists. Its language Vadalog is an extension of the rule-based language Datalog [1], and can naturally capture SQL (through support for the SQL operators), ontological reasoning in OWL 2 QL[14] and SPARQL (through the use of existential quantifiers), and graph analytics (through non-trivial support for recursion and aggregation). The declarative nature of the language makes the code concise, manageable, and self-explanatory. The engine is fully extensible through its bindings to different data sources and libraries. Data extensions provide access to relational data stored in Postgres or MySQL, for example, or to graph data stored in neo4j or Janus, or to web data using OXPath [24]. Library extensions allow the integration of state-of-the-art machine learning tools such as Weka, scikit-learn, or Tensor-Flow. Additional integration with libraries for string similarities and regular expressions allows for defining complex entity resolution workflows. The engine also supports reasoning with probabilistic data and probabilistic rules, which makes it ideal for handling uncertainty stemming from the different stages of the data scientist's workflow. Finally, the Vadalog engine seamlessly integrates with Jupyter: a well-known platform for data analysts and scientists with a convenient interface for data processing and visualisation.

The paper is organised as follows. Section 2 provides an overview of the core language. Section 3 provides a system overview of the Vadalog engine. Section 4 describes the various features of the system within a typical data scientist's workflow in Jupyter. Section 5 demonstrates the engine's integration with machine learning on typical use cases. Finally, Sect. 6 describes in more detail the support of the system for probabilistic reasoning.

This paper includes, in abbreviated form, material from a number of previous papers on the topic [7–10]. The Vadalog system is Oxford's contribution to VADA [34], a joint project of the universities of Edinburgh, Manchester, and Oxford. We reported first work on the overall VADA approach to data wrangling in [25]. In this paper, we focus on the Vadalog system at its core. Currently, our system fully implements the core language and is already in use for a number of industrial applications.

2   Core Language

Vadalog is a Datalog-based language. It belongs to the Datalog$^\pm$ family of languages that extends Datalog by existential quantifiers in rule heads, as well as by other features, and at the same time restricts its syntax in order to achieve decidability and data tractability; see, e.g., [14–17]. The logical core of the Vadalog language corresponds to *Warded Datalog$^\pm$* [4,29], which captures plain Datalog as well as SPARQL queries under the entailment regime for OWL 2 QL [28] and is able to perform ontological reasoning tasks. Reasoning with the logical core of Vadalog is computationally efficient. Vadalog is obtained by extending

---

[14] https://www.w3.org/TR/owl2-profiles/.

Warded Datalog$^\pm$ with additional features of practical utility. We now illustrate the logical core of Vadalog, more details about extensions can be found in [7].

The logical core of Vadalog relies on the notion of wardedness, which applies a restriction on how the "dangerous" variables of a set of existential rules are used. Note that existential rules are also known as tuple-generating dependencies (tgds), i.e., Datalog rules where existential quantification is allowed in the head. Intuitively, a "dangerous" variable is a body-variable that can be unified with a labelled null value when the chase algorithm is applied, and it is also propagated to the head of the rule. For example, given the set Σ consisting of the rules

$$P(x) \rightarrow \exists z\, R(x, z) \quad \text{and} \quad R(x, y) \rightarrow P(y),$$

the variable y in the body of the second rule is "dangerous" (w.r.t. Σ) since starting, e.g., from the database $D = \{P(a)\}$, the chase will apply the first rule and generate $R(a, \nu)$, where ν is a null that acts as a witness for the existentially quantified variable z, and then the second rule will be applied with the variable y being unified with ν that is propagated to the obtained atom $P(\nu)$.

Note that, throughout this paper, we will mix the "logical" notation shown above that is often used in papers, and the "code"-like notation that is used in systems, such as the Vadalog system. The above example would be given as follows in Vadalog notation:

```
r(X,Z) :- p(X).
p(Y) :- r(X,Y).
```

The goal of wardedness is to tame the way null values are propagated during the construction of the chase instance by posing the following conditions: (i) all the "dangerous" variables should coexist in a single body-atom α, called the *ward*; (ii) the ward can share only "harmless" variables with the rest of the body, i.e., variables that are unified only with database constants during the construction of the chase.

Warded Datalog$^\pm$ consists of all the (finite) sets of warded existential rules. As an example of a warded set of rules, the following rules encode part of the OWL 2 direct semantics entailment regime for OWL 2 QL (see [4,29]):

$$\underline{\text{Type}(x, y)}, \text{Restriction}(y, z) \rightarrow \exists w\, \text{Triple}(x, z, w)$$
$$\underline{\text{Type}(x, y)}, \text{SubClass}(y, z) \rightarrow \text{Type}(x, z)$$
$$\underline{\text{Triple}(x, y, z)}, \text{Inverse}(y, w) \rightarrow \text{Triple}(z, w, x)$$
$$\underline{\text{Triple}(x, y, z)}, \text{Restriction}(w, y) \rightarrow \text{Type}(x, w).$$

It is easy to verify that the above set is warded, where the underlined atoms are the wards. Indeed, a variable that occurs in an atom of the form $\text{Restriction}(\cdot, \cdot)$, or $\text{SubClass}(\cdot, \cdot)$, or $\text{Inverse}(\cdot, \cdot)$, is trivially harmless. However, variables that appear in the first position of Type, or in the first/third position of Triple can be dangerous. Thus, the underlined atoms are indeed acting as the wards.

Reasoning in Warded Datalog$^\pm$ is PTIME-complete in data complexity [4, 29]. Although polynomial time data complexity is desirable for conventional applications, PTIME-hardness can be prohibitive for "Big Data" applications. One such example is towards building knowledge graphs that consider huge elections in the area of computational social choice [20]. Yet, in fact, this is true even for linear time data complexity. This is discussed in more detail in [7].

This core language has a number of extensions to make it practical, among them data types, arithmetic, (monotonic) aggregation, bindings of predicates to external data sources, binding function symbols to external functions, and more.

We will discuss *monotonic aggregation* here. Vadalog supports aggregation (*min, max, sum, prod, count*), by means of an extension to the notion of monotonic aggregations [44], which allows adopting aggregation even in the presence of recursion while preserving monotonicity w.r.t. set containment. Such functionality is crucial for performing graph analytics, an example of which is shown in Sect. 4.

We will discuss some of these extensions throughout this paper. One of the extensions that are planned is more support consistency, in particular consistent query answering [3,5] as well as view updates [13,31].

3   Core System

The functional architecture of the Vadalog system, our KGMS, is depicted in Fig. 1. The knowledge graph is organised as a repository, a collection of Vadalog rules. The external sources are supported by means of *transducers*, intelligent adapters that integrate the sources into the reasoning process.

The Big Data characteristics of the sources and the complex functional requirements of reasoning are tackled by leveraging the underpinnings of the core language, which are turned into practical execution strategies. In particular, in the reasoning

Fig. 1. KGMS reference architecture [7]

algorithms devised for Warded Datalog$^\pm$, after a certain number of chase steps (which, in general, depends on the input database), the chase graph [15] (a directed acyclic graph where facts are represented as nodes and the applied rules as edges) exhibits specific periodicities and no new information, relevant to query answering, is generated. The Vadalog system adopts an *aggressive recursion and termination control* strategy, which detects such redundancy as early as possible by combining compile-time and runtime techniques. In combination with a highly engineered architecture, the Vadalog system achieves high performance and an efficient memory footprint.

At compile time, as wardedness limits the interaction between the labelled nulls, the engine rewrites the program in such a way that joins on specific values of labelled nulls will never occur. This exploits work on schema mapping composition and optimisation [32, 33, 38, 42].

The Vadalog system uses a pull stream-based approach (or pipeline approach), where the facts are actively requested from the output nodes to their predecessors and so on down to the input nodes, which eventually fetch the facts from the data sources. The stream approach is essential to limit the memory consumption or at least make it predictable, so that the system is effective for large volumes of data. Our setting is made more challenging by the presence of multiple interacting rules in a single rule set and the wide presence of recursion. We address this by means of a specialised buffer management technique. We adopt pervasive local caches in the form of wrappers to the nodes of the access plan, where the facts produced by each node are stored. The local caches work particularly well in combination with the pull stream-based approach, since facts requested by a node successor can be immediately reused by all the other successors, without triggering further backward requests. Also, this combination realises an extreme form of multi-query optimisation, where each rule exploits the facts produced by the others, whenever applicable. To limit memory occupation, the local caches are flushed with an eager eviction strategy that detects when a fact has been consumed by all the possible requestors and thus drops it from the memory. Cases of actual cache overflow are managed by resorting to standard disk swap heuristics (e.g., LRU, LFU).

More details on the Vadalog system can be found in [10]. The system includes many other features, such as data extraction with OXPath, which is in use with our collaborators at dblp [36].

4   Supporting the Data Science Workflow

As the importance of data science constantly increases, the Vadalog system can support the entire spectrum of data science tasks and processes to a certain extent. It does not however replace tools specialists like to use, but rather conveys a universal platform to integrate various approaches and tools into a unified framework. All integrations are realised in terms of *data binding primitives* and *functions*.

One such key example is the use of the UI/development platform, where Jupyter was chosen as a platform that data scientists are familiar with. The Vadalog system has seamless integration with JupyterLab with the use of a Vadalog extension and kernel (see Fig. 2). JupyterLab is a well-known platform for data analysts and scientists with a convenient interface for data processing and visualisation. It has a multi-user support, in which dedicated resources and the environment are associated with a concrete user. The Vadalog extension and kernel for JupyterLab give data scientists the possibility to evaluate the correctness of the program, run it, and analyse the derivation process of interesting output facts. All output is rendered in JupyterLab's output area.

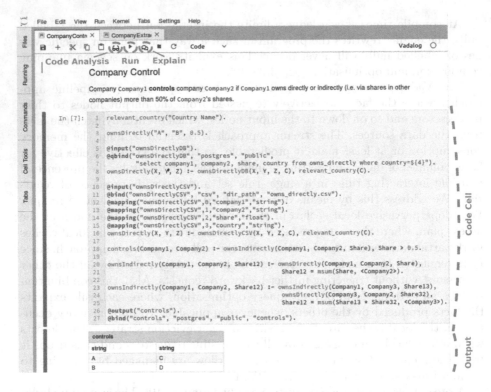

Fig. 2. Example of the Vadalog program for inferring a company control indicator

Data Binding Primitives. Bindings give one a possibility to connect an automatic reasoning workflow with external systems for data exchange. An external system can represent a database, framework, library or information system. Currently Vadalog supports relational databases, such as Postgres and MySQL, and graph databases, such as neo4j. It also has seamless integration with machine learning tools, e.g., Weka and scikit-learn (see Sect. 5.1), and a web data extraction tool, OXPath [24] (see Fig. 3). Other integrations are included or can be easily integrated. Data sources and targets can be declared by adopting @input and @output annotations. Annotations are special facts augmenting sets of existential rules with specific behaviours. @input and @output define the direction of facts into and from the Vadalog program, respectively. Additional @bind annotation defines means for interacting with an external system. A query bind annotation @qbind is a special modification of @bind. It supports binding predicates to queries against inputs and outputs in the external language (e.g., SQL-queries for a data source or target that supports SQL). The first parameter of @bind and @qbind specifies a predicate the external resource is bound to; the second parameter defines a type of the target (e.g., "postgres"). In case the schema of an external resource cannot be derived automatically, or should be overridden, additional @mapping annotation can be used to define mapping strategy for tuples between Vadalog and an external system.

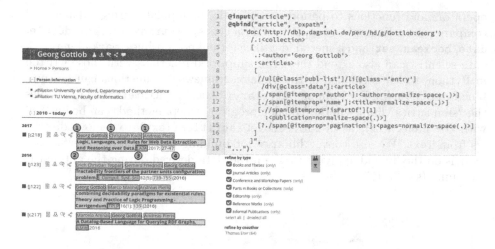

Fig. 3. Integration of OXPath, a web data extraction tool

In Fig. 2, we give a synthetic example of a Vadalog program to infer a company control indicator. It can be formulated as follows: *A company A "controls" company B if A owns directly or indirectly (i.e., via shares in other companies) more than 50% of B's shares* (lines 18–25). As we can see, various strategies for binding external resources can be used in the Vadalog program. For example, data tuples `ownsDirectly` can be propagated into the program from the parametric `@qbind` (lines 6–7 for Postgres via tuples `ownsDirectlyDB`) or `@bind` (line 11 for CSV via tuples `ownsDirectlyCSV`). For `@qbind` SQL query is instantiated with the parameter from the predicate `relevant_country` (line 8). The query instantiation is realised within the join, in which the parameter C from the `relevant_country` predicate is propagated into the fourth term of the predicate `ownsDirectlyDB`. In contrast, in case of `@bind`, all data is streamed into the Vadalog system and filtered on-the-fly by only selecting information regarding the "relevant country" (line 16). `ownsDirectly` tuples can also be specified within the program in terms of facts (line 3). During the evaluation of the program, each derived tuple `controls` is streamed into a Postgres database as it is specified in lines 26–27.

In Fig. 3, we illustrate an example of binding with OXPath. OXPath [24] is a web data extraction language, an extension of XPath 1.0 for interacting with web applications and extracting data from them. In this example, the OXPath binding streams all articles of Georg Gottlob from dblp website into the Vadalog program. Extracted articles can be represented as a relation `article(authors, title, publication, pages)`. Integration with machine learning tools is discussed in the next section.

Functions. Besides bindings, functions provide a data scientist with a rich set of value transformations and operations for different data types supported in Vadalog. A user can write expressions of different complexity with the use of operators and functions to perform arithmetic, manipulate strings, dates, and compare values. Examples of supported data types are `string`, `integer`, `double`, `date`, `boolean`, `set`, and a special identifier for unknown values, `marked null`. A data scientist can also extend the set of supported functions with those written in Python, which is enabled in the Vadalog framework. Functions can be combined into *libraries*. For example, `@library("sim:", "simmetrics")`. enables the "simmetrics" library in the Vadalog program, where methods can be invoked with the prefix `sim:`, as in `sim:removeDiacritics(Text)` to remove diacritics from `Text`. We also convey libraries for building regression or classification models on-the-fly and applying those on the data derived during the automatic reasoning (see Sect. 5.1).

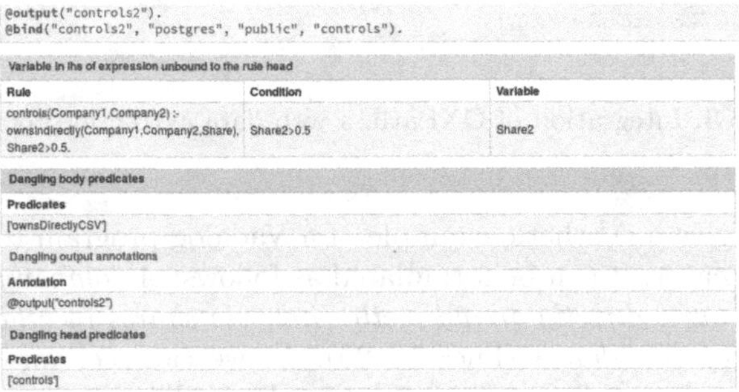

Fig. 4. A screenshot depicting code analysis for an altered Vadalog program in the company control example

Code Analysis. The correctness of the program is assessed with the use of the code analysis functionality (see Fig. 4). It checks whether there are essential or well-known error patterns in the program. For example, in Fig. 4, we altered the original program illustrated in Fig. 2. The parameter `Share` of the condition in the line 18 was replaced with `Share2`, lines 10–15 were commented, leaving `ownsDirectlyCSV` without the binding, and the output `controls` was changed to `controls2`.

Fact Derivation Analysis. The analysis of derivations can be performed with the use of *explanations* (see Fig. 5). It gives an explanation of how a certain fact has been derived within the program and which rules have been triggered.

Bindings and functions make data analytics both more effective and efficient. Vadalog directly interacts with various data sources regardless of their nature, be it a database or the Web. Furthermore, with rich reasoning capabilities it can lift the analysis up from basic values, tuples or relations within databases to semantically rich structures, e.g., from property graphs such as of neo4j to concepts of a domain ontology. This makes the code more concise and self-explanatory.

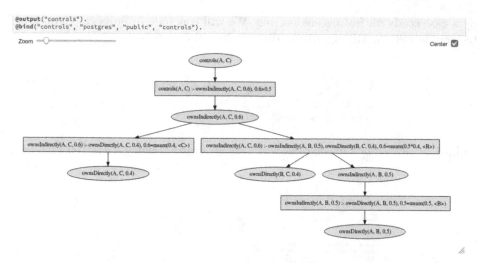

Fig. 5. A screenshot of the output depicting a "yes"-explanation for the fact `controls("A", "C")` in the company control example

The Vadalog system is a universal tool which can reconcile two opposite paradigms of data scientists and domain experts, so-called "inductive" (or bottom-up) and "deductive" (or top-down) approaches. An inductive paradigm goes along with a statement that "patterns emerge before reasons for them become apparent" [21]. It certainly refers to data mining and machine learning approaches which are used for deriving new knowledge and relations from data. As all data scientists face in practice, "all models are wrong and some are useful" [12, p. 208], which explains problems of finding the best model given a dataset. Furthermore, limitations related to labour intensive labelling for some machine learning algorithms can also cause incorrect or incomplete results. Thus, knowledge of a domain expert with a deductive approach is important to correct potential errors propagated from generated models.

5 Integrating Machine Learning

In this section, we will discuss how to integrate machine learning directly. We will focus on one of the approaches to machine learning integration, schematically illustrated in Fig. 6. In the first subsection, we will concretely talk about Weka and scikit-learn integration. The system's TensorFlow integration is similar in style to the scikit-learn integration. This will be followed in Subsect. 5.2

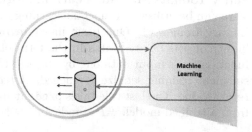

Fig. 6. Schematic view of the interaction between machine learning and reasoning

by a case study on feature engineering. We will conclude in Subsect. 5.3 on how
to include custom ML algorithms directly into the system.

```
1  j48(X1, X2, X3, X4, Class) :- training_data(X1, X2, X3, X4, Class).
2  @bind("j48", "wekaj48", "iris", "file_path").
3  @mapping("j48", 0, "sepallength", "double").
4  @mapping("j48", 1, "sepalwidth", "double").
5  @mapping("j48", 2, "petallength", "double").
6  @mapping("j48", 3, "petalwidth", "double").
7  @mapping("j48", 4, "class", "string").
```

Fig. 7. A snippet of Vadalog code, which demonstrates training a J48 Weka model

```
1  classified_data(X1,X2,X3,X4,Class) :- data(X1,X2,X3,X4), j48Model(M), j48(M,X1,X2,X3,X4,Class).
2
3  @input("j48").
4  @qbind("j48", "weka", "{'4'='Iris-setosa,Iris-versicolor,Iris-virginica'}",
5      "{model="${1}", tuple="(${2},${3},${4},${5})", class="${6}"}").
6  @mapping("j48", 0, "model", "string").
7  @mapping("j48", 1, "sepallength", "double").
8  @mapping("j48", 2, "sepalwidth", "double").
9  @mapping("j48", 3, "petallength", "double").
10 @mapping("j48", 4, "petalwidth", "double").
11 @mapping("j48", 5, "class", "string").
```

Fig. 8. A snippet of Vadalog code, which demonstrates the classification phase with a
trained J48 Weka model

5.1   Direct Integration

Weka. Integration with a machine learning framework, Weka, is demonstrated
in Figs. 7 and 8. Figure 7 illustrates the J48 model generation example for the Iris
dataset. Training data is propagated to the bound decision tree classifier associated with the predicate j48. Mapping annotations specify attributes and the
class of tuples streamed into the underlying machine learning algorithm. Figure 8
depicts an example of the classification process given a model M. Attributes of
the tuple data to be classified and the generated model are streamed into the
underlying Weka framework via the predicate j48. The results of the classification are instantiated in a relation classified_data. In the @qbind expression,
the third parameter defines nominal attributes, a class in our case, which had
index 4 in the training phase. The fourth parameter of @qbind defines parameter
propagation template from the predicate j48 into the underlying model.

SciPy Toolkits Machine Learning. An external Python library such as scikit-
learn can be utilised for machine learning tasks over predicates, through Vadalog
Library framework. One basic linear regression example is shown below. The
input consists of predicates in the form of $training\_set(ID, X, Y)$. The $sk{:}fit$
function feeds input data one by one and returns current training set size. Once
sufficient training set size is reached, $sk{:}train$ function is called with a boolean
return value. The last rule takes predict inputs one by one and retrieves output
from a trained model. $\#T$ stands for boolean value true.

```
@library("sk:", "sklearn").
training_set("ID1", [1, 1], 2).
training_set("ID1", [2, 2], 4).
training_set("ID1", [3, 3], 6).
predict("ID1", [17, 17]).


training_size(ID, C) :- training_set(ID, In, Out), C=sk:fit(ID, In, Out).
classified(ID, R) :- training_size(ID, C),C>=3,R = sk : train(ID).
result(ID, In, Out) :-
    predict(ID, In), classified(ID, #T), Out = sk:predict(ID, In).
```

5.2 Case Study: Feature Engineering

We consider a case study of implementing a supervised machine learning framework and post-classification reasoning with Vadalog. Our implementation consists of three phases: (i) feature extraction with Vadalog, (ii) interaction between
Vadalog and a serialised classifier, (iii) post-classification reasoning. We assume
that the classifier has already been trained and serialised and for the reasons
of brevity omit the description of representing a training corpus and training
the classifier with Vadalog, as it can be done through a simple extension of the
framework. The schematic view of the framework we implement in this case
study is given in Fig. 6.

Feature Extraction with Vadalog. Consider the problem of identifying semantic
blocks on a web page, such as pagination bars, navigation menus, headers, foot-
ers, and sidebars [26, 35]. The page is represented by the DOM tree and CSS
model. We represent all information contained both in the DOM and CSS as
DOM facts, which are Vadalog edb predicates. An example of three DOM facts
representing the (i) font size of a DOM tree element with ID 100, (ii) its background colour, (iii) and the coordinates, width, and height of the corresponding
CSS box is listed below.

```
dom__css__fontSize("e_100", "16px").
dom__css__backgroundColor("e_100", "rgb(229, 237, 243)").
dom__css__boundingBox("e_100", 150, 200, 450, 400, 300, 200).
```

In the code snippet below we extract the feature, which computes the average
font size of the sub-tree rooted at a given DOM node N, used in the navigation
menu classifier, i.e., the average font size computed on a set unifying node N
and all of its descendant nodes (calculated through the Start and End indices of
DOM nodes).

```
@output("feature").

descendant(N,D) :-
    dom_element(N, Start, End), dom_element(D, StartD, EndD),
    Start < StartD, EndD < End.

feature("averageFontSize", N, FontSize) :- dom_css_fontSize(N, FontSize).

feature("averageFontSize", N, FontSize) :-
    descendant(N,D), dom_css_fontSize(D, FontSize).

@post("feature", "avg(3)").
```

Note that we use the `feature` namespace for the predicate, which computes this particular feature, as well as all other features used by classifiers. The feature predicates are the output of this feature extraction phase of the framework, so that they can be further passed on as input to a serialised classifier.

Interaction with a Serialised Classifier. All extracted features are passed on to a serialised classifier through the @bind operator. For the case of web block classification, we use Weka as the machine learning library and J48 decision tree as the classifier, but the implementation of the framework in Vadalog is both library and classifier agnostic, e.g., we can seamlessly integrate Vadalog with scikit-learn, as demonstrated in Subsect. 5.1, and the J48 decision tree classifier can also be seamlessly changed to any other classifier, e.g., an SVM. The classifications produced by the classifier are then passed back to Vadalog, also through the @bind operator. These classifications are in the `classification` namespace, e.g., `classification(e_200,"navigation_menu")` that classifies DOM node with ID 200 as a navigation menu.

Post-classification Reasoning. We can now apply post-classification reasoning that cannot be easily represented by machine learning classifiers to the classifications computed in the previous phase. For example, given serialised header and footer classifiers and classifications computed in the previous phase, we can impose a constraint that a header and a footer cannot overlap.

```
header_footer_overlap_constraint(N, M) :-
    classification(N, "header"), classification(M, "footer"),
    no_overlap(N, M).
```

5.3 Direct Use of Algorithms

In case no external support is available, or users want to adapt and tie their algorithms closer to the knowledge graph, a number of Machine Learning algorithms can be directly implemented in Vadalog. Note that this is a complementary alternative – in case algorithms should be used out-of-the-box based on existing systems and approaches, and no modification or close interaction with the knowledge graph is required, it is certainly a good idea to use such external systems and algorithms as described in Sect. 5.1. Taking advantage of the declarative programming paradigm, it requires only concisely expressing the logic of the definition, instead of explicitly describing the exact algorithm. As a result, the program is easy for modification, verification or parallel execution. The application areas include but are not limited to clustering, anomaly detection, and weekly supervised learning.

We will use DBSCAN (Density-based spatial clustering of applications with noise) algorithm as a simple example [22]. Two main parameters of DBSCAN are *eps* (distance threshold) and *minPts* (minimal number of points for a dense region). The input is a set of points $p(ID, X, Y)$, ID is a sequential number representing an identifier.

$$eps(0.11), \; minPts(5),$$
$$p(1, 0.697, 0.460), \; p(2, 0.774, 0.376), \; \ldots$$

Two points are in a *neighbourhood* if their Euclidean distance is less than *eps*. The *neighbourhood number* is obtained through aggregation as below.

$p(A, X_A, Y_A), p(B, X_B, Y_B), C = \sqrt{(X_A - X_B)^2 + (Y_A - Y_B)^2}$
$\rightarrow point\_pairs(A, B, C).$
$point\_pairs(A, B, C), eps(E), C <= E \rightarrow neighbourhood(A, B).$
$neighbourhood(A, B), J = mcount(B) \rightarrow neighbourhood\_count(A, J).$
$neighbourhood\_count(A, J), K = max(J) \rightarrow neighbourhood\_number(A, K).$

Different types of points, i.e., core, border and noise, are defined as follows.

$neighbourhood\_number(A, K), minPts(M), K >= M \rightarrow core\_point(A).$
$\neg core\_point(A), core\_point(B), neighbourhood(A, B) \rightarrow border\_point(A).$
$neighbourhood\_number(A, K), \neg core\_point(A), \neg border\_point(A)$
$\rightarrow noise\_point(A).$

Notions of *density reachability* and *connectivity* are defined below.

$core\_point(A), neighbourhood(A, B) \rightarrow directly\_reachable(A, B).$
$directly\_reachable(A, B) \rightarrow reachable(A, B).$
$reachable(A, C), directly\_reachable(C, B) \rightarrow reachable(A, B).$
$reachable(C, A), reachable(C, B) \rightarrow connected(A, B).$

The goal of density clustering process is to find point pairs that satisfy both *connectivity* and *maximality properties*, respectively:

$$connected(A, X) \rightarrow cluster(A, X).$$
$$reachable(A, X) \rightarrow cluster(A, X).$$

The cluster is identified by the point (from this cluster) which has the minimal ID number. This is achieved by the post-processing instruction, @post, which takes the minimum value for the second term (position) of the relation *cluster*, grouping by the first term (position).

@output("cluster"). @post("cluster", "min(2)").
Output Example: cluster(1,1). cluster(2,1). cluster(3,3).

6   Probabilistic Reasoning

In the design of winning data science solutions, it is more and more clear that completely neglecting domain knowledge and blindly relying only on inductive models (i.e., with parameters learnt from data) easily leads to sub-optimal results, subject to overfitting when not to wrong conclusions. Thus, data scientists tend to integrate inductive reasoning with deductive approaches, complementing and when it is the case overruling machine learning models with domain knowledge.

In the Vadalog system, we introduce *probabilistic knowledge graphs*, a valuable tool to craft a new kind of data science solutions where statistical models incorporate and are driven by the description of the domain knowledge.

Combining uncertainty and logic to describe rich uncertain relational structures is not new and has been the primary focus of Statistical Relational Learning (SRL) [27,40]. One prominent representative of this area is Markov Logic Networks (MLN) [41], which allow to describe relational structures in terms of first-order logic. A number of algorithms for exact and approximate reasoning in MLNs and other SRL models [6,23] have been proposed, and systems built such as Alchemy [41], Tuffy [37] and SlimShot [30]. MLNs have been successfully applied in natural language processing [39], ontology matching [2], record linkage [45], and so on. Yet, one common limitation of SRL models is their logical reasoning side: logic in SRL is not utilised for deducing new knowledge, but rather serves the role of a constraint language. Systems that can be built on top of these models are hence of very limited applicability in data science tasks.

Consider the following example.

Example 1. Let G be a knowledge graph, which contains the following facts about the ownership and link relationships between companies, augmented with a Vadalog program composed of rules (1) and (2):

$$\text{Own}(a, b, 0.4), \text{Own}(b, c, 0.5), \text{Own}(a, d, 0.6), \text{Own}(d, c, 0.5),$$
$$\text{Linked}(a, b), \text{Linked}(a, d), \text{Linked}(b, c), \text{Linked}(d, c).$$

(1) $\text{Own}(x, y, s), s > 0.2 \rightarrow \text{Linked}(x, y).$

(2) $0.8 :: \text{Own}(x, y, s), \text{Own}(y, z, t), w = \text{sum}(s \cdot t) \rightarrow \text{Own}(x, z, w).$

Rule (1) expresses that company x is linked to y if x owns directly or indirectly more than 20% of y's shares. Rule (2) is a recursive rule with an aggregate operator and expresses indirect shareholding: when x owns a number of companies y, each holding a different share t_y of z, then x owns $\sum_y (s \cdot t_y)$ of z.

An example of a "traditional" logical reasoning task is answering the following question over G: *"which companies are linked to a?"*. The result of the reasoning task is the companies b and d, as directly specified by G, and, additionally, c, which is implied by the program. Indeed, by Rule (2) we first derive the fact $Own(a, c, 0.5)$, as $0.4 \times 0.5 + 0.6 \times 0.5 = 0.5$, and thus, by Rule (1), we deduce $Linked(a, c)$.

However, here we are in an uncertain setting: Rule (2) is not definitive but holds with a certain probability. We say that G is a *probabilistic knowledge graph*. Probabilistic reasoning on G would then consist in answering queries over such uncertain logic programs, i.e., when we can only access a distribution of the entailed facts. The answer to the question —which companies are linked to a— would contain companies b and d with probability one and c with some probability p depending on the "ownership distance" between a and c.

In spite of its high relevance, surprisingly, none of the exiting KGMSs allow for uncertain reasoning, crucial in many contexts. The Vadalog system aims at filling this gap.

The Vadalog system provides a form of hybrid logic-probabilistic reasoning, where logical inference is driven and aided by statistical inference. We adopt the novel notion of *probabilistic knowledge graph*, and propose Soft Vadalog, an extension to Vadalog with soft, weighted rules (such as the ones used in Example 1) for representing and supporting uncertain reasoning in the Vadalog system. A Soft Vadalog program is a template for a reason-tailored statistical model, namely the *chase tree*, the semantics of which is based on a probabilistic version of the *chase* procedure, a family of algorithms used in databases to enforce logic rules by generating the entailed facts.

In particular, the system adopts the *MCMC-chase* algorithm: a combination of a Markov chain Monte Carlo method with the chase. The application of the chase is guided by the MCMC, so that logical and statistical inference are performed in the same process. We will report about these achievements soon.

Acknowledgements. This work is supported by the EPSRC programme grant EP/M025268/1. The Vadalog system is IP of the University of Oxford.

References

1. Abiteboul, S., Hull, R., Vianu, V.: Foundations of Databases. Addison-Wesley, Boston (1995)
2. Albagli, S., Ben-Eliyahu-Zohary, R., Shimony, S.E.: Markov network based ontology matching. J. Comput. Syst. Sci. **78**(1), 105–118 (2012)
3. Arenas, M., Bertossi, L.E., Chomicki, J.: Consistent query answers in inconsistent databases. In: PODS, pp. 68–79. ACM Press (1999)
4. Arenas, M., Gottlob, G., Pieris, A.: Expressive languages for querying the semantic web. In: PODS, pp. 14–26 (2014)
5. Arming, S., Pichler, R., Sallinger, E.: Complexity of repair checking and consistent query answering. In: ICDT, LIPIcs, SD-LZI, vol. 48 (2016)
6. Bach, S.H., Broecheler, M., Huang, B., Getoor, L.: Hinge-loss Markov random fields and probabilistic soft logic. J. Mach. Learn. Res. (JMLR) **18**(109), 1–67 (2017)

7. Bellomarini, L., Gottlob, G., Pieris, A., Sallinger, E.: Swift logic for big data and knowledge graphs. In: IJCAI, pp. 2–10 (2017)
8. Bellomarini, L., Gottlob, G., Pieris, A., Sallinger, E.: Swift logic for big data and knowledge graphs. In: Tjoa, A.M., Bellatreche, L., Biffl, S., van Leeuwen, J., Wiedermann, J. (eds.) SOFSEM 2018. LNCS, vol. 10706, pp. 3–16. Springer, Cham (2018)
9. Bellomarini, L., Gottlob, G., Pieris, A., Sallinger, E.: Swift logic for big data and enterprise knowledge graphs. In: AMW, The Vadalog System (2018)
10. Bellomarini, L., Sallinger, E., Gottlob, G.: The Vadalog system: datalog-based reasoning for knowledge graphs. PVLDB **11**(9), 975–987 (2018)
11. Bizer, C., et al.: Dbpedia - a crystallization point for the web of data. J. Web Sem. **7**(3), 154–165 (2009)
12. Box, G.E.P., Hunter, J.S., Hunter, W.G.: Statistics for Experimenters: Design, Innovation, and Discovery, 2nd edn. Wiley, Hoboken (2005)
13. Buneman, P., Khanna, S., Tan, W.C.: On propagation of deletions and annotations through views. In: PODS, pp. 150–158. ACM (2002)
14. Calì, A., Gottlob, G., Kifer, M.: Taming the infinite chase: query answering under expressive relational constraints. J. Artif. Intell. Res. **48**, 115–174 (2013)
15. Calì, A., Gottlob, G., Lukasiewicz, T.: A general datalog-based framework for tractable query answering over ontologies. J. Web Sem. **14**, 57–83 (2012)
16. Calì, A., Gottlob, G., Lukasiewicz, T., Marnette, B., Pieris, A.: Datalog+/-: a family of logical knowledge representation and query languages for new applications. In: LICS, pp. 228–242 (2010)
17. Calì, A., Gottlob, G., Pieris, A.: Towards more expressive ontology languages: the query answering problem. Artif. Intell. **193**, 87–128 (2012)
18. Christen, P.: Data Matching - Concepts and Techniques for Record Linkage, Entity Resolution, and Duplicate Detection. Data-Centric Systems and Applications. Springer, Heidelberg (2012). https://doi.org/10.1007/978-3-642-31164-2
19. The UniProt Consortium: UniProt: the universal protein knowledgebase. Nucleic Acids Res. **45**(Database-Issue), D158–D169 (2017)
20. Csar, T., Lackner, M., Pichler, R., Sallinger, E.: Winner determination in huge elections with MapReduce. In: AAAI, pp. 451–458. AAAI Press (2017)
21. Dhar, V.: Data science and prediction. Commun. ACM **56**(12), 64–73 (2013)
22. Ester, M., Kriegel, H.-P., Sander, J., Xu, X. et al.: A density-based algorithm for discovering clusters in large spatial databases with noise. In: KDD, vol. 96, pp. 226–231 (1996)
23. Fierens, D., et al.: Inference and learning in probabilistic logic programs using weighted Boolean formulas. TPLP **15**(3), 358–401 (2015)
24. Furche, T., Gottlob, G., Grasso, G., Schallhart, C., Sellers, A.J.: OXPath: a language for scalable data extraction, automation, and crawling on the deep web. VLDB J. **22**(1), 47–72 (2013)
25. Furche, T., Gottlob, G., Neumayr, B., Sallinger, E.: Towards a lingua franca for data wrangling. In: AMW, Data Wrangling for Big Data (2016)
26. Furche, T., Grasso, G., Kravchenko, A., Schallhart, C.: Turn the page: automated traversal of paginated websites. In: ICWE, pp. 332–346 (2012)
27. Getoor, L., Taskar, B.: Introduction to Statistical Relational Learning (Adaptive Computation and Machine Learning). The MIT Press, Cambridge (2007)
28. Glimm, B., et al.: SPARQL 1.1 entailment regimes. W3C Recommendation, 21 March 2013
29. Gottlob, G., Pieris, A.: Beyond SPARQL under OWL 2 QL entailment regime: rules to the rescue. In: IJCAI, pp. 2999–3007 (2015)

30. Gribkoff, E., Suciu, D.: Slimshot: in-database probabilistic inference for knowledge bases. PVLDB **9**(7), 552–563 (2016)
31. Guagliardo, P., Pichler, R., Sallinger, E.: Enhancing the updatability of projective views. In: AMW, CEUR Workshop Proceedings, vol. 1087. CEUR-WS.org (2013)
32. Kolaitis, P.G., Pichler, R., Sallinger, E., Savenkov, V.: Nested dependencies: structure and reasoning. In: PODS, pp. 176–187. ACM (2014)
33. Kolaitis, P.G., Pichler, R., Sallinger, E., Savenkov, V.: Limits of schema mappings. Theory Comput. Syst. **62**(4), 899–940 (2018)
34. Konstantinou, N., et al.: The VADA architecture for cost-effective data wrangling. In: SIGMOD. ACM (2017)
35. Kravchenko, A., Fayzrakhmanov, R.R., Sallinger, E.: Web page representations and data extraction with BERyL. In: Proceedings of MATWEP 2018, p. 8 (2018, in Press)
36. Michels, C., Fayzrakhmanov, R.R., Ley, M., Sallinger, E., Schenkel, R.: Oxpath-based data acquisition for dblp. In: JCDL, pp. 319–320. IEEE CS (2017)
37. Niu, F., Ré, C., Doan, A.H., Shavlik, J.W.: Tuffy: scaling up statistical inference in markov logic networks using an RDBMS. PVLDB **4**(6), 373–384 (2011)
38. Pichler, R., Sallinger, E., Savenkov, V.: Relaxed notions of schema mapping equivalence revisited. Theory Comput. Syst. **52**(3), 483–541 (2013)
39. Poon, H., Domingos, P.M.: Unsupervised ontology induction from text. In: ACL, pp. 296–305 (2010)
40. De Raedt, L.: Logical and Relational Learning: From ILP to MRDM (Cognitive Technologies). Springer, Heidelberg (2008). https://doi.org/10.1007/978-3-540-68856-3
41. Richardson, M., Domingos, P.M.: Markov logic networks. Mach. Learn. **62**(1–2), 107–136 (2006)
42. Sallinger, E.: Reasoning about schema mappings. In: Dagstuhl Follow-Ups, Data Exchange, Information, and Streams, vol. 5, pp. 97–127. SD-LZI (2013)
43. Sarawagi, S.: Information extraction. Found. Trends Databases **1**(3), 261–377 (2008)
44. Shkapsky, A., Yang, M., Zaniolo, C.: Optimizing recursive queries with monotonic aggregates in deals. In: ICDE, pp. 867–878 (2015)
45. Singla, P., Domingos, P.M.: Entity resolution with Markov logic. In: ICDM, pp. 572–582 (2006)
46. Vrandecic, D., Krötzsch, M.: Wikidata: a free collaborative knowledgebase. Commun. ACM **57**(10), 78–85 (2014)

Databases

NoSQL Databases – Seek for a Design Methodology

Chaimae Asaad[✉] and Karim Baïna[✉]

Alqualsadi, Rabat IT Center, ENSIAS, Mohammed V University, Rabat, Morocco
chaimaeasaad.email@gmail.com, karim.baina@um5.ac.ma

Abstract. NoSQL has emerged as a novel approach to bypass the rigidity and limits that traditional Databases presented when modeling real world features. Its heterogeneity, the variety of models it introduced and its several technical advantages helped NoSQL conquer the industrial and business world. NoSQL Databases are mostly conceived at physical design level, following a set of storage and structural rules regulated by each specific database. As NoSQL thrived, so did NoSQL data modeling. Research into unified approaches for NoSQL Databases at all design levels has been widely pursued in the last decade or so. This paper presents a survey of the various proposals aiming to unify all or most NoSQL Databases under a uniform design methodology. We also present the different data models of each NoSQL Database type, and the numerous approaches existing in the literature to designing and modeling them, in addition to an evaluation system for NoSQL design methodologies.

Keywords: NoSQL · Database modeling
NoSQL design methodology · Data models

1 Introduction

NoSQL has become the go-to database type for complex real-life representation usage. It abolished the outdated concept of one-solution-for-all, and instead, brought forward a huge number of various, powerful and efficient databases. The growing interest in NoSQL has first been pushed by industrial powerhouses, but, research has been catching up in the last decade or so, resulting in a new wave of published papers presenting different proposals related to NoSQL's data models, applications and implementations. Although research into NoSQL Design Methodologies is fairly new, many promising outcomes have emerged. The literature presents a number of proposed data models to unify all or most NoSQL databases. The heterogeneity that characterizes NoSQL is considered a significant advantage point, however, in data modeling, it represents a major constraint considered debatebly a direct cause behind the lack of a NoSQL unified model. Researchers have nevertheless managed to group three of the major NOSQL databases (Key-Value Stores, Column Family Stores, Document-Oriented Databases) under the aggregate data model, and consequently unify

© Springer Nature Switzerland AG 2018
E. H. Abdelwahed et al. (Eds.): MEDI 2018, LNCS 11163, pp. 25–40, 2018.
https://doi.org/10.1007/978-3-030-00856-7_2

to some extent their design methodology. To the best of our knowledge, only two papers so far have managed to present a unifying methodology and include Graph Databases in their proposal for a NoSQL Design Methodology, which leaves a huge gap in the field, and presents a goldmine of potential possibilities for more research into NoSQL to flourish. The main contribution of this paper is to realize a comprehensive review of NoSQL design methodologies existing in the literature and propose a subjective evaluation method for NoSQL data models. The remaining part of this paper is organized as follows. Section 2 presents the various proposals aiming to unify NoSQL Databases. Section 3 includes a brief literature review of NoSQL design methodologies relating to each specific category of NoSQL databases. Section 4 proposes an evaluation system for NoSQL data models. Section 5 is a case study. Conclusions and perspectives are given in Sect. 6.

2   NoSQL Design Methodologies

NoSQL Data Modeling has been approached from different perspectives. Intuitively, researchers try to find commonalities between the different data models in order to conceptualize an abstraction for NoSQL databases. In [1], the authors state that NoSQL database design can be devised into the same three levels as Relational database design, namely: A Conceptual Level, A Logical Level and a Physical Level. Both the first two phases are system-independent and only the last is specifically related to the choice of database. [1] adds that in the logical level, databases from the same type or family are modeled following the same design methodology, whilst in the conceptual phase, only the high-level data structure is represented. This section will present the different approaches aiming to develop an abstraction through a common conceptual or logical model in order to unify all or most NoSQL databases under a uniform design methodology. The specific data models for target NoSQL databases are implemented on the physical design level, which is beyond the scope of this paper. The grouping of Key-Value (e.g. Dynamo, Redis, Scalaris), Column-Family (e.g. Hbase, MonetDB) and Document (e.g. CouchDB, MongoDB, SimpleDB) databases under the Aggregate Data Model represents a huge breakthrough in NoSQL modeling. [2] states that the aggregate data model is formally defined as a forest of independent aggregates. The term *aggregate* in the scope of NoSQL data modeling defines a rich structure of closely related data that makes sense to be stored as a unit, which is the case in the aforementioned NoSQL database types. In what follows, we will present the various unifying Design Methodologies for NoSQL databases.

2.1   Ontology-Driven NoSQL Data Model (ODNSDM)

This proposal was presented in [3] and explored further in [5] and represents a unifying approach to NoSQL data modeling. To the best of our knowledge, it's one of two proposals managing to include Graph Databases in its unified approach to NoSQL data modeling, and therefore include ALL NoSQL database types. The authors state that [3] has been proposed to conceptualize data representation facets over heterogeneous types of databases by providing a common conceptual abstraction level based on semantically enriched formal vocabularies. They define ontology as the explicit specification of shared conceptualization in terms of concepts, relationships amongs concepts and axioms. The authors of [3] propose an ontology driven meta-model called ODNSDM (Ontology Driven NoSQL Data Model) which they claim capable of providing a universal perception at conceptual level to handle different types of databases, preserving strong semantics in knowledge exchange, representing hierarchical, non-hierarchical, symmetric and n-array relationships, and conforming to the CAP model. The ODNSDM is a proposed conceptualization composed of a set of constructs and relationships along with their properties. It consists of three inter-related layers, where each layer has their recognizable construct types making it distinct. The three main layers and their respective constructs are *Collection(Col)*, *Family(FA)* and *Attribute(AT)*. The authors of [3] have formally specified and explained the different construct types and relationships attached to them in their paper where further details can be found. They also included algorithms for transformations from their proposed model to both schema-based and schema-less databases. The (shema-less db) algorithm was applied on the NoSQL Document-Oriented database MongoDB. This proposal represents a unified data model leveraging the commonalities of schema-based and schema-less databases and including their differences in order to achieve a data modeling specification based on mathematical logic to create a balance in the variations at physical level implementations and thus facilitate and conceptualize their design. This model was validated initially with an ontology editorial tool called Protégé based on OWL [3].

2.2   Logical Unified Modeling for NoSQL databases (UMLtoNoSQL)

[4] is a recent article proposing a novel (Model Driven Architecture) MDA-based process transforming a conceptual data model describing Big Data into several physical models, with the aim of assisting developers in implementing Big Data on NoSQL systems, and allowing them the choice of system. This approach was illustrated using a case study in the Healthcare field. The authors of [4] propose an approach for defining, specifying and automating a process for storing Big Data on NoSQL systems. They named their process UMLtoNoSQL. They claim that this process can automatically transform a conceptual model represented as a UML class diagram into the physical model of a NoSQL system of choice. They introduce a logical level between conceptual and physical levels in which they develop a generic model. The novelty of this proposal is its compatibility with Graph Databases, a challenge which many approaches have not managed to overcome. The authors excluded Key-Value stores because "Column-Oriented, Document-Oriented and Graph-Oriented extend the concepts of Key-Value systems" [4]. Applications of this approach were conducted successfully on Cassandra, MongoDB and Neo4j [4].

2.3   Query-Oriented Data Modeling Approach (QODM)

A query-oriented data modeling approach for NoSQL databases was presented in [6]. This approach aims at designing both the data model (defining the entities and relationships) and data schema (defining the data structure) of an application for NoSQL databases. The authors of this paper claim that their contributions consist of: defining a methodology of data query requirements representation; designing a meta-model of the platform-independent data schema for NoSQL DB; and proposing an approach for generating both the data model and data schema based on particular requirements. The authors developed a framework for their query-oriented modeling approach consisting of three phases. Firstly, a description of the stored data structure in the problem domain and the data query requirements of the application. Then, using the stored data structure and data query requirements as a basis for the QODM-analyzer to generate the data model for NoSQL databases. And lastly, based on that data model, the QODM-analyzer generates the data schema for NoSQL databases. The authors provide an algorithm for generating the data model [6]. As for the data schema, adapting to different NoSQL databases imposes having a platform-independent model from which transformation to specific databases can be conducted. The QODM approach was evaluated using ElasticInbox as a case study [6]. This approach, although only viable for aggregate-oriented NoSQL databases, presents a novel way to tackle the data modeling problem. By being query-oriented, it manages to adapt to the heterogeneous nature of NoSQL, without locking the user to any specific database. The authors realize the difference that Graph databases present, and how their inclusion could prove to be inherently difficult, but believe their approach to have the potential to be revolutionary in the NoSQL data modeling world.

2.4   The Save Our Systems Platform (SOS)

The SOS platform [7] was proposed as a common programming interface for NoSQL systems, with the aim of supporting application development by hiding the specific details of the various systems. This platform is based on a meta-modeling approach, i.e., the specific interfaces of individual systems are mapped to a common one [7]. This proposal is one of the pioneering ones aiming to unify NoSQL data models, and has inspired many other proposals based on its main idea. The authors' goals and motivation behind this approach was to "alleviate the consequences of the heterogeneity" that NoSQL systems present. They state that SOS is a programming environment where non-relational (i.e., NoSQL databases) can be uniformly defined, queried and accessed by an application program. The basis for this programming model is a generic and extensible meta-layer representing a theoritical unifying structure to be implemented in the specific database [7]. The paper presented a discussion around the implementation of the approach in three aggregate-oriented NoSQL databases. The architecture of the SOS system is organized following three modules: the common interface representing the core of the system and offering the primitives to interact with NoSQL stores; the meta-layer storing the form of the involved data; and the specific handlers generating the appropriate calls to the specific database system. The approach was illustrated using a case study consisting of defining a simplified version of Twitter, and generating implementations for Redis, MongoDB and HBase [7].

2.5 The NoSQL Abstract Data Model (NoAM)

In a series of papers [8–10], Atzeni et al. present NoAM, a "logical approach to the NoSQL database design problem, with initial activities that are independent of the specific target system". The approach aims to exploit the commonalities of various NoSQL systems, and represents an intermediate abstract data model designed to represent application data as collections of aggregate objects. [8] states that database design in the NoSQL world is often widely based on best practises and guidelines, and systematically related to the specific chosen database and thus completely relaying on physical level characteristics. The authors of [8] proclaim that the aim of NoAM is to fill the gap in the design methodology of NoSQL. This approach manages to unify the aggregate-oriented NoSQL databases, and does so by defining a proposal consisting of four main phases, namely: *Aggregate Design, Aggregate Partitioning, High-level NoSQL Database Design,Implementation* [8]. The NoAM data model can be defined as follows [9]: A NoAM *Database*: A set of *collections*, where each collection has a distinct name. A Collection: A set of *blocks*, where each block is identified by a unique-within-the-collection *block key*. A Block: A non-empty set of *entries*, where each entry is a pair of (entry-key, entry-value). The approach is applied on a running example of an online social game [9]. In [10], the previously specified NoAM data model is further explored and more details are included to illustrate the conceptual level of the proposal and its use and experimental results are also presented. Implementation steps are also further detailed with respect to a single elected representative of each NoSQL database, namely: Oracle NoSQL for KV Stores; DynamoDB for Extensible Record Stores; and MongoDB for Document-Oriented databases. Graph Databases remain, as in the two other papers, beyond the scope of the approach, since they are not aggregate-oriented databases and represent entirely different data models [10].

2.6 MDE-based Reverse Engineering Approach

[11] proposes an MDE-based reverse engineering approach designed to infer the schema of aggregate-oriented NoSQL databases, and uses the obtained schemas to build database utilities in order to tackle problems relating to the use of implicit schemas. The authors note that although the schema-less nature of NoSQL (or rather the lack of explicit schema specification) might be the most "attractive" feature of NoSQL databases, it has contributed immensely in making database design in NoSQL a particularly error-prone task. Their approach has been designed, as mentioned previously, for NoSQL systems following an aggregate data model. The authors of [11] state that their proposal represents a

strategy aiming to infer the implicit schemas in NoSQL databases, taking into account the different versions of entities, and call them *Versioned Schemas*, and proclaim that their usefulness can be illustrated through both schema visualization and automated generation of data validators. The contributions of [11] as claimed by its authors are twofold. It is a novel approach inferring conceptual schemas from NoSQL databases and including all versions of entities and relationships. And, it presents a road map to using the versioned schemas to automatically generate different software artifacts. The authors validated their approach for the MongoDB, CouchDB and HBase databases [11]. The authors of [11] state that their approach, although only viable for aggregate-oriented databases, represents a useful tool in generating specifications that describe the data accurately, and takes into account each version of each entity, thus completely defining the structure of the data and illustrating the high-level relationships. Graph databases are beyond the scope of this approach.

3 NoSQL Databases Specific Design Methodologies

The heterogeneity of NoSQL databases can be seen even within each type. The variety and volume of databases existing contributes to the lack of a unified modeling approach, as we have discussed in the previous section, most works only manage to propose a uniform approach for aggregate-oriented NoSQL databases, since they present an inherently similar layout, even if their characteristics differ immensly. Although research into NoSQL data models is somewhat recent, various works have been conducted to explore the design methodologies of NoSQL database types, as well as specific data models for target NoSQL databases. In what follows, we present a brief survey of the various papers and proposals discussing the modeling of each distinct NoSQL database type presented in the literature.

3.1 Key-Value Databases

Key-Value stores (or Tuple Stores) are considered somewhat the simplest NoSQL databases. They consist of a unique key and a "bucket" containing any data the user wishes to store. The value content of the said bucket is schema-less and doesn't need to be consistent. This content usually consists of unstructured or semi-structured data. The buckets have a huge storage ability for quite large entries, incuding BLOBs (Basic Large OBjects). The values can be read by knowing the key and bucket. Key Value Stores are row-based systems designed to efficiently return data for an entire bucket (interpreted as a row or record) in as few operations as possible. Essentially, all Key Value Stores run in batch mode and are therefore used for analytic or caching projects as opposed to transactional operations [12].

- Dynamic Distributed Dimenstional Data Model (D4M):
The D4M data model was presented in [13] as a somewhat technical perspective aiming to provide a mathematically rich interface to tuple stores by allowing linear algebra to be readily applied to databases. The goal of this approach is to combine the advantages of tuple stores to create a database and computation system that solves the challenges associated with Big Data. Key-Value Stores (e.g. HBase, Accumulo) are implementations leveraging the Google BigTable model, and as such, the one-to-one mapping that the D4M associative arrays provide onto the tables in a tuple store makes complex manipulations simple to code. To illustrate the model, the authors use D4M for a facet search on a Document Keyword Table, and claim that the results are consistent and deliver near the theoritical performance level of the hardware [13].

3.2 Document-Oriented Databases

Document Oriented Databases are based on the paradigm Key-Value, where the Value is a JSON or XML document. Consequently, one key can get access to a structured set of information easily. In other words, Document Oriented databases take the data and aggregate it into documents using a specific format (e.g. JSON) [14]. Many approaches for the data modeling of this specific NoSQL type can be found in the literature. The most pertinent might be:

- [15] presents a *Workload-Driven Logical Design Approach for NoSQL Document Databases* consisting of a process aiming to convert a conceptual model into efficient logical representations for a NoSQL Document database. This proposed conversion process considers the expected workload of the application. The approach was validated with an example of e-commerce application.
- [16] proposes a standard for NoSQL data modeling by using NoQSL Document-Oriented databases to introduce modeling techniques. The contribution of this paper is presented in its proposal for viewing Document Databases, and how it is used to build a conceptual data model regulated by a few assumptions and constraints. The proposal was evaluated on a case study related to identifying and comparing expression levels of human kidney and liver RNA sequenced samples [16].
- [17] proposes a NoSQL data modeling standard by introducing techniques to be used on Document-Oriented databases and including geographical features. The authors justify their choice of NoSQL by stating that some non-functional aspects are common features of both NoSQL databases and spatial data treatement. This approach uses [16] and adapts the conceptual model to geospatical features and integrates them using MongoDB.

3.3 Column-Family Databases

A Columnar database is called as such when the smallest information unit to be manipulated is a column. It represents a two-level data aggregation structure. Just like in Key-Value databases, the first level is a key identifying an aggregation of interest. The difference remains in the second level containing several columns that can hold either simple or complex values. In addition, these columns can be accessed either all at once or one at a time. Column-Family databases somehow neglect the conceptual design phase, making their data modeling a very difficult one, which explains the gap in modeling proposals in the literature [18].

- [18] proposes an approach for logical design of Columnar databases as a way to contribute to filling the void between abstract methodologies and the physical level and technological advances in the NoSQL world. The authors state that their proposal represents a reconcilitation approach between the classical database design approach and Columnar databases, contributing with a logical design process that considers the semantics of the application domain in order to achieve an optimized conversion from a conceptual schema to a logical columnar schema.

3.4   Graph Databases

As mentioned in the previous sections, Graph databases are seldom included in attempts to conceptualize a unifying NoSQL design methodology, because of their non-conformity to the aggregate-oriented data model, and for their very different nature compared to the other NoSQL families. However, Graph databases remain debatebly the most well modeled NoSQL databases. Their mathematical background and the rich history of research into different uses of graphs in many disciplines resulted in rich literature presence. [21] presents a survey of the different data models for Graph databases. In this section, we will not discuss those models, but rather the novel proposals present in the literature to map or use this highly representative type of databases.

- [22] proposes an approach defining a test model for graph database applications, taking into account the data model of the graph database systems, and presents a framework placing model-based testing into the model-driven architecture context in order to automate the derivation of the test cases and the evaluation of their adequacy. The authors proclaim that their contributions consist of defining a framework that integrates model-based testing (MBT) into the model-driven architecture (MDA) paradigm, and presenting a formal definition of a test model for graph database applications relying on both the underlying conceptual data model and the system specification [22].
- [23] proposes a model-driven, system-independent design methodology for Graph databases. The proposed approach starts from a conceptual Entity-Relationship representation of the interest domain, and proposes a strategy to devise a graph database in which the data accesses for answering queries is minimized. The authors state that their methodology relies a logical model for Graph databases, and demonstrate the effectiveness of their approach with a number of experimental results over various Graph Database Management Systems [23].

– [24] describes a mapping approach from UML(Unified Modeling Language)/OCL(Object Constraint Language) conceptual schemas to *Blueprints*, an abstraction layer built on top of a variety of Graph Databases. The authors also present, via an intermediate Graph metamodel, Gremlin: a graph traversal language. The novelty of this approach is the presentation of the UML-toGraphDB framework to translate conceptual schemas expressed using UML into a graph representation and generate database-level queries [24].

4   Discussion

4.1   Evaluation Process

The various NoSQL design methologies existing in the literature address the conceptual and logical steps to NoSQL modeling from different angles and following different approaches. In this paper, we presented the ones proposing a unified design methodology for NoSQL databases and their types. In what follows, we will present a comparison based on numerous criteria to evaluate the approaches aforementioned in an attempt to seek the "best" design methodology for NoSQL. To the best of our knowledge, a set of formally defined and agreed upon criteria for evaluating NoSQL design methodologies has not yet been introduced in the literature. Consequently, the following deductions were made in an ad-hoc manner and inferred based on a methodology paradigm chosen by the authors. In this section, we will combine a number of previous research contributions and use evaluation criteria introduced as means to compare Relational Data Models, and adjust them according to the NoSQL conceptualization standards.

The data modeling phase represents the pillar of the entire design system, since its impact on the final result's quality is undeniably great. However, it shouldn't be described as a deterministic process of uncovering the "right" model. The choice of the most appropriate data model is inherently based on common sense and experience, and there are generally no guidelines for the evaluation of different models [26]. [26,27] presented each a set of evaluation criteria for design methodologies. The former introduced a framework for objective evaluation and improvement of data models, while the latter proposed a number of qualifying norms for design methodologies. Evidently, these proposals weren't specifically tailored after the NoSQL model, however, we will be adapting their definitions according to our models in order to form a group of only the salient, adequate and specifically influencing criteria for NoSQL.

4.2   Evaluation Criteria

The following is a combination of different criteria proposed by [26,27], some redefined or readjusted with respect to our best judgement.

1. *Simplicity:* references the size of the model and the complexity of the methodology. Simpler approaches are often better, their complexity has a direct correlation with the complexity of the resulting system. A simpler NoSQL Design Methodology will simplify the modeling process and therefore simplify the next database design steps.

2. *Completeness:* expresses resolvability and relates to the smooth transitioning from different levels of abstraction without omitting any logical steps or having any gaps in the mapping process. The transition from the NoSQL logical and conceptual levels to the specific NoSQL physical design level should be well established and not lacking any crucial steps.

3. *Flexibility:* expresses the adaptability of the model to changes in user requirements and to automated design tools. The NoSQL model should be flexible and high-level enough to handle new additions or omissions in the physical level without changing the original data model.

4. *Consistency:* describes the coherence of the entire methodology. The approach's various steps shouldn't contradict one another. Consistency can also include the methodology's support of CAP/BASE aspects.

5. *Understandability:* defines the level of ease that the users of the data model deal with. [26] notes that one of the major purposes of using data models is as means of communicating between business specialists and technical specialists. Therefore, for a NoSQL methodology to be 'understandable', it has to be 'simple' enough for users to grasp its main concepts and structures.

6. *Scope of the model:* specifies the level of inclusion of the methodology. For a NoSQL design methodology to abide by this criterion, it needs to include the different data models that NoSQL introduces, or most of them.

7. *Implementability:* emphasizes the feasibility of the realization of the transition to the physical design and its implementation. Although a NoSQL design methodology carries no assumptions of physical requirement specifications, it should contain practical guidelines to implement the model in target systems.

4.3 Synthesis

In the absence of empirical validation for the criteria, and since measuring the complexity of models is beyond the scope of this paper, we used approximations based on common sense and our understanding of the methodologies at hand. The models included in this work are distinguished in their completeness since they represent somewhat clear and logical design steps. Intuitively, they comply with the flexibility criterion, since they are proposing a design for a highly variant group of databases. The methodologies differ in their understandability levels, and some of them take special knowledge of a few concepts (e.g. Ontology) for users to fully grasp them. All methodologies have shown proof of concept and of implementability by including different case studies. *QODM* presented a data model based on query requirements but failed to mention a description of schema-less data. *NoAM* proposed a common data model to specify system-independent realization of the application data, however, dynamically inserted data into NoSQL databases was overlooked. Most approaches are "good" design

Table 1. Evaluation of NoSQL Methodologies (O = Yes, ~ = Average, ∀ = All, A = Aggregate-oriented DB)

Methodology \ Criterion	Simplicity	Completeness	Flexibility	Consistency	Understandability	Scope	Implementability
ODNSDM	~	O	O	O	~	∀	O
UMLtoNoSQL	~	O	O	O	~	∀	O
QODM	~	O	O	O	~	A	O
SOS	~	O	O	O	O	A	O
NoAM	~	O	O	O	~	A	O
MDE-RE	~	O	O	O	~	A	O

methodologies within their scope, but don't provide a formalism able to deal with the semantics of data [3]. Table 1 illustrates the results of the aforementioned methodologies with respect to the criteria specified earlier. Scope-Wise, '∀' means the approach unifies all NoSQL Databases, and 'A' means that it unifies only the Aggregate-Oriented NoSQL databases.

Evidently, the "perfect" design methodology for NoSQL has not seen the light yet, but the different proposals discussed in this paper present a steady stepping stone and fertile ground for more research. A hybrid design methodology based on two or more of these proposals seems like the right answer, however, due to differences in perspectives, logical and conceptual designs, it would probably add unecessary complexity to the design mapping. Based on the criteria, we can identify ODNSDM [3] as the "best" design methodology for NoSQL primarily for its wide *scope, its logical model and its strenght in capturing the semantics of the data.* This approach has its limits, however, a hybridization with other models can prove fruitful in polyglot persistence or a multimodel database.

4.4   Limitations and Perspectives

The evaluation criteria we proposed in the previous sections represents a path to a more concise and precise framework for the evaluation of NoSQL design methodologies. Some of the most serious deficiencies in the existing literature relating to the quality of data models is that very few approaches are empirically validated in practise. Most are either, theoritically or experientially justified, which leaves a considerable margin of error due to subjective and biased interpretations. Furthermore, there are relatively few guidelines for evaluating the quality of data models, and little agreement even among experts on what makes a 'good' model [28]. Our evaluation system suffers the same limitations. It combines a number of quality factors to compare different NoSQL design methodologies, without testing or validation. As [29] notes, defining quality criteria is not enough to ensure quality in practice, since different individuals will have different interpretations of the meaning of those criteria. In this sense, we are aware of our process's need for empirical validation and practical testing. Our work can be improved by introducing metrics to quantify the different criteria aforementioned, with the purpose of improving the evaluation system. These metrics will provide a purely objective and mathematical measure in order to determine what a 'good' model is, and aid in the comparison between different NoSQL models. However, it is worth mentioning that this might prove to be difficult given the notion of *conceptual manageability* (i.e., difficulty to synthesise a large number of metrics into an overall picture of the quality of the model), and also since subjective ratings and textual descriptions of quality issues have been proven in such cases to provide a more holistic view of the quality of the model, in addition to the fact that requirements analysis is more of an "art" than a science, due to the difficulty of measuring the quality of a logical specification in comparison to physical database design (for which quantitative measurements exist, such as storage space, speed of access and CPU requirements) [29]. The focus of our research was not to develop a framework of quantitative measures to evaluate the quality of NoSQL data models, but rather to attempt to lay the groundwork and serve a quideline for our future work into a hybrid approach combining quantitative measures with subjective criteria to evaluate the quality of NoSQL design methodologies and help improve them by pinpointing their deficiencies.

5   Case Study

In this section, we present a simplified and practical study illustrating both the mapping process of UMLtoNoSQL and the ODNSDM approach in the case of a blood bank donation system. The purpose of this case study is to exemplify how UMLtoNoSQL and ODNSDM can be applied for NoSQL data modeling. The reason for choosing to apply the case study on these two models is their compatibility with all NoSQL Databases. Figure 1 represents the UML Class Diagram of a blood donation system [30] which will be mapped into a generic model and then used to infer a physical Cassandra model Fig. 2 to illustrate the UMLtoNoSQL approach. Experiments on real code generation for this mapping can be carried out using Eclipse Modeling Framework (EMF), the metamodeling language Ecore, the XML based standard for metadata interchange (XMI) and the OMG standard for models transformation QVT [4]. The same blood donation system will be used to illustrate ODNSDM. Figure 3 represents the resulting Ontology Graph. It is worth mentioning that due to space issues the graph was simplified by omitting a few Families and Attributes. In this blood donation system, and as shown in the ontology graph in Fig. 3, blood tests are conducted on every donor's blood, and the results determine whether the blood will be accepted for donation or rejected. Furthermore, these blood results along with the donor's medical history do not have a predefined schema (in our example) since they may differ from one case to the other. Consequently, they are to be inserted dynamically in the database. Accordingly, [3] notes that when some features of the data at hand are not predefined and can dynamically change, a high irregularity and required flexibility in representation are implied, which results in a requirement for schema-less databases rather than schema-based ones.

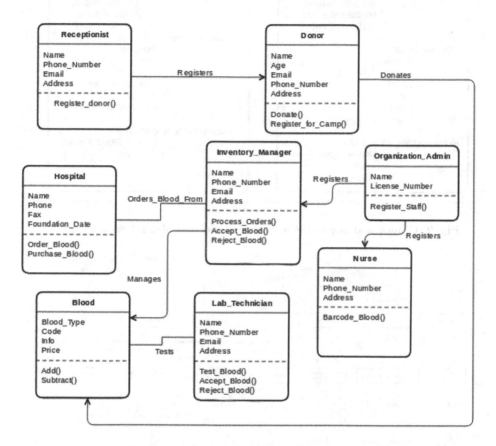

Fig. 1. UML class diagram of a blood donation system [30]

In our case study and as shown in Fig. 3, we can distinguish the three ODNSDM layers: Collection (Donate), Family (Top-most level: Donor, Hospital, Blood; Bottom-most level: Nurse, Receptionist, etc.), Attribute (Email, Phone, etc.). Different relationships can be found in the ontology graph. For instance, *Inter Containment* relationships join the collection Donate and the top-most families Donor, Hospital and Blood. *Inter Inverse Containment* relationships attach an Attribute element with a Family element (e.g. relationship between Receptionist and Recep_pers_info), *Intra Containment* relationships represent the level hierarchy between top-most families and their respectively attached adjacent lower-level families (e.g. relationship between Hospital and Nurse or

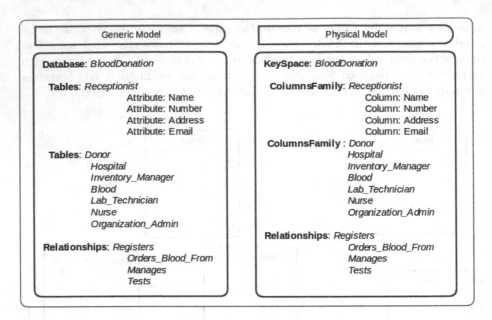

Fig. 2. Generic and physical (Cassandra) model of a blood donation system

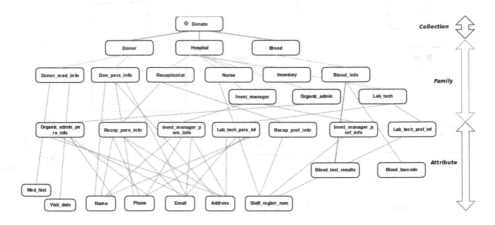

Fig. 3. ODNSDM ontology graph for blood donation case study

between Blood and Blood_info, etc.), and *Intra Inverse Containment* illustrates the relationships between elements of the same layer (e.g. relationship between two families). To denote relationships required to represent dynamically inserted data which has no predefined schema, the *Inverse Containment* relationship is used (e.g. between Blood_info and Blood_test_results). Additional details about other types of relationships can be found in [3] along with a conversion algorithm that can be applied to our resulting ODNSDM to convert it and implement it in a schema-less database (e.g. MongoDB).

6   Conclusion

NoSQL Databases differ in both their structural nature and their modeling. Various approaches have been proposed, thus enriching the literature of NoSQL design methodologies. In this paper, we cited the different models unifying all NoSQL databases, along with those unifying each NoSQL database category. Furthermore, we introduced an evaluation system based on various criteria inspired from evaluation frameworks of relational databases. A case study was used to illustrate the two main NoSQL design methodologies unifying all NoSQL databases. Future work will be directed towards classifying the approaches by their design level and also towards developing a more precise framework for the evaluation of the quality of NoSQL data models.

References

1. Shin, K., Hwang, C., Jung, H.: NoSQL database design using UML conceptual data model based on Peter Chens framework. Int. J. Appl. Eng. Res. **12**(5), 632–636 (2017)
2. Jovanovic, V., Benson, S.: Aggregate data modeling style. SAIS **2013**, 70–75 (2013)
3. Banerjee, S., Sarkar, A.: Ontology driven meta-modeling for NoSQL databases: a conceptual perspective. Int. J. Softw. Eng. Its Appl. **10**(12), 41–64 (2016)
4. Abdelhedi, F., Brahim, A.A., Atigui, F., Zurfluh, G.: Logical unified modeling for NoSQL DataBases. In: 19th International Conference on Enterprise Information Systems (ICEIS 2017) p. 249, April 2017
5. Banerjee, S., Sarkar, A.: Modeling NoSQL databases: from conceptual to logical level design. In: 3rd International Conference Applications and Innovations in Mobile Computing (AIMoC 2016), Kolkata, India, February, pp. 10–12 (2016)
6. Li, X., Ma, Z., Chen, H.: QODM: a query-oriented data modeling approach for NoSQL databases. In: 2014 IEEE Workshop on Advanced Research and Technology in Industry Applications (WARTIA), pp. 338–345. IEEE, September 2014
7. Atzeni, P., Bugiotti, F., Rossi, L.: Uniform access to non-relational database systems: the SOS platform. In: Ralyté, J., Franch, X., Brinkkemper, S., Wrycza, S. (eds.) CAiSE 2012. LNCS, vol. 7328, pp. 160–174. Springer, Heidelberg (2012). https://doi.org/10.1007/978-3-642-31095-9_11
8. Bugiotti, F., Cabibbo, L., Atzeni, P., Torlone, R.: A logical approach to NOSQL databases (2013). http://cabibbo.dia.uniroma3.it/pub/noam.pdf
9. Bugiotti, F., Cabibbo, L., Atzeni, P., Torlone, R.: Database design for NoSQL systems. In: Yu, E., Dobbie, G., Jarke, M., Purao, S. (eds.) ER 2014. LNCS, vol. 8824, pp. 223–231. Springer, Cham (2014). https://doi.org/10.1007/978-3-319-12206-9_18
10. Atzeni, P., Bugiotti, F., Cabibbo, L., Torlone, R.: Data modeling in the NoSQL world. Comput. Stand. Interfaces (2016)
11 Sevilla Ruiz, D., Morales, S.F., García Molina, J.: Inferring versioned schemas from NoSQL databases and its applications. In: Johannesson, P., Lee, M.L., Liddle, S.W., Opdahl, A.L., López, Ó.P. (eds.) ER 2015. LNCS, vol. 9381, pp. 467–480. Springer, Cham (2015). https://doi.org/10.1007/978-3-319-25264-3_35
12. Vorhies, B.: Lesson 5: key value stores (Aka Tuple stores) (2014). http://data-magnum.com/lesson-5-key-value-stores-aka-tuple-stores. Accessed 14 May 2018

13. Kepner, J., et al.:. Dynamic distributed dimensional data model (D4M) database and computation system. In: 2012 IEEE International Conference on Acoustics, Speech and Signal Processing (ICASSP), pp. 5349–5352. IEEE, March 2012

14. Issa, A., Schiltz, F.: Document Oriented Databases, ULB, Faculty of Science, INFO-H415-Advanced database, October 2015. http://cs.ulb.ac.be/public/_media/teaching/infoh415/student_projects/couchdb.pdf. Accessed 14 May 2018

15. de Lima, C., dos Santos Mello, R.: A workload-driven logical design approach for NoSQL document databases. In: Proceedings of the 17th International Conference on Information Integration and Web-based Applications & Services, p. 73. ACM, December 2015

16. Vera, H., Wagner Boaventura, M. H., Guimaraes, V., Hondo, F.: Data modeling for NoSQL document-oriented databases. In: CEUR Workshop Proceedings, vol. 1478, pp. 129–135, September 2015

17. Boaventura Filho, W., Olivera, H.V., Holanda, M., Favacho, A.A.: Geographic data modeling for NoSQL document-oriented databases. In: GEOProcessing **2015**, 72 (2015)

18. Poffo, J.P.: A Logical Design Process for Columnar Databases. In: ICIW 2016, p. 10 (2016)

19. Chebotko, A., Kashlev, A., Lu, S.:. A big data modeling methodology for Apache Cassandra. In: 2015 IEEE International Congress on Big Data (BigData Congress), pp. 238–245. IEEE, June 2015

20. Wang, G., Tang, J.: The nosql principles and basic application of cassandra model. In: 2012 International Conference on Computer Science & Service System (CSSS), pp. 1332–1335. IEEE, August 2012

21. Angles, R., Gutierrez, C.: Survey of graph database models. ACM Comput. Surv. (CSUR) **40**(1), 1 (2008)

22. Blanco, R., Tuya, J.: A test model for graph database applications: an MDA-based approach. In: Proceedings of the 6th International Workshop on Automating Test Case Design, Selection and Evaluation, pp. 8–15. ACM, August 2015

23. De Virgilio, R., Maccioni, A., Torlone, R.: Model-driven design of graph databases. In: Yu, E., Dobbie, G., Jarke, M., Purao, S. (eds.) ER 2014. LNCS, vol. 8824, pp. 172–185. Springer, Cham (2014). https://doi.org/10.1007/978-3-319-12206-9_14

24. Daniel, G., Sunyé, G., Cabot, J.: UMLtoGraphDB: mapping conceptual schemas to graph databases. In: Comyn-Wattiau, I., Tanaka, K., Song, I.-Y., Yamamoto, S., Saeki, M. (eds.) ER 2016. LNCS, vol. 9974, pp. 430–444. Springer, Cham (2016). https://doi.org/10.1007/978-3-319-46397-1_33

25. Braimniotis, M.: A Transformation from ORM Conceptual Models to Neo4j Graph Database (Doctoral dissertation, Institute of Computing) (2017)

26. Moody, D.L., Shanks, G.G.: What makes a good data model? Evaluating the quality of entity relationship models. In: Loucopoulos, P. (ed.) ER 1994. LNCS, vol. 881, pp. 94–111. Springer, Heidelberg (1994). https://doi.org/10.1007/3-540-58786-1_75

27. Buchmann, A.P., Dale, A.G.: Evaluation criteria for logical database design methodologies. Comput. Aided Des. **11**(3), 121–126 (1979)

28. Moody, D.L., Shanks, G.G.: Improving the quality of data models: empirical validation of a quality management framework. Inf. Syst. **28**(6), 619–650 (2003)

29. Moody, D.L.: Measuring the quality of data models: an empirical evaluation of the use of quality metrics in practice. In: ECIS 2003 Proceedings, p. 78 (2003)

30. Denzel, D.: Blood bank system Class Diagram (2012). https://creately.com/diagram/example. Accessed 18 May 2018

Mortadelo: A Model-Driven Framework for NoSQL Database Design

Alfonso de la Vega(✉), Diego García-Saiz, Carlos Blanco, Marta Zorrilla, and Pablo Sánchez

Software Engineering and Real-Time, University of Cantabria, Santander, Spain
{delavegaa,garciasad,blancobc,zorrillm,p.sanchez}@unican.es

Abstract. In big data contexts, the performance of relational databases can get overwhelmed, usually by numerous concurrent connections over large volumes of data. In these cases, the support of ACID transactions is dropped in favour of NoSQL data stores, which offer quick responses and high data availability. Although NoSQL systems solve this concrete performance problem, they also present some issues. For instance, the NoSQL spectrum covers a wide range of database paradigms, such as key-value, column-oriented or document stores. These paradigms differ too much from the relational model, provoking that it is not possible to make use of existent, well-known practices from relational database design. Moreover, the existence of that paradigm heterogeneity makes difficult the definition of general design practices for NoSQL data stores. We present Mortadelo, a framework devised for the automatic design of NoSQL databases. Mortadelo offers a model-driven transformation process, which starts from a technology-agnostic data model and provides an automatically generated design and implementation for the desired NoSQL data store. The main strength of our framework is its generality, i.e., Mortadelo can be extended to support any kind of NoSQL database. The validity of our approach has been checked through the implementation of a tool, which currently supports the generation of column family data stores and offers preliminary support of document-based ones.

Keywords: NoSQL · Database design · Model-driven engineering

1 Introduction

In the Big Data era [25], NoSQL databases [13] have arisen as a solution for contexts where many clients perform a massive number of requests over previously unseen quantities of data. Examples of these contexts are social network databases like Facebook and Twitter or international online stores such as Amazon. NoSQL is not just a technology, but a global term that comprises different database paradigms, including document, key-value or column family-based stores [6,17].

A common characteristic of NoSQL databases is that they are mainly used when the support of ACID transactions [14] from traditional Relational

© Springer Nature Switzerland AG 2018
E. H. Abdelwahed et al. (Eds.): MEDI 2018, LNCS 11163, pp. 41–57, 2018.
https://doi.org/10.1007/978-3-030-00856-7_3

DataBase Management Systems (RDBMSs) is not vital and, for instance, some temporal inconsistencies in data are tolerable [7]. Dropping the support of ACID transactions allows NoSQL databases, among other things, to scale well against large volumes of data, and to offer an adequate service for a very high number of end users [15].

Another common and important characteristic is that the design of databases for many NoSQL technologies is highly dependent on how the stored data is accessed [8,21]. In these databases, the structure of the data can be denormalized, in order to offer low latencies and high efficiency for the workload towards which they are prepared [24]. In contrast, this denormalization is not usually done in RDBMSs, where performance optimizations are obtained by other means, such as indexes or materialized views [1].

Unfortunately, the differences between NoSQL and RDBMSs shown above come with some losses for the NoSQL part, being the biggest one the inability to apply the well-known and heavily-tested design practises of relational databases to the definition of NoSQL data stores. These practises are based on conceptual models, such as the Entity-Relationship (ER) model [9] or UML relational specifications [20], from which many existing CASE tools can automatically infer the final database implementation [2]. In addition to this lost, the differences among NoSQL technologies provoke that the design of a NoSQL database may even vary depending on the paradigm we wish to employ [6]. For instance, the design decisions would not be the same if we were targeting a column family-based or a document-based data store [3].

Numerous works about NoSQL design exist in the literature [8,11,19,21]. Nevertheless, due to the heterogeneity of NoSQL, these works usually only focus on a concrete technology. A high-level and conceptual solution for the design of NoSQL data stores, such as the ones available for relational systems, would be beneficial for the centralization of existent, concrete works into a common framework.

Based on this context, we present Mortadelo, a framework that generates NoSQL designs for the data store of our choice. By providing a technology-agnostic data structure model that also includes details about how data are going to be accessed, our framework is able to automatically generate an implementation adapted to the specificities and benefits of the targeted NoSQL database. Mortadelo defines a transformation process which, through a series of steps, transforms first the provided conceptual model into a logical model dependant on the used NoSQL paradigm, and then generates the implementation scripts that would instantiate the targeted NoSQL technology from that paradigm.

The main strength of Mortadelo can be found in its model-driven, modular architecture, which can be extended to support any new NoSQL paradigm or technology. This architecture has been developed employing de facto modeling standards such as the Eclipse Modeling Framework [23], with the objective of offering an homogeneous treatment of different NoSQL paradigms sustained over well-known technologies and foundations. With the development of Mortadelo, we expect to cover the existent gap in NoSQL design practices and, to offer analogous methodologies to the ones that can be employed for relational-based systems.

The validity of Mortadelo has been tested through the implementation of an homonymous tool, which currently supports the generation of specifications for column family-based systems, with concrete transformations for Cassandra [5]. The support of column-family data stores has supposed the development of a metamodel for the logical design of this kind of databases, and also the definition of a set of rules to transform the data structure model to this logical model and to the final implementation in the concrete technology. Additionally, we briefly introduce how we are working in the support of document-based data stores, including an example for MongoDB [10].

The remaining of the paper is structured as follows. In Sect. 2 we detail the different phases of the transformation process followed by Mortadelo to generate NoSQL databases. It includes the description of the different metamodels that intervene in the process and the rules employed in the transformation. In Sect. 3, we present the prototype tool which implements our framework. Next, in Sect. 4, related works in NoSQL design are discussed. Finally, we expose our conclusions and future work in Sect. 5.

2 Framework Description

We start by giving an overview of the transformation process supported by Mortadelo. Then, successive sections describe Mortadelo's components with more detail.

2.1 Transformation Process Overview

Figure 1 shows the transformation process supported by Mortadelo. In this process, an input model is transformed in a succession of steps to obtain an implementation of certain target NoSQL data store technology. Next paragraphs comment on these steps.

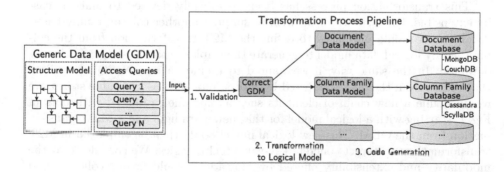

Fig. 1. Transformation process of Mortadelo.

As introduced before, Mortadelo follows a model-driven approach. Therefore, the input of the transformation process is a model, which conforms to a meta-model that we have denoted as the *Generic Data Model (GDM)* (Fig. 1, left). An instance of the GDM represents a conceptual definition of the database provided by the user. The GDM is composed of two blocks: (i) the *Structure Model*, which contains the information about domain entities and their relationships; and (ii) the *Access Queries*, which define how data from the structure model are going to be requested. The GDM is intentionally platform-independent, so it can be used seamlessly as input for different NoSQL paradigms. We give more details about the GDM components in Sect. 2.3.

The transformation process starts by validating the provided GDM instance to assess that it contains no mistakes (Fig. 1, step 1). For instance, if an entity present in an access query is not defined in the GDM, the validation process would indicate an error.

In step 2, a model-to-model (M2M) transformation translates the conceptual GDM model into a logical NoSQL specification by the application of a set of transformation rules. Due to the heterogeneity of NoSQL, in Mortadelo a logical metamodel and an associated M2M transformation has to be defined for each NoSQL paradigm. In the figure, two logical metamodels are shown: a column family data model and a document data model. These metamodels are intermediate representations, which contain information specific to the paradigm they represent. For instance, the column family data model allows defining the column families that should be instantiated in the final database. However, these specifications are still abstracted from any implementation details, i.e., the logical model of a paradigm can be employed to represent technologies that belong to the same paradigm.

Finally, the third step of the transformation process consists in a model-to-text (M2T) transformation. The obtained logical model from the M2M transformation of step 2 is used to automatically generate an implementation script for the targeted technology. Continuing with the column family example, a M2T generation from a logical model could be performed to obtain a physical implementation for Cassandra, a database from this paradigm. An analogous example could be made for a document data model and a MongoDB implementation.

This transformation process has been specifically devised to make it easily extensible. For instance, if we wish to support another column family-based database, we would only need to define the M2T transformation from the column family logical data model to generate the implementation script of this new database. In the same way, if we wanted to include a new NoSQL paradigm that differs from the ones supported by Mortadelo, such as key-value stores, we would define a new chain of elements such as the one presented with dots in Fig. 1, starting with a logical model for that new paradigm and a M2M transformation from the GDM. This new logical model could then be employed in M2T transformations to target concrete key-value technologies. We consider that the modularity and extensibility offered by Mortadelo would favour cohesion and reuse of existent components, such as logical models and transformation rules.

Next sections detail the GDM metamodel and describe concrete examples of the transformation process for column family and document-based stores.

2.2   Generic Data Model (GDM)

As mentioned in the previous section, we use instances of the *Generic Data Model (GDM)* as input for Mortadelo. Figure 2 shows the GDM metamodel. This metamodel contains both the *Structure Model* and the *Access Queries* elements, which are described below.

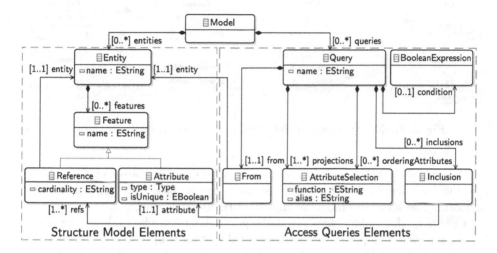

Fig. 2. Fragment of the Generic Data Model metamodel.

The *Structure Model* (Fig. 2, left) is defined in a UML-like fashion. This is a well-known notation both in the modeling and database research areas, which presents adequate for the specification of the structure of domain data. Moreover, it is independent of any database technology, which is one of the requirements of the presented process. The data structure is defined by the specification of *entities*. These entities contain *features* of two kinds: (i) primitive *attributes* which store values of a certain type, and (ii) *references* to other related entities. The references of an entity can have variable cardinality, e.g., 1, 2, 4 or unlimited.

The *Access Queries* (Fig. 2, right) represent the requests that are going to be performed over the database. These queries are defined in the GDM over entities from the structure model. Queries are defined through a SQL-like structure, which facilitates their later specification with a textual notation. A *Query* is executed over a main entity, captured by a *From* element. Any reference from that entity can be included in the query through an *Inclusion* element. Inclusions work in the same way as a conventional join of a relational SQL query. In addition, entities referenced by those that have been included previously can also be included, i.e., inclusions can be recursively added as long as there are references available. The set of projection attributes that are retrieved by the query is specified as a list of *AttributeSelection* elements. This list can contain attributes coming from the *From* or the *Inclusion* entities. The *condition* of a query is captured with a *BooleanExpression*, which allows to declare any desired restrictions. The notation for boolean expressions is not shown in this article for the sake of simplicity and brevity, as this syntax is probably known by the reader. Finally, ordering can be specified through a set of *AttributeSelections*, again coming from the entities selected by the *From* and *Inclusion* elements.

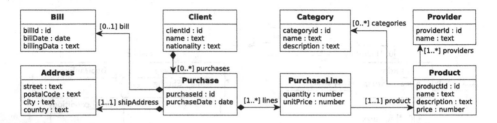

Fig. 3. GDM's Structure Model of the e-commerce platform example.

We now show a concrete instantiation of the GDM metamodel through an example. We have selected a database that stores data from an e-commerce platform. The structure model of this platform is shown in Fig. 3.

Clients of this online shop can make purchases of products. Each *Purchase* has an associated shipping *Address* and a *Bill*, which is optional. A *Product* can belong to different *Categories*, and it can be purchased from different *Providers*. The *PurchaseLine* entity allows to include different products in the same purchase.

```
01 query Q3_productsByCategory:
02   select prod.name, prod.description, prod.price, cat.name
03   from Product as prod
04   including prod.categories as cat
05   where cat.name = "?"
06   order by prod.price
```

Fig. 4. Example of a GDM access query over entities of the structure model.

Continuing with the GDM instance definition, in Fig. 4 an example of how an access query from our GDM can be textually specified is shown. This query retrieves all products of a given category ordered by their prices. The instantiation of the query in the GDM would be as follows. The *From* entity would be Product (line 3), and an *Inclusion* is defined to add the *Category* entity through the *categories* reference (line 4). From these entities, the retrieved attributes are the *name*, *description* and *price* of the products, and the category *name* (line 2). The aliases *prod* and *cat* are employed to simplify the attribute selection. A condition is defined in line 5 through an equality that restricts the shown products to those belonging to a specific category, which is indicated by its name. Lastly, in line 6, an *order by* clause specifies that the products should be ordered by their price.

In this section, we have seen how input databases can be specified by the instantiation of the structure data model and the access queries of the Generic Data Model. GDM specifications do not contain NoSQL details, which allows employing them as input for any NoSQL technology. Next section shows the logical model for column family data stores, and how Mortadelo can perform the transformations that generate a physical implementation of a Cassandra database from a GDM instance.

2.3   Transformations for Column Family-Based Stores

Figure 5 shows the logical metamodel for column family-based stores. Any provided GDM instance model can be automatically transformed with Mortadelo to conform to these metamodel through a model-to-model transformation.

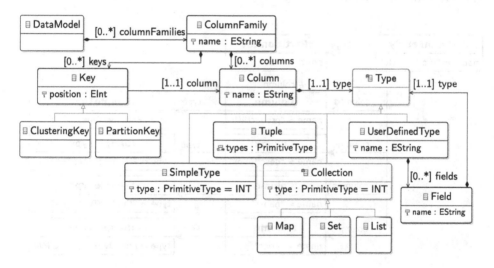

Fig. 5. Metamodel for the logical modeling of column family-based databases.

In this kind of NoSQL databases, information is stored in structures denoted *Column Families (CFs)*, which are collections of rows that contain *Column* values. These rows are uniquely identified by a *key*, which is defined by a selection of columns from the CF. For some CF databases, like Cassandra, the columns that conform are organized in two subsets: (i) the *partition key* and (ii) the *clustering key*. The partition key is used to distribute the data of a CF into different physical nodes or machines. Rows with the same partition key are stored together. The clustering key allows to indicate the physical ordering of the CF rows inside each partition.

In this kind of column family databases, because querying rows from different physical locations would be inefficient, only data from a CF partition can be queried each time, this is, only a concrete value for the partition key can be requested on each query. This provokes that the redundancy of having different CFs storing the same data is not only recommended, but a necessary mechanism in order to query these data with different conditions.

Columns of a CF can have an assigned *type*, which can be *simple*, a *collection* of simple elements, or *user defined*. These last type is a composition of other types that can help to perform data denormalizations, an operation that is common in this kind of data stores.

Continuing with the online shop example presented in the previous section, we could define a CF for the storage of products. In Fig. 6, an instantiation of this CF with the logical metamodel notation is shown. The CF is denoted *ProductById*. It is composed of four simple columns: *productId*, *description*, *name* and *price*. The key is composed of a single column, the *productId*, which acts as the partition key. This means that each partition would contain data of a single product, and that each query would have to specify the productId of the concrete product of interest.

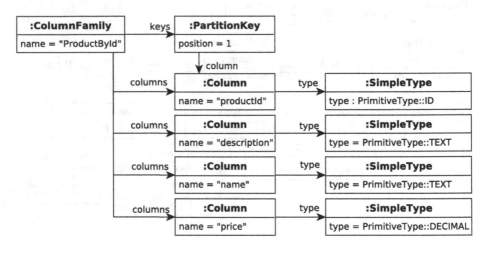

Fig. 6. Example column family from the logical model that stores products data.

Next, we show how Mortadelo can generate a database for Cassandra NoSQL technology, traversing through the column family logical model. The input GDM of this example is composed of the *Structure Model* shown in Fig. 3, while the following queries conform the GDM's *Access Queries*:

Q1 *Products* data, given their *productId*.
Q2 *Products* data, together with the data from their associated *categories*, given the product *name*.
Q3 *Products* data, given their *categories' names*, and ordered by *price*.

Q4 *Purchases* data, with their associated *bills*, given the purchase *year*, and ordered by *purchaseDate*.

Q5 *Purchase* data, with their *purchase lines*, the *client's name* and the *products* data, given the *nationality* of the *client*, and ordered by *purchaseDate*.

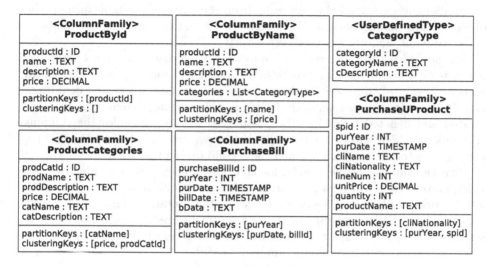

Fig. 7. Logical model of the sample database for column family databases.

Figure 7 shows the logical model generated by our framework when applying a M2M transformation to the provided GDM instance. As instances of logical models can become too verbose if displayed graphically (e.g. all the elements of Fig. 6 only represent a column family), we show the *column families* definition in a more compact format, where CFs are specified with the <ColumnFamily> stereotype, and <UserDefinedType> does the same for user defined types. The complete logical model, which follows the format shown in Fig. 6, can be visualized in the GitHub repository of our tool, Mortadelo[1].

The first query (*Q1*) only requests data from one entity, so a simple transformation rule is applied to generate the *ProductById* column family from Fig. 6 described above. For the query *Q2*, which involves *Product* and *Category* entities, the column family *ProductByName* is created, which contains product and category columns. Given that none of the *Category* columns belongs to the CF key, a user defined type denoted *categoryType* is created, which holds data about categories. Then, the *ProductByName* CF stores the categories of a product as a list of type *categoryType*.

Although query Q3 involves the same entities than Q2, i.e. *Product* and *Category*, in this case the *categories' names* are part of the *partition key*. Moreover, the *products' price* belong to the *clustering key*, in order to introduce ordering.

---

[1] https://github.com/alfonsodelavega/mortadelo

Requiring different keys provokes that a new CF must be created, and this time no user-defined type can be employed. The generated CF is *ProductCategories*, which contains as columns the attributes from both entities, as shown in Fig. 7. Also, given that the two columns used in the query, i.e. category *name* and product *price*, do not guarantee row uniqueness, an extra field denoted *idprodcat* has been added at the end of the *clustering key*.

Similar rules are applied to generate, from the rest of the sample queries, the other column families shown. For details about the complete transformations rules, we remit again to our tool's repository.

We show in Fig. 8 the resulting database implementation for Cassandra, which is obtained by our framework in a code generation step from the logical model. Cassandra offers a SQL-like language for database query and definition, called Cassandra Query Language (CQL). In this language, column families are treated and denoted as *tables*. The *primary key*, which includes the columns that uniquely identifies the *rows*, is divided in two sets of columns: the first set corresponds to the *partition key* and the second one to the *clustering key*.

The current logical metamodel for column families shown in Fig. 5 is also valid, in its current form, for generating code for other databases, like ScyllaDB, which works similarly to Cassandra. However, this metamodel may contain certain concepts that are specific of the Cassandra technology, e.g., the CF keys structure. We plan to abstract these concepts in future iterations, in order to ease the support of other column family data stores.

```
CREATE TABLE ProductById(
productId uuid, name text,
price decimal, description text,
PRIMARY KEY(productid))


CREATE TABLE ProductByName(
productId uuid,
name text,
price decimal,
description text,
categories
  List<frozen <categoryType>>,
PRIMARY KEY((name), price))


CREATE TABLE PurchaseBill(
purchaseBillId uuid,
purYear int, purDate timestamp,
billDate timestamp, bData text,
PRIMARY KEY((purYear),
      purDate, salebillid))
```

```
CREATE TYPE categoryType(
categoryId uuid,
categoryName text,
cdescription text)


CREATE TABLE PurchaseUProduct(
spid uuid, purYear int,
purDate timestamp, cliName text,
cliNationality text, lineNum int,
unitPrice decimal, quantity int,
productName text,
PRIMARY KEY((cliNationality),
      purYear, spid))


CREATE TABLE ProductCategories(
prodCatId uuid, prodName text,
price decimal, prodDescription text,
catName text, catDescription text,
PRIMARY KEY((catName),
      price, prodcatid))
```

Fig. 8. Cassandra CQL implementation of the sample database.

2.4   Towards Transformations for Document-Based Stores

In this section, we show the current state of our work for the generation of document-based data stores. These stores are generally schema-less. However, as the purpose of Mortadelo is the provision of NoSQL designs based on the storage and data access requirements of the end users, this framework generates a set of collections, whose objective is to store documents, along with a proposed structure to which these documents should conform in order to better support the end user needs. The set of collections and their suggested structure for the documents is defined in a logical document data model. Figure 9 shows an example of this model.

As introduced, a document data model is composed of *Collections*, which have a *name* that identifies them. Each collection will be used to store documents. The structure of these documents is captured in a *DocumentType* element. At the moment, collections in Mortadelo are only used to store one kind of document, i.e., they only have one associated instance of *DocumentType*. However, if we later find out that, for some use cases, it is beneficial to store several types of documents in the same collection, the model will be updated accordingly. A *DocumentType* element defines the structure of documents as a collection of *Fields*. These fields can be *Primitive* elements, *Arrays* of elements, or even nested *DocumentTypes* inside the main one. In addition, as some document databases allow defining indexes over these fields to improve performance, we have included this functionality in the metamodel (Fig. 10).

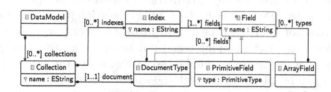

Fig. 9. Metamodel for the logical modeling of document-based stores.

```
{
    productid: 103,
    name: "LCD-IPS Monitor",
    price: 129.99,
    description: "Monitor for PC",
    categories:
        [{name: "Electronics", description: "Electrical Appliances"},
         {name: "Computers", description: "Computer Devices"}]
}
```

Fig. 10. Example of a denormalized collection in MongoDB that answers query *Q2*.

For this kind of databases, the *Access queries* of the GDM can be used to determine whether the logical model must follow a more normalized design, with each collection representing a different entity of the *Structural Model*; or a more de-normalized one, by embedding some entities into another. Figure 9 shows an example of a document that represents a *product* in MongoDB. Each product contains an embedded array to store the data of the *categories* to which it belongs. When following this structure, categories are repeated several times, one for each product belonging to them, which introduces data redundancy in the system. On the other hand, this de-normalization could be useful to make the sample query *Q2* more efficient, since all the required information is contained in a single collection, instead of being necessary to consult several of them (e.g. consulting the categories referenced by a product). We are working in more mechanisms to adapt the provided GDM and transformations to the specificities of document databases.

3   Implementation

We have implemented a prototype of Mortadelo to assess the transformation process presented in the previous section. This implementation has been made available under a free licence in an external repository[2]. Next paragraphs summarize the main components of this repository.

The metamodels presented in Sect. 2 can be found in the corresponding projects of the repository in *Ecore* [23] format. Precisely, the GDM, column family, and document metamodels are included. In addition, the projects also contain the model-to-model and model-to-text specifications that conform the transformation process. Conventionally, M2M transformations are specified through model-to-model languages such as ETL or ATL. These languages are useful when each input element of a certain type is transformed into one or more output elements. However, this strict mapping could not be appropriate when generating NoSQL designs. For instance, it could be the case that two queries of the GDM's *Access Queries* can be answered through the same column family of a Cassandra data store, instead of generating one column family for each query. Therefore, the data structure and access queries have to be treated all at once in the transformation, instead of in a one-by-one basis. For this reason, we decided to employ an imperative language for the M2M transformation process. We selected *Xtend*[3], which is a Java-based language that offers advanced model manipulation capabilities. In the case of M2T transformations, they have been specified with EGL (Epsilon Generation Language) [22].

For the GDM metamodel, a textual Domain-Specific Language (DSL) [18] for the manipulation of GDM instances is also provided. This DSL has been implemented with Xtext [12], which provides a full-featured and easily configurable editor. Figure 11 shows a screenshot, where the online shop case study is manipulated through the DSL editor. The left window shows the syntax of the DSL, which allows to define and validate entities and queries over these entities. On the top right window, the corresponding GDM instance model of the processed

---

[2] https://github.com/alfonsodelavega/mortadelo.
[3] https://www.eclipse.org/xtend/.

Fig. 11. Editor of the provided GDM textual DSL.

"onlineShop.gdm" file is shown. This instance would be the input of Mortadelo's transformation process. Below, in the Properties view, individual details of concrete elements from the model can be consulted, such as the *AttributeSelection* object selected in the figure.

Finally, an examples project is included, which contains the specifications and resulting NoSQL schemas for the online shop running example of this paper.

4 Related Work

As we mentioned in the introduction, well-known practises of the design process of relational databases are not suitable for NoSQL systems because of the differences between them and RDBMSs [3, 21].

There are works in the literature that face the challenge of NoSQL database design. However, because of the heterogeneity present in NoSQL technologies, most of these works limit their efforts to a concrete paradigm, such as column families [8, 21], key-value [19] or graph-based [11] stores. For instance, Mior et al. [21] present NoSE (NoSQL Schema Evaluator), an initially generic tool for obtaining NoSQL schemas. However, this work focuses on column family databases and, as the authors state in their conclusions, "NoSE may require significant changes to fully exploit the capabilities of different data models".

Nonetheless, the lack of generality of these works does not make them unusable for our purposes. As mentioned in Sect. 2.2, one of the steps performed by our framework is the transformation of a generic conceptual model to the logical model of a concrete NoSQL paradigm. So, it is possible to include the described process of individual works for a specific paradigm into Mortadelo, therefore contributing to the homogenisation of these works under the same framework. As an example, for column family databases, we have taken as base transformation rules the ones included in NoSE. Also, we have improved them by overcoming some of their limitations, such as for example the lack of support for User Defined Types and Collections that are useful for the design of certain column families.

Instead of by abstracting the design stage, other approaches bring the generality to the application level by presenting high-level interfaces to access underlying data stores. Authors of [4] present one of these interfaces, denoted as *SOS (Save Our Systems)*, which offers a common data access layer for the interconnection with different NoSQL physical storage systems.

There are two works that require special comments, as their objectives relate to the ones of Mortadelo. In the first one, Herrero et al. [16] present a NoSQL design process for analytical workloads. This process, as the one defined by Mortadelo, is divided in three phases, where a conceptual model is first used as input to obtain a logical model, which later gets instantiated in a physical implementation. One of the main differences with respect to our proposal is that, rather than performing manual steps, we seek to automatically generate the NoSQL schemas from the provided generic data model. However, authors of the mentioned work take into account important factors for the analytical workloads they support, such as data variability. These factors could be included in a future to improve Mortadelo's transformation process.

The second of these works, authored by Atzeni et al. [3], presents NoAM (NoSQL Abstract Metamodel), a design metamodel that does not focus on any particular NoSQL technology but on giving support to all of them. An instance of this metamodel represents a technology-agnostic NoSQL schema through high-level concepts, which have been generalized from the characteristics of existent NoSQL paradigms.

When we started working on Mortadelo, we studied the possibility of using NoAM as the intermediate logical model that is employed in the transformation process, prior to the code-generation step into a concrete NoSQL solution. Nevertheless, we detected that more information than the one contained in NoAM models was necessary to perform the final transformations for some of the NoSQL databases. For instance, in the case of column family data stores like Cassandra, an extra differentiation between partition and clustering keys is necessary for the final instantiation. We compared the overhead of using a combination of NoAM plus this extra information against the definition of logical metamodels for each NoSQL paradigm, and decided than the latter option was simpler in our case. This is why we employ a column family metamodel and a document metamodel in Sect. 2, instead of a single intermediate model such as NoAM. The use of a logical model for each paradigm or family of NoSQL data stores allows Mortadelo to remain agnostic of concrete details of technologies such as Cassandra or MongoDB until it is necessary (i.e. when the code generation templates for concrete systems are executed). Moreover, these logical models can be reused between technologies of the same paradigm, such as MongoDB and CouchDB for document stores.

5 Conclusions and Future Work

This paper has presented Mortadelo, a framework for the generation of NoSQL databases. The main contribution of Mortadelo is that, following a model-driven approach, it can be used to automatically obtain the implementation of a targeted NoSQL database, by using as input a technology-agnostic data structure model that also includes the description of how data are usually accessed. An advantage offered by this framework is its modular structure, which eases the inclusion of support for new database paradigms or technologies.

We have shown how Mortadelo can be used to generate databases for column family data stores, with a full example for the Cassandra database. We have detailed all the steps of the proposed framework for this example: (i) the implementation of a conceptual data model to specify the data structure in a technology-agnostic way; (ii) the development of an intermediate logical meta-model that captures details of column family databases; and (iii) the implementation of a set of rules to automatically transform the data structure model to the logical model, and this logical model to the implementation code in Cassandra. Also, we have established the first steps to extend our framework for the support of document-based databases, like MongoDB or CouchDB.

As an additional contribution, we have implemented an homonymous prototype tool of Mortadelo. The development of this tool is active, and the meta-models and transformations explained throughout the paper are available in the tool's repository.

We are currently working towards offering full support for document-based data stores. As future work, we will study the expansion of the framework to support other kind of NoSQL paradigms, like key-value stores or graph databases. This will also involve researching how to extend the technology-agnostic data structure model in order to take into account other components in the transformation process. After the functionality of Mortadelo has been tested, it is also important to consider the non-functional requirements that usually affect the design of NoSQL data stores. Issues such as scalability, security, consistency, technology/storage restrictions, or workload frequency will be taken into account for future improvements.

Acknowledgements. This work has been partially funded by the Government of Cantabria (Spain) under the doctoral studentship program from the University of Cantabria, and by the Spanish Government under grant TIN2014-56158-C4-2-P (M2C2) and TIN2017-86520-C3-3-R.

References

1. Agrawal, S., Chaudhuri, S., Narasayya, V.: Automated selection of materialized views and indexes in SQL databases. In: 26th Conference on Very Large Data Bases, pp. 496–505 (2000)
2. Alur, N.: IBM Infosphere Datastage Data Flow and Job Design. Vervante (2008)

3. Atzeni, P., Bugiotti, F., et al.: Data Modeling in the NoSQL World. Comput. Stand. Interfaces (2016)
4. Atzeni, P., Bugiotti, F., Rossi, L.: Uniform access to NoSQL systems. Inf. Syst. **43**, 117–133 (2014)
5. Carpenter, J., Hewitt, E.: Cassandra: The Definitive Guide: Distributed Data at Web Scale. O'Reilly, Modesto (2016)
6. Cattell, R.: Scalable SQL and NoSQL Data Stores. SIGMOD Records **39**(4), 12–27 (2011)
7. Chandra, D.G.: BASE analysis of NoSQL database. Futur. Gener. Comput. Syst. **52**, 13–21 (2015)
8. Chebotko, A., Kashlev, A., Lu, S.: A big data modeling methodology for apache Cassandra. In: International Congress on Big Data, pp. 238–245. IEEE (2015)
9. Chen, P.P.S.: The entity relationship model – toward a unified view of data. ACM Trans. Database Syst. **1**(1), 9–36 (1976)
10. Chodorow, K.: MongoDB: The Definitive Guide: Powerful and Scalable Data Storage. O'Reilly Media, Sebastopol (2013)
11. Daniel, G., Sunyé, G., Cabot, J.: UMLtoGraphDB: mapping conceptual schemas to graph databases. In: Comyn-Wattiau, I., Tanaka, K., Song, I.-Y., Yamamoto, S., Saeki, M. (eds.) ER 2016. LNCS, vol. 9974, pp. 430–444. Springer, Cham (2016). https://doi.org/10.1007/978-3-319-46397-1_33
12. Eysholdt, M., Behrens, H.: Xtext: implement your language faster than the quick and dirty way. In: 25th Annual Conference on Object-Oriented Programming, Systems, Languages, and Applications, pp. 307–309 (2010)
13. Gessert, F.: NoSQL database systems: a survey and decision guidance. Comput. Sci. Res. Dev. **32**(3), 353–365 (2017)
14. Haerder, T., Reuter, A.: Principles of transaction-oriented database recovery. ACM Comput. Surv. **15**, 287–317 (1983)
15. Hecht, R., Jablonski, S.: NoSQL evaluation: a use case oriented survey. In: International Conference on Cloud and Service Computing (CSC), pp. 336–341. IEEE (2011)
16. Herrero, V., Abelló, A., Romero, O.: NOSQL design for analytical workloads: variability matters. In: Comyn-Wattiau, I., Tanaka, K., Song, I.-Y., Yamamoto, S., Saeki, M. (eds.) ER 2016. LNCS, vol. 9974, pp. 50–64. Springer, Cham (2016). https://doi.org/10.1007/978-3-319-46397-1_4
17. Hills, T.: NoSQL and SQL Data Modeling: Bringing Together Data, Semantics, and Software. Technics Publications, Basking Ridge (2016)
18. Kleppe, A.: Software Language Engineering: Creating Domain-Specific Languages Using Metamodels. Addison-Wesley Professional, Upper Saddle River (2008)
19. Li, C.: Transforming relational database into HBase: a case study. In: IEEE International Conference on Software Engineering and Service Sciences. pp. 683–687, July 2010
20. Li, L., Zhao, X.: UML specification and relational database. J. Object Technol. **2**(5), 87–100 (2003)
21. Mior, M.J., Salem, K.: NoSE: schema design for NoSQL applications. IEEE Trans. Knowl. Data Eng. **29**(10), 2275–2289 (2017)
22. Rose, L.M., Paige, R.F., Kolovos, D.S., Polack, F.A.C.: The epsilon generation language. In: Schieferdecker, I., Hartman, A. (eds.) ECMDA-FA 2008. LNCS, vol. 5095, pp. 1–16. Springer, Heidelberg (2008). https://doi.org/10.1007/978-3-540-69100-6_1
23. Steinberg, D., Budinsky, F., Paternostro, M., Merks, E.: EMF: Eclipse Modeling Framework, 2nd edn. Addison-Wesley Professional, Reading (2009)

24. Vajk, T., Fehr, P., et al.: Denormalizing data into schema-free databases. In: 4th International Conference on Cognitive Infocommunications, pp. 747–752. IEEE (2013)
25. Walker, S.J.: Big data: a revolution that will transform how we live, work, and think. Int. J. Advert. **33**(1), 181–183 (2014)

Towards OntoUML for Software Engineering: Experimental Evaluation of Exclusivity Constraints in Relational Databases

Zdeněk Rybola[✉] and Michal Valenta

Faculty of Information Technology, Czech Technical University in Prague,
Prague, Czech Republic
{zdenek.rybola,michal.valenta}@fit.cvut.cz
http://ccmi.fit.cvut.cz

Abstract. Model-driven development approach to software engineering requires precise models defining as much of the system as possible. OntoUML is a conceptual modelling language based on Unified Foundational Ontology, which provides constructs to create ontologically well-founded and precise conceptual models. In the approach we utilize, OntoUML is used for making conceptual models of software application data and this model is then transformed into its proper realization in a relational database. In these transformations, the implicit constraints defined by various OntoUML universal types and relations are realized by database views and triggers. In this paper, we specifically discuss the realization of *phase partitions* of *Phase* types from the OntoUML model by *exclusive associations* and provide an experimental evaluation of this approach.

Keywords: MDD · Transformation · OntoUML
Relational database · Exclusivity constraints · Evaluation

1 Introduction

Software engineering is a demanding discipline that deals with complex systems [6]. The goal of software engineering is to ensure high-quality software implementation of these complex systems. To achieve this, various software development approaches have been formulated. One of these approaches is the Model-Driven Development (MDD), which is based on elaborating models and transformations between them [12].

To ensure high quality of a software system, high-quality expressive conceptual models are necessary to define all requirements and constraints for the system [6]. As OntoUML is based on Unified Foundational Ontology (UFO), it is domain-agnostic and it provides mechanisms to create ontologically well-founded conceptual models [7], it qualifies for creating precise conceptual models of application data. However, it should hold for the MDD transformations that more

© Springer Nature Switzerland AG 2018
E. H. Abdelwahed et al. (Eds.): MEDI 2018, LNCS 11163, pp. 58–73, 2018.
https://doi.org/10.1007/978-3-030-00856-7_4

specific models preserve the constraints defined in the more abstract models [7]. Therefore, it is necessary to transform such OntoUML model into its realization properly, without losing the implicit constraints OntoUML introduces.

This paper is part of a series, where the usage of OntoUML for Software Engineering is investigated. As conceptual data modelling is the most popular part of the MDD approach and the relational database management systems (RDBMSs) are still the most popular type of data storage[1], we focus primarily on the proper realization of the OntoUML conceptual models in relational databases (see, e.g., [17] for the introduction to our approach, or [18,19] for the transformation of anti-rigid and rigid Sortals, respectively). In this paper, we discuss explicitly the transformation of the *phase partitions* from an OntoUML model into its proper realization in the RDBMS by means of *exclusive associations* as proposed in [18] and we justify the approach by an experimental evaluation.

The structure of the paper is as follows: in Sect. 2, the background to our approach is presented; in Sect. 3, the gradual transformation of the *phase partitions* is presented; in Sect. 4, the experiments justifying our approach are presented; and finally, in Sect. 5, the conclusion of the paper results is provided.

2   Background

In this section, we outline the background and related work to our paper.

2.1   OntoUML

OntoUML is a conceptual modelling language focused on building ontologically well-founded models. It was formulated in Guizzardi's PhD Thesis [7] as a lightweight extension of UML based on UML profiles. The language is based on *Unified Foundational Ontology* (UFO) [9], which is in turn based on cognitive science and modal logic. Thanks to this fact, it provides expressive and precise constructs for modellers to capture the domain of interest.

UFO and OntoUML address many problems in conceptual modelling, such as the distinction between universals and individuals, the identity principle and the rigidity of properties [7], the concept of roles [10] or part-whole relations [8].

2.2   Our Approach

As OntoUML is based on UFO and supports creation of ontologically well-founded models, it seems to be well-suited for creating precise conceptual models. Such model can be also used for modelling conceptual data models of the developed application, defining various constraints and restrictions for the domain objects simply by specifying the appropriate universal and relation types (Kinds,

---

[1] According to the ranking published on https://db-engines.com/en/ranking in February 2018, 7 of 10 most popular DBMSs are relational.

Subkinds, Roles, Phases, etc.). The principles of OntoUML also guide the modeller to think about many important aspects of the domain objects like their identity, rigidity and dependencies (both existential and relational). However, in order to use such conceptual models in the MDD approach, these models must be transformed into their realizations in such a way, that the implicit constraints defined by the individual universal and relation types used in the OntoUML model are not lost.

In [17], an approach to the transformation of such conceptual data models in OntoUML into their proper realization in a relational database was introduced. In this approach, the transformation is divided into three consecutive steps:

1. transformation of the initial OntoUML conceptual model (OntoUML PIM) into a UML platform-independent model (UML PIM),
2. transformation of the resulting UML PIM into a relational platform-specific model (RDB PSM),
3. and finally the transformation of the resulting RDB PSM into an implementation-specific model consisting of SQL DDL scripts (SQL ISM).

In the first step, the initial OntoUML PIM with various universal and relation types is transformed into a pure UML PIM consisting of standard UML classes and relations. Since OntoUML applies certain constraints to the types based on the kind of universal represented by each particular type, these constraints are carried over to the other consecutive models by utilizing OCL constraints, where it is not possible to express them by the means of the well-known UML Class diagram notation.

In the second step, the resulting UML PIM with the constraints derived from the initial OntoUML PIM is transformed into an RDB PSM consisting of the definitions of tables, references and FOREIGN KEY constraints. Additional OCL constraints are derived to define the constraints that cannot be defined by the standard means of a relational schema.

In the final step, the resulting RDB PSM from the previous step is transformed into an SQL ISM, which consists of the SQL DDL scripts. We also deal with the proper realization of the OCL constraints derived in the previous steps to preserve the semantics of the model in the database and prevent creating and querying data violating the constraints.

Although the transformation could be done in a single step, i.e., by generating the SQL DDL scripts directly from the OntoUML model, our approach brings several advantages. First, the existing know-how for the transformation of UML models into relational databases may be utilized (see, e.g., [11,20]), as well as the existing tools supporting this transformation (e.g., Enterprise Architect[2], which we use for the diagrams in this paper). Second, the first step of the transformation may be used as a part of the transformation into any other platform, such as a pure object model of Smalltalk, an object-oriented data model of EJB[3], etc.

---

[2] Enterprise Architect is a popular commercial CASE tool used for creating models, http://www.sparxsystems.com.au/products/ea/index.html.

[3] Enterprise Java Beans, http://www.oracle.com/technetwork/java/javaee/ejb/index. html.

And, finally, after each of the transformation steps, the resulting model may be analysed and refactored, in order to optimize the model, simplify it and remove redundancies and duplicities.

2.3 Related Work

In the past, various approaches like the OO-Method [15], Model-Driven Architecture [13] or Model-Driven Development in general [12] have been developed to overcome the distinction between the conceptual and solution models by precisely defined transformations.

In our approach, we utilize OntoUML for the conceptual modelling. The idea of similar approach was introduced already in [3], where the author proposes a transformation of an OntoUML conceptual model into an object-oriented implementation model in UML. Similar approach is also presented in [16]. There are also other works dealing with the transformation of OntoUML into other languages, such as Alloy [2] and OWL [23].

Regarding the transformation of the UML PIM into a relational database, it is a well-known process documented for instance in [11]. However, in order to realize the original OntoUML PIM properly, it is necessary to properly transform and realize also the OCL constraints derived from the universal and relation types used in the OntoUML conceptual model, as well as other constraints such as special multiplicities of associations or meta-properties *isDisjoint* and *isCovering* of the generalization sets, which are usually ignored by the documented transformations. In our approach, we focus on the proper realization of these constraints.

In [20], an approach for the realization of special multiplicity constraints in a relational database was proposed. The approach was inspired by DresdenOCL Toolkit[4], where OCL constraints are transformed into database views querying data violating the constraints. It was also inspired by the realization of inverse referential integrity constraints used in IIS*Case tool [1]. In our approach, we build up on these approaches and use the views and triggers for the realization of the OntoUML constraints.

There are also several other approaches for the realization of OCL constraints in a relational database. In [14], the authors present their approach to checking constraints by incremental SQL queries that select the violating data. In [22], the author describes an extension plugin for Enterprise Architect that generates the SQL code realizing OCL constraints. His approach is based on translating OCL expressions into SQL queries and realizing the constraints by database functions used to detect the constraint violation. Another related work can be found in [5], where the authors transform OCL constraints into stored procedures. In contrast to them, we focus on enforcing the constraints directly for any DML operations by using triggers to minimize the special handling by the application using the database.

---

[4] https://github.com/dresden-ocl/dresdenocl.

3   Transformation of Phase Partitions

In this section, the transformation of the *Phase* univerals and their partitions defined in the OntoUML PIM as proposed in [18] is explained in detail. For creating the illustrating diagrams, we use the mentioned Enterprise Architect case tool.

3.1   OntoUML PIM

As discussed in [7], the backbone of the whole OntoUML model is formed by the *Kind* universals and their specializing *Subkind* universals, which define the types of individuals with unique identity principles. While *Kinds* define a new unique identity principles and provide it to their instances, the *Subkinds* inherit the basic identity principle from their rigid ancestor (another *Kind* or *Subkind*) and extend it, providing this extended identity principle to their instances. Therefore, being an instance of a *Subkind* type automatically means the individual is also an instance of the supertype with all its properties. Moreover, as both *Kinds* and *Subkinds* are rigid, the identity of an individual provided by one of them cannot change in the individual's lifetime.

In contrast to *Kinds* and *Subkinds*, *Phase* universals are anti-rigid [7], and thus the individuals can change the fact of being its instance. Still, all instances of a *Phase* type must follow the same identity principle. This means, that each instance of a *Phase* type must also be an instance of a rigid sortal type defining the identity principle (called *identity bearer* in this paper) - for instance, an *available copy* is a *copy*, which is in the state of being available. This fact is modelled by the generalization relation between the *Phase* types and the *identity bearer* type. Moreover, the *Phase* types always form *phase partitions* – {disjoint,complete} generalization sets of the *identity bearer* type. Thanks to the *completeness* and *disjointness*, each instance of the *identity bearer* type must always be an instance of exactly one of the *Phase* types, but thanks to the anti-rigidity, the instance of the *Phase* type can change in time. Because of these properties of *Phases*, they are used to model all the possible states or stages of instances of certain type, defining the properties and relations of such an instance in each particular phase.

In Fig. 1, an example of a PIM of the book copies in a library organization is shown using the OntoUML notation. The information about the availability of the particular book copy is represented by the *Phase* types Available, Borrowed and Discarded, which define the only possible states of each copy.

3.2   Transformation of OntoUML PIM into UML PIM

Both *Kind* and *Subkind* universals are rigid. Therefore, when transforming an OntoUML PIM into the UML PIM, each *Kind* and *Subkind* type can be simply transformed into a standard UML class in the UML PIM. Also, the generalization sets of the *Subkind* types can be realized by standard UML generalization sets with the same meta-properties *isDisjoint* and *isCovering* [19].

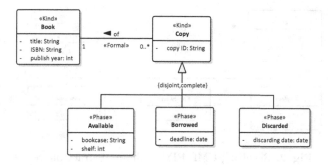

Fig. 1. PIM of the availability of book copies in a library modelled using the OntoUML notation

Similar to the *Kind* and *Subkind* types, the *Phase* types from the OntoUML PIM can also be transformed into standard UML classes in the UML PIM. However, as the *Phases* are anti-rigid, the generalization relation between the *Phase* types and their *identity bearer* type cannot be transformed into standard UML generalization, which is always rigid. Instead, this relation must be transformed into an association to allow the changes of related *Phase* instances to any *identity bearer* instance [18]. Moreover, as the *Phase* types form the *phase partitions*, they must be treated together to correctly preserve the *disjointness* and *completeness* of the partition.

According to the approach presented in [18], there are two general ways to realize a *phase partition* in the UML PIM: *abstract phase* and *exclusive associations*.

Abstract Phase. A new artificial *abstract phase* class is generated. This class is related by mandatory one-to-one association with the transformed *identity bearer* class. Additionally, the *abstract phase* class is specialized by the {`disjoint,complete`} generalization set of the transformed *phase* classes. Together, the mandatory association enforces the mandatory variable relation between the *identity bearer* and its *phase*, while the generalization set specifies the possible states [18]. The resulting UML PIM created by applying this approach to the OntoUML PIM shown in Fig. 1 is shown in Fig. 2.

This approach is in accordance to the Open-Closed Principle (OCP) [4], however, it introduces an additional concept not existing in the original domain. Moreover, as discussed in [18], the realization of the abstract *phase* class and its generalization set leads into more complicated model of referencing tables (also, the generalization set meta-properties should be properly realized!). After certain optimizations discussed for instance in [21], the transformation results in almost the same model as in the case of the approach based on *exclusive associations*. As this paper focuses on the realization by *exclusive associations*, the reader is kindly referred to [18] for more details about this realization.

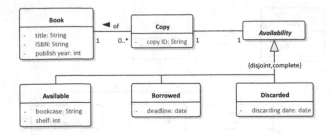

Fig. 2. Resulting UML PIM with an abstract phase

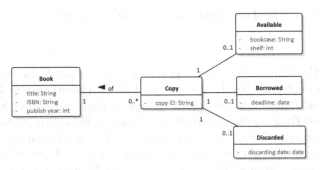

Fig. 3. Resulting UML PIM with exclusive phases

Exclusive Associations. Following this approach, the *phase partition* is transformed into a set of one-to-one associations between the *identity bearer*'s class and the individual transformed *phase* classes. The associations are mandatory on the side of the *identity bearer* class, but they are optional on the side of the related *phase* classes. Additionally, to maintain the exclusivity defined by the {complete, disjoint} *phase partition*, a special *exclusivity constraint* must be defined for this set of relations, checking that exactly one of the relations exists between the instances [18]. In our approach, we use OCL invariants for defining such constraints that cannot be defined directly in the UML diagrams. The resulting UML PIM created by applying this approach to the OntoUML PIM shown in Fig. 1 is shown in Fig. 3 and the required *exclusivity constraint* is shown in Constraint 1.

With this realization, there is no abstract concept with no reflection in the reality as it is in the case of the *abstract phase* approach. Also, although not following the OCP, it is absolutely viable model on the conceptual level, which the UML PIM in our approach is. Moreover, the realization is much simpler on

---

Constraint 1 OCL invariant for the exclusivity constraint in UML PIM

---

context c : Copy **inv** Copy_Availability :
c . available ◇OclVoid XOR c . borrowed◇OclVoid XOR c . discarded◇OclVoid

---

the PSM level as discussed below. The remaining of the paper further discusses only the transformation based on the *exclusive associations* approach.

3.3 Transformation of UML PIM into RDB PSM

In the second step of the transformation, the resulting UML PIM is transformed into the RDB PSM. During this transformation, the classes with attributes are transformed into tables with columns (in the examples in this paper, we use Oracle as the target DBMS, therefore we use the Oracle data types) and the associations between the classes are transformed into the references restricted by the FOREIGN KEY constraints [17].

According to this approach, the *phase partition* realized by the *exclusive associations* can be transformed very easily into exclusive references. According to the multiplicities of the associations, the references are created in the tables representing the individual *phase* classes, referencing records in the *identity bearer* table [20]. The example of the transformed UML PIM shown in Fig. 3 is shown in Fig. 4.

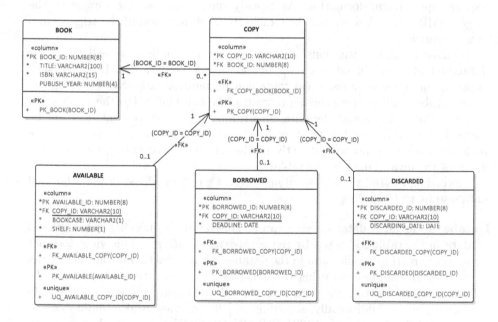

Fig. 4. Resulting RDB PSM with exclusive references

The only complication lies in the realization of the *exclusivity constraint* for the associations between the individual *Phase* classes and their *identity bearer* class. The OCL constraint defined in context of the *identity bearer* class is transformed into an equivalent OCL constraint defined in the context of the *identity bearer* table and the references from the other *Phase* tables. An example of the transformed OCL constraint shown in Constraint 1 is shown in Constraint 2.

Constraint 2 OCL invariant for the exclusivity constraint in RDB PSM

```
context COPY inv Copy_Availability:
def Available_Instance: Boolean =
  AVAILABLE. allInstances()->exists(a|a.COPY_ID = self.COPY_ID)
def Borrowed_Instance: Boolean =
  BORROWED. allInstances()->exists(b|b.COPY_ID = self.COPY_ID)
def Discarded_Instance: Boolean =
  DISCARDED. allInstances()->exists(d|d.COPY_ID = self.COPY_ID)

Available_Instance XOR Borrowed_Instance XOR Discarded_Instance
```

3.4 Transformation of RDB PSM into SQL ISM

The last step of the transformation consists of generating SQL DDL scripts for creating all the elements defined in the RDB PSM. For each table, a CREATE TABLE statement is generated, including all its columns, UNIQUE, PRIMARY KEY and FOREIGN KEY constraints. However, the additional OCL constraints defining the exclusivity of the references realizing the original *phase partition* requires special transformation. As already mentioned, we use Oracle as the target DMBS, therefore we use the Oracle PL/SQL notation of the triggers and other constructs.

In most common situations, such constraint is usually not realized in the database and it is enforced by the application using the database. However, such approach brings several risks: (a) there can be multiple applications using the same database, all of them having to realize the constraint; (b) the application may not fully understand the data constraints; (c) the constraint may not be correctly realized, allowing to store invalid data. Therefore, we focus on the realization of the constraint directly in the database, preventing creation and usage of the invalid data in the tables.

According to [18], the *exclusivity constraint* can be realized in the relational database by the following constructs:

Database views. A database view can be generated for querying only the valid data in the table restricted by the *exclusivity constraint*. This view does not prevent creating invalid data in the database, but hides them from the queries used by the application using the database. Moreover, the view can also be joined when selecting the data from the related tables representing the individual *phases*. Additionally, according to [19], the view is also updatable and can be defined with the WITH CHECK OPTION clause. Such a view can be then used for DML operations on the table while checking the updated data to meet the condition of the view. The example of such a view for the constraint shown in Constraint 2 is shown in SQL 1.

Still, the *exclusivity constraint* can be violated by DML operations on the *Phase* tables, and thus the view can reliable be used only for the queries. Moreover, the views are not mandatory and the original tables can still be used in the queries to access even the invalid data. Therefore the application must use them explicitly.

Even when using the view just for querying the data, it results in slowing down the query operations, as the constraint condition is checked to filter out all invalid records. Therefore, we present the experiments evaluating the efficiency of the queries with and without such a view in Section 4.

CHECK constraint. According to the specification of SQL:1999, a CHECK constraint might be used to restrict the possible PK values in the *identity bearer* table to values correctly referenced from exactly one *Phase* table. However, as the body of the CHECK constraint would be based on selecting data from multiple tables, it cannot be really used in practice, because the contemporary database engines do not support subqueries in CHECK constraints.

Triggers. Triggers can be used to perform complex data validations and manipulations when various DML operations are performed on a table. Thanks to that, a set of triggers can be generated to check all the operations that can cause violation of the *exclusivity constraint*. In total, the following situations can cause the violation:

S1 Inserting a new record into the *identity bearer* table without referencing records in exactly one of the exclusively related *phase* tables.

S2 Updating a record in the *identity bearer* table and changing its PRIMARY KEY value to a value, which is not referenced from exactly one of the exclusively related *phase* tables. However, as changing the PRIMARY KEY value constitutes the change of the identity of the instance, such operation should not be allowed at all and we do not check it in regards with the *exclusivity constraint*.

S3 Inserting a new record into some of the exclusively related *phase* tables, referencing a record referenced from another of the exclusively related tables (thus making it referenced by records in multiple tables).

S4 Updating a record in one of the exclusively related *phase* tables and changing its reference value referencing a record in the constrained *identity bearer* table. However, as the referenced *identity bearer* instance defines the identity of the *phase* instance and the identity should be always immutable, this operation should not be allowed at all and we do not check it in regards with the *exclusivity constraint*.

S5 Deleting the last record from the exclusively related *phase* table, which is referencing an existing record in the constrained *identity bearer* table (thus making it referenced by no related record).

The situation S1 can be checked by a trigger defined on the *identity bearer* table for the INSERT operation. The trigger needs to check, that for the inserted record, there is a referencing record in exactly one of the exclusively related *phase* tables. As the trigger is based on the new value of the affected record, it should be executed before each such DML operation and throw an application error, if the checked constraint is violated. The example of such trigger for the constraint shown in Constraint 2 is shown in SQL 2.

To allow the correct insertion of the referencing record into the particular *phase* table before inserting the referenced record into the *identity bearer* table, the FOREIGN KEY constraint of this reference must be defined as

---

SQL 1 Updatable view definition for the exclusivity constraint in SQL ISM

```
CREATE OR REPLACE VIEW COPY_VALID AS
SELECT * FROM COPY c WHERE (
(EXISTS (SELECT 1 FROM AVAILABLE a WHERE a.COPY_ID = c.COPY_ID)
   AND NOT EXISTS (SELECT 1 FROM BORROWED b WHERE b.COPY_ID = c.COPY_ID)
   AND NOT EXISTS (SELECT 1 FROM DISCARDED d WHERE d.COPY_ID = c.COPY_ID))
 OR (NOT EXISTS (SELECT 1 FROM AVAILABLE a WHERE a.COPY_ID = c.COPY_ID)
   AND EXISTS (SELECT 1 FROM BORROWED b WHERE b.COPY_ID = c.COPY_ID)
   AND NOT EXISTS (SELECT 1 FROM DISCARDED d WHERE d.COPY_ID = c.COPY_ID))
 OR (NOT EXISTS (SELECT 1 FROM AVAILABLE a WHERE a.COPY_ID = c.COPY_ID)
   AND NOT EXISTS (SELECT 1 FROM BORROWED b WHERE b.COPY_ID = c.COPY_ID)
   AND EXISTS (SELECT 1 FROM DISCARDED d WHERE d.COPY_ID = c.COPY_ID)))
WITH CHECK OPTION;
```

DEFERRABLE. Then, the reference value is checked at the end of the transaction, and thus the referencing *phase* record can be inserted first, then the *identity bearer* record is inserted and checked by the trigger, and at the end of the transaction, the reference is checked by the deferred FOREIGN KEY constraint.

Similarly, the situation S3 can be checked by a trigger defined on each of the exclusively related *phase* tables for the INSERT operation. These triggers need to check, that for the inserted record, there is no record in the other exclusively related *phase* tables with the same reference value. As the trigger is based on the new value of the affected record, it should be executed before each such DML operation and throw an application error, if the checked constraint is violated. The example of such trigger for the constraint shown in Constraint 2 and the **AVAILABLE** table is shown in SQL 3. Similar triggers should be also defined for the other *phase* tables.

The situation S5 cannot be actually checked by a trigger. The reason is that it is necessary to allow the change of the *phase* for any *identity bearer* instance. Because of the trigger checking the situation S3, the new *phase* record cannot be inserted while the old *phase* record exists. Therefore, it is necessary to first delete the old *phase* record, violating the *exclusivity constraint* as described in situation S5, and then insert the new *phase* record making the data valid again. As the triggers cannot be executed for a set of DML operations on different tables at once, this *change of phases* cannot be checked using triggers. Therefore, the DELETE operation must be allowed and the view should be always used for ensuring the query of only the valid data, hiding the data eventually violated by this operation (situation S5).

Beside the views and triggers, there are also other options: (a) stored procedures and functions manipulating with data in multiple tables at the same time (e.g., removing one phase record and creating a different phase record); (b) instead of triggers; or (c) cascading operations (e.g., deleting any phase record upon deleting the identity bearer record). However, such solutions require the application to use special database constructs. Moreover, the procedures and functions are dependent on the exact structure of the tables and any extension requires update of the procedures as well as the application using them. There-

SQL 2 Trigger definition for checking the exclusivity constraint in situation S1

```
CREATE TRIGGER EX_COPY_AVAILABILITY
BEFORE INSERT ON COPY FOR EACH ROW
DECLARE
 l_count NUMBER;
BEGIN
 SELECT COUNT(1) INTO l_count FROM DUAL WHERE (
  (EXISTS (SELECT 1 FROM AVAILABLE a WHERE a.COPY_ID = :new.COPY_ID)
   AND NOT EXISTS
    (SELECT 1 FROM BORROWED b WHERE b.COPY_ID = :new.COPY_ID)
   AND NOT EXISTS
    (SELECT 1 FROM DISCARDED d WHERE d.COPY_ID = :new.COPY_ID))
  OR (NOT EXISTS
    (SELECT 1 FROM AVAILABLE a WHERE a.COPY_ID = :new.COPY_ID)
   AND EXISTS (SELECT 1 FROM BORROWED b WHERE b.COPY_ID = :new.COPY_ID)
   AND NOT EXISTS
    (SELECT 1 FROM DISCARDED d WHERE d.COPY_ID = :new.COPY_ID))
  OR (NOT EXISTS
    (SELECT 1 FROM AVAILABLE a WHERE a.COPY_ID = :new.COPY_ID)
   AND NOT EXISTS
    (SELECT 1 FROM BORROWED b WHERE b.COPY_ID = :new.COPY_ID)
   AND EXISTS (SELECT 1 FROM DISCARDED d WHERE d.COPY_ID = :new.COPY_ID)
 ));

 IF l_count = 0 THEN raise_application_error
  (-20101, 'OCL constraint EX_Copy_Availability violated!');
 END IF;
END;
```

fore, our goal is to let the application manipulate the data without any special care, using standard SQL DML statements and queries.

4 Experiments

In order to justify our approach to the realization of the *exclusivity constraints*, we made a series of experiments. The goal of these experiments is to prove, that although the realization of the constraints in the database slows down some of the DML or query operations, this slowdown is not substantial. On the other hand, this slowdown is paid off by increasing the database consistency and preventing invalid data usage.

The whole experiment was performed on a dedicated database server (a virtual managed by WMware) used for courses of database systems on our faculty (4 Intel Xeon E5-2630 CPUs with x86_64 architecture, 2.3 GHz, 8 GB of RAM, CentOS Linux 7 operating system). On the server, Oracle 12c DBMS runs. The database buffer cache size of the Oracle instance is approximately 500 MB, the whole SGA (Shared Global Area) consumes approximately 2 GB.

The experiments were executed under a specially created user with unlimited profile settings. The user had its own tablespace on a common filesystem. Data generators and measurements are written in the form of PL/SQL procedures. It guarantees that all the code runs on the server and hence the whole measurement is client independent. We used built-in and Oracle-recommended procedure dbms_utility.get_time for the time measurement and dbms_random

SQL 3 Trigger definition for checking the exclusivity constraint in situation S2

```
CREATE TRIGGER EX_COPY_AVAILAB_AVAIL_INS
BEFORE INSERT ON AVAILABLE FOR EACH ROW
DECLARE
  l_count NUMBER;
BEGIN
  SELECT COUNT(1) INTO l_count FROM DUAL WHERE (
    (EXISTS (SELECT 1 FROM BORROWED b WHERE b.COPY_ID = :new.COPY_ID)
    OR EXISTS (SELECT 1 FROM DISCARDED d WHERE d.COPY_ID = :new.COPY_ID)
  ));

  IF l_count > 0 THEN raise_application_error
    (-20101, 'OCL constraint EX_Copy_Availability violated!');
  END IF;
END;
```

package for the data generation and construction of measurement sets (see bellow).

The experiments were made for the model shown in Fig. 4 with five tables: BOOK, COPY, AVAILABLE, BORROWED, and DISCARDED. We simulated the situation when there are also incorrect data in the tables, i.e., copies without a phase and copies having 2 or 3 phases at the same time. There is a view COPY_VALID (see SQL 1) which presents only the valid copies and there are four triggers (see SQL 2 and SQL 3) to check that the inserting copy and its phase are valid. Let us note, that for the reason of measurements, we had to change the triggers in a way that they do not raise an application error if the constraint is violated, instead they just perform the check and provide a **null** statement instead of the **raise_application_error** statement.

The strategy of the measurement is described in the following sections.

4.1   Generating Data Sets for the Measurements

The testing data of different sizes were generated, containing both valid and invalid data. We chose to generate 85% of valid copies, 5% copies without a phase, 5% copies with two phases, and 5% with three phases. We used a random generator in order to simulate situation when there are different number of copies for a book and also to derive the phases of the copies (available, borrowed, discarded).

The following sizes of the data sets were generated for the individual measurements: 100 k, 500 k, 1 M, 2 M, 4 M, 8 M, and 16 M of COPY records. For the sizes 100 k, 500 k and 1 M, the described generator was used. For the other sizes, the INSERT INTO table SELECT ... FROM table statement was used to multiply the records in the table, because the running time for the generator was too long. Each measurement described below was repeated 30 times, each time with a new randomly generated data set of the same size.

4.2 SELECT Measurement

In this measurement, a set of 100 SELECT statements from the COPY table, each
for a single record selected at random by the COPY_ID value, was measured by the
get_time procedure. In the set, we targeted 90 valid copies, 4 copies without the
state, 3 with two states, and 3 with three states. Let us note, that for each round
of measurements, a new data set was generated. Two variants were measured:

- Querying directly the COPY table: The result contains both valid and invalid
  records. This measurement is labelled COPY in Table 1.
- Querying the view COPY_VALID: The result contains only valid data checked by
  the realized constraint. This measurement is labelled COPY_VALID in Table 1.

4.3 INSERT Measurement

In this measurement, the time for 100 sets of INSERT statements was measured.
In each such set, an INSERT statement for a single copy and variable number
of states were generated, following the same distribution as for the SELECT
measurement (90, 4, 3, 3). Two variants were measured:

- Without the triggers: The operation results in inserting invalid data into the
  tables. This measurement is labelled INSERT in Table 1.
- With the triggers: No invalid data are inserted into the tables. This measurement is labelled INSERT_VALID in Table 1.

4.4 Results of the Experiments

The results of the measurements are shown in Table 1. We can see that the query
time for only the valid copies using the view is approximately 5–6 times slower
than the direct access to the table with possibly invalid data. The slowdown
caused by the triggers checking the constraint during the insert process is really
small, less than 20%.

Table 1. Measurement results.

db size[#copies]	COPY [ms]	COPY_VALID [ms]	INSERT [ms]	INSERT_VALID [ms]
100,000	80	430	170	170
500,000	80	450	150	180
1,000,000	80	440	150	180
2,000,000	80	440	150	190
4,000,000	80	450	160	200
8,000,000	80	450	160	180
16,000,000	80	450	160	180

In both cases, the slowdown is independent of the database size. It may look
strange for the first look, but it is not - in the view and the triggers, the violation

of the constraint is checked by searching for the referencing records by their FK values, which are restricted by a UNIQUE index. Therefore, the DBMS uses this index to find them efficiently using its B*tree structure. As the depth of the index B*tree is 3 even for 16M of records, there is no impact on the time.

However, this result can be applied only to the realization of the *phase partitions*, which are automatically related by *one-to-one* references. In other cases, there would be no UNIQUE indexes and the slowdown would be much bigger unless there is another index structure explicitly defined.

5 Conclusions

In this paper, we discussed the transformation of a *phase partition* of *Phase* types from an OntoUML PIM into its proper realization in a relational database. We specifically discussed the realization by *exclusive associations* in the intermediate UML PIM and its implementation in the actual database using a view and a set of triggers. In order to justify this approach, we made a set of experiments, measuring the times of SELECT and INSERT operations and comparing the times with and without the realization of the *exclusivity constraint*.

As shown by the results of the measurements, the operations are slowed down, however, the absolute slowdown is rather small. On the other hand, the view and the triggers help a lot with the enforcement of the constraint satisfaction by the data and prevents creating and querying invalid data violating the constraint. Therefore, it helps with improving the database consistency in exchange for a small decrease in efficiency.

References

1. Aleksić, S., Ristić, S., Luković, I., Čeliković, M.: A design specification and a server implementation of the inverse referential integrity constraints. Comput. Sci. Inf. Syst. **10**(1) (2013)
2. Benevides, A.B., Guizzardi, G., Braga, B.F.B., Almeida, J.P.A.: Assessing modal aspects of OntoUML conceptual models in alloy. In: Heuser, C.A., Pernul, G. (eds.) ER 2009. LNCS, vol. 5833, pp. 55–64. Springer, Heidelberg (2009). https://doi.org/10.1007/978-3-642-04947-7_8
3. Carraretto, R.: Separating ontological and informational concerns: a model-driven approach for conceptual modeling. Master thesis, Federal University of Espirito Santo (2012)
4. COMPSCI: The Open-Closed Principle. https://www2.cs.duke.edu/courses/fall07/cps108/papers/ocp.pdf (2007)
5. Egea, M., Dania, C.: SQL-PL4OCL: an automatic code generator from OCL to SQL procedural language. Softw. Syst. Model. (2017)
6. Ghezzi, C., Jazayeri, M., Mandrioli, D.: Fundamentals of Software Engineering, 2nd edn. (2002)
7. Guizzardi, G.: Ontological Foundations for Structural Conceptual Models, vol. 015. University of Twente, Enschede (2005)

8. Guizzardi, G.: The problem of transitivity of part-whole relations in conceptual modeling revisited. In: van Eck, P., Gordijn, J., Wieringa, R. (eds.) CAiSE 2009. LNCS, vol. 5565, pp. 94–109. Springer, Heidelberg (2009). https://doi.org/10.1007/978-3-642-02144-2_12

9. Guizzardi, G., Wagner, G.: A unified foundational ontology and some applications of it in business modeling. In: CAiSE Workshops, pp. 129–143 (2004)

10. Guizzardi, G.: Agent roles, qua individuals and *the Counting Problem*. In: Garcia, A., Choren, R., Lucena, C., Giorgini, P., Holvoet, T., Romanovsky, A. (eds.) SELMAS 2005. LNCS, vol. 3914, pp. 143–160. Springer, Heidelberg (2006). https://doi.org/10.1007/11738817_9

11. Kuskorn, W., Lekcharoen, S.: An adaptive translation of class diagram to relational database. In: International Conference on Information and Multimedia Technology, ICIMT 2009, pp. 144–148, December 2009

12. Mellor, S.J., Clark, A.N., Futagami, T.: Model-driven development. IEEE Softw. **20**(5) (2003)

13. OMG: MDA guide revision 2.0, June 2014. http://www.omg.org/cgi-bin/doc?ormsc/14-06-01. Accessed 19 July 2018

14. Oriol, X., Teniente, E.: Incremental checking of OCL constraints through SQL queries. In: Proceedings of the 14th International Workshop on OCL and Textual Modelling, pp. 23–32 (2014)

15. Pastor, O., Gómez, J., Insfrán, E., Pelechano, V.: The OO-Method Approach for Information Systems Modeling: From Object-oriented Conceptual Modeling to Automated Programming. Inf. Syst. **26**(7) (2001)

16. Pergl, R., Sales, T.P., Rybola, Z.: Towards OntoUML for software engineering: from domain ontology to implementation model. In: Cuzzocrea, A., Maabout, S. (eds.) MEDI 2013. LNCS, vol. 8216, pp. 249–263. Springer, Heidelberg (2013). https://doi.org/10.1007/978-3-642-41366-7_21

17. Rybola, Z., Pergl, R.: Towards OntoUML for software engineering: introduction to the transformation of OntoUML into relational databases. In: Pergl, R., Molhanec, M., Babkin, E., Fosso Wamba, S. (eds.) EOMAS 2016. LNBIP, vol. 272, pp. 67–83. Springer, Cham (2016). https://doi.org/10.1007/978-3-319-49454-8_5

18. Rybola, Z., Pergl, R.: Towards OntoUML for software engineering: transformation of anti-rigid sortal types into relational databases. In: Bellatreche, L., Pastor, Ó., Almendros Jiménez, J.M., Aït-Ameur, Y. (eds.) MEDI 2016. LNCS, vol. 9893, pp. 1–15. Springer, Cham (2016). https://doi.org/10.1007/978-3-319-45547-1_1

19. Rybola, Z., Pergl, R.: Towards OntoUML for software engineering: transformation of kinds and subkinds into relational databases. Comput. Sci. Inf. Syst. (2017)

20. Rybola, Z., Richta, K.: Possible realizations of multiplicity constraints. Comput. Sci. Inf. Syst. **10**(4), 1621–1646 (2013)

21. Rybola, Z., Pergl, R.: Towards OntoUML for software engineering: optimizing kinds and subkinds transformed into relational databases. In: Enterprise and Organizational Modeling and Simulation, Tallinn, Estonia, June 2018

22. Sobotka, P.: Transformation from OCL into SQL. Master thesis, Charles University, Prague, Czech Republic, May 2012. https://is.cuni.cz/webapps/zzp/download/120076745

23. Zamborlini, V., Guizzardi, G.: On the representation of temporally changing information in OWL. In: 2010 14th IEEE International Enterprise Distributed Object Computing Conference Workshops (EDOCW), pp. 283–292. IEEE (2010)

Ontology and Model Driven Engineering

Scrum and V Lifecycle Combined with Model-Based Testing and Model Driven Architecture to Deal with Evolutionary System Issues

Imane Essebaa[✉] and Salima Chantit

Computer Science Laboratory of Mohammedia, Faculty of Sciences and
Technologies, Hassan 2 University of Casablanca, Casablanca, Morocco
Imane.essebaa@gmail.com, Salima.chantit@gmail.com

Abstract. Model Driven Engineering (MDE) and Agile Methods (AM) are two
principal domains that are in the way of improvement and evolution in order to
facilitate the realisation of IT projects. However, these areas evolve separately
despite the great number of researches that focus on improving realisation
project' techniques. Thus, our approach aims to provide an approach that
combines two variants of MDE, Model Driven Architecture approach and
Model-Based Testing with the V development lifecycle used in every scrum
Agile Methodology sprint to deal with system evolution. In order to well
illustrate this approach, we apply it on Rental Car Agency System realisation
using Scrum methodology with some requirements' evolution.

Keywords: Model Driven Architecture · Model-Based Testing
V incremental lifecycle · Scrum agile methodology · Model transformations
Test generation · Evolutionary system

1 Introduction

Software Development has become more and more important in different application
domains and evolves in a fast manner. To deal with this issue two main areas were
proposed: MDE and Agile Methodologies.

Model Driven Engineering (MDE) is an Object Management Group (OMG) proposition to deal with this issue. MDE is a paradigm based on the use of models throughout
the life cycle of an application as it enhances every step of software development from
design until code and testing, by defining different variants as Model Driven Architecture
(MDA) which is based on transformations between models of different levels of
abstraction, and Model-Based Testing (MBT) that aims to generate automatically test
cases from Models. The other domain is Agile methodologies that focus on best practices
information programming and their integration in the development process. It is an
approach that defines a disciplined management of software development projects:
Agility recommends iterative and incremental method to develop software systems.

We note that both, MDE and Agile Methodologies (AM) aim to easily manage
frequent requirements changes; AM focus on a methodological aspect that defines the

© Springer Nature Switzerland AG 2018
E. H. Abdelwahed et al. (Eds.): MEDI 2018, LNCS 11163, pp. 77–91, 2018.
https://doi.org/10.1007/978-3-030-00856-7_5

process to develop and test the system while MDE is more concerned by an architectural aspect that aims to automatically generate test cases from requirements models.

Several works have been made on these two domains that allow them to evolve but separately. However, few works have focused on how to combine MDE and Agility, which constitutes the main idea of this paper where we aim to combine MDE with its two variants MDA and MBT inside V development lifecycle that is used to develop all sprints in scrum agile methodology.

This paper is organized as follow, in the second section we summarize concepts elaborated in this paper. In the third section, we present and discuss some previous works made in this context. The following section (Sect. 4) describes our proposed approach that will be illustrated in the fifth section with a case study of Rental Car Agency system, and we finish by a conclusion and some of our future works.

2   Overview of Context

2.1   Model Driven Architecture

The MDA (Model Driven Architecture) is an initiative of the OMG (Object Management Group) released in 2000 [1]. The basic idea of the MDA approach is the separation of the functional system specifications and its implementation on a particular platform. The MDA approach lies in the context of the Model Driven Engineering which involves the use of model and metamodels in the different phases of development lifecycle [2], thus MDA defines three viewpoints

- CIM (Computation Independent Model): the objective of this model is to represent the application in their environment independently of any computation information.
- PIM (Platform Independent Model): the role of the PIM is to give a static and dynamic vision of the application regardless of the technical conception of it.
- PSM (Platform Specific Model): This model depends on technical platforms; it represents a template of code that facilitates code generation.

2.2   Model Transformations

The transition from one level to another is realized by applying transformations to source elements, to generate target elements. There are two types of model transformations; Model to Model transformation (M2M) that are used to move from CIM to PIM, and from PIM to PSM. The second type is Model to Text (M2T) which is used for the generation of source code from PSM (PSM to Code).

2.3   Model-Based Testing

Testing a system is an activity performed to identify software problems and failures in order to improve the quality of a program. The Model-Based Testing (MBT) is a variant of test techniques that are based on explicit behaviour models, describing the expected behaviours of the System Under Test (SUT), or the behaviour of its environment, built from functional requirements. The MBT is an evolutionary approach that aims to generate automatically from models, test cases to apply on the developed software application [3].

2.4 V Life Cycle

Typical V-model shows Software Development activities on the Left-hand side of the model and the Right-hand side of the model describes actual Testing phases that can be performed: Unit testing, Integration testing, Validation testing.

2.5 Scrum

The 'Agile Manifesto' published in February 2001 [4] based on analysis of previous experiences that allow to propose good practices to developers, the agile principle introduced by the agile manifesto is related to time invested in analysis and design [5, 6].

Scrum is a subset of Agile. It is a lightweight process for agile development, and the most widely-used one. Scrum is most often used to manage complex software and product development, using iterative and incremental practices. Scrum significantly increases productivity and reduces time to benefits relative to classic "waterfall" processes.

3 Related Works

Being aware of the importance of Model Driven Engineering with its both variant MDA and MBT, agile methodologies and development lifecycles, many works were made on these domains in order to improve development process considering managing system changes. However, we note that these domains evolve separately and their combination was discussed in few works that are presented in the following of this section.

Caceres et al. propose in their paper [7] a case study of an Agile Model Driven Development integrated in MIDAS framework which combines Model Driven Architecture approach and Agile practices based on eXtreme Programming (XP). MIDAS is a model driven methodology for Web Information Systems (WIS) agile development. We mention that authors in this paper detail the architecture of the MIDAS framework while it does not explain how the Agility is integrated in the process of MIDAS tool. Moreover, we note that the XP practices are specifically dedicated to the development phase during the software system realisation, which allows us to note that this approach does not implement all the aspect of the MDA approach.

In their paper [8], Nakicenovic presents an Agile Model Driven Development process developed in consideration of lean and agile practices. This paper aims to provide an approach that shows that MDD and agility can work together exploiting the benefits of each domain. The proposed approach is applied on both forward and reverse engineering in order to respond to two issues; accelerating the re-engineering process of the MDD solution and benefiting from agility and lean while producing MDD solution within a short time frame. The paper describes an approach that combines MDD and agility based on lean, the approach implementation was made on the Market Server Capabilities (MSC) project proposed by SunGard company.

Kulkarni et al. discuss and argue in their paper [9] why agile methodology can't be used with Model Driven Engineering, then they propose a modification to make on agile methodologies in order to combine them with MDE. Indeed, this paper describes a new Software Development process that combines Scrum and MDE. In this approach authors proposed the use of Meta-Sprints that run in parallel to Sprints in order to validate models, they suggest two to three months as timescales for meta sprints where clients must provide feedback on models and prototyping, which is opposite to agility principles. As a matter of fact, that agility recommends that the feedback of clients must be in period less than what was proposed in this approach.

Alfraihi in his paper [10] analyses the challenge of combining Agility and Model Driven Development, the paper describes an approach that aims to increase the adaptability of these domains by proposing a framework that facilitate Agility and MDD, this approach proposes recommendations, guidelines, and procedure to use Agile MDD in practice. We note that even if this approach proposes some practices to implement the Agile MDD but it does not take account of the architecture of the MDD, Model Driven Architecture, and how to benefit from the different abstraction levels to produce sustainable software systems.

In the paper, Wegener [11] presents a study made on the context of the combination of agility and Model Driven Development, then to propose issues that show how this combination affect organizations, process and architecture, this paper presents a comparison of different approaches proposed to use Agility and Model Driven Development.

In their paper [12], Mahé et al. presents their first reflections about the fusion of the MDA and Agility in order to have a combination with improved properties than the additions of the two approaches, they propose a canvas based on processes and agile practices in both modelling and meta-modelling level.

In their paper [13], the authors present an implementation tool using Model-Based Testing that deal with system evolutions. In their work, they consider different test suites to test SUT after evolution (Evolution, stagnation, regression and deletion). For each test suite, they propose a rule to define it. For the generation of these test suites, they use TestDesigner which is based on Class Diagram and State Machine Diagram with OCL constraints. Using OCL constraints to generate tests does not allow to validate all the system, the paper does not describe how to define a set of tests to apply to SUT after evolution.

Pretschner et al. present in their paper [14] the importance to deal with evolution of systems in testing phases. They also present their Autofocus tool which implement Model-Based Testing and that aim to generate test cases. The paper describes some evolution development process. However, this paper does not propose any method or approach to how system requirements should be modelled neither how Autofocus generate test cases and from which model. We note also that this paper does not explain how to deal with evolution of system using Model-Based Testing.

In the paper [15], the authors discuss how organizations use specific model-based tools and evolved their existing engineering processes to develop and test applications.

The paper highlights challenges and best practices of Model-Based Testing and its integration in developments life cycles, however, it does not present which model to use to generate tests.

For the two-last presented works in this section, we note that the use of scrum methodology does not allow to test all system in its different phases, but only the validation step to confirm if the developed system satisfies all customer requirements. Most of works that are based on agile methodologies especially scrum combine it with a development life cycle in each iteration (Such as V or Y life cycle).

Another point of view on the modelling of software system was presented in Osis et al.'s book [18], where they presented a method based on Topological Functioning Modelling (TFM) that was detailed in other works [19, 20].

In order to well manage all development phases, in next sections of this paper, we will focus on V life cycle and we will show how to combine it with Model Driven Architecture and Model-Based Testing in Scrum.

4 Proposed Approach

Our approach is a combination between two important areas that aim to improve software engineering technics to deal with system evolution; Model Driven Engineering represented by different level of its variant Model Driven Architecture and Agile Methodologies. In this paper we focus on Scrum as an agile method with V development lifecycle in each iteration.

This approach is divided into three main parts: At the first part we aim to automate transformations in MDA approach between all levels; from CIM to PIM, then from PIM to PSM until code generation. The second part is the integration of Model-Based Testing in V development lifecycle based on MDA approach, while the third part is the combination of all previous elements following V lifecycle process in each sprint of scrum methodology to deal with system' evolutive requirements.

4.1 Transformations Automatization Between MDA Levels

Models transformation is the core of MDA approach. Our approach, that aims to automate these transformations, consists on:

- Describing system requirements in CIM level by a structured English using SBVR.
- Transforming automatically Business Vocabulary and Business Rules of SBVR into Use Case Diagram (UCD) in CIM level [16].
- Applying transformation rules to generate Business Class Diagram (BCD) and System Sequence Diagram (SSD) from SBVR and UCD of CIM level to represent the PIM level [17].
- Generating PSM level of MVC architecture represented by Detailed Class Diagram (DCD) and Detailed Sequence Diagram (DSD) from PIM level using automatic transformation rules.
- Generating application source code from PSM level.

We mention that the automation of the two last steps of the approach will be implemented as an eclipse plugin which is the continuity of the previous one.

Choosing previous diagrams to model MDA levels is depending on different aspects that each level should cover according to OMG specifications:

- For CIM level, we define three aspects; Static and Dynamic that are covered by SBVR, while the Functional aspect is covered by UCD.
- For PIM level, we define two aspects; Structural aspect covered by BCD and Dynamic one covered by SSD.
- For PSM level, we define in our approach 4 aspects; Static aspect covered by Model classes of DCD, Structural one covered by Class Diagram, Dynamic aspect covered by Controller classes and Behavioural one represented by DSD.

In this approach, we automate the two types of transformations Model-to-Model (M2M) and Model-to-Text (M2T). For M2M, we use QVT language while for M2T we use Acceleo transformation language. Transformation rules between the different levels of MDA are implemented as an Eclipse plugin to ensure automaticity and traceability of transformation rules.

The Fig. 1 below describes an overview of our approach:

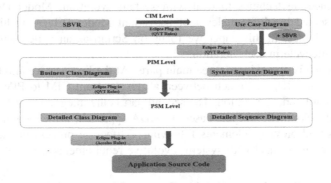

Fig. 1. Overview of MDA transformation approach

4.2 Approach of Integration Model-Based Testing in V Life Cycle Based on Model Driven Architecture

In this section, we present in the first part our approach to model system requirements using MDA approach integrated with V life cycle and their combination with MBT; the second part is to present some rules that we aim to use in order to automate test generation.

4.3 Modelling System Requirements in V Lifecycle Using MDA Approach

To well manage system requirements evolution, we aim to combine V process and MBT. Our approach consists on:

- Covering Requirements and functional specifications steps in V life cycle by CIM level of MDA which is represented in our approach by SBVR. The UCD and Business Rules generated at the CIM level are then used generate "Validation tests" to validate if the developed system responds to described requirements.
- Generating the High-level design represented in our approach by the PIM level which is generated automatically from CIM level (To generate PIM level from CIM one, we use our approach defined in our previous works (Essebaa et al. 2017). This step is represented by BCD and SSD for each use case element. We then generate "Integration tests" from these diagrams (BCD and SSD) to test the correct functioning between different elements of the system.
- Generating the low-level design represented by PSM level which is modelled by CD and DSD (The approach we propose to automate transformations between PIM and PSM levels will be discussed in our future works). We generate "Unit tests" from this level to test the generated code.

Figure 2 describes the presented approach:

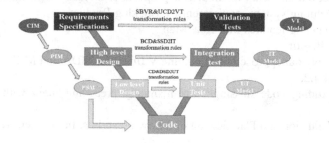

Fig. 2. Overview of a combination of MBT in V lifecycle using MDA approach

Test Generation Rules

To generate tests from Models in our approach, we defined three main rules that are detailed in our previous work [16];

Rule 1: Generate Validation tests from CIM level: Validation tests are generated from SBVR and Use Case Diagram.

Rule 2: Generate Integration tests from PIM level: Integration tests are generated from PIM level which is represented using Class Diagram and System Sequence Diagram.

Rule 3: Generate Unit tests from PSM level: Unit tests in our approach are generated from PSM level using Detailed Sequence Diagram and Detailed Class Diagram.

The Table 1 below summarize these rules:

Table 1. Test generation rules

Rule	Model	Target
SBVR&UCD2VT	Use Case Element	Requirement to validate
	Fact Type	Sub feature to test
	Business rules of a fact type	Validation tests
BCD&SSD2IT	Actor and DataObject lifecycle	Classes to test
	Relationship between classes	Integration tests
DCD&DSD2UT	Messages	Operation to test
	Operation in classes	Unit tests

4.4   Combining MDA, MBT and V Process in Scrum

In the two previous parts we present how we automate transformations in MDA and combine it with MBT in V lifecycle to generate different type of tests, in this part we will present our approach of managing evolutions of system using MDA and MBT inside a V lifecycle in scrum method. Our proposal is divided into 5 main steps:

Step 1: Defining system requirement by Backlog Product.

Step 2: Planning features in a RoadMap.

Sprint to Begin:

Step 3: Apply our approach that combine V lifecycle, MDA and MBT presented in Sects. 4.1 and 4.2.

Step 4: Adding code missing parts manually preceding them with "@added" annotation.

Step 5: Validation and Planification of following sprints. In this step we define two cases:

- If there is no system evolution:
  - Restart from step 3 for the next sprint
- If there is an evolution:
  - Restart from step 1 and keep the old code except the parts preceded by "@added" annotation of features that still exist in the system (added code of deleted features is deleted automatically after the new execution)

In the Fig. 3 below we describe an overview of the presented approach in this paper:

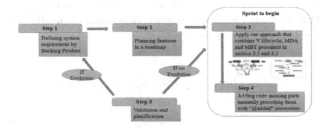

Fig. 3. Overview of a combination of MDA, MBT, V lifecycle in scrum

5 Case Study

To well illustrate our approach and transformation rules defined, we present in this section their application on a Rental Car Agency system. The application has three users' profiles that have different privileges:

- Customer: A person who can view the cars available in the agency, rates and promotions and may subscribe. A client must register and authenticate in the system to search for available cars and book a car by indicating the reservation date and time.
- Manager: A Manager must also authenticate to view all cars, add, edit or remove cars. He can also view the bookings made by customers waiting for validation to decide to accept or refuse them.
- Administrator: Once authenticated into the system, the administrator has the privilege of modifying and deleting a customer account, as well as the management of managers account (add, change or delete).

We can also define some management rules as below:

- A customer can rent at least 1 car.
- A car can be rented by at least 1 customer.
- A manager can manage at least 1 car.
- A car is managed by at least 1 manager.
- An administrator can manage at least 1 customer account.
- An administrator can manage at least 1 manager account.

In the following part we present an application of our approach' steps on Rental Car Agency System example:

Defining a Backlog Product by System Requirements

After analysing system requirements, the first step in our approach is to define the backlog product of the project then plan the Roadmap that describes different sprints of first project' requirement before any evolution, in this example we plan three sprints to develop the system, we define 3 sprints where each one takes 2 weeks.

Figure 4 describes the roadmap of Rental Car Agency system:

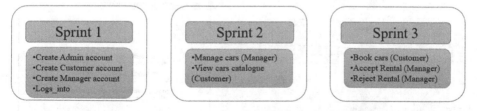

Fig. 4. Scrum RoadMap of Rental Car Agency System

Modelling User Stories of the First Sprint by SBVR and UCD to Cover CIM Level of MDA

The next step after dispatching features on sprints is to describe CIM level of first sprint by Business Vocabulary and Business Rules using SBVR standard as described in following Figs. 5 and 6.

```
account
login
    General_concept: text
password
    General_concept: text
account has login
    Synonymous_form: login is_property_of account

account has password
    Synonymous_form: password is_proprty_of account

customer owns account
    Synonymous_form: account is_owned_by customer

customer manages account
    Synonymous_form: account is_managed_by customer

admin owns account
    Synonymous_form: account is_owned_by admin

admin manages account
    Synonymous_form: account is_managed_by admin

manager owns account
    Synonymous_form: account is_owned_by manager
```

```
It is possible that customer owns at most 1 account.
It is possible that admin owns at most 1 account.
It is permitted that admin manages account.
It is possible that manager owns at most 1 account.
```

Fig. 5. Examples of SBVR of the first sprint of Rental Car agency

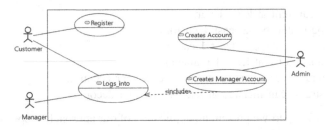

Fig. 6. UML Use Case Diagram of the first sprint of Rental Car Agency System

In the same level of MDA, we apply horizontal transformation rules, implemented as an eclipse plugin, to automatically generate UCD from SBVR. The Fig. 7 below represents the generated UCD of the first sprint for Rental Car Agency system.

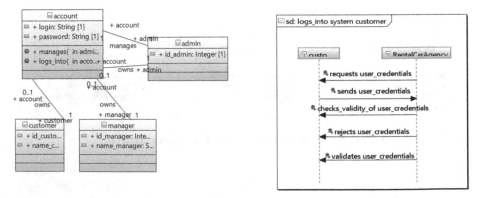

Fig. 7. Generated BCD and SSD of the first sprint of Rental Car Agency

Generating Validation Tests from CIM

As in our approach we use V lifecycle process combined with MDA, after defining CIM level, we can generate Validation tests from this level as described for "Logs-into" feature in Table 2 below.

Table 2. Validation tests generation from PSM level

Source			Target		
UseCase element	Fact type	Business rule	Requirement	Sub feature	Validation test
Logs_into	System requests user credential	It is obligatory that the system requests user credential if customer logs into system	The system must allow customer to "logs_into" the system	Requests user credential	The system must request user credential if a customer try to logs into the system

Applying Transformation Rules on CIM to Generate BCD and SSD of PIM Level

Generating PIM level is the first vertical Model-to-Model transformation that aims to automatically generate BCD and SSD from CIM level for Sprint 1 using our Eclipse plugin that implements transformation rules, the figure below represents a PIM level of Rental Car Agency system.

Generating Integration Tests from PIM

According to V lifecycle used in our approach, Integration Tests are automatically generated from PIM level that covers high level design of V lifecycle, the Table 3 below describes Integration test for "logs_into" feature in sprint 1.

Applying Transformation Rules to Generate DCD and DSD of PSM Level from PIM

The last level before code is PSM level, which is the result of M2M transformations applied on PIM level to automatically generate DCD and DSD, Fig. 8 defines diagrams of PSM level of sprint 1.

Generating Unit Tests from PSM

Unit tests in our approach are generated from low level design step of V lifecycle covered by PSM level, the Table 4 below describes example of Unit test of "logs_into" feature in sprint 1:

Generating Application Source Code

The last transformation in our approach is automatic code generation which is the result of M2T transformations that takes as an input a DCD and DSD of PSM to generate as an output source code for MVC web application.

Table 3. Integration tests generation from PIM level

Source		Target	
Requirements	SD Connection	Classes	Integration tests
Logs_into	The operation requires connection between "Customer" and "Account"	Customer	Customer owns 1 account
		Account	Account belongs to 1 customer

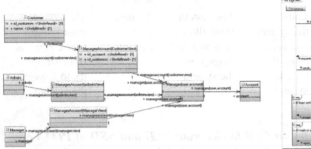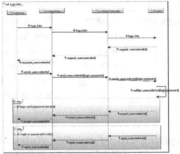

Fig. 8. Generated MVC-DCD and MVC-DSD of the first sprint of Rental Car Agency

Table 4. Unit tests generation from PSM level

Source		Target	
Requirements	SD Messages	Operation to test	Unit tests
Logs_into	System requests User_credential	Request (User_credential)	Test "requests" operation
	Customer sends User_credential	Sends (User_credential)	Test "sends" operation
	System verifies User_credential	Verifies (User_credential)	Test "verifies" operation
	System accepts User_credential	Accepts (User_credential)	Test "accepts" operation
	System rejects User_credential	Rejects (User_credential)	Test "rejects" operation

Evolution of Rental Car Agency System' Requirements. In this section we will make some evolutions to the system (addition, deletion and modification of features) in order to visualize the process of models' transformation and test generation in V lifecycle combined in scrum, the evolution will be as follow:

- *Modifications:* "View car catalogue" feature will be available for all users not only customers, this modification engender a new actor *"User"* that it will be a generalization of "Customer" actor, this modification requires changing the actor of *"register"* method too.

- *Addition:* In the new system, "Customer" will be able to validate its rental by *"payment"*, The addition of a feature may engender some modifications to old ones, for example the verification of car availability will be made automatically by a system.

- *Deletion:* The addition of *"payment"* feature requires to delete *"manage rental"* feature of *"Manager"* that allowed him to accept or reject the rental, in the new system the customer can validate its rental from the system, before proceeding to payment option the system must be able to check if the chosen car is available for date specified by the customer.

After studying system requirements' evolution, we have to make another feature dispatching on next sprints as presented in Fig. 9:

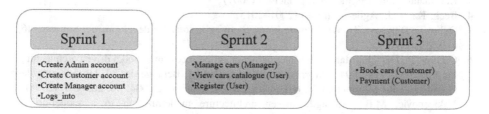

Fig. 9. Scrum Roadmap of Rental Car Agency system after requirements' changes

After the new RoadMap planification, the sequence of the following steps is done in the same way presented earlier: we start by the CIM description of the new sprint thus the generation of the following levels up to the generation of the code. The new set of tests is also automatically generated according to the rules presented in the previous sections.

6   Conclusion

The primary objectives of this paper are to introduce a scrum approach that combines two important variants of Model Driven Engineering; MDA and MBT, with V lifecycle to manage every sprint in order to ensure the quick and performing development process.

Indeed, in this first work we chose to combine these methods and approaches to deal with system changing issues and features, we define in this paper, three types of backlog product evolution; modification or suppression of existing features, and addition of new features.

As well as saving time, the proposed approach can also make future evolutions and maintenance easier. This allows team members to concentrate their effort on analysing and describing the business features of the application.

In our future works we plan to:

- Propose Metamodel of tests and automate test generation from MDA levels.
- Apply our approach on other case studies to improve it.
- Extend our approach to cover all agile methodologies.

References

1. Miller, J., Mukerji, J.: MDA Guide version 1.0.1. (2003)
2. Soley, R.: Model driven architecture (MDA) (2000). http://www.omg.org/cgibin/doc?omg/00-11-05
3. Utting, M., Legeard, B.: Practical Model-Based Testing: A Tools Approach. Morgan Kaufmann Publishers Inc., San Francisco (2007)
4. Beck, K., et al.: Agile manifesto (2001–2015)
5. Dyba, T., Dingsoyr, T.: What do we know about agile software development? Software 46, 6–9. IEEE (2009)
6. Caceres, P., Díaz, F., Marcos, E.: Integrating an agile process in a model driven architecture. In: INFORMATIK 2004 - Informatik verbindet, Band 1, Beitrage der 34. Jahrestagung der Gesellschaft fur Informatik e.V. (GI), Ulm, 20–24. September 2004, pp. 265–270 (2004)
7. Nakicenovic, M.B.: An agile driven architecture modernization to a model-driven development solution. Int. J. Adv. Softw. 5(3, 4) (2012)
8. Kulkarni, V., Barat, S., and Ramteerthkar, U.: Early experience with agile methodology in a model-driven approach. In: 14th International Conference Model Driven Engineering Languages and Systems, MODELS 2011, Wellington, New Zealandpages, pp. 578–590 (2011)
9. Alfraihi, H.: Towards improving agility in modeldriven development. In: Joint Proceedings of the Doctoral Symposium and Projects Showcase Held as Part of STAF 2016 Co-located with Software Technologies: Applications and Foundations (STAF 2016) (2016)
10. Wegener, H.: Agility in model-driven software development? Implications for organization, process, and architecture (2002)
11. Mahe, V., Combemale, B., Cadavid, J.: Crossing model driven engineering and agility – preliminary thoughts on benefits and challenges (2010)
12. Bouquet, et al.: A model-based testing approach for evolution (2011)
13. Pretschner, et al.: Model based testing in evolutionary software development (2001)
14. Blackburn et al.: Life cycle integration of model-based testing tools (2005)
15. Essebaa, I., Chantit, S.: Tool support to automate transformations from SBVR to UML use case diagram. In: Proceedings of the 13th International Conference on Evaluation of Novel Approaches to Software Engineering (2018)
16. Essebaa et al.: Tool support to automate transformations between CIM and PIM levels. In: Proceedings of the 12th International Conference on Evaluation of Novel Approaches to Software Engineering (2017)
17. Essebaa, I., Chantit, S.: A combination of V development life cycle and model-based testing to deal with software system evolution issues. In: Proceedings of the 6th International Conference on Model-Driven Engineering and Software Development (2018)

18. Osis, Janis, Donins, Uldis: Topological UML Modeling: An Improved Approach for Domain Modeling and Software Development, 1st edn. Elsevier Sci. Pub, Amsterdam (2017)
19. Nazaruka, E., Osis, J.: Determination of natural language processing tasks and tools for topological functioning modelling. In: Proceedings of the 13th International Conference on Evaluation of Novel Approaches to Software Engineering (2018)
20. Nazaruks, V., Osis, J.: Retrieving the topology from the knowledge frame system for composition of the topological functioning model. In: Proceedings of the 13th International Conference on Evaluation of Novel Approaches to Software Engineering (2018)

Adaptive Algorithms for Computing Ontologies Metrics Through Processing of RDF Graphs

Jean Vincent Fonou-Dombeu[1]([✉]) and Yannick Kazela Kazadi[2]

[1] School of Mathematics, Statistics and Computer Science,
University of KwaZulu-Natal, Private Bag X01, Scottsville, Pietermaritzburg 3209,
South Africa
fonoudombeuj@ukzn.ac.za
[2] Saratoga Software, 4 Greenwich Groove Station road rondebosch,
Cape Town 7700, South Africa
yan.kazela@gmail.com

Abstract. The advent of the Semantic Web has increased the number of ontologies representing domains knowledge on the internet. These ontologies are available in the form of thousands of Resource Description Framework (RDF) or Web Ontology Language (OWL) statements which are difficult to read and understand by a human being. On the one hand, several tools have been developed to enable the semi-automatic or automatic access and exploitation of RDF and OWL ontologies. On the other hand, several metrics have been defined to theoretically measure the complexity of RDF and OWL ontology graphs. However, implementing computer programs for the empirical analysis of ontology complexity metrics through the automatic exploration of RDF or OWL graphs remains challenging. This study proposes a set of generic algorithms for computing ontology complexity metrics through the processing of RDF graphs. The algorithms are applied on a set of 25 biomedical ontologies and provide promising results.

Keywords: Algorithm · Biomedical ontologies · BioPortal
Ontology complexity metrics · RDF Graphs

1 Introduction

The past years have witnessed the proliferation of ontologies on the Semantic Web (SW) due to the advent of Linked Data, ontologies libraries as well as the adoption of semantic technologies in various application domains. These ontologies are available on the internet in the form of thousands of Resource Description Framework (RDF) and Web Ontology Language (OWL) statements which are difficult to read and understand by human beings.

On the one hand, several tools such as Swoogle [1], Watson [2], BioPortal [3], etc. have been developed to enable the semi-automatic or automatic access and exploitation of RDF and OWL ontologies. However, the metadata of ontologies

© Springer Nature Switzerland AG 2018
E. H. Abdelwahed et al. (Eds.): MEDI 2018, LNCS 11163, pp. 92–106, 2018.
https://doi.org/10.1007/978-3-030-00856-7_6

such as the number of classes, properties and instances, obtained with existing tools are the basic characteristics of ontologies and are insufficient for the analysis of the complexity of an ontology [4].

On the other hand, in [5], it is argued that the quantitative measurement of the complexity of ontology can improve the understanding of its structure and semantic to ontologies users/developers, thereby, allowing them to better evaluate the design of ontology and control its development process. Furthermore, Yang et al. [4] added that ontology evaluation enables developers to determine the fundamental characteristics of ontologies in order to improve the quality, estimate cost and reduce future maintenance. To this end, research has proposed various theoretical metrics for evaluating the complexity of ontologies [4–7]. In [6] three metrics, namely, the number of root classes, the number of leaf classes, and the average depth of inheritance tree are presented to measure the cohesiveness of an ontology. Another study in [5] used the concept of software metrics to propose a suite of ontology metrics including the size of vocabulary, edge node ratio, tree impurity, entropy of ontology graph, number of children, depth of inheritance, class in-degree and class out-degree for the analysis of the design complexity of ontologies. In [4] a suite of metrics for measuring the complexity of an ontology are presented. These metrics examined the quantity, ratio and correlativity of concepts and relationships in the ontology. Another study in [8] introduced a prototype to assess the quality of ontologies via an online web platform, using the so-called semiotic-influenced metrics to grade ontology quality. However, implementing computer programs for the empirical analysis of the abovementioned ontology complexity metrics through the automatic exploration of RDF or OWL graphs remains challenging. This drawback may hamper the widespread reuse of existing Semantic Web ontologies in the scientific community.

This study proposes a set of algorithms for computing ontology complexity metrics through the processing of RDF graphs. The algorithms are designed to comprehensively compute existing ontology complexity metrics including the entropy of ontology graph, tree impurity [5], average number of paths per class, class richness, relationship richness [7], average path length of a concept and average path length of ontology [4]. The proposed algorithms are generic and could be applied in any knowledge domain to analyze the complexity of ontologies based on the abovementioned ontology complexity metrics. The study applies the proposed algorithms on 25 biomedical ontologies and displays promising results.

The rest of the paper is structured as follows. Section 2 discusses related research. The materials and methods used in the study are described in Sect. 3. Section 4 presents the proposed algorithms. The experiments and results are presented and discuss in Sect. 5. A conclusion is drawn in the last section.

2 Related Work

Automatically exploring ontologies has been of interest to many researchers. Two platforms for exploring ontologies, namely, OntoQuest and OntoXpl are presented in [10,11], respectively. The interfaces of both platforms enable users to access metadata information on ontologies such as the list of concepts, instances and properties, instances of a particular concept, the domain and range of properties, and so on. Although both platforms are useful for viewing ontologies structures, the metadata information provided are considered to be only basic features of these ontologies [4,5,7]. The existing metrics for measuring the complexity of ontologies are not provided in these platforms [5].

Another study in [12] proposed a set of SPARQL-based algorithms that implement a so called advanced faceted search on a RDF graph. The Faceted search is defined as an approach for querying RDF documents through the application of filters called facets [13]. Although, the ouputs of these algorithms provide insights on the semantic structure of ontologies, i.e., how concepts of the ontologies are semantically related to each other, they were not designed to explore RDF graphs and compute existing metrics for measuring the complexity of ontologies.

The proximity and the Jaccard similarity distance between two nodes/concepts of ontology are computed in [14,15] to measure the semantic relatedness of concepts and perform concepts alignment between two ontologies, respectively. The algorithms in [14,15] did not tackle the issue of exploring RDF graphs of ontologies to compute their complexity metrics as it is done on this study.

3   Materials and Methods

3.1   Definition

This section defines the underlying concepts used for processing of RDF graphs in this study. An RDF graph is a collection of triples (subject, predicate and object) that can be seen as a directed multigraph, that is, two nodes can be connected by more than one edge; where classes and properties are the nodes and edges, respectively. An RDF graph G is a tuple $<C, P>$ where C and P are the sets of classes/nodes and properties/edges, respectively. The inheritance hierarchy of the RDF graph G is a subgraph G'. G' is also a tuple $<C', P'>$ where C' is the set of classes and P' the set of properties in G'.

A path t between two nodes c_0 and c_n in G is represented as in Eq. 1 and is defined as a sequence of unrepeated nodes connected by edges (properties) from c_0 to c_n; the length pl_t of this path is the number of edges on the path.

$$t = C_0 \rightarrow C_1 \rightarrow C_2 \rightarrow ... \rightarrow C_n \tag{1}$$

A path between a root node and a node c_i $(0 \leq i \leq n)$ is called path of c_i. The total number of paths (p_i) between the root node and other nodes c_i is determined using the function p on C as in Eq. 2.

$$p : C \rightarrow \mathbb{N}, p(C_i) = p_i \tag{2}$$

The set of subclasses of a node c_i is determined through the function h in Eq. 3.

$$h : C \rightarrow C, h(c_i) = \{c \in C, c \text{ is subclass of } c_i\} \tag{3}$$

The set of superclasses of a node c_i is obtained with h^{-1}, the inverse of h as in Eq. 4.

$$h^{-1} : C \rightarrow C, h^{-1}(c_i) = \{c \in C, c \text{ is superclass of } c_i\} \tag{4}$$

The degree $E(c_i)$ of a node c_i is the sum of its number of superclasses and subclasses in G and is given in Eq. 5.

$$E(c_i) = card(h(c_i)) + card(h^{-1}(c_i)) \tag{5}$$

where $card(X)$ represents the cardinality of number of elements of the set X.

3.2   Complexity Metrics of Ontologies

Many authors have developed metrics for the quantitative measurement of the design complexity of ontologies [4–7]. The complexity metrics reviewed below are those computed by the proposed algorithms in this study Sect. 4. The authors used a purposive sampling method [16] to chose these metrics amongst the existing ontology complexity metrics. In the purposive sampling method, the authors use his own judgement to chose the suitable set metrics for the studies.

1. The average number of paths per concept (ANP): This metric indicates the average connectivity degree of a concept to the root concept in the ontology inheritance hierarchy [4]. This metric is defined as in Eq. 6:

$$ANP = \frac{\sum_{i=1}^{m} p_i}{|C|} \tag{6}$$

   where p_i is the number of paths of a given concept.

2. Tree Impurity (TIP): This metric is used to measure how far an ontology inheritance hierarchy deviates from a tree, and it is given in Eq. 7:

$$TIP = |P'| - |C'| + 1 \tag{7}$$

   where P' and C' represent the sets of relations and concepts in the inheritance hierarchy, respectively.

3. Average path length of a concept (APL_{C_i}): this metric provides the average number of ancestors of a specific concept in each of its path. This metric is defined in Eq. 8:

$$APL_{C_i} = \frac{\sum_{k=1}^{p_i} p_{i,k}^l}{p_i} \tag{8}$$

where, $p_{i,k}^l$ represents the length of the kth path for the ith concept.

4. The average path length of the ontology (APL): This metric indicates the average number of concepts in a path. It is defined as in Eq. 9:

$$APL = \frac{\sum_{i=1}^{m}\sum_{k=1}^{p_i} p_{i,k}^{l}}{\sum_{i=1}^{m} p_i} \tag{9}$$

were $p_{i,k}^{l}$ and p_i are the path length and number of paths of each concept, respectively.

5. Entropy of ontology graph (EOG): This metric is the application of the logarithm function to a probability distribution over the ontology graph to provide a numerical value that can be used as an indicator of the graph complexity [2]. It is defined as in Eq. 10:

$$EOG = \sum_{i=1}^{n} p(i)log_2(p(i)) \tag{10}$$

where $p(i)$ is the probability for a concept to have i relations.

6. Relationship Richness (RR): This metric provides an indication of the distribution of relations in an ontology. It is defined in Eq. 11:

$$RR = \frac{|R|}{|SR| + |R|} \tag{11}$$

where $|R|$ and $|SR|$ represent the number of relations between classes and the number of subclass relations, respectively.

7. Class Richness (CR): the value of this metric provides an indication of the distribution of individuals across the ontology classes. It is defined as in Eq. 12:

$$CR = \frac{|C'|}{|C|} \tag{12}$$

3.3   Data Structures and Design

The design of the proposed algorithms relies on the Apache Jena library, a Semantic Web Application Programming Interface (API) and toolkit for Java developers [9]. In fact, the Jena API features including the set of object classes and interfaces for creating and managing RDF graphs are used in the design of the algorithms. Furthermore, various Java constructs including arrays, queues and lists are used in the design of the algorithms. The proposed algorithms are presented in the next section.

4   Proposed Algorithms

This section presents the proposed algorithms for computing ontology complexity metrics in Eqs. 6 to 12. There are in total nine algorithms grouped into three main groups, namely, path-related, entropy, and class and relation richness algorithms as presented in the following subsections.

4.1 Path-Related Algorithms

This subsection presents four algorithms developed for the computation of the average number of paths per class, the average path length and the tree impurity. To compute the average number of paths per class and the average path lengths of concept and ontology, Algorithm 1 that uses Algorithms 2, 3 and 4 is used.

Algorithm 1: FINDNUMBPATHS
1. **Input:** Jena Ontology Model (M), depth,
2. **Output:** averageNumbPath, averagePathLength, treeImpurity
3. **Begin**
4.   Create setOfPaths
5.   Create listOfPaths
6.   countSubClassOfRelation←0, classtree←0, rootclass←0
7.   **For** each class c_i of M **Do**
8.   If card($h^{-1}(c_i)$)=0 **Then**
9.   rootclass←rootclass+1
10.   Create pathNode
11.   pathNode.add (c_i)
12.   setOfPaths.add (pathNode)
13.   **EndIf**
14. **EndFor**
15. listOfPaths ← TOTALPATHS (setOfPaths, M, depth)
16. listOfPaths ← DUPLICATE (listOfPaths)
17. **For** each class c_i of M **Do**
18.   pathResult← PATH (listOfPaths, c_i, depth)
19.   averageLengthC$_i$←pathResult[1]/pathResult[0]
20.   pathLength[0]=pathLength[0]+pathResult[0]
21.   pathLength[1]=pathLength[1]+pathResult[1]
22. **EndFor**
23. **For** each ontology statement S in M **Do**
24.   If S ∈ R' **Then**
25.   countSubClassOfRelation← countSubClassOfRelation + 1
26. **EndFor**
27. **For** each class c_i of M **Do**
28.   If c_i∈ C' **Then**
29.   classtree← classtree+1
30.   **EndIf**
31. **EndFor**
32. averageNumbPath=pathLength / |C|
33. averagePathLength = pathLength[0]/pathLength[1]
34. treeImpurity = (countSubClassOfRelation – classtree) + rootclass + 1
35. **End**

Algorithm 1 (FINDNUMBPATHS) processes the ontology Model and the depth of inheritance (obtained from Bioportal together with the ontology) to obtain a set of paths of leaf nodes in the RDF graph of ontology (FINDNUMB-PATHS from line 4 to line 16). The resulting set of paths is used to get the average number of paths per class and the average path length (lines 17–21 and 32–33 of FINDNUMBPATHS). The tree impurity is obtained through the counting of the root nodes, subclass of relations and nodes belonging to the inheritance hierarchy (FINDNUMBPATHS lines 8–9, 23–25, 28–29 and 34).

Formally, Algorithm 1 works as follows: A set of paths (SetOfPaths) is created (FINDNUMBPATHS from line 4), and each subset of SetOfPaths is initialized with a root node (FINDNUMBPATHS from line 4 to line 12). SetOfPaths is then used along with the Jena Model of the ontology and the value of the depth of inheritance (line 15 of FINDNUMBPATHS) as parameters to Algorithm 2

(TOTALPATHS) which returns another set of paths ListOfPaths. ListOfPaths is further passed as a parameter to Algorithm 3 (DUPLICATE) to remove the duplicated sets of nodes from the list of paths (line 16 of FINDNUMBPATHS). The ontology classes in ListOfPaths returned by DUPLICATE are fed together with the value of the depth of inheritance to Algorithm 4 (PATH) which returns an array containing the number of paths of input class and the sum of lengths of its paths.

The outputs of PATH are then used to determine the average path length of the class (FINDNUMBPATHS lines 19), the sum of the number of paths of all the classes (FINDPATHS lines 20) and the sum of the lengths of all the paths (FINDNUMBPATHS lines 21).

Algorithm 2: TOTALPATHS

1. **Input:** Jena Model (M), setOfPaths, depth
2. **Output:** L
3. **Begin**
4.   **While** ¬Empty (setOfPaths)
5.   setOfNodes ← remove last element of setOfPaths
6.   listOfPaths.add(setOfNodes)
7.   **If** Size of setOfNodes < depth **Then**
8.   Node= last element (setOfNodes)
9.   I= h(Node)
10.   **For each** $s \in I$ **Do**
11.   setOfPaths.add(setOfNodes.add(subject(s))
12.   **EndFor**
13.   **EndIf**
14.   **EndWhile**
15.   **Return** (listOfPaths)
16. **End**

Algorithm 2 (TOTALPATHS) receives three parameters which are the Jena Model of the ontology, the set of paths SetOfPaths created in FINDNUMB-PATHS algorithm and the depth of inheritance of the ontology.

From line 4 to 14 of TOTALPATHS, a loop is used to determine different routes from the root nodes to the leaf nodes in the Jena Model (RDF graph) of the ontology. At each iteration of the While-loop in TOTALPATHS, the last element of SetOfPaths (a set of nodes) is removed and assigned to SetOfNodes (in line 5) which is then added to the list of paths ListOfPaths in line 6. If the size (number of nodes) of SetOfNodes is less than the depth of inheritance (line 7) a group of instructions from line 8 to 13 are executed to find the subclasses of the last element of SetOfNodes (line 8 and line 9). Each subclass of the last element is added to SetOfNodes, which in turn is added to SetOfPaths in line 11.

Algorithm 3: DUPLICATE

1. **Input**: listOfPaths
2. **Output**: listOfPaths
3. **Begin**
4.   For i←0 to i<= size of listOfPaths – 1 **Do**
5.   j← i+1
6.   **While** j<= size of listOfPaths or f=false
7.   **If** listOfPaths (i) is contained into listOfPaths (j)
8.   Delete listOfPaths (i) from listOfPaths
9.   f←true
10.   **EndIf**
11.   j← j+1
12.   **EndWhile**
13.   **EndFor**
14.   **Return** (listOfPaths)
15. **End**

Algorithm 3 (DUPLICATE) removes from the list of paths ListOfPaths returned by TOTALPATHS the set of duplicated nodes. DUPLICATE uses an iterative process from line 4 to line 13. Two counters are used at each iteration to test and remove duplicated nodes (line 4 to 11).

Algorithm 4: PATH

1.   **Input**: listOfPaths, a class c_i, depth
2.   **Begin**
3.   countNumbPaths← 0, countPathsLength←0
4.   Create pathsc$_i$
5.   i← 0
6.   **For each** p ∈ listOfPaths **Do**
7.   **If** p contains c_i **Then**
8.   pathsc$_i$.add(p)
9.   **EndIf**
10.   **EndFor**
11.   **While** i<= depth
12.   Create posPathsc$_i$
13.   **For each** p ∈ pathsc$_i$ **Do**
14.   **If** p.(i)= c_i **Then**
15.   posPathsc$_i$.add(p)
16.   **EndIf**
17.   **EndFor**
18.   **For** j←0 to j<= card(posPathsc$_i$) - 1
19.   **For** k←j+1 to k<= card(posPathsc$_i$)
20.   **If** ((SubSet (posPathsc$_i$(j),i))=(SubSet (posPathsc$_i$(k),i)))
21.   Delete posPathsc$_i$(k) from posPathsc$_i$
22.   **EndIf**
23.   **EndFor**
24.   **EndFor**
25.   countPathsLength = countPathsLength +(card(posPathsc$_i$)*i)
26.   countNumbPaths = countNumbPaths + card(posPathsc$_i$)
27.   i←i+1
28.   **EndWhile**
29.   pathLength[0]← countPathsLength
30.   pathLength[1]← countNumbPaths
31.   **Return** pathLength
32. **End**

Algorithm 4 (PATH) is executed with the list of paths without duplicates listOfPaths returned by the DUPLICATE, a class c_i and the depth of inheritance. For every class $c_i \in C'$ a set of instructions is executed from line 6 to line 27 to determine the number of paths and sum of path lengths. In line 4 a set of paths pathsc$_i$ is created and filled with elements of listOfPaths containing the current class c_i (line 8). In line 11 a loop is executed until the value of a counter is equal to the depth of the ontology. Within the loop another set of paths $posPathsc_i$ is created (line 12) and filled with elements of $pathsc_i$ where there is a match with classes at the position of the loop counter (line 15). Thereafter, iterations are executed from line 18 to line 24 to remove the duplicated paths from $posPathsc_i$.

4.2 Entropy Algorithms

These set of algorithms include Algorithms 5 to 8. Algorithm 5 (ENTROPY) calls the Algorithm 6 (NUMBEDGES) which in turn calls Algorithms 7 (MAXNUMBEDGES) and 8 (TOTALEDGES). The ENTROPY receives as input the number of classes and the Jena Model of the ontology; it uses the list returned by NUMBEDGES (ENTROPY line 4) to compute the entropy of the ontology graph (line 5 to 12).

Algorithm 5: ENTROPY
1.   **Input**: number of classes (n), Jena Ontology Model (M)
2.   **Begin**
3.   Create a List of Integer (F)
4.   F← NUMBEDGES (M)
5.   For j←0 to j<= size of F **Do**
6.   If (F.get(j)>0)
7.   P← F.get(j)/n //Probability for a class to have j edges
8.   V← Log₂ P
9.   entropy←entropy+P*V
10.   **EndIf**
11.   **EndFor**
12.   Return (entropy *(-1))
13. **End**

Algorithm 6: NUMBEDGES
1.   **Input**: Jena Ontology Model (M)
2.   **Begin**
3.   max← MAXNUMBEDGES (M)
4.   Create a List of Integer (F) with size max+1
5.   For i←0 to i<= max **Do**
6.   For each class cᵢ in M **Do**
7.   totalNumberEdges← TOTALEDGES (M, cᵢ)
8.   F.set(totalNumberEdges, F.get(totalNumberEdges) + 1)
9.   **EndFor**
10.   **EndFor**
11.   **Return F**
End

The ENTROPY starts by creating a list of integers in line 3; this list is populated by NUMBEDGES (ENTROPY line 4). An iterative process is executed (ENTROPY lines 5 to 11) to test the value of each edge of the ontology graph (ENTROPY line 6); this value is then divided by the number of classes to obtain the probability for a class c_i to have i relations in the ontology (ENTROPY line 7). In lines 8 and 9 the calculation of the entropy of the ontology graph is completed and its value is multiplied by -1 and returned in line 12.

In Algorithm 6 (NUMBEDGES) the total number of edges (max) in the ontology graph is obtained with Algorithm 7 (MAXNUMBEDGES) in line 3. This number is then used to create a list of integers with the size equal to max plus one (line 4). Thereafter, an iterative process is applied (lines 5 to 9) to determine the degree of each class c_i, $E(c_i)$ with Algorithm 8 (TOTALEDGES). MAXNUMBEDGES determines the maximum degree value in the ontology graph. An iterative process from line 4 to 9 determines the degree $E(c_i)$ of each class c_i in the ontology graph using TOTALEDGES (MAXNUMBEDGES lines 4 and 5); the values obtained are iteratively compared amongst themselves to determine the bigger one (MAXNUMBEDGES lines 6 and 7).

The TOTALEDGES is executed with two parameters the Jena Model of the ontology and a class c_i of this ontology; it determines and return the degree $E(c_i)$ of the class c_i.

Algorithm 7: MAXNUMBEDGES
1. Input: Jena Ontology Model (M)
2. Begin
3.   maxEdges←0
4.   For each class c_i in M Do
5.   totalNumberEdges← TOTALEDGES (M, c_i)
6.   If (maxEdges < totalNumberEdges) Then
7.   maxEdges← totalNumberEdges
8.   End If
9.   EndFor
10.   Return maxEdges
11. End

Algorithm 8: TOTALEDGES
1. Input: Jena Ontology Model (M), ontology class (c_i)
2. Begin
3.   noSuperClasses←0
4.   noSubClasses←0
5.   K ← M.listStatements() //statements in M where c_i is an Object
6.   For each statement in K Do
7.   noSubClasses += 1
8.   EndFor
9.   K ← M.listStatements() //statements in M where c_i is a Subject
10.   For each statement in K Do
11.   noSuperClasses += 1
12.   EndFor
13.   Return (noSuperClasses + noSubClasses)
14. End

4.3   Class and Relation Richness Algorithm

Algorithm 9 (RICHNESS) counts the number of instances of classes in the ontology graph (lines 4 to 8); this number is further divided by the total number of classes in the ontology to obtain the value of the class richness (RICHNESS line 9). The computation of the relation richness (RR) starts in line 10 of the RICHNESS by collecting all the statements in the ontology. These statements are then tested in lines 11 to 17. The test determines and counts the subclassOf relations (RICHNESS line 12) and the relations other than subclassOf which are restrictions (RICHNESS line 15). The number of subclassOf and other relations are accumulated in line 19 and used to compute the RR in line 20 of RICHNESS.

Algorithm 9: RICHNESS
1.   Input: number of classes (nClasses), Jena Ontology Model (M)
2.   Output: class richness, relationship richness
3.   Begin
4.   For each class c_i of M Do
5.   If c_i has an instance Then
6.   countInstances ← countInstances+1
7.   EndIf
8.   EndFor
9.   classRichness← countInstances/nClasses
10.   For each ontology statement S in M Do
11.   If S is a SubclassOf relation Then
12.   subClassOfRel← subClassOfRel + 1
13.   Else
14.   If S is a Restriction Then
15.   otherRel← +1
16.   EndIf
17.   EndIf
18.   EndFor
19.   relations← otherRel+ subClassOfRel
20.   relationRichness←relations/(relations+ subClassOfRel)
21.   End

5   Experiments and Evaluation

5.1   Dataset

A set of 25 biomedical OWL ontologies downloaded from the Bioportal repository [3] is used in the experiments. For each ontology in the dataset, Table 1 provides the index, number of classes, size (in kilobytes) and execution times (in milliseconds) of the path-related, entropy and richness algorithms.

Table 1. Execution time of the algorithms on 25 biomedical ontologies

Ontology index	Number of classes	Size (KB)	Execution time (MS)		
			Path-related	Entropy	Richness
O_1	51346	21731	3299702	659	50
O_2	6544	2629	15991	291	8
O_3	9795	6310	90309	297	55
O_4	8850	6115	823512	113	21
O_5	3003	2304	70937	486	23
O_6	5278	3462	56742	182	7
O_7	4326	4288	4095	188	32
O_8	16377	23938	1020351	210	15
O_9	2366	1977	30466	76	5
O_{10}	9484	21268	37845	148	52
O_{11}	42241	60987	2714577	542	41
O_{12}	3165	2146	8193	79	6
O_{13}	108063	171095	6599404	1713	130
O_{14}	5930	2968	82256	212	17
O_{15}	67663	20597	4348298	868	66
O_{16}	4186	2862	20695	113	7
O_{17}	10580	3977	50105	600	21
O_{18}	4612	3947	13188	130	5
O_{19}	2520	828	18573	77	5
O_{20}	4530	2813	7717	155	6
O_{21}	2339	852	4287	61	11
O_{22}	3066	1708	3697	220	6
O_{23}	3593	2146	2500	18	18
O_{24}	1734	842	1322	93	5
O_{25}	746	510	733	45	3

5.2   Computer and Software Environments

The experiments were carried out on a computer with the following characteristics: 64-bit Genuine Intel (R) Celeron (R) CPU 847, Windows 8 release preview, 2 GB RAM and 300 GB hard drive. The algorithms for computing and analysing the complexity metrics were implemented in Java Jena API configured in Eclipse Integrated Development Environment (IDE) Version 4.2.

5.3   Performance Analysis

The performance analysis concerns the main algorithms including: FINDPATHS, ENTROPY and RICHNESS. The analysis consists of determining the asymptotic behaviour of the function $f(n)$ of the execution time of these 3 algorithms. The asymptotic behaviour of a function $f(n)$ of the execution time of an algorithm refers to the growth of $f(n)$ as n gets larger with n representing the size of the input to the algorithm [17]. The asymptotic behaviour of the 3 above-mentioned algorithms is based on the $Big - O$ notation which considers only the variable n with its highest order while ignoring other low-order terms in $f(n)$ [17].

Asymptotic Behaviour of FINDPATHS Algorithm. Based on the rule of thumb from the algorithm complexity theory related to the number of loops in an algorithm [17], the function $f(n)$ of the FINDPATHS algorithm is $O(n)$; this is due to the fact that FINDPATHS has three simple loops (not nested). Further, based on the rule of the worst-case or highest number of iterations of a loop [17] n is considered as the number of classes of the ontology evaluated. Figure 1 presents the results of the execution time of the FINDPATHS algorithm on the dataset. The results in Fig. 1 show that the execution time of FINDPATHS on the dataset is higher on the ontologies with a large number of classes (e.g. O_1, O_{11}, O_{13} and O_{15}) and smaller on the ontologies with a low number of classes (e.g. O_5, O_{10}, O_{16} and O_{25}). This is an indication that the execution time of FINDPATHS depends on the number of classes of the ontology.

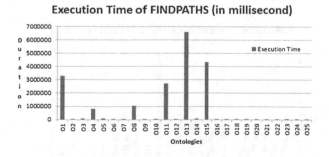

Fig. 1. Execution time FINDPATHS algorithm

Asymptotic Behaviour of ENTROPY Algorithm. The ENTROPY algorithm is mainly based on a loop that processes a list of integers where each value corresponds to the number of classes with $E(c_i)$ equal to the position of the value in the list. Therefore, one can deduce that the $f(n)$ of ENTROPY is $O(n)$ with the worst-case corresponding to case where for 2 classes c_i and c_j, $E(c_i) \neq E(c_j)$. Figure 2 presents the results of the execution time of the ENTROPY on the dataset. Once more the findings presented in Fig. 2 suggests that running ENTROPY over the ontologies with a larger number of classes (e.g. O_1, O_{11}, O_{13} and O_{15}) takes more time than running it on ontologies with a smaller number of classes (e.g. O_4, O_{10}, O_{16} and O_{25}).

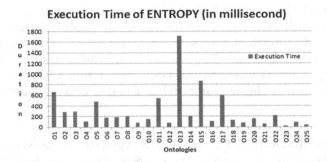

Fig. 2. Execution time of ENTROPY algorithm

Asymptotic Behavior of RICHNESS Agorithm. The RICHNESS algorithm mainly relies on two loops to processes every class and every statement of the ontology. Therefore, the function $f(n)$ of RICHNESS is $O(n)$ with the worst-case being when a higher number of classes lead to a higher number of statements in the ontologies. The results in the Fig. 3 show that for the ontologies in the dataset with a large number of classes (e.g. O_1, O_{13} and O_{15}), the execution time for RICHNESS is greater than on the ontologies with lower number of classes (e.g. O_4, O_{12}, O_{16} and O_{25}).

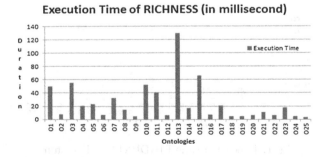

Fig. 3. Execution time of RICHNESS algorithm

The above analysis shows that the execution times of the proposed algorithms are linear $O(n)$ and proportional to the size of the input ontologies. This suggests that the proposed algorithms are efficient and could be used in real world applications.

6 Conclusion

This study proposed a set of algorithms for computing the complexity metrics of ontologies through the automatic exploration of RDF/OWL graphs. These algorithms were implemented using the Apache Jena library and executed on a set of 25 biomedical ontologies in order to assess their time complexity performance. The experiments showed that the execution times of the proposed algorithms are linear and proportional to the size of the input ontologies. This is a promising results as the proposed algorithms may be implemented in real world applications. In future we intend to develop a framework that would help classify ontologies based on their level of complexity. The framework will rely on the algorithms implemented in this study and on a module that implements a decision making process for ranking ontologies.

References

1. Ding, L., et al.: Swoogle: a search and metadata engine for the semantic web. In: 13th ACM Conference on Information and Knowledge Management, Washington, DC, USA, pp. 652–659 (2004)
2. d'Aquin, M., Motta, E.: Watson, more than a Semantic Web search engine. Seman. Web J. **2**, 1–9 (2011)
3. Rubin, D.L., Moreira, D.A., Kanjamala, P.P., Musen, M.A.: BioPortal: a web portal to biomedical ontologies. In: AAAI Spring Symposium: Symbiotic Relationships between Semantic Web and Knowledge Engineering, Palo Alto, California, USA, pp. 74–77 (2008)
4. Yang, Z., Zhang, D., Ye, C.: Evaluation metrics for ontology complexity and evolution analysis. In: Proceedings of the IEEE International Conference on e-Business Engineering, Shanghai, China, pp. 162–170 (2006)
5. Zhang, H., Li, Y.F., Tan, H.B.K.: Measuring design complexity of semantic web ontologies. J. Syst. Soft. **83**, 803–814 (2010)
6. Yao, H., Orme, A.M., Etzkorn, L.: Cohesion metrics for ontology design and application. J. Comput. Sci. **1**, 107–113 (2005)
7. Tartir, S., Arpinar, B., Moore, M., Sheth, A., Aleman-Meza, B.: OntoQA: metric-based ontology quality analysis. In: Proceedings of IEEE Workshop on Knowledge Acquisition from Distributed, Autonomous, Semantically Heterogeneous Data and Knowledge Sources, USA, pp. 45–53 (2005)
8. Myneni, S., Amith, M., Geng, Y., Tao, C.: Towards an ontology-driven framework to enable development of personalized mHealth solutions for cancer survivors' engagement in healthy living. Stud. Health Technol. Inform. **216**, 113–117 (2015)
9. Carroll, J., Dickinson, I., Dollin, C., Reynolds, D., Seaborne, A., Wilkinson, K.: Jena: implementing the semantic web recommendations. In: Proceedings of the 13th International World Wide Web Conference on Alternate Track Papers & Posters, New York, NY, USA, pp. 74–83 (2004)

10. Chen, L., Martone, M., Gupta, A., Fong, L.: OntoQuest: exploring ontological data made easy. In: Proceedings of the 32nd International Conference on Very Large Databases, Korea, pp. 1183–1186 (2006)
11. Haarslev, V., Lu, Y.: ONTOXPL-intelligent exploration of OWL ontologies. In: Proceedings of International Conference on Web Intelligence, China, pp. 45–66 (2004)
12. Aranas, M., Grau, B.C., Kharlamov, E., Marciuska, S., Zheleznyakov, D.: Faceted search over ontology enhanced RDF data. In: Proceedings of Conference on Information and Knowledge Management, China, pp. 939–948 (2014)
13. Tunkelang, D.: Faceted search. In: Synthesis Lectures on Information Concepts, Retrieval, and Services, vol. 1, pp. 1–80. Morgan & Claypool Publishers (2009)
14. Leal, J.P.: Using proximity to compute semantic relatedness in RDF graphs. Comput. Sci. Inf. Syst. **10**, 1727–1746 (2013)
15. Tongchim, S., Kruengkrai, C., Sornlertlamvanich, V., Srichaivattana, P., Isahara, H.: Analysis of an iterative algorithm for term-based ontology alignment. In: Dale, R., Wong, K.-F., Su, J., Kwong, O.Y. (eds.) IJCNLP 2005. LNCS (LNAI), vol. 3651, pp. 346–356. Springer, Heidelberg (2005). https://doi.org/10.1007/11562214_31
16. Palys, T.: Purposive sampling. In: Given, L.M. (ed.) The Sage Encyclopedia of Qualitative Research Methods, vol. 2, pp. 697–698 (2008)
17. Arora, S., Barak, B.: Computational Complexity: A Modern Approach, 1st Edn. Cambridge University Press (2009)

CRank: A Novel Framework for Ranking Semantic Web Ontologies

Jean Vincent Fonou-Dombeu$^{(\boxtimes)}$ and Serestina Viriri

School of Mathematics, Statistics and Computer Science,
University of KwaZulu-Natal, Durban, South Africa
{fonoudombeuj,viriris}@ukzn.ac.za

Abstract. To support the reuse of ontologies on the Semantic Web (SW), various approaches have been proposed to rank these ontologies to help the users or ontology engineers to choose the appropriate ones that suit their needs. However, although some of the existing approaches for ranking ontologies are very effective, they all have been designed with a complete disregard of the degree or level of complexity of the ontologies on the SW. In fact, it is argued that the study of the complexity of ontologies in a domain provide useful information for the selection of the appropriate ones for reuse. This study proposes the CRank framework for ranking ontologies on the SW based on their degree or level of complexity. The CRank framework consists of two phases, namely, the pre-processing and ranking. In the pre-processing phase, the graph of each ontology in the dataset is processed to compute seven complexity metrics that measure the design complexity of ontologies. Thereafter, a decision making algorithm is applied in the ranking phase to rank the ontologies in the dataset by aggregation of their complexity metrics. The CRank framework was applied on a set of 100 ontologies of the biomedical domain and displayed promising results.

Keywords: Ontology · Semantic web · Complexity metrics
Decision making · Ontology ranking

1 Introduction

The semantic web was launched by Berners-Lee et al. [1] as an improvement of the current World Wide Web (WWW). In semantic web, the content of the WWW is enhanced with semantic annotations to enables both humans and computers to understand and process it. The semantic annotation of the Web content is done with ontology. Ontology is an abstract and simple view of a domain through its concepts, entities and objects, and the relationships between them [2]. Ontology is further represented in logic-based syntax in standard languages such as Resource Description Framework (RDF) and Web Ontology Language (OWL) to enable the automatic interpretation and processing of Web content by computers.

© Springer Nature Switzerland AG 2018
E. H. Abdelwahed et al. (Eds.): MEDI 2018, LNCS 11163, pp. 107–121, 2018.
https://doi.org/10.1007/978-3-030-00856-7_7

Since the inception of the semantic web, ontology has been widely adopted in various domains as a technology for realising the integration and interoperability of heterogeneous systems on the internet. Furthermore, the advent of Linked Data has increased the use of ontologies on the Web and many initiatives have been undertaken to create ontology libraries [3] to store in dedicated locations the ontologies of various domains, to promote their access sharing and reuse on the semantic web.

Despite the increase in the number of ontologies on the semantic web, building ontology remain a challenging task due to the time, cost and domain expert knowledge required [4]. Therefore, the trend is towards the reuse of existing ontologies in new applications rather than building a new ontology de novo [5]. Ontology reuse would require the users or ontology engineers to be able to select the appropriate ontology amongst the existing ontologies, for their applications.

To this end, various approaches have been proposed to rank the ontologies on the semantic web [6–8] to help the users or ontology engineers to choose the appropriate ones that suit their needs. The existing approaches for ranking ontologies are based on two main criteria including the structural features of concepts [6,7] and semantic relations and hierarchy of classes [6,8]. None of the previous studies has attempted to rank ontologies on the semantic web based on their design complexity. However, it is argued that the study of the design complexity of ontologies in a domain provide useful information for the selection of the appropriate ontologies for reuse [9].

This study proposes the CRank framework for ranking ontologies on the SW based on their degree or level of complexity. The CRank framework consists of two phases, namely, the pre-processing and ranking. In the preprocessing phase, the graph of each ontology in the dataset is processed to compute seven complexity metrics that measure the design complexity of ontologies. Thereafter, decision making algorithms are applied in the ranking phase to rank the ontologies in the dataset by aggregation of their complexity metrics. The CRank framework was applied on a set of 100 ontologies of the biomedical domain and displayed promising results.

The rest of the paper is structured as follows. Section 2 provides the background of the study. The CRank framework is designed and specified in Sect. 3. Section 4 presents the experimental results of the study and a conclusion ends the paper in Sect. 5.

2   Related Work

The task of ranking ontologies on the semantic web has been of interest to many researchers in the past years [4,5,7,8,10–12]. Alani et al. [4] argued that the task of ranking a set of ontologies should be done based on multidimensional criteria. The authors then proposed the AKTiveRank system which uses four criteria, namely, centrality, class match, density and betweenness to rate and rank ontologies on the semantic web.

Another study in [8] proposed an approach, namely, ARRO for ranking ontologies on the semantic web based on the semantic relations and hierarchy structure of classes in ontologies. Like the AKTiveRank system [4], the ARRO approach ranks each ontology based on its relevance to the user's query terms. A similar approach to ARRO, namely, OntologyRank was proposed in [5]. Like the ARRO approach, the OntologyRank measures the semantic relationships between the classes of ontologies to weight and rank them; the classes considered are those that match the user's query terms.

The ARRO approach was improved in [10] to develop the OS_Rank approach for ranking ontologies. The OS_Rank approach uses three criteria including the class name, ontology structure and semantic relations to measure the coverage of a user's concept by the ontologies. The weight of each ontology class that matches a user's concept is calculated as a weighted sum of the values of the three criteria for that class. The rank of an ontology in OS_Rank is obtained as a weighted sum of the weights of all the classes that match the concepts/terms from a user's query.

Jones and Alani [11] proposed a content-based method for ranking ontologies. The ranking scores of ontologies are obtained by matching the classes to a predetermined corpus of terms extracted from Google and expanded in WordNet; the corpus is built based on a user's query. The content-based ranking method differ from the AKTiveRank and ARRO in that the classes of ontologies are not directly matched to the user's query terms but to a corpus that best represent the domain of interest.

The content-based [11] and OntologyRank [5] methods are combined in [12] to create the Content-OR method for ranking ontologies. The Content-OR method takes advantage of the strong ranking measures developed in OntologyRank to further rank the ontologies that best represent a domain of interest to the users or knowledge engineers, outputted by the content-based method. In fact, in the Content-OR, the content-based method is first applied to rank the ontologies; thereafter, the output of the content-based is used as input to the OntologyRank to perform the final ranking of the ontologies.

A recent approach for ranking ontologies on the semantic web, namely, DWRank was proposed in [7]. Two measures, namely, centrality and authority are computed for each concept of an ontology that match a user's query term. The centrality of a concept is related to the connectivity of this concept to other concepts in the ontology, whereas, the authority of a concept represents its relationship with other concepts in the ontology. Thereafter, a ranking model based on a Learning to rank algorithm is applied to learn the weights of concepts/classes based on their centrality and authority values and rank the ontologies.

None of the previous ranking methods discussed above has dealt with the complexity of the output ranked ontologies. The interest of authors of the previous ranking methods have been mainly to find and rank ontologies that match the user's or knowledge engineer's query terms. However, an inexperienced user may want to use a less complex ontology from the list of ranked ontologies or an experienced knowledge engineer may want to use a complex or less complex ontology from the list of ranked ontologies, based on the application at hand.

Furthermore, ontology libraries have been developed in the past years to store ontologies of specific domains; for instance, the BioPortal, oeGov, AgroPortal libraries [3] store the ontologies of the biomedical, e-government and agriculture domains, respectively. For these ontology libraries that include ontologies that best describe their respective domains, some of the current ranking algorithms may not be useful. The ranking of the ontologies in the libraries requires new ranking techniques like the CRank framework proposed in this study to assist the users or knowledge engineers in the choice of the appropriate ontologies for reuse in a domain. The proposed CRank framework is suitable for ranking ontologies representing a domain based on their degree or level of complexity. The CRank framework may also be used as a complement to existing ontology ranking methods to further rank the output ontologies from these methods to provide additional help to users or ontology engineers in the choice of suitable ontologies for reuse.

3   Design of the CRank Framework

In this section, the architecture of the proposed CRank framework is presented. Thereafter, the theoretical background on the metrics for measuring the design complexity of ontologies and the decision-making algorithms are described. Finally, the platform utilised in the CRank to parse the ontologies is presented.

3.1   Architecture of the CRank Framework

Figure 1 shows the overall architecture of the CRank framework. The framework operates offline in two phases including the pre-processing and ranking phases. In the pre-processing phase, each ontology in the ontology repository is parsed and its complexity metrics are computed. The ontologies stored in the ontology repository of the CRank framework are from either the existing ontologies libraries [3] or the outputs of other lexical-based ontologies ranking methods [4,5,7,8,10–12]. In fact, the existing lexical-based ontologies ranking methods output a ranked list of ontologies in the form of Uniform Resource Identifiers (URIs). These URIs are utilised to download these ontologies from the internet and load them into the ontology repository of the CRank framework.

As mentioned earlier, the ontology libraries keep the ontologies of the same domain in a dedicated location on the internet. Therefore, the ontologies are downloaded from websites on the Internet and loaded into the ontology repository of the CRank framework. After the parsing of an ontology, the pre-processing phase of the CRank framework ends with the computation of the complexity metrics of the ontology. All the complexity metrics of ontologies are submitted as input to the ranking phase. In the ranking phase of the CRank framework, a decision-making algorithm is applied on the ontologies indexes and their complexity metrics to rank the ontologies. The theoretical background on the metrics for measuring the design complexity of ontologies and the decision-making algorithm are presented in the next subsections.

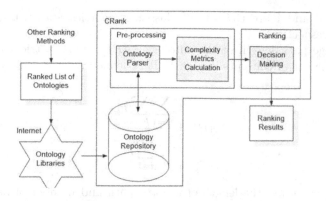

Fig. 1. Architecture of the CRank framework

3.2 Complexity Metrics of Ontologies

Many authors have developed metrics for the quantitative measurement of the design complexity of ontologies [9,13–15]. The complexity metrics reviewed below are those computed for each ontology in the pre-processing phase of the CRank framework in Fig. 1 and used in the ranking phase to rank the ontologies.

1. The average number of paths per concept (ANP): This metric indicates the average connectivity degree of a concept to the root concept in the ontology inheritance hierarchy [13]. This metric illustrates the average level of inheritance of concepts in the ontology. A higher ANP shows that a class inherits from many other classes; it also shows that there is a great number of interconnections between classes. This metric is defined as in Eq. 1:

$$ANP = \frac{\sum_{i=1}^{m} p_i}{|C|} \qquad (1)$$

   where p_i is the number of paths of a concept and C the set of concepts/classes in the ontology. The value ANP for any ontology must be greater or equal to 1; a $ANP = 1$ indicates that an ontology inheritance hierarchy is a tree.

2. Tree Impurity (TIP): This metric is used to measure how far an ontology inheritance hierarchy deviates from a tree, and it is given in Eq. 2:

$$TIP = |P^{'}| - |C^{'}| + 1 \qquad (2)$$

   where $P^{'}$ and $C^{'}$ represent the set of relations and concepts in the inheritance hierarchy, respectively.

3. Size of vocabulary (SOV): This metric defines the total number of named classes, properties and instances in the ontology; it is defined as in Eq. 3:

$$SOV = |P| + |C| + |I| \qquad (3)$$

where C, P and I are the sets of classes, properties and instances in the ontology, respectively.

4. The average path length of the ontology (APL): This metric indicates the average number of concepts in a path. It is defined as in Eq. 4:

$$APL = \frac{\sum_{i=1}^{m}\sum_{k=1}^{p_i} p_{i,k}^l}{\sum_{i=1}^{m} p_i} \quad (4)$$

were $p_{i,k}^l$ and p_i are the length of the kth path and number of paths of the ith concept, respectively.

5. Entropy of ontology graph (EOG): This metric is the application of the logarithm function to a probability distribution over the ontology graph to provide a numerical value that can be used as an indicator of the graph complexity [9]. It is defined as in Eq. 5:

$$EOG = \sum_{i=1}^{n} p(i) log_2(p(i)) \quad (5)$$

where $p(i)$ is the probability for a concept to have i relations.

6. Relationship Richness (RR): This metric provides an indication of the distribution of relations in an ontology. It is defined in Eq. 6:

$$RR = \frac{|R|}{|SR| + |R|} \quad (6)$$

where $|R|$ and $|SR|$ represent the number of relations between classes and the number of subclass relations, respectively.

7. Class Richness (CR): the value of this metric provides an indication of the distribution of individuals across the ontology classes [15]. It is defined as in Eq. 7:

$$CR = \frac{|C'|}{|C|} \quad (7)$$

The value of the CR is a percentage that indicates the amount of instantiation of classes in the ontology.

3.3   Decision Making Process

To rank the ontologies in the CRank framework based on their complexity metrics, a multi-attributes decision making (MADM) algorithm, namely, Weighted Linear Combination Ranking Technique (WLCRT) is used. A MADM algorithm has several parameters including the alternatives, attributes/criteria, criteria weights and decision matrix [16,17]. These parameters are explained below.

Alternatives. They are the different choices of action available to the decision maker. Usually, the set of alternatives is assumed to be finite, ranging from several to hundreds. They are supposed to be screened, prioritized and eventually ranked. In a decision making problem the set of M alternatives is defined as a set $A = \{A_1, A_2, A_3, ..., A_M\}$.

Attributes or Criteria. They represent the different dimensions from which the alternatives can be viewed. In a decision making problem the set of N criteria is defined as a set $C = \{C_1, C_2, C_3, ..., C_N\}$.

Criteria Weights. MADM algorithms determine and use the weights or importance levels of each of the criteria. The criteria weights indicate how an attribute is important than another. The set of criteria weights is given by the vector $W = (w_1, w_2, w_3, ..., w_N)$. Usually the sum of the criteria weights is equal to 1 as in Eq. 8.

$$\sum_j w_j = 1 \tag{8}$$

Decision Matrix. A MADM problem with M alternatives and N criteria is usually represented in the form of a matrix called decision matrix. A decision matrix D is a matrix of $M \times N$ dimensions where each element d_{ij} corresponds to the performance of the alternative A_i when it is evaluated in terms of decision criterion C_j, $(for\ i = 1, 2, 3, ..., M, and\ j = 1, 2, 3, ..., N)$.

In this study, the alternatives are the ontologies in the dataset, whereas, the attributes or criteria are the complexity metrics of these ontologies. The MADM algorithm applied in the ranking phase of the CRank framework is presented in the next subsection.

3.4   Weighted Linear Combination Ranking Technique

The Weighted Linear Combination Ranking Technique (WLCRT) is based on the linear combination of matrix algebra calculations [18]. The WLCRT algorithm uses the Pearson correlation coefficients and the eigenvector method to calculate the criteria weights. The steps of the WLCRT algorithm are explained below.

Construction of the Normalized Decision Matrix. The normalized decision matrix D' in WLCRT is obtained by transforming the decision matrix D in two steps. The first step consists of computing the elements d'_{ij} of D' from the elements of D with Eq. 9.

$$d'_{ij} = \frac{d_{ij} - d_{jmin}}{d_{jmax} - d_{jmin}} \ (for\ i = 1, 2, 3, ..., M, and\ j = 1, 2, 3, ..., N) \tag{9}$$

The second step consists of computing the normalized decision matric R of D based on D' as in Eq. 10.

$$r_{ij} = 0.1 + 0.8d'_{ij} \ (for\ i = 1, 2, 3, ..., M, and\ j = 1, 2, 3, ..., N) \tag{10}$$

Elicitation of Criteria Weights. The determination of the criteria weights begins with the calculation of the Pearson correlation coefficients from the normalised decision matrix R. The Pearson correlation coefficient $correl(x, y)$ of two discrete variables $x = [x_1, x_2, ..., x_{n-1}, x_n]$ and $y = [y_1, y_2, ..., y_{n-1}, y_n]$ is a value that expresses the distance (or linear dependence) between these variables [19]. It is used to determine whether 2 variables are related. The Pearson correlation coefficients are calculated with Eq. 11.

$$correl(x, y) = \frac{\sum_i^n (x_i - \overline{x}).(y_i - \overline{y})}{\sqrt{\sum_i^n (x_i - \overline{x})^2}.\sqrt{\sum_i^n (y_i - \overline{y})^2}} \tag{11}$$

where $-1 \leq correl(x, y) \geq 1$; $\overline{x} = \frac{1}{n}\sum_i^n x_i$ and $\overline{y} = \frac{1}{n}\sum_i^n y_i$. Therefore, if each column of the normalized decision matrix R is a discrete variable, the Pearson correlation coefficients between M criteria of R form a proximity matrix $C(M \times M)$ [18]. The proximity matrix C expresses a set of observations on how correlated the criteria are. According to Chou [18], the weights of the criteria represent the priorities of the elements of the principal diagonal of the proximity matrix; these weights are the absolute values of the eigenvectors that correspond to the maximum eigenvalue λ_{max}. Given a linear transformation (or linear matrix) P, a non-zero vector w is defined as an eigenvector of C if there is a scalar λ that satisfies the Eq. 12.

$$Pw = \lambda w \tag{12}$$

where, the scalar λ is called the eigenvalue of C for the eigenvector w [20]. Given the set of eigenvectors and their corresponding eigenvalues, one can obtain a diagonal matrix where each element of the diagonal corresponds to an eigenvalue [18]. This matrix is given in Eq. 13.

$$W^{-1}.P.W = diagonal\{\lambda_1, \lambda_2, ---, \lambda_{max}\} \tag{13}$$

Where, W is a matrix composed of the eigenvectors of P and W^{-1} the inverse of W.

Aggregation of the Preference or Alternative Information. The aggregation of preference or alternatives consists in transforming a set of numerical values into a unique representative value of an alternative [21]. An aggregation is a continuous function $h : [0, 1]^n \rightarrow [0, 1]$ that determines the unique value of an alternative [21]. Given the weights of criteria of a decision-making process, the aggregation operator h in the WLCRT method is defined as in Eq. 14; it is a parametric function called the weighted generalised mean.

$$h_\alpha(A_i) = (\sum_j^N w_j.r_{ij})^{\frac{1}{\alpha}} \ (for \ i = 1, 2, 3, ..., M, and \ j = 1, 2, 3, ..., N) \tag{14}$$

where, A_i is an alternative, w_j the weight of criterion C_j and r_{ij} the performance of the alternative A_i to a criterion C_j. $\alpha(-\infty < \alpha < +\infty)$ is a non-zero real number, it is the parameter of the aggregation operator h. The score of the alternative A_i corresponds to the mean or average of h_α [18] and it is calculated as in Eq. 15.

$$\overline{h_\alpha} = \frac{\int_a^b h_\alpha d\alpha}{b-a} \tag{15}$$

where, $\overline{h_\alpha}$ is the mean value of h_α, a and b the beginning and end of an arbitrary interval $[a, b] \subseteq [-\infty, +\infty]$. The trapezoidal rule is used to approximate the value of $\int_a^b h_\alpha d\alpha$ as in Eq. 16.

$$\int_a^b h_\alpha d\alpha \approx \Delta\alpha.[\frac{h_a + h_b}{2} + \sum_{i=1}^{u-1} h_{\alpha_i}] \tag{16}$$

where, u is an arbitrary number of the subinterval of $[a, b]$, $a + b = 0$, $\Delta\alpha = \frac{b-a}{u}$ and $\alpha_i = a + i.\Delta\alpha$. Equation 16 can be further written as in Eq. 17 [18].

$$\int_a^b h_\alpha d\alpha \approx \frac{b-a}{2u}(h_a + 2h_{a+\Delta\alpha} + 2h_{a+2\Delta\alpha} + ... + 2h_{b-2\Delta\alpha} + 2h_{b-\Delta\alpha} + h_b) \tag{17}$$

By substituting Eq. 17 into Eq. 15 one obtains a new representation of $\overline{h_\alpha}$ as in Eq. 18.

$$\overline{h_\alpha} = \frac{1}{2u}(h_a + 2h_{a+\Delta\alpha} + 2h_{a+2\Delta\alpha} + ... + 2h_{b-2\Delta\alpha} + 2h_{b-\Delta\alpha} + h_b) \tag{18}$$

Ranking of Alternatives. Alternatives are ranked based on their respective mean values calculated with Eq. 18. The last step of the WLCRT algorithm is the sensitivity analysis.

Sensitivity Analysis. The sensitivity analysis of a decision-making problem consists in determining the set of criteria for which the smallest change of their weights will impacts the ranking order of alternatives [22]. As the sum of criteria weights is always equal to 1, a change to one criterion weight will lead to a change of other criteria weights. Let?s assume the weight w_i is changed into w_i', the change of another criterion weight w_k into w_k' is expressed as in Eq. (19).

$$w_k' = \frac{1 - w_i'}{1 - w_i}.w_k \tag{19}$$

3.5   Ontology Parser

To parse and process ontologies in the CRank framework, a semantic web library, namely, Jena API is used. It is an open source library for developing Semantic

Web applications through extraction and manipulation of RDF graphs of ontologies. The Jena API library includes interfaces for RDF and OWL ontologies, a SPARQL engine and RDF parsers. In Jena, a RDF graph is represented by the Model interface which represents the set of statements of RDF ontology. The Model interface also provides functions for retrieving and saving RDF graphs from and to files as well as functions for creating resources, properties and literals, and the statements for linking them [23].

4   Experiments

This section presents and discusses the experimental results of the study. The dataset, the computer and programming environments as well as the calculated complexity metrics of ontologies in the dataset are presented. Thereafter, the ranking results of the CRank framework applied on the ontologies in the dataset is presented and discussed.

4.1   Dataset

The dataset in this study is constituted of 100 biomedical ontologies downloaded from the BioPortal Repository [24]. Due to space constraint, the list of these ontologies could not be provided in this paper. However, the 100 ontologies are encoded $O_i, 1 \leq i \leq 100$, to ease the reference to them in the discussions. The ontologies in the dataset are the semantic modelling of different branches of the biomedical domain. The computer and software environments that was used to conduct the experiments in this study is presented next.

4.2   Computer and Software Environments

The experiments were carried out on a computer with the following characteristics: 64-bit Genuine Intel (R) Celeron (R) CPU 847, Windows 8 release preview, 2 GB RAM and 300 GB hard drive. The implementation of the CRank framework was done in Java Jena API library [23] configured in Eclipse Integrated Development Environment (IDE) Version 4.2.

4.3   Experimental Results

Amongst the 100 ontologies in the dataset, only the codes of 70 were successfully parsed in Jena API to enable the calculation of their complexity metrics. Table 1 presents the ranking results of the 70 ontologies that were successfully processed by the parser of the CRank framework. The complexity metrics (Eqs. 1 to 7) of the ontologies were computed in the pre-processing phase of the CRank framework. Thereafter, WLCRT decision making algorithm was applied to the complexity metrics of the ontologies along with their indexes $(O_i, 1 \leq i \leq 100)$ in the ranking phase of the CRank framework to rank the ontologies. In Table 1 the ranking results is provided in increasing order from 1 to 70. Due to the

Table 1. Ranking results of the CRank framework

Index	Rank	Index	Rank	Index	Rank	Index	Rank	Index	Rank	Index	Rank
O_{44}	1	O_{48}	13	O_{45}	25	O_{76}	37	O_{56}	49	O_{57}	61
O_{66}	2	O_{53}	14	O_{17}	26	O_{42}	38	O_{21}	50	O_{16}	62
O_{97}	3	O_{91}	15	O_2	27	O_{75}	39	O_{26}	51	O_{24}	63
O_{34}	4	O_{80}	16	O_{73}	28	O_{60}	40	O_{95}	52	O_{11}	64
O_{88}	5	O_{28}	17	O_{86}	29	O_{50}	41	O_{100}	53	O_{85}	65
O_{96}	6	O_{69}	18	O_{71}	30	O_{18}	42	O_{54}	54	O_{78}	66
O_{43}	7	O_{63}	19	O_{51}	31	O_{98}	43	O_{36}	55	O_{70}	67
O_{94}	8	O_{55}	20	O_9	32	O_1	44	O_{82}	56	O_{14}	68
O_{99}	9	O_3	21	O_{84}	33	O_{49}	45	O_8	57	O_{29}	69
O_{30}	10	O_{40}	22	O_{90}	34	O_{12}	46	O_{72}	58	O_4	70
O_{13}	11	O_{89}	23	O_{35}	35	O_{20}	47	O_{61}	59		
O_5	12	O_{32}	24	O_7	36	O_{33}	48	O_{46}	60		

large number of ontologies involved in the ranking, patterns of information are looked at in three regions in the ranking results, namely, the first, middle and last 10 positions; these are the ranges of positions: 1 to 10, 31 to 40 and 61 to 70. Tables 2, 3 and 4 presents the complexity metrics of the ontologies in the three ranges including the ANP, APL, TIP and SOV.

In [25], it is demonstrated that ontologies with high values for the complexity metrics including: ANP, APL and TIP are highly complex. The analysis of the complexity metrics of the first 10 ontologies in the CRank ranking Tables 1 reveals that they have lower values for the ANP, APL and TIP Table 2. This is an indication that the first 10 ontologies in the CRank ranking results are less

Table 2. Complexity metrics of the first 10 ontologies in the CRank ranking results

Index	Ranges of complexity metrics of ontologies in the dataset			
	$[1 \leq ANP \leq 133]$	$[1 \leq APL \leq 6]$	$[1 \leq TIP \leq 58741]$	$[150 \leq SOV \leq 112377]$
O_{44}	4	1	2	7510
O_{66}	4	1	715	582
O_{97}	3	1	2	990
O_{34}	1	1	5	796
O_{88}	5	1	1	284
O_{96}	5	1	20	528
O_{43}	3	1	2507	4105
O_{94}	3	1	98	937
O_{99}	3	1	257	638
O_{30}	3	1	1048	3719

Table 3. Complexity metrics of the last 10 ontologies in the CRank ranking results

Index	Ranges of complexity metrics of ontologies in the dataset			
	$[1 \leq ANP \leq 133]$	$[1 \leq APL \leq 6]$	$[1 \leq TIP \leq 58741]$	$[150 \leq SOV \leq 112377]$
O_{57}	1	1	907	211
O_{16}	71	3	30562	42382
O_{24}	45	5	5176	4267
O_{11}	44	5	2919	31554
O_{85}	50	5	39915	11482
O_{78}	13	2	781	4151
O_{70}	7	2	455	4530
O_{14}	49	6	1533	2465
O_{29}	75	6	2644	4502
O_4	75	6	122	20279

Table 4. Complexity metrics for the middle 10 ontologies in the CRank ranking results

Index	Ranges of complexity metrics of ontologies in the dataset			
	$[1 \leq ANP \leq 133]$	$[1 \leq APL \leq 6]$	$[1 \leq TIP \leq 58741]$	$[150 \leq SOV \leq 112377]$
O_{51}	9	2	248	210
O_9	9	2	610	3602
O_{84}	37	1	249	298
O_{90}	10	2	47	240
O_{35}	11	1	1368	4235
O_7	31	2	899	5952
O_{76}	9	1	1340	2333
O_{42}	12	2	359	1056
O_{75}	9	2	332	1239
O_{60}	19	5	635	1619

complex compared to the rest of the ontologies in the dataset. This finding is supported in [25] where it is shown that these ontologies have low number of classes and properties.

The last 10 ontologies in the CRank ranking have higher values for the complexity metrics: ANP, APL and TIP Table 3 compared to the first 10 ontologies Table 2. This indicates their high level of complexity [9, 25]. This finding is also supported by the high size of vocabulary (SOV) of these ontologies (rightmost column of Table 3).

Table 4 shows that the middle 10 ontologies in the CRank ranking have higher values for the complexity metrics including ANP, APL and TIP, than those in the first 10 positions Table 2; furthermore, these metrics are lower than that of the ontologies in the last 10 positions Table 3. This finding suggests that the CRank framework has successfully ranked the ontologies in the dataset in increasing order on their level or degree of complexity.

Compared to other ontology ranking approaches, Alani et al. [4] suggested that a multi-dimensional approach in which all possible features of an ontology is considered should be adopted to address the task of ranking ontologies on the semantic web. This multi-dimensional ranking approach would give the users or ontology engineers the freedom to control all ranking criteria as required [4]. Therefore, the CRank framework is a complement to existing ontology ranking methods in that it can be applied to further rank the output ontologies from these methods based on their degree or level of complexity, thereby, providing additional help to the users or ontology engineers in the choice of suitable ontologies for reuse.

5   Conclusion

This study proposed a novel framework for ranking ontologies on the semantic web. The framework namely, CRank offers two phases for ranking semantic web ontologies. In its pre-processing phase, the CRank framework parses each ontology in the dataset and computes its complexity metrics. The resulting complexity metrics of ontologies are submitted as input to the ranking phase of the CRank framework. In the ranking phase, the WLCRT decision-making is applied on the complexity metrics of the ontologies to rank them. The CRank framework was successfully applied to parse and rank 70 ontologies of the biomedical domain in increasing order on the aggregation of their complexity metrics. The ranking results constitute important guidelines for the selection and reuse of biomedical ontologies in the dataset. The CRank framework is suitable for ranking ontologies from existing ontology libraries. Furthermore, the CRank framework can also be used as a complement to existing ontology ranking methods to further rank the outputs ontologies from these methods to provide additional help to users or ontology engineers in the choice of suitable ontologies for reuse. In future, the authors intend to investigate the use of Machine Learning algorithms in the ranking phase of the CRank framework to classify ontologies based on their complexity metrics.

References

1. Berners-lee, T., Hendler, J., Lassila, O.: The Semantic Web. Sci. Am., 29–37 (2001)
2. Gruber, T.R.: Toward principles for the design of ontologies used for knowledge sharing. Int. J. Hum.-Comput. Stud. **43**, 907–928 (1995)
3. Naskar, D., Dutta, B.: Ontology libraries: a study from ontofier and ontologist perspectives. In: 19th International Symposium on Electronic Theses and Dissertations, Lille, France, pp. 1–12 (2016)
4. Alani, H., Brewster, C., Shadbolt, N.: Ranking ontologies with AKTiveRank. In: 5th International Conference on the Semantic Web, Athens, Greece, pp. 1–15 (2006)
5. Park, J., Ohb, S., Ahn, J.: Ontology selection ranking model for knowledge reuse. Expert Syst. Appl. **38**, 5133–5144 (2011)

6. Sridevi, K., Umarani, R.: Ontology ranking algorithms on semantic web: a review. Int. J. Adv. Res. Comput. Commun. Eng. **2**, 3471–3476 (2013)
7. Butt, A.S., Haller, A., Xie, L.: DWRank: learning concept ranking for ontology search. Semant. Web **7**, 447–461 (2016)
8. Yu, W., Cao, J., Chen, J.: A novel approach for ranking ontologies on the semantic web. In: 1st International Symposium on Pervasive Computing and Applications, Urumchi, Xinjiang, China, pp. 608–612 (2006)
9. Zhang, H., Li, Y.F., Tan, H.B.K.: Measuring design complexity of semantic web ontologies. J. Syst. Softw. **83**, 803–814 (2010)
10. Yu, W., Chen, J.: Ontology ranking for the semantic web. In: 3rd International Symposium on Intelligent Information Technology Application, NanChang, China, pp. 573–574 (2009)
11. Jones, M., Alani, H.: Content-based ontology ranking. In: 9th International Protg Conference, Stanford, CA, USA, pp. 1–4 (2006)
12. Subhashini, R., Akilandeswari, J., Haris, S.: An integrated ontology ranking method for enhancing knowledge reuse. Int. J. Eng. Technol. (IJET) **6**, 1424–1431 (2014)
13. Yang, Z., Zhang, D., Ye, C.: Evaluation metrics for ontology complexity and evolution analysis. In: IEEE International Conference on e-Business Engineering, UK, pp. 162–170 (2006)
14. Manso, M.E., Genero, M., Piattini, M.: No-redundant metrics for UML class diagram structural complexity. In: Eder, J., Missikoff, M. (eds.) CAiSE 2003. LNCS, vol. 2681, pp. 127–142. Springer, Heidelberg (2003). https://doi.org/10.1007/3-540-45017-3_11
15. Tartir, S., Arpinar, B., Moore, M., Sheth, A., Aleman-Meza, B.: OntoQA: metric-based ontology quality analysis. In: IEEE Workshop on Knowledge Acquisition from Distributed, Autonomous, Semantically Heterogeneous Data and Knowledge Sources, USA, pp. 45–53 (2005)
16. Triantaphyllou, E., Shu, B., Nieto Sanchez, S., Ray, T.: Multi-criteria decision making: an operations research approach. In: Webster, J.G. (ed) Encyclopedia of Electrical and Electronics Engineering, vol. 15, pp. 175–186. Wiley, New York (1998)
17. Chen, S., Hwang, C.: Fuzzy Multiple Attribute Decision Making Methods and Applications. Lecture Notes in Economics and Mathematical Systems, vol. 375. Springer, Heidelberg (1992)
18. Chou, J.R.: A weighted linear combination ranking technique for multi-criteria decision analysis. S. Afr. J. Econ. Manage. Sci. Spec. **16**, 28–41 (2013)
19. Hauke, J., Kossowski, T.: Comparison of values of Pearsonś and Spearmanś correlation coefficients on the same sets of data. Quaestiones Geographicae **30**, 87–93 (2011)
20. Pentland, A., Moghaddam, B., Starner, T.: A view-based and modular eigenspaces for face recognition. In: IEEE Internation Conference on Computer Vision and Pattern Recognition, pp. 84–91 (1994)
21. Smilikova, R., Wachiowak, M.P.: Aggregation operator for selection problems. J. Fuzzy Sets Syst. Spec. Issue Soft Decis. Anal. **131**, 23–34 (2002)
22. Wallace, S.W.: Decision making under uncertainty: is sensitivity analysis of any use? Oper. Res. **48**, 20–25 (2000)
23. McBride, B.J.: Implementing the RDF model and syntax. Specification. In: 2nd International Workshop on the Semantic Web - SemWeb 2001, Hong Kong, China, pp. 1–6 (2001)

24. Noy, N.F., et al.: BioPortal: ontologies and integrated data resources at the click of a mouse. In: International Conference on Biomedical Ontology, New York, USA, p. 197 (2009)

25. Kazadi, Y.K., Fonou-Dombeu, J.V.: Analysis of advanced complexity metrics of biomedical ontologies in the bioportal repository. Int. J. Biosci. Biochem. Bioinf. **7**, 20–32 (2017)

Data Fusion, Classification and Learning

A New Way of Handling Missing Data in Multi-source Classification Based on Adaptive Imputation

Ikram Abdelkhalek[1(✉)], Afef Ben Brahim[2], and Nadia Essousi[1]

[1] Institut Supérieur de Gestion de Tunis, LARODEC, Université de Tunis,
Tunis, Tunisia
ikram.abdelkhalek28@gmail.com
[2] Tunis Business School, LARODEC, Université de Tunis, Tunis, Tunisia

Abstract. Data fusion is an interesting methodology for improving the classification performance. It consists in combining data acquired from multiple sources for more informative decision and better decision making. This latter is a challenging task due to many issues. The main of these issues arises from the data to be fused. Missing data presents one of the issues, their presence affects the performance of the algorithms and results on a misleading prediction. Appropriately handling missing data is crucial for accurate inference. Several approaches have been proposed in the literature to deal with multi-source classification problems, however they neglect the presence of missingness in the data and assume that the data are complete which is not the case in real life. Other approaches use directly simple data imputation before the learning process, which is not always enough to obtain a reliable learning and prediction model. In this paper, we propose a new approach to deal with missing data in multi-source classification problem. In our approach, we avoid the direct imputation when the concerned feature is not important, but we also adjust the predictions fusion process based on the missing data rate in each data source and in the new instance to classify. This approach is used with Random Forests as an ensemble classifier, and it has shown improved classification performance compared to existing approaches.

Keywords: Data fusion · Missing data · Classification
Random forests

1 Introduction

In several disciplines, information underlying the same problem can be acquired from different sources. For intelligent decision making, taking advantage of all the data available is important to consolidate different concepts. Data fusion is well suited to solve this problem as it combines data acquired from multiple heterogenous sources and leads therefore for a better decision making [1]. There are mainly three types of fusion strategies [2], namely data fusion (low level fusion),

E. H. Abdelwahed et al. (Eds.): MEDI 2018, LNCS 11163, pp. 125–136, 2018.
https://doi.org/10.1007/978-3-030-00856-7_8

feature fusion (intermediate level fusion), and decision fusion (high level fusion). In the low level raw data provided from multiple sources are combined into new raw data that is expected to be more synthetic and informative. However, this level suffers from the alignment problem since the data are presented in different way and it is difficult to provide a general frame. Feature fusion requires the extraction and combination of different features to remove redundant and irrelevant ones. The disadvantage here, is that this reduction may affect the performance of the learning algorithm. Decision fusion uses a set of classifiers and combines their outputs by various methods for better and unbiased result. Several methods of decision fusion exist like Majority voting [3], weighted majority voting [4] and Dempster-Shafer evidence theory [5], etc. In our work, we are interested in the decision fusion level since it the most appropriate for multi-source data merging, it can deal with multiple learning algorithm and the most important multiple combination techniques. It is also advantageous because of its feasibility and its low computational complexity.

Significant research efforts for robust fusion of information and for making combined decisions from these sources are being pursued at a rapid pace. Ensemble methods have been heavily applied for this purpose in many areas and they have proven their effectiveness. In [6] a methodology is developed for combining multi-season Landsat and ancillary data using the Random Forests algorithm. It has shown improved accuracy result compared with state of the art. Authors in [7] proposed a classifier fusion approach using two data sources.

Most of these works have been primarily focused on the cases where the data is complete across all the different sources and can not effectively integrate sources in the presence of missing data. However, the multitude and diversity of the sources of acquisition gives rise to a large amount of data of different nature, characterized by incompleteness, incoherence, noise, etc. This makes the data fusion a challenging task. Missing data presents one of the challenges, their presence affects the performance of the algorithm and leads to a misleading prediction. Thus, it is important to appropriately handling them [8].

In this paper, we propose a new fusion method for incomplete data based on adaptive imputation. This method is able to deal with missing data in a new way through an adaptive imputation and its main aim is to improve the prediction performance in multi-source classification. The object to classify is committed to an imputation only if the missing values concern features that are relevant. We applied the weighted majority voting as a fusion rule. Since there will be still some bias associated with the filling of the missing data no matter what imputation method is chosen, we propose a new weight assignment formula in the decision fusion process which takes into account if an imputation process has been performed during the prediction phase or not. Also, it consider the percentage of missing values in each data source.

The reminder of the paper is organized as follows. Section 2 presents the related work of missing data imputation methods in multi-source classification. We describe our proposed approach in Sect. 3. In Sect. 4, we conduct an experimental study on two data sets and with comparison to existing approaches. Section 5 concludes this paper.

2   Related Work

Process of filling in the missing data is an intimidating task, which has almost always to be confronted in data mining. There are several approaches that can be used to fill in the missing data, depending on the type and amount of missing data.

One of the approaches to deal with missing data is to discard the instances which contain missing values [9]. This is the case deletion method and it is the easiest solution to deal with missing data, however, the problem here is that important information may be lost. This method is useful for datasets containing small amount of missing values, Acuna et al. [10] demonstrated that in this case there is no significant difference between case deletion and other imputation approaches. The other approach is feature selection, it concerns the deletion of non relevant feature that contain missing values. A feature is considered to be irrelevant if it correlates poorly with the class attribute. The third approach which is the frequently used to treat missing data is the imputation of missing values. The method chosen depends on the type of variable and the amount of missing data, i.e. for missing numerical data, mean or median are used instead of mode. Those methods are detailed in [10].

For missing data in multi-source problem, Yuan et al. propose an incomplete Multi-Source Feature learning method in Alzheimer's patients classification problem [11]. In their approach, they first divide the samples to many blocks according to the different combinations of available data sources, and learn shared sets of features based on a multi-task problem. After that, they combine the results from all data blocks to obtain a consistent feature learning result without necessarily estimating before the missing values.

In [12], authors propose the Heterogeneous boosting (HBOOST), an extension of AdaBoost algorithm that exploits complete and partial information from multiple data sources. To ensure improved accuracy, the HBOOST method boosts the decisions from the individual sources using a modification to AdaBoost. This modification concerns the reweighting, where the importance of an object present in only one source out of n sources will be increased.

The described methods focus on dealing with missing data, but do not take into account whether an imputation process has been applied or not during the multi-source learning model building, nor during the classification of new data.

In our proposed approach, we avoid the direct imputation when the feature is not important, but we also adjust the prediction process based on the missing data rate in each source. We use both the feature selection and the imputation method to benefit from the advantages of each one according to our needs.

3   Our Proposed Approach

To ensure the improved classification accuracy when combining incomplete data from multiple sources, we propose to deal with missing values by adaptive imputation based on feature selection. It is followed by a learning process where a classification ensemble model is built from different data sources. Then, a fusion process is done where the ensemble decisions are combined. In the latter step, the predictions are adjusted by a coefficient calculated based on the missingness rate in each data source and in the new instance to classify. The proposed approach is named Fusion Method based on Adaptive Imputation (FMAI) and it consists of three phases namely: the learning phase, the prediction phase, and the fusion phase. These phases are detailed in what follows.

3.1   Learning Phase

The aim of the first phase is to build the models from the different sources, where a source represents a dataset, to be used in the next phase to classify an object. Before the building process step FMAI computes the percentage of missing data in the sources which will be used further in the fusion phase since it has an important impact on the reliability assigned to that source.

Then, an imputation process is performed on different datasets using the rough method. This method works one of two ways. If the variable being imputed is numeric, it is roughly imputed by its median value. If it is categorical, then the most common class of the variable that is being imputed is selected as the imputed value. Computationally, this method is not expensive, it is fast. In addition, it gives good performance [13]. Thereafter, the building process is performed using a classification algorithm able to learn from multiple sources. We choose Random Forests (RF) algorithm as it is known to be efficient for input data with heterogeneous types, and is able to solve feature selection problem on which we are also interested [6], thus we used RF for classification but also for identifying relevant features.

Random Forests

RF is a popular decision tree ensemble famous for its robustness and good performance in relation with other algorithms.

As a decision tree ensemble, RF needs to create several different decision trees. In order to do so, each tree is built iteratively based on a bootstrap sample from the original training data. Then to determine the split at each node, a random selection of features is applied. To classify a new instance classifiers outputs are combined using the majority vote [7].

We apply the RF algorithm for different sources and based on the model built, the relevant features are ranked in a vector. We can easily remark that a feature selection occurs into the random forests algorithm, by selecting features which improve the most the predictive performance to put them in the tree nodes. In [14], authors discussed the use of random forests in feature selection. Relevant features play a main role for achieving an accurate classification. Therefore, selecting them is a crucial step in this phase since they are the pieces on which we will rely on in the prediction phase. In order to find relevant features, we get an essential need to quantify the feature importance. RF offer this possibility. The most used score of importance is the increasing in mean of the error of a tree, misclassification rate for classification problems. With RF to calculate the importance of a specific feature, the observed values of this feature are randomly permuted in the (Out Of Bag) OOB sample (instances that are not included in the bootstrap sample used to build the tree t). Such method for measuring feature importance is called random forests permutation importance and it is described in [14].

All those steps are performed for each data source separately. Algorithm (1) represents the different steps of this phase.

Algorithm 1. Model building

1: **Input**: $source_i$: Dataset from $source_i$
2: **Output**: PM: Percent of missing values in the dataset, $Model_i$: Built model, IF: vector of important features
3: **Begin**
4: PM = **Compute MV**($source_i$)   Calculate the percent of missing value in the dataset
5: Complete data =**Imput**($source_i$)   Filling in the missing value with the rough method
6: Model = **Random Forest**(Attribute class, learning set =$source_i$, Nbtree)
7: IF = Importance(Model)
8: **End**

3.2 Prediction Phase

The next phase consists in classifying a new instance. It takes as input the information about the new instance to classify and the outputs of the previous phase and gives as result the initial class according to each source through an adaptive imputation. Three possible cases occurs: (i) the new object contains missing values for attributes that are important, then an imputation is performed to allow the prediction of the class, (ii) the missing values concern also features that are not important, in this case the prediction is performed based only on the other available features. Note here that we avoid the imputation of irrelevant features to reduce the risk of mis-prediction because an irrelevant feature with approximative estimation of its value has a higher risk of giving misleading prediction later in the classification phase. Another reason for not considering irrelevant features is to reduce the complexity and the execution time when it is about high dimensional data. (iii) There are no missing values, a classification is performed directly. Since we deal with multi source classification, the instance to classify has multiple source of information. Each information source is represented by a vector V_i which contains the information about this instance from $source_i$, where i = 1..n and n denotes the number of data sources. Algorithm (2) provides a description of this procedure.

Algorithm 2. Initial class prediction process

1: **Input:** $Model_i$: Built model from $source_i$, V_i: the information about
the instance to classify from $source_i$, IF_i: vector of important features of
$source_i$;
2: **Output:** Predicted initial class C
3: Tab = **Evaluate**(V_i);
4: **If**(Tab is null)   The matrix does not contain missing features
C = Predict($Model_i$,V_i)
Else If(Tab $\in IF_i$)   There is missing important features in the matrix
$NewV_i$ = Impute(V_i)
C = Predict($Model_i$,$NewV_i$)
Else   There is missing features but they are not important
$NewV_i$ = Eliminate(V_i)   Discard missing features
C = Predict($Model_i$,V_i)   Prediction performed based only on available
features

3.3 Fusion Phase

In the last phase, the final class is obtained by combining the different initial
classes based on a weighted majority voting. It is obvious from the literature
that the imputation gives only approximative estimation of missing values no
matter what imputation method is chosen and researchers are still working on
improving the imputation methods. For this reason in our proposed method, the
assigned weight checks if an imputation has been performed during the prediction
phase or not. It is important to check the completeness of the information about
the instance to be classified since it influences the prediction. An instance with
complete information has more chance to be classified correctly since there will
be still some bias associated with filling of the missing values. Also, we take
into account the amount of missing data in each source since this latter has an
impact on the performance of the classifier. Thus, the proposed weight for each
model by our method is computed as follows:

$$W_i = \frac{Accuracy(Model_i)}{\beta_i + \varepsilon}$$

where β_i is the sum of PM_i (the percentage of the missing values in $source_i$) and
pm (the percentage of missing values in the new instance) and ε is a value very
close to zero (e.g.: 0,001) used to avoid the division by zero error in case there
are no missing values in all the data sources. Figure 1 presents the flowchart of
our proposed approach.

4   Experimental Study

In this section we report the experimental setup and results of our fusion method
proposed in Sect. 3. This method is applied to two data sets described in Sect. 4.1.
We use the Holdout protocol for our experiments, which splits the whole data

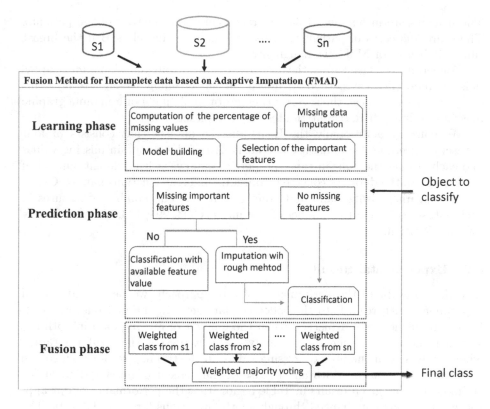

Fig. 1. Flowchart of the proposed method

set into a training and a test set. Also, we evaluate our method in terms of accuracy, Specificity, F-measure, Recall and precision which are the main evaluation measures.

4.1 Datasets

In our frame, FMAI considers heterogenous sources of data for the same problem. The heterogeneity concerns the source of acquisition. Hence it is tested on two datasets that contain data acquired from different information sources for the same problem. These datasets are available at the UCI Machine Learning Repository.

The first dataset allows the diagnosis of the breast cancer disease. The data are acquired from three heterogenous sources where the second and third contain missing values. The first source represents the cell nucleus characteristics that were created from digitized image of a fine needle aspiration of a breast mass. This dataset consists of 569 instances and 32 features. Each property was ranged between 0 and 1 (0 if it is malignant and 1 if it is benign). The second source represents the clinical cases reported for each patient exhibiting breast cancer.

The features are in number of 34 and represent the properties of the patients. There are 198 cases of patients in this dataset involving class B if the breast cancer is benign or M if it is malignant.

Concerning the last source, the data are acquired from digital mammography. It is the most effective method for breast cancer screening available today. This dataset is used to check the severity (benign or malignant) of a mammographic mass lesion from BI-RADS attributes and the patient's age.

We consider additionally the Heart disease dataset that consists of four datasets concerning heart disease diagnosis. All of them contain missing values and each one has the same instance properties, however with different number of objects. Since the data are collected from four different locations namely Cleveland, Hungarian, Switzerland and Long Beach VA. The number of features in each dataset is 76 and the number of instances is 303, 294, 123, 200 respectively for each location.

4.2 Experimental Results

In order to evaluate the performance of our approach, we performed several experiments with regards to the collected data sets. In the first one, we studied the robustness of our method when the amount of missing data in both the learning and test set increase gradually. Table 1, present the results obtained when increasing the number of missing values in the training set for each source (*10) at each iteration. With an increase of the percent of missing data in the training set. The given results in Table 1 show that the performance of our approach almost has not changed throughout the iterations for both datasets. The method gives good learning results in terms of accuracy, F-measure, Recall and precision. A slight change has been performed in the specificity measure for the breast cancer dataset, since it has decreased. This means that the features of the observations having negative class in this data sources were incorrectly estimated, since the specificity measures how effectively a classifier identifies negative labels. However, the increase of the missing values in the test set provides different impact on the performance of the method. In Table 2 we can notice that the accuracy decreased on a small scale at each iteration until it becomes stable from the 5th iteration to 0.79 for breast cancer dataset and 0.81 for heart disease datasets. This decrease is quite normal because with a large amount of missing data in the sources of the object to be classified the performance of the model can be affected. However, our method can be considered robust to missing data because the decrease of the accuracy remains in a small scale in both datasets. Mainly, the results prove the robustness of our method facing the increase in the amount of missing values in both the training and test set. Consequently, it proves the reliability of our method independently of the amount of missingness in the data.

Our algorithm FMAI proposes two contributions: first a new adaptive imputation of missing data, and second an adjustment of the fusion' results based on the data missingness rate. Thus, to prove the effectiveness of our algorithm, we compared it to different settings where we first vary the fusion method, and

Table 1. The impact of missing values on the FMAI performance

Percentage of missing value in training set	Accuracy	F-measure	Specificity	Recall	Precision
Results given by the Breast cancer datasets					
20%	0,86	0,81	0,73	0,88	0,76
30%	0,86	0,80	0,69	0,84	0,78
40%	0,85	0,80	0,84	0,83	0,78
50%	0,84	0,79	0,76	0,83	0,76
60%	0,84	0,78	0,67	0,82	0,75
70%	0,83	0,78	0,63	0,81	0,72
Results given by the Heart disease datasets					
20%	0,87	0,80	0,72	0,88	0,74
30%	0,86	0,80	0,79	0,82	0,77
40%	0,86	0,80	0,85	0,82	0,77
50%	0,85	0,79	0,76	0,83	0,76
60%	0,85	0,78	0,77	0,82	0,75
70%	0,84	0,78	0,73	0,81	0,72

Table 2. The impact of missing value in the test set on the performance of FMAI

Percentage of missing value in test set	Accuracy	F-measure	Specificity	Recall	Precision
Results given by the Breast cancer datasets					
20%	**0,84**	0,81	0,74	0,89	0,75
30%	**0,84**	0,80	0,74	0,82	0,77
40%	**0,84**	0,82	0,72	0,84	0,79
50%	**0,79**	0,76	0,72	0,81	0,74
60%	**0,79**	0,78	0,71	0,82	0,75
70%	**0,79**	0,78	0,71	0,81	0,72
Results given by the Heart disease datasets					
20%	**0,85**	0,81	0,74	0,89	0,75
30%	**0,87**	0,80	0,74	0,82	0,77
40%	**0,86**	0,80	0,74	0,82	0,77
50%	**0,82**	0,77	0,72	0,81	0,74
60%	**0,81**	0,78	0,73	0,82	0,75
70%	**0,81**	0,77	0,73	0,80	0,71

then vary the imputation techniques. For all these settings, RF is used as an ensemble classifier.

First, Table 3 shows the performance of the fusion method in FMAI compared to the simple majority vote rule. For FMAI, the number of data sources is not a constraint. However, it is obvious from the literature that the simple majority voting rule can be used only under the condition that the number of classifiers is odd. For this reason, to compare with our approach, we only tested on the breast cancer datasets since this latter consists of three sources while the heart disease consists of four datasets. The obtained results in Table 3 show the effectiveness of FMAI in improving the classification results, and another advantage concerning our method is that it can deal with any number of data sources.

Then, to focus on evaluating the performance of the adaptive imputation proposed with our method, we compared FMAI to the classic setting where a simple imputation process is used to deal with missing data. For comparisons, we tested two different imputation methods which are the mean and the K-Nearest Neighbors (KNN) imputation [15]. The results are given in Table 4 and they show that our approach gives promising results in terms of all evaluation measures for both datasets. It also outperforms other settings where simple imputation methods are applied. Based on Tables 3 and 4, we can also deduce that for breast dataset, the fusion technique in FMAI outperforms the simple majority vote independently of the applied imputation method. This explains the advantage of adjusting the predictions' fusion process based on the missing data rate in each data source and in the new instance to classify.

Table 3. Classification results for Breast cancer datasets with FMAI and Simple majority voting

	Accuracy	F-measure	Specificity	Recall	Precision
FMAI	**0,86**	0,80	0,77	0,88	0,74
Simple majority voting	**0,73**	0,72	0,66	0,71	0,76

To further evaluate our proposed approach, Table 5 reports it classification results compared with The Heterogenous boosting (HBOOST) method [12] described in Sect. 2, since the two methods address the same problem of classifying multi-source data with missing information. Let's remind that FMAI is based on RF ensemble classifier while HBOOST is based on AdaBoost. Given the results in Table 5 the proposed approach FMAI outperformed the HBOOST method with higher accuracy, specificity, precision, recall and F-measure scores. Furthermore, we can observe that the HBOOST based method results did not exceed a specificity of 0.69, a recall of 0.72 and an accuracy of 0.77. Thus, our goal of improving the classification quality is achieved using FMAI and RF.

Table 4. Classification results using FMAI imputation and simple imputation techniques

	Accuracy	F-measure	specificity	Recall	Precision
Results given by the Breast cancer datasets					
FMAI	0,86	0,83	0,77	0,88	0,77
Method using Mean imputation	0,74	0,74	0,68	0,73	0,78
Method using KNN imputation	0,75	0,75	0,69	0,74	0,79
Results given by the Heart disease datasets					
FMAI	0,86	0,84	0,78	0,88	0,78
Method using Mean imputation	0,77	0,76	0,69	0,74	0,80
Method using KNN imputation	0,74	0,74	0,68	0,74	0,78

Table 5. Comparison of the different measures for FMAI and the HBOOST

Method	Accuracy	F-measure	Specificity	Recall	Precision
Breast cancer datasets					
FMAI	0,86	0,82	0,73	0,88	0,76
HBOOST	0.71	0.78	0.69	0,72	0,77
Heart disease datasets					
FMAI	0,84	0,80	0,71	0,88	0,74
HBOOST	0.76	0.80	0.66	0,74	0,79

5   Conclusion

We propose a new fusion method for incomplete data, FMAI, based on adaptive imputation. The objective is to take benefits of the information acquired from multiple sources and combine them for improved prediction. Our proposed approach shows encouraging results both for improving the classification performance and for dealing with missing data in multi-source classification. Experiments on two datasets show that our proposed approach FMAI improves the classification quality in terms of accuracy, specificity, precision, recall and F-measure compared to different settings using existing imputation and fusion methods. Experiments show also the robustness of our proposed method regarding the missing data rate. In the future work, the method can be extended by studying conflicting and noisy data in order to enhance learning results. Another direction is to adapt it to scale in the case of big dimensionality.

References

1. Hall, D.L., Llinas, J.: An introduction to multisensor data fusion. Proc. IEEE **85**(1), 6–23 (1997)
2. Dasarathy, B.V.: Decision Fusion. IEEE Computer Society Press, Los Alamitos (1994)
3. Kittler, J., Hatef, M., Duin, R.P., Matas, J.: On combining classifiers. IEEE Trans. Pattern Anal. Mach. Intell. **20**(3), 226–239 (1998)
4. Littlestone, N., Warmuth, M.K.: The weighted majority algorithm. Inf. Comput. **108**(2), 212–261 (1994)
5. Shafer, G.: A Mathematical Theory of Evidence. Princeton University Press, Princeton (1976)
6. Ghosh, A., Sharma, R., Joshi, P.K.: Random forest classification of urban landscape using Landsat archive and ancillary data: combining seasonal maps with decision level fusion. Appl. Geogr. **48**, 31–41 (2014)
7. Wang, Y., Dunham, M.H., Waddle, J.A., Mcgee, M.: Classifier fusion for poorly-differentiated tumor classification using both messenger RNA and microRNA expression profiles. In: Proceedings of the 2006 Computational Systems Bioinformatics Conference (CSB 2006), Stanford, California (2006)
8. Lahat, D., Adali, T., Jutien, C.: Multimodal data fusion: an overview of methods, challenges, and prospects. Proc. IEEE **103**(9), 1449–1477 (2015)
9. Momeni, A., Pincus, M., Libien, J.: Imputation and missing data. Introduction to Statistical Methods in Pathology, pp. 185–200. Springer, Cham (2018). https://doi.org/10.1007/978-3-319-60543-2_8
10. Acuna, E., Rodriguez, C.: The treatment of missing values and its effect on classifier accuracy. In: Banks, D., McMorris, F.R., Arabie, P., Gaul, W. (eds.) Classification, Clustering, and Data Mining Applications, pp. 639–647. Springer, Heidelberg (2004). https://doi.org/10.1007/978-3-642-17103-1_60
11. Yuan, L., Wang, Y., Thompson, P., Narayan, V., Ye, J.: Multi-source feature learning for joint analysis of incomplete multiple heterogeneous neuroimaging data. NeuroImage **61**(3), 622–32 (2012)
12. Aziz, M.S., Reddy, C.K.: Robust prediction from multiple heterogeneous data sources with partial information. In: Proceedings of the 19th ACM International Conference on Information and Knowledge Management, pp. 1857–1860 (2010)
13. Williams, G.: Random forests. Data Mining with Rattle and R, pp. 245–268. Springer, New York (2011). https://doi.org/10.1007/978-1-4419-9890-3_12
14. Genuer, R., Poggi, J.M., Tuleau-Malot, C.: Variable selection using random forests. Pattern Recogn. Lett. **31**(14), 2225–2236 (2010)
15. Batista, G.E., Monard, M.C., et al.: A study of k-nearest neighbour as an imputation method. In: Proceedings of the International Conference on Hybrid Intelligent Systems, pp. 251–260 (2002)

Feedback-Oriented Assessor Model

Application: Allocation of Submissions in Online Peer Assessment

Mohamed-Amine Abrache[(⊠)], Khalid Megder,
and Chihab Cherkaoui

IRF-SIC Laboratory, FSA - Ibn Zohr University, Agadir, Morocco
mohamed-amine.abrache@edu.uiz.ac.ma

Abstract. Ensuring effective feedback for learners is an important factor in the success of the learning experience. In the context of MOOCs, instructors are unable to provide feedback to a big, heterogeneous community of participants. Different platforms and tools have adopted peer assessment to solve this problem. However, they have been faced with a large number of learners who do not have enough capacity to generate accurate assessments and meaningful feedback. This finding leads to relying on the intelligence of the mass in order to generate more valid and effective feedback. At this level, one limitation of most tools and platforms is that they create random groups of assessors without considering the individual characteristics of its members. For this reason, this article proposes an updated assessor model that focuses on the characteristics of learners related to assessment capacity and their ability to provide correct, objective and useful feedback for their peers. Based on this feedback-oriented assessor model, we consider the aforementioned characteristics in the context of an algorithm that creates groups of assessors and allocates submissions in order to optimize peer feedback.

Keywords: Online learning · MOOC · Online assessment · Peer feedback
Peer assessment · Assessor model · Allocation of submissions

1 Introduction

Within the context of modern online learning, especially in MOOCs, the formative and timely feedback is a key factor in achieving the objectives of the learning process [1, 2]. Yet, due to the massiveness of such environments, instructors lack the ability to conduct formative assessment along with providing effective feedback [3].

In order to include the formative element of assessment, many MOOCs use the automatically evaluated multiple-choice questions (MCQs), although this tool does not capture enough information about the current performance of participants, which may cause a lack of the provided effective feedback [4].

Besides, the assessment of open-ended questions and problem-based tests can be used for measuring the achievement of some deeper educational objectives, such as

© Springer Nature Switzerland AG 2018
E. H. Abdelwahed et al. (Eds.): MEDI 2018, LNCS 11163, pp. 137–149, 2018.
https://doi.org/10.1007/978-3-030-00856-7_9

critical analysis and synthesis skills [5]. Aspects that cannot be reliably assessed through MCQs [6].

On the other hand, the traditional view of learning experience considers assessment as a task whereby instructors exercise their usual judgmental authority over the learner's performance. However, the advances in the fields of information technology and modern education have contributed to fundamental shifts in the design of the evaluation process. In fact, instructors tend to consider a more active participation of learners in the task of evaluating and judging their own achievements and those of their fellow students.

Moreover, the more interaction with learners the more they develop trust and positive attitude toward the course content [7]. Peer assessment (PA) is a solution that fosters the engagement and the interaction of students within the activities of assessment [8].

PA also reduces the burden of evaluation for teachers [3] and can be applied to different forms of assessment as the aforementioned open-ended questions and problem-based tests.

PA is a task in which the learner evaluates the nature of her\his peers work in terms of quality, level or value [9]. PA can combine formative and summative purposes. However, Sluijsmans [10] emphasized that the benefit of peer assessment is more effectively realized in the context of a formative approach. Being a summative tool, PA is limited to the measurement of the failure or success of the students in achieving learning expectations [11]. On the other hand, the formative approach includes comments of learners in which they identify the qualities of peers' work, as well as suggestions on how to improve their performance. These generated comments are called "Peer Feedback" (PF) [12].

PF fosters the contribution and the retention of participants as long as it is relevant and organized [13]. The instructors are keen to reap the benefits of PF for learners, even if they still question the ability of this exercise to be a source of meaningful and helpful information about the learner's performance and progression, which is due to a variety of factors and variables that influence the generation of comments and then its acceptance by students.

In the context of this paper, we introduce an updated assessor model that gathers different characteristics that shape the learner's assessment quality and mainly her\his capacity to provide effective feedback. We also propose an application of this model in the context of an algorithm for the allocation of submissions that considers assessors' characteristics.

The remainder of this paper is organized as the following; Sect. 2 represents a brief overview of the features of peer feedback, Sect. 3 introduces the feedback-oriented assessor model. In Sect. 4, we describe an application of the assessor model within the allocation of submissions in the context of a MOOC; the last section emphasizes the conclusion and the perspectives for future work.

2   Peer Feedback

Peer feedback (PF) is an element of a perspective of human learning that emphasizes the active involvement of students in the process of knowledge construction more than its simple acquisition [14].

According to Flachikov [15], peer feedback can be part of the learning process because it encourages students to think and build their self-confidence. It also urges them to take responsibility for learning and to understand the educational materials.

PF represents a key element of the collaborative learning along with providing learners with an increased motivation, reduced anxiety, a clearer view of how learning works, and consequently a development of their constructive critical thinking [16].

Moreover, the feedback provided by a group of assessors may be as valid as expert comments [17]. PF can be applied at the end of the course as part of the summative evaluation or for formative purposes with the progress of learning activities.

Furthermore, through the generation of feedback, learners-as-assessors benefit from an experience that helps them enhance their cognitive abilities such as analyzing problems and developing logical arguments. They also profit from an opportunity that allows developing their meta-cognitive skills in order to self-regulate their learning [9, 18].

At the same time, by the means of the received feedback, learners-as-assessees perceive their work's strengths and weaknesses along with receiving guidance to improve their performances and behaviors [19]. In fact, students tend to be more motivated when they manage and understand their learning process [20–22].

The peer assessment can take the form of written comment, face-to-face or online discussions, and possibly audio or video records.

Table 1 shows a summary of why, when, and how the peer feedback is taking part in the learning process mainly in online environments.

Table 1. Why? When? How? to feedback.

Peer feedback	
Why?	• To provide learners with their current level of performance • To supply arguments related to learners awarded rating and include guidance for improvement • To improve the independence and the motivation of learners as well as their understanding of the educational content • To make the student able to criticize her\his own work besides the work of her\his peers
When?	• As a summative measurement of the learner performance at the end of the course units • As a formative tool with the progress in learning activities
How?	• In a form of written comments, face-to-face or online discussions, audio or video records

The application of peer assessment underlines PF in some online assessment tools that stimulate the active participation of learners. For instance, Peerceptiv is an online evaluation platform that aims to improve the critical thinking of learners [23]. It asks learners to comment on the work of peers effectively and encourages them to evaluate the level of the helpfulness of their received feedback. Similarly, Moodle Workshop allows learners to rate the comments that have been received [24]. The rating of the assessor feedback takes part of her\his overall score.

Besides, the assessment in Aropä online platform relies more on peer feedback than on peer grading, which is due to the fact that learners tend to provide comments instead of rating the work of peers [10]. Aropä includes an algorithm that compares learners comments in order to improve the validity of the assessment [25].

Moreover, a number of complementary controls are adopted in order to limit the impact of subjective factors in peer feedback, such as ensuring the anonymity of the assessor and the assessee, which aims to support the acceptance of criticism and the making of effective comments [26]. Indeed, the characteristics of online learning environments help students to supply anonymous ratings and feedback without time or space constraints [16, 27, 28].

In addition, to compensate for deficiencies in the expected results of the peer-based assessment, some procedures are undertaken prior to the start of the assessment process. For instance, before allocating peers' submissions to assessors, several online assessment platforms provide guidelines and training for assessors in order to foster the understanding of the assessment criteria and improve the ability to identify errors and gaps in knowledge [29].

Some other systems have chosen to intervene at the end of the assessment process in order to correct the result of peer assessment. Piech et al. [30] proposed a statistical model that assumes the existence of observed variables like the peer's assigned score, along with other latent (unobservable) variables that have to be estimated such as the true score and the potential level of subjectivity of assessment.

Goldin [31] who developed an experiment on a small group of 28 students proposes a similar but slightly different model. He collected the results of exams assessed by students, as well as those evaluated by teachers, so the model can provide an estimation of the actual student homework scores and learner assessment errors.

Furthermore, the Fuzzy Constraint Networks (FCN) are generally used for defining inaccurate knowledge. Then, in order to reduce the subjectivity and improve the quality of the assessment, Lai's et al. [32] model represents learner assessment in the form of two fuzzy constraints: the scores and the satisfaction rate. Considering the prejudices and subjective aspects related to the character of the assessor, the importance or representativeness of the assessment of each student might be different. Thus, the model adjusts the assessment of students according to their characteristics.

Yet, the three above-mentioned models that function at the end of the assessment process are highly interested in the accuracy and the reliability of the summative grading more than the formative aspect of providing effective feedback; even if Lai's et al. model includes a component that encourages providing rich feedback.

Besides, monitoring and intervening in the middle of peer assessment tasks are possibly achieved within online learning environments. By way of example, Staubitz et al. [33] have adopted a principle of submission priority to motivate learners to become more involved in the context of evaluation and feedback. This principle consists of placing a higher priority on the submissions of learners who have completed their assigned assessment tasks. Thus, the work of these learners is assigned first when allocating submissions.

The next section describes the assessor model that represents the individual factors related to the learner rating and feedback generating experience.

3 Feedback-Oriented Assessor Model

The assessor model is a representation of the parameters that influence the assessor experience in the context of peer assessment. It considers learners' personal factors that determine the ability to perform the assessment task, in addition to those that are affected by the practice of this exercise.

Learners may lack sufficient knowledge and skills in a particular field of study to enable them to evaluate their peers fairly. Yet, peer feedback may be biased not only because of the inadequate knowledge and performance of the assessor but also because of different parameters that affect its providence whether they are learning or thinking styles [32, 34], preferences, or social interactions, etc.

Learners feel the power of their peers and doubt of their abilities [35]. This kind of feeling may cause a negative attitude toward this assessment exercise. Besides, the perception of the assessment and the context in which it takes place are also parameters that influence the quality of peer feedback. If learners work in competitive situations, their assessment may be weak or unfair and not reflect the performance of learners, unlike students who view peer feedback as a cooperative learning situation [27].

Moreover, Panadero [19] has separated the aspects related to the assessment exercise on three basic categories: intra-individual factors, interpersonal aspects, cognitive aspects. Where the intra-individual factors represent the perception of the individual assessor in terms of motivation, emotions, level of fairness and sense of comfort \discomfort.

The interpersonal aspects are part of collaborative learning. For instance, the psychological safety refers to which extent the learner feels safe when providing or receiving effective feedback. The cognitive aspects represent the confidence of the learner in her\his own and peers' assessment capacities, besides the sense of commitment over the evaluation process and the degree of dependence between the two parties of the assessment task.

Figure 1 represents the assessor model that considers the aforementioned factors besides others that were presented on our first model of the assessor [36, 37]. The actual model has been enriched with parameters that are mainly related to the generation of feedback. Among these factors and parameters, we can mention:

- **The level of competency in writing effective feedback, which is also linked to the language proficiency:**
  Effective feedback helps in reducing the rejection of peer-based assessment [38]. The quality of feedback depends heavily on language proficiency and writing

ability, which are parameters that also affect the comprehension of the educational material and peers' assignments [39].

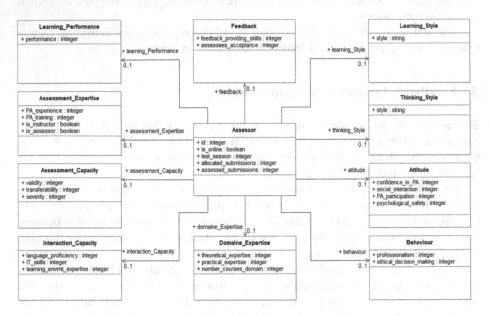

Fig. 1. Feedback oriented assessor model

- **The training and the expertise of learners over peer feedback and peer grading:**
  Finding difficulties in generating feedback is a common feature of most learners [40]. More trained assessors with assessment guidance have more ability to provide effective and meaningful feedback [41].
- **The number of assessment tasks that have been affected to learners:**
  Peer feedback is associated with numerous pedagogical benefits. However, it is noteworthy that this activity can be time-consuming [15], which implies that the allocation of the submitted assignments must be performed in a way that does not impose an overwhelming assessment load on students.

  The number of assigned assessment tasks may represent a parameter that influences the quality of the learner rating and feedback besides the motivation and engagement within the process.
- **The learning and thinking styles that may shape some characteristic of learner feedback:**
  In their peer assessment model, Lan et al. [32] have emphasized a correspondence between learning styles and the ability to provide assessment according to some specific assessment criteria. Besides, receiving holistic or specific feedback also has a different influence on the performance of learners with respect to their thinking styles [34, 42].

- **Different behavior patterns affect the participation of learners in peer assessment** [43]:

  The more learner has a sense of professionalism and ethical decision-making the more she\he tends to provide fair, non-biased grading and feedback.

  The next section represents an algorithm for the allocation of submissions within the context of peer assessment that stands on the feedback-oriented assessor model.

4 Application Within an Algorithm for the Allocation of Submissions in Online Peer Assessment

In different online learning platform as Peerceptiv, Turnitin PeerMark, PeerScholar, and Calibrated Peer Review (CPR) [26, 44–46], the making of assessors groups is performed randomly. Thus, we believe that making heterogeneous groups of assessors according to their capacity of providing effective feedback may have a positive influence on the quality of feedback.

Haddadi et al. [47] stand on the same convictions to provide a technic of clustering assessors according to their profiles (performances, certificates, and preferences). From our side, we propose an algorithm for the allocation of submissions (formation of assessors groups) based on an indicator of the learner's assessment capacity, which we called the assessor score (AS).

Our proposed algorithm classes learners with similar assessing capacities into categories of assessors, and for each submitted homework, the system takes a member of each category to form the heterogeneous assessment group.

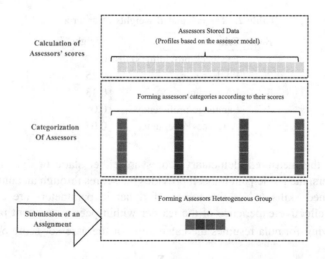

Fig. 2. The process of the algorithm of submissions allocating

Figure 2 summaries the process of the algorithm that consists of three basic stages:

(1) Calculation of assessors' scores.
(2) Grouping assessors with convergent levels into categories.
(3) Composing assessment groups by selecting an assessor from each category.

The assessor score is a measure of the capacity of learners to assess peers work and provide feedback. This AS is calculated by determining a number of elementary scores, each of which represents a qualitative measure of the skill level for the corresponding characteristic of the assessor model.

However, these characteristics do not have the same importance and impact on the assessor's overall capacity, which implies the need to provide each character with a weight that represents its level of significance in terms of rating capacity and feedback.

The weight determination of the characteristics can be considered as part of a multiple-criteria decision analysis problem. Indeed, through a study of the related literature, we have chosen SWARA (Step-wise Weight Assessment Ratio Analysis) [48] to calculate the weights reflecting the impact of the characteristics on the assessor capacity.

The SWARA process consists of two main stages. The first is to rank the criteria (the characteristics) according to their importance by a comity of experts of the field in question. In the second stage, the low-importance criteria are excluded by reference to the expert ranking, and then the weights of the remaining criteria are determined based on a calculation algorithm.

Motivated by the interest in the learner capability to provide effective feedback, our research team gave a higher ranking for the parameters with the higher impact on the generation of feedback. Table 2 represents the calculated weights for these criteria using SWARA.

Table 2. The calculated weights of criteria

Rank	Criterion	Weight
1	Feedback providing skills	0.47
2	PA Expertise	0.25
3	PA training	0.13
4	Language proficiency	0.08
5	Assessees acceptance	0.07

Moreover, the measured elementary scores are either static or dynamic. For the static parameters, the participant himself provides the scores through an auto-estimation of the concerned skills, while the scores of dynamic parameters are collected by observing the effective experience of the learner within peer assessment process.

The following formula resumes the calculation of the assessor score $\hat{S}_i$:

$$\hat{S}_i = W^T \times S_i = \sum_{j=1}^{n} W_j \times S_{ij} \tag{1}$$

With *n* the number of the selected criteria (characteristics).

S_i is the matrix of the elementary scores obtained by the assessor *i*.

W is the matrix of the calculated weights of the criteria.

On the other hand, according to their scores, the system performs the classification phase by grouping the assessors into four categories with an equal number of members. The first category consists of the assessors considered expert according to their higher scores; the second is formed of the advanced assessors and so on for the remaining two categories (intermediates and beginners). The equal number of categories members allows a fair workload for each assessor.

When a new assignment is submitted, the system checks the number of submissions allocated to each assessor. Then, it assigns this assignment to a member of each category (making of the group) in order to provide more credibility for/the assessment and a higher probability of receiving meaningful and effective feedback per submission. Figure 3 represents the results of the allocation of submissions in the context of a simulation.

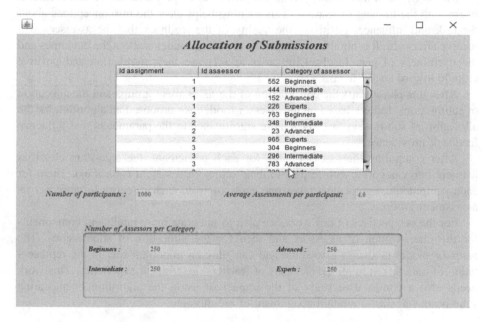

Fig. 3. Results of the simulation of the algorithm of submissions allocating

The results of the simulation showed that the created groups of assessors consist of members belonging to the four different categories. This is accompanied by an equal number of tasks assigned to the participants in a manner that guarantees that no major burden is placed on each assessor.

5 Conclusion

Peer feedback is reflected in observations, critiques, and recommendations made by learners for their peers in the context of an assessment exercise. It provides many educational benefits to the participants in their roles of assessors or assessees.

PF helps improve the cognitive and metacognitive abilities of individuals, as well as their interpersonal expressions. However, many instructors and learners fundamentally wonder about its purpose and the importance of its use.

Much research has focused on the outcomes of adopting peer feedback within an evaluation strategy, along with developing its process by introducing methods that help to obtain peer-based assessments that identify learner performance correctly.

In the same sense, we presented in the context of this contribution a feedback-oriented assessor model that stands on the factors that shape the capacity of an assessor to provide effective feedback. Different characteristic has been considered within this model such as the level of validity of assessors, their assessment expertise, their language proficiency and their attitudes, etc.

Monitoring and intervening within the processes of peer assessment and feedback begin with the training of learners. This training helps clear the misconceptions about the task and influences positively the quality of the feedback that the assessees will receive afterward. It is highly recommended to inform students about the outcomes and the usefulness of peer feedback in order to increase their motivation and positive attitude toward such exercise.

After this phase starts the construction of the assessment groups and the allocation of submissions. Indeed, based on the assessor model, we proposed an algorithm for the allocation of submission that gives more significance to the parameters that influence feedback providence.

After computing the assessor score for each participant, the algorithm classifies learners into categories with respect to their scores (assessment capacities). Then, for each submitted assignment, it takes one assessor from each category to construct its assessment group.

For the perspectives of this work, we plan to integrate more intelligent components for the classification of assessors and then for the allocation of submissions. The assessor model is always extendible and can play an important role in the representation of data linked to all the elements of learners' assessment experience. This work needs also a comparative study of the impact of using the algorithm of allocating submissions against a random assignment of submissions.

References

1. Wanner, T., Palmer, E.: Formative self-and peer assessment for improved student learning: the crucial factors of design, teacher participation and feedback. Assess. Eval. High. Educ. **43**, 1–16 (2018)
2. Mills, J., Glover, C., Stevens, V.: Using assessment within course structures to drive student engagement with the learning process. In: Proceedings of the 2005 13th International Symposium Improving Students Learning: Improving Student Learning Through Assessment, Refocusing feedback. Alden Press, Oxford (2006)
3. Suen, H.K.: Peer assessment for massive open online courses (MOOCs). Int. Rev. Res. Open Distrib. Learn. **15**(3), 312–327 (2014)
4. Anand, I.M., Djoudi, L.A.: Assessment issues for MOOCs and large scale examinations and robust, objective testing with reverse multiple-choice. In: Proceedings of the International Conference on e-Learning, e-Business, Enterprise Information Systems, and e-Government (EEE) (2015). The Steering Committee of the World Congress in Computer Science, Computer Engineering and Applied Computing (WorldComp)
5. Krathwohl, D.R.: A revision of Bloom's taxonomy: an overview. Theor. Pract. **41**(4), 212–218 (2002)
6. Herman, J.L., Klein, D.C., Wakai, S.T.: American students' perspectives on alternative assessment: do they know it's different? Assess. Educ.: Principles Policy Pract. **4**(3), 339–352 (1997)
7. Bendou, A., Abrache, M.-A., Cherkaoui, C.: Contribution of pedagogical agents to motivate learners in online learning environments: the case of the PAOLE agent. In: Ben Ahmed, M., Boudhir, A.A. (eds.) SCAMS 2017. LNNS, vol. 37, pp. 344–356. Springer, Cham (2018). https://doi.org/10.1007/978-3-319-74500-8_32
8. Yuan, J., Kim, C.: The effects of autonomy support on student engagement in peer assessment. Educ. Technol. Res. Develop. **66**(1), 25–52 (2018)
9. Topping, K.J.: Peer assessment. Theor. Pract. **48**(1), 20–27 (2009)
10. Sluijsmans, D.M., et al.: Peer assessment in problem based learning. Stud. Educ. Eval. **27**(2), 153–173 (2001)
11. Topping, K.J., et al.: Formative peer assessment of academic writing between postgraduate students. Assess. Eval. High. Educ. **25**(2), 149–169 (2000)
12. Gielen, S., et al.: Improving the effectiveness of peer feedback for learning. Learn. Instr. **20**(4), 304–315 (2010)
13. Choi, B., et al.: Socialization tactics in wikipedia and their effects. In: Proceedings of the 2010 ACM Conference on Computer Supported Cooperative Work. ACM (2010)
14. Ertmer, P.A., et al.: Using peer feedback to enhance the quality of student online postings: an exploratory study. J. Comput.-Mediated Commun. **12**(2), 412–433 (2007)
15. Falchikov, N.: Peer feedback marking: developing peer assessment. Program. Learn. **32**(2), 175–187 (1995)
16. Arch-Int, N.: Multidimensional assessment of open-ended questions for enhancing the quality of peer assessment in e-Learning environments. In: Handbook of Research on Applied e-Learning in Engineering and Architecture Education, p. 263 (2015)
17. Cho, K., MacArthur, C.: Student revision with peer and expert reviewing. Learn. Instr. **20**(4), 328–338 (2010)
18. Casey, G.: Students as "assessors" and "assessees" in an era of social media. In: Assessment in Online and Blended Learning Environments, p. 55 (2015)
19. Panadero, E.: Is it safe? social, interpersonal, and human effects of peer assessment. In: Handbook of Human and Social Conditions in Assessment, p. 247 (2016)

20. Topping, K.: Peer assessment between students in colleges and universities. Rev. Educ. Res. **68**(3), 249–276 (1998)

21. Van Gennip, N., et al.: Reactions to 360 feedback: the role of trust and trust-related variables. Int. J. Hum. Resour. Develop. Manage. **10**(4), 362–379 (2010)

22. Elliott, N., Higgins, A.: Self and peer assessment–does it make a difference to student group work? Nurse Educ. Pract. **5**(1), 40–48 (2005)

23. Cho, K., Schunn, C.D.: The SWoRD is mightier than the pen: scaffolded writing and rewriting in the discipline. In: 2004 Proceedings of IEEE International Conference on Advanced Learning Technologies. IEEE (2004)

24. Using Workshop – MoodleDocs (2017). https://docs.moodle.org/29/en/Using_Workshop#Grade_for_assessment

25. Purchase, H.C., Hamer, J.: Peer review in practice: eight years of experiences with Aropä. School of Computing Science University of Glasgow, 31 January 2017

26. Cho, K., Schunn, C.D.: Scaffolded writing and rewriting in the discipline: a web-based reciprocal peer review system. Comput. Educ. **48**(3), 409–426 (2007)

27. Lin, S.S.-J., Liu, E.-F., Yuan, S.-M.: Web based peer assessment: attitude and achievement. IEEE Trans. Educ. **44**(2), 13 (2001)

28. Li, L.: The role of anonymity in peer assessment. Assess. Eval. High. Educ. **42**(4), 645–656 (2017)

29. Sluijsmans, D., Dochy, F., Moerkerke, G.: Creating a learning environment by using self-, peer-and co-assessment. Learn. Environ. Res. **1**(3), 293–319 (1998)

30. Piech, C., et al.: Tuned models of peer assessment in MOOCs. arXiv preprint arXiv:1307.2579 (2013)

31. Goldin, I.M.: Accounting for peer reviewer bias with bayesian models. In: Proceedings of the Workshop on Intelligent Support for Learning Groups at the 11th International Conference on Intelligent Tutoring Systems. Citeseer (2012)

32. Lan, C.H., Graf, S., Lai, K.R.: Enrichment of peer assessment with agent negotiation. IEEE Trans. Learn. Technol. **4**(1), 35–46 (2011)

33. Staubitz, T., et al.: Improving the peer assessment experience on MOOC platforms. In: Proceedings of the Third ACM Conference on Learning@ Scale. ACM (2016)

34. Lin, S.S., Liu, E.Z.-F., Yuan, S.-M.: Web-based peer assessment: feedback for students with various thinking-styles. J. Comput. Assist. Learn. **17**(4), 420–432 (2001)

35. Liu, N.-F., Carless, D.: Peer feedback: the learning element of peer assessment. Teach. High. Educ. **11**(3), 279–290 (2006)

36. Abrache, M., Qazdar, A., Cherkaoui, C.: Involvement of learners' characteristics within the allocation of submissions in the context of peer assessment in MOOCs. Int. J. Comput. Appl. **168**(12), 7–11 (2017)

37. Abrache, M.-A., Qazdar, A., Bendou, A., Cherkaoui, C.: The allocation of submissions in online peer assessment: what can an assessor model provide in this context? In: Ben Ahmed, M., Boudhir, A.A. (eds.) SCAMS 2017. LNNS, vol. 37, pp. 276–287. Springer, Cham (2018). https://doi.org/10.1007/978-3-319-74500-8_25

38. Brown, G.A., Bull, J., Pendlebury, M.: Assessing Student Learning in Higher Education. Routledge, londin (2013)

39. Fini, A.: The technological dimension of a massive open online course: the case of the CCK08 course tools. Int. Rev. Res. Open Distrib. Learn. **10**(5), 6 (2009)

40. Kulkarni, C., et al.: Peer and Self Assessment in Massive Online Classes, in Design Thinking Research, pp. 131–168. Springer, Cham (2015). https://doi.org/10.1007/978-3-319-06823-7_910

41. Ngoon, T.J., et al.: Interactive Guidance Techniques for Improving Creative Feedback (2018)

42. Van Zundert, M., Sluijsmans, D., Van Merriënboer, J.: Effective peer assessment processes: research findings and future directions. Learn. Instr. **20**(4), 270–279 (2010)
43. Cook, S., et al.: Going'massive': learner engagement in a MOOC environment. THETA 2015-Create, Connect, Consume-Innovating today for tomorrow (2015)
44. Prescott, T.: How does using Turnitin in a formative way change student attitudes towards plagiarism (2012). plagiarismadviceorg/documents/Prescott_fullpaper.pdf. Accessed 4 Oct 2014
45. Paré, D.E., Joordens, S.: Peering into large lectures: examining peer and expert mark agreement using peerScholar, an online peer assessment tool. J. Comput. Assist. Learn. **24** (6), 526–540 (2008)
46. Russell, J., et al.: Variability in students' evaluating processes in peer assessment with calibrated peer review. J. Comput. Assist. Learn. **33**(2), 178–190 (2017)
47. Lynda, H., et al.: Peer assessment in MOOCs based on learners' profiles clustering. In: 2017 8th International Conference on Information Technology (ICIT). IEEE (2017)
48. Karabasevic, D., et al.: An Approach to criteria weights determination by integrating the DELPHI and the adapted SWARA methods. management. J. Sustain. Bus. Manage. Solutions Emerg. Econ. 17 (2017)

Communication and Information Technologies

A Gamification and Objectivity Based Approach to Improve Users Motivation in Mobile Crowd Sensing

Hasna El Alaoui El Abdallaoui[✉], Abdelaziz El Fazziki,
Fatima Zohra Ennaji, and Mohamed Sadgal

Computing Systems Engineering Laboratory (LISI),
Cadi Ayyad University, Marrakesh, Morocco
h.elalaoui@edu.uca.ac.ma, {elfazziki,sadgal}@uca.ma,
f.ennaji@edu.uca.ma

Abstract. The advent of new communication and information technologies offers great potential for capturing and transmitting information related to mobility. The use of these technologies makes it possible to collect information and transmit it in a participative production (crowdsourcing) perspective for organizational government services such as suspect investigation. The objective of this work is to improve the process of identifying suspects by combining collective intelligence with mobile devices. To do this, this article proposes an approach for the development of a framework based on the gathering of information by the crowd (crowd sensing), their filtering and their analysis. This framework increases the user participation by integrating the gamification technique as a motivation approach. The reliability of the crowd sensed information, in turn, is provided by an objectivity analysis algorithm. The experimental results of the case study, carried out through AnyLogic simulations, show that the methods and technologies incorporated in the suspect identification procedures accelerated the search and location process by ensuring high system performance as well as by improving the quality of the sensed data.

Keywords: Crowd sensing · Gamification · Objectivity analysis
Suspect investigation · User motivation

1 Introduction

Crowdsourcing is a concept that was described by J. Howe and M. Robinson in 2006 [1] that can literally be translated as participatory production. It is based on the use of the expertise and skills of a large audience or crowd to perform certain tasks, solve problems or collect information. Depending on the type of skills required, the tools used and the type of problems to be solved, a crowdsourcing activity can take many forms. In some situations, participants are only asked to carry out the detection and the collection of relevant information, a form known as crowd sensing (CS) [2]. The deployment of this mechanism has become possible through the new technologies of the Internet, mobile platforms and telecommunications. Mobile Crowd Sensing (MCS) is, therefore, a new form of data collection exploiting the crowd of intelligent

© Springer Nature Switzerland AG 2018
E. H. Abdelwahed et al. (Eds.): MEDI 2018, LNCS 11163, pp. 153–167, 2018.
https://doi.org/10.1007/978-3-030-00856-7_10

terminals already deployed around the world to massively collect data. The principle is that each contributor is a potential data sensor. Mobile phones with their ability to determine a position (based on GPS, WiFi or 3G/4G) offer the ideal sensor for collecting data on mobility.

From these observations, we can note the huge potential of crowd sensing, but also its limits and its risks. Recurring questions about the concept of participant motivation and the accuracy of the information provided by the crowd can be raised. First, the success of a CS operation relies on the participation of the crowd, specifically on the participation of a number of individuals large enough to benefit from their diversity. It is therefore for the actors of the CS initiative to encourage the participation of the crowd. Indeed, the attraction ability of the crowd and relationship management in a CS activity has been the subject of several research works [3–7]. These approaches distinguish the intrinsic motivations related to the satisfaction associated with the task or its social dimension (leisure, pleasure, interest, etc.) [3] and the extrinsic motivations encouraged by all the external incentives offered by the crowdsourcer (monetary benefits, price, etc.) [3].

Secondly, even if the user motivation management allows the guarantee of a large participation and a massive collection of data, it does not manage all the detection information provided by the crowd and ensure or verify their reliability. With the large-scale data that a crowdsourcing activity provides, it is difficult to determine the veracity of each piece of information received. Several approaches worked in this direction and proposed a set of methods [8–11]. For example, the authors in [12], categorized three methods to explain the general principle of this analysis: iterative methods that are easier to understand and to implement, optimization-based methods and PGM-based solutions (Probabilistic Graphical Model) that are more difficult to assimilate.

This work includes the concept of crowdsourcing as a new paradigm used by institutions to solve many organizational problems, we will focus mainly on locating, tracking, and identifying suspects using human mobility. It will also discuss issues related to participant motivation by integrating gamification techniques into CS platforms and proposing an algorithm for objectivity analysis as a method to improve the quality of the sensed data. To sum up, the aim of this research is the development of a crowd sensing framework that facilitates to the authorities, the collecting, the analysing and the interpretation of data provided by citizens. This framework is mainly based on these points:

- The use of mobile crowd sensing to collect information from the public.
- The verification of the collected data credibility using an objectivity analysis.
- The crowd participation will be encouraged by means of the integration of gamification techniques in the crowd sensing application.

The rest of this paper is organized as follows: Sect. 2 presents a literature review about the most important concepts used in this paper. The proposed approach is detailed in Sect. 3 including its process and architecture. The concepts of the objectivity analysis and the gamification mechanisms used in this paper are also structured in Sect. 4. Section 5 introduces a case study of a suspect investigation using the proposed framework and presents the experiment results. Finally, we conclude with a discussion and a conclusion sections.

2 Literature Review

2.1 Crowdsourcing and Suspect Tracking

Several founding works are mainly based on the techniques to be incorporated into the investigation process, but few of them have focused on the human potential or to promote the crowdsourcing concept. Table 1 below summarizes their functionalities and presents their advantages and limitations.

Table 1. Tracking systems comparison

Literature document	Tool(s) used	System description	Advantages	Limitations
[13]	CCTV Systems	Image taken from live streaming CCTV is compared to a criminal database and information are displayed if a matching exists	*Automatic system *Crime prevention	Effectiveness not reliable and is affected by many factors
[14]	Semantic Web + 3D models	Tracking suspects and their activities around the globe by referring to the social networks and the semantic data	*Help officials to have an idea about a suspect's behaviour *Avert crimes and terrorist attacks	Not all information can be available or shared on semantic web
[15]	GIS	*Decision support system that provides spatial and non-spatial information *Identify police stations closest to the crime scene and determine the shortest paths	*Useful system and quick response *Suspect tracking	The system identifies large evacuation areas and not the exact position of the suspect
[16]	Artificial Intelligence + Natural Language Processing	Promoting generic reporting while automating the process of crime detection, summarisation and delegation	*Newer in-formation sharing techniques *Sophisticated sensors *Responsive feedback	Application of technology to mitigate existing issues and less citizen implication

Our study of the literature allowed us to explore some of the other issues with such systems like the negligence of citizens' involvement. The framework we are presenting will mainly take advantage of crowdsourcing, specifically mobile crowd sensing, to identify and to detect the exact position of a suspect and this will form the contribution of this paper.

2.2 Objectivity Analysis in a CS Initiative

In the era of information explosion, we are continuously generating data through various channels, blogs, social media, crowdsourcing platforms, etc. Hence, the major problem with current crowdsourcing environments is the lack of manageability. As a result of the openness of Web based platforms, where anybody can join and participate, quality assurance becomes challenging.

Thereby, numerous researches have tried to tackle this challenge using different approaches as described in [12]. They estimate the reliability of each source and the credibility of the information it provides using quality assurance (QA) or truth discovery (TD) methods [8–10]. In [10], the authors proposed a fuzzy-based system to enhance the quality of human computation in crowdsourcing applications. Likewise, the authors in [17] proposed an approach to further improve the efficiency and safety in the trust discovery process.

The authors in [12] presented a comprehensive comparison between different methods depending on the input data and the source reliability. Their examination was done under 5 different aspects and they concluded that more directives should be deployed for large-scale data.

2.3 Crowd Motivation Techniques: Gamification

The users' motivation is the key factor that determines the contribution quality and/or quantity in a crowdsourcing context. In this work, we focused mainly on the users' motivation while performing a CS activity. The approach to be adopted is gamification. It is the transfer of game mechanics into serious areas that have nothing to do with gaming (making activities which are not considered as games more playful [18]). It is thus based on the observation of the mechanics allowing to build a "good" game, and on the study of the players' behaviour.

In crowdsourcing, the gamification became an effective approach for increasing crowdsourcing participation: Organizations make crowdsourcing activities more like a game to motivate participants or allow the creation of positive motivations [18].

The most modest and classic way to design a gamified crowdsourcing application is to incorporate the most often used mechanics from the game world as part of a gamification approach; for example: the attribution of a score, the attribution of a status linked to a level or time of use, ranking, the use of quizzes, the use of the notion of mission, leader boards, etc. [18].

3   The Proposed Approach

3.1   A General Overview

Although the law enforcement domain has constantly evolved and incorporated new techniques that have improved investigation's effectiveness, crowd's collaboration has often been a necessity. It has always led the investigation towards successful paths better than depending only on the latest technologies. With the emergence of mobile technologies, many applications have largely enabled the crowd to collect real time data. Mobile Crowd Sensing (MCS), has recently been widely applied by decision-makers who use citizens and their mobile devices as an important source of information in situations like suspect identification. The presence of several built-in sensors in smart phones can capture information about the user's environment. This data is then transferred to the database servers. The data is usually geo-stamped and time-stamped and may include multimedia content.

Besides the aforementioned suspect investigation's improvement, particular challenges must be faced: striking a balance between crowd's participation and the information correctness is crucial. The objective behind this work is threefold: (i) to involve as many people as possible in helping the authorities to identify and locate the suspect through the use of a gamified crowdsourcing application that will play a key role in increasing the motivation of participants (ii) then, to use the crowd and their mobile devices as an important large-scale data sources. This will help the authorities to gather as much information as possible. (iii) These collected data will be verified using the algorithm of objectivity analysis (OA) that will keep only the relevant data and will eliminate any data likely to disturb the process of investigation. Figure 1 summarizes the structure of the proposed approach.

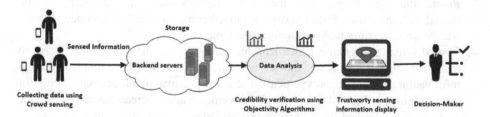

Fig. 1. The mobile crowd sensing approach infrastructure

3.2   The Suspect Investigation Process

The proposed suspect investigation process begins after the authorities receive an alert about an assault or an aggression. Figure 2 describes the steps that the framework follow starting from collecting information about the suspect to his tracking and localization.

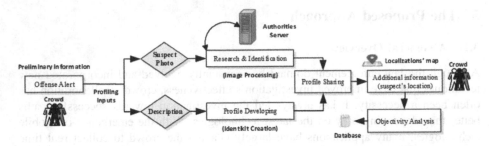

Fig. 2. The suspect investigation proposed process

The framework is based on four generic steps including methods and techniques developed to solve the problems discussed previously:

1. **Profiling inputs collecting.** The victims and the witnesses present at the time of the offense are a real source of information that must be exploited to collect useful information about the suspect (profiling inputs). In addition to the description of the suspect, digital exhibits can be retrieved like surveillance cameras videos or crowd mobile devices visuals.
2. **Data analysis.** The objective behind this step is to ensure the identity of the suspect by performing his profile.

   - Research and identification: image processing techniques are exploited to search, in the authority databases, for a profile that matches with the suspect one (from an image taken by the crowd or video from surveillance cameras).
   - Profile developing: If no video or picture of the suspect was taken, a sketch generation will be established.

3. **Profile sharing.** The profile of the suspect realized during the last steps will be shared with the crowd. Social networks and other media, like TVs and newspapers, will be an interesting tool to hugely disseminate the profile.
4. **Crowd sensing for suspect localization.** This solution allows the participants to mark the suspect's position and all relevant information (date, time, additional information such as transport vehicle). The result is a map (made accessible only for the authorities) where all the suspect's movements and whereabouts are displayed. They are first checked by the OA algorithm before getting stored in a database.

3.3   The Framework Structuring

In this section, we will present the overall structure of the framework consisting of six components schematized with their interactions in Fig. 3.

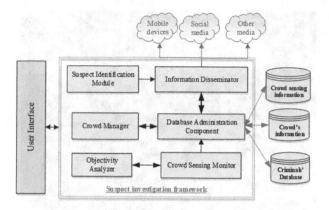

Fig. 3. The framework structuring

- Database Administration Component (DAC): It keeps data updated in the database. It is linked to the authorities' database that stores a set of important data.
- Objectivity Analyzer (OA): Responsible for checking the trustworthiness of the crowd sensing data. Any information that is sensed by the crowd must firstly be verified by the objectivity analysis algorithm implemented in this module.
- The Crowd Manager (CM): Responsible for managing the crowd activities and participations on the gamified mobile application (dashboards, scores, rewards).
- The Information Disseminator Module (IDM): It is using the adequate algorithms and APIs to broadcast the suspect profile to mobile devices and social media.
- The Crowd Sensing Monitor (CSM): Associated to the OA module, this component monitors the localization data provided by the crowd in the framework. Once a localization information is validated by the OA module, it is then transferred to the DAC to be stored in the database. All suspect's localizations are then assembled by this module in a single map perceptible by all police officers.
- The Suspect Identification Module (SIM): It incorporates the whole forensic investigation procedure that emphasizes the suspect video/image analysis process in addition to the sketch generation development.

4 The Framework Implementation Methods

4.1 The Objectivity Analysis

An objectivity analysis algorithm is proposed in this paper to verify the trustworthiness of the information provided by the crowd (suspect localization). For starters, the locations reported by the crowd are grouped together in the same cluster if they are close in time. This step was performed by the K-means algorithm. The different colors of the markers illustrated in Fig. 4 indicate the different clusters obtained after performing K-means algorithm. Then, we apply the algorithm of the objectivity analysis presented below for each group or cluster.

Fig. 4. The grouping of close localizations into the same location (cluster)

By fixing a time $T = t \pm \Delta t$, we define some parameters for the credibility computation as follows:

- S: the number of participants (the crowd).
- L: set of sensed information reported at the time T where $L = \{l_0, l_1 \ldots l_n\}$ and l_i is the ith group of localizations (a cluster) at the time T and n the number of clusters.

Algorithm 1: The objectivity analysis algorithm

Input: the information $L = \{l_0, l_1 \ldots l_n\}$ and the number of participants S

Output: Identified credible locations and their scores

   For l_0 to l_n *do*

$$OS(l_i) = \frac{|S_{l_i}|}{|S|} \qquad \sum_{i=0}^{n} OS(l_i) = 1 \qquad S_{l_i} \text{ is the number of people who}$$

reported the location l_i

   End for

Return: the cluster l_i with the highest objectivity score OS.

For each location l_i, the Algorithm 1 infers the objectivity score of the cluster l_i based on the current estimation. At the end of n iterations, it returns the cluster with the highest score, which indicates the most trustworthy information.

4.2   Crowd Motivation: Gamification in Crowdsourcing

Application analysis. The first step is to determine the functionalities that a user can achieve with the application in a given context (summarized in Table 2 below).

Table 2. Game's contexts and corresponding actions

Context	Actions
Installation & registration	-User downloads and installs the application on his/her mobile device. -User registers anonymously to the application by entering a nickname and a password
Authentication	-If first authentication, the user can customize his/her game avatar. -User can access his/her profile to edit account's information (nickname, password) -User can access his/her dashboard to visualize his/her scores (points, badges, etc.)
Suspect identification	-User can provide real picture of the suspect instead of his/her identikit -User can provide a video containing the suspect recorded while committing a criminal act -User can provide any important information concerning the suspect (name, address, etc.)
Suspect localization	-User can report the suspect's localization on the map -User can report, in addition to the localization, the date and time of localization -User can report, in addition to the previous data, additional information concerning the suspect (vehicle, clothes, persons accompanying him/her, etc.)

Designing. This step consists of defining the system of points, scores and rewards awarded to a player once s/he completes a task in the application. For example, if the user (the player) reports the localization of the suspect, 5 points will be offered. Whereas if s/he records, in addition to the localization, the date and the time, s/he will be able to earn 10 points instead of 5. The daily authentication will allow players to

Table 3. Player's levels and their corresponding badges

Level	Cadet	Police Officer	Detective	Sergeant	Lieuten-ant	Captain	Inspector
Badge	Silver Shield	Golden Shield	Silver Medallion	Golden Medal-lion	Laurel with a star	Laurel with 2 stars	Lion Medal-lion
Pic-ture							
Rule	Registra-tion	Score ≥50	Score ≥150	Score ≥300	Score ≥450	Score ≥500	Score ≥650

accumulate a large number of points and to receive bonuses (e.g. new accessories). Along with the points, the game offers badges to the players. Table 3 presents the badge attributed to a participant when reaching a given score in the game.

5   Case Study

Due to the unavailability of real data or the possibilities to test the proposed solution in the real world, we decided to simulate a scenario close to the reality using a simulation software; the AnyLogic[1] simulator. It helped to reflect the crowd's behavior in the case of an aggression by modelling the process we proposed in this paper.

The second part of the case study will present a first prototype of the gamified application including some screenshots of the player's board.

Finally, for the automatic face analysis (image and video processing), we used the OpenCV[2] library in Java and the FBI Faces software for the identikit generation.

5.1   Experimental Results

The implementation is illustrated by the Anylogic simulation. Using Anylogic, we simulate the aggression environment. In this environment, different agents exist: a crowd of men, women and children randomly walking in this environment, police officers set in separate places and a suspect who moves among the crowd to chase his victim. Figure 5-a shows the aggression scene taken by a camera following the suspect and Fig. 5-b his escape between the crowds (the suspect is enclosed by a yellow circle).

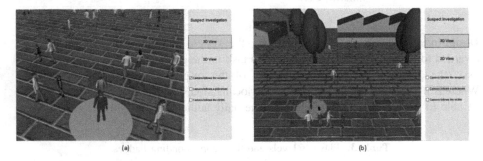

Fig. 5. The aggression (a) and the suspect's escape after the aggression (b)

---

[1] https://www.anylogic.com/.

[2] http://opencv.org/.

People near the assault's location provide the closest police officer with the suspect's profiling inputs as shown in Fig. 6-a. These profile inputs will be summarized and archived in order to be broadcasted later. Then, if a person identifies the suspect, s/he uses the gamified application to report all the localization's information (Fig. 6-b).

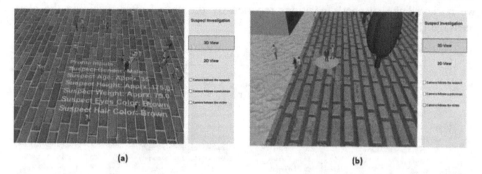

Fig. 6. (a) Collecting suspect's profile inputs and (b) suspect detection

The gamified application. It essentially allows the crowd to report any information about the suspect or his location easily. Figure 7-a shows the interface enabling the avatar customization. New body, face, hair features, wardrobe and accessories are available at each new level. Another important gamification technique integrated in this application is the player board where all his/her obtained scores, badges and rewards are displayed (Fig. 7-b).

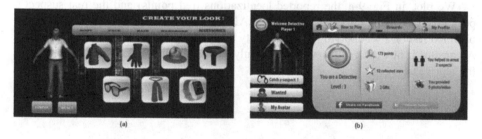

Fig. 7. (a) Avatar customization and (b) Player board (rewards, badges, score, etc.)

Face recognition and identikits. The aim is to test the crowd accuracy in comparison to the machine's performance in the case of face recognition from a profile image and a digital sketch. To do so; we carried out, in a previous work [19], a set of experiments: the crowd's wisdom were experienced by asking 83 people to answer a google form.

All the automatic face analysis experiments and comparisons with human intelligence are available in [19] and proved that crowd intelligence has largely exceeded the capabilities of the machine especially in cases where some facial properties were imperceptible or the picture quality was poor.

5.2 Results

We took into consideration the human error margin during the implementation of the Anylogic simulation. Therefore, the analysis module of the Anylogic tool allowed the extraction of data representing the movement of the suspect according to the X and Y coordinates of the created environment from the aggression time (t = 25). In parallel, we retrieved the suspect's positions reported by the crowd after receiving the alert message (Fig. 8).

Projects	Palette 🖾	▭ ◻	datasets_log 🖾					
	Analysis	▦ ▨		agent_type	agent	name	index	x	y
				▼	▾	▼	▾	↑▾	▼
🕐	▾ Data		1	Female	females[18] : 283	dataset1	8	59.001	62.021
🧍	🔘 Data Set		2	Female	females[58] : 323	dataset1	8	59.465	349.119
▥	📊 Statistics		3	Female	females[0] : 265	dataset1	8	59.567	438.72
🚗	📊 Histogram Data		4	Female	females[40] : 305	dataset1	34	85.662	173.827
💧	📊 Histogram2D Data		5	Female	females[36] : 301	dataset1	55	107.955	371.683
	🅖 Output		6	Female	females[71] : 336	dataset1	70	122.036	324.496
🔾	▾ Charts		7	Female	females[8] : 273	dataset1	84	135.69	358.741
🔵	📊 Bar Chart		8	Female	females[57] : 322	dataset1	84	136.62	533.023
	▥ Stack Chart		9	Female	females[4] : 269	dataset1	117	168.793	482.697
🔴	🥧 Pie Chart		10	Female	females[1] : 266	dataset1	124	175.456	21.714
🍴	📈 Plot		11	Female	females[49] : 314	dataset1	124	176.23	434.232
	📉 Time Plot		12	Female	females[3] : 268	dataset1	128	179.479	399.706
📊	📉 Time Stack Chart		13	Female	females[21] : 286	dataset1	127	179.523	559.415
	📉 Time Color Chart		14	Female	females[28] : 293	dataset1	142	193.134	470.658
📊	📊 Histogram		15	Female	females[13] : 278	dataset1	143	194.144	489.224
	📊 Histogram2D		16	Female	females[49] : 314	dataset1	200	251.265	305.166
			17	Female	females[43] : 308	dataset1	200	251.805	88.576

Fig. 8. The suspect's localizations reported by the crowd

We plot, in Fig. 9-a, the reported localizations (red points) and the real suspect's positions (the blue curve) using MATLAB simulator, while Fig. 9-b shows the obtained results after applying the objectivity analysis algorithm. The application of the Algorithm 1, however, allowed to retain only the most reliable data and the closest to the real values.

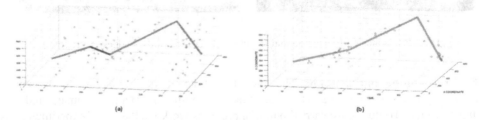

(a)   (b)

Fig. 9. MATLAB results (Color figure online)

6 Discussion

This work raised an important question: would the use of the crowd and new technologies increase the capacities of the authorities to control and monitor the population? This paper leans towards to show that the answer is positive. The bursting of urban space and the rise of local agencies (private and public security), engaged in the contest against insecurity, have resulted in a fragmentation of knowledge acquired through technical devices used to monitor and/or protect people. More fundamentally, the spread of smartphones, crowd sensing and video surveillance in urban areas marks the emergence of a new "economy of visibility" in the exercise of public order which is characterized by a decentralized power tracking without release malicious or even ordinary citizens.

The reorganization of the legal field and the management of public order are not without impact on the very nature of their exercise in the urban spaces. As a result, there is a little more to do with "public order" because the managers of the surveillance systems work primarily for the clients who employ them, when they are not simply working to defend their own interests. This means that security has changed imperceptibly by nature: from a right recognized by all and guaranteed by the state, it has become a good of market value, a good that only the richest (individuals, businesses, communities, etc.) can afford. In the same way, with regard to local authorities, the mapping of the surveillance systems implementation in the territory suggests a distribution determined essentially by the wealth of the municipalities which must be able to raise the funds necessary for the installation of the device but also to its daily operation.

Has the spread of these devices in the territories of a city led to increased surveillance by the police of the population? If we mean all the forms of control and standardization organized and provided by authorities and private companies, the answer is negative. This hyperspecialization limits the prospects of the information sharing and confrontation of knowledge acquired in different places and by different operators. It is very hopeful to think that private and public security management will respond relentlessly to the needs - especially expectations and the demands of the public interest. Why not have the necessary human and technical resources to act autonomously in all public areas? This is undoubtedly one of the main features of this new strategy of visibility: a surveillance exercised by a multiplicity of "people", in charge of the whole territory and animated by a logic and a gamification to motivate the defense of the common interest.

7 Conclusion

Advances in mobile computing and social networking services are enabling people to probe the dynamics of a public interest. In this paper, we addressed the problem of locating, tracking, and identifying suspects by using crowd sensing concept with, human mobility. Unlike existing suspicious tracking methods, we identify suspects based on the routing behavior of people in an urban area. The suspect tracking system can benefit both private and public areas. On the other hand, this work studies the gamification mechanisms and their application for the promotion of participatory urban detection. Participatory detection, which uses users' smartphones, focuses on an effective and economical detection mechanism for large areas. However, continuing to motivate many participants for a long time is difficult. In addition, financial incentives are generally limited. To solve these problems, gamification mechanisms are considered as a promising technique because they have the potential to suppress financial incentives by maintaining participants' motivation.

Crowdsourcing offers a great potential for the field of forensic investigations and the search for suspects. In this paper, we were interested in exploiting the concept of Mobile Crowd Sensing (MCS), for the collection of relevant data on a suspect by the crowd and their mobile devices. Building on the strength of modern technologies, the proposed framework provides answers to the following questions:

1. How can crowdsourcing be adopted in the context of suspect investigations and how can the authorities benefit from collective intelligence?
2. How to strengthen the participation of the crowd to capture their potential value?
3. How to trust the data delivered by the crowd or verify their reliability?

Through the experimental results presented in this paper, we have demonstrated that collective intelligence can be very useful and achieve goals that even the most powerful machines cannot achieve, such as the case of identifying a suspect via a surveillance image or video.

In order to increase the participation of the crowd, the CS actors have a range of motivations on which they can rely on by setting up various stimuli such as the interest of the task, the remuneration and/or the intrinsic valorisation. In this article, we have chosen gamification as a motivation approach widely used in crowdsourcing initiatives. Making the search for a suspect an attractive game is an innovative contribution in the e-government field.

Finally and to answer the last sub-question, this article has highlighted a simple and powerful objectivity analysis algorithm to clean the information received from the crowd from any noisy data that can hinder the investigation process progress. The simulations of this paper have proved that this algorithm gives very satisfactory results and quite close to the real values.

References

1. Howe, B.J.: The Rise of Crowdsourcing. Wired Mag. **14**(6), 1–4 (2006)
2. Guo, B., Wang, Z., Yu, Z., et al.: Mobile crowd sensing and computing: the review of an emerging human-powered sensing paradigm. ACM Comput. Surv. **48**(1), 1–31 (2015). http://dl.acm.org/citation.cfm?doid=2808687.2794400
3. Hossain, M.: Users' motivation to participate in online crowdsourcing platforms. In: 2012 International Conference on Innovation, Management and Technology Research, ICIMTR 2012, pp. 310–315 (2012). https://doi.org/10.1109/ICIMTR.2012.6236409
4. Kamar, E., Horvitz, E.: Incentives for truthful reporting in crowdsourcing. In: 11th International Conference on Multiagent Systems, pp. 1329–1330 (2012). http://dl.acm.org/citation.cfm?id=2343988

5. Hossain, M.: Crowdsourcing: activities, incentives and users' motivations to participate. In: 2012 International Conference on Innovation, Management and Technology Research, ICIMTR 2012, pp. 501–506 (2012). https://doi.org/10.1109/ICIMTR.2012.6236447
6. Yang, G., He, S., Shi, Z., Chen, J.: Promoting cooperation by the social incentive mechanism in mobile crowdsensing. IEEE Commun. Mag. **55**(3), 86–92 (2017)
7. Shen, X., Lee, M.K.O., Cheung, C.M.K.: Computers in human behavior exploring online social behavior in crowdsourcing communities: a relationship management perspective. Comput. Hum. Behav. **40**, 144–151 (2014). https://doi.org/10.1016/j.chb.2014.08.006
8. Ye, C., Wang, H., Gao, H., Li, J., Xie, H.: Truth discovery based on crowdsourcing. In: International Conference on Web-Age Information Management, pp. 453–458 (2014). https://doi.org/10.1007/978-3-319-08010-9_48
9. Huang, C., Wang, D., Chawla, N.: Towards time-sensitive truth discovery in social sensing applications. In: Proceedings - 2015 IEEE 12th International Conference on Mobile Ad-hoc and Sensor Systems, MASS 2015, pp. 154–162 (2015)
10. Folorunso, O., Mustapha, O.A.: A fuzzy expert system to trust-based access control in crowdsourcing environments. Appl. Comput. Inform. **11**(2), 116–129 (2015). https://doi.org/10.1016/j.aci.2014.07.001
11. Howard, C., Jones, D., Reece, S., Waldock, A.: Learning to trust the crowd: validating "crowd" sources for improved situational awareness in disaster response. Procedia Eng. **159**, 141–147 (2016). https://doi.org/10.1016/j.proeng.2016.08.141%0A
12. Li, Y., Gao, J., Meng, C., et al.: A survey on truth discovery. ACM SIGKDD Explor. Newsl. **17**(2), 1–16 (2016). https://doi.org/10.1145/2897350.2897352
13. Mali, P., Rahane, V., Maskar, S., Kumbhar, A., Wankhade, S.V.: Criminal tracking system using CCTV. Imp. J. Interdiscip. Res. **2**(7) (2016). http://www.onlinejournal.in
14. Mathew, A., Sheth, A., Deligiannidis, L.: SemanticSpy: suspect tracking using semantic data in a multimedia environment. In: Mehrotra, S., Zeng, D.D., Chen, H., Thuraisingham, B., Wang, F.-Y. (eds.) ISI 2006. LNCS, vol. 3975, pp. 492–497. Springer, Heidelberg (2006). https://doi.org/10.1007/11760146_46
15. El-Aziz, E.M.A., Mesbah, S., Mahar, K.: GIS-based decision support system for criminal tracking. In: International Conference on Computer Theory and Applications, ICCTA, pp. 30–34. IEEE (2012)
16. James, A.B.: Crime intelligence 2.0: reinforcing crowdsourcing using artificial intelligence and mobile computing (2017). https://cloudfront.escholarship.org/dist/prd/content/qt39s3k7bw/qt39s3k7bw.pdf
17. Xu, G., Li, H., Tan, C., Liu, D., Dai, Y., Yang, K.: Achieving efficient and privacy-preserving truth discovery in crowd sensing systems. Comput. Secur. **69**, 114–126 (2017). https://doi.org/10.1016/j.cose.2016.11.014
18. Morschheuser, B., Werder, K., Hamari, J., Abe, J.: How to gamify? A method for designing gamification. In: Proceedings 50th Annual Hawaii International Conference on System Sciences (HICSS), Hawaii, USA, 4–7 January 2017, pp. 1–10 (2017). https://doi.org/10.24251/HICSS.2017.155
19. El Alaoui El Abdallaoui, H., Ennaji, F.Z., El Fazziki, A.: An image processing based framework using crowdsourcing for a successful suspect investigation. In: Abraham, A., Haqiq, A., Muda, A.K., Gandhi, N. (eds.) SoCPaR 2017. AISC, vol. 737, pp. 70–80. Springer, Cham (2018). https://doi.org/10.1007/978-3-319-76357-6_7

Modeling and Evaluating Cross-layer Elasticity Strategies in Cloud Systems

Khaled Khebbeb[1,2]([✉]), Nabil Hameurlain[2], and Faiza Belala[1]

[1] LIRE Laboratory, Constantine 2 University – Abdelhamid Mehri,
Constantine, Algeria
{khaled.khebbeb, faiza.belala}@univ-constantine2.dz,
khaled.khebbeb@univ-pau.fr
[2] LIUPPA Laboratory, University of Pau, Pau, France
nabil.hameurlain@univ-pau.fr

Abstract. Clouds are complex systems that provide computing resources in an elastic way. Elasticity property allows their adaptation to input workload by (de) provisioning resources as the demand rises and drops. However, due to the numerous overlapping factors that impact their elasticity and the unpredictable nature of the workload, providing accurate action plans to manage cloud systems' elastic adaptations is a particularly challenging task. In this paper, we propose an approach based on *Bigraphical Reactive Systems* (BRS) to model cloud structures and their elastic behavior. We design elasticity strategies that operate at service and infrastructure cloud levels to manage the elastic adaptations. Besides, we provide a Maude encoding to permit generic executability and formal verification of the elastic behaviors. One step ahead, we show how the strategies can be combined at both levels to provide different high-level elastic behaviors. Finally, we evaluate the different cross-layer combinations using *Queuing Theory*.

Keywords: Cloud Computing · Elasticity · Cross-layer elastic behavior
Modeling · Bigraphical Reactive Systems · Maude

1 Introduction

Cloud computing [25] is a recent paradigm that has known a great interest in both industrial and academic sectors. It consists of providing a pool of virtualized resources (servers, virtual machines, etc.) as on-demand services. These resources are offered by cloud providers according to three fundamental service models: infrastructure as a service (IaaS), platform as a service (PaaS), and software as a service (SaaS). The most appealing feature that distinguishes the cloud from other models is the elasticity property [16]. Elasticity [11] allows to efficiently control resources provisioning according to workload fluctuation in a way to maintain an adequate quality of service (QoS) while minimizing operating cost. Such a behavior is implemented by an elasticity controller: an entity usually based on a closed control loop [18] that decides of the elasticity actions to be triggered to adapt to the demand. In fact, managing a cloud system's elasticity can be particularly challenging. Elastic behaviors rely on many overlapping factors such as the available resources, current workload, etc. Managing

© Springer Nature Switzerland AG 2018
E. H. Abdelwahed et al. (Eds.): MEDI 2018, LNCS 11163, pp. 168–183, 2018.
https://doi.org/10.1007/978-3-030-00856-7_11

these dependencies significantly increases the difficulty of modeling cloud systems' elasticity controller. To address this challenge, formal methods characterized by their efficiency, reliability and precision, present an effective solution to deal with these numerous factors.

In this paper, we provide a formal modeling approach that reduces the complexity of designing cloud systems and the elasticity controller behavior. We adopt *Bigraphical Reactive Systems* (BRS) [26] as a *meta-model* for specifying structural and behavioral aspects of elastic cloud systems. Bigraphs are used to model the structure of cloud systems and the elasticity controller. Bigraphical reaction rules describe the elastic behavior of a cloud system. We focus on the infrastructure (IaaS) and service (SaaS) levels to define reactive elasticity strategies for provisioning and deprovisioning cloud resources in a cross-layered way. A strategy provides the logic that governs resources provisioning. It enables the elasticity controller to manage the cloud system's elastic behavior. It consists of a set of actions (bigraphical reaction rules) that are triggered according to the specified conditions (i.e., reactive strategies take the form: *if condition(s) then action(s)*).

Furthermore, we turn to Maude [23] as a semantic framework to encode the BRS modeling approach and to provide a generic executable solution of cloud elastic behavior. Maude is a formal tool environment based on rewriting logic. It can be used as a declarative and executable formal specification language, and as a formal verification system. It provides good representation and verification capabilities for a wide range of systems including models for concurrency. This enables us to easily map the BRS specifications into Maude modules and to manage the *non-determinism* that characterizes cloud systems' elastic behavior.

Finally, we present a way to combine different strategies at both infrastructure and service levels to enable different high level elastic behaviors. We propose a queuing-based approach as an analytical support for the elastic behavior. Precisely, we conduct experimental simulations of different execution scenarios to provide a quantitative evaluation of the multiple cross-layer elasticity strategies combinations.

The remainder of the paper is structured as follows. In Sect. 2, we present our vision of cloud systems and explain how their elastic behavior is managed by the elasticity controller. In Sect. 3, we introduce and use BRS formalism to provide a modeling approach for cloud systems. We model the elasticity controller and define elasticity strategies. In Sect. 4, we encode the bigraphical specifications of elastic cloud systems into Maude. We provide a quantitative evaluation of the elasticity strategies combinations using a queuing approach in Sect. 5. In Sect. 6, we review the state of art on elasticity and formal specification of elastic cloud systems. Finally, Sect. 7 summarizes and concludes the paper.

2   Cloud Systems and Elasticity

At a high level of abstraction, an elastic cloud system can be divided in three parts: the *front-end* part, the *back-end* part and the *elasticity controller*. The front-end represents the client interface that is used to access the cloud system and to interact with it. The back-end part refers to the cloud system's *hosting environment*, i.e., the set of computing resources (servers, virtual machines, service instances, etc.) that are deployed in the system and that are provided to satisfy its incoming workload. Cloud systems offer their computing resources in an elastic way. *Elasticity* is property that was defined as *"the degree in which a system is able to adapt to workload changes by provisioning and deprovisioning resources in an autonomic manner such that at each point in time the available resources match the current demand as closely as possible."* [13].

Elastic cloud systems usually work according to the closed-loop architecture shown in Fig. 1, where the elastic cloud system receives *end-users'* requests through its client interface. The amount of received requests (i.e., the *input workload*) can oscillate in an unpredictable manner. The growing workload, thus the *system's load* can cause users *Quality of Experience (QoE)* degradations (e.g. performance drop). The *cloud infrastructure provider* hosts the controlled system (i.e., the cloud *hosting environment*). It provides costs to the cloud *service provider* according to the provisioned resources (that are allocated to the service provider's running applications). When the input workload drops, the eventually unnecessarily allocated resources are still billed. The *elasticity controller* monitors the controlled system and determines its adaptation (i.e., its *elastic behavior*). The adaptation actions (i.e. (de)provision cloud resources) are triggered to satisfy high-level policies that are set by the service provider such as *minimize costs, maximize performance*, etc.

The behavior of an elastic system can be intuitively described as follows. During its runtime, the system's load can increase. Which might lead to overload the provisioned resources. To avoid the saturation, an elastic system stretches, i.e., it scales by provisioning more computing resources. Conversely, when the system load decreases, some resources might become underused. To reduce costs, the elastic system contracts, i.e., it scales by deprovisioning the unnecessarily allocated resources [4]. However, due to the complexity of cloud systems and the multiplicity of the overlapping factors that impact their elasticity, specifying and implementing the elastic behavior is a particularly tedious task. Elasticity is specified by strategies that are designed to satisfy the high-level policies in an autonomic way. In this paper, we address this challenge by relying on formal methods. We provide a BRS based modeling of cloud systems' structure and the elasticity controller's behavior. Then we encode the proposed specification into Maude language to provide an executable solution of the elastic behaviors.

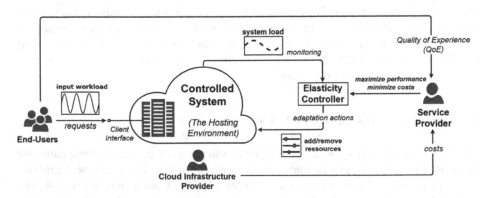

Fig. 1. High level view of cloud systems' elastic behavior

3   BRS Based Specification of Elastic Cloud Systems

Bigraphical reactive systems (BRS) are a recent formalism introduced by Milner [26, 27], for modeling the temporal and spatial evolution of computation. It provides an algebraical model that emphasize both *connectivity* and *locality* via a *link graph* and a *place graph* respectively. A BRS consists of a set of *bigraphs* and a set of *reaction rules*, which define the dynamic evolution of the system by specifying how the set of bigraphs can be reconfigured.

3.1   Bigraphical Modeling of Cloud Systems

A cloud system is represented by a bigraph *CS* including all cloud architectural elements. The sorting logic introduces mapping rules and expresses all the constraints and formation rules, that *CS* needs to satisfy, to ensure proper and accurate encoding of the cloud semantics into BRS concepts. Formal definitions are given in what follows.

Definition 1. Formally, a cloud system is defined by a bigraph *CS*, where:

$$CS = \left(V_{CS}, E_{CS}, ctrl_{CS}, CS^P, CS^L \right) : I_{CS} \rightarrow J_{CS}$$

- V_{CS} and E_{CS} are sets of nodes and edges of the bigraph *CS*.
- $ctrl_{CS} : V_{CS} \rightarrow K_{CS}$ a control map that assigns each node $v \in V_{cs}$ with a control $k \in K_{cs}$.
- $CS^P = (V_{CS}, ctrl_{CS}, prnt_{CS}) : m_{CS} \rightarrow n_{CS}$ is the place graph of *CS* where $prnt_{CS} : m_{CS} \uplus V_{CS} \rightarrow V_{CS} \uplus n_{CS}$ is a parent map. m_{CS} and n_{CS} are the number of sites and regions of the bigraph *CS*.
- $CS^L = (V_{CS}, E_{CS}, ctrl_{CS}, link_{CS}) : X_{CS} \rightarrow Y_{CS}$ represents link graph of *CS*, where $link_{CS} : X_{CS} \uplus P_{CS} \rightarrow E_{CS} \uplus Y_{CS}$ is a link map, X_{CS} and Y_{CS} are respectively inner and outer names and P_{CS} is the set of ports of *CS*.
- $I_{CS} = \langle m_{CS}, X_{CS} \rangle$ and $J_{CS} = \langle n_{CS}, Y_{CS} \rangle$ are the inner and outer interfaces of the cloud system bigraph *CS*.

Nodes V_{CS} represent the physical (servers) or logical (VM and service instances) elements of the cloud system. Edges E_{CS} represent the links (e.g. communication canals) that connect the nodes via their ports P_{CS}. Control map $ctrl_{CS}$ associate semantics to the nodes. The place graph CS^P gives the hierarchical construction of the system basing on the parent map $prnt_{CS}$ for nodes and regions (e.g. a server node is a parent for a VM node, or hosts is). Regions represent the different parts of the system (e.g. the hosting environment). Sites are used to neglect parts of the system that are not included in the model. The link graph CS^L gives the link map $link_{CS}$ that show all the connections between ports and names. Inner and outer interfaces I_{CS} and J_{CS} give the openness of the system to its external environment (other bigraphs). Inner and outer names X_{CS} and Y_{CS} give labels to different parts of the system for interfacing purposes.

Definition   2. The   sorting   discipline   associated   to   *CS*   is   a   triple $\Sigma_{CS} = \{\Theta_{CS}, K_{CS}, \Phi_{CS}\}$.

Where Θ_{CS} is a non-empty set of sorts. K_{CS} is its signature, and Φ_{CS} is a set of formation rules associated to the bigraph. Table 1 gives for each cloud concept the mapping rules for BRS equivalence. It consists of the control associated to the entity, its arity (number of ports) and its associated sort. *Sorts* are used to distinguish node types for structural constraints while *controls* identify states and parameters a node can have. For instance, a server noted SE has control SE^L when it is overloaded and SE^U when unused but all nodes representing servers are of sort *e*.

Table 1. The sorting discipline of the bigraph *CS*

Cloud element	Control	Arity	Sort
Server	SE	2	e
Overloaded server	SE^L	2	e
Unused server	SE^U	2	e
Virtual machine	VM	2	v
Overloaded VM	VM^L	2	v
Unused VM	VM^U	2	v
Service instance	S	1	s
Overloaded service instance	S^L	1	s
Unused service instance	S^U	1	s
Request	q	0	r

Table 2 gives the formation rules that define construction constraints over the bigraphical model. Rule $\Phi 0$ specifies that servers are at the top of the hierarchical order of the deployed entities in the bigraph. Rules $\Phi 1$–3 give the structural disposition of the hosting environment where a server hosts VMs, a VM runs service instances and a service instance handles requests. All connections are port-to-port links to illustrate possible links between the different cloud entities. In $\Phi 5$–6, we use the name *w* (for workload) to illustrate the connection the cloud system has with its abstracted front-end part. A server is linked to its hosted VMs and a VM is linked to the service instances it is running [19]. Rule $\Phi 4$ gives the active elements, i.e., that may take part in reactions.

Table 2. Construction constraints Φ_{CS} of the bigraph *CS*

	Rule description
$\Phi 0$	All children of a 0-region (hosting environment) have sort e
$\Phi 1$	All children of a e-node have sort v
$\Phi 2$	All children of a v-node have sort s
$\Phi 3$	All children of a s-node have sort q
$\Phi 4$	All $\widetilde{evsq}$-nodes are active
$\Phi 5$	In an e-node, one port is always linked to a w-name and the other may be linked to v-nodes
$\Phi 6$	In a v-node, one port is always linked to a e-node and the other may be linked to s-nodes

3.2   The Elasticity Controller as a Behavioral Entity

The elasticity controller determines the adaptations of the cloud system's hosting environment. In our modeling approach, we consider this entity as the set of reaction rules that describe the system's behavior and the logic that governs the rules' triggering. This logic is implemented as *strategies* that describe different adaptations of the cloud system in a *cross-layered* manner (i.e., at infrastructure and service cloud levels).

Reaction Rules. A reaction rule Ri is a pair (R, R'), where *redex R* and *reactum R'* are bigraphs that have the same interface. The evolution of the cloud bigraph *CS* is derived by checking if R is a match in *CS* and by substituting it with R' to obtain a new system *CS'*. This is made with triggering the suitable reaction rule Ri. The evolution is noted $CS \xrightarrow{Ri} CS'$.

Table 3 gives the algebraic description of the different reaction rules that implement the adaptation actions of the elasticity controller. Sites (expressed as d) are used to neglect the elements that are not included in the reaction. The specified rules define the *horizontal scale* elasticity actions at different cloud levels. Reaction rules are applied for provisioning (R1–2) and deprovisioning (R3–4) resources by *scaling-out* and *scaling-in* the hosting environment. Rules R5–6 specify migration actions for service instances and requests, which are used to balance the system's load.

Table 3. Reaction rules describing adaptation actions

Adaptation action	Reaction rule algebraic form
Scale-Out	
Replicate service instance	$R1 \stackrel{def}{=} SE.((VM.(S.d2)|d1)|d0)|id \rightarrow SE.((VM.(S.d2)|S)|d1)|d0)|id$
Replicate VM instance	$R2 \stackrel{def}{=} SE.((VM.(S.d2)|d1)|d0)|id \rightarrow SE.(((VM.(S.d2)|d1)|(VM))|d0)|id$
Scale-In	
Consolidate service instance	$R3 \stackrel{def}{=} SE.((VM.(S.d3)|(S.d2)|d1)|d0)|id \rightarrow SE.((VM.(S.d2)|d1)|d0)|id$
Consolidate VM instance	$R4 \stackrel{def}{=} SE.(((VM.(S.d3)|d2)|(VM.d1))|d0)|id \rightarrow SE.((VM.(S.d2)|d1)|d0)|id$
Load Balancing	
Migrate service instance	$R5 \stackrel{def}{=} SE.(((VM.(S.d3)|d2)|(VM.d1))|d0)|id$ $\rightarrow SE.(((VM|d2)|(VM.(S.d3)))|d0)|id$
Transfer request	$R6 \stackrel{def}{=} SE.((VM.(S.q|d4)|d3)|(VM.(S.d2)|d1)|d0)|id$ $\rightarrow SE.((VM.(S.d4)|d3)|(VM.(S.q|d2)|d1)|d0)|id$

Elasticity Strategies. As explained before, the specified strategies define the logic that governs the elastic behavior of the controlled cloud system. We use reactive strategies to make decisions about the elastic adaptations of the deployed entities by reasoning on their states. A reactive strategy takes the form: *IF Condition(s) THEN Action(s)* where conditions are expressed in *predicates logic* and actions are reaction rules. Table 4 defines the scaling (out/in) policies at both service and infrastructure levels.

Infrastructure Level. We introduce two strategies to express different provisioning policies for VM instances, as follows.

- *Strategy V1:* ensures VM instances' *high availability*. It states that the system *scales out*, i.e., provision a new VM instance, by executing rule R2 when at least one VM is overloaded, i.e., when it reaches its upper threshold of hosted service instances. In other terms, when it has control VM^L.
- *Strategy V2:* is designed to ensure the *limited availability* in terms of VM instances. It states that scale-out adaptations (provisioning VM instances) are triggered when all available VMs are overloaded.
- Both *V1* and *V2* specify that the system *scales-in*, i.e., deprovisions an empty VM instance (of control VM^U) by executing rule R4, if one is detected and no overloaded VM is available. This choice prevents having contradictory adaptation loops.

Service *Level.* We define two strategies to describe the system's service instances provisioning behaviors, as follows.

- *Strategy S1*: ensures service instances' *high availability*. It states that a new instance of service is provisioned by executing rule R1, when at least one available instance is overloaded (when it has control S^L).
- *Strategy S2:* defines service instances' *limited availability*. It states that *scale-out* adaptations (provisioning service instances) are triggered when all available service instances are overloaded.
- Strategies *S1* and *S2* specify that the system *scales in*, i.e., deprovisions an empty service instance (which has control S^U) by executing rule R3, when one is detected, and no overloaded instance is available.

Table 4. Scaling strategies at service and infrastructure levels

Strategy	Scale-Out	Scale-In
	Infrastructure level	
V1	*IF $\exists v \in V_{CS} \, ctrl_{CS}(v) = VM^L THEN \, R2$*	*IF $\forall v \in V_{CS} \exists v' \in V_{CS} \, ctrl_{CS}$*
V2	*IF $\forall v \in V_{CS} \, ctrl_{CS}(v) = VM^L THEN \, R2$*	$(v) \neq VM^L \wedge ctrl_{CS}(v') = VM^U THEN \, R4$
	Service level	
S1	*IF $\exists s \in V_{CS} \, ctrl_{CS}(s) = S^L THEN \, R1$*	*IF $\forall s \in V_{CS} \exists s' \in V_{CS} \, ctrl_{CS}(s) \neq S^L \wedge ctrl_{CS}(s')$*
S2	*IF $\forall s \in V_{CS} \, ctrl_{CS}(s) = S^L THEN \, R1$*	$= S^U THEN \, R3$

In addition, we define two strategies for the system's load balancing at both service and infrastructure levels as follows.

- *Strategy LB-V*: describes the system load balancing at infrastructure level, it states that service instances are migrated from loaded VMs to less loaded ones (executing rule R5) to reach a VMs load equilibrium.
- *Strategy LB-S*: states that requests are transferred from loaded service instances to less loaded ones (by applying rule R6) to achieve load balancing at service level.

Modeling the Elastic Behavior with LTL. Modeling the introduced elastic behavior with *Linear Temporal Logic* allows the specification of formulas to verify the system's elastic adaptations. To this purpose, we define a model of temporal logic with a *Kripke structure* A_{CS}, as follows.

Definition 3. Given a set AP_{CS} of *atomic propositions*, we consider the Kripke structure $A_{CS} = (A, \rightarrow_A, L_{CS})$. Where A is the *set of states*, $\rightarrow_A$ is the *transition relation*, and $L_{CS} : A \rightarrow AP_{CS}$ is the *labeling function* associating to each state $a \in A$, the set $L_{CS}(a)$ of the atomic propositions in AP_{CS} that hold in the state a. $LTL(AP_{CS})$ denotes the formulas of the *propositional linear temporal logic*. The semantics of $LTL(AP_{CS})$ is defined by a *satisfaction relation*: $A_{CS}, a \models \varphi$, where $\varphi \in LTL(AP_{CS})$.

We consider the set $AP_{CS} = \{Stable, Overloaded, Underused, LBTrue, M\}$ of the atomic propositions that describe the hosting environment's states. For the sake of simplicity, these states are symbolic and relate to the elastic behavior of the system. The system is considered *Overloaded/Underused* when at least one entity (VM, Service) is overloaded/unused. It is *Stable* otherwise. *LBTrue* is a non-exclusive proposition that can hold together with *Stable, Overloaded* or *Underused* (that are exclusive) when load balancing at VM or Service levels is applicable. M holds when the system is being monitored. In other terms, different structural states of the system in A (i.e., configurations) can be gathered (i.e., labeled) in the same class of equivalence with respect to the global symbolic state of the system in AP_{CS}.

The *non-deterministic finite-state automaton* in Fig. 2 shows the transitions *Scale-Out, Scale-In* and *LB* (for *Load Balancing*) that represent the adaptation actions that are executed by the elasticity controller. The transitions *Input* and *Output* stand for receiving and releasing end-users' requests. Initially, the controlled system is in the monitoring phase. When monitored, it can be at any elastic state.

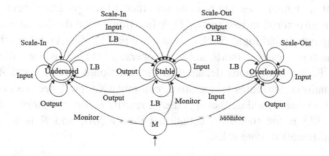

Fig. 2. Elastic behavior non-deterministic finite-state automaton

Note that the evolution of the system's state depends on its elastic constraints (bounded resources capacity introduced by thresholds, triggering predicates, etc.). Thus, reaching the stable state is not always possible (i.e., all elastic states can be final).

To describe the elastic behaviors that are triggered by the elasticity controller in LTL, we introduce the set $LTL(AP) = \{Scale-Out, Scale-In, LoadBalance\}$ of the propositional formulas, as follows.

- $Scale-Out \equiv G(Overloaded \rightarrow F\ Stable)$
- $Scale-In \equiv G(Underused \rightarrow F\ Stable)$
- $LoadBalance \equiv G(LBTrue \rightarrow F \sim LBTrue)$

Where the formulas $Scale-Out$ and $Scale-In$ state that a given system that is $Overloaded/Underused$ will eventually reach its $Stable$ state. $LoadBalance$ formula ensures that the system will eventually apply load balancing as long as it is possible. We use the symbol $\sim$ for negation. The symbols G and F are LTL operators that respectively stand for "*always*" and "*eventually*".

4   Principles of Maude Encoding and Property Verification

To verify the correctness of the introduced elasticity strategies and to watch the aimed cross-layered elasticity, it is important to provide an executable solution for the specified elastic behaviors. Theoretically, BRS provide good *meta-modeling* bases to specify cloud systems' structure and their elastic behavior. As for their executable capabilities, the few existing tools built around BRS as BigraphER [5] and BPL Tool [14] are limited and only suitable for some specific application domains. Furthermore, the BRS *model-checker* BigMC [30] that was used in [32], allows formal verification of safety properties. However, the possible verifications rely on very limited predefined predicates. These tools lack of providing concurrent and autonomic executability of the specified BRS models. In this paper, we turn to Maude language to tackle these limitations and to provide a generic executable solution of elasticity strategies together with their verification.

4.1   Motivating the Use of Maude

Maude [9] is a high-level formal specification language based on equational and rewriting logics. A Maude program is a *logical theory* and a Maude computation is *logical deduction* which uses the axioms specified in the program/theory. A Maude specification is structured in two parts. (1) A functional module that specifies a *theory* in membership equational logic. Such a theory is a pair $(\Sigma, E \cup A)$, where the *signature* Σ specifies the type structure (sorts, subsorts, operators etc.). E is the collection of the (possibly conditional) equations declared in the functional module, and A is the collection of equational attributes (associative, commutative, etc.) declared for the operators. (2) And a system module that specifies a *rewrite theory* as a triple $(\Sigma, E \cup A, R)$. Where $(\Sigma, E \cup A)$ is the module's equational theory part, and R is a collection of (possibly conditional) rewrite rules.

The Bigraphical specifications for cloud systems' structure (in Sect. 3.1) can be encoded in a functional module. Where the declared operations and equations define the constructors that build the system's elements. Similarly, BRS dynamics (in Sect. 3.2) that describe the elasticity controller's behavior can be encoded in a system module. Where the elasticity strategies are described as conditional rewrite rules. The set of rewrite rules R express the bigraphical reaction rules. Their triggering conditions expressed as equations from the functional module encode the strategies' predicates.

4.2 Setting up Elastic Cloud Systems

To encode the BRS modeling approach for cloud structures and their elastic behavior in Maude, we first map the BRS model into Maude language as shown in Table 5.

Structure Encoding. In the functional module, the bigraph sorts e, v and s (i.e., server, VM and service) are defined as CS, VM and S. Note that we enriched Maude sorts with additional information as the maximum hosting thresholds and the entities states. A sort is built according to its associated constructor. For instance, a cloud server is built by the term CS < x, y, z/VML:state >, where x, y and z are naturals that encode upper hosting thresholds at server, VM and service levels. VML is a list of VMs, this relationship is expressed by the declaration of sort VM as a subsort of sort VML. The element state gives a state out of the constructors (overloaded, unused, stable, etc.). To enable horizontal scale strategies according to configurable preferences, we define the sort HSCALE(V i, S j) :: cs. Where the parameters $i, j \in [1, 2]$ indicate which strategies are applied at infrastructure (*V1* or *V2*) and service (*S1* or *S2*) levels of the cloud system cs.

Table 5. Encoding the BRS cloud model into Maude

Bigraphical model	Maude specification
	Functional module
Sorting discipline (*structure construction*)	sorts HSCALE CS VM S VML SL state . subsort VM < VML . subsort S < SL . op HSCALE (V_ , S_) :: _ : Nat Nat CS -> HSCALE [ctor] . op CS<_,_,_/_:_> : Nat Nat Nat VML state -> CS [ctor] . op VM{_,_:_} : Nat SL state -> VM [ctor] . op S[_,_:_] : Nat Nat state -> S [ctor] . ops stable over under idle : -> state [ctor] . op nilv : -> VML [ctor] . op _|_ : VML VML -> VML [ctor assoc comm id: nilv] . op nils : -> SL [ctor] . op _+_ : SL SL -> SL [ctor assoc comm id: nils] . ...
System state predicates (*self-aware property*)	ops isStable(_) isOverloaded(_) isUnderused(_) AoverV(_) EoverV(_) EunV(_) AoverS(_) EoverS(_) EunS(_) LBVpred(_) LBSpred(_) : CS -> Bool . ...
	System module
Reaction rules and elasticity strategies (*self-adaptive property*)	Conditional rewrite rules of the form: crl [rewrite-rule-name] : term => term' if condition(s) .

System State Predicates Encoding. We define a set of system predicates in the functional module that give information about the managed cloud system configuration (that we express as a cloud server in Maude). For instance, *AoverV()* is a predicate for "*all VMs are overloaded*" and *EunS()* is a predicate for "*there exists an unused service instance*". We also encode system state predicates *isStable(), isOverloaded()* and *isUnderused()* that are true if the cloud system is stable, overloaded or underused.

Elasticity Strategies Encoding. Strategies are encoded as conditional rewrite rules in the system module. Their conditions are the states and monitoring predicates and their actions (bigraph reaction rules) are encoded as Maude functional computation. For instance, load-balancing strategy at VM level is specified as the following rewrite rule: `crl[LB-VM-level]:cs => LBV(cs) if LBVpred(cs)`. Where `cs` is a given cloud system, `LBV(cs)` is an equation that reduces the term `cs` in such a way to apply load-balancing at VM level and `LBVpred(cs)` is a predicate that is true if load-balancing at VM level in `cs` is possible. *LBV()* and *LBVpred()* are defined as equations in the functional module.

Formal Verification of Elasticity. To verify the elastic behavior of the system as encoded in the system module, we define a Maude property specification based on *Linear Temporal Logic*. Maude allows associating *Kripke* structures to the rewrite theory specified in the system module. The semantics introduced by the Kripke structure A_{CS} in Sect. 3.2 allowed us to define a generic LTL model checking that can reason on any system configuration. For instance, determining that a cloud configuration is stable in terms of elasticity is specified with: `cs ⊨ Stable = true if isStable(cs) == true`. Where `cs` is a given cloud configuration. `Stable` is a proposition $\in AP_{CS}$ that represent the symbolic elastic state "*stable*". And `isStable(cs)` is a predicate for "*the cloud system cs is stable*" which is defined in the functional module.

We execute Maude's LTL model-checker with, as parameters, a cloud configuration as an initial state and a property formula in $LTL(AP_{CS})$ to verify. The model-checker can give counter examples showing the succession of the triggered rewrite rules that are applied on the initial state of the system, in such a way to verify the given property according to the specified elasticity strategies.

5   A Queuing Approach for Quantitative Evaluation

As its input workload rises, the congestions that may result in a system are in fact waiting queues that indicate the insufficiency of the provisioned resources. For this reason, we advocate that a queuing approach is a relevant support to study the elastic behavior of a system and to evaluate the performance of elasticity strategies. To proceed to a quantitative evaluation of the introduced strategies, we perform queuing-based offline simulations of elastic cloud systems.

Queuing Model. We consider a *queuing model*, defined by a set of parameters as introduced by the *Kendall* notation: A/S/C/Q/N/D [3], where C is the number of service instances. A is the *arriving process* describing how the requests arrive into the system.

D is the *serving discipline* describing how the requests are processed (e.g., *first come first served*). The *service process* S gives the amount of time required to process the requests. Q is the maximum number of requests that the system can hold, and N is the number of requests expected to arrive into the system. In our evaluation, we consider that Q and $N = \infty$. We consider that A is a *Poisson process* which gives an exponential distribution of the received requests (at each time unit) with the average value of λ. S also follows an exponential law with the average value of μ to give the number of requests that are processed by service instances. The essence of elasticity being the adaptations, we use a queuing model with on-demand number C of service instances, inspired from [15], to show how the system adapts to its varying input workload by (de)provisioning resources at service and infrastructure levels.

Experiment. To evaluate elasticity, we consider the example of a cloud-based voting service where initially one VM is provisioned in which one service instance is deployed. We define the upper-bound hosting thresholds $v = 2$, $s = 2$ and $w = 40$, for the cloud system, the VMs and the service instances respectively in terms of VMs, service instances and requests. We simulate the execution of a cloud system from the same initial configuration according to the defined strategies, for both infrastructure (*V1, V2*) and service (*S1, S2*) levels. The simulations are performed within 50 time units over a scenario where $\lambda = 50$ and $\mu = 35$. The results give the system's average *resources provisioning*, *performance* and *efficiency*. Introducing thresholds makes the systems bounded in terms of hosting capabilities. Thus, the displayed rates are given in function of the maximum capacity of service/VM instances and their average recorded deployment. Idem for the system load (i.e., the processed requests per time unit). The delay represents the ratio between the pending requests and those being served.

Knowing that load balancing (*LB-V, LB-S*) is applied when possible, the graphs in Fig. 3 show the cross-layer behaviors resulting from combining the scaling strategies introduced in Sect. 3.2.

Intuitively, combining high availability for both infrastructure and service levels (*V1, S1*) leads to *high-performance*, i.e., low processing delay (1%), but also brings high provisioning costs, i.e., high hosting environment deployment (93% service and 100% VM instances capacity).

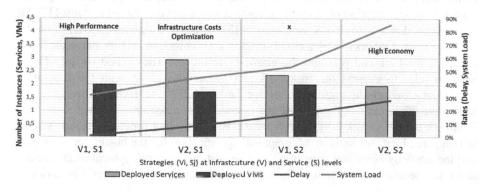

Fig. 3. Evaluation of cross-layer elasticity strategies

Inversely, applying limited availability at both levels ($V2$, $S2$) implies low costs i.e., *high economy* but also low performance, i.e., high processing delay (28%).

The combination ($V2$, $S1$) ensures *infrastructure costs optimization*, i.e., new VMs are provisioned only when the available ones are fully loaded (by scaling-out at service level). It brings better overall optimization than ($V1$, $S1$) with less average service deployment and better average system load (with respectively 73% and 44% service instances provisioning and usage rate for combination (VS, $S1$) versus 93% and 32% for combination ($V1$, $S1$)), yet with lower performance (i.e., higher delay).

The combination ($V1$, $S2$) doesn't seem to describe a specific behavior (labeled "x") in this simulation. It leads to mediocre rentability of the VMs and to consequent delay regarding the recorded usage rate of the Service instances.

To conclude this evaluation, we want to emphasize the fact that the concept of "good" strategy is not absolute. It depends on the case study (i.e., the system config-uration, workload tendencies, available resources, etc.) and on the preferences set by the cloud service provider [29]. Indeed, having strategies that describe different high-level behaviors gives a certain range of possibilities to endow the managed cloud system with the desirable elastic behaviors.

6 Related Work

There have been several researches in the literature about cloud systems' elasticity such as [1, 7, 10, 21, 33]. However, only a few works like [12, 20, 22, 28] were proposed to study elasticity property using formal methods.

In the context of modeling cloud systems and their elastic behaviors, authors in [4] adopted the temporal logic named CLTLt(D) (Timed Constraint LTL) to model some properties related to cloud systems such as elasticity, resource management and quality of service. In their work, they considered cloud resources as virtual machines and did not address service level. In [2] authors proposed a Petri Nets based formalization to describe cloud-based business processes' elastic behaviors. They introduced elasticity strategies for routing, duplicating and consolidating cloud components at service level. They focused on the application layer of a cloud configuration but did not address the cloud infrastructure in their model. As for our adopted formalism, BRS were proven useful in the specification of ubiquitous, context aware and distributed systems [17, 24] and in other domains [6]. BRS were used in [31] to provide a generic model of elastic cloud systems. Authors modeled cloud structures with bigraphs in three parts: the front-end part, the back-end part and the elasticity controller. They relied on bigraphical reaction rules to express the front/back-end interactions along with the adaptation actions of cloud configurations at service and infrastructure levels. However, they lacked providing elasticity strategies that operate in an autonomic manner.

In our previous work [19], we proposed a BRS modeling for elastic cloud systems in two parts. First, we defined a bigraphical specification for the hosting environment and the elasticity controller structures. And second, we used bigraphical reaction rules to model the adaptation actions, which describe the elasticity controller's behavior.

In this present paper, we propose a different approach. We use a bigraphical modeling to describe the structural aspect of a cloud system's hosting environment *only*; and we model the elasticity controller as a behavioral entity. The controller is modeled using bigraphical reaction rules alongside with the logic that triggers the reactions. This logic is represented by elasticity strategies that specify the elastic behavior of the cloud system in a *cross-layered* manner (i.e., at service and infrastructure levels). This new approach enables seeing the elasticity controller as an intrinsic entity of the cloud system. Therefore, monitoring tasks over the controlled cloud system enables considering it as "*self-aware*"; and the adaptation actions that are triggered in function of its state enables considering it as "*self-adaptive*" [8]. In addition, we propose a way to combine the different designed strategies to provide multiple cross-layer elastic patterns. We evaluate the combinations to highlight the resulting high-level elastic behaviors.

Besides, *Control Theory* was used for resources management in distributed [35] and cloud [34] systems. One of the main limitations of this approach is the non-linearity of most inter-relationships in computing systems [36]. This requires designing nonlinear and adaptive controllers that are difficult to understand and implement. In this paper, we inspire from closed-loop based approaches to design our elasticity controller. It aims at having the controlled cloud system reach a "stable" global state (which is defined in predicates logic) by relying on elasticity strategies we specified using BRS. Maude encoding of these behaviors ensures autonomic and concurrent execution of the elastic adaptations. And Maude's LTL model-checking enables verifying the correctness of the adaptations regarding the reachability of the "stable" state.

7   Conclusion

In this paper, we provided a modeling approach for cloud systems' structure and elastic behaviors based on Bigraphical Reactive Systems. We use bigraphs and bigraphical reactive rules to express both aspects respectively. These behaviors implement the elasticity controller and are described by elasticity strategies. We propose different strategies for horizontal scale (de)provisioning of cloud system resources and for load balancing at service and infrastructure levels. Strategies describe the logic that enables the elasticity controller to reason over the entire cloud system's state and manage its elastic adaptations.

One step further, we encoded the modeling approach into Maude language to provide a generic executable solution for elasticity in cloud systems. We also provided formal verification of elasticity property using the LTL model-checker integrated in Maude.

Besides, we presented an original way to compose different elasticity strategies at both service and infrastructure levels to provide multiple high-level elastic behaviors.

Finally, we proposed a queuing-based approach to conduct experimental simulations of the different elasticity strategies combinations in order to provide a quantitative evaluation of the adaptations.

As on-going work, we aim to enlarge the specifications of cloud system's elastic behavior. Our goal is to provide a more complete solution that considers vertical scale elasticity for cloud resources management.

References

1. Ali-Eldin, A., Tordsson, J., Elmroth, E.: An adaptive hybrid elasticity controller for cloud infrastructures. In: 2012 IEEE Network Operations and Management Symposium, Maui, HI, pp. 204–212 (2012)
2. Amziani, M.: Modeling, evaluation and provisioning of elastic service-based business processes in the cloud. Thesis. Institut National des Télécommunications, 2015. English. < NNT: 2015TELE0016 > . < tel-01217186>
3. Baynat, B.: Théorie des files d'attente. Hermès Science publications, Paris (2000). http:// books.google.fr/books?id=NWWgMQEACAAJ
4. Bersani, M., Bianculli, D., et al.: Towards the formalization of properties of cloud based elastic systems. In: Proceedings of the 6th International Workshop on Principles of Engineering Service-oriented and Cloud Systems – PESOS 2014, Hyderabad, pp. 38–47 (2014)
5. Sevegnani, M., Calder, M.: BigraphER: rewriting and analysis engine for bigraphs. In: Chaudhuri, S., Farzan, A. (eds.) CAV 2016. LNCS, vol. 9780, pp. 494–501. Springer, Cham (2016). https://doi.org/10.1007/978-3-319-41540-6_27
6. Calder, M., Sevegnani, M.: Modeling IEEE 802.11 CSMA/CA RTS/CTS with stochastic bigraphs with sharing. Form. Asp. Computing. **26**(3), 537–561 (2014)
7. Chatziprimou, K., Lano, K., Zschaler, S.: Runtime infrastructure optimization in cloud iaas structures. CloudCom **1**, 687–692 (2013)
8. Chen, T., Bahsoon, R., Yao, X.: A survey and taxonomy of self-aware and self-adaptive cloud autoscaling systems. ACM Comput. Surv. **51**(3), 61:1–61:40 (2018)
9. Clavel, M., Duran, F., et al.: Maude Manual V 2.7.1 (2017)
10. Copil, G., Moldovan, D., et al.: "Multi-level elasticity control of cloud services. In: Service-oriented Computing, 2013, pp. 429–436 (2013)
11. Dustdar, S., Guo, Y., Satzger, B., Truong, H.: Principles of elastic processes. IEEE Internet Comput. **15**, 66–71 (2011)
12. Freitas, L., Watson, P.: Formalizing workflows partitioning over federated clouds: Multi-level security and costs. International Journal of Computer Mathematics, **91**(5), 881–906 (2014)
13. Galante, G., Bona, L.: A survey on cloud computing elasticity. In: 2012 IEEE Fifth International Conference on utility and Cloud Computing, Chicago, Il, 2012, pp. 263–270 (2012)
14. Glenstrup, A.J., Damgaard, T.C., et al.: An implementation of bigraph matching". Technical Report 2010-135. ITUniversitetet Kobenhavn, Copenhagen (2010)
15. Gurtov, A., Mazalov, V.: Queueing system with on-demand number of servers. Math. Appl. **40**(2), 1–12 (2012)
16. Herbst, N., Kounev, S., Reussner, R.: Elasticity in cloud computing: What it is, and what it is not. In: Proceedings of the 10th International Conference on Autonomic Computing, San Jose, CA: uSENIX (2013)
17. Wang, J., Xu, D., Lei, Z.: Formalizing the structure and behaviour of context-aware systems in bigraphs. In: First ACIS International Symposium on Software and Network Engineering (2011)

18. Jacob, B.: A Practical Guide to the IBM Autonomic Computing Toolkit. IBM, International Technical Support Organization, Raleigh (2004)
19. Khebbeb, K., Sahli, H., Hameurlain, N., et al.: A BRS Based Approach for Modeling Elastic Cloud Systems. In: Service-Oriented Computing – ICSOC 2017 Workshops, pp. 5–17
20. Kikuchi, S., Hiraishi, K.: Improving reliability in management of cloud computing infrastructure by formal methods. In: Network Operations and Management Symposium (NOMS) pp. 1–7 (2014)
21. Letondeur, L.: Planification pour la gestion autonomique de l'élasticité d'applications dans le cloud. Computer Science [cs]. Thesis at Joseph Fourier University, (2014). French. < tel-01140128>
22. Rady, M.: Formal definition of service availability in cloud computing using OWL. In: Moreno-Díaz, R., Pichler, F., Quesada-Arencibia, A. (eds.) EUROCAST 2013. LNCS, vol. 8111, pp. 189–194. Springer, Heidelberg (2013). https://doi.org/10.1007/978-3-642-53856-8_24
23. Clavel, M., et al.: All About Maude - A High-Performance Logical Framework. LNCS, vol. 4350. Springer, Heidelberg (2007). https://doi.org/10.1007/978-3-540-71999-1
24. Mansutti, A., Miculan, M., Peressotti, M.: Multi-agent systems design and prototyping with bigraphical reactive systems. In: DAIS 2014, pp. 201–208 (2014)
25. Mell, P., Grance, T.: The NIST definition of cloud computing. In: National Institute of Standards & Technology, Special Publication, 2011, pp. 800–145 (2011)
26. Milner, R.: Bigraphs and their algebra. Electron. Notes Theor. Comput. Sci. **209**, 5–19 (2008)
27. Milner, R.: The space and motion of communicating agents. Cambridge University Press, Cambridge (2009)
28. Naskos, A., Stachtiari, E., et al.: Cloud elasticity using probabilistic model checking. CoRR, vol. abs/1405.4699 (2014)
29. Netto, M., Cardonha, C., et al.: Evaluating auto-scaling strategies for cloud computing environments. In: 2014 IEEE 22nd International Symposium on Modelling, Analysis & Simulation of Computer and Telecommunication Systems (2014)
30. Perrone, G., Debois, S., Hildebrandt, T.: A model checker for bigraphs. In: Proceedings of the 27th ACM Symposium in Applied Computing ACM-SAC 2012 (2012)
31. Sahli, H., Hameurlain, N., Belala, F.: A bigraphical model for specifying elastic cloud systems and their behaviour. Int. J. Parallel Emergent Distrib. Syst. (2016). https://doi.org/10.1080/17445760.2016.1188927
32. Sahli, H., Belala, F., Bouanaka, C.: Model-checking cloud systems using BigMC. In: 8th International Workshop on Verification and Evaluation of Computer and Communication Systems. Bejaïa, Algeria, September 2014
33. Trihinas, D., Sofokleous, C., Loulloudes, N., Foudoulis, A., Pallis, G., Dikaiakos, M.D.: Managing and monitoring elastic cloud applications. In: Casteleyn, S., Rossi, G., Winckler, M. (eds.) ICWE 2014. LNCS, vol. 8541, pp. 523–527. Springer, Cham (2014). https://doi.org/10.1007/978-3-319-08245-5_42
34. Mendieta, M., Martin, C., et al.: A control theory approach for managing cloud computing resources: a proof-of-concept on memory partitioning. In: IEEE Second Ecuador Technical Chapters Meeting (ETCM) (2017)
35. Liu, X., Zhu, X., et al.: Adaptive entitlement control of resource containers on shared servers. In: 9th IFIP/IEEE International Symposium on Integrated Network Management (2005)
36. Zhu, X., Uysal, M., et al.: What does control theory bring to systems research? ACM SIGOPS Oper. Sys. Rev. **43**(1), 62–69 (2009)

Thing Federation as a Service: Foundations and Demonstration

Zakaria Maamar[1]([✉]), Khouloud Boukadi[2], Emir Ugljanin[3], Thar Baker[4], Muhammad Asim[5], Mohammed Al-Khafajiy[4], Djamal Benslimane[6], and Hasna El Alaoui El Abdallaoui[7]

[1] Zayed University, Dubai, UAE
zakaria.maamar@zu.ac.ae
[2] Sfax University, Sfax, Tunisia
[3] State University of Novi Pazar, Novi Pazar, Serbia
[4] Liverpool John Moores University, Liverpool, UK
[5] National University of Computer and Emerging Sciences, Islamabad, Pakistan
[6] Université Lyon 1, Lyon, France
[7] Cadi Ayyad University, Marrakesh, Morocco

Abstract. This paper presents the design and implementation guidelines of thing federation-as-a-service. The large and growing number of things compliant with the Internet-of-Things (IoT) principles need to be "harnessed" so, that, things' collective over individual behaviors prevail. A federation gathers necessary things together according to the needs and requirements of the situation that this federation is tasked to handle. Two types of federations exist: planned whose things are all known at design-time and ad-hoc whose things are known after a competitive selection at run-time. In this paper, federations handle situations about emergency services that involve different stakeholders with different backgrounds raising the complexity of ensuring a successful delivery of these services. A system for patient emergency transfer following a tunnel closure is implemented demonstrating the technical doability of thing federation-as-a-service.

Keywords: Federation-as-a-Service · Internet of Things
Emergency services

1 Introduction

According to Gartner (www.gartner.com/newsroom/id/3165317), 6.4 billion connected things were in use in 2016, up 3% from 2015, and will reach 20.8 billion by 2020. It is, also, predicted that the total economic impact of the Internet-of-Things (IoT) will reach between \$3.9 trillion and \$11.1 trillion per year by the year 2025 [3]. This large and growing number of things need to be "harnessed" so, that, among other benefits, collective over individual behaviors prevail. A promising way of achieving this benefit is to put-in-place federations that would gather relevant things together according to the needs and requirements of the

© Springer Nature Switzerland AG 2018
E. H. Abdelwahed et al. (Eds.): MEDI 2018, LNCS 11163, pp. 184–197, 2018.
https://doi.org/10.1007/978-3-030-00856-7_12

situations that these federations will be tasked to handle. In this paper, we exemplify situations with emergency services that involve different stakeholders with different backgrounds raising the complexity of ensuring a successful delivery of these services.

Contrarily to system/cloud/identity federations that are "thoroughly" investigated by the ICT community (Sect. 2.1), thing federation remains, to the best of our knowledge, overlooked (or barely touched) for different reasons. The ICT community's current concern is to tackle challenges that hinder the operations of individual things (acting as silos). These challenges result from the diversity and multiplicity of things' development and communication technologies [1], users' reluctance and sometimes rejection because of privacy invasion caused by things [7], lack of killer applications that would justify the existence of things [6], lack of an IoT-oriented software engineering discipline that would guide thing analysis, design, and development [13], and, finally, passive nature of things that primarily act as data suppliers (with limited actuating capabilities) [3]. Thing federation requires a different thinking by, for instance, identifying those things that would have the necessary capabilities in support of other available things in the same federation.

We advocate for 2 types of federations that would be associated with the same situations: planned and ad-hoc. The former is formed ahead of time and has its thing constituents already identified (i.e., known) with respect to a situation's needs and requirements. Contrarily, the latter is formed on-the-fly when none of the existing planned federations can handle a situation and, hence, necessary thing constituents that will satisfy this situation's needs and requirements, need to be identified. In either way, a set of criteria for selecting things among similarly-functional things are deemed necessary and will constitute what we refer to, in this paper, as Quality-of-Thing (QoT) model[1]. We, also, discuss, in this paper, how ad-hoc federations evolve into planned federations over time.

Our contributions are manifold: (i) definition of QoT model in support of thing identification and selection, (ii) definition of federations in preparation to handling situations, (iii) development of planned versus ad-hoc federations, and (iv) technical demonstration of federation use using a case study. The rest of this paper is organized as follows. Section 2 presents some related work and a case study. Section 3 is about the core concepts and principles of thing federations. Some implementation details are, also, included in this section. Conclusions and future work are drawn and listed in Sect. 4, respectively.

2   Background

This section first, discusses federations in other ICT domains like cloud and identity, and, then, presents a case study requiring emergency services.

---

[1] QoT is similar to Quality-of-Service (QoS) that is adopted in other disciplines like service computing [9] and uses non-functional properties like reliability and latency.

2.1 Related Work

Despite the growing interest in IoT [10], there are not, to the best of our knowledge, dedicated works that particularly examine thing federation. The below related-work paragraphs discuss the concept of federation from device, cloud, and identity perspectives.

Heil et al. define IoT as a context-aware federation of devices [5]. The objective of setting-up such a federation is to support users access, connect, and locate arbitrary devices according to their functionalities. Heil et al.'s thing federation is different from ours in the sense that we advocate for gathering devices/things together in response to specific situations' needs, and, not, for accessing these devices/things, only. Heil et al.'s approach takes advantage of the concept of Federated Devices Assemblies (FDX) for integrating real-world devices into service federations. This integration encapsulates and exposes devices' capabilities for external use in terms of operations, status variables, and events. According to the authors, FDXs are already designed to communicate among each other irrespectively of the hardware addressed underneath.

Mathlouthi and Ben Saoud discuss cloud federation to enable a flexible composition of System of Systems (SoS) [8]. A SoS is about the cooperation of several constituents that are complex, heterogenous, autonomous, and independently governed, but capable of working cooperatively to achieve common goals. These constituents' characteristics raise concerns with respect to interoperability, fault tolerance, continuous monitoring, etc. Because these systems are deployed over different clouds, the federation of clouds at the software level (SaaS where the 1st S could be SoS) is deemed necessary. In line with Mathlouthi and Ben Saoud, we will show later that thing federation could benefit from cloud federation in the sense that thing federations could be deployed over multiple clouds when handling complex situations.

*aaS where everything is software, platform, infrastructure, data, or thing federation[2] is a model that exposes "resources" to the external world through services for different reasons thoroughly discussed in the literature [11]. In support of exposing thing federation as a service, Celesti et al. discuss IoT as a service (IoTaaS) in conjunction with the development that cloud computing is being subject to and that is leading to IoT cloud and cloud federation [2]. The authors suggest 3 stages towards a true IoT cloud federation. The first stage, "monolithic IoT clouds", is the current stage where IoT clouds are independent; IoT devices interact with a remote cloud system that is in charge of collecting the sensed and actuated data coming from heterogenous IoT devices. The second stage, "vertical supply chain", requires a smart, improved coordination system for enabling the cooperation of different involved IoT cloud providers. Finally, the third stage is about IoT cloud federation that calls for a logical layer between the physical infrastructure and services. 2 types of clouds are identified in the federation: home IoT and foreign IoT. The former is a provider that needs extra external sensing and actuating capabilities and, consequently, forwards federation requests to the latter with the purpose of elastically enlarging

---

[2] With the first three defining the essence of cloud computing.

its IoT infrastructure. It is worth noting that an IoT cloud provider could simultaneously be home cloud and foreign cloud. Finally, Celesti et al. recommend a 3 layer cloud federation reference-architecture that would meet 3 requirements: automatism and scalability, interoperable resource provisioning, and interoperable security. These layers are virtualization, virtual infrastructure manager, and cloud manager. The latter is capable of providing IoTaaS in the form of IaaS, PaaS, and SaaS.

The aforementioned paragraphs discuss federation from different perspectives but overlook the perspective of things forming federations. Despite the latest IoT development [12], today's things' limited capabilities call for their grouping into federations capable of handling complex situations.

2.2   Case Study

We consider a temporarily-closed tunnel resulting from a car accident. In compliance with the emergency procedures and in response to the tunnel-closure situation, a federation of back-up cameras is automatically activated so, that, live images are broadcasted to the rescue teams while meeting their non-functional requirements (e.g., upload speed and resolution quality). To handle the closed-tunnel situation, 2 cases are possible:

1. 1st time tunnel-closure: an ad-hoc camera federation is formed (by some engineers) after selecting the necessary cameras with respect to the rescue teams' non-functional requirements. Once the closure is over, the ad-hoc camera federation becomes a planned camera federation that could be initiated in the future, should a similar situation happen along with similar non-functional requirements.
2. Recurrent tunnel-closure: a planned camera federation, among those that were initiated in the past, is selected with respect to the rescue teams' non-functional requirements. If the selection is unsuccessful, then the case is treated as 1st time tunnel-closure.

Over time, tunnel-closure situation becomes associated with different planned camera federations, each satisfying this situation's changing non-functional requirements (i.e., one time the focus was on streaming quality, and on another time the focus was on streaming reliability). The pool storing all planned camera federations permits to benchmark things in federations and federation as well using our proposed QoT model (Sect. 3.4).

Questions that we would like to address in this work are, but not limited to, the following: how to define the QoT model in support of thing selection, how to define federations in preparation to assigning them situations, how to develop planned *versus* ad-hoc federations, and how to technically demonstrate the use of federations using a case study?

3   Concepts and Operations of Thing Federations

This section is about the core concepts and operations of defining, forming, managing, and deploying federations.

3.1   Definitions

Federation is about gathering multiple things into the same virtual space. Things become members of a federation because of their capabilities that permit to satisfy the needs and requirements of the situation assigned to this federation for handling. To this end, things are to be described, discovered, and, then, selected before they sign-up in federations.

From a management perspective, a federation could make a thing sign-off if its QoT-driven performance (e.g., unreliable data and recurrent failure) does not meet its expectations that are, in fact, related to meeting situations' non-functional requirements. A thing can, also, willingly leave a federation if the business in the federation is no longer appealing (e.g., data-sharing rate among the members drops below a threshold). To avoid unexpected departures from federations, incentives (monetary or in-kind) could be used to ensure that things remain committed to the same federations, assuming that there is still some "work" to do.

To distinguish planned from ad-hoc federations, we define abstract *versus* concrete things. The latter instantiates the former at run-time and executes operations related to the under-handling situation.

- A planned federation has, at both design- and run-time, all its concrete thing members already identified and ready to act, should this federation be selected.
- An ad-hoc federation has, at design-time, its abstract thing members identified prior to looking for concrete things that will instantiate them, at run-time. After execution, the ad-hoc federation is inserted, as planned, into the pool of planned federations linked to a particular situation.

3.2   Architecture

Figure 1 represents our ecosystem of things and federations hosting things. Federations, whether planned or ad-hoc, are expected to transition through certain stages that are assembling, storage, either activation or instantiation, and ultimately disassembling.

- Assembling is about identifying things that will populate federations. Things are either concrete in the context of planned federations or abstract in the context of ad-hoc federations. The assembling, also, calls for specifying the collaboration among things in the federation according to the situation to handle.
- Storage is about grouping planned federations in a dedicated pool in preparation for their selection and then activation, and, also, grouping ad-hoc federations in another dedicated pool in preparation for their loading and then instantiation. Over time, a situation becomes associated with several planned federations and one ad-hoc federation.

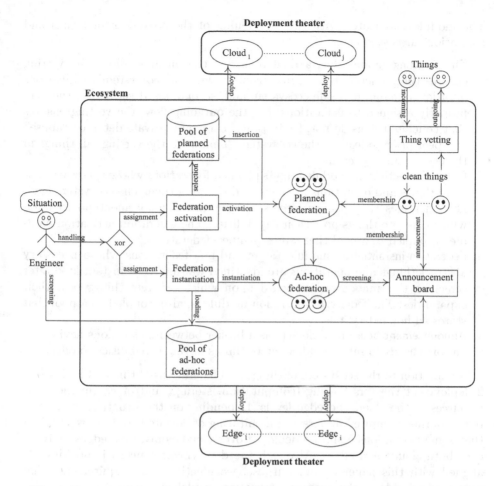

Fig. 1. Representation of the ecosystem of things and federations hosting things

– **Activation** is about initiating the execution of a planned federation following its selection from the pool of planned federations with respect to a situation's non-functional requirements. The planned federation's concrete things are already known and now need to be activated.

  xor

  Instantiation is about searching for concrete things that correspond to abstract things referred to in the ad-hoc federation's specification. The search and selection of concrete things is driven by a situation's non-functional requirements.

– **Disassembling** is about putting an end to a planned federation after reviewing its performance like limited competitiveness compared to other planned federations all linked to the same situation. We recall that upon instantiating an ad-hoc federation, this one becomes a planned federation and is inserted into the pool of planned federations. Thus, disassembling targets planned federations, only.

The modules associated with the functioning of the ecosystem of things and federations are listed below (Fig. 1):

1. Thing-vetting module has a dual role. For the incoming flow, the vetting ensures that concrete things, first, comply with the ecosystem's regulations in order to maintain a safe ecosystem and, second, are described so they are properly assigned to federations. For the outgoing flow, the vetting ensures that concrete things do not, for instance, carry any private detail or "abuse" any peer prior to leaving the ecosystem. Thanks to the vetting, all things in the ecosystem are "clean".
2. Federation-activation module targets planned federations whose necessary concrete things and operations are identified ahead of time. The ecosystem engineer identifies these things after screening the announcement board upon which concrete things post their capabilities. The federation-activation module is coupled to a pool that stores planned federations.
3. Federation-instantiation module targets ad-hoc federations whose necessary abstract things and operations are identified waiting to be instantiated after screening the announcement board upon which concrete things post their capabilities. The federation-initiation module is, also, coupled to a pool that stores ad-hoc federations.
4. Announcement-board module acts as a broker between federations having situations' needs to satisfy and concrete things having capabilities to offer.

In addition to the ecosystem of things and federations of things, Fig. 1 shows 2 deployment theaters hosting (computation, storage, and/or communication) resources at the cloud and edge levels. Depending on the situations to handle (e.g., transfer of injured drivers and monitoring of deviated traffic), we consider that some federations could be deployed over clouds, only, over edges, only, or over both clouds and edges. Although the deployment concern is not directly aligned with this paper's main purpose, we identify some requirements that would help decide on the relevant deployment model as follows:

1. Frequency is about the rate of data transfer from thing federations to fog/-cloud nodes. In the case of high frequency, we recommend transferring data of things to fog nodes, first, for any initial storage and/or processing and, then, to cloud nodes, if necessary. This 2-stage transfer should help guarantee data freshness since the edge nodes are "close" to things producing data.
2. Sensitivity is about the nature of data exchanged between thing federations and fog/cloud nodes. Highly-sensitive data of things should not be exposed longer on networks during the exchange and, hence, we recommend transferring such data to fog nodes, first, and, then, cloud nodes, if necessary. Securing sensitive data could happen at the level of edge nodes compensating the limited processing capabilities of things.
3. Volume is about the amount of data that thing federations produce and need to be stored. In the case of high volumes, we recommend sending data of things to cloud nodes, first, for any initial storage and/or processing and, then, sharing whatever data (with or without processing) is required with the edge nodes, if necessary.

Applying the 3 requirements to the situation of transferring injured patients would privilege edge over cloud. Indeed, during the transfer, patients' vitals need to be frequently and securely sent to rescue teams. Contrarily, monitoring deviated traffic would feature volume over sensitivity, and, hence, cloud over edge would be privileged.

3.3   Federation Formation

According to Sect. 3.2, the handling of a situation (s_i) could be assigned to either (1) one of the multiple Planned Federations ($PF^{s_i}_{j=1}...$) whose necessary Concrete Things ($CT^{s_i}_{j,k=1}...$) are already identified for each federation, or (2) an ad-Hoc Federation (HF^{s_i}) whose necessary Abstract Things ($AT^{s_i}_{k=1}...$) are already identified, too. At run-time, the abstract things are instantiated by making them bind to concrete things. This binding is driven by the situation's non-functional requirements and concrete things' non-functional properties (reported in their respective QoT models).

In addition to the close-tunnel situation (s_1), let us consider another situation that is traffic monitoring (s_2). The federation of things to put in place includes a traffic light, a speed-limit sign, and a mobile radar. Assuming that this is the 1st time that traffic-monitoring situation happens, HF^{s_2} is formed as per the following details: $HF^{s_2} = \{AT^{s_2}_1, AT^{s_2}_2, AT^{s_2}_3\}$ where AT_1 is traffic light, AT_2 is speed-limit sign, and AT_3 is mobile radar. After instantiation, HF^{s_2} becomes $PF^{s_2}_1$ having the following concrete things $\{CT^{s_2}_{1,1}, CT^{s_2}_{1,2}, CT^{s_2}_{1,3}\}$ where $CT^{s_2}_{1,1}$ is traffic light$_{AA}$ corresponding to AT_1, $CT^{s_2}_{1,2}$ is speed-limit sign$_{BB}$ corresponding to AT_2, and $CT^{s_2}_{1,3}$ is mobile radar$_{CC}$ corresponding to AT_3. It should be noted that $CT^{s_2}_{1,1}$, $CT^{s_2}_{1,2}$, and $CT^{s_2}_{1,3}$ are selected based on their QoT models meeting the non-functional requirements of traffic-monitoring situation.

After several rounds of handling traffic-monitoring situation, a pool of planned federations is formed ($PF^{s_2}_{1,2,3,...}$, Fig. 1). Each time there is a need of handling this situation again, this pool is checked first. If none of the planned federations meets the traffic-monitoring situation's new non-functional requirements, the ad-hoc federation is loaded from the pool of ad-hoc federations in preparation for its instantiation (Fig. 1).

3.4   Quality-of-Things Model

Defining a QoT model for IoT-compliant things is in line with the trend of defining similar models in other ICT contexts. We cite the quality model for cloud service selection [4]. Eisa et al. refer to this model as a degree to which a set of attributes/properties of a service fulfils stated requirements. Eisa et al. base their definition on ISO9000 and ISO9000:2015 statements about quality.

To allow a competitive selection of (concrete) things with respect to situations' non-functional requirements, we resort to developing properties that would constitute a thing's QoT model. This model would revolve around 3 core features describing the operation of any IoT ecosystem (Fig. 2): sensing (in the sense of collecting/capturing data), actuating (in the sense of processing data), and communicating (in the sense of sharing/distributing data). According to Fig. 2, (*i*) a thing is meant for sensing the surroundings (whether virtual or physical), so, that, it generates some outcomes; (*ii*) a thing is meant for actuating outcomes with focus on the outcomes that result from sensing; and (*iii*) a thing is meant for communicating with the surroundings (whether virtual or physical) the outcomes that result from both sensing and actuating. It is worth noting that sensing and actuating have an impact how their respective outcomes will be communicated. Communicating, only, relays what is available for distribution/sharing.

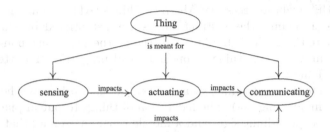

Fig. 2. Features defining a thing's QoT model

In the following, we propose some QoT properties with respect to the features of sensing, actuating, and communicating:

1. QoT properties for assessing sensing include:
   - *Frequency of sensing* (e.g., continuous *versus* intermittent).
   - *Quality of sensed outcome* that determines for instance, the accuracy and validity of the outcome (e.g., high *versus* low accuracy; high-accuracy outcome would not require any further verification).
   - *Resource* (e.g., energy, CPU, and storage) consumption during sensing (e.g., high *versus* low energy).
2. QoT properties for assessing actuating include:
   - *Quality of actuated outcome* that determines for instance, the accuracy and validity of the outcome.
   - *Resource* (e.g., energy, CPU, and storage) consumption during actuating (e.g., high *versus* low).
3. QoT properties for assessing communicating include:
   - *Reception rate of sensed and/or actuated outcome* (incoming flow) that determines for instance, data loss, data volume with respect to a bandwidth, etc.
     - *Acceptance rate of received outcome* is about the outcome that has been accepted for distribution; some received outcome could be rejected.
   - *Delivery rate of sensed and/or actuated outcome* (outgoing flow) that determines data loss, data volume with respect to a bandwidth, etc.

- *Acceptance rate of delivered outcome* is about the outcome that has been accepted after distribution at the recipient end; some delivered outcome could be rejected.
  - *Resource* (e.g., energy and bandwidth) consumption during communicating (e.g., high *versus* low bandwidth).

In Fig. 2, sensing, actuating, and communicating features constitute 4 independent life cycles listed below:

1. Sensing ⇒ actuating ⇒ communicating: the outcomes of sensing are passed on to actuating whose outcomes are passed on to communicating.
2. Sensing ⇒ actuating: the outcomes of sensing are passed on to actuating whose outcomes are finals.
3. Sensing ⇒ communicating: the outcomes of sensing are passed on to communicating for distribution.
4. Actuating ⇒ communicating: the outcomes of actuating are passed on to communicating for distribution.

The established life cycles point out how some QoT properties in a feature could impact some QoT properties in other features. For instance, a high-quality actuated outcome should lead to a better acceptance of this outcome by potential recipients that communicating will distribute to these recipients.

3.5   Testbed Setup and Experiment Scenarios

Our testbed shown in Fig. 3 includes a Lenovo Ideapad laptop (i5 1.8 GHz CPU, 8 GB RAM) connected to the Internet over Ethernet cable and fitted with an HD Lenovo EasyCamera Webcam with 0.92 MP. In addition to the laptop, a traffic light, Raspberry PI 3 -model B (RPI) (Quad Core 1.2 GHz CPU, 1 GB RAM) connected to the Internet over Ethernet cable, has 2 LED diodes (Green and Red) wired through the breadboard to the RPI. The traffic light receives signals over Message Queuing Telemetry Transport (MQTT) protocol via the subscribed topic[3] "*dev/traffic*" upon which it changes to green or red. Finally, the testbed's message sign display is a Wemos D1 R1 (ESP8266) microcontroller connected to the Internet via WiFi, and has a 16×2 LED display connected via the breadboard. The message sign display subscribes to MQTT topic "*dev/message*" and uses message payload to show appropriate messages.

Our experiment includes 4 things: ambulance carrying injured drivers from the tunnel, camera broadcasting live images from the way to the tunnel, traffic light regulating the access to the tunnel, and message sign display warning drivers. To detect ambulances, we developed an in-house Python image recognition program that processes RGB images and sends 14 frames/second using an Open Source Computer Vision (OpenCV, opencv.org) Library. Upon ambulance detection via a nearby camera to the tunnel, the program sends a message to the traffic light, to stop the traffic to the tunnel, over MQTT protocol via

---

[3] A topic is a UTF-8 String that MQTT broker uses to decide on which client receive which message.

Fig. 3. Devices used during the experiment

topic *"dev/traffic"* requesting to set the traffic light sign to red. In the same vein, the program posts relevant messages on the sign display via topic *"dev/message"* in JSON format (e.g., "type":"warning","message":"Car accident in the tunnel"). When the ambulance leaves the tunnel, the traffic light is changed to green and the message sign displays other messages inviting vehicles' owners to use the tunnel again.

For evaluation needs, 2 simulation scenarios were carried out as per the following details:

Scenario$_1$: we considered a planned federation of 2 things namely 1 camera, camera$_1$, and 1 traffic light and measured the total time required to execute this federation. Camera$_1$ detects ambulances heading to the tunnel where the accident has taken place and sends a signal to the traffic light. During the same execution lifecycle, we set the detection to 10 times (i.e., 10 ambulances), 50 times, and 100 times. The objective was to observe how the testbed behaves with respect to the number of detected ambulances and number of messages exchanged. Figure 4 reports the results of the process of recording and recognizing objects, detecting if these objects are ambulances, alerting the traffic light, and finally switching the light to red.

Scenario$_2$: we expanded scenario$_1$'s planned federation to 3 things namely 2 cameras, camera$_1$ and camera$_2$, and 1 traffic light and measured the total time required to execute this federation compared to the initial federation of 2 things, only. In this scenario, the vision of camera$_1$, which is located in the tunnel entrance, is obscured by an object (e.g., another vehicle parked on the roadside or stopped on hard shoulder of the tunnel to allow the ambulance to overtake) and could not verify whether the passed vehicle was an ambulance or not. In this case, camera$_1$ requests (in ad-hoc way) a confirmation from camera$_2$ so that the traffic light (in planned way) is properly notified. We run this scenario 6 times along with increasing the number of ambulances so that federation$_1$ refers to 1 ambulance, federation$_2$ refers to 2 ambulances, etc.

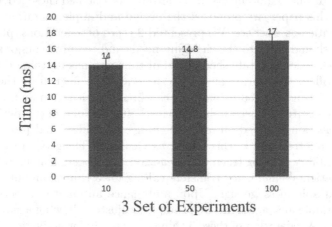

Fig. 4. Execution time per number of detected ambulances

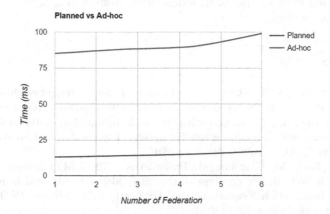

Fig. 5. Execution time related to planned *versus* ad-hoc federation

We checked how the testbed behaves when ad-hoc things (here camera$_2$) are added to a planned federation. Figure 5 illustrates the results showing cases of different federations; it took between 80 ms to 1.1s to execute ad-hoc federations and between 14 ms to 17 ms to execute planned federations.

4 Conclusion

Gartner is expecting a remarkable growth reaching 20.8 billion of connected things by 2020. This growth highlights the importance of combining things so, that, collective over individual behaviors emerge. A promising way of achieving this combination is to form federations that would gather relevant things according to the needs and requirements of the situations assigned these federations for handling. In this paper, we proposed the design and implementation guidelines of thing federation-as-a-service. We presented 2 types of federations, planned and ad-hoc, that should cater to the changing needs and requirements of situations. A planned federation is established ahead of time and has its thing constituents already identified. Contrarily, an ad-hoc federation is formed on-the-fly when none of the existing planned federations can handle a situation and, hence, necessary thing constituents need to be identified after a round of competitive selection. This selection is based on a set of things' non-functional properties that form what is referred tom in this paper, as Quality-of-Thing (QoT) model. The technical feasibility of thing federation-as-a-service has been demonstrated with a system for patients' emergency transfers calling for 3 things: ambulance, traffic light, and variable message sign. Upon ambulance automatic detection, traffic lights and variable message signs are promptly adjusted allowing a smooth transfer of patients. A federation of these 3 things was ready for activation. In term of future work, we would like to examine federation use and federation comparison. The former helps adapt existing (planned) federations to new situations and the latter helps rank existing (planned) federations. Refining the QoT model is also part of our future work.

References

1. Androèc, D., Tomaš, B., Kišasondi, T.: Interoperability and lightweight security for simple IoT devices. In: Proceedings of the Information Systems Security Conference (ISS 2017) Held in Conjunction with the 40th Jubilee International Convention on Information and Communication Technology, Electronics, and Microelectronics (MIPRO 2017), Opatija, Croatia, May 2017
2. Celesti, A., Fazio, M., Giacobbe, M., Puliafito, A., Villari, M.: Characterizing cloud federation in IoT. In: Proceedings of the 2016 30th International Conference on Advanced Information Networking and Applications Workshops (WAINA 2016), Crans-Montana, Switzerland (2016)
3. DZone: The Internet of Things, application, protocols, and best practices. Technical report (2017). https://dzone.com/guides/iot-applications-protocols-and-best-practices. Accessed May 2017

4. Eisa, M., Younas, M., Basu, K.: Analysis and representation of QoS attributes in cloud service selection. In: Proceedings of the 32nd International Conference on Advanced Information Networking and Applications (AINA 2018), Cracow, Poland (2018)

5. Heil, A., Knoll, M., Weis, T.: The Internet of Things - context-based device federations. In: Proceedings of the 40th Hawaii International Conference on System Sciences (HICSS 2007), Hawaii, USA (2007)

6. Leppänen, T., Riekki, J.: A lightweight agent-based architecture for the Internet of Things. In: Proceedings of the WEICE Workshop on Smart Sensing, Wireless Communications, and Human Probes, Wuxi, China, March 2013

7. Martínez-Ballesté, A., Pérez-Martínez, P.A., Solanas, A.: The pursuit of citizens' privacy: a privacy-aware smart city is possible. IEEE Commun. Mag. **51**(6), 136–141 (2013)

8. Mathlouthi, W., Saoud, N.B.B.: Flexible composition of system of systems on cloud federation. In: Proceedings of the 2017 IEEE 5th International Conference on Future Internet of Things and Cloud (FiCloud 2017), Prague, Czech Republic (2017)

9. Menascé, D.A.: QoS issues in web services. IEEE Internet Comput. **6**(6), 72–75 (2002)

10. Perera, C., Liu, C.H., Jayawardena, S., Chen, M.: A survey on Internet of Things from industrial market perspective. IEEE Access **2**, 1660–1679 (2014)

11. Rittinghouse, J.W., Ransome, J.F.: Cloud Computing: Implementation, Management, and Security. Taylor & Francis (2009)

12. Taivalsaari, A., Mikkonen, T.: A roadmap to the programmable world: software challenges in the IoT era. IEEE Softw. **34**(1), 72–80 (2017)

13. Zambonelli, F.: Key abstractions for IoT-oriented software engineering. IEEE Softw. **34**(1), 38–45 (2017)

Formalizing Reusable Communication Models for Distributed Systems Architecture

Quentin Rouland[1], Brahim Hamid[1(✉)], and Jason Jaskolka[2]

[1] IRIT, University of Toulouse, Toulouse, France
{quentin.rouland,brahim.hamid}@irit.fr
[2] Systems and Computer Engineering Carleton University Ottawa, Ontario, Canada
jaskolka@sce.carleton.ca

Abstract. Building distributed computing systems involves complex concerns integrating a multitude of communication styles, technologies (IoT, cloud and big data...), stakeholders (architects, developers, integrators, etc.) and addressing a multitude of application domains (smart cities, health, mobility, etc.). Existing architectural description languages fail to rigorously bridge the gap between the abstract representation of communication styles and those supported by existing execution infrastructures. In this paper, we aim at specifying software architecture of distributed systems using an approach combining semi-formal and formal languages to build reusable model libraries to represent communication solutions. Our contribution is two fold. First, we propose a metamodel to describe high level concepts of architecture in a component- port-connector fashion focusing on communication styles. Second, we attempt to formalize those concepts and their semantics following some properties (specifications) to check architectural conformance. To validate our work, we provide a set of reusable connector libraries within a set of properties to define architectures for systems with explicit communications models like message passing and remote procedure calls, that are common to most distributed systems.

Keywords: Component · Connector · Communication · Reuse
Meta-modeling · Formalization

1 Introduction

The shift from traditional computer systems towards the Internet of Things, i.e. devices connected via the Internet, Machine-to-Machine communication (M2M), wireless communication or other interfaces requires a reconsideration of complex software-dependent and distributed systems engineering processes. In fact, this reconsideration introduces new types and levels of risks, including those inherited from the underlying technologies like communication, virtualization and containerization. This is especially true for industrial systems, as they exist in many use cases, and systems using web applications with the recent growth of

© Springer Nature Switzerland AG 2018
E. H. Abdelwahed et al. (Eds.): MEDI 2018, LNCS 11163, pp. 198–216, 2018.
https://doi.org/10.1007/978-3-030-00856-7_13

more applications in cloud-based computing systems. Many of these systems belong to critical infrastructure, on which other economic and social aspects are based on. The foundation for comprehensive rigorous systems engineering facing strong non-functional requirements such as security [21,26], is a comprehensive understanding of modern communication systems and technologies and their implications on the underlying critical infrastructure [3]. We took this need towards software engineering for distributed software systems, focusing on the problem of integrating communication styles at the level of architecture design to foster reuse. We employ Model-Driven Engineering (MDE) [25] and attempt to add more formality to improve parts of the system design.

When we study distributed systems, we often use models to denote some abstract representation of a distributed system. To encode distributed computing (programs) in such systems, we use a common means of communication [3], where system components have only local vision of the system and interact only with their neighbors with explicit communications models like message passing, remote procedure calls and distributed shared memory, common to most distributed systems. The program executed at each node consists of a set of variables (state) and a finite set of actions. A component can write to its own variables and interact with its neighbors following a specific communication style. In our context, we model software architectures with message passing and remote-procedure call styles that we expect the architectural description to adhere to. The aim of this modeling and verification is to check if the architecture models satisfy all the desired properties such as security properties and do not hold any undesired property such as deadlock property.

In this paper, we present a formal framework to support the rigorous design of software architectures focusing on the communication aspects at the architecture level. It is based on the definition of a metamodel to describe high level concepts of architecture in a component- port- connector fashion focusing on communication styles and a formal definition of those concepts and their semantics following some properties (specifications). The former offers a transparent structural definition of communication styles (mainly message passing and remote procedure call mechanisms). The latter supports the application designer in the rigorous development process to model and analyze architectural communication styles. In the scope of this paper, we propose to use Alloy [10] for formalizing those communication styles and verifying conformance of the communication style at the model level. The formal specification and verification of a software architecture is represented through an Alloy module based on a set of reusable models, namely connectors corresponding to each of the considered communication styles. We provide a set of reusable connector libraries within a set of properties to define architectures for systems with explicit communications model such as message passing and remote procedure calls.

The remainder of the paper is organized as follows. Section 2 compares our work with related work. Section 3 presents our component based architectural metamodel. Section 4 describes the communication style semantics through finite state machine models. Then, Sect. 5 presents our approach for supporting the formalization and verification of these communication models using Alloy. Section 6 provides a motivating example that models a software architecture for a web application. Finally, Sect. 7 concludes and sketches directions for future work.

2   Related Work

Recent times have seen a paradigm shift in terms of software architecture design [22] by combining multiple software engineering paradigms, namely, Component-Based Development [4], Model-Driven Engineering(MDE) [25] and formal methods [23]. In the spirit of using multi-paradigms, many description languages and formalisms for modeling complex distributed systems have been proposed in the literature. A significant proportion of these works have aimed to capture the communication, concurrency, and some non-functional properties of the components that make up a given system. Examples of these existing works include those using process algebras (e.g., CSP [9]), architectural modeling languages (e.g., CCM [13], AADL [24], MARTE [16], SysML [14], and the recent OMG initiative UCM [18]), architectural formal languages (e.g., OCL [15], Wright [2], labeled transition systems [20]).

While each of the above mentioned modeling formalisms and modeling languages have already been successful in many application domains, in this paper we build a new communication-based architectural formal modeling language using Alloy for the structural and behavioral specification and analysis of distributed systems. Closely related to this vision is the approach of Khosrav et al. [11] which provides a modeling and analysis of the Reo connectors using Alloy and the approach of Garlan [5] that describes a formal modeling and analysis of software architectures built in terms of the concepts of components, connectors and events. Alloy is a lightweight modeling language, based on first-order relational logic. It provides support for reuse through a separation between the definition of connectors as modules from the description of the software architecture using them. The Alloy formal language is supported by an efficient tool called Alloy Analyzer [1] that will serve as the analysis tool in our experimentations. We provide support for specifying systems at various levels of abstraction by combining the characteristics of both state-based and trace-based models, offering a flexible and verifiable view of communication where several non-functional requirements could be specified and treated in a fine-grained fashion. In contrast to our work, other modeling and formal languages for capturing the communication and non-functional requirements of complex distributed systems do not directly provide such a simple and understandable view.

3   Software Architecture Metamodel

In the context of reliable distributed systems, a connection between distributed components should perform a reliable and trusted communication. While this could be done with standard specification of distributed component-based applications, such as those based on CCM [13,15] and ADL-like [2,24], it would be

impossible to configure and control the reliability and trustworthiness of communication connections at design time. This motivates the usage of the connector
concept to embed specific interaction semantics and multiple implementations
of the semantics within distributed computing systems. The basic idea of this
extension is that the semantics of an interaction is defined by a certain port type
and that one or more connectors can support this port type. The port types are
already fixed at component design time, whereas the choice of a connector (and
a specific communication style) is also constrained by the deployment characteristics.

A connector has certain similarities with a component. The main difference
is that it is dedicated for communication purposes. Since a connector is responsible for incoming, outgoing, intercepting, and blocking data and messages, it
is an ideal place for the integration of security and dependability mechanisms.
However, connectors are still *non-standard* interaction mechanisms. For instance
there is no corresponding concept in the architecture description languages used
in industrial contexts, i.e., containing an UML-like [17] vocabulary.

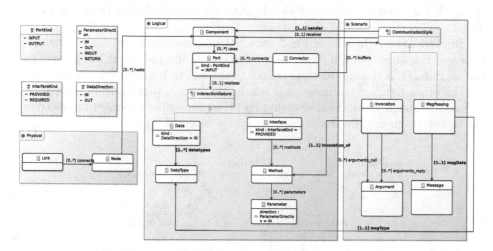

Fig. 1. Component-port-connector metamodel

We propose to build a modeling framework to define architectural models
that are conceptually close to the industrial practice, i.e., containing an UML-
like and an UCM-like vocabulary. Figure 1 visualizes a metamodel as a class
diagram. The metamodel provides concepts for describing software architectures
in terms of different views [12], with a focus on:

1. *Logical view* to capture the functional architecture of the system in terms of
   components.
2. *Physical view* to describe the deployment of the software onto the hardware
   taking into account the distributed aspects.
3. *Scenario view* which builds upon the logical and the physical views, describing
   the behavioral aspects of the system.

4 Modeling

In order to verify any communication style formally, it is mandatory to model that style carefully. Therefore, in modeling each communication style, each of the two communication parties (client and server) and the channel (connector connecting two ports) between them are described as a finite state machine.

4.1 Message Passing

In the message passing communication style (MPS), a channel is used for sending a message from a client to a server. The message is simply transmitted without any acknowledgement. The communication channel is modeled as a set of fixed length for messages offering two operations: (a) *push* to add an element in the set and (b) *pull* to remove an element from the set.

The left side of Fig. 2 shows the states of a client for sending a message. It is shown that if the state is sent (0) and a send event occurs when the buffer is not full ($\sim (\#buf = max)$), it changes its state from 0 to 1 for sending [1]. On the other hand, if the buffer is full ($\#buf = max$), it remains at state 0. It also shows that if the state is sending and the message is in the buffer ($mess\_in\_buf$), it changes its states from 1 to 0 for sent.

Similarly, the right side of Fig. 2 shows the states of a server for receiving a message. It is shown that if the state is received (0) and the buffer has a message ($mess\_in\_buf$), it changes its state from 0 (received) to 1 for receiving a message. On the other hand, if the message is not in the buffer, it remains at state 0. It also shows that if the state is receiving and the message is no longer anymore in the buffer, it changes its states from 1 to 0 for received.

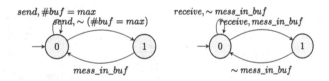

Fig. 2. States of a client (resp. server) for sending (resp. receiving) messages

Figure 3 shows the states of a connector for pulling and pushing a message. It is shown that if the state is 0 for waiting to receive messages from a caller and a message is pushed into the buffer, it changes its state from 0 to 1. If the current state 1 for waiting to receive message from a caller or retrieving a message from a receiver, it shows that if an event push or pull is executed and the buffer has more than one message but is not full ($max > \#buf > 1$), then it stays in the state 1. Otherwise, if a pull occurs and the buffer only has one message ($\#buf = 1$), it changes its states from 1 to 0. But if a push occurs and the buffer is full minus 1 message ($\#buf = max - 1$), it changes its state from

---

[1] $\sim Q$ denotes the negation of the statement Q and $\#A$ denotes the cardinality of the set A.

1 to 2 for retrieving messages from a receiver. Finally, it shows that to change from state 2 to 1 only a pull event is required.

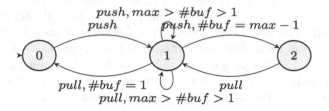

Fig. 3. States of a MPS connector

4.2   Message Passing with FIFO Ordering

The message passing with FIFO (First-in-first-out) ordering communication style is identical to message passing with a preservation of the order from the perspective of a sender. If a sender sends one message before another, it will be delivered in this order at the receiver. Here, the communication channel is modeled as a queue of fixed length for messages offering two operations: (a) *push* to add an element in the head of the queue and (b) *pop* to remove the element at the tail of the queue.

The left side of Fig. 4 shows the states of a client for sending a message. It is shown that if the state is sent and a send event occurs when the buffer is not full, it changes its state from 0 (Send) to 1 for sending. On the other hand, if the buffer is full, it remains at state 0. It also shows that if the state is sending and the message is at the head of the buffer (*mess_head_buf*), it changes its states from 1 to 0 for sent.

Similarly, the right side of Fig. 4 shows the states of a server for receiving a message. It is shown that if the state is received and a message is at the tail of the buffer (*mess_tail_buf*) it changes its state from 0 (received) to 1 for receiving a message. On the other hand, if the message is not at the tail of the buffer, it remains at state 0. It also shows that if the state is receiving and the message is no longer in the buffer, it changes its states from 1 to 0 for received.

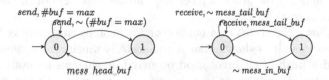

Fig. 4. States of a client (resp. server) for sending (resp. receiving) messages

Figure 5 shows the states of a connector for popping and pushing messages. It is shown that if the state is 0 for waiting to receive a message from a caller and a message is pushed into the buffer, it changes its states from 0 to 1. If its current state is 1 for waiting to receive a message from a caller or retrieving a message from a receiver, it shows that if an event pop or pull happens and the buffer has more than one message but is not full, then it stays in the state 1. Otherwise, if a pop occurs and the buffer only has one message, it changes its state from 1 to 0. But if a push occurs and the buffer is full minus 1 message, it changes its state from 1 to 2 for retrieving messages from a receiver. Finally, it shows that to change from state 2 to 1 only a pop event is required.

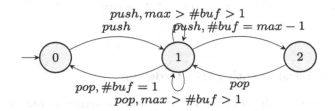

Fig. 5. States of a MPS FIFO connector

4.3   Remote Procedure Call

In the typical remote procedure call (RPC) communication style [3], a channel is used for sending invocation (request) messages from a client to a server and for receiving acknowledgement (reply) messages from a server to a client. The communication channel is modeled as a queue of fixed length for both request and reply messages from a client and a server respectively. Note that RPC is a special case of the general message-passing model.

Figure 6 shows the states of a client for sending invocation messages and receiving reply messages. It is shown that if the state for send is sending and the buffer is not full, it changes its state from 0 (invocation sent) to 1 for waiting for a reply. On the other hand, if the state is sending and the buffer is full, it remains at state 0. It is also shown that if the state is waiting to receive a reply (1) and the reply is in the buffer, it changes its state from 1 to 2 for receiving a reply. Otherwise, if the reply is not yet in the buffer, it remains at state 1. On the other hand, if the state is receiving and the reply is not in the buffer, it changes its state from 2 to 0.

Figure 7 shows the states of a connector for pushing and pulling invocation and reply messages. It is shown that if the state is waiting to receive from the caller (0) and a push of an invocation occurred, it changes its state from 0 to 1. The connector stays in state of retrieving an invocation to the receiver (1) until a pull of an invocation which changes its state from 1 to 2 for waiting for a reply. Figure 7 also shows also that the connector remains in this new state until a push of a reply occurs then it changes its states from 2 to 3 indicating that it is receiving a reply. Finally, it changes its state from 3 to 0 if a pull of a reply occurred.

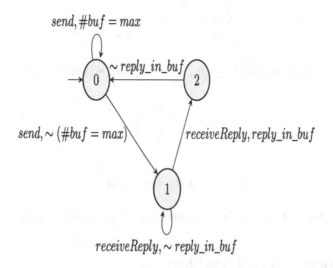

Fig. 6. States of a client for invocation/receiving reply messages

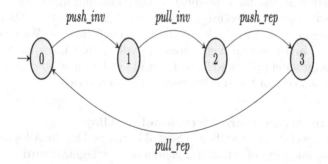

Fig. 7. States of a RPC connector

Figure 8 shows the states of a server for receiving invocation and sending reply messages. It is shown that if the state is waiting to receive an invocation and an event *receiveInvocation* occurs in the case that an invocation is present in the buffer it changes it state from 0 to 1. Otherwise, if the invocation is absent it remains in the same state. It also shows that after the execution when an event reply, if the buffer is not full it changes its state from 1 to 2. Otherwise, if the buffer is full it stays in state 1. Finally, from state 2 it returns to state 0 when a reply is in the buffer.

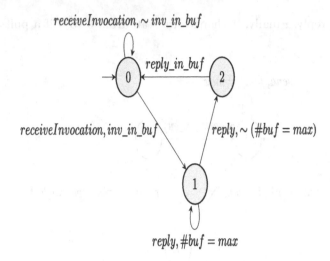

Fig. 8. States of a server for receiving invocation/sending reply message

5   Formalization and Verification

In this section, we discuss the definition of our software architecture metamodel in Alloy, followed by the specification and verification of the connectors. It consists of a set of definitions, facts, predicates, assertions and functions. We attempt to formalize software architecture models and their semantics following some properties (specifications) to check architectural conformance. We facilitate this by providing an architectural meta model in Alloy, that incorporates the concepts of the metamodel presented in Sect. 3 and involves new concepts to capture the behavioral aspects of the specific communication styles.

5.1   Software Architecture Metamodel in Alloy

A software architecture as described in Sect. 3 is mapped to our Alloy meta model as follows. The mapping of structural elements is straightforward. An architectural component, port, connector, interface, methods, and data are mapped to their namesake types in Alloy, as are nodes and links. Before two (or more) components can interact, we assume that a connector must be present between them. We used the Time module provided within Alloy, where time is explicitly modeled as a set of discrete, ordered Time instances. Therefore, associations (such as the set of ports connected by one connector) can be made by adding a relationship with the Time set (i.e., the connects relationship that relates connector to port is a relationship from connector over port to Time). Furthermore, if a connector exists between components on different nodes, then there must be a corresponding link between those nodes to host the Connector.

A component is connected to a connector through a number of ports. The three basic concepts in the model are components, ports and connectors that are represented as a set of Alloy signatures as depicted in Listing 1.1. With regard to the scenario view, we defined two additional concepts: *MsgPassing* and *Invocation*. Each of them is created by the client and consumed by the server. For instance, once a send is executed by the sender component, *MsgPassing* is buffered in a connector. When it is received by the receiving component, it is removed from the connector.

```
sig Port {}
sig Component {
  uses: set Port
}
abstract sig Connector {
  connects: set Port -> Time
}{
  all disj c1,c2:Component,t:Time {
    c1.uses + c2.uses in connects.t implies
      some n1,n2:Node {
        c1 in n1.hosts.t
        c2 in n2.hosts.t
        n1 = n2 or some l:Link | n1+n2 in l.connects.t
      }
  }
}
abstract sig Channel extends Connector {
  disj portI,portO: one Port
}{
  all t:Time | connects.t = portI + portO
}
abstract sig CommunicationArtifact {
  client: one Component,
  server: one Component
}{
  client != server
}
sig MsgPassing extends CommunicationArtifact {
  msgData: one Message
  msgType: one DataType
}
sig Invocation extends CommunicationArtifact {
  invocation_of: one Method,
  arguments_call: set Argument,
  arguments_reply: set Argument -> Time
}
```

Listing 1.1. Software architecture metamodel in Alloy

5.2 Formal Specification of the Connectors

Listings 1.2, 1.3 and 1.4 depict an excerpt of the formalization of the three studied connectors, respectively *message passing connector*, *message passing with FIFO ordering connector* and *remote procedure call connector*. The semantics of these connectors are the same as those of the modeling presented in Sect. 4. To specify the behavior of a connector, we use traces of computation which is a common technique in Alloy. For each connector we define a trace of computation as a sequence of states. To model a trace in Alloy, we reuse the Alloy standard ordering module which creates a single linear ordering over the instances of the signature provided as its input. Therefore, we provide a fact that puts a constraint on the behavior of the connector. For example, in Listing 1.2, the fact constrains the acceptable state transitions of the message passing connector to form a valid executable trace.

```
sig ConnectorMPS extends Channel{
  buffer : set MsgPassing -> Time,
  capacity: Int
}
pred MPS_init [t: Time] {
  all c:ConnectorMPS | # c.buffer.t = 0
}
pred MPS_push [t, t': Time, c:ConnectorMPS, mp:MsgPassing] {
  #c.buffer.t < c.capacity
  c.buffer.t' = c.buffer.t + mp
```

```
}
pred MPS_pull [t, t': Time, c: ConnectorMPS, mp: MsgPassing] {
  mp in c.buffer.t
  c.buffer.t' = c.buffer.t - mp
}
fact traces {
  MPS_init [TO/first]
  all t: Time - TO/last | let t' = TO/next[t] |
  some c: ConnectorMPS, mp: MsgPassing | MPS_push [t, t', c, mp]
  or MPS_pull [t, t', c, mp]
}
```

Listing 1.2. Message passing connector

```
sig QMessage extends QElem {
  message: one MsgPassing
}
sig ConnectorMPSFIFO extends Channel{
  buffer : one Queue,
}
pred MPSFIFO_init [t: Time] {
  all c: ConnectorMPSFIFO | QEmpty[t, c.buffer]
}
pred MPSFIFO_push [t, t': Time, c: ConnectorMPSFIFO, mp: MsgPassing] {
  one qm: QMessage | qm.message = mp and QEnq[t, t', c.buffer, qm]
}
pred MPSFIFO_pop [t, t': Time, c: ConnectorMPSFIFO, mp: MsgPassing] {
  QLast[t, c.buffer].message = mp
  QDeq[t, t', c.buffer]
}
fact traces {
  MPSFIFO_init [TO/first]
  all t: Time - TO/last | let t' = t.next |
  some mp: MsgPassing, c: ConnectorMPSFIFO | MPSFIFO_push [t, t', c, mp]
  or MPSFIFO_pop [t, t', c, mp]
}
```

Listing 1.3. Message passing with FIFO ordering connector

```
sig ConnectorRPC extends Channel{
  buffer : Invocation lone -> Time
}
pred RPC_Init[t: Time] {
  all c: ConnectorRPC | c.buffer.t = none
}
pred RPC_push [t, t': Time, c: ConnectorRPC, i: Invocation] {
  c.buffer.t = none
  c.buffer.t' = i
}
pred RPC_pull [t, t': Time, c: ConnectorRPC, i: Invocation] {
  c.buffer.t = i
  c.buffer.t' = none
}
pred RPC_pushInvocation  [t, t': Time, c: ConnectorRPC, i: Invocation] {
  # c.buffer.t.arguments_reply.t = 0
  RPC_push[t,t',c,i]
}
pred RPC_pullInvocation  [t, t': Time, c: ConnectorRPC, i: Invocation] {
  # c.buffer.t.arguments_reply.t = 0
  RPC_pull[t,t',c,i]
}
pred RPC_pushReply  [t, t': Time, c: ConnectorRPC, r: Invocation] {
  # c.buffer.t.arguments_reply.t' != 0
  RPC_push[t,t',c,r]
}
pred RPC_pullReply  [t, t': Time, c: ConnectorRPC, r: Invocation] {
  # c.buffer.t.arguments_reply.t != 0
  RPC_pull[t,t',c,r]
}
fact traces {
  RPC_Init [TO/first]
  all t: Time - TO/last | let t' = TO/next[t] |
  some c: ConnectorRPC, i: Invocation, r: Invocation
  | RPC_pushInvocation [t, t', c, i] iff not RPC_pullInvocation [t, t', c, i]
  iff not RPC_pushReply [t, t', c, r] iff not RPC_pullReply [t, t', c, r]
}
```

Listing 1.4. Remote procedure call connector

5.3   Formal Specification of the Communication Primitives

Moreover, we define the corresponding communication primitives associated with each of the corresponding communication styles. The semantics of these primitives are the same as those of the modeling presented in Sect. 4.

Message Passing Communication. Communication in the message passing communication style is performed using the *send()* and *receive()* primitives. The *send()* primitive requires the name of the receiver component, the transmitted data and the expected data types as parameters, while the *receive()* primitive requires the name of the anticipated sender component and should provide storage variables for the message data and the expected data types (see Listing 1.5).

In spite of blocking primitives that are often chosen, for the sake of easier realization, here we consider the semantics of a non-blocking primitives to capture the more general asynchronous communication paradigm. The non-blocking *send(receiver, data)* returns control to the sender immediately and the message transmission process is then executed concurrently with the sender process. The sender executes a *send(receiver, data)* which results in the communication system constructing a message and sending it to the receiver through the corresponding connector. The receiver executes a *receive(sender, data)* which causes the receiver to be blocked, awaiting a message from the sender. When the message is received, the communication system removes the message from the corresponding connector, extracts the data from the message and delivers it to the receiver. As a prerequisite, we added the *check_type_interaction_data* predicate to ensure that message's types are supported at both the sending and receiving components. Without data type checking, the support of the message type is only verified at execution time.

```
pred check_type_interaction_data [mp: MsgPassing]{
    one  di : Data, p:mp. client . uses |  di in p. realizes and di. kind = DATA_OUT and
    mp. msgType in di. DataType
    one di : Data, p:mp. server . uses |  di in p. realizes and di. kind = DATA_IN and
    mp. msgType in di. DataType
}
pred Component. send [ receiver : Component, d: Message, typ : DataType, t : Time] {
    some mp: MsgPassing{
    mp. client = this
    mp. server = receiver
    mp. msgData = d
    mp. msgData. msgType= typ
    check_type_interaction_data [mp]
    one  t ': t . next |  let c = { c : ConnectorMPS |  c. portO in mp. client . uses and
    c. portI in mp. server . uses} |  MPS_push [ t , t ' , c , mp]
    }
}
pred Component. receive [ sender : Component, d: Message, typ : DataType, t : Time] {
some mp: MsgPassing{
    mp. client = sender
    mp. server = this
    mp. msgData = d
    mp. msgData. msgType= typ
    check_type_interaction_data [mp]
    one t ': t . next |  let c = { c : ConnectorMPS |  c. portO in mp. client . uses and
    c. portI in mp. server . uses} |  MPS_pull [ t , t ' , c , mp]
    }
}
```

Listing 1.5. Message passing communication

Remote Procedure Call Communication. Communication in the remote procedure call communication style is performed using the *call()*, *executeCall()*, *reply()* and *executeReply()* primitives. As depicted in Listing 1.6, the *call()*

primitive executed at the caller component requires the name of the callee component providing the invoked method, the method being invoked and the associated arguments as parameters. The *executeCall*() primitive requires the name of the anticipated caller component, the corresponding invoked method and its input and output arguments. The *reply*() primitive requires the name of the anticipated caller component, the corresponding invoked method and its result parameters. The *executeReply*() primitive requires the name of the anticipated callee component, the corresponding invoked method and its result parameters.

The semantics of RPC in distributed systems are the same as those of a local procedure call in a non distributed systems: The caller component calls and passes input arguments to the remote procedure and it blocks at the *call(callee, method, input, result)* while the remote procedure executes (*executeCall(caller, method, input, result)*). When the remote procedure completes, the callee component can return result parameters to the calling component (*reply(caller, method, result)*) and the caller becomes unblocked and continues its execution (*executeReply(callee, meth, result)*). As a prerequisite, we added the *check_type_interaction_interface* predicate to ensure that operations are present at the sending and receiving components before an invocation is executed. Without interface type checking, the presence of the invoked operation is only verified at execution time.

```
pred check_type_interaction_interface[i:Invocation]{
    one if:Interface , p:i.client.uses | if in p.realizes and if.kind = REQUIRED and  i.
        invocation_of in if.methods
    one if:Interface , p:i.server.uses | if in p.realizes and if.kind = PROVIDED and i.
        invocation_of in if.methods
}
pred Component.call[callee:Component, meth: Method, in: set Argument, out:set
        Argument, t:Time]{
    some i : Invocation{
    i.client = this
    i.server = callee
    i.invocation_of = meth
    i.arguments_call = in
    # i.arguments_reply.t = 0
    check_type_interavtion_interface[i]
    one t':t.next | let c = { c:ConnectorRPC | c.portO in i.client.uses
    and c.portI in i.receiver.uses} | RPC_pushInvocation[t,t',c,i]
    }
}
pred Component.executeCall[caller:Component, meth: Method, in: set Argument, out:set
        Argument, t:Time] {
    some i : Invocation{
    i.client = caller
    i.server = this
    i.invocation_of = meth
    i.arguments_call = in
    # i.arguments_reply.t = 0
    check_type_interaction_interface[i]
    one t':t.next | let c = { c:ConnectorRPC | c.portO in i.client.uses
    and c.portI in i.server.uses}
    | RPC_pullInvocation[t,t',c,i] and c.buffer.t'.arguments_reply.t' = args_out
    }
}
pred Component.reply[caller:Component, meth: Method, out:setArgument, t:Time] {
    some r : Invocation{
    r.client = caller
    r.server = this
    i.invocation_of = meth
    i.arguments_call = in
    i.arguments_reply = out
    check_type_interaction_interface[i]
    one t':t.next | let c = { c:ConnectorRPC | c.portO in r.client.uses
    and c.portI in r.server.uses}
    | RPC_pushReply[t,t',c,r]
    }
}
pred Component.executeReply[callee:Component, meth: Method, in: set Argument,out:set
        Argument, t:Time] {
    some r : Invocation{
    r.client = this
```

```
r.server = callee
i.invocation_of = meth
i.arguments_call = in
i.arguments_reply = out
check_type_interaction_interface[i]
one t':t.next | let c = { c:ConnectorRPC | c.portO in r.client.uses
and c.portI in r.server.uses}
| RPC_pullReply[t,t',c,r]
}
}
```

Listing 1.6. Remote procedure call communication

5.4   Formal Verification and Results

To analyze the connectors, the modeling formalism developed in this work allows to specify the properties to be checked in terms of first-order predicate logic formulas. Then, the Alloy Analyzer automatically checks the properties using a SAT solver. Among the set of possible and yet specified characteristics of the behaviors of the message passing and remote procedure call communication styles, a subset of them are encoded in terms of properties as predicates and assertions and the results of their verification are stated below.

Some of the properties that are specified and verified reflect typical liveness properties of concurrent and communicating systems. In order to ensure that such systems are dependable, liveness properties such as property (a) given below for both message passing and remote procedure call communication are vital to ensuring reliable communications and system behaviors.

– *Message passing communication.*
  - (a) "once the client $c1$ sends a message to server $s1$, eventually that server receives it".

```
pred send_eventually_received{
  one t:Time | one t':t.nexts | some c1,c2:Component | some d:Message | some
    typ:DataType |
  c2.send[c1,d,typ,t'] => c1.receive[c2,d,typ,t]
}
```

  - (b) "once the server $s1$ receives a message, it must already have been sent by a certain client $c1$".

```
assert recieve_must_be_sent{
  one t:Time | one t':t.nexts | some c1,c2:Component | some d:Message | some
    typ:DataType |
  c2.receive[c1,d,typ,t'] => c1.send[c2,d,typ,t]
}
```

  - (c) "messages sent from the client $c1$ to the server $s1$ reach the server $s1$ in the same order as they were sent from $c1$".

```
assert is_FIFO {
  all disj c1,s1:Component | all disj d1,d2: Message | some typ1,typ2:
    DataType | all ts1:Time | let ts2 = ts1.nexts | all tr1:Time | all tr2:
    Time |
  (c1.send[s1,d1,typ1,ts1] and c1.send[c2,d2,typ2,ts2]
    and s1.receive[c1,d1,typ1,tr1]
    and s1.receive[c1,d2,typ2,tr2])
    => tr2 in tr1.nexts
}
```

The Alloy Analyzer shows that properties (a) and (b) hold for both types of message passing connector (simple and FIFO). It also shows that property (c) does not hold for a simple message passing connector. Since the property does not hold, Alloy produces a counter example, which shows the main reason why the specified property does not hold. However, the Alloy analyzer shows that this property holds for a FIFO ordered message passing connector.

– *Remote procedure call communication.*

- (a) "Once the caller $c1$ sends an invocation to callee $c2$, the caller eventually receives an acknowledgement from that callee".

```
pred send_is_eventually_replied {
    one t:Time | one t':t.nexts |  some c1,c2:Component |  some m:Method
    | some args_in:Argument | some args_out:Argument |
    c1.call[c2,m,args_in ,args_out ,t] => c1.executeReply[c2,m,args_in ,args_out
        ,t ']
}
```

- (b) "Once the caller $c1$ receives results corresponding to an invocation of a method m at a certain server $c2$ and the caller $c1$ starts the next invocation of the same method at the same server, the callee $c1$ is eventually executing that invocation".

```
pred reply_and_call_is_eventually_received{
    one t:Time | one t':t.nexts | one t'':t'.next |
    some c1,c2:Component  | some m:Method |
    some disj args_in1 ,args_out1 ,args_in2 ,args_out2  :Argument |
    c2.reply[c1 ,m,args_in1 ,args_out1 ,t] and c1.call[c2,m,args_in2 ,args_out2 ,t
        '] =>
    c2.executeCall[c1 ,m,args_in2 ,args_out2 ,t '']
}
```

The Alloy Analyzer shows that both properties (a) and (b) hold for a RPC connector.

6   Use Case

We use a college library website system [19] to exemplify the proposed approach. Figure 9 shows the overall architecture description of the web application. It consists of a the following software components: a client, a web server and a database server. The website provides online services for searching for and requesting books. The users are students, college staff and librarians. Staff and students will be able to log in and search for books, and staff members can request books. Librarians will be able to log in, add books, add users, and search for books. We use a UML class diagram to describe the high level architecture model of the web application, where software components are represented by classes, and connectors between these components are represented by associations. However, effective realizations of these connectors are not modeled in the UML class diagram; they may be subject to certain changes and/or adaptations (e.g., new solutions, deletions, modifications of realization), verifications (e.g., formal verification) and reuse (e.g., in the same domain or across domains) while the structure of the main software architecture can be maintained. Each connector represents a communication pattern which rigorous software developers, mainly architects would like software modeling and analysis languages to easily express.

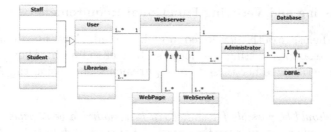

Fig. 9. A web application example in UML

6.1   Expressing the Architecture of a Web Application Example

Listing 1.7 depicts the Alloy specification of the web application architecture described in Fig. 9. We start by defining the component types, and the interfaces and connectors as simple extensions to the concepts of our software architecture metamodel. Then, we reuse our connector models, the corresponding communication primitives and their associated properties to specify the structure and the behavior of the software architecture describing the example in Alloy.

```
one sig UserBrowser extends Component {
}{
    uses = PortInterfaceBrowser
}
one sig Webserver extends Component {
}{
    uses = PortInterfaceWebserver + PortDataWebserver
}
one sig Database extends Component {
}{
    uses = PortDataDatabase
}
one sig InterfaceBrowser extends Interface {
}{
    getBook in methods
}
one sig InterfaceWebserver extends Interface {
}{
    getBook in methods
}
one sig DataWebserver extends Data {
}
one sig DataDatabase extends Data {
}
one sig PortInterfaceBrowser extends Port {
}{
    realizes = InterfaceBrowser
}
one sig PortInterfaceWebserver extends Port {
}{
    realizes = InterfaceWebserver
}
one sig PortDataWebserver extends Port {
}{
    realizes = DataWebserver
}
one sig PortDataDatabase extends Port {
}{
    realizes = DataDatabase
}
one sig BrowerWebserverConnector extends ConnectorRPC {
}{
    portO = PortInterfaceBrowser
    portI = PortInterfaceWebserver
}
one sig DatabaseWebserverConnector extends ConnectorMPS {
}{
    portO = PortDataDatabase
    portI = PortDataWebserver
}
```

Listing 1.7. A web application example in Alloy

6.2   Expressing and Verifying Functional Requirements

To illustrate the usage of the developed model, we studied two functional requirements of the example. Listing 1.8 depicts their encoding in Alloy. Then, the architect can verify whether these two requirements hold using the Alloy analyzer.

– *Req_1. It should be possible for somebody to visualize a book page.*
– *Req_2. It should be possible for the database to transmit data to the Webserver.*

```
pred Req_1{
    some ws:Website,  bw:Browser,  op:getBook,  args_in , args_out:  set Argument,  t:Time,
            t ':t.nexts |
    bw . call [ws,op , args_in , args_out ,t] and
    bw . executeReply [ws,op , args_in , args_out ,t ']
}
pred Req_2 {
    some  ws:Webserver,  db:Database,  c:Message,  typ:DataType,  t:Time,  t ':t.nexts
            |
    db . send [ws,c,typ,t] and
    ws . receive [db,c,typ,t ']
}
```

Listing 1.8. Examples of requirements of a web application

The Alloy analyzer shows that both *Req_1* and *Req_2* hold, within the specified scope. This check enforces that the model is complete w.r.t. the current level of design.

7   Concluding Remarks and Future Works

Formalization and verification techniques are useful in the rigorous development of computer-based systems. In this paper, our experience in verifying message passing and RPC communication styles using Alloy is presented. Here, we have verified some most common properties of these two styles of communication and found that the properties hold. Thus from our experience we can say that the connectors and the software architecture using them are verifiable for building reliable distributed systems. Our next goal is to improve our Patten Based System Engineering (PBSE) framework [7] considering security and safety requirements within software architectures built on-top of these communication styles. We plan to transform our PBSE pattern modeling concepts to Alloy specifications to ensure semantic validation. In addition, we aim at refining our modeling framework with properties and reasoning of Security Modeling Framework (SeMF) [6]. Our starting point is modeling security patterns in Alloy from [8]. Moreover, some timing and/or other resource constraints can also be enforced to verify the architecture models.

References

1. Alloy Analyzer. http://alloy.mit.edu. Accessed June 2017
2. Allen, R., Garlan, D.: A formal basis for architectural connection. ACM Trans. Softw. Eng. Methodol. **6**(3), 213–249 (1997)
3. Coulouris, G., Dollimore, J., Kindberg, T., Blair, G.: Distributed Systems: Concepts and Design, 5th edn. Addison-Wesley Publishing Company, Boston (2011)
4. Crnkovic, I.: Component-based software engineering for embedded systems. In: Proceedings of the 27th International Conference on Software Engineering, ICSE 2005, pp. 712–713. ACM (2005)
5. Garlan, D.: Formal modeling and analysis of software architecture: components, connectors, and events. In: Bernardo, M., Inverardi, P. (eds.) SFM 2003. LNCS, vol. 2804, pp. 1–24. Springer, Heidelberg (2003). https://doi.org/10.1007/978-3-540-39800-4_1
6. Hamid, B., Gürgens, S., Fuchs, A.: Security patterns modeling and formalization for pattern-based development of secure software systems. Innov. Syst. Softw. Eng. **12**(2), 109–140 (2016)
7. Hamid, B., Perez, J.: Supporting pattern-based dependability engineering via model-driven development: approach, tool-support and empirical validation. J. Syst. Softw. **122**, 239–273 (2016)
8. Heyman, T., Scandariato, R., Joosen, W.: Reusable formal models for secure software architectures. In: Joint Working IEEE/IFIP Conference on Software Architecture and European Conference on Software Architecture, pp. 41–50 (2012)
9. Hoare, C.A.R.: Communicating sequential processes. Commun. ACM **21**(8), 666–677 (1978)
10. Jackson, D.: Software Abstractions: Logic, Language, and Analysis. The MIT Press, Cambridge (2006)
11. Khosravi, R., Sirjani, M., Asoudeh, N., Sahebi, S., Iravanchi, H.: Modeling and analysis of Reo connectors using alloy. In: Lea, D., Zavattaro, G. (eds.) COORDINATION 2008. LNCS, vol. 5052, pp. 169–183. Springer, Heidelberg (2008). https://doi.org/10.1007/978-3-540-68265-3_11
12. Kruchten, P.: Architectural blueprints - the "4+1" view model of software architecture. IEEE Softw. **12**(6), 42–50 (1995)
13. OMG: CORBA Specification, Version 3.1. Part 3: CORBA Component Model (2008). http://www.omg.org/spec/CCM. Accessed Nov 2009
14. OMG. OMG Systems Modeling Language (OMG SysML), Version 1.1 (2008). http://www.omg.org/spec/SysML/1.1/,. Accessed Jan 2013
15. OMG: Object Constraint Language (OCL), Version 2.2 (2010). http://www.omg.org/spec/OCL/2.2. Accessed Jan 2013
16. OMG: UML profile for Modeling and Analysis of Real-Time and Embedded Systems (MARTE), Version 1.1 (2011). http://www.omg.org/spec/MARTE/1.1/. Accessed Jan 2013
17. OMG: Unified Modeling Language (UML), Version 2.4.1 (2011). http://www.omg.org/spec/UML/2.4.1. Accessed Jan 2013
18. OMG: Unified Component Model for Distributed, Real-Time And Embedded Systems, Version 1.0 (2017). http://www.omg.org/spec/UCM/20170601/. Accessed Jan 2018
19. OWASP: Application threat modeling (2017). https://www.owasp.org/index.php/Application_Threat_Modeling. Accessed Dec 2017

20. Alur, R., Dill, D.: The theory of timed automata. In: de Bakker, J.W., Huizing, C., de Roever, W.P., Rozenberg, G. (eds.) REX 1991. LNCS, vol. 600, pp. 45–73. Springer, Heidelberg (1992). https://doi.org/10.1007/BFb0031987
21. Ravi, S., Raghunathan, A., Kocher, P., Hattangady, S.: Security in embedded systems: design challenges. ACM Trans. Embed. Comput. Syst. **3**(3), 461–491 (2004)
22. Taylor, R.N., Medvidovic, N.: Software Architecture: Foundation, Theory, and Practice. Wiley, Hoboken (2010)
23. Rodano, M., Giammarc, K.: A formal method for evaluation of a modeled system architecture. Procedia Comput. Sci. **20**, 210–215 (2013)
24. SAE: Architecture Analysis & Design Language (AADL) (2009). http://www.sae.org/technical/standards/AS5506A. Accessed Jan 2011
25. Selic, B.: The pragmatics of model-driven development. IEEE Softw. **20**(5), 19–25 (2003)
26. Zurawski, R.: Embedded systems in industrial applications - challenges and trends. In: International Symposium on Industrial Embedded Systems (SIES). IEEE (2007)

Safety and Security

A Valid BPMN Extension for Supporting Security Requirements Based on Cyber Security Ontology

Mohamed El Amine Chergui[1]($\boxtimes$) and Sidi Mohamed Benslimane[2]

[1] EEDIS Laboratory, Djillali Liabes University, Sidi Bel Abbès, Algeria
amine.chergui@univ-sba.dz
[2] LabRI-SBA Laboratory, Ecole Superieure en Informatique,
Sidi Bel Abbes, Algeria
s.benslimane@esi-sba.dz

Abstract. Business Process Model and Notation (BPMN) is the de facto standard for business process modeling. One of the most important aspect of business process models is security. Since most business processes revolve around the exchange of information, the security of such information assets becomes a critical factor for the success of the overall business process. Therefore, it is very important to capture the security requirements at conceptual level in order to identify the security needs in the first place. There is a need for an integrated tools and methodology that allows for specifying and enforcing compliance and security requirements for business process-driven enterprise systems. Furthermore, BPMN do not support the specification of security requirements along the business process modelling. This will increase the vulnerability of the system and make the future development of security for the system more difficult. In this paper, we extend the BPMN language to explicitly support the specification of security requirements derived from cyber security ontology. We incorporate visual constructs for modeling security requirements. In order to provide a commonly usable extension, these enhancements were implemented as a valid BPMN extension. An application example from the healthcare domain is used to demonstrate our approach. The experimentation denotes that the authors' approach achieves better results in terms comprehensive understanding of incorporated security requirements.

Keywords: BPMN extension · Security in business process
Business process modeling

1 Introduction

Modern enterprise systems are often process-driven. Adopting business process modeling standards to express and design the functional requirements of their business. Business process models are used for communication business requirements between system experts and business experts. Modern business processes combine human tasks with automated tasks (e.g., implemented by web services), a business process

E. H. Abdelwahed et al. (Eds.): MEDI 2018, LNCS 11163, pp. 219–232, 2018.
https://doi.org/10.1007/978-3-030-00856-7_14

modelling language needs to bridge the gap between the language used by business experts and the language used by system experts (Brucker et al. 2012).

Integrating high level security and compliance requirements into process models are a major concern for designing and running business process driven systems. In addition, security requirements have been recognized as an important preoccupation among system developers and users. Based on these facts, the association between business process and security is inevitable. Empirical studies shows that those who model the business process i.e. business domain expert are able to specify security requirements at high level of abstraction i.e. while designing the system (Rodriguez et al. 2007).

Many software development methods often treat security, separately at later stage. Business process modelling is the most appropriate layer to describe security requirements (Menzel et al. 2009). Business process modelling is normally performed in a modelling language such as UML or BPMN. However in practice, business domain expert mainly focus on the functionality because business domain expert is not a security expert (Rodriguez et al. 2007). These modelling languages do not support natively annotation security, which may result in significant problems regarding the comprehensibility and maintainability of these ad hoc models. Several approaches have been proposed to model the security requirements along the business process model. However, those approaches remain theoretical and miss many important security concepts (Maines et al. 2016). BPMN is used as a modelling language for our work; which is an industry standard for business modelling (Rodriguez et al. 2007). Current BPMN-security extensions have made attempts, but they are being constructed unsystematically, without any empirical evidence to support their choice of concepts (Leitner et al. 2013) and most extensions are not compliant with the BPMN standard (Braun et al. 2014).

The main goal of this paper is to assess the design and modeling of security concepts in business processes. An ontology-based extension approach is proposed to model security requirements through business process. We will summarize our BPMN extension for modeling secure business process through Business Process Diagrams, and we will apply this approach to case study business process. This security annotative business process model will facilitate the security expert while defining concrete security implementation.

The remaining part of the paper is organized as follows: In Sect. 2, the most related work is briefly reviewed. Section 3 introduces fundamentals in terms of general extensibility of BPMN. In Sect. 4 we present the proposed extension that support security annotation. Section 5 provide an illustration with use case to demonstrate integration of security concepts. Finally, Sect. 6 concludes the paper and outlines directions for future work.

2 Literature Review

There are several research papers that are related to analyzing security requirements for designing security extensions in BPMN, we briefly review the most related work.

(Wolter et al. 2009) have introduced an approach to express security goals at the business process level. The foundation constitutes their generic security model that specifies security goals, policies, and constraints based on a set of basic entities, such as objects, attributes, interactions, and Effects. The concepts they specify are confidentiality, authentication, authorisation, integrity, traceability and auditing, and availability. (Rodriguez et al. 2007) have presented a BPMN metamodel with core element and extension that allow incorporating security requirements into Business Process Diagrams that will increase the scope of the expressive ability of business analysts. They used concepts as nonrepudiation, attack/harm detection, integrity, privacy, access control, security role, and security permissions. We note the lack of availability concept; it is a necessary requirement that should have been included.

(Mulle et al. 2011) present a rich language to represent security constraints for business processes and provide security support from the modelling to the runtime phase of a business-process lifecycle. Serval's concept introduced as confidentiality and integrity, authorization, authentication, auditing.

(Basin et al. 2011) introduce a new approach to aligning security and business objectives for information systems. Using CSP, they modeled a system at two levels of abstraction: the control-flow level, modeling a system's business objectives, and the task execution level, modeling who executes which tasks. Furthermore, they presented a novel approach to scope SoD and BoD constraints to subsets of task instances using release points.

(Brucker et al. 2012) proposed a model-based approach for designing and operating business-process-driven systems that integrates security and compliance requirements on the design-time modeling as well as the run-time enforcement of security and compliance requirements. The authors focuses on access control but also provides support for the other concepts: separation of duty, binding of duty and need to know.

(Saleem et al. 2012) presented a DSL, to model the security requirements along the business process model. They emphasise the need for specifying security requirements at design-time. In their approach, only core concepts (Confidentiality, integrity and availability) are used (Salnitri et al. 2014) introduced a framework that enables specifying information systems in SecBPMN, a security-oriented extension of BPMN. There are several concepts used in their framework as accountability, auditability, authenticity, availability, confidentiality, integrity non-repudiation and privacy. These concepts derived from the Reference Model of Information Assurance and Security (RMIAS) (Cherdantseva et al. 2013).

In (Altuhho et al. 2013), they propose a structured approach that extended BPMN to represents security risks. They specifies different colors for representing different resources. In addition, Tasks elements are used to model security activities, such as to authenticate users. However, those approaches miss many important security concepts. (Labda et al. 2014) proposes a novel extension to the visual notation of BPMN towards supporting privacy concerns. The extension focuses on representing privacy requirements about personal data. Their extension focus on privacy the concepts included focusing only on specifics sections of cyber security: separation of tasks, access control, binding of tasks, necessity to know and user consent.

(Maines et al. 2015) propose a new comprehensive ontology including all concepts potentially modellable in BPMN related to cyber security. The diagram also illustrates

Table 1. Overview of security-related BPMN extension

		Rodriguez et al	Brucker et al	Saleem et al	Salmitri et al	Wolter et al	Labda et al	Mulle et al	Sang et al	Altuhhova et al	Basin et al	Maines et al	Argyropoulos et al
Standard Conformity	Year	2007	2012	2012	2014	2009	2014	2011	2015	2013	2011	2016	2017
	Definition	Own Ext	Own Ext	Own Ext	None	Own Ext	Own Ext	None	Own Ext	Own Ext	Own Ext	None	Own Ext
	Abstract Syntax	UML, OCL	UML	UML	None	UML	UML	None	UML	UML	UML	None	UML
	Concrete Syntax	Explicit	None	Explicit	Explicit	Implicit	Explicit	Implicit	Explicit	Explicit	Explicit	Implicit	Implicit
	Process Model / MDA	No	No	No	No	Yes	No	No	No	No	No	No	No
Cyber Security Concept													
Access control	Access, control / Authenticity	✓	✓		✓		✓		✓		✓	✓	
	Authentication					✓		✓	✓				✓
	Authorisation					✓		✓	✓				✓
	Trust policy							✓					
	Security permissions	✓											
Accountability	Assignment mechanism							✓					
	Accountability	✓			✓							✓	
	Non-repudiation	✓			✓								
	Auditability/Traceability				✓	✓							
	Availability			✓	✓				✓	✓		✓	✓
Privacy	Privacy	✓		✓	✓	✓		✓	✓				
	Confidentiality		✓				✓	✓				✓	✓
	Necessity/Need to know						✓	✓					
	User consent						✓	✓					
Integrity	Integrity	✓		✓	✓	✓		✓	✓	✓		✓	✓
	Security role	✓						✓					
	Delegation												
	Separation of duty		✓				✓	✓			✓		
	Binding of duty		✓				✓	✓			✓		
	Separation of tasks								✓				
	Attack/harm detection	✓										✓	

the relationships between each class (concept) and their respective subclasses. However, the approach remains theoretical.

(Sang et al. 2015) provide a solution to model the security concepts in BPMN by extending it with new designed security elements, which can be integrated with the BPMN diagram. It provides the opportunity to improve and raise the security awareness in the healthcare process.

(Maines et al. 2016) propose the application of a third dimension to BPMN as a means of representing cyber security requirements. They include all concepts potentially modellable in BPMN related to cyber security. However, the approach remains theoretical and not valid BPMN extension.

(Argyropoulos et al. 2017) introduce an approach for the verification of security in business process models based on structural properties of the workflow of the process. To that end, they added a series of attributes to existing BPMN 2.0 concepts and algorithms for checking the compliance of a process model against the most common security requirements.

Table 1 displays BPMN security extensions found in the literature review. Each extension was analyzed with respect to the cyber security concepts and the standard conformity criterion regarding the syntactical and semantic correctness of the extension in the light of the BPMN standard (Braun et al. 2014). There is no single extension incorporating all security concepts. It is remarkable, that extensions listed are not compliant with the BPMN standard (not use BPMN extension mechanism).

3 Fundamentals

This section presents fundamentals in terms of general extensibility of BPMN and outlines the extension method of (Stroppi et al. 2011) as well domain analysis.

BPMN provides a "extension by addition" mechanism that enables the definition and integration of domain-specific concepts and ensures the validity of the BPMN core elements. The following elements are defined for the specification of valid BPMN extensions: An Extension Definition is a named group of new attributes that can be used by BPMN elements. Thus, new elements can be built implicitly. An Extension Definition consists of several Extension Attribute Definitions that define the particular attributes. Values of these Extension Attribute Definitions can be defined by the Extension Attribute Value class. Therefore, primitive types from the Meta Object Facility (MOF[1]) can be used.

The element Extension binds the entire extension definition and its attributes to a BPMN model definition. By doing so, all extension elements are accessible for existing BPMN elements. Despite the fact that BPMN offers a well-defined extension interface, only very few BPMN extensions make use of it. Instead, most extensions are only defined graphically. This hampers both comprehensibility and comparability between developed extensions and impedes the straightforward integration of extensions in

---

[1] http://www.omg.org/spec/MOF/.

BPMN modeling tools due the missing compliances with the BPMN metamodel. One reason for that is the missing procedure model for building extensions in the BPMN specification. Although extension elements are defined, methodical guidance for their creation is missing (Braun et al. 2014).

According to our research, Stroppi's approach (Stroppi et al. 2011) is the only one that address the stated problem. They define a model-transformation based procedure model for the methodical development of valid BPMN extensions. The procedure model consists of the following steps:

1. Conceptualizing the domain by defining a Conceptual Domain Model of the Extension (CDME) as UML class diagram.
2. Transformation of the CDME into a valid BPMN extension model by using UML profiles (BPMN+X).
3. Transformation of the BPMN+X into a XML Schema Extension Definition Model.
4. Transformation of the XML Schema Extension Definition Model into a XML Schema Extension Definition Document.

For our approach, we used a cyber-security ontology (Maines et al. 2015) in the domain analysis step to clarify the concepts (Stroppi et al. 2011). The concrete syntax of the extension will be defined in a final step within the development process.

4   Cyber Security Ontology-Based BPMN Extension

In this section, we provide a BPMN extension with complete set of security concepts derived from cyber security ontology to enable the modelling of the security requirements. The design of the extension is presented gradually below.

4.1   Domain Analysis

There is a need for specifying accurately cyber security requirements within BPMN. We propose the use of new comprehensive ontology, which includes all concepts

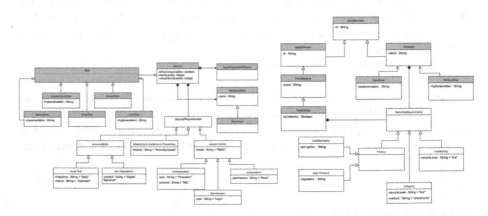

Fig. 1. Domain model for BPMN extension

potentially modellable in BPMN related to cyber security. Current BPMN-security extensions are being constructed unsystematically, without any empirical evidence to support their choice of concepts (Leitner et al. 2013). A common problem when creating security extensions lies with the lack of clear, predetermined concepts to be modelled. To address this problem, an ontology of cyber security for security extensions was created by (Maines et al. 2015). The main objective being to ensure any cyber security requirement a user may wish to model within BPMN is present within the ontology. We conceptualizing the domain by defining a Conceptual Domain Model of the Extension (CDME) (Fig. 1).

4.2 BPMN Extension Model (BPMN+X)

The second step is accomplished by developing a BPMN+X model based on the CDME resulting of the first step. BPMN+X is a language developed by (Stroppi et al. 2011) as a UML profile. Thus, it can be supported by existing UML tools. Another benefit of defining BPMN+X as a profile is that its learning curve will be more effective as UML it's a popular modeling language. The semantics and the abstract syntax of the BPMN +X elements are based on the specification of the BPMN extension mechanism (Fig. 2).

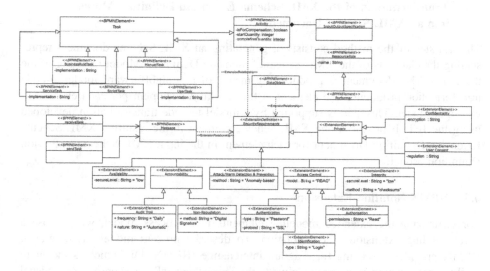

Fig. 2. BPMN+X extension model

The BPMN+X model is enhanced with stereotypes. The ExtensionDefinition stereotype describes a container and corresponds to the respective class in the MOF extensibility mechanism. The ExtensionElement stereotype is defined in the BPMN-X UML profile and matches the ExtensionAttributeValue class of the MOF extensibility mechanism. This allows representing the various elements as class objects for the next transformation step.

4.3   BPMN Transformation of the BPMN+X Model into an XML Schema Extension Definition Model

The third step consists of transforming the BPMN+X model into an XML Schema Extension Definition Model that is an instance of a MOF metamodel representing the concepts of the XML Schema specification.

- An ExtensionElement element is transformed into a ComplexTypeDenition element.
- An ExtensionEnum element is transformed into a SimpleTypeDenition element.
- BPMNElement and BPMNEnum elements are not transformed into any kind of XML Schema element. This is because the generated Schema imports the BPMN specification so the BPMN elements can be referenced by the other elements defined in the ExtensionModel (Stroppi et al. 2011).

The third step of the method is supported by a model-to-model transformation by using the QVT. This transformation takes a BPMN+X model and returns an XML Schema Extension Definition Model, which is an instance of an Ecore representation of XML Schema.

4.4   Transformation of the XML Schema Extension Definition Model into an XML Schema Document

The last step of the method consists of generating an XML Schema document representing the elements of the XML Schema Extension Definition Model resulting of the third step. This document is produced by means of a straightforward model-to-code transformation producing one element in the resulting document per each element in the input model. This step is supported by a model-to-code transformation developed using the JET. It produces one XML Schema element in the resulting XML Schema Extension Definition Document for each element in the input XML Schema Extension Definition Model.

4.5   BPMN Notation Extension

For visualizing the extended modeling elements in a process model, we propose a corresponding extension of the notation. To describe process models as diagrams, BPMN provides a schema for diagram interchange (BPMN: DI) which is meant to facilitate interchange between modeling tools. This schema allows specifying the visual attributes of a process model in its XML representation (Schultz and Radloff 2014). In this regard, the BPMN specification provides neither guidelines for the graphical representation of extension elements nor an extensibility mechanism for new notation elements. The notation has to be implemented separately to the semantics in a modeling tool (Stroppi et al. 2011). In general, the notation of an extension must not alter the BPMN notation and should be as close as possible to it (look and feel). Our notation extends the shapes of the BPMN Activity respectively the BPMN Task, Message and Data Object. We add an icon to the shape as shown in Table 2.

Table 2. Notation for security extension

Concept	Representation	Concept	Representation
Attack/harm detection and prevention		Authorization	
Audit Trail		Integrity	
Non-Repudiation		User-Consent	
Confidentiality		Authentication	
Availability		Identification	

5   Case Study

To demonstrate the using of our BPMN extension approach, we annotate a typical business process of admitting a patient to a hospital (Rodriguez et al. 2007). Three Pools describe the business process (see Fig. 3). Patient represents individuals who receives medical care. Administration Area is divided into two Lanes, where the Medical Institution records details about costs and insurances. Finally, the Pool Medical Area is divided into Lanes (Medical Evaluation and Exams) where preadmission tests, exams, evaluations and complete clinical data collecting are carried out. Security requirements are included in this business process specification. We considered several aspects of security. We define confidentiality for activity admission request, with the aim of preventing the disclosure of sensitive information about Patients.

- Non-repudiation has been defined over the message flow that goes from the pool Patient to the pool administration with the aim of avoiding the denial of the "Admission Request.
- Authentication has been defined for activity "review admission request".
- Audit Trail specification has been added to activity "fill out cost'. This implies that it must register role name, date and time of all events related to the update of cost.

Integrity (high) requirement has been specified for Data Object "Clinical Information" and "Accounting data".

– Finally, we specified Attack Harm Detection for "Medical Evaluation" with audit
requirement. All events related to attempt or success of attacks or damages must be
registered.

As illustrated, the example shows how our security extensions improve the current
BPMN standard in order to support the security requirements specification in the
process of modelling.

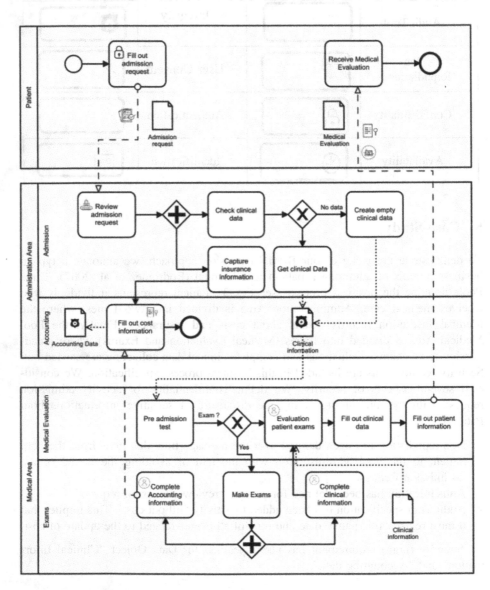

Fig. 3. Business process of admitting a patient to a hospital

Considering current approaches to security extensions and modelling languages in general, our solution offer complete set of security concepts with their graphical presentation to simplify modeling security requirements.

6 Experimental Evaluation

In a design science research project, the evaluation step tries to observe and measure how well the designed artifact supports a solution for the addressed problem (Schultz and Radloff 2014). In order to evaluate the BPMN security extension, we designed an experiment involved a comprehension task. Participants were shown a business process diagram. They were then asked 10 questions to test their understanding of some elementary semantics of the security concepts.

6.1 Design and Measures

A 1×2 between-group experiment is designed. Three dependent measures were used as in (Bodart et al. 2001):

- Accuracy: Participants were asked 10 questions about the semantics underlying the security concepts. We evaluate their response as either correct or incorrect. Their accuracy score was the total number of questions that they answered correctly.
- Time: We recorded the time taken (in seconds) by a participant to answer each question. Their time score was the total time taken for them to answer the 10 questions.
- Normalized accuracy: Where accuracy and time are performance measures, it is well known that participant may make tradeoffs—for example, they may compromise accuracy in their responses for increased response speed. Accordingly, a normalized accuracy score was calculated, which is a participant's accuracy score divided by their time score. A participant's normalized accuracy score on each trial is the number of accurate answers they provided per elapsed second.

6.2 Materials and Participants

Materials were based upon a student enrolment process. Two business process diagrams were created. The first was a diagram enhanced with security-related information based on the previously presented BPMN extension (group BPMN+C). The second was a traditional BPMN diagram with security matrix concepts (separately from the process models).

Participants in the experiment were 50 computer science students, recruited through Djillali Liabes University, who have taken at least one conceptual modelling course in which they had studied the BPMN (thus, they were second-year computer science students and above). Furthermore, 15 teachers from the same University are asked for voluntary participation.

6.3   Procedures

The two groups receive the same business process of student enrolment process and related security concepts. One group obtains information on security concepts (security matrix) separately from the process models (group BPMN). The other group has access to process models that are enhanced with security concepts. Their goal was to answer these questions as accurately and completely as possible.

In this evaluation, we focus on model interpretation. For evaluating the quality of model interpretation two perspectives are discussed: Accuracy (how faithfully does the interpretation of the model supports the reader to understand the domain semantics included in the model?) and normalized accuracy (comprehension task efficiency) (Burton-Jones et al. 2009). In our experiment following hypothesis are tested:

- H1: accuracy is positively affected by using the BPMN extension for representing security concepts in process models.
- H2: normalized accuracy is positively affected by using the BPMN extension for representing security concepts in process models.

The experiment took place entirely online using the Qualtrics research suite[2].

6.4   Results

Table 3 shows the results for the three performance measures.

Table 3. Performance statistics

	Accuracy	Time	Normalized accuracy
Group with BPMN security extension	6.077	82.38	0.080
Group BPMN	4.462	90.14	0.052

The BPMN Security extension group outperformed the BPMN group in terms of accuracy and normalized accuracy. The two groups did not differ so much in terms of time. The experimental results indicate that the BPMN extension has a positive effect on accuracy with regard to the representation and the assessment of security concepts in process models. One potential interpretation is that the integrated security concepts reduces the cognitive load for model interpretation. We believe that the presented extension meet security experts needs for modelling all security concepts clearly.

---

[2] https://www.qualtrics.com/fr/.

7 Conclusions and Perspectives

In this paper, we evaluated existing BPMN security extensions. From this literature review, we were able to highlight the key problems current extensions have that our solution aims to solve. We conservatively extend BPMN to address the many short-comings that it exhibits when it comes to describing security requirements in the first place by applying the (Stroppi et al. 2011). In order to ensure a reasonable design of extension elements, we provide a valid BPMN extension with complete set of security concepts derived from cyber security ontology to enable the modelling of the security requirements, which will extensively improve the system's security analysis capability. The usage of the security extensions is illustrated with a simple example (admission of patients in hospital).

A university experiment with 65 participants showed that the extension increases interpretational efficiency compared to a separated security requirements documentation.

With this extension, business analysts will be able to express security requirements from their own perspective and be able to improve and raise the security awareness.

To evolve the contribution of this paper, we plan to enrich the security requirements specifications, and assess the learnability and usability of our extension model by applying it to different domains. Afterwards, we aim to tackle the development a comprehensive security-aware business process modeling and execution framework to enforce security constraints during runtime.

References

Menzel, M., Thomas, I., Meinel, C.: Security requirements specification in service-oriented business process management. In: International Conference on Availability, Reliability and Security, ARES 2009, pp. 41–48 (2009)

Rodriguez, A., Fernandez-Medina, E., Piattini, M.: A BPMN extension for the modeling of security requirements in business processes. IEICE Trans. Inf. Syst. E90–D(4), 745–752 (2007)

Brucker, A.D., Hang, I., Lückemeyer, G., Ruparel, R.: SecureBPMN. In: Proceedings of the 17th ACM symposium on Access Control Models and Technologies - SACMAT 2012, pp. 123–126 (2012)

Qaiser, S.M., Jaafar, J.B., Hassan, M.F.: A domain-specific language for modelling security objectives in a business process models of SOA applications. Int. J. Adv. Inf. Sci. Serv. Sci. 4 (1), 353–362 (2012)

Salnitri, M., Dalpiaz, F., Giorgini, P.: Modeling and verifying security policies in business processes. In: Bider, I., et al. (eds.) BPMDS/EMMSAD -2014. LNBIP, vol. 175, pp. 200–214. Springer, Heidelberg (2014). https://doi.org/10.1007/978-3-662-43745-2_14

Cherdantseva, Y., Hilton, J.: A reference model of information assurance and security. In: 2013 International Conference on Availability, Reliability and Security, pp. 546–555 (2013)

Wolter, C., Menzel, M., Schaad, A., Miseldine, P., Meinel, C.: Model-driven business process security requirement specification. J. Syst. Architect. 55(4), 211–223 (2009)

Labda, W., Mehandjiev, N., Sampaio, P.: Modeling of privacy-aware business processes in BPMN to protect personal data. In: Proceedings of the 29th Annual ACM Symposium on Applied Computing - SAC 2014, pp. 1399–1405 (2014)

Mülle, J., Stackelberg, S.V., Böhm, K.: A security language for BPMN process models. In: Karlsruhe Reports in Informatics (2011)

Maines, C.L., Llewellyn-Jones, D., Tang, S., Zhou, B.: A cyber security ontology for BPMN-security extensions. In: The IEEE International Conference on Computer and Information Technology, Ubiquitous Computing and Communications, Dependable, Autonomic and Secure Computing, Pervasive Intelligence and Computing, pp. 1756–1763 (2015)

Sang, K.S., Zhou, B.: BPMN security extensions for healthcare process. In: The IEEE International Conference on Computer and Information Technology, Ubiquitous Computing and Communications, Dependable, Autonomic and Secure Computing, Pervasive Intelligence and Computing, pp. 2340–2345 (2015)

Altuhhov, O., Matulevičius, R., Ahmed, N.: An extension of business process model and notation for security risk management. Int. J. Inf. Syst. Model. Des. 4(4), 93–113 (2013)

Basin, D., Burri, S.J., Karjoth, G.: Obstruction-free authorization enforcement: aligning security with business objectives. In: 2011 IEEE 24th Computer Security Foundations Symposium, pp. 99–113 (2011)

Maines, C.L., Zhou, B., Tang, S., Shi, Q.: Adding a third dimension to BPMN as a means of representing cyber security requirements. In: 2016 9th International Conference on Developments in eSystems Engineering (DeSE), pp. 105–110 (2016)

Argyropoulos, N., Mouratidis, H., Fish, A.: Attribute-based security verification of business process models. In: 2017 IEEE 19th Conference on Business Informatics (CBI), pp. 43–52 (2017)

Braun, R., Esswein, W.: Classification of domain-specific BPMN extensions. In: Frank, U., Loucopoulos, P., Pastor, Ó., Petrounias, I. (eds.) PoEM 2014. LNBIP, vol. 197, pp. 42–57. Springer, Heidelberg (2014). https://doi.org/10.1007/978-3-662-45501-2_4

Stroppi, L.J.R., Chiotti, O., Villarreal, P.D.: Extending BPMN 2.0: method and tool support. In: Dijkman, R., Hofstetter, J., Koehler, J. (eds.) BPMN 2011. LNBIP, vol. 95, pp. 59–73. Springer, Heidelberg (2011). https://doi.org/10.1007/978-3-642-25160-3_5

Braun, R., Schlieter, H., Burwitz, M., Esswein, W.: BPMN4CP: design and implementation of a BPMN extension for clinical pathways. In: 2014 IEEE International Conference on Bioinformatics and Biomedicine (BIBM), pp. 9–16 (2014)

Leitner, M., Miller, M., Rinderle-Ma, S.: An analysis and evaluation of security aspects in the business process model and notation. In: 2013 International Conference on Availability, Reliability and Security, pp. 262–267 (2013)

Schultz, M., Radloff, M.: Modeling concepts for internal controls in business processes – an empirically grounded extension of BPMN. In: Sadiq, S., Soffer, P., Völzer, H. (eds.) BPM 2014. LNCS, vol. 8659, pp. 184–199. Springer, Cham (2014). https://doi.org/10.1007/978-3-319-10172-9_12

Bodart, F., Patel, A., Sim, M., Weber, R.: Should optional properties be used in conceptual modelling? a theory and three empirical tests. Inf. Syst. Res. 12(4), 384–405 (2001)

Burton-Jones, A., Wand, Y., Weber, R.: Guidelines for empirical evaluations of conceptual modeling grammars. J. Assoc. Inf. Syst. 10(6), 495–532 (2009)

A Correct-by-Construction Model
for Attribute-Based Access Control

Hania Gadouche$^{(\boxtimes)}$, Zoubeyr Farah, and Abdelkamel Tari

LIMED Laboratory, Faculty of Exact Sciences, University of Bejaia, Béjaïa, Algeria
gad.hania@gmail.com, zoubeyr.farah@gmail.com, tarikamel59@gmail.com

Abstract. In this paper, a formal specification approach of the Attribute-Based Access Control (ABAC) is proposed using the Event-B method. We apply an a-priori formal verification to build a correct model in a stepwise manner. Correctness of the specification model is insured during the construction steps. The model is composed of abstraction levels that are generated through refinement operations. A set of ABAC properties is defined in each level of refinement starting from the highest abstract level to the most concrete one. These properties are preserved by proofs with the behavior specification.

Keywords: ABAC · A priori verification · Correct-by-Construction
Event-B · Formal methods · Proof and refinement
Specification and validation

1   Introduction

In safety-critical systems, serious vulnerabilities can result from incorrect access definition to sensitive data. Access Control Policies (ACP) are a common solution for controlling access to resources. Hence, several access control models have been proposed in the literature [1–4], namely the Mandatory Access Control (MAC), the Discretionary Access Control (DAC), the Role Based Access Control (RBAC) and the Attribute Based Access Control (ABAC). Each access model has been designed to meet specific security requirements. Moreover, research on the MAC, DAC, RBAC and ABAC has proven that an access control model, which can express the RBAC policies is also capable of enforcing both MAC and DAC policies, as well that ABAC can express RBAC policies. The ABAC model improves RBAC since it enables fine-grained access control by defining the notion of attributes. The additional use of attributes when defining access control rules overcome the met shortcomings and make the handled objects more reachable in a secured way.

Validating and ensuring correctness of ACP specifications generally involve the use of systematic verification [5] which consists of checking absence of inconsistency and incompleteness in the built model. Regardless of used formalism, many specification and verification approaches are based on testing, simulation

© Springer Nature Switzerland AG 2018
E. H. Abdelwahed et al. (Eds.): MEDI 2018, LNCS 11163, pp. 233–247, 2018.
https://doi.org/10.1007/978-3-030-00856-7_15

or model checking. These latter implement a-posteriori verification techniques [6] but are generally restricted to the following limitations:

- The state-space explosion problem;
- The checking is performed when the model instantiation is achieved.

Most of the existing literature approaches have used the XACML (eXtensible Access Control Markup Language) [7] which is a standard for specifying ABAC policies. XACML as a practical standard of OASIS has been covered in many testing and verification researches. However, the XACML complexity make these testing and verification methods limited. To overcome this, we propose an Event-B based approach to build a valid ABAC model free from specification inconsistencies and errors. Specification approaches that are based on formal methods, such as Event-B [8], are widely used to model faultless critical systems. The use of formal methods has significantly improved the quality of computer systems [9], including analysis and design of software, also, verification of hardware and embedded systems. Similar improvements can be achieved by integrating formal methods into the development of secure systems [10,11]. Using formal methods requires understanding the system behavior and the relations between its components. Several works in the literature have used the Event-B method to specify the RBAC standard [12,13], but to the best of our knowledge, no work has addressed ABAC using the Event-B method.

We use the Event-B formal method, since it allows the specification of systems according to a correct-by-construction methodology, additionally, it provides a large selection of tools and techniques for specifying, validating and checking properties of systems. The proposed specification approach is based on refinement and gives a multilevel view of the access control model. The refinement starts from a high abstract level of specification to the most concrete one. The specification consistency is preserved through all its levels as the model properties are linked to the behavior. Indeed, defining properties of the model according to its behavior allows to get an a priori verification of the specification correctness. Thus, our approach is based on an a priori formal verification process, similarly to the one proposed to validate communicating systems in [14,15]. When the model is instantiated, all proved properties of the generic model remain valid thanks to the correct-by-construction approach. RODIN platform [8] is used to develop and validate the model.

The key features of our proposal are as follows:

- The approach is progressive and based on proving refinement, accordingly it avoids the combinatorial explosion.
- The behavior and properties of the model are correctly specified following a correct-by-construction approach, consequently the consistency of the specification is proved in the overall refinement levels.
- The approach allows specific views of the model rather than a global integrated one which simplifies the model analysis.

The remainder of the paper is organized as follows: Sect. 2 gives a presentation of the ABAC standard. Section 3 describes the Event-B formal method. Section 4 gives a browse of each level of the proposed Event-B specification approach. Proof obligations of the model are mentioned in Sect. 5. Related works are discussed in Sect. 6. Finally, the conclusion and some research perspectives are given in Sect. 7.

2 ABAC

In this section, an overview of ABAC is given. In the special publication [16] the NIST gives the following official definition of ABAC: "An access control method where a subject requests to perform operations on objects are granted or denied based on assigned attributes of the subject, assigned attributes of the object, environment conditions, and a set of policies that are specified in terms of those attributes and conditions".

Accordingly, we identify the following components for ABAC (Fig. 1):

- Policy: is a set of rules that determine if a requested access should be allowed, given the values of the attributes of the subject, object, and probably environment conditions or other constrains. A policy is created and owned by the resource administrator and plays a crucial role in the operation of ABAC.
- Subjects: is a set of entities requesting to perform permissions upon objects. Subjects are characterized by a set of attributes.
- Objects: is a set of system resources, such as devices, files, records, tables, processes, programs, networks . . . etc. Objects are the entities to be protected from unauthorized use. The objects attributes are provided by their owners.
- Permissions: known as authorizations, access rights, or privileges. A permission consists of granting rights to a subject request on an object according to policy rules.

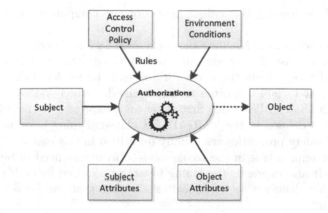

Fig. 1. ABAC basic architecture

- Attributes: are characteristics of subjects, objects, or environment conditions. Attributes allow administrators to apply access control policies for unlimited number of subjects that might require access without prior knowledge of them. Thus, new subjects can join the system without modifying the rules and objects. Each attribute can be either atomic or set of values.
- Environmental conditions: consist of the operational or situational context in which access requests to objects are formulated. Environmental conditions are characterized by a set of attributes.

3 Event-B Method

Event-B is a formal method used to model and analyze systems. An Event-B development model [17] is based on components of two kinds: Contexts and Machines. Contexts contain the static parts (axiomatization and theories) of the model, whereas the Machines implement the dynamic parts (states and transitions). Machines and contexts have various relations: a machine can be "refined" by another one, and a context can be "extended" by another one. Moreover, a machine can "see" one or several contexts. A Context is defined by a set of clauses as follows:

- CONTEXT represents the name of the component that should be unique in a model.
- EXTENDS declares the Context(s) extended by the described Context.
- SETS describes a set of abstract and enumerated types.
- CONSTANTS represents the constants used by a model.
- AXIOMS describes, in first-order logic expressions, the properties of the defined elements in the CONSTANTS and SETS clauses. Types and constraints are described in this clause as well.
- THEOREMS are logical expressions that can be deduced from the axioms.

Similarly to Contexts, Machines are defined by a set of clauses:

- MACHINE represents the unique name of the component in an Event-B model.
- REFINES declares the Machine that is refined by the described Machine.
- SEES gives the list of Contexts imported by the described Machine.
- VARIABLES represents the state variables of the model. Refinement may introduce new variables in order to enrich the described system.
- INVARIANTS describes, using first-order logic expressions, the properties of the variables defined in the VARIABLES clause. Typing information, functional and safety properties are usually described in this clause. These properties must remain true in the whole model. Invariants need to be preserved by events. It also expresses the gluing invariant required by each refinement.
- THEOREMS defines a set of logical expressions that can be deduced from the invariants.
- VARIANT introduces a natural number or a finite set that the "convergent" events must strictly make smaller at every execution.

Table 1. Structure of an Event-B development

Context ctxt_a Extends ctxt_b
Sets s, Constants c
Axioms A(s,c), Theorems T(s,c)
End
	Machine mach_a Refines mach_b
	Sees ctxt_a
	Variables v, Invariants I(s,c,v)
	Theorems T(s,c,v), Variants V(s,c,v)
	Events evt= Any x
	    Where G(s,c,v,x)
	    Then v:=BA(s,c,v,x,v')
	    End
	End

The general structure of an Event-B development is illustrated in the Table 1, where s denotes sets, c denotes constants and v denotes the declared variables of the machine. Axioms are denoted by $A(s,c)$ and theorems by $T(s,c)$, whereas invariants are denoted by $I(s,c,v)$ and local theorems by $T(s,c,v)$. For an event evt, its guards are denoted by $G(s,c,v,x)$ and its actions by the before-after predicate $BA(s,c,v,x,v')$. The clause defines a list of events (transitions) that can occur in a given model. Each event is characterized by its guards and is described by a set of actions (substitutions). Each machine must contain an initialization event. The events occurring in an Event-B model affect the state described in clause. An event consists of the following clauses:

- Refines: declares a list of events refined by the described event.
- Any: lists a set of the event parameters.
- Where: expresses a set of guards for the event. An event can be fired when its guard turns to true. If several guards of events become true, only a single event is fired.
- Then: contains a set of actions of the event that are used to modify variables.

Event-B is based on a refinement methodology, it allows the system developer to start with an abstract model of the system considering its context, and gradually add details to the model. This process leads to a sequence of concrete models until the final implementation is reached. A number of proof obligations are generated through this process, which guarantees the correctness of the model as well as any desired invariants (properties) that the model should preserve. Proof obligations can then be proved by automatic or interactive theorem provers or model-checking tools and the model itself can be simulated in runtime. Proving obligations, checking invariants and model simulating are functions that are supported by tools such as ProB [18] which is available in RODIN platform. The latter, made for the Rodin project, supplies a set of tools to support Event-B development. It also provides effective support for refinement and mathematical proofs.

4   Event-B Specification of ABAC

The proposed ABAC specification is detailed in this section. In the suggested approach, properties of the model are given in conjunction with the behavior specification. The model is developed in a way to link up between behavior and properties of ABAC components. We define a correct-by-construction approach following an a-priori verification. Consequently, the validity and the correctness of the ABAC model are guaranteed through the specification steps. The developed Event-B model contains one context that forms the static part of the specification, and four machines that form the dynamic part. Each machine expresses a level of the ABAC properties specification. Figure 2 gives the structure of the proposed Event-B model.

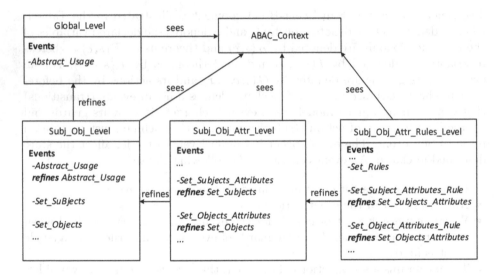

Fig. 2. Architecture of the ABAC specification

The Global_Level gives the general authorization structure to be provided by the access model. The subjects and the requested objects are introduced and detailed in the Subj_Obj_Level which refines the Global_Level. Attributes of subjects and requested objects are introduced in the Subj_Obj_Attr_Level in order to decide the appropriate privileges to assign since access decisions are granted based on attribute values. The access rules, defined in the last level Subj_Obj_Attr_Rules_Level, manage access to resources according to ABAC entities attributes (subjects, objects, environment,... etc.) Environment attributes and privileges are detailed in this level. We detail each specification level in the following:

- ABAC_Context: The basic elements of ABAC are introduced in the static part of the specification. These elements are reported in the CONTEXT named ABAC_Context. All the required static definitions to operate the dynamic part of the model are declared in this context (see Table 2).

In ABAC-Context, the declared working sets are: SUBJECTS, OBJECTS, attributes of subjects(SUBJ_ATTRIBUTES), attributes of objects (OBJ_ATTRIBUTES), attributes of the system environment (ENV_ATTRIBUTES) and PRIVILEGES of the access model. The required conditions when defining these sets are stated as axioms: The sets must be finite and not empty.

- Global_Level: The dynamic specification starts with a level that gives a global and high view of ABAC. It is expressed by the machine Global_Level as depicted in the Table 3. In this level, details are not important; the ABAC structure has just to be in a brief and perceivable view. The ABAC policy is expressed by the variable Authorizations. The considered properties in this level are about the typing of authorizations and the definition of relationships between their components. Authorizations are manipulated in the event Abstract_Usage that generates abstract view of the access model. To preserve the abstraction, non-deterministic assignment ($:\in$) is used. This affectation will gradually be determined in the refinement process.

- Subj_Obj_Level: This level provides more precision on the access requesters subjects and the requested objects. Subjects and Objects are introduced in the model in the events depicted in the Table 4. A precision concerning the subjects and the objects involved in the authorization is brought in this level by the refinement of the event Abstract_Usage as depicted in the Table 5.

- Subj_Obj_Attr_Level: The key feature of ABAC is the use of attributes to decide the suitable authorizations to grant. In this level, subject and object attributes are introduced to define the rules composing the concrete authorizations in the next refinement level. Attributes of subjects are introduced by refining the event Set_Subjects in the event Set_Subjects_Attributes as depicted in the Table 6. In the refinement of the Set_Subjects event, a witness relation is used to ensure that every Subject is given its own attributes. In the same way, the event Set_Objects is refined in Set_Objects_Attributes. To preserve consistency between the introduction of subjects and objects and their attributes, some invariants are given (see Table 7).

- Subj_Obj_Attr_Rules_Level : In this level, the defined rules are used to concretize the authorizations variable. A rule matches attributes of subjects to requested objects attributes, as well as the system environment attributes, to establish a privilege assignment. The event Set_Rules is given in the Table 8. To preserve consistency between the subjects and objects attributes and their definition in the context of a rule, two invariants are added (see Table 9).

Table 2. ABAC context

ABAC_Context	
SETS	
SUBJECTS	all possible Subjects of the application
OBJECTS	all possible Objects of the application
SUBJ_ATTRIBUTES	all possible Attributes of the Subjects
OBJ_ATTRIBUTES	all possible Attributes of the Objects
ENV_ATTRIBUTES	all possible Environmental Attributes
PRIVILEGES	all possible Privileges
AXIOMS	
axm1:	$SUBJECTS \neq \varnothing \wedge finite(SUBJECTS)$
axm2:	$OBJECTS \neq \varnothing \wedge finite(OBJECTS)$
axm3:	$SUBJ\_ATTRIBUTES \neq \varnothing \wedge finite(SUBJ\_ATTRIBUTES)$
axm4:	$OBJ\_ATTRIBUTES \neq \varnothing \wedge finite(OBJ\_ATTRIBUTES)$
axm5:	$ENV\_ATTRIBUTES \neq \varnothing \wedge finite(ENV\_ATTRIBUTES)$
axm6:	$PRIVILEGES \neq \varnothing \wedge finite(PRIVILEGES)$
END	

Table 3. Global-Level machine

MACHINE Global_Level
SEES ABAC_Context
VARIABLES
Authorizations
INVARIANTS
inv1: $Authorizations \subseteq SUBJECTS \times OBJECTS \times ENV\_ATTRIBUTES \times PRIVILEGES$
EVENTS
INITIALISATION:
THEN
act1: $Authorizations := \varnothing$
END

Abstract_Usage:
THEN
act1: $Authorizations :\in \mathbb{P}1(SUBJECTS \times OBJECTS \times ENV\_ATTRIBUTES \times PRIVILEGES)$
END
END

Table 4. Subject and Object introduction events

MACHINE
Subj_Obj_Level
REFINES
Global_Level
SEES ABAC_Context

...

Set_Subjects:
ANY   subject
WHERE $grd1 : subject \in SUBJECTS$
THEN $act1 : Subjects := Subjects \cup \{subject\}$
END

Set_Objects:
ANY   object
WHERE $grd1 : object \in OBJECTS$
THEN $act1 : Objects := Objects \cup \{object\}$
...

Table 5. Refinement of the Abstract-Usage event

...
Abstract_Usage
REFINES Abstract_Usage
WHERE
$grd1 : Subjects \neq \varnothing$
$grd2 : Objects \neq \varnothing$
THEN
$act1 : Authorizations :\in \mathbb{P}1(Subjects \times Objects \times ENV\_ATTRIBUTES \times PRIVILEGES)$
...

Table 6. Subject attributes definition

...
Set_Subjects_Attributes:
REFINES Set_Subjects
ANY   subject_attribute
WHERE
$grd1 : subject\_attribute \in SUBJECTS \times SUBJ\_ATTRIBUTES$
WITH
$subject : subject \in dom(\{subject\_attribute\})$
THEN
$act1 : Subj\_Attributes := Subj\_Attributes \cup \{subject\_attribute\}$
END

...

Table 7. Invariants of the attributes level introduction

MACHINE	Subj_Obj_Attr_Level
REFINES	Subj_Obj_Level
...	
INVARIANTS	
inv4:	$Subj\_Attributes \subseteq SUBJECTS \times SUBJ\_ATTRIBUTES$
inv5:	$Obj\_Attributes \subseteq OBJECTS \times OBJ\_ATTRIBUTES$
inv6:	$\forall s.s \in Subjects \Rightarrow s \in dom(Subj\_Attributes)$
inv7:	$dom(Subj\_Attributes) = Subjects$
inv8:	$\forall o.o \in Objects \Rightarrow o \in dom(Obj\_Attributes)$
inv9:	$dom(Obj\_Attributes) = Objects$

Table 8. The Set_Rules event

Set_Rules:	
ANY	
$attr\_subj, attr\_obj, attr\_env, privilege$	
WHERE	
grd1:	$attr\_subj \in SUBJ\_ATTRIBUTES$
grd2:	$attr\_obj \in OBJ\_ATTRIBUTES$
grd3:	$attr\_env \in ENV\_ATTRIBUTES$
grd4:	$privilege \in PRIVILEGES$
THEN	
act1:	$Rules := Rules \cup \{attr\_subj \mapsto attr\_obj \mapsto attr\_env \mapsto privilege\}$
END	

Table 9. Invariants of rules introduction

MACHINE Subj_Obj_Attr_Rules_Level	
REFINES Subj_Obj_Attr_Level	
INVARIANTS	
inv10:	$Rules \subseteq$
	$SUBJ\_ATTRIBUTES \times OBJ\_ATTRIBUTES \times ENV\_ATTRIBUTES \times PRIVILEGES$
inv11:	$\forall s\_attr.s\_attr \in ran(Subj\_Attributes) \Rightarrow$
	$s\_attr \in dom(dom(dom(Rules)))$
inv12:	$\forall o\_attr.o\_attr \in ran(Obj\_Attributes) \Rightarrow$
	$o\_attr \in ran(dom(dom(Rules)))$

5 Proofs of the Model

The initial Event-B model presented above has been developed within the Rodin platform. This latter generates automatically Proof Obligations in the form of sequences [17]. The automatic Prover of RODIN can discharge automatically many of the POs, the remainder of non-discharged POs can be tackled by the interactive Prover. The developed model led to 24 proof obligations. 21 were proved automatically and three needed few interactive proof steps. Table 10 details the statistic proofs of the initial model.

Table 10. Statistic of proofs

Model components	Proof obligations	Automatic proofs	Interactive proofs
Global_Level	1	1	0
Subj_Obj_Level	2	2	0
Subj_Obj_Attr_Level	14	12	2
Subj_Obj_Attr_Rules_Level	7	6	1

The adopted specification approach engendered a reduced number of POs since the properties of the ABAC were expressed with the model behavior as events properties. Accordingly, many POs were automatically proved.

6 Related Works

Several approaches in the literature address the ABAC model specification and verification; most of them have used the XACML.

A work that addresses the logic programming is presented in [19], where a stratified framework for ABAC is defined based on computable and hereditarily set theory to represent policies making them consistent, complete and transformable to perform faster runtimes.

The authors in [20] present a model-checking algorithm for the access control policies evaluation. Which consists of ensuring that the authorized users are granted enough permissions to achieve their goal, also, to avoid the achievement of malicious goals from unauthorized users. The algorithm consists of two modes: the assessing mode and the intrusion detection mode.

In [21] the authors define a formal model to specify access to resources using XACML. Their approach define access control properties in many ordering relations and translate them into Boolean satisfiability problems. To grant access decisions and verify automatically the access control properties, the authors used the SAT solver. However, they admit that their approach has some limitations in terms of correctness of the access decisions issued from the Boolean problems.

The authors in [22] propose an approach based on mutation for the assessment of policy properties quality and its verification. A policy mutate into several variants called mutant policies with a single fault for each one. The verification process identifies the fault of the mutant policy in case of properties are not preserved.

Authors in [23] investigate a two-step approach to validate a non-specific ACP using Event-B. The first step constructs the secured system from combining the unsecured system and the desired security. The second step performs a verification on the resulting combined system against safety temporal properties. The combination is based on many levels of abstraction and refinement where each level expresses a class of properties. For illustration, they apply the approach on a banking system. Although the specification of the two parts of the system is done by design, the combination step includes a verification process to ensure absence of combining specification errors.

[24] define a method to efficiently detect the conflicts in ABAC policies using the formal notions of semantically equivalent policies and statically conflicting rules. The proposed method is based on two optimization techniques: The first technique reduces the semantically equivalent rules into a set of compact, then the binary-research technique is applied to detect conflicts in the set of the reduced rules.

In [25] the authors develop a tool named ACPT (Access Control Policy Testing) for the correct modeling, implementation and verification of XACML access control policies. The developed tool supports both of the static and the dynamic verification in order to decrease policies faults.

Authors in [26] present an abstraction-refinement-based approach to verify ACP. The principle is to define a bounded model-checker by computing an approximate size of the policy to be verified, then, fix a bound of checking operations to perform where any error can be detected. This allows to reduce verification complexity since the access errors research is not exhaustive. They demonstrate that the proposed approach scales better when input policies increase in size. They apply their approach on ARBAC model, which is a variant of ABAC. Although this technique scales well, the detection of all possible errors is not always assured and the correctness of the specification model is not fully guaranteed.

Most of the specification and verification of ABAC models follow an a-posteriori verification technique. Whether it is testing, simulation or model-checking based, the use of the a-posteriori verification becomes inappropriate when the access model increases in size and functionality. Indeed, testing techniques can be performed when an implementation of the model is available, furthermore, they can only be used to prove the existence of some specific errors, for the simulation and model-checking techniques they are limited by the state explosion problem. In this paper, a correct-by- construction specification approach is proposed to overcome the aforementioned limitations. Indeed, unlike existing approaches defined to specify and validate ABAC models, the correctness of the model behavior is ensured by proofs during the specification steps, which means that we define an a-priori approach to specify a correct behavior in a stepwise manner. Additionally, we adopt a specification methodology where ABAC components are progressively introduced by refinement. Consequently, the specification process is simplified and will not be affected when the system scales in size and functionality.

7   Conclusion

In this paper an Event-B formal specification approach for ABAC is presented. Due to the limitation of the a-posteriori based specification and verification of ABAC and in order to deal with large-scale systems, an a-priori formal approach is proposed. Accordingly, we construct an Event-B model of ABAC where all the properties are validated and the correct behavior is proved. The main advantages of the solution are:

- The model complexity of the system is decreased since the model is built step-by-step with refinements and proving based specification.
- The approach generates a model with different abstraction views which simplify the observation and analysis of the specified model.
- All the validated properties of the general model remain valid after instantiation independently of the size of the model component instances.

As future work, the aim would be to:

- Complete the model in order to illustrate it through an application on a case study.
- Improve the model in order to support access system reconfigurations.

References

1. Osborn, S., Sandhu, R., Munawer, Q.: Configuring role-based access control to enforce mandatory and discretionary access control policies. ACM Trans. Inf. Syst. Secur. (TISSEC) **3**(2), 85–106 (2000)
2. Yong, J., Bertino, E., Roberts, M.T.D.: Extended RBAC with role attributes. In: PACIS 2006 Proceedings, p. 8 (2006)
3. Mammass, M., Ghadi, F.: Access control models: State of the art and comparative study. In: 2014 Second World Conference on Complex Systems (WCCS), pp. 431–435. IEEE (2014)
4. Hu, V.C., Kuhn, D.R., Ferraiolo, D.F.: Attribute-based access control. Computer **48**(2), 85–88 (2015)
5. Hu, V.C., Kuhn, R., Yaga, D.: Verification and test methods for access control policies/models. NIST Spec. Publ. **800**, 192 (2017)
6. Heljanko, K., Junttila, T., Keinänen, M., Lange, M., Latvala, T.: Bounded model checking for weak alternating Büchi automata. In: Ball, T., Jones, R.B. (eds.) CAV 2006. LNCS, vol. 4144, pp. 95–108. Springer, Heidelberg (2006). https://doi.org/10.1007/11817963_12

7. Anderson, A., et al.: eXtensible Access Control Markup Language (XACML) version 1.0. OASIS (2003)
8. Abrial, J.R., Butler, M., Hallerstede, S., Hoang, T.S., Mehta, F., Voisin, L.: Rodin: an open toolset for modelling and reasoning in Event-B. Int. J. Softw. Tools Technol. Transf. **12**(6), 447–466 (2010)
9. Romanovsky, A., Thomas, M. (eds.): Industrial Deployment of System Engineering Methods. Springer, Heidelberg (2013). https://doi.org/10.1007/978-3-642-33170-1
10. Voas, J., Schaffer, K.: Whatever happened to formal methods for security? Computer **49**(8), 70 (2016)
11. Chong, S., et al.: Report on the NSF workshop on formal methods for security. Technical report, USA (2016)
12. Huynh, N., Frappier, M., Mammar, A., Laleau, R., Desharnais, J.: A formal validation of the RBAC ANSI 2012 standard using B. Sci. Comput. Program. **131**, 76–93 (2016)
13. Idani, A., Ledru, Y.: B for modeling secure information systems. In: Butler, M., Conchon, S., Zaïdi, F. (eds.) ICFEM 2015. LNCS, vol. 9407, pp. 312–318. Springer, Cham (2015). https://doi.org/10.1007/978-3-319-25423-4_20
14. Farah, Z., Ait-Ameur, Y., Ouederni, M., Tari, K.: A correct-by-construction model for asynchronously communicating systems. Int. J. Softw. Tools Technol. Transf. **19**(4), 465–485 (2017)
15. Benyagoub, S., Ouederni, M., Aït-Ameur, Y., Mashkoor, A.: Incremental construction of realizable choreographies. In: Dutle, A., Muñoz, C., Narkawicz, A. (eds.) NFM 2018. LNCS, vol. 10811, pp. 1–19. Springer, Cham (2018). https://doi.org/10.1007/978-3-319-77935-5_1
16. Hu, C.T.: Attribute based access control (ABAC) definition and considerations. Technical report (2014)
17. Abrial, J.R.: Modeling in Event-B: System and Software Engineering. Cambridge University Press, Cambridge (2010)
18. Leuschel, M., Butler, M.: ProB: a model checker for B. In: Araki, K., Gnesi, S., Mandrioli, D. (eds.) FME 2003. LNCS, vol. 2805, pp. 855–874. Springer, Heidelberg (2003). https://doi.org/10.1007/978-3-540-45236-2_46
19. Wang, L., Wijesekera, D., Jajodia, S.: A logic-based framework for attribute based access control. In: Proceedings of the 2004 ACM Workshop on Formal Methods in Security Engineering, pp. 45–55. ACM (2004)
20. Zhang, N., Ryan, M., Guelev, D.P.: Evaluating access control policies through model checking. In: Zhou, J., Lopez, J., Deng, R.H., Bao, F. (eds.) ISC 2005. LNCS, vol. 3650, pp. 446–460. Springer, Heidelberg (2005). https://doi.org/10.1007/11556992_32
21. Hughes, G., Bultan, T.: Automated verification of access control policies using a sat solver. Int. J. Softw. Tools Technol. Transf. **10**(6), 503–520 (2008)
22. Martin, E., Hwang, J., Xie, T., Hu, V.: Assessing quality of policy properties in verification of access control policies. In: Computer Security Applications Conference, ACSAC 2008. Annual, pp. 163–172. IEEE (2008)
23. Hoang, T.S., Basin, D., Abrial, J.R.: Specifying access control in event-b. Technical report 624 (2009)

24. Shu, C., Yang, E.Y., Arenas, A.E.: Detecting conflicts in ABAC policies with rule-reduction and binary-search techniques. In: IEEE International Symposium on Policies for Distributed Systems and Networks, POLICY 2009, pp. 182–185. IEEE (2009)

25. Hwang, J., Xie, T., Hu, V., Altunay, M.: ACPT: a tool for modeling and verifying access control policies. In: 2010 IEEE International Symposium on Policies for Distributed Systems and Networks (POLICY), pp. 40–43. IEEE (2010)

26. Jayaraman, K., Tripunitara, M., Ganesh, V., Rinard, M., Chapin, S.: Mohawk: abstraction-refinement and bound-estimation for verifying access control policies. ACM Trans. Inf. Syst. Secur. (TISSEC) 15(4), 18 (2013)

Algorithmics and Text Processing

Voronoi-Diagram Based Partitioning for Distance Join Query Processing in SpatialHadoop

Francisco García-García[1], Antonio Corral[1(✉)], Luis Iribarne[1], and Michael Vassilakopoulos[2]

[1] Department of Informatics, University of Almeria, Almeria, Spain
{paco.garcia,acorral,luis.iribarne}@ual.es

[2] Department of Electrical and Computer Engineering, University of Thessaly, Volos, Greece
mvasilako@uth.gr

Abstract. SpatialHadoop is an extended MapReduce framework supporting global indexing techniques that partition spatial data across several machines and improve query processing performance compared to traditional Hadoop systems. SpatialHadoop supports several spatial operations efficiently (e.g. k Nearest Neighbor search, spatial intersection join, etc.). Distance Join Queries (DJQs), e.g. k Nearest Neighbors Join Query, k Closest Pairs Query, etc., are important and common operations used in numerous spatial applications. DJQs are costly operations, since they combine joins with distance-based search. Therefore, performing DJQs efficiently is a challenging task. In this paper, a new partitioning technique based on Voronoi Diagrams is designed and implemented in SpatialHadoop. A new kNNJQ MapReduce algorithm and an improved kCPQ MapReduce algorithm, using the new partitioning mechanism, are also developed for SpatialHadoop. Finally, the results of an extensive set of experiments are presented, demonstrating that the new partitioning technique and the new DJQ MapReduce algorithms are efficient, scalable and robust in SpatialHadoop.

Keywords: Data partitioning · k Nearest Neighbors Join
k Closest Pairs · SpatialHadoop · MapReduce

1 Introduction

In the age of smart cities and mobile environments, the increase of the volume of available spatial data (e.g. location, routing, etc.) is huge all over the world. Recent developments of spatial big data systems have motivated the emergence of novel technologies for processing large-scale spatial data on shared-nothing clusters in a distributed environment. SpatialHadoop [8] is a disk-based Distributed

---

Work funded by the MINECO research project [TIN2017-83964-R].

© Springer Nature Switzerland AG 2018
E. H. Abdelwahed et al. (Eds.): MEDI 2018, LNCS 11163, pp. 251–267, 2018.
https://doi.org/10.1007/978-3-030-00856-7_16

Spatial Data Management System (DSDMS) based on Hadoop-MapReduce that allows users to work on distributed spatial data without worrying about computation distribution and fault-tolerance. SpatialHadoop is a full-fledged MapReduce [6] framework with native support for spatial data.

Data partitioning is a powerful mechanism for improving efficiency of data management systems, and it is a standard feature in modern database systems. Aside from the fact that data partitioning improves the overall manageability of large datasets, it also improves query performance. By partitioning such datasets into smaller units, it enables processing of a query in parallel and reduces the I/O activity by only scanning a few partitions that contain relevant data for the query constraints. Spatial data partitioning, however, is challenging, especially due to several important properties that are particular to spatial data and query processing, like spatial data skew and boundary object handling [1]. SpatialHadoop [7] supports seven partitioning strategies to handle large-scale spatial data [7]. They are classified as space-based (Grid and Quadtree), data-based (STR, STR+ and k-d tree) and space filling curve-based (Z-curve and Hilbert-curve) partitioning strategies. The incorporation of a distance-based partitioning technique (based on Voronoi Diagrams) in SpatialHadoop may be worth for improving the performance of distance join queries.

Distance Join Queries (DJQs) in spatial databases have received considerable attention from the database community, due to their importance in numerous applications, such as geographical information systems (GIS), location-based systems, continuous monitoring in streaming data settings and road network constrained data, among others. DJQs are costly queries because they combine two datasets, taking into account a distance metric. Two of the most representative and known DJQs are the k Nearest Neighbor Join Query (kNNJQ) and the k Closest Pairs Query (kCPQ). Given two point datasets $\mathbb{P}$ and $\mathbb{Q}$, the kNNJQ finds, for each point of $\mathbb{P}$, its k nearest neighbors in $\mathbb{Q}$. The kCPQ finds the k closest pairs of points from $\mathbb{P} \times \mathbb{Q}$ according to a certain distance function. Several research works have been devoted to improve the performance of these DJQs by proposing efficient algorithms in centralized environments [3–5]. However, with the fast increase in the scale of the big input datasets, processing large-scale data in parallel and distributed fashions is becoming a popular practice. For this reason, a number of parallel DJQ algorithms in MapReduce have been designed and implemented for kNNJQ [12,13,16]. A kCPQ [9,10] algorithm has been also developed particularly in SpatialHadoop.

The contributions of this paper are the following:

- We design and implement an efficient partitioning technique based on Voronoi Diagrams in SpatialHadoop.
- We present a new kNNJQ MapReduce algorithm in SpatialHadoop and improve the existing kCPQ MapReduce algorithm [9,10], both using the new partitioning mechanism.
- We execute an extensive set of experiments, studying efficiency and scalability, to compare the proposed distance-based partitioning technique with the existing ones in SpatialHadoop, using big real-world spatial datasets.

This paper is organized as follows. In Sect. 2, we review related work on partitioning techniques and provide the motivation for this paper. In Sect. 3, we present preliminary concepts related to DJQ, SpatialHadoop and partitioning techniques based on Voronoi Diagrams. Section 4 proposes a partitioning technique based on Voronoi Diagrams in SpatialHadoop. In Sect. 5, the parallel and distributed algorithms for processing kNNJQ and kCPQ in SpatialHadoop are proposed. In Sect. 6, we present the most representative results of the experiments that we have performed, using real-world datasets, for comparing the new partitioning technique in SpatialHadoop. Finally, in Sect. 7, we provide the conclusions arising from our work and discuss related future work directions.

2   Related Work and Motivation

In [1], an extension of SATO [15], that is a spatial data partitioning framework for scalable query processing, is presented. The main objective of [1] is to provide a comprehensive guidance for spatial data partitioning to support scalable and fast spatial data processing in distributed computing environments such as MapReduce. To accomplish this, the authors provide a systematic evaluation of six spatial partitioning methods with a set of different partitioning strategies, and study their implications on the performance of spatial queries in MapReduce. In particular, the proposed spatial partitioning algorithms were Binary Split Partitioning (BSP), Fixed Grid Partitioning (FG), Strip Partitioning (SLC), Boundary Optimized Strip Partitioning (BOS), Sort-Tile-Recursive Partitioning (STR) and Hilbert Curve Partitioning (HC). The most important results are the runtime cost of the partitioning algorithms (there are three categories: fast -FG, BSP-, medium -HC, STR- and slow -SLC, BOS-) and spatial join query performance between two datasets, where BSP and STR have the best performance in terms of running time and, FG and HC are the worst.

In [7], seven different *spatial partitioning techniques* in SpatialHadoop are presented, and an extensive experimental study on the quality of the generated index and the performance of range and spatial join queries is reported. These seven partitioning techniques are also classified in two categories according to boundary object handling: *replication-based techniques* (Grid, Quadtree, STR+ and k-d tree) and *distribution-based techniques* (STR, Z-Curve and Hilbert-Curve) [7]. The *distribution-based techniques* assign an object to exactly one overlapping cell and the cell has to be expanded to enclose all contained points. The *replication-based techniques* avoid expanding cells by replicating each point to all overlapping cells, but the query processor has to employ a duplicate avoidance technique to account for replicated elements. The most important conclusions of [7] for distributed join processing, using the *overlap* spatial predicate, are the following: (1) the smallest running time is obtained when the same partitioning technique is used for the join processing, (2) Quadtree outperforms all other techniques with respect to running time, since it minimizes the number of overlapping partitions between the two files by employing a regular space partitioning, (3) Z-Curve reports the worst running times, and (4) k-d tree gets very similar results to STR.

The most representative papers that adopt the Voronoi-Diagram based partitioning technique within MapReduce are [2,11,12]. In [2], this partitioning is used to answer range search and kNN search queries in 2d spaces. In [12], the problem of answering the kNNJ using MapReduce is studied. This is accomplished by exploiting the Voronoi-Diagram based partitioning method, that divides the input datasets into groups, such that kNNJ can answer by only checking object pairs within each group. Moreover, several pruning rules to reduce the shuffling cost as well as the computation cost are developed in the PGBJ (Partitioning and Grouping Block Join) algorithm, which works with two MapReduce phases. Finally, in [11], the vector projection pruning technique is proposed to process efficiently kNNJ, since it enables to prune non-kNN points and reduce the cost of distance computation. A new algorithm, kNN-MR, using this new pruning technique, that performs better than PGBJ, is presented.

Apart of [11,12], other parallel and distributed kNNJ algorithms that do not use the Voronoi-Diagram based partitioning technique has been published in the literature. The most remarkable ones are [13,14,16]. In [16], novel (exact and approximate) algorithms in MapReduce to perform efficient parallel kNNJQ on large datasets are proposed, and they use the R-tree and Z-value-based partition joins to implement them. In [14], the existing solutions that perform the kNNJ operation in the context of MapReduce are reviewed and studied from the theoretical and experimental point of view. Finally, the only DJQ algorithm already included in SpatialHadoop is the kCPQ MapReduce algorithm [9,10], that consists of a MapReduce job, adopting the plane-sweep technique and improving the computation of an upper bound of the distance value of the k-th closest pair from sampled data as a global preprocessing phase.

Based on the previous observations, the incorporation of a new partitioning technique (based on Voronoi Diagrams) in SpatialHadoop which could lead to efficient algorithms for processing the kNNJQ and kCPQ over large-scale spatial datasets is a promising research direction and the motivation for this paper.

3   Preliminaries and Background

In this section, we first present the basic definitions of the kNNJQ and kCPQ, followed by a brief introduction of preliminary concepts of SpatialHadoop, and finally the main concepts and properties of the Voronoi Diagrams.

3.1   Distance Join Queries

To introduce the details of the semantics of the DJQs studied in this paper, we define the kNNJ and kCP queries. Moreover, we also define the distance-based query that is the basis of kNNJQ, the k Nearest Neighbor (kNN) query, where just one dataset is processed.

Given one points dataset, the kNNQ discovers the k closest points to a given query point (i.e. it reports only the top k points). It is one of the most important and studied spatial operations, where one spatial dataset and a distance function are involved. The formal definition of the kNNQ for points is the following:

Definition 1. k-Nearest Neighbor query, kNN query

Let $\mathbb{P} = \{p_0, p_1, \cdots, p_{n-1}\}$ a set of points in E^d (d-dimensional Euclidean space), a query point q in E^d, and a number $k \in \mathbb{N}^+$. Then, the result of the k Nearest Neighbor Query with respect to the query point q is an ordered collection, $kNN(\mathbb{P}, q, k) \subseteq \mathbb{P}$, which contains the k ($1 \leq k \leq |\mathbb{P}|$) different points of $\mathbb{P}$, with the k smallest distances from q:

$kNN(\mathbb{P}, q, k) = (p_1, p_2, \cdots, p_k) \in \mathbb{P}$, such that for any $p_i \in \mathbb{P} \setminus kNN(\mathbb{P}, q, k)$ we have $dist(p_1, q) \leq dist(p_2, q) \leq \cdots \leq dist(p_k, q) \leq dist(p_i, q)$.

When two datasets ($\mathbb{P}$ and $\mathbb{Q}$) are combined, two of the most studied DJQs are the k Nearest Neighbor Join (kNNJ) and the k Closest Pairs (kCP) queries.

The kNNJQ, given two points datasets ($\mathbb{P}$ and $\mathbb{Q}$) and a positive number k, finds for each point of $\mathbb{P}$, its k nearest neighbors in $\mathbb{Q}$. The formal definition of this kind of DJQ is given below.

Definition 2. kNearest Neighbor Join query, $kNNJ$ query

Let $\mathbb{P} = \{p_0, p_1, \cdots, p_{n-1}\}$ and $\mathbb{Q} = \{q_0, q_1, \cdots, q_{m-1}\}$ be two set of points in E^d, and a number $k \in \mathbb{N}^+$. Then, the result of the k Nearest Neighbor Join query is a set $kNNJ(\mathbb{P}, \mathbb{Q}, k) \subseteq \mathbb{P} \times \mathbb{Q}$, which contains for each point of $\mathbb{P}$ ($p_i \in \mathbb{P}$) its k nearest neighbors in $\mathbb{Q}$:

$kNNJ(\mathbb{P}, \mathbb{Q}, k) = \{(p_i, q_j) : \forall p_i \in \mathbb{P}, q_j \in kNN(\mathbb{Q}, p_i, k)\}$

On the other hand, the kCPQ discovers the k pairs of points formed from two datasets ($\mathbb{P}$ and $\mathbb{Q}$) having the k smallest distances between them (i.e. it reports only the top k pairs). The formal definition of this DJQ is as follows.

Definition 3. k Closest Pairs query, kCP query

Let $\mathbb{P} = \{p_0, p_1, \cdots, p_{n-1}\}$ and $\mathbb{Q} = \{q_0, q_1, \cdots, q_{m-1}\}$ be two set of points in E^d, and a number $k \in \mathbb{N}^+$. Then, the result of the k Closest Pairs query is an ordered collection, $kCP(\mathbb{P}, \mathbb{Q}, k) \subseteq \mathbb{P} \times \mathbb{Q}$, containing k different pairs of points ordered by distance, with the k smallest distances between all possible pairs:

$kCP(\mathbb{P}, \mathbb{Q}, k) = ((p_1, q_1), (p_2, q_2), \cdots, (p_k, q_k)), (p_i, q_i) \in \mathbb{P} \times \mathbb{Q}, 1 \leq i \leq k$, such that for any $(p, q) \in \mathbb{P} \times \mathbb{Q} \setminus kCP(\mathbb{P}, \mathbb{Q}, k)$ we have $dist(p_1, q_1) \leq dist(p_2, q_2) \leq \cdots \leq dist(p_k, q_k) \leq dist(p, q)$.

3.2 SpatialHadoop

SpatialHadoop [8] is a full-fledged MapReduce framework with native support for spatial data. It is an efficient disk-based distributed spatial query processing system. Note that MapReduce [6] is a scalable, flexible and fault-tolerant programming framework for distributed large-scale data analysis (i.e. MapReduce is a shared-nothing platform for processing large-scale datasets). A task to be performed using the MapReduce framework consists of two phases: the *map* phase which is specified by a *map function* that takes input typically from Hadoop Distributed File System (HDFS) files, possibly performs some computations on this input, and distributes the result to worker nodes; and the *reduce* phase which processes these results as specified by a *reduce function*. An important aspect of MapReduce is that both the input and the output of the *map* step are represented as *key/value pairs*, and that pairs with the same key will be processed as one group by the *reducer*. Additionally, a *combiner function* can be used to run on the output of the *map* phase and perform some filtering or aggregation to reduce the number of keys passed to the *reducer*.

SpatialHadoop is a comprehensive extension to Hadoop that injects spatial data awareness in each Hadoop layer, namely, the language, storage, MapReduce, and operations layers. *MapReduce* layer is the query processing layer that runs MapReduce programs, taking into account that SpatialHadoop supports spatially indexed input files. The *Operation* layer enables the efficient implementation of spatial operations, considering the combination of the spatial indexing in the storage layer with the new spatial functionality in the *MapReduce* layer. In general, a spatial query processing in SpatialHadoop consists of four steps [8–10]: (1) *Preprocessing*, where the data is partitioned according to a specific spatial index (partitioning), generating a set of partitions or cells (indexing). (2) *Pruning*, when the query is issued, where the master node examines all partitions and prunes (by a *filter function*) those ones that are guaranteed not to include any possible result of the spatial query. (3) *Local Spatial Query Processing*, where a local spatial query processing is performed on each non-pruned partition in parallel on different machines. And finally, (4) *Global Processing*, where the results are collected from all machines in the previous step and the final result of the concerned spatial query is computed. A *combine* function can be applied in order to decrease the volume of data that is sent from the *map* task. The *reduce* function can be omitted when the results from the *map* phase are final.

3.3 Partitioning Technique Based on Voronoi Diagrams

For the sake of brevity, let $\mathcal{R} = \{r_0, r_1, \cdots, r_{r-1}\}$ be a set of r distinct points in the plane; these points can be called generators or *pivots*. We define the *Voronoi Diagram* of $\mathcal{R}$ as the subdivision of the plane into r cells, one for each pivot in $\mathcal{R}$, with the property that a point p lies in the cell corresponding to a pivot r_i if and only if $dist(p, r_i) < dist(p, r_j)$ for each $r_j \in \mathcal{R}$ with $j \neq i$. We can denote the Voronoi Diagram generated by $\mathcal{R}$ as $VD(\mathcal{R})$. The cell of $VD(\mathcal{R})$ that corresponds to a pivot r_i is called the Voronoi Cell of r_i and is denoted by $VC(r_i)$. The Voronoi Diagram has also the following property: $VD(\mathcal{R}) = \bigcup_{i=0}^{r-1} VC(r_i)$ and $\bigcap_{i=0}^{r-1} VC(r_i) = \emptyset$.

According to [12], given a dataset $\mathbb{P}$, the main idea of *Voronoi-Diagram based partitioning* technique is to select a set $\mathcal{R}$ of points (which may not necessarily belong to $\mathbb{P}$) as *pivots*, and then split the points of $\mathbb{P}$ into $|\mathcal{R}|$ disjoint partitions, where each point is assigned to the partition of its closest pivot r_i. In the case of multiple pivots that are closest to a particular point, then that point is assigned to the partition with the smallest number of points. In this way, the whole data space is split into $|\mathcal{R}|$ disjoint Voronoi Cells. Let $\mathcal{R}$ be the set of pivots selected, $\forall r_i \in \mathcal{R}$, $\mathcal{P}_i^{\mathbb{P}}$ denotes the set of points from $\mathbb{P}$ that has r_i as its closest pivot. In addition, we denote $U(\mathcal{P}_i^{\mathbb{P}})$ and $L(\mathcal{P}_i^{\mathbb{P}})$ as the maximum and minimum distance from the pivot r_i to the points of $\mathcal{P}_i^{\mathbb{P}}$, respectively. That is, $U(\mathcal{P}_i^{\mathbb{P}}) = \max\{dist(p, r_i) : \forall p \in \mathcal{P}_i^{\mathbb{P}}\}$ and $L(\mathcal{P}_i^{\mathbb{P}}) = \min\{dist(p, r_i) : \forall p \in \mathcal{P}_i^{\mathbb{P}}\}$.

4 Voronoi-Diagram Based Partitioning Technique in SpatialHadoop

In SpatialHadoop, the *Partitioning* phase of the indexing algorithm runs in three steps [1]. The first step computes the number of desired partitions x based on file size and HDFS block capacity, which are both fixed for all partitioning techniques. The second step reads a random sample (*Sampling*), with a sampling ratio ρ, from the input file and uses this sample to partition the space (*Space subdivision*) into x cells/partitions, such that the number of sample points in each cell is at most $\lfloor s/x \rfloor$, where s is the sample size. Finally, the third step partitions the file by assigning each point to one or more cells (*Indexing*). Actually, SpatialHadoop supports seven spatial partitioning techniques: Grid, Quadtree, STR, STR+, k-d tree, Z-Curve and Hilbert-Curve.

Similarly, to include into SpatialHadoop the new partitioning technique based on Voronoi-Diagram, we have implemented the following steps: (1) Initially, SpatialHadoop provides a random sample, $\mathcal{S}$, from a dataset $\mathbb{P}$ and the values of the parameters x and $s = |\mathcal{S}|$ (*Sampling*). (2) A set $\mathcal{R}$ of *pivots* is obtained from the random sample $\mathcal{S}$ (*Space subdivision*), using some pivot selection technique such as *random selection* or *k-means* algorithm as described in [12]. For the former, $\lfloor s/x \rfloor$ random sets of pivots are generated and the set with the largest sum of distances between each pair of pivots is chosen. For the latter, an standard k-means algorithm is initialized using a random set of x pivots from the random sample $\mathcal{S}$ and a threshold distance is used as the convergence criterion of the algorithm to reduce partitioning time, especially when a larger number of elements is partitioned. (3) Finally, the points are assigned to their closest pivot $r_i \in \mathcal{R}$ (*Indexing*) and some properties of the pivot are calculated, such as the number of elements, the minimum bounding rectangle *MBR*, $U(\mathcal{P}_i^{\mathbb{P}})$ and $L(\mathcal{P}_i^{\mathbb{P}})$.

5 DJQ MapReduce Algorithms in SpatialHadoop

In this section, we first present a new MapReduce algorithm for kNNJQ in SpatialHadoop, and next, an existing kCPQ MapReduce algorithm in SpatialHadoop is briefly reviewed and improved by Voronoi-Diagram based partitioning.

5.1 kNNJQ MapReduce Algorithm in SpatialHadoop

From the definition of kNNJQ, we can observe that it can be formulated on the basis of kNNQ. In [8], a kNNQ operation on SpatialHadoop was presented. The proposed kNNQ MapReduce algorithm is composed of the three steps: the *initial answer*, the *correctness check* and the *answer refinement*. Keeping this in mind, to develop a kNNJQ MapReduce algorithm in SpatialHadoop, we have followed the kNNJQ algorithm presented in [13]. The proposed kNNJQ algorithm in [13], on two datasets $\mathbb{P}$ and $\mathbb{Q}$, consists of a series of phases of MapReduce jobs: *information distribution* phase, *primitive computation* phase, *update lists* phase and *unify lists* phase. In the *information distribution* phase, a uniform partitioning of the dataset $\mathbb{Q}$ is made and the number of elements from $\mathbb{P}$ that are inside the partitions of $\mathbb{Q}$ are counted. Then, in the *primitive computation* phase, an initial response is provided by calculating the kNNQ for each point p_i of $\mathbb{P}$ with the points of $\mathbb{Q}$ of the partition in which p_i is located. Once this phase is completed, it is necessary to refine these initial kNN lists for each point of $\mathbb{P}$, if there have been found less than k neighbors, or if there are nearby cells that overlap with the distance to each k-th nearest neighbor. All this refinement is done in the *update lists* phase where new non final kNN lists are obtained. Finally, in the *unify lists* phase, the merge of the all the kNN lists resulting from previous phases is performed, obtaining the final answer.

To adapt and implement the previous kNNJQ MapReduce algorithm in SpatialHadoop, we have to carry out several extensions and improvements that are the following: (1) The *information distribution* phase is implemented using the indexing methods provided by SpatialHadoop, allowing us to use non-uniform partitions such as STR, Quadtree, Hilbert, etc. with the different improvements and particularities that they can offer. (2) The *information distribution* phase is performed only once for each dataset and is reused for further kNNJ queries. (3) SpatialHadoop indices are used in each of these phases to accelerate the processing of the partitions. (4) An implementation of new kNNQ based on a plane-sweep algorithm is carried out, which reduces the number of operations and calculations obtaining a higher performance join operation. (5) Finally, a new repartitioning phase is added as a first step to speed up the algorithm. This new phase uses Grid or Quadtree partitioning so as to split the largest partitions in smaller ones, dealing with skew problems and getting smaller tasks.

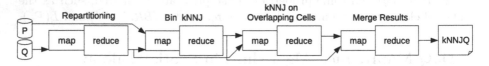

Fig. 1. Overview of the kNNJQ MapReduce algorithm in SpatialHadoop.

Figure 1 shows the phases of the proposed kNNJQ MapReduce algorithm in SpatialHadoop: *Repartitioning, Bin kNNJ, kNNJ on Overlapping Cells* and *Merge Results*. First phase, called *Repartitioning*, uses an existing partitioning technique, e.g. Grid or Quadtree, to subdivide the largest partitions from dataset $\mathbb{Q}$ and saves the information for further use in subsequent phases. Then in the *Bin kNNJ* phase (*information distribution* and *primitive computation* in [13]), a Bin-Spatial Join of the input datasets, in which the join operand is the kNNQ, is accomplished. In the *map* function of the *Bin kNNJ* phase, each point of $\mathbb{P}$ is combined with the partition in which it is located in the dataset $\mathbb{Q}$, so that in the *reduce* function, the plane-sweep kNNQ of that point with the points of $\mathbb{Q}$ in the same partition is executed. The result of this phase is a *kNN list* for each point of $\mathbb{P}$. Then a completeness check is made to find which of the previous kNN lists are not final and therefore it is necessary to continue with their processing. For the *kNNJ on Overlapping Cells* phase (*update lists* in [13]), in the *map* function is checked if the previous kNN lists for each point of $\mathbb{P}$ contain less than k results and also if there are neighboring cells that overlap with the circular range, centered on p and with radius the distance to the current k-th nearest neighbor. These points are then sent together with the calculated neighboring cells to the *reduce* phase where another plane-sweep kNNQ will be performed for each cell. Finally, the *Merge Results* phase (*unify lists* in [13]) consists of collecting the non final kNN lists of the two previous phases, obtaining the final kNNQ results for each point.

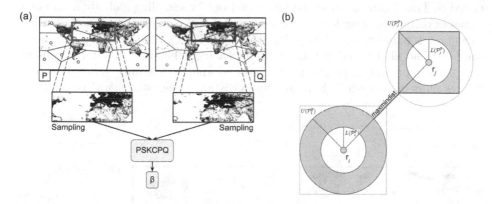

Fig. 2. Using Voronoi-Diagram based partitioning on the *initial partitioning* of the datasets (a) and in the *repartitioning* and *kNNJ on Overlapping Cells* phases (b).

Voronoi-Diagram based partitioning can be incorporated, as shown in Fig. 2(a), into the proposed kNNJQ MapReduce algorithm in two ways: (a) performing the *initial partitioning* of the datasets, and/or (b) subdividing the partitions from $\mathbb{Q}$ in the *repartitioning phase* individually and then using its properties on the *kNNJ on Overlapping Cells* phase. With the first one, we can take advantage of the characteristics of this technique globally, using the defaults parameters given by SpatialHadoop, in the same way that it is done for any built-in query. For the second one, we can accelerate the kNNJQ processing by decomposing the initial partitioning, which can use another partitioning technique, in smaller partitions given a maximum number of elements to solve skew data problems and reduce the number and size of the tasks of the *Bin kNNJ* and *kNNJ on Overlapping Cells*. Furthermore, when calculating the overlapping cells the coordinates of each pivot r_i and the $U(\mathcal{P}_i^{\mathbb{P}})$ and $L(\mathcal{P}_i^{\mathbb{P}})$ values can be used to get greater performance and accuracy than using only the *MBR* of each partition. Figure 2(b) shows that only the shaded part can contain points within the MBR of a $\mathcal{P}_i^{\mathbb{P}}$ partition and therefore there is no overlap with the distance of the current k-th nearest neighbor of p_i.

5.2 kCPQ MapReduce Algorithm in SpatialHadoop

In general, the kCPQ MapReduce algorithm [9,10] in SpatialHadoop consists of a MapReduce job. The *map* function aims to find the kCP between each local pair of partitions from $\mathbb{P}$ and $\mathbb{Q}$ with a plane-sweep kCPQ algorithm and the result is stored in a binary max heap (called *LocalKMaxHeap*). The *reduce* function aims to examine the candidate pairs of points from each *LocalKMax-Heap* and return the final set of the k closest pairs in another binary max heap (called *GlobalKMaxHeap*). To improve this approach, for reducing the number of possible combinations of pairs of partitions, we need to find in advance an upper bound of the distance value of the k-th closest pair of the joined datasets, called β. This β computation can be carried out by sampling globally from both datasets or by sampling locally for an appropriate pair of partitions and, then executing a plane-sweep kCPQ algorithm (PSKCPQ, see Fig. 3(a)) over both samples. The *filter* function takes as input each combination of pairs of cells in which the input set of points are partitioned and the distance value β, and it prunes pairs of cells which have minimum distances (*mindist_mbrs*) larger than β.

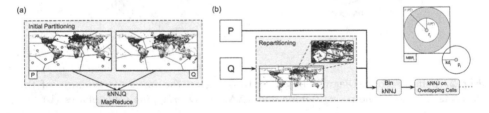

Fig. 3. β computation using Voronoi-Diagram based partitioning by sampling locally from both datasets (a) and partition refinement by its MBR, $U(\mathcal{P}_i^{\mathbb{P}})$ and $L(\mathcal{P}_i^{\mathbb{P}})$ properties and maximum minimum distance calculation (b).

Using Voronoi-Diagram based partitioning, as shown in Fig. 3(a), the kCPQ MapReduce algorithm can be improved by modifying its local β computation and *filter* function. For the former, the most appropriate partitions, where an initial kCPQ is performed, are those whose pivots are closer to each other and have both higher density of points and area of intersection. Figure 3(b) shows that for each partition of this partitioning technique, we have both its MBR and its $U(\mathcal{P}_i^{\mathbb{P}})$ and $L(\mathcal{P}_i^{\mathbb{P}})$ values, allowing to detect areas of the former in which there are no points. Moreover, for the *filter* function a new distance metric can be used, the minimum distance between pivots (*mindist_pivots*) defined as the distance between pivots minus their $U(\mathcal{P}_i^{\mathbb{P}})$ values. Therefore, as shown in

Fig. 3(b), this function prunes pairs of partitions which have maximum minimum distance ($minmaxdist = max\{mindist\_mbrs, mindist\_pivots\}$) larger than β.

6 Experimentation

In this section, we present the most representative results of our experimental evaluation. We have used real-world 2d point datasets to test our DJQ algorithms in SpatialHadoop. We have used datasets from OpenStreetMap[1]: *LAKES* (*L*) which contains 8.4M records (8.6 GB) of boundaries of water areas (polygons), *PARKS* (*P*) which contains 10M records (9.3 GB) of boundaries of parks or green areas (polygons), *ROADS* (*R*) which contains 72M records (24 GB) of roads and streets around the world (line-strings), *BUILDINGS* (*B*) which contains 115M records (26 GB) of boundaries of all buildings (polygons), and *ROAD_NETWORKS* (*RN*) which contains 717M records (137 GB) of road network represented as individual road segments (line-strings) [8]. To create sets of points from these five spatial datasets, we have transformed the MBRs of line-strings into points by taking the center of each MBR. In particular, we have considered the centroid of each polygon to generate individual points for each kind of spatial object. The main performance measure that we have used in our experiments has been the total execution time (i.e. total response time).

All experiments were conducted on a cluster of 12 nodes on an OpenStack environment. Each node has 4 vCPU with 8 GB of main memory running Linux operating systems and Hadoop 2.7.1.2.3. Each node has a capacity of 3 vCores for MapReduce2/YARN use. Finally, we used the latest code available in the repositories of SpatialHadoop[2].

Our first experiment aims to compare our new proposed Voronoi-Diagram based partitioning algorithms, using *k-means* (*Voronoi$_k$*, V_k) and *random selection* (*Voronoi$_R$*, V_R), with the *Quadtree* (Q) built-in partitioning technique which has shown to obtain the best performance results with the different queries present in SpatialHadoop [7–10]. In Fig. 4, the partitioning of different datasets is shown with respect to the execution time, for both the *Space subdivision* and *Indexing* phases. The first conclusion is that the execution times for *Voronoi$_R$* and *Quadtree* grow similarly as the size of the datasets is increased. On the other hand, for *Voronoi$_k$* the increase in execution times is much higher, since a *k-means* algorithm is used in the *Space subdivision* phase. This *k-means* algorithm takes longer times to converge towards a solution as the size of the datasets increases, despite using a threshold value as convergence criterion to accelerate it. Finally, *Voronoi$_R$* presents the fastest execution times, mainly because it consumes the smallest time in the *Indexing* phase of the data, since in the *Space subdivision* phase the times are very similar to those of *Quadtree*. In Table 1, we can observe information of data distribution (points per partition) about the partitioning of *RN* dataset for each technique. On one hand, *Quadtree* presents a higher mean value due to having a slightly lower number of partitions than the

---

[1] Available at http://spatialhadoop.cs.umn.edu/datasets.html.
[2] Available at https://github.com/aseldawy/spatialhadoop2.

Voronoi-Diagram based techniques. On the other hand, $Voronoi_k$ has a much lower standard deviation that allows better handling of data skew problems by having a more proportional distribution.

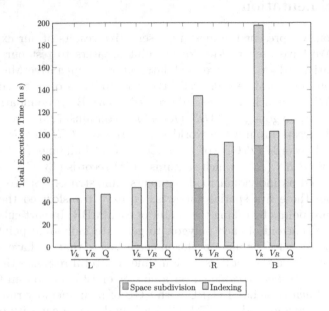

Fig. 4. Partitioning cost (total execution time) per phase, considering different partitioning techniques and datasets.

Table 1. Information of data distribution of RN dataset per partitioning techniques.

	MEAN	MIN	MAX	STDEV
$Voronoi_k$	1400486	19914	3684694	623909
$Voronoi_R$	1400486	42921	10225199	1092866
$Quadtree$	1667555	218	4275451	1130277

In Fig. 5, left chart, the kCPQ for a fixed $k = 100$ and for real spatial datasets ($L \times P$, $P \times R$, $R \times B$ and $B \times RN$) is shown with respect to the execution time for the different partitioning techniques ($Voronoi_k$, $Voronoi_R$ and $Quadtree$). We can observe that the execution times in all partitioning techniques grow almost linearly as the size of the datasets is increased. For kCPQ, the best partitioning technique is $Quadtree$, which is approximately 18% faster than $Voronoi_k$. Moreover, for the combinations of $L \times P$ and $P \times R$, $Voronoi_k$ is slightly faster than $Quadtree$ (e.g. for $P \times R$ $Voronoi_k$ is just 2 s faster than Quadtree), but for the combinations of the biggest datasets ($R \times B$ and $B \times RN$) $Quadtree$ is the fastest, e.g. for $B \times RN$ $Quadtree$ is 18% (278 s) faster than

Voronoi$_k$. That is, *Voronoi$_k$* exhibits smaller runtime values for smaller dataset sizes, since it produces a slightly larger number of partitions (e.g. 24 vs 23 partition pairs for $L \times P$) that are better distributed in tasks for this cluster of nodes. But for big dataset sizes, *Quadtree* is the fastest for kCPQ, since it minimizes the number of partitions for each dataset and the number of the ones that overlap between each other. Finally *Voronoi$_R$* shows the worst results, noting that the indexing time of *Voronoi$_k$* is much higher. Figure 5, right chart, shows the effect of increasing the k value for the combination of the biggest datasets ($BUILDINGS \times ROAD\_NETWORKS$) for kCPQ. This experiment shows that the total execution time grows slowly as the number of results to be obtained (k) increases. All partitioning techniques report very stable execution times, even for large k values (e.g. $k = 10^5$), although, we can see that *Quadtree* still has the lowest execution times.

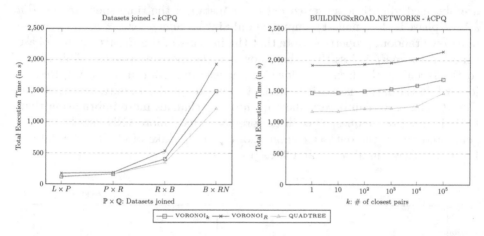

Fig. 5. Total execution time of kCPQ, considering different partitioning techniques (left) and varying the k values (right).

The last experiment compares the three repartitioning techniques *Voronoi$_k$*, *Voronoi$_R$* and *Quadtree* for the kNNJQ in SpatialHadoop, based on the execution time, of each of the phases. In Fig. 6, left chart, the kNNJQ for the combination of different datasets ($L \times P$, $L \times R$, $L \times B$ and $L \times RN$) is shown for each repartitioning technique and for a fixed $k = 10$. We can observe that the *Voronoi$_k$* repartitioning technique exhibits the best performance. Moreover, *Quadtree* is much slower, especially in the *kNNJ on Overlapping Cells* phase. This is due to the fact that with both *Voronoi* techniques, every point of $\mathbb{P}$ is assigned to $\mathbb{Q}$ partition that contains at least k elements, so after the *Bin kNNJ* phase there are more final kNN lists and therefore the processing time of the next phase is reduced. Note that the *kNNJ on Overlapping Cells* phase is usually more expensive if the number of final kNN lists, from the previous phase, is lower, because when the range query on the nearby cells is executed, there is a large growth of the number of partitions to search for kNN candidates. Moreover, this same behaviour can be observed in Fig. 6, right chart, where as the k value is increased for the combination of the datasets, $LAKES \times PARKS$, the execution time of the *kNNJ on Overlapping Cells* phase is also higher. Continuing with the left chart of Fig. 6, the differences in execution time between the three repartition techniques are reduced with the combination of the larger dataset, $L \times RN$, mainly because the *Quadtree* technique returns more final kNN lists. As the volume and size of $\mathbb{Q}$ are much greater, the volume of points of $\mathbb{P}$ that fall into partitions of $\mathbb{Q}$ is also greater, obtaining final results that reduce the execution time of the algorithm. Another conclusion that can be obtained from the results is that *Quadtree* is the fastest while $Voronoi_k$ is the slowest for the *Repartitioning* phase. This is due to the use of an algorithm based on k-means that makes the time increase considerably larger, in the same way to the *Indexing* time in previous experiment. However, thanks to this processing, the best results are obtained, due to less skewed data (for instance, the time spent in the *Bin kNNJ* phase is the smallest), improved only by $Voronoi_R$ for $L \times R$ and because of its own random properties. Note that the increase of the *Repartitioning* phase time for $Voronoi_k$ is less than that shown in the indexing process. This is due to the fact that the former is done within each partition using a MapReduce job, while the latter is carried out in the master node. Finally, in the *Merge Results* phase, we can observe how *Quadtree* exchanges more information than both *Voronoi* techniques, since in the previous phase more kNN lists have been generated for all the dataset combinations. For the sake of clarity, the data of Fig. 6 are shown in Tables 2 and 3, respectively.

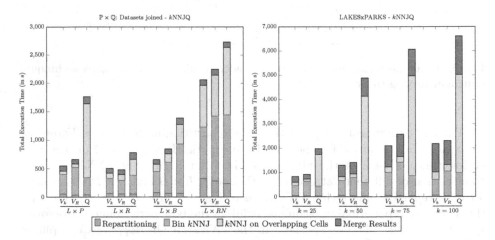

Fig. 6. Total execution time of kNNJQ, considering different partitioning techniques (left) and varying the k values (right).

Table 2. kNNJQ cost (in sec), varying the combination of datasets and considering different partitioning techniques.

	$L \times P$			$L \times R$			$L \times B$			$L \times RN$		
	V_k	V_R	Q	V_k	V_R	Q	V_k	V_R	Q	V_k	V_R	Q
Repartitioning	53	34	38	61	53	50	77	63	65	325	282	235
Bin kNNJ	347	488	303	266	241	330	372	548	870	905	1142	1210
kNNJ on Over.	59	61	1299	92	101	284	130	150	342	737	721	1192
Merge Results	90	78	121	85	83	116	80	86	113	98	103	95
Total	549	661	1761	504	478	780	659	847	1390	2065	2248	2732

Table 3. kNNJQ cost (in sec) for the combination of the datasets, $LAKES \times PARKS$, considering different partitioning techniques and varying the k values.

	$k = 25$			$k = 50$			$k = 75$			$k = 100$		
	V_k	V_R	Q	V_k	V_R	Q	V_k	V_R	Q	V_k	V_R	Q
Repartitioning	49	39	36	58	35	37	66	43	38	61	35	35
Bin kNNJ	413	601	406	613	757	562	940	1380	832	657	1019	958
kNNJ on Over.	142	97	1303	165	159	3546	232	238	4105	306	268	4033
Merge Results	229	188	233	466	465	742	865	913	1092	1162	981	1590
Total	833	925	1978	1302	1416	4887	2103	2574	6067	2186	2303	6616

The main conclusions extracted for this set of experiments on the proposed Voronoi-Diagram based partitioning techniques are the following: (1) the partitioning execution times for $Voronoi_R$ are the smallest and grow almost linearly as the size of the datasets, while, for $Voronoi_k$, this increment is much higher duc to its k-means based pivot selection algorithm. (2) $Quadtree$ outperforms all other techniques with respect to the execution time for the kCPQ (it follows a global query processing schema), although both $Voronoi$ techniques present only slightly lower performance, especially, for the smaller datasets combinations. (3) For kNNJQ (it follows a multiple nearest neighbor query processing schema), both Voronoi-Diagram partitioning techniques are faster than $Quadtree$, because they deal better with data skew and they get more final results in the Bin $kNNJ$ phase. And (4), being the $Repartitioning$ phase a MapReduce job, it is worth using $Voronoi_k$ instead of $Voronoi_R$, since the loss of time in the k-means pivot selection is compensated by the gain in performance in later phases.

7 Conclusions and Future Work

Distance Join Queries (DJQs) are important and common operations used in numerous spatial applications. DJQs are costly operations, since they combine joins with distance-based search. and therefore, the execution of DJQs efficiently is a challenging task. For this reason, in this paper, a new partitioning technique based on Voronoi Diagrams in SpatialHadoop is designed and implemented. A new kNNJQ algorithm and an improved kCPQ MapReduce algorithm, using this new partitioning mechanism, with two pivot selection algorithms, *random selection* (V_R) and k-*means* (V_k), have also been proposed. The execution of a set of experiments has demonstrated that both algorithms using Voronoi-Diagram based partitioning have shown good results in terms of running times, compared to other spatial partitioning techniques implemented already in SpatialHadoop. For kCPQ, *Quadtree* shows slightly better performance than V_k and V_R. However, in the case of kNNJQ, the use of these new techniques to repartition the data leads to a great improvement in performance, especially through the use of k-*means*. Our proposal is a good foundation for the development of further improvements, such as implementing the k-*means* pivot selection algorithm in MapReduce in order to speed it up. Other future work might include improvements of our kNNJQ MapReduce algorithm, exploiting properties of Voronoi-Diagram based partitioning, similarly to how these were exploited in [12] and the comparison with other MapReduce algorithms.

References

1. Aji, A., Vo, H., Wang, F.: Effective spatial data partitioning for scalable query processing. CoRR abs/1509.00910 (2015)
2. Akdogan, A., Demiryurek, U., Kashani, F.B., Shahabi, C.: Voronoi-based geospatial query processing with MapReduce. In: CloudCom Conference, pp. 9–16 (2010)
3. Böhm, C., Krebs, F.: The k-nearest neighbour join: turbo charging the KDD process. Knowl. Inf. Syst. **6**(6), 728–749 (2004)
4. Corral, A., Manolopoulos, Y., Theodoridis, Y., Vassilakopoulos, M.: Closest pair queries in spatial databases. In: SIGMOD Conference, pp. 189–200 (2000)
5. Corral, A., Manolopoulos, Y., Theodoridis, Y., Vassilakopoulos, M.: Algorithms for processing k-closest-pair queries in spatial databases. Data Knowl. Eng. **49**(1), 67–104 (2004)
6. Dean, J., Ghemawat, S.: MapReduce: simplified data processing on large clusters. In: OSDI Conference, pp. 137–150 (2004)
7. Eldawy, A., Alarabi, L., Mokbel, M.F.: Spatial partitioning techniques in spatial hadoop. PVLDB **8**(12), 1602–1613 (2015)
8. Eldawy, A., Mokbel, M.F.: SpatialHadoop: a MapReduce framework for spatial data. In: ICDE Conference, pp. 1352–1363 (2015)
9. García-García, F., Corral, A., Iribarne, L., Vassilakopoulos, M., Manolopoulos, Y.: Enhancing SpatialHadoop with closest pair queries. In: Pokorný, J., Ivanović, M., Thalheim, B., Šaloun, P. (eds.) ADBIS 2016. LNCS, vol. 9809, pp. 212–225. Springer, Cham (2016). https://doi.org/10.1007/978-3-319-44039-2_15
10. García-García, F., Corral, A., Iribarne, L., Vassilakopoulos, M., Manolopoulos, Y.: Efficient large-scale distance-based join queries in SpatialHadoop. GeoInformatica **22**(2), 171–209 (2018)
11. Kim, W., Kim, Y., Shim, K.: Parallel computation of k-nearest neighbor joins using MapReduce. In: Big Data Conference, pp. 696–705 (2016)
12. Lu, W., Shen, Y., Chen, S., Ooi, B.C.: Efficient processing of k nearest neighbor joins using MapReduce. PVLDB **5**(10), 1016–1027 (2012)

13. Nodarakis, N., Pitoura, E., Sioutas, S., Tsakalidis, A., Tsoumakos, D., Tzimas, G.: kdANN+: a rapid AkNN classifier for big data. In: Hameurlain, A., Küng, J., Wagner, R., Decker, H., Lhotska, L., Link, S. (eds.) Transactions on Large-Scale Data- and Knowledge-Centered Systems XXIV. LNCS, vol. 9510, pp. 139–168. Springer, Heidelberg (2016). https://doi.org/10.1007/978-3-662-49214-7_5
14. Song, G., Rochas, J., Beze, L.E., Huet, F., Magoulès, F.: K nearest neighbour joins for big data on mapreduce: a theoretical and experimental analysis. IEEE Trans. Knowl. Data Eng. **28**(9), 2376–2392 (2016)
15. Vo, H., Aji, A., Wang, F.: SATO: a spatial data partitioning framework for scalable query processing. In: SIGSPATIAL Conference, pp. 545–548 (2014)
16. Zhang, C., Li, F., Jestes, J.: Efficient parallel kNN joins for large data in MapReduce. In: EDBT Conference, pp. 38–49 (2012)

Graph Pattern Matching Preserving Label-Repetition Constraints

Houari Mahfoud[(✉)] [ID]

LRIT Laboratory, Abou-Bekr Belkaid University, Tlemcen, Algeria
houari.mahfoud@gmail.com

Abstract. Graph pattern matching is a routine process for a wide variety of applications such as social network analysis. It is typically defined in terms of subgraph isomorphism which is NP-COMPLETE. To lower its complexity, many extensions of graph simulation have been proposed which focus on some topological constraints of pattern graphs that can be preserved in polynomial-time over data graphs. We discuss the satisfaction of a new topological constraint, called *Label-Repetition constraint*. To the best of our knowledge, existing polynomial approaches fail to preserve this constraint, and moreover, one can adopt only subgraph isomorphism for this end which is cost-prohibitive. We present first a necessary and sufficient condition that a data subgraph must satisfy to preserve the *Label-Repetition constraints* of the pattern graph. Furthermore, we define matching based on a notion of *triple simulation*, an extension of graph simulation by considering the new topological constraint. We show that with this extension, graph pattern matching can be performed in polynomial-time, by providing such an algorithm. We extend our solution to deal with edges that have counting quantifiers of the form "$\geq p$".

Keywords: Subgraph isomorphism · Triple simulation
Label-Repetition constraint

1 Introduction

Modeling data with graphs is one of the most active topics in the database community these days. This model has recently gained wide applicability in numerous domains that find the relational model too restrictive, such as social networks [6], biological networks, Semantic Web, crime detection networks and many others. Indeed, it is less complex and also most natural for users to reason about an increasing number of popular datasets, such as the underlying networks of Twitter, Facebook, or LinkedIn, within a graph paradigm. In emerging applications such as social networks, edges of data graphs (resp. pattern graphs) can be typed [7] to denote various relationships such as marriage, friendship, recommendation, co-membership, etc. Moreover, pattern graphs can define multi-labeled vertices [18] to look, e.g., for persons with different possible profiles.

Given a data graph G and a pattern graph Q, the problem of *graph pattern matching* is to find all subgraphs of G that satisfy both the labeling properties

© Springer Nature Switzerland AG 2018
E. H. Abdelwahed et al. (Eds.): MEDI 2018, LNCS 11163, pp. 268–281, 2018.
https://doi.org/10.1007/978-3-030-00856-7_17

and topological constraints carried by Q. Matching here is expressed in terms of subgraph isomorphism which consists to find all subgraphs of G that are *isomorphic* to Q. Graph pattern matching via subgraph isomorphism is an NP-COMPLETE problem as there are possibly an exponential number of subgraphs in G that match Q. To tackle this NP-COMPLETENESS, graph simulation has been adopted for graph pattern matching [17] to preserve child-relationships only. Unlike subgraph isomorphism which requires a *bijective* mapping function from pattern nodes to data nodes, graph simulation is defined by a simple *binary* relation which can be computed in quadratic time. A cubic-time extension of graph simulation, called *strong simulation*, has been proposed [14] by enforcing two additional conditions: *duality* to preserve child and parent relationships of the pattern graph; and *locality* to overcome excessive matching by considering only subgraphs that have radius bounded by the diameter of the pattern graph. Nonetheless, strong simulation may return incorrect matches as shown below.

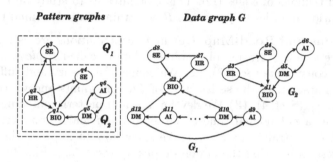

Fig. 1. Querying a recommendation network.

Example 1. Consider the real-life example taken from [14]. A headhunter (**HR**) wants to find a biologist (**BIO**) to help a group of software engineers (**SE**) analyze genetic data. To do this, she uses the network G depicted in Fig. 1. In G, nodes denote persons with different profiles, and edges indicate recommendations between these persons. The cycle between the nodes d_9 and d_{12} contains many **DM** (data mining specialist) that are all connected to the **BIO** represented by the node d_2. The biologist **BIO** to find is specified with the pattern graph Q_1 of Fig. 1. Intuitively, the **BIO** has to be recommended by: (a) an **HR** person since the headhunter trusts the judgment of a person with the same occupation; (b) at least two **SE** that are recommended by the same **HR** person (to increase incredibility), that is, the **BIO** has a strong experience by working with different **SE**s; and (c) a **DM**, as data mining techniques are required for the job. Moreover, there is an artificial intelligence expert (**AI**) who recommends the **DM** and is recommended by a **DM**. When strong simulation is adopted, the subgraph G_2 of G is returned as the only match of Q_1 in G. However, the **BIO** of this match, represented by the node d_1, is recommended by only one **SE**, which is incorrect w.r.t Q_1. To make search less restrictive, one can look for a **BIO** with the same constraints specified by Q_1 excepting that this **BIO** can be recommended by only one **SE**. This search is specified by the pattern graph Q_2 of the same figure. In this case, strong simulation returns G_2 as the only match of Q_2 in G, which is a correct. Notice however that strong simulation does not make difference between Q_1 and Q_2 since they are matched over G to the same match result.

The pattern graph Q_1 illustrates a new kind of topology called *Label-Repetition* (*LR*) constraint: nodes that have the same label but not necessarily the same set of children and parents (see Example 5). Graph simulation [17] and its counterparts [8,14] fail to preserve this constraint in the sense that some nodes of the pattern query, that have the same label l and supposed to be different, may be matched to only one data node that is labeled with l. One can adopt subgraph isomorphism to preserve *LR* constraints during graph pattern matching. The challenge is that subgraph isomorphism is NP-COMPLETE and real-life data graphs are often big, e.g., the social graph of Facebook has billions of nodes and trillions of edges [12]. This motivates us to study an extension of graph simulation in order to preserve *LR* constraints in polynomial-time.

Contributions and Road-Map. Our main contributions are as follows:[1] **(1)** We introduce a new extension of graph simulation, called *triple simulation*, to preserve *LR* constraints (Sect. 3). **(2)** We define a necessary and sufficient condition that characterizes the satisfaction of *LR* constraints and we compute its time complexity (Sect. 4). **(3)** We develop a graph pattern matching algorithm which requires a polynomial time to preserve *Child* and *Parent* relationships, as well as *LR* constraints (Sect. 5.1). We show how to improve the quality of our match results by using the notion of locality (Sect. 5.2). Finally, we discuss an extension of our approach to deal with simple counting quantifiers on edge (Sect. 6).

Related Work. We categorize related work as follows.

Polynomial-time graph pattern matching: Traditional matching is by subgraph isomorphism, which is NP-Complete [4] and found often too restrictive to capture sensible matches [8]. To loosen the restriction, one direction is to adopt *graph simulation* [17]. Matching based on graph simulation preserves only child relationships of the pattern graphs, which makes it useful for some applications like Web sites classification [2]. In other applications however, e.g. social network analysis, the result of such matching may have a structure drastically different from that of the pattern graph, and often very large to analysis and understand. To handle this, *strong simulation* is proposed [14] to capture child and parent relationships (notion of *duality*), and to make match results bounded by the diameter of the underlying pattern graph (notion of *locality*). This approach has proven efficient since it is in PTIME. However, it can not preserve *LR* constraints.

Quantified pattern graphs: Closer to our work is [11] that introduces *quantified pattern graphs* (**QGPs**), an extension of pattern graphs by supporting simple

---

[1] Proofs and other details are available in the full version [16].

counting quantifiers on edges. A **QGP** naturally expresses numeric and ratio aggregates, and negation besides existential and universal quantification. Notice that any ratio aggregate can be translated into numeric aggregate. They show that quantified matching (based on subgraph isomorphism) is NP-Complete in the absence of negation and DP-Complete for general **QGPs**.

2 Background

We review here some graph pattern matching approaches.

Graphs. A *directed graph* (or simply a *graph*) is defined with $G(V, E, \lambda)$ where: (1) V is a finite set of nodes; (2) $E \subseteq V \times V$ is a finite set of edges in which (u, u') denotes an edge from nodes u to u'; and (3) λ is a labeling function that maps each node $u \in V$ to a label $\lambda(u)$ in a set $\sum(G)$ of labels. We simply denote G as (V, E) when it is clear from the context.

In this paper, both data graphs and pattern graphs are specified with the previous graph structure. Moreover, we assume that pattern graphs are connected, as a common practice.

Distance and Diameter [14]. The *distance* from nodes n to n' in a graph G, denoted by $dist(n, n')$, is the length of the shortest undirected path from n to n' in G. The *diameter* of a connected graph G, denoted by d_G, is the longest shortest distance of all pairs of nodes in G, that is, $d_G = max(dis(n, n'))$ for all nodes n, n' in G.

Graph Pattern Matching. A data graph $G(V, E, \lambda)$ may match a pattern graph $Q(V_Q, E_Q, \lambda_Q)$ via different methods.

(A) Subgraph isomorphism: A subgraph $G_s(V_s, E_s, \lambda_s)$ of G matches Q via *subgraph isomorphism*, denoted $G_s \prec_{iso} Q$, if there exists a *bijective function* $f : V_Q \rightarrow V_s$ s.t.: *(1)* for each node $n \in V_Q$, $\lambda_Q(n) = \lambda_s(f(n))$; and *(2)* for each edge $(n, n') \in E_Q$, there exists an edge $(f(n), f(n')) \in E_s$.

(B) Graph simulation: G matches Q via *graph simulation* [17], denoted $Q \prec G$, if there exists a *binary match relation* $S \subseteq V_Q \times V$ s.t.: *(1)* For each $(u, v) \in S$, $\lambda_Q(u) = \lambda(v)$; and *(2)* For each node $u \in V_Q$, there exists a node $v \in V$ where: *(a)* $(u, v) \in S$; and *(b)* for each edge $(u, u') \in E_Q$, there exists an edge $(v, v') \in E$ with $(u', v') \in S$.

Intuitively, graph simulation preserves only child relationships.

(C) Dual simulation: G matches Q via *dual simulation* [14], denoted $Q \prec_D G$, if there exists a *binary match relation* $S_D \subseteq V_Q \times V$ s.t.: *(1)* For each $(u, v) \in S_D$, $\lambda_Q(u) - \lambda(v)$; and *(2)* for each node $u \in V_Q$, there exists a node $v \in V$ where: *(a)* $(u, v) \in S_D$; *(b)* for each edge $(u, u') \in E_Q$, there exists an edge $(v, v') \in E$ with $(u', v') \in S_D$; and moreover *(c)* for each edge $(u', u) \in E_Q$, there exists an edge $(v', v) \in E$ with $(u', v') \in S_D$.

Dual simulation enhances graph simulation by imposing the condition (c) in order to preserve both child and parent relationships. As mentioned in [14], the graph pattern matching via graph simulation (resp. dual simulation) is to find the *maximum* match relation S (resp. S_D). Ma et al. [14] show that graph/dual simulation may do excessive matching of pattern graphs which makes the graph result very large and difficult to understand and analysis. For this reason, they propose *strong simulation*, an extension of dual simulation by imposing the notion of *locality*. This notion requires that each subgraph of the final match result must have a radius bounded by the diameter of the pattern graph.

(D) Strong simulation: G matches Q via *strong simulation*, denoted $Q \prec_D^L G$, if there exists a node $v \in V$ and a subgraph G_s of G centered at v s.t.:

1. The radius of G_s is bounded by d_Q, i.e., for each node v' in G_s, $dist(v, v') \leq d_Q$;
2. $Q \prec_D G_s$ with the maximum match relation S_D.

Informally, rather than matching the whole data graph G over Q we extract, for each node $n \in V$, a subgraph G_s of G centered at n and which has a radius equals to d_Q. Then, we match G_s over Q via dual simulation. In this way, the match result will be composed of subgraphs of reasonable size that satisfy both child and parent relationships of Q.

Match Results. *(A)* When $Q \prec_{iso} G$ then the *match result* $\mathcal{M}_{iso}(Q, G)$ is the set of all subgraphs of G that are isomorphic to Q. *(B)* When $Q \prec G$ with the maximum match relation S then the *match result* $\mathcal{M}(Q, G)$ w.r.t S is each subgraph $G(V_s, E_s)$ of G in which: (1) a node $n \in V_s$ iff it is in S; and (2) an edge $(v, v') \in E_s$ iff there exists an edge $(u, u') \in E_Q$ with $(u, v) \in S$ and $(u', v') \in S$. *(C)* When $Q \prec_D G$ then the *match result* $\mathcal{M}_D(Q, G)$ is defined similarly to graph simulation but w.r.t the maximum match relation S_D. *(D)* When $Q \prec_D^L G$ then the *match result* $\mathcal{M}_D^L(Q, G)$ is defined with $\bigcup_i \mathcal{M}_D(Q, G_i)$ where each G_i is a subgraph of G that satisfies the conditions of strong simulation.

Potential Matches. Given a data graph $G(V, E, \lambda)$ and a pattern graph $Q(V_Q, E_Q, \lambda_Q)$. For any node $u \in V_Q$, we call *potential match* each node $v \in V$ that has the same label as u (i.e. $\lambda_Q(u) = \lambda(v)$). Moreover, SIM$(u)$ refers to the set of all potential matches of u in G.

Example 2. Consider the data graph G and the pattern graph Q_2 of Fig. 1. With dual simulation, both G_1 and G_2 are found as matches of Q_2 in G. Remark that the cycle of two nodes **AI** and **DM** in Q_2 is matched with the long cycle $d_9 \rightarrow \cdots \rightarrow d_{12} \rightarrow d_9$ in G_2, which may be hard to analysis. With the notion of locality, strong simulation returns G_1 as the only match of G over Q_2 and ignores G_2 since it represents an excessive matching.

3   Triple Simulation

We start first by presenting a new topological constraint that one would like to preserve during graph pattern matching. We then define a new extension of graph simulation by imposing this constraint. We compare our extension with only strong simulation [14] since this is the more expressive graph pattern matching approach that requires a polynomial-time. Notice that another polynomial-time approach exists [8], called *bounded simulation*, which imposes constraints on edges. However, our extension concerns nodes constraints.

Given a data graph G and consider the pattern graphs $Q_1 = a \rightarrow b$ and $Q_2 = b \leftarrow a \rightarrow b$. It is obvious that these two patterns are not equivalent: Q_1 requires that each node v in G that matches a must have **at least one** child node labeled with b, however, Q_2 requires that v must have **at least two** child nodes labeled with b. Strong simulation fails to make this difference and considers Q_1 and Q_2 as equivalent patterns (as illustrated by Example 1).

Definition 1. *Given a data graph $G(V,E)$ and a pattern graph $Q(V_Q, E_Q)$. A Label-Repetition (**LR**) constraint defined over a node $u \in V_Q$ with label l specifies that: (1) there is a maximum subset $C_u = \{u_1, \ldots, u_K\}$ $(K \geq 2)$ of children (resp. parents) of u that are all labeled with l; and (2) any match v of u in G must have a subset $C_v = \{v_1, \ldots, v_K\}$ of children (resp. parents) ordered in such a way that allows to match each v_i to a child u_i of u.*

Intuitively, a *LR* constraint concerns a repetition of some label either among children or among parents of some node in Q. If children (resp. parents) of each node in Q have distinct labels, then Q is defined with only child and parent relationships and, thus, can be matched correctly via strong simulation. The limitation of this latter is observed when some children (resp. parents) of the same node are defined with the same label.

Example 3. Consider the pattern graph Q_1 of Fig. 1. There is an *LR* constraint defined over the node q_2 with label **SE**. It specifies that each node of the data graph that matches q_2 must have at least two children labeled **SE** s.t. one of them matches the node q_3 and the other one matches the node q_4.

We propose next a new extension of graph simulation in order to satisfy *LR* constraints.

Definition 2. *A data graph $G(V, E, \lambda)$ matches a pattern graph $Q(V_Q, E_Q, \lambda_Q)$ via triple simulation, denoted by $Q \prec_T G$, if there exists a binary match relation $S_T \subseteq V_Q \times V$ s.t.:*

- *For each $(u, v) \in S_T$, $\lambda_Q(u) = \lambda(v)$.*
- *For each $u \in V_Q$ there exists $(u, v) \in S_T$.*
- *For each $(u, v) \in S_T$ and for all edges $(u, u_1), \ldots, (u, u_n) \in E_Q$, there exists **at least n distinct children** $v_1, \ldots, v_n$ of v in G s.t.: $(u_1, v_1), \ldots, (u_n, v_n) \in S_T$.*
- *For each $(u, v) \in S_T$ and for all edges $(u_1, u), \ldots, (u_n, u) \in E_Q$, there exists **at least n distinct parents** $v_1, \ldots, v_n$ of v in G s.t.: $(u_1, v_1), \ldots, (u_n, v_n) \in S_T$.*

$\mathcal{M}_T(Q, G)$ *is the match result that corresponds to the maximum match relation S_T.*[2]

---

[2] This match result can be defined similarly to graph (dual) simulation.

Intuitively, if a node u in Q has n children (resp. parents) then each match v of u in G must have at least n distinct children (resp. parents) s.t. we can match, w.r.t some order, each child (resp. parent) of v to only one child (resp. parent) of u. This new restriction imposed by conditions (3) and (4) prevents matching of distinct children (resp. parents) of some node u in Q to the same node in G, as may be done by strong simulation. Notice that triple simulation preserves also child and parent relationships and not only LR constraints.

Example 4. Consider the data graph G and the pattern graphs Q_1 and Q_2 of Fig. 1. The node q_1 with label **BIO** in Q_1 has two parents, q_3 and q_4, that have the same label **SE**. Remark that d_1 and d_2 are potential matches of q_1 in G. According to triple simulation, d_1 (resp. d_2) must have at least two distinct parents s.t. one can match q_3 and the other one can match q_4. This is not the case since d_1 (resp. d_2) has only one parent labeled **SE**. Thus, we can conclude that no subgraph in G satisfies the LR constraint of Q_1, and then, $\mathcal{M}_T(Q_1, G) = \emptyset$. When triple simulation is adopted for Q_2 over the subgraph G_2, we obtain the following maximum match relation: $S_T = \{(q_1, d_1), (q_2, d_3), (q_4, d_4), (q_5, d_5), (q_6, d_6)\}$. The match result that corresponds to S_T is the whole subgraph G_2, which is correct.

We use **CPL** *relationships* to refer to *Child* and *Parent* relationships (called *duality* properties), as well as relationships based on *LR* constraints. Our motivation is to preserves *CPL* relationships in polynomial-time.

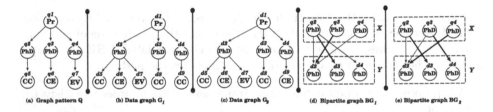

Fig. 2. Problem of preserving LR constraints.

4   Satisfy LR Constraints

We first present the problem of satisfying LR constraints and show that a naive approach may lead for exponential cost. Next, we define a necessary and sufficient condition to satisfy LR constraints and which can be checked in polynomial-time.

Example 5. Consider the graphs depicted in Fig. 2. The pattern graph Q looks for each professor (**Pr**) which has supervised at least three **PhD** thesis in topics related respectively to *Cloud Computing* (**CC**), *Collaborative Editing* (**CE**) and *Electronic Vote* (**EV**). The node d_1 in G_1 is a potential match of q_1. To satisfy the condition (3) of triple simulation (Definition 2), d_1 must have at least three child nodes which is the case, and there must be some order that allows to match each child of d_1 to a child of q_1. However remark that: if we match q_2 with d_2 then we can not have match neither for q_3 nor for q_4; and moreover, if we match q_2 with d_3 then we can match either q_3 with d_2 or q_4 with d_2. Clearly, there is no order over the children d_2, d_3, d_4 of d_1 that allows to match all the children q_2, q_3, q_4 of q_1 in Q. Therefore, the data graph G_1 does not satisfy the LR constraint of Q. The data graph G_2 matches correctly Q: there is an order that allows to match each child of d_1 to a child of q_1, i.e., q_2, q_3, q_4 can be matched respectively with d_3, d_4, d_2. Thus, the LR constraint of Q is satisfied over G_2.

Given the aboves, one can think that checking LR constraints may lead to exponential cost (since we must consider all orders over some data nodes). However, we show later that this process can be done in polynomial-time.

Definition 3. *Given a data graph $G(V, E)$ and a pattern graph $Q(V_Q, E_Q)$. Consider all the LR constraints defined over children (resp. parents) of some node $u \in V_Q$, and let $v \in V$ be a potential match of u. The bipartite graph $BG(X \cup Y, E)$ that inspects these LR constraints w.r.t v is defined as follows:*

- *$X \subseteq V_Q$ contains each child (resp. parent) of u that is concerned by an LR constraint.*
- *$Y \subseteq V$ contains each child (resp. parent) of v that (potentially) matches some node in X.*
- *$(u', v') \in E$ if $u' \in X$ is (potentially) matched with $v' \in Y$.*

A complete matching over BG is a maximum matching [5] that covers all nodes in X.

Consider only the LR constraints defined over children of u. The set X of the bipartite graph BG contains all children of u that are concerned by some LR constraint, and the set Y contains each child of v that (potentially) matches some child u' of u, provided that u' is concerned by an LR constraint (i.e. $u' \in X$). Moreover, an edge in $E \subseteq X \times Y$ denotes some child of u in X that can be (potentially) matched with some child of v in Y. For LR constraints defined over parents of u, the bipartite graph that inspects them is defined in the same manner (i.e. X is a subset of parents of u, and Y is a subset of parents of v).

Example 6. Consider the graphs Q, G_1 and G_2 depicted in Fig. 2. Recall that there is an LR constraint defined over the children of the node q_1 in Q. The bipartite graph BG_1 that inspects this LR constraint, w.r.t the potential match d_1 of q_1 in G_1, is depicted in Fig. 2(d). Moreover, w.r.t the potential match d_1 of q_1 in G_2, the corresponding bipartite graph BG_2 is given in Fig. 2(e).

The next theorem states our main contribution which is a *necessary and sufficient* condition to satisfy LR constraints.

Theorem 1. *Given a data graph $G(V, E)$, a pattern graph $Q(V_Q, E_Q)$, and a node $u \in V_Q$ with a potential match $v \in V$. Let BG be the bipartite graph that inspects all the LR constraints defined over children (resp. parents) of u w.r.t v. These LR constraints are satisfied by some children (resp. parents) of v iff there is a complete matching over BG. Moreover, this can be decided in at most $O(|V_Q||V|\sqrt{|V_Q| + |V|})$ time.*

We emphasize that for each node u in Q and each potential match v of u in G, we construct at most two bipartite graphs to inspect respectively LR constraints defined over children of u and those defined over parents of u.

Example 7. As seen in Example 5, the LR constraint defined over the children of q_1 in Q is not satisfied by the children of its potential match d_1 in G_1. This is confirmed by the bipartite graph BG_1 of Fig. 2(d) which has a maximum matching of size 2 (does not cover the set X). Thus, no complete matching exists over BG_1 and, according to Theorem 1, we can conclude that the underlying LR constraint is not satisfied by the children of d_1. Consider the bipartite graph BG_2 of Fig. 2(e) that inspects the same LR constraint w.r.t d_1 of G_2. Bold edges in BG_2 represent a maximum matching of size 3. Thus, a complete matching exists over BG_2 which implies that the LR constraint, defined over the children of q_1 in Q, is satisfied by the children of its potential match d_1 of G_2.

5   An Algorithm for Triple Simulation

5.1   Description and Complexity

Our algorithm, referred to as **TSim**, is shown in the Fig. 3. Given a pattern graph Q and a data graph G, **TSim**(Q, G) returns the match result $\mathcal{M}_T(Q, G)$, if $Q \prec_T G$, and $\emptyset$ otherwise. This match result contains each subgraph of G that satisfies all CPL relationships of Q.

First, we compute for each node $u \in V_Q$, the set $\text{SIM}(u)$ of all its potential matches in V [line 1–3]. In order to preserve efficiently the CPL relationships of Q over G, we define four auxiliary structures [line 4] as follows. For any node $u \in V_Q$, $\mathbf{CP}(Q, u)$ contains all children and parents of u that are concerned by $Child$ and/or $Parent$ relationships; and $\mathbf{LR}(Q, u)$ contains those concerned by some LR constraints. Moreover, for any query node u and a data node v, **ChildAsMatch**(Q, G, v, u) returns the number of v's children that are potential matches of u in G (i.e. each child v' of v with $v' \in \text{SIM}(u)$); and **ParentAsMatch**(Q, G, v, u) returns the number of v's parents that are potential matches of u in G.

Algorithm **TSim** preserves the $Child$ and $Parent$ relationships of Q [line 6–15] as follows. Given a node $u \in V_Q$, a potential match v of u is kept in $\text{SIM}(u)$ unless: (1) u has a child $u' \in \mathbf{CP}(Q, u)$ but v has no child that matches u' (i.e. **ChildAsMatch**$(Q, G, v, u')=0$); or (2) u has a parent $u' \in \mathbf{CP}(Q, u)$ but v has no parent that matches u' (i.e. **ParentAsMatch**$(Q, G, v, u')=0$). If one of these two conditions is satisfied then v is an incorrect match of u, w.r.t duality properties, and is removed from $\text{SIM}(u)$ [line 8 + 13]. The checking of LR constraints [line 17–19] is done through the procedure **LR_Checking** given in Fig. 4. Given a node $u \in V_Q$ with a potential match $v \in V$. According to Definition 3, the procedure **LR_Checking** constructs two bipartite graphs: BG_1 that inspects all the LR constraints defined over the children of u [line 2–7]; and BG_2 that inspects those defined over the parents of u [line 8–13]. If a complete matching exists over BG_1 and another one exists over BG_2 then, according to Theorem 1,

Algorithm TSim(Q, G)
Input: Graph pattern $Q(V_Q, E_Q, \lambda_Q)$, data graph $G(V, E, \lambda)$.
Output: The match result $\mathcal{M}_T(Q, G)$ if $Q \prec_T G$ and $\emptyset$ otherwise.

```
 1: for each u ∈ V_Q do                  /* POTENTIAL MATCHES OF EACH NODE IN Q */
 2:     SIM(u) := {v | v ∈ V and λ_Q(u)=λ(v)};
 3: end for
 4: initAuxStruct(Q, G);
 5: do
 6:     for each (u, v) with v ∈ SIM(u) do
 7:         for each child u' of u with u' ∈ CP(Q, u) do
 8:             if (ChildAsMatch(Q, G, v, u')= 0) then
 9:                 SIM(u) := SIM(u)\{v}; UpdateStruct(G, u, v);
10:             end if
11:         end for
12:         for each parent u' of u with u' ∈ CP(Q, u) do
13:             if (ParentAsMatch(Q, G, v, u')= 0) then
14:                 SIM(u) := SIM(u)\{v}; UpdateStruct(G, u, v);
15:             end if
16:         end for
17:         if (LR_Checking(Q, G, u, v)=false) then
18:             SIM(u) := SIM(u)\{v}; UpdateStruct(G, u, v);
19:         end if
20:         if (SIM(u) = ∅) then return < ∅, ∅ > ; end if
21:     end for
22: while there are changes;
23: S_T := {(u, v) | u ∈ V_Q and v ∈ SIM(u)};
24: Construct the match result M_T(Q, G) that corresponds to S_T;
25: return M_T(Q, G);
```

Fig. 3. Algorithm for triple simulation.

we conclude that: *(a)* all the LR constraints defined over the children of u are satisfied by some children of v; and *(b)* all the LR constraints defined over the parents of u are satisfied by some parents of v. Thus, the procedure returns *true* only if these two complete matching exist over BG_1 and BG_2. If the procedure returns *false* then there is at least one LR constraint defined over the children (resp. parents) of u which is not satisfied by the children (resp. parents) of v. In this case, v is an incorrect match of u, w.r.t LR constraints, and is removed from SIM(u) [line 18]. The procedure *CompleteMatch*[3] is an implementation of the algorithm of Hopcroft and Karp [13].

---

[3] This procedure finds the maximum matching over BG_1 (resp. BG_2), using the algorithm of Hopcroft et al. [13], and then checks whether the size of this maximum matching is equals to $|X_1|$ (resp. $|X_2|$).

Procedure UpdateStruct(Q, G, u, v)
Input: A pattern graph Q, data graph $G(V, E)$, a query node u with a removed potential match v.
Output: Updates the auxiliary structures **ChildAsMatch** and **ParentAsMatch**.

1: **for each** $(v', v) \in E$ **do**
2:    **ChildAsMatch**$(Q, G, v', u) :=$ **ChildAsMatch**(Q, G, v', u) - 1;
3: **end for**
4: **for each** $(v, v') \in E$ **do**
5:    **ParentAsMatch**$(Q, G, v', u) :=$ **ParentAsMatch**(Q, G, v', u) - 1;
6: **end for**

Procedure LR_Checking(Q, G, u, v)
Input: Pattern $Q(V_Q, E_Q)$, data graph $G(V, E)$, a node $u \in V_Q$ with its match $v \in V$.
Output: If LR constraints defined over u are satisfied by children and/or parents of v.

1: $BG_1 := (X_1 \cup Y_1, E_1)$; $BG_2 := (X_2 \cup Y_2, E_2)$; where $X_1 = Y_1 = X_2 = Y_2 = E_1 = E_2 = \emptyset$;
2: **for each child** u' of u **with** $u' \in \mathbf{LR}(Q, u)$ **do**
3:    $X_1 := X_1 \cup \{u'\}$;
4:    **for each** $v' \in \text{SIM}(u')$ **with** $(v, v') \in E$ **do**
5:       $Y_1 := Y_1 \cup \{v'\}$; $E_1 := E_1 \cup \{(u', v')\}$;
6:    **end for**
7: **end for**
8: **for each parent** u' of u **with** $u' \in \mathbf{LR}(Q, u)$ **do**
9:    $X_2 := X_2 \cup \{u'\}$;
10:    **for each** $v' \in \text{SIM}(u')$ **with** $(v', v) \in E$ **do**
11:       $Y_2 := Y_2 \cup \{v'\}$; $E_2 := E_2 \cup \{(u', v')\}$;
12:    **end for**
13: **end for**
14: **return** *true* only if ($\mathbf{CompleteMatch}(BG_1)$ & $\mathbf{CompleteMatch}(BG_2)$);

Fig. 4. The procedures used by **TSim**.

Each time a data node v is removed from $\text{SIM}(u)$, the cardinalities stored by the structures **ChildAsMatch** and **ParentAsMatch** are updated according to the couple (u, v). This is done by the procedure **UpdateStruct** given in Fig. 4. The two phases discussed above (checking of *duality* properties and LR constraints) are repeated until there are no more changes [line 5–22]. Finally, the corresponding match result $\mathcal{M}_T(Q, G)$ is constructed and returned.

Theorem 2. *For any pattern graph* $Q(V_Q, E_Q)$ *and data graph* $G(V, E)$, *algorithm* **TSim** *takes at most* $O(|Q||G| + |V_Q|^3 |V|^2 \sqrt{|V_Q| + |V|})$ *time to decide whether* $Q \prec_T G$ *and to find the match result* $\mathcal{M}_T(Q, G)$. *Moreover, it takes* $O(|Q||G|)$ *time if* Q *has no LR constraint.*[4]

---

[4] Given a graph $G(V, E)$, $|G| = |V| + |E|$.

The worst-case time complexity of **TSim** is bounded by $O(|Q|^2|G|^{1.5})$. As opposed to the NP-COMPLETENESS of its traditional counterpart via subgraph isomorphism [11], triple simulation preserves LR constraints in polynomial-time.

5.2 TSim with Locality

The next example suggests to incorporate the notion of locality [14] into our algorithm **TSim** in order to overcome excessive matching and thus to improve the quality of our match results.

Example 8. Consider the graphs depicted in Fig. 1. We extend the subgraph G_1 with the following relationships: $d_1 \leftarrow d_{13} \leftarrow d_7$ where d_{13} is a new node labeled with **SE**. Let G_1' be the subgraph that results from this modification. When triple simulation is adopted, **TSim** returns G_1' as the only match of Q_1 in G. The **BIO** found in G_1' (node d_2) is recommended by two **SE** (d_8 and d_{13}) as specified by Q_1. However, **TSim** returns an excessive match of the cycle **AI** $\leftrightarrows$ **DM**, i.e. the cycle $d_9 \rightarrow \cdots \rightarrow d_{12} \rightarrow d_9$ in G_1', that one does not want.

Next, we extend triple simulation with the notion of locality.

Definition 4. *A data graph G matches a pattern graph Q via triple simulation and under locality, denoted $Q \prec_T^L G$, if there exists a subgraph G_s of G centered at some node v that satisfies the following conditions: (a) the radius of G_s is bounded by d_Q, i.e., for each node v' in G_s, dist$(v, v') \leq d_Q$; and (b) $Q \prec_T G_s$ with the maximum match relation S_T.*
The match result $\mathcal{M}_T^L(Q, G)$ is defined with $\bigcup_i \mathcal{M}_T(Q, G_i)$ where each G_i is a subgraph of G that satisfies the previous conditions.

To implement the Definition 4, one can replace only the procedure **dualSim** in the algorithm **Match** [14] with our algorithm **TSim**. Let **Match**$^+$ be the algorithm that results from this combination. Given a data graph G and a pattern graph Q. Algorithm **Match**$^{+}$[5] extracts a subgraph G_v over each node v in G, provided that its radius does not exceed d_Q. It then matches G_v over Q via triple simulation (instead of dual simulation). The match found on each subgraph has a reasonable size and satisfies all the CPL relationships of Q.

Theorem 3.[6] *For any pattern graph $Q(V_Q, E_Q)$ and data graph $G(V, E)$, algorithm **Match**$^+$ takes at most $O(|V|^2 + |Q||G||V| + |V_Q|^3|V|^3\sqrt{|V_Q| + |V|})$ time to decide whether $Q \prec_T^L G$ and to find the corresponding match result $\mathcal{M}_T^L(Q, G)$.*

The complexity of **Match**$^+$ is bounded by $O(|Q|^2|G|^2)$ while that of **Match**[14] is bounded by $O(|Q||G|^2)$. This promises that combining our results with existing orthogonal approaches will not increase drastically the complexity.

---

[5] Not given here since its definition is trivial.
[6] This result is a combination of our Theorem 2 and Theorem 4.1 of Ma et al. [14].

6 Deal with Simple Counting Quantifiers

We study the case of pattern graphs that contain simple counting quantifiers on edges. We show that matching of this kind of pattern graphs can be done in polynomial-time by extending our solution for LR constraints.

Definition 5. *A pattern graph with counting quantifiers, called* quantified pattern graph *(**QGP**), is defined with $Q(V, E, \lambda, C)$ where V, E, and λ are the same as their conventional counterparts; and C is a function s.t., for each edge $e \in E$, $C(e)$ is a counting quantifier (**CQ**) of the form "$\geq p$" $(p \geq 1)$.*

Notice that conventional pattern graphs are a special case where for each edge e, $C(e)=$"≥ 1". We omit $C(e)$ from e in this case. The semantic of CQs is stated intuitively as follows. The QGP $A \xrightarrow{\geq p} B \to C$ specifies that: (1) each data node v that matches A must have *at least* p child nodes that match B; and (2) *all* these p nodes must have at least one child node that matches C. An LR constraint, however, specifies the minimum number of children (resp. parents) that must have some node such that they have the same label but not necessarily the same topological properties (see the graph pattern Q of Example 5).

Proposition 1. *Given a QGP $Q(V_Q, E_Q, \lambda_Q, C)$, a data graph $G(V, E)$, and a node $u \in V_Q$ with a potential match $v \in V$. Each CQ defined over some child of u can be transformed into an LR constraint. Moreover, children of v satisfy this CQ iff they satisfy its equivalent LR constraint.*

Based on the above proposition, we show next that matching $QGPs$ is in PTIME when it is treated as an extension of graph simulation, contrary to the NP-Completeness found in [11] when subgraph isomorphism is considered.

Theorem 4. *Given a QGP $Q(V_Q, E_Q, \lambda_Q, C)$ with possible LR constraints and a data graph $G(V, E)$. Let p be the largest cardinality of counting quantifiers in Q. It takes at most $O(|Q||G|+p.|V_Q|^3|V|^2\sqrt{p.|V_Q| + |V|})$ time to decide whether G matches Q and to find the corresponding match result.*

The overall time complexity of our approach in case of $QGPs$ is bounded by $O(p^{1.5}|Q|^2|G|^{1.5})$. Notice that p is very small in practice [1]. This result can be extended easily to deal with counting quantifiers of the form $A \xrightarrow{\geq p\%} B$[7].

7 Conclusion

We have discussed pattern graphs with LR constraints that existing approaches do not preserve [8,14] or preserve in exponential time [11]. To tackle this NP-Completeness, we have showed that LR constraints can be preserved in polynomial-time when treated as maximum matching in bipartite graphs, and

---

[7] See [11] for the semantic.

we proposed an algorithm to implement this result. We are to stduy other constraints that can be preserved in polynomial-time, e.g., *negation* and *optional edges*. The polynomial-time of our algorithm may make graph pattern matching infeasible when conducted on graphs with millions of nodes and billions of edges (e.g. Facebook [12]). To boost the matching on large data graphs, we plan to extend our work with some optimization techniques: *(1) incremental graph pattern matching* [10], *(2) pattern matching on distributed data graphs* [3,19], and *(3) pattern matching on compressed data graphs* [9,15]. These techniques are orthogonal, but complementary, to our work.

References

1. Arias, M., Fernández, J.D., Martínez-Prieto, M.A., de la Fuente, P.: An empirical study of real-world SPARQL queries. CoRR (2011)
2. Cho, J., Shivakumar, N., Garcia-Molina, H.: Finding replicated web collections. In: Proceedings of SIGMOD (2000)
3. Cong, G., Fan, W., Kementsietsidis, A.: Distributed query evaluation with performance guarantees. In: Proceedings of SIGMOD (2007)
4. Cordella, L.P., Foggia, P., Sansone, C., Vento, M.: A (Sub)Graph isomorphism algorithm for matching large graphs. IEEE Trans. Pattern Anal. Mach. Intell. **26**, 1367–1372 (2004)
5. Cormen, T.H., Leiserson, C.E., Rivest, R.L., Stein, C.: Introduction to Algorithms, 3rd edn. MIT Press, Cambridge (2009)
6. Fan, W.: Graph pattern matching revised for social network analysis. In: Proceedings of ICDT (2012)
7. Fan, W., Li, J., Ma, S., Tang, N., Wu, Y.: Adding regular expressions to graph reachability and pattern queries. In: Proceedings of ICDE (2011)
8. Fan, W., Li, J., Ma, S., Tang, N., Wu, Y.: Graph pattern matching: from intractable to polynomial time. Proc. VLDB Endow. **3**, 264–275 (2010)
9. Fan, W., Li, J., Wang, X., Wu, Y.: Query preserving graph compression. In: Proceedings of SIGMOD (2012)
10. Fan, W., Wang, X., Wu, Y.: Incremental graph pattern matching. ACM Trans. Database Syst. **38** (2013)
11. Fan, W., Wu, Y., Xu, J.: Adding counting quantifiers to graph patterns. In: Proceedings of SIGMOD (2016)
12. Grujic, I., Dinic, S.B., Stoimenov, L.: Collecting and analyzing data from e-government facebook pages (2014)
13. Hopcroft, J.E., Karp, R.M.: An n5/2 algorithm for maximum matchings in bipartite graphs. SIAM J. Comput. **2**, 225–231 (1973)
14. Ma, S., Cao, Y., Fan, W., Huai, J., Wo, T.: Strong simulation: capturing topology in graph pattern matching. ACM Trans. Database Syst. **39** (2014)
15. Maccioni, A., Abadi, D.J.: Scalable pattern matching over compressed graphs via dedensification. In: Proceedings of SIGKDD, pp. 1755–1764 (2016)
16. Mahfoud, H.: Graph pattern matching preserving label-repetition constraints. CoRR (2018)
17. Milner, R.: Communication and Concurrency (1989)
18. Shemshadi, A., Sheng, Q.Z., Qin, Y.: Efficient pattern matching for graphs with multi-labeled nodes. Knowl. Based Syst. **109**, 256–265 (2016)
19. Tung, L.-D., Nguyen-Van, Q., Hu, Z.: Efficient query evaluation on distributed graphs with hadoop environment. In: Proceedings of SoICT (2013)

Standard and Dialectal Arabic Text Classification for Sentiment Analysis

Mohcine Maghfour[✉] and Abdeljalil Elouardighi

LM2CE Laboratory, FSJES, Hassan 1st University, Settat, Morocco
maghfour.mohcin@gmail.com, abdeljalil.elouardighi@uhp.ac.ma

Abstract. In social networks, the users tend to express more themselves by sharing publicly their opinions, emotions and sentiments, the benefits of analyzing such data are eminent, however the process of extracting and transforming these raw data can be a very challenging task particularly when the sentiments are expressed in Arabic language. Two main categories of Arabic are massively used in social networks, namely the modern standard Arabic, which is the official language, and the dialectal Arabic, which is itself, subdivided to several categories depending on countries and regions. In this paper, we focus on analyzing Facebook comments that are expressed in modern standard or in Moroccan dialectal Arabic; therefore we put these two language categories under the scope by testing and comparing two approaches. The first one is the classical approach that considers all Arabic text as homogeneous. The second one, that we propose, require a text classification beforehand sentiment classification, based on language categories: the standard and the dialectal Arabic. The idea behind this approach is to adapt the text preprocessing on each language category with more precision. In supervised classification, we have applied two of the most reputed classifiers in sentiment analysis applications, Naive Bayes and SVM. The results of this study are promising since good performance were obtained.

Keywords: Sentiment analysis · Natural language processing
Supervised classification · Language classification
Modern standard Arabic · Moroccan dialectal Arabic
Facebook comments

1 Introduction

The increasing number of social network users and the frequency of their daily use reflects the importance and interest attributed to these platforms. In the light of this progress, the volume of information generated has also increased. Among the shared information the personal thought, sentiments and opinions represents an interesting raw material for which a big effort was made in order to develop methods necessary for extracting these information and therefore the creation of knowledge [15].

© Springer Nature Switzerland AG 2018
E. H. Abdelwahed et al. (Eds.): MEDI 2018, LNCS 11163, pp. 282–291, 2018.
https://doi.org/10.1007/978-3-030-00856-7_18

Sentiment analysis (SA), or opinion mining, is a field of study that analyzes people's opinions and sentiments that are expressed via web platforms in a text format. These sentiments are consequently very broad and changing in time because they may concern various topics, products, organizations, individuals, events, etc. [8]. SA is a special application of text mining, indeed, the linguistic aspects and proprieties are imposing the mean difficulties in this analysis. Specifically the Arabic language is considered one of the most challenging languages in term of its processing, because of its complex morphology and its dialectal varieties.

The modern standard Arabic (MSA), which is the official form, is distinguished by a compact morphology since the words has more attachment and concatenation capabilities. Otherwise, the dialectal Arabic (DA) is a variety of vernacular languages spoken in the daily life within a country or a region, such as the Moroccan dialectal Arabic (MDA), the Egyptian Arabic, the Saudi Arabic, etc. [20]. The challenges of the DA resides mostly in the spelling variation, as one word may be written differently depending on the writer, in addition the adopted habits and styles of writing in social networks introduce more ambiguity to the text because of misspelling, the interaction between users and topic shifting and divergence [9].

MSA and DA are both used in social networks jointly, however despite the common aspects shared between them in term of structure and vocabulary, every dialect possess its own specificities, which require a more extended and advanced processing.

This work is focus on SA based on Arabic comments that are shared in MSA and in MDA, thus we aim to compare two different SA approaches, in the first one we treat all the Arabic texts (whether they are in MSA or in MDA) as one homogeneous corpus on which we apply the same preprocessing. In the second approach we proceed by classifying the Arabic corpus depending on the language beforehand sentiment classification, in this case we apply on each sub-corpus the correspondent preprocessing.

The rest of this paper is organized as follow: in the next section we introduce some related work and present their proposed approaches and results, in Sect. 3 we present the proposed approaches of this study, then in Sect. 4 we discuss the obtained results and finally we conclude this work by summarizing its important findings and its perspectives.

2   Related Work

Several works have addressed SA based on standard and dialectal Arabic text. They have proposed and tested many preprocessing tasks and classification approaches to deal with the complexity and challenges of Arabic language. Medhaffar et al. [10] collected and annotated a Tunisian dialoct corpus of 17.000 comments from Facebook, then they have developed and tested a SA system for Tunisian dialect based on three classification algorithms SVM, NB, and MLP (multi-layer perceptron). The results shows better performance of their system compared to models trained on other dialects or MSA dataset.

In [16] Rafee and Risier raised some encountered challenges, when analyzing opinions from twitter, such as language varieties and topic shifting, they have collected a dataset composed from 3000 multidialectal Arabic tweets, then the SVM algorithm was applied in sentiment classification stage. The results showed good performance with cross-validation; however, it has significantly decreased when evaluating the models on a test set that was collected later in time.

Hammad et al. [7] led a study to examine how different configurations of the Bag of Words model and text representation scheme affect the results of the supervised classification by applying three classifiers, namely SVM, Compliment Naive Bayes, and Multinomial Naive Bayes. Their experimentation concerned three datasets from twitter with different dialects, Saudi dataset (11000 +), an Egyptian dataset and a multidialectal dataset that was used in [16]. Their results showed no significant improvement when simple processing task like cleaning and normalization were applied, however, when they have applied a light stemmer or a dialectal stemmer the performance have improved.

Shoukry and Rafea [19] conducted their study on tweets that comes in standard Arabic and in Egyptian dialect. The major issues outlined concerned the dialectal aspects, because preprocessing tasks that were developed specifically for the MSA tend to fail with a dialectal Arabic text. Therefore, the authors have proposed their own stemming solution in order to resolve these issues.

In their work, Salamah and Elkhlifi [17] have proposed a Microblogging Opinion Mining Approach for Kuwaiti Dialect based on four stages, collecting, preprocessing, opinion extraction and supervised classification using SVM and decision trees. At the processing stage, the collected tweets were segmented into sentences before tokenization. The obtained results yielded an average value of precision and recall of 76% and 61% respectively.

Alomari et al. [3] carried out a SA study on tweets in MSA and Jordanian dialect; their experimental framework covered filtering stemming, light stemming and no stemming, the results showed better scores of root stemming when SVM was used. On the contrary, the better performance was obtained when the light stemmer was tested with NB.

Nabil et al. [11] presented an Arabic sentiment tweets dataset (ASTD) which is a corpus composed 10000 tweets published mostly in MSA and Egyptian dialect. In The experimentation, after they exposed the statistical properties of the studied data set, they have tested a wide range of standard classifiers including SVM, KNN, MNB on balanced and unbalanced data. Their conclusions shows the difficulty encountered in sentiment classification with balanced data and the outperformance of SVM when compared to other algorithms.

In [1] Al-Kabi et al. led a sentiment analysis study on MSA and multidialectal Arabic comments (4625 comment) collected from Yahoo!-Maktoob. In the preprocessing step, the stemming task was applied. Moreover, they have exploited two of the most reputed classifiers in sentiment classification, namely SVM and NB. The experimentation stage was based two dataset balanced and unbalanced. The overall results were under expected because the best accuracy did not exceed 70%.

Several SA works dealt with Arabic corpus that includes both standard and dialectal Arabic. Some of them proposed additional natural language processing that are specific to the dialect in question [10,19]. Their approaches were based on all documents without the categorization between those published in standard Arabic and the dialectal ones, in our work we aim to focus exactly on this idea.

3   Two-Step Arabic Text Classification for Sentiment Analysis

3.1   Dataset Description

The first step toward a SA is data collection. In this work, we have collected Arabic Facebook comments (in MSA and MDA) that concern broad and various topics in Morocco, including politics, economy, sport, religion, society and others. The main source of the collected comments was the public Facebook pages of Moroccan online news. A double annotation task was performed on a total of 9901 collected comment. Each comment was annotated as positive or negative and at the same time classified in two classes MSA or MDA. Table 1 provides a dataset description depending on the sentiment and the language.

Table 1. The dataset composition

	Positive	Negative	Total
MSA	2221	4138	6359
MDA	0684	2858	3542
Total	2905	6996	9901

3.2   The Proposed Approach

In social networks, one of the main challenges of the SA based on Arabic corpus is the presence of standard Arabic text and at least one dialect. MSA and MDA shares many common aspects; however, the differences exist at the level of morphology and vocabulary. The essential complexity of the MSA is reflected in the concatenation capabilities of its words [6]. The MDA also possesses this aspect but in addition, the lack of the standardization in its writing amplify in advance the morphological complexity of the dialect [2].

In this work, we aim to inspect if it is helpful to classify in advance the Arabic corpus depending on the language forms, standard or dialectal, before the sentiment classification step. Thus, two schemes were tested and compared. One-step classification (Fig. 1) is a straightforward sentiment classification. All the Arabic text is considered as one same corpus; in this case, the same preprocessing tasks are applied on all the document. Two-step classification (Fig. 2): is based on an additional step of standard/dialectal classification, followed by the specific preprocessing applied on each sub-corpus. The preprocessing is intended to reduce the embedded noise in the text, furthermore the shared text via social network may contain more irregularities and anomalies [9].

In this context preprocessing tasks such as cleaning, normalizing and tokenizing are applied in prior to sentiment classification. These tasks can be considered as basic because they are required independently of the used language. Therefore, we have applied them in both schemes, at one level in Fig. 1, and at three levels in Fig. 2 before each classification stage: MDA/MSA sentiment classification, MDA sentiment classification and MSA sentiment classification.

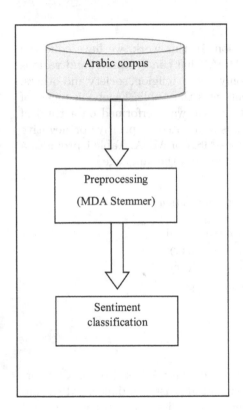 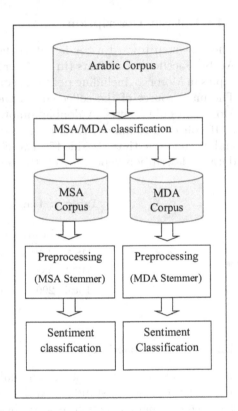

Fig. 1. One-step classification approach   **Fig. 2.** Two-step classification approach

Despite the MSA and the MDA diverge on a morphological level, yet helpfully they still share mostly the same word stems. For example the word اعرفهم in MSA (I know them) and its equivalent in MDA كنعرفهم are based on the same stem عرف (know). Thus, a relevant stemming that considers both the MSA and MDA specificities is expected yielding to better performance when applied to a corpus containing texts in MSA and in MDA . The unavailability of such tools adapted to process the MDA texts had led us to develop and to implement a new Arabic light stemmer through which we have tried to deal with the complexities of this dialect. The dialectal stemmer provides two stemming options: MSA or MDA, where the MDA stemming option incorporates almost all the MSA operations, moreover it include also the specific tasks to process the MDA. In Fig. 1 we have applied MDA light stemming since the standard-dialectal discrimination was ignored in the corpus. In Fig. 2, the MDA and the MSA stemmers were applied respectively to each correspondent sub-corpus.

3.3 Supervised Classification

The performance of text categorization application is heavily influenced by the specificity of the studied dataset such as language, topic, text length, etc. [13]. Therefore, we have tested four configurations of feature representation with the combination of weighting schemes and extraction schemes:

- TF/Unigram
- TF/Unigram + Bigram
- TF-IDF/Unigram
- TF-IDF/Unigram + Bigram

At the classification stage, we have applied two most used classification algorithms for text classification in SA: Naive Bayes (NB) and SVM with linear kernel. These classifiers have shown good performance in many SA works based on English corpus [4,5,12]. With the four adopted configuration, each dataset was randomly split into two subsets. The learning subset with 75% of the observations, in which we have applied 10 folds cross-validation and parameters optimization. The subset with 25% of unseen data for testing the performance of the developed models. The Fscore was chosen as evaluation metric [18]. We have used python programming language in preprocessing and scikit-learn library [14] in the classification step.

4 Results and Discussion

In this work, for analyzing the effect of Arabic language on SA, we have proposed and tested two approaches. The first one is the one step-classification approach (Fig. 1) which is the classical one. Table 2 presents the obtained results with the classifiers NB and SVM for two level of preprocessing.

At first, the basic preprocessing that includes cleaning, normalizing etc. was used. Then, in addition to these tasks, the dialectal stemmer was applied beforehand the sentiment classification. In overall, these results show the important contribution of the stemming in the improvement of the sentiment classification. The best Fscore was obtained under NB classifier with Unigram+Bigram/ TF configuration (84.10%). Whit two step-classification, the best performance at the level of language classification (Table 3) was registered under NB classifier through the configuration Unigram/TF (Fscore = 85.79%).

Table 2. One-step classification results

MSA+MDA	NB		SVM	
	Basic processing	MDA stemmer	Basic processing	MDA stemmer
1 g/TF	81.33%	83.94%	79.15%	82.89%
1+2 g/TF	81.33%	84.10%	79.15%	83.13%
1 g/TFIDF	78.63%	82.04%	80.07%	83.20%
1+2 g/TFIDF	78.90%	82.42%	80.36%	83.37%

Table 3. Two step classification results: language classification

	NB	SVM
Unigram/TF	**85.79%**	78.89%
Uni+Bigram/TF	85.57%	78.71%
Unigram/TFIDF	84.49%	79.34%
Uni+Bigram/TFIDF	84.93%	79.41%

Table 4. Two-step classification results: sentiment classification of MDA comments

MDA	NB		SVM	
	Basic processing	MDA stemmer	Basic processing	MDA stemmer
1 g/TF	77.96%	81.25%	75.61%	77.99%
1+2 g/TF	78.44%	81.83%	74.78%	78.36%
1 g/TFIDF	74.78%	75.82%	74.98%	78.55%
1+2 g/TFIDF	76.56%	78.78%	75.22%	78.94%

At the stage of sentiment classification, the dialectal light stemmer was applied on the MDA corpus. Table 4 presents the obtained results.

The obtained results were less good than those obtained with the one step-classification approach (Table 2). These can be explained by two factors: on one hand the complexity of the MDA, on the other hand the dataset size, which is smaller (3542 comments). Although the effect of stemming is still significant, because the best Fscore in this case, was yielded by NB classifier with the configuration Unigram+Bigram/TF (Fscore = 81.83%).

When the MSA corpus was processed independently (Table 5), the results of the sentiment classification have increased compared with those obtained with the one-step classification approach where the corpus contained both standard and dialectal texts. Indeed, the reason behind this improvement was determined by the best precision of the stemming. The best Fscore was obtained with NB classifier using the configuration Unigram/TF.

In summary, despite the two-step classification is more expensive due to the double annotation at the level language and sentiment classification, it shows precisely the effect of preprocessing on sentiment classification with each sub-corpus. Otherwise, one-step classification tend to have more stemming error because of the linguistically heterogeneous texts contained in the corpus (standard and dialectal texts), but this approach benefits from the cumulative effect of

Table 5. Two-step classification results: sentiment classification of MSA comments

MSA	NB		SVM	
	Basic processing	MSA stemmer	Basic processing	MSA stemmer
1 g/TF	81.57%	84.56%	78.98%	83.30%
1+2 g/TF	81.43%	84.30%	78.65%	83.53%
1 g/TFIDF	80.12%	82.57%	80.15%	83.46%
1+2 g/TFIDF	80.24%	82.67%	79.98%	84.33%

the dataset size. We can say that the two classification approaches are effective. To choose which approach to adopt many criteria might be considered, such as the data set size, the weight of language categories, and the possible relationship between the text language and sentiment polarity.

Similar SA works were based on other arabic dialects, in [17] Salamah and Elkhlifi collected a dialectal Kuwaiti corpus, The Fscore found was equal to 70.55%, which is slightly less than the score obtained in our study.

Mdhaffar et al. [10] led their SA on facebook comments that have been written in Tunisian dialectal Arabic, they adopted the error rate as a performance measure, the best obtained score was 23%, which has some similarity to our finding, although the measure is different than we have applied (Fscore). At the end, these results show that the nature and properties of the analyzed dataset influence the quality of sentiment classification.

5 Conclusion

Arabic content in the web continue to increase specially in social networks and enclose a lot information that is valuable for decisions making. To take the advantage of this content and make it valuable, analysis techniques must be applied. In social networks, one of the main challenges of the SA based on Arabic text is the presence of the modern standard and the dialectal Arabic text. Several SA works dealt with corpus including both standard and dialectal Arabic. Some of them proposed additional natural language processing that are specific to the Arabic. However, their analysis focused on all documents without distinction between those published in modern standard or in dialectal Arabic. In this paper, we have dealt with the SA for Facebook comments written and shared in MSA or in MDA. Our main objective is to inspect if it is useful to classify at first the Arabic corpus according to its forms: MSA or MDA before the sentiment classification step. For this, we have tested and compared two schemes of Arabic SA. The first scheme was the classical method where the basic preprocessing that includes cleaning, normalizing etc. was used. In addition to these tasks, the Arabic dialectal stemmer was applied beforehand the sentiment classification. In the second scheme, we have incorporated an additional text classification step for all corpus according to its forms: MSA or MDA, followed by the specific preprocessing applied on each sub-corpus. At the stage of sentiment classification, the dialectal light stemmer was applied on the MDA corpus. The obtained results with the MDA corpus were less good than those obtained with the classical schemes. This is mainly due to the complexity of the Arabic dialectal processing and the dataset size used. The obtained results whit the MSA corpus were better. This variance in the obtained results give us the opportunity for improvements. In the future work, we believe that there is a promising trend to obtain the best results for Arabic SA. As we have seen, most of the work in the field of Arabic SA has focused on the use of supervised learning techniques and lexicon-based approaches. We intend to propose and develop a new hybrid method using deep learning technique and big data technique such as Hadoop and MapReduce to solve some of the existing problems in MDA for SA.

References

1. Al-Kabi, M.N., Abdulla, N.A., Al-Ayyoub, M.: An analytical study of Arabic sentiments: Maktoob case study. In: 2013 8th International Conference for Internet Technology and Secured Transactions (ICITST), pp. 89–94. IEEE (2013)
2. Al-Sabbagh, R., Girju, R.: Yadac: yet another dialectal arabic corpus. In: LREC, pp. 2882–2889 (2012)
3. Alomari, K.M., ElSherif, H.M., Shaalan, K.: Arabic tweets sentimental analysis using machine learning. In: Benferhat, S., Tabia, K., Ali, M. (eds.) IEA/AIE 2017. LNCS (LNAI), vol. 10350, pp. 602–610. Springer, Cham (2017). https://doi.org/10.1007/978-3-319-60042-0_66
4. Dave, K., Lawrence, S., Pennock, D.M.: Mining the peanut gallery: opinion extraction and semantic classification of product reviews. In: Proceedings of the 12th International Conference on World Wide Web, pp. 519–528. ACM (2003)
5. Go, A., Bhayani, R., Huang, L.: Twitter sentiment classification using distant supervision. CS224N Project Report, Stanford 1(12) (2009)
6. Habash, N.Y.: Introduction to arabic natural language processing. Synth. Lect. Hum. Lang. Technol. 3(1), 1–187 (2010)
7. Khalil, T., Halaby, A., Hammad, M., El-Beltagy, S.R.: Which configuration works best? An experimental study on supervised Arabic twitter sentiment analysis. In: 2015 First International Conference on Arabic Computational Linguistics (ACLing), pp. 86–93. IEEE (2015)
8. Liu, B.: Sentiment analysis and opinion mining. Synth. Lect. Hum. Lang. Technol. 5(1), 1–167 (2012)
9. Liu, B.: Sentiment Analysis: Mining Opinions, Sentiments, and Emotions. Cambridge University Press, New York (2015)
10. Medhaffar, S., Bougares, F., Esteve, Y., Hadrich-Belguith, L.: Sentiment analysis of Tunisian dialects: linguistic resources and experiments. In: Proceedings of the Third Arabic Natural Language Processing Workshop, pp. 55–61 (2017)
11. Nabil, M., Aly, M., Atiya, A.: ASTD: Arabic sentiment tweets dataset. In: Proceedings of the 2015 Conference on Empirical Methods in Natural Language Processing, pp. 2515–2519 (2015)
12. Pang, B., Lee, L., Vaithyanathan, S.: Thumbs up? Sentiment classification using machine learning techniques. In: Proceedings of the ACL-02 Conference on Empirical Methods in Natural Language Processing, vol. 10, pp. 79–86. Association for Computational Linguistics (2002)
13. Pang, B., Lee, L.: Opinion mining and sentiment analysis. Found Trends Inf. Retr. 2(1–2), 1–135 (2008)

14. Pedregosa, F., et al.: Scikit-learn: machine learning in Python. J. Mach. Learn. Res. **12**, 2825–2830 (2011)
15. Pozzi, F.A., Fersini, E., Messina, E., Liu, B.: Sentiment Analysis in Social Networks. Morgan Kaufmann, San Francisco (2016)
16. Refaee, E., Rieser, V.: An Arabic twitter corpus for subjectivity and sentiment analysis. In: LREC, pp. 2268–2273 (2014)
17. Salamah, J.B., Elkhlifi, A.: Microblogging opinion mining approach for Kuwaiti dialect. In: The International Conference on Computing Technology and Information Management (ICCTIM2014), pp. 388–396. The Society of Digital Information and Wireless Communication (2014)
18. Sebastiani, F.: Machine learning in automated text categorization. ACM Comput. Surv. (CSUR) **34**(1), 1–47 (2002)
19. Shoukry, A., Rafea, A.: Preprocessing Egyptian dialect tweets for sentiment mining. In: The Fourth Workshop on Computational Approaches to Arabic Script-based Languages, p. 47 (2012)
20. Zaidan, O.F., Callison-Burch, C.: Arabic dialect identification. Comput. Linguist. **40**(1), 171–202 (2014)

A Graph-Based Model for Tag Recommendations in Clinical Decision Support System

Sara Qassimi[✉], El Hassan Abdelwahed, Meriem Hafidi, and Rachid Lamrani

Laboratory ISI, Cadi Ayyad University, Marrakesh, Morocco
{sara.qassimi,meriem.hafidi,rachid.lamrani}ced.uca.ma,
abdelwahed@uca.ac.ma

Abstract. The healthcare providers use clinical decision support systems to manage the patients' electronic health records. In this paper, we aim to enhance the computer-aided diagnosis in medical imaging. We developed a graph-based tag recommendations approach that suggests relevant diseases and pathologies by analysing the tagged medical images. Healthcare providers can rapidly get an improved diagnostic value of radiographs using the graph-based tag recommendations that enable discovering common and relevant diseases used within the patient's community, his related images and semantically tied tags. The dataset ChestX-Ray14 has been conducted to evaluate the accuracy and effectiveness of our proposal. Futures works will address the online evaluation of the suggested tags by exploiting the healthcare providers' feedback.

Keywords: Tag recommendations · Graph-based model
Network analysis · Electronic health record · Clinical decision support

1 Introduction

The use of electronic health record EHR has been widely implemented in healthcare systems worldwide. The Clinical Decision Support System CDSS benefits from the wealth of information provided by the EHRs in order to deliver efficient healthcare organizations. For instance, the CDSS optimizes patients' care by including patients' follow up, reminders, warning systems, and diagnostic suggestions [1]. The EHRs are presented in structured and unstructured forms like free-text documentation "clinical notes" medical histories, imaging results, laboratory test results and physician reports. Even though the structured information enables a faster data analysis, it does not consistently facilitate communication of patients' information. Moreover, the majority of clinicians do not trust the EHR structured information and prefer verbal communication as a means to gather and convey important information about their patients [2]. However, it is time-consuming to enter free-text electronic notes and not easily accessed for viewing [3]. In fact, physicians spend two hours of desk work on documenting a patient's

© Springer Nature Switzerland AG 2018
E. H. Abdelwahed et al. (Eds.): MEDI 2018, LNCS 11163, pp. 292–300, 2018.
https://doi.org/10.1007/978-3-030-00856-7_19

EHR for each hour of clinical consulting [4]. Besides, physicians prefer to read succinct and brief medical notes. Therefore, it is crucial to managing textual notations and encourage the use of shortcut "Tags" presenting well-defined and meaningful information. Actually, physicians need to be involved in generating succinct and easily readable notes that contain essential information [5]. Tags are descriptive annotations that define the commonly used clinical terms. The use of tags will capture sharable information in an efficient and timely manner. Moreover, tagging EHRs will meet the patients' consent to exchange some parts of their medical record, like diagnosed pathologies, but not their other personal parts.

In this paper, consideration has been given to tagging medical images where tags represent the common diseases or pathologies. Tagging approach, a representation of semantic interpretations, has proven benefits in managing, searching and discovering pictures for specific use [8]. It will facilitate diagnosis of diseases by reducing loosely labelled or undescribed medical images. However, it is still very difficult to achieve clinically relevant computer-aided detection and diagnosis in chest X-ray images [6]. Therefore, this paper proposes a graph based tag recommendations aiming to describe and organize the patients' medical images. The recommender system of tags will aid the CDSS to detect further diagnosis on medical images in order to execute high-quality patient-centred care. Indeed, the primary interest is not about getting correct CDSS pieces of advice but rather is the extent to which the CDSS improve the diagnostic hypotheses of clinicians and suggest relevant clinical findings [7]. The suggestion of tags -diseases- will not only help healthcare providers to generate relevant interpretation reports summarizing the findings and impressions but will also enable them to navigate and retrieve the right tag before creating or reading a patient's EHR.

The rest of the paper is organized as follows: Sect. 2 provides some backgrounds and related research papers. Section 3 depicts the proposed approach of graph-based tag recommendations. The experimental results and evaluation are described in Sect. 4. Finally, the conclusion and future directions are delineated in Sect. 5.

2 Background and Related Work

The term "tag" has emerged with the arrival of the social web to describe the web resources [10]. In the clinical activity, tags are the commonly used medical terms. The clinical text contains various type of information (e.g., radiology reports) that can be used to improve CDSS performances. The authors [11] proposed a de-identified corpus of clinical text annotated to support information extraction from the free text notes. Some machine learning techniques for text mining are used for the pre-processing of free-text breast cancer pathology reports [12]. The authors [6] provided a chest X-ray database "ChestX-ray8" that compromises frontal view X-ray images of unique patients with fourteen diseases in form of labels. The image labels represent diseases' keywords (tags) extracted from the radiological reports using NLP. However, a golden training set of an adequate annotated clinical text notes is required for the off-the-shelf NPL tools using machine learning-based methods. Tag recommendation is beneficial for the tagging process. It has multiple recommender techniques, like, content-based, tag co-occurrence based and graph-based [9]. The graph-based tag recommendation method extract tags based on the neighbourhood of the target item (or user). A hypergraph-based method is proposed for image tagging that exploits the image content and geo-localisation [13]. Various multi-label classification methods exploit label correlations in order to annotate multi-label images [14]. A coverage of the multi-label classification is beyond the scope of this paper. Our motivation position is to achieve clinically relevant computer-aided detection and diagnosis of medical images. We aim to make a great use of the extracted diagnostic labels (tags) from the free text report to enhance the categorisation and annotation of medical images using a graph-based recommender system of tags.

3   Proposed Approach

The tag recommendations will help healthcare providers making clinical decisions by detecting diagnosis in medical images and facilitate their interpretation. The proposed approach is based on graphs generated by analyzing previously tagged medical images of the community of patients. The graphs modeling (see Fig. 1) is derived from three interconnected layers, namely the patients, images and tags layers. Therefore, three associative networks are generated. A simple network is a single-layer network, represented by a graph. A graph is a tuple $G = (V, E)$, where V is the set of nodes and $E \subseteq V \times V$ is the set of edges connecting the pair of nodes.

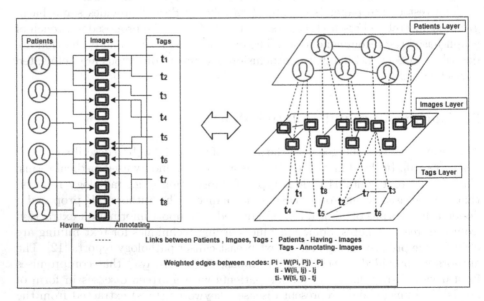

Fig. 1. Graphs modeling of the tripartite relationship among patients, images and tags

A community of patients P have a set of images I annotated with a set of tags T. $P = \{P_1, ..., P_l\}$ $I = \{I_1, ..., I_k\}$ $T = \{t_1, ..., t_n\}$ Where, l, k and n are respectively the number of patients, images and tags. Three weighted undirected graphs are defined, namely patients, images and tags graphs, denoted by G_P, G_I and G_T. The instances of patients, images and tags are respectively the nodes of G_P, G_I and G_T, related with weighted edges. Besides, we have considered identifying the most central nodes in network analysis. The centrality measures address the insights concerning a node within the whole network. With regard to the nature of the generated networks, we consider weighted degree centrality measure because the node strength takes into consideration the weights of ties. The weighted degree centrality of a node is computed by summing the weights across all its related nodes.

The weighted edge of the graph of images is denoted by $W(i_{Pi}, j_{Pi})$, where i_{Pi}, j_{Pi} are images belonging to the same patient $P_i \in P$.

The tag recommendation method based on the graph of images (Algorithm 1, procedure RecommendationGraphImages) recommends the previously assigned tags corresponding to the patient P_i in order to remind the healthcare providers about his already detected diseases.

The creation of communities is processed by grouping a set of similar patients having the same diseases. The community of patients is an undirected graph whose nodes are patients tied with the weighted edges. For patients P_i, $P_j \in P$, the weighted edge is $W(P_i, P_j) = \frac{Number\ of\ same\ tags\ annotating\ images\ of\ P_i\ and\ P_j}{Number\ of\ tags\ in\ the\ corpus}$. The weighed degree centrality of the patient P_i is $w_c(P_i) = \sum_{j}^{l} W(P_i, P_j)$. The method of community graph-based tag recommendation (Algorithm 1, procedure RecommendationGraph-Community) suggests tags assigned to the k most related patients P_j of the target patient P_i.

A tag is relevant - well spread and common diseases - if it is annotating important amount of medical images corresponding to active patients (who have a great number of medical images). The weighted edge of two tags t_i, $t_j \in T$ is denoted by $W(t_i, t_j) = W_P(t_i, t_j) \times W_I(t_i, t_j)$. It considers the patient based weight $W_P(t_i, t_j) = \frac{Number\ of\ patients\ having\ images\ annotated\ by\ t_i\ and\ t_j}{Number\ of\ patients\ with\ annotated\ images}$ and the image based weight $W_I(t_i, t_j) = \frac{Number\ of\ images\ annotated\ by\ t_i\ and\ t_j}{Number\ of\ annotated\ images}$. Each tag t_i has its weighted degree centrality $w_c(t_i) = \sum_{j}^{n} W(t_i, t_j)$.

The graph of tags will enhance the recommendation of tags by suggesting the semantically close tags within the graph. The Tags' graph based recommendation of tags (Algorithm 1, procedure RecommendationGraphTags) recommends related tags to the suggested tags of either the graph of images or the community graph based tag recommendation. Otherwise, the graph of tags suggests the strongly related tags in order to solve the cold start problem.

Algorithm 1. Graph-based tag recommendations

P_i, $P_j \in P$; $I_{Pi} \subset I$; $T_{Pi}, T_{Pj} \subset T$; $t_j \in T$; $t_{Pi} \in T_{Pi}$; $t_{Pj} \in T_{Pj}$; i_{Pi}, $j_{Pi} \in I_{Pi}$; Rti_{Pi}, Rtc_{Pi}, $Relt_{Pi} \subset T_{Pi}$

Rti_{Pi} : a set of recommended tags based on the images' graph

Rtc_{Pi} : a set of recommended tags based on the patients' community graph

$Relt_{Pi}$: a set of recommended tags based on the tags' graph

procedure RECOMMENDATIONGRAPHIMAGES(P_i, i_{Pi})

    for W(i_{Pi}, j_{Pi})=1 **do**

        Rti_{Pi} ←list of t_{Pj} annotating i_{Pj}

    end for

    return Rti_{Pi}

end procedure

procedure RECOMMENDATIONGRAPHCOMMUNITY(P_i)

    for $P_j \in P$ **do**

        if W(P_i, P_j) > 0 **then**

            ω ←W(P_i, P_j)× $w_c(P_j)$

            Rtc_{Pi} ←list of t_{Pj} ranked by ω limit k

        end if

    end for

    return Rtc_{Pi}

end procedure

procedure RECOMMENDATIONGRAPHTAGS(P_i, i_{Pi}, t_{Pi})

    Rti_{Pi} ←RecommendationGraphImages(P_i, i_{Pi})

    Rtc_{Pi} ←RecommendationGraphCommunity(P_i)

    if $t_{Pi} \in T_{Pi}$ OR $t_{Pi} \in Rti_{Pi}$ OR $t_{Pi} \in Rtc_{Pi}$ **then**

        for $t_j \in T$ **do**

            ω ←W(t_{Pi}, t_j)× $w_c(t_j)$

            if ω > threshold **then**

                $Relt_{Pi}$ ←list of t_j ranked by ω

            end if

        end for

    end if

    return $Relt_{Pi}$

end procedure

---

4 Experimental Results and Evaluation

Our experimental dataset was taken from the "ChestX-ray8" chest X-ray database [6]. In our experiments, we used a number of 1000 patients having 3663 images with 14 pathologies categories considered as tags (Atelectasis, Consolidation, Infiltration, Pneumothorax, Edema, Emphysema, Fibrosis, Effusion, Pneumonia, Pleural_thickening, Cardiomegaly, Nodule, Mass and Hernia). The dataset generates 1000 patients nodes related with 63627 edges and 14 tags nodes tied with 339 edges (see Fig. 2). To evaluate our proposed approach of the graph based tag recommendations, we have considered 9 patients to whom the tag recommendations were performed in order to suggest tags for their X-ray images (10 distinct X-ray images) (see Table 3). The evaluation of tag recommendations

Table 1. Tag recommendations

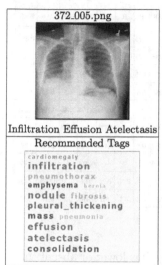

372_005.png
Infiltration Effusion Atelectasis
Recommended Tags
cardiomegaly **infiltration** pneumothorax **emphysema** hernia **nodule** fibrosis **pleural_thickening** **mass** pneumonia **effusion** **atelectasis** **consolidation**

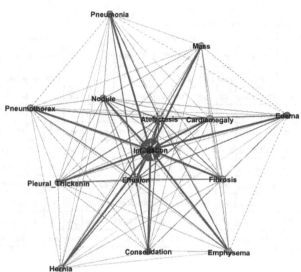

Fig. 2. Tags weighted network using Gephi

is performed using the automatic or offline evaluation that considers the previously assigned tags (used tags) as the ground truth (true positive). The common accuracy metrics are calculated from the number of tags that are either used or unused and either recommended or not (see Table 2).

Table 2. Confusion matrix accumulating the possible results of tag recommendations

	Used	Not used
Recommended	True-positive (Tp)	False-positive (Fp)
Not recommended	False-negative (Fn)	True-negative (Tn)

Precision P $= \frac{Tp}{Tp+Fp}$ represents the probability that a recommended tag is the used tag. Recall R $= \frac{Tp}{Tp+Fn}$ represents the probability that a used tag is recommended. The F1-measure F $= \frac{2 \times P \times R}{P+R}$ combines precision and recall into a single score. Accuracy A $= \frac{Tp+Tn}{Tp+Fp+Fn+Tn}$ is the number of all correct predictions (the recommended used tags and the not recommended unused tags) divided by the total number of the recommended and not recommended tags. The false positive rate FPR $= \frac{Fp}{Fp+Tn}$ is the probability that an unused tag is recommended. The false negative rate of FNR $= \frac{Fn}{Tp+Fn}$ is the probability that a used tag is not recommended.

Table 3. Evaluation

Patient ID	X-ray Image	Community Graph							Images Graph							Tags Graph						
		P	R	F	FPR	FNR	A	ERR	P	R	F	FPR	FNR	A	ERR	P	R	F	FPR	FNR	A	ERR
13	13_030.png	0.384	1	0.555	0.888	0	0.428	0.571	0.5	1	0.666	0.555	0	0.643	0.357	0.25	0.2	0.222	0.231	0.8	0.611	0.388
372	372_005.png	0.231	1	0.375	0.909	0	0.286	0.714	0.428	1	0.6	1	0	0.714	0.286	0.75	1	0.857	0.09	0	0.928	0.0714
4	4_000.png	0.154	1	0.266	0.916	0	0.214	0.786	-	0	-	-	1	0.875	0.125	0.25	0.5	0.333	0.231	0.5	0.733	0.266
132	132_004.png	0.384	1	0.555	0.888	0	0.428	0.571	0.5	1	0.666	0.4	0	0.714	0.286	0.5	0.5	0.5	0.166	0.5	0.75	0.25
132	132_005.png	0.385	1	0.555	0.888	0	0.428	0.571	0.571	0.8	0.666	0.3	0.2	0.733	0.266	0.5	0.4	0.444	0.166	0.6	0.705	0.294
208	208_000.png	0.231	1	0.375	0.909	0	0.285	0.714	-	0	-	0	1	0.777	0.222	0.5	0.666	0.571	0.166	0.333	0.8	0.2
211	211_006.png	0.357	1	0.526	1	0	0.357	0.643	0.5	1	0.666	0.555	0	0.643	0.357	0.5	0.4	0.444	0.166	0.6	0.706	0.294
10	10_000.png	0.083	1	0.154	0.846	0	0.0214	0.756	-	0	-	0	1	0.933	0.066	0	0	-	0.214	1	0.733	0.266
282	282_000.png	0.307	1	0.470	0.9	0	0.357	0.643	-	0	-	0	1	0.777	0.222	0.75	0.75	0.75	0.09	0.25	0.8666	0.133
32	32_034.png	0.333	1	0.5	0.8	0	0.428	0.571	0.5	1	0.666	0.4	0	0.714	0.286	0.5	0.5	0.5	0.166	0.5	0.75	0.25

The evaluation table shows that an untagged image has lower or absent measures' scores in the images graph based tag recommendation, for example, the X-ray images "208_000.png" and "282_000.png". Which underlines the use of tags recommended by the graph of tags and the community graph. Otherwise, the scores of the precision, recall and F1-measure are generally high. The recall $R = 1$ means that the community graph and images graph based tag recommendations always recommend the used tags (previously assigned tags). In the community graph based tag recommendation, all the healthcare providers' used tags are recommended that the reason why the $FNR = 0$. For instance, the patient "372" who has the X-ray image "372_005.png" previously tagged with three tags (diseases) "Infiltration; Effusion; Atelectasis" (see Table 1) has higher measures scores using the tag graph based tag recommendation which indicates that these three previously used tags are strongly related within the graph of tags. Even though the accuracy is lower for the graph of community compared to the graph of tags, the recommender system can be moderated by adding the recommended unused tags. Despite the low cost, coverage and scalability in large-scale tag recommendations, the offline evaluation still lowers the effectiveness of the recommendations compared to the online one. Some of the recommended tags, the unused recommended tags or false positive, might be considered relevant tags for the online evaluation that relies on healthcare stakeholders to evaluate manually the suggested tags describing pathologies detected in the X-ray image.

5   Conclusion and Perspectives

To achieve clinically relevant computer-aided detection and diagnosis in medical images (e.g. the chest X-rays), we have developed a graph-based recommender system of tags that suggests relevant diseases (or pathologies) to annotate the medical images and improve their interpretation. Three graphs are generated namely a graph relating different diseases (tags), a graph of images and another graph of patients' community. Therefore, the system of recommendation will aid the radiologists to detect and interpret invisible diseases of the underlying anatomical structure. It may also help in early revealing and diagnosis of cancerous lung nodules from chest X-ray images. The experimental evaluation has shown relevant results attesting the effectiveness of our approach. However, we aim to call for healthcare providers' online evaluation. To foster our future research, we aim to apply other centrality measures to detect the centrality of nodes for each graph. Also, we will expand the community of patients in order to support consistent and meaningful testing on a larger dataset. Future perspectives will focus on capturing, integrating and investigating other additional information (e.g. context, the patient's personal information) to adjust the semantic relationships among the graphs and enhance the nodes' clustering. In future works, we will promote the interactions within a network by recommending divers items in the different domain of interest (e.g. the collaborative learning and the valorization of cultural heritage).

References

1. Castaneda, C., Nalley, K., Mannion, C.: Clinical decision support systems for improving diagnostic accuracy and achieving precision medicine. J. Clin. Bioinform. **5**, 4 (2015)
2. Finn, C.: Narrative nursing notes in the electronic health record: a key communication tool. Online J. Nurs. Inform. (OJNI) **19**(2) (2015)
3. Moss, J., Andison, M., Sobko, H.: An analysis of narrative nursing documentation in an otherwise structured intensive care clinical information system. In: AMIA Annual Symposium Proceedings, pp. 543–547 (2007)
4. Sinsky, C., Colligan, L., Li, L., Prgomet, M., Reynolds, S., Goeders, L.: Allocation of physician time in ambulatory practice: a time and motion study in 4 specialties. Ann. Intern. Med. **165**, 753–760 (2016)
5. Han, H., Lopp, L.: Writing and reading in the electronic health record: an entirely new world. Med. Educ. Online **18** (2013). https://doi.org/10.3402/meo.v18i0.18634
6. Wang, X., Peng, Y., Lu, L., Lu, Z., Bagheri, M., Summers, R.: Chestx-ray8: hospital-scale chest x-ray database and benchmarks on weakly-supervised classification and localization of common thorax diseases. In: Proceedings of the CVPR, pp. 3462–3471 (2017)
7. Hasman, A., Safran, C., Takeda, H.: Quality of health care: informatics foundations. Methods Inf. Med. **42**, 509–518 (2003)
8. Chiu, M.P., Cheng, W., Chu, K., Lin, C., Yeung, S.: Do medical professionals tag images differently from non-medical professionals? An implication of retrieving user-generated images of everyday medical situations. Proc. Assoc. Info. Sci. Tech. **53**, 1–5 (2016)
9. Belém, F., Almeida, J., Gonalves, M.: A survey on tag recommendation methods. J. Assoc. Inf. Sci. Technol. **68**(4), 830–844 (2016)
10. Ouhammou, Y., Ivanovic, M., Abelló, A., Bellatreche, L. (eds.): MEDI 2017. LNCS, vol. 10563. Springer, Cham (2017). https://doi.org/10.1007/978-3-319-66854-3

11. Savkov, A., Carroll, J., Koeling, R., Cassell, J.: Annotating patient clinical records with syntactic chunks and named entities: the Harvey Corpus. Lang. Resour. Eval. **50**, 1–26 (2016)
12. Napolitano, G., Marshall, A., Hamilton, P., Gavin, A.T.: Machine learning classification of surgical pathology reports and chunk recognition for information extraction noise reduction. Artif. Intell. Med. **70**, 77–83 (2016)
13. Pliakos, K., Kotropoulos, C.: Simultaneous image tagging and geo-location prediction within hypergraph ranking framework. In: Proceedings of the IEEE International Conference on Acoustic, Speech and Signal Processing, pp. 6894–6898 (2014)
14. Tan, Q., Liu, Y., Chen, X., Yu, G.: Multi-label classification based on low rank representation for image annotation. Remote Sens. **9**(2), 109 (2017)

Spatial Batch-Queries Processing Using xBR+-trees in Solid-State Drives

George Roumelis[1], Michael Vassilakopoulos[1(✉)], Antonio Corral[2],
Athanasios Fevgas[1], and Yannis Manolopoulos[3]

[1] Data Structuring & Engineering Lab., Department of Electrical and Computer
Engineering, University of Thessaly, Volos, Greece
{groumelis,mvasilako,fevgas}@uth.gr
[2] Department of Informatics, University of Almeria, Almeria, Spain
acorral@ual.es
[3] Faculty of Pure and Applied Sciences, Open University of Cyprus, Nicosia, Cyprus
yannis.manolopoulos@ouc.ac.cy

Abstract. Efficient query processing in spatial databases is of vital importance for numerous modern applications. In most cases, such processing is accomplished by taking advantage of spatial indexes. The xBR+-tree is an index for point data which has been shown to outperform indexes belonging to the R-tree family. On the other hand, Solid-State Drives (SSDs) are secondary storage devices that exhibit higher (especially read) performance than Hard Disk Drives and nowadays are being used in database systems. Regarding query processing, the higher performance of SSDs is maximized when large sequences of queries (batch queries) are executed by exploiting the massive I/O advantages of SSDs. In this paper, we present algorithms for processing common spatial (point-location, window and distance-range) batch queries using xBR+-trees in SSDs. Moreover, utilizing small and large datasets, we experimentally study the performance of these new algorithms against processing of batch queries by repeatedly applying existing algorithms for these queries. Our experiments show that, even when the existing algorithms take advantage of LRU buffering that minimizes disk accesses, the new algorithms prevail performance-wise.

Keywords: Spatial indexes · xBR+-trees · Query processing
Solid-State Drives

1 Introduction

Nowadays, the volume of available spatial data (e.g. location, routing, navigation data, etc.) is continuously increasing world-wide. To exploit these data, efficient processing of spatial queries is of great importance due to the wide area of applications that may address such queries. The most common spatial queries where points are involved are point-location, window, distance-range and K nearest-neighbor queries (PLQs, WQs, DRQs and KNNQs, respectively, in the sequel).

© Springer Nature Switzerland AG 2018
E. H. Abdelwahed et al. (Eds.): MEDI 2018, LNCS 11163, pp. 301–317, 2018.
https://doi.org/10.1007/978-3-030-00856-7_20

At a higher level, such queries have been used as the basis of many complex operations in advanced applications, for example, geographical information systems (GIS), location-based systems (LBS), geometric databases, CAD, etc.

The use of efficient spatial indices is very important for performing spatial queries and retrieving efficiently spatial objects from datasets according to specific spatial constraints [5]. Hierarchical indices are useful due to their ability to focus on the interesting subsets of data. This focusing results in an efficient representation and execution times on query processing and thus, it is particularly useful for performing spatial operations. An example of such indices is the Quadtree [20], which is based on the principle of recursive decomposition of space and has become an important access method for spatial applications [21].

The External Balanced Regular (xBR)-tree [23] is a secondary memory structure that belongs to the Quadtree family (widely used in GIS applications, which is suitable for storing and indexing points and, in extended versions, line segments, or other spatial objects). We use an improved version of xBR-tree, called xBR$^+$-tree [19], which is also a disk-resident structure. The xBR$^+$-tree improves the xBR-tree in the node structure and in the splitting process. The node structure of the xBR$^+$-tree stores information which makes query processing more efficient. In addition, the xBR$^+$-tree outperforms R*-tree and R$^+$-tree (in terms of I/O activity and execution time) for the most common spatial queries, like PLQs, WQs, DRQs, KNNQs, etc. [18].

The advent of non-volatile memories (NVM) has enabled a brand-new class of storage devices with exciting features that will prevail in the storage market in the near future. Their high read and write speeds, small size, low power consumption and shock resistance are some of the reasons that made them storage medium of choice. NAND flash is undoubtedly the most popular NVM today. Storage devices based on NAND Flash are found both in consumer devices and enterprise data-centers. However, upcoming technologies, such as 3D XPoint from Intel and Micron, make possible even more efficient devices [6]. At the very beginning, raw Flash memory chips were embedded in mobile devices and other electronics. However, soon enough, the increasing needs for efficient storage drove the emergence of Solid-State Drives (SSDs). SSDs are composed by Flash chips, embedded controllers and DRAM [3]. Contemporary devices incorporate from a few to many NAND chips, supplying capacities even of tens of terabytes in high-end systems. Flash controller, usually a 32-bit embedded CPU, executes the firmware that controls SSD operation, while DRAM is utilized to store metadata, information regarding address mapping and for user data caching. Firmware is fundamental for SSD operation [2]. Its main responsibility is to map virtual addresses, as they are seen by the host, to physical addresses in flash chips. For this reason is also known as Flash Translation Layer (FTL). FTL performs tasks for garbage collection, wear leveling and management of bad blocks. SSDs exhibit higher write and especially read performance than Hard Disk Drives. This performance advantage is maximized when issuing commands that massively write to/read from SSDs large sequences of consecutive pages (due to exploiting the internal parallelism of SSDs), instead of issuing commands that write to/read from SSDs the pages of such sequences in small subsequences, or even, one-by-one [12].

In this paper, we present new algorithms for processing large sequences of common spatial queries (PLQs, WQs, DRQs) using xBR$^+$-trees in SSDs. These algorithms are especially designed to massively read from SSDs large sequences of pages needed for answering such queries. Such large sequences of queries (batch queries) appear frequently in applications. Moreover, using small and large datasets, we experimentally study the performance of these new algorithms against processing of batch queries by repeatedly applying existing algorithms for these queries. In addition, several experiments have been executed, showing that the new algorithms are performance winners.

The sequel is organized as follows. In Sect. 2 we review related work on spatial query processing over xBR-trees, as well as, on indices taking advantage of SSDs performance and provide the motivation of this paper. In Sect. 3, we describe the most important characteristics of the xBR$^+$-tree. Section 4 presents new algorithms for batch queries processing using xBR$^+$-tree in SSDs. The results of our experiments are discussed in Sect. 5. Finally, Sect. 6 provides the conclusions arising from our work and discusses future work directions.

2 Related Work and Motivation

In this section, we first briefly review the xBR-tree family. Then, the most representative spatial indexes, taking advantage of SSD performance, are revised. Finally, the main motivation of this work is exposed.

2.1 The xBR-tree Family

The xBR-tree was initially proposed in [23] as a secondary-memory pointer-based structure that belongs to the Quadtree family. The original xBR-tree was enhanced in [15]. The xBR$^+$-tree [18,19] is a further improved extension of the xBR-tree regarding performance of tree creation and spatial query processing. Bulk-loading and bulk-insertion methods for xBR$^+$-trees are presented in [16] and [17], respectively.

In [18], an exhaustive performance comparison (I/O activity and execution time) of xBR$^+$-trees (non-overlapping trees of the Quadtree family), R$^+$-trees (non-overlapping trees of the R-tree family) and R*-trees (industry standard belonging to the R-tree family) is performed. In this comparative study, several performance aspects are studied, like tree building and processing single point dataset queries (PLQs, WQs, DRQs and KNNQs) and distance-based join queries (DJQs), using medium and large spatial (real and synthetic) datasets. As a conclusion, the xBR$^+$-tree is a clear winner for tree building and query performance. The excellent building performance of the xBR$^+$-tree is due to the regular subdivision of space that leads to much fewer and simpler calculations. The higher query performance of the xBR$^+$-tree is due to the combination of the regular subdivision of space, the additional representation of the minimum rectangles bounding the actual data objects, the algorithmic improvements of certain spatial queries and the storage order of the entries of internal nodes.

2.2 Spatial Indexes for Flash SSDs

NAND Flash provides superior performance compared to traditional magnetic disks but has some intrinsic characteristics. It exhibits asymmetry in the read, write, and erasure speeds and a page must be erased first before being re-programmed. Erase operations take place at block level, while reads and writes are performed at page level. SSDs inherit some of these characteristics, thus in most devices read operations are faster than writes, while difference exist among the speeds of sequential and random I/Os as well. Especially, random writes may initiate garbage collection which is impacts the efficiency of the device. On the other hand, the high degree of internal parallelism of latest SSDs substantially contributes to the improvement of I/O performance [13]. Many research efforts have been made for Flash efficient database indexes. The works for spatial data processing mostly concern the R-tree.

The RFTL [24] is the first effort towards a flash efficient implementation of the R-tree. It is based on recording deltas for update operations. An in-memory buffer is utilized to hold the deltas before be persisted in batches. The same method has also been applied for the Aggregated R-tree in [11].

The LCR-tree [10] exploits a small section of SSD to log update operations. In contrary to other works it accumulates all the deltas for a particular node to one page in Flash. This way it ensures only one additional page reading to reach a tree node. The LCR-tree exhibits better performance than the original R-tree and the RFTL in mixed search/insert experimental scenarios. In the FOR-tree [7] authors aim to reduce small random writes by introducing overflow nodes to the R-tree. They propose new search and insert algorithms and a buffering algorithm for efficient caching of original and overflow nodes.

Regarding to non R-tree spatial indexes, the F-KDB [8] is a log-structured implementation of the K-D-B-tree for Flash, the MicroGF [9] is a 2D Grid File like structure for raw Flash, that is embedded in wireless sensor nodes, while a first effort towards to an efficient Grid-File for SSDs is presented in [4].

Furthermore two generic frameworks for spatial indexing have been proposed so far, which can encapsulate different data structures. FAST [22] utilizes the original insertion and update algorithms, buffers updates in RAM and flashes them to the SSD at once. eFIND [1] is a newer generic framework that provides better performance than FAST.

MPSearch [13,14] is a multi-path search algorithm for the B^+-tree that performs batch searches considering the characteristics of SSDs to accelerate performance. To the best of our knowledge, there are not any works concerning spatial batch-queries processing for Flash SSDs. Motivated by this observation, in this paper, we develop new algorithms for processing common spatial batch queries (PLQs, WQs, DRQs), using xBR^+-trees in SSDs. These algorithms are designed for maximizing performance by exploiting the internal parallelism of SSDs.

3   The xBR$^+$-tree Structure

In this section, for the sake of self-containment of the paper, we present the basics of the xBR$^+$-tree. The xBR$^+$-tree [19] is a hierarchical, disk-resident Quadtree-based index for multidimensional points (i.e. it is a totally disk-resident, height-balanced, pointer-based tree for multidimensional points). For 2d space, the space indexed is a *square* and is recursively subdivided in 4 equal subquadrants. The tree nodes are disk pages of two kinds: *leaves*, which store the actual multidimensional data and *internal nodes*, which provide a multiway indexing mechanism.

Internal node entries in xBR$^+$-trees contain entries of the form (*Shape*, *qside*, *DBR*, *Pointer*). Each entry corresponds to a child-node, having a region related to a subquadrant of the original space. *Shape* is a flag that determines if this region is a complete or non-complete square (the area remaining, after one or more splits; explained later in this subsection). This field is heavily used in queries. *qside* is the side length of the subquadrant of the original space that corresponds to this child-node. *DBR* (Data Bounding Rectangle) stores the coordinates of the rectangular subregion of this child-node region that contains point data (at least two points must reside on the sides of the *DBR*), while *Pointer* points to this child-node.

The subquadrant of the original space related to a child-node is expressed by an *Address*. This *Address* (which has a variable size) is not explicitly stored in the xBR$^+$-tree, although it is uniquely determined and can be easily calculated using *qside* and *DBR*. Here, we depict the *Address* only for demonstration purposes. Each *Address* represents a subquadrant that has been produced by Quadtree-like hierarchical subdivision of the current space (of the subquadrant of the original space related to the current node). It consists of a number of directional digits that make up this subdivision. The NW, NE, SW and SE subquadrants of a quadrant are distinguished by the directional digits 0, 1, 2 and 3, respectively. For example, the *Address* 1 represents the NE quadrant of the current space, while the *Address* 12 the SW subquadrant of the NE quadrant of the current space.

The actual region of the child-node is, in general, the subquadrant of its *Address* minus a number of smaller subquadrants, i.e. the ones corresponding to the next entries of the internal node. The entries in an internal node are saved in sequential groups, consisting of subgroups. The first entry of each group is the parental entry of the rest entries of this group. Each entry of a group is a descendant of the entry on its left, or it is the parent of a new (sub)group. For example, in Fig. 1 an internal node (a root) that points to 5 internal nodes that point to 15 leaves is depicted. The region of the root is the original space, which is assumed to have a quadrangular shape with origin (0,0) on the upper left corner and side length 1. The region of the rightmost entry (220*) is the NW subquadrant of the SW subquadrant of the SW quadrant of the original space (the * symbol is used to denote the end of a variable size *Address*). The flag *shape* is set at the value 'S' which expresses that this subquadrant is a complete square and thus, no part of its region will be found anywhere in the index, except for the child nodes of the subtree rooted at this entry. The region of the next (on the left) subquadrant is the SW subquadrant of the SW quadrant of the whole space. For this subbquadrant, the *Address* is 22* (non-complete square, denoted by 'noS'). The next two (on the left) entries cover the whole space of the NE quadrant (1*) and the NW quadrant (0*) of the whole space, respectively. Finally, the first entry in the root of this example expresses the whole space minus the four descendant regions (0*, 1*, 22* and 220*), and of course it is a non-complete square area. During a search, or an insertion of a data element with specified coordinates, the appropriate leaf and its region is determined by descending the tree from the root.

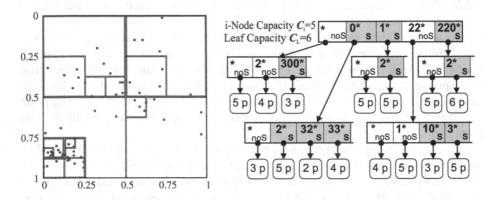

Fig. 1. A collection of 64 points, its grouping to xBR$^+$-tree nodes and its xBR$^+$-tree.

External nodes (leaves) of the xBR$^+$-tree simply contain the data elements and have a predetermined capacity C_L. When C_L is exceeded, due to an insertion in a leaf, the region of this leaf is partitioned in two subregions.

An example that demonstrates split of a leaf and an internal node follows. In the left upper part of the Fig. 2, an xBR$^+$-tree having one internal (root) node with 5 entries (its cardinality equals the maximum capacity of internal nodes, $C_i = 5$) is depicted. The 5 entries point to 5 leaves containing the first 25 points of the total number of 64 points of the dataset of Fig. 1. The next (26th) point p must be inserted in a leaf that already contains 6 points and is pointed by the first entry of the root (*) . Since $C_L = 6$, this leaf overflows and is split in two (itself and a new leaf). The new leaf covers the region of the subquadrant 2* and holds 3 points (left lower part of Fig. 2). The other 4 points remain in the existing leaf (*). An entry for the new leaf (2*) must be inserted in the root node which is already full. The root overflows and is split in two internal nodes (itself and a new node). In order to maintain the cohesion of the tree, a new root node having 2 entries is created. The first entry (*) points to the old root node and the second entry points to the new node (0*). The resulting xBR$^+$-tree, consisting of 3 internal nodes with 6 entries pointing to 6 leafs, is depicted in the right part of Fig. 2. The final tree, after inserting the rest of the 64 points and the space partitioning of the xBR⁺-tree are shown in Fig. 1. Details on the algorithms for splitting leaf and internal nodes appear in [19].

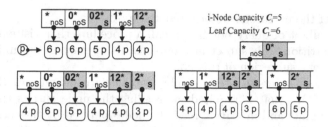

Fig. 2. Up-left: an xBR⁺-tree root pointing to 5 leaves. Down-left: an overflown xBR⁺-tree root pointing to 6 leaves. Right: the resulting xBR⁺-tree after splitting of the root.

4   Algorithms for Batch-Queries Processing

In the following, we present algorithms for processing the batch versions of three common single-dataset queries, using xBR⁺-trees in SSDs. These algorithms are designed for maximizing performance when applied on SSDs. They make use of a main memory area (denoted by M in the following), group read accesses needed by several queries of the batch, reorder the pages to be read and, at the same time, avoid unnecessary re-reading of the same pages and issue massive read operations of large sequences of consecutive pages (exploiting the internal parallelism of SSDs).

4.1   Algorithm for Processing of Batch Point-Location Queries

In this subsection, we present our new processing method for Batch Point-Location Queries ($BPLQ$) using xBR⁺-trees in SSDs. The definition of this query is as follows: Given an index $\mathcal{I}_P$ of a dataset P of points and a set of query points Q, the **BPLQ** returns the largest subset $R \subseteq Q$ such that $R = \{p : p \in Q \land p \in P\}$. The basic idea is as follows. We use the main memory area M (the size of M is defined by the system administrator and its size, a few MBs, is not significant in comparison to the size of the datasets) and we divide Q in subsets such that of each subset can be processed within M. Hierarchically, we visit the tree nodes and partition the query points in groups such that each group uniquely falls within one subregion of the current node and massively read the nodes corresponding to the resulting subregions into M. This process continues down to the leaf level, where we read the leaves corresponding to the resulting subregions into M. For each leaf, we determine all the query points of Q that exist in this leaf. The algorithm is described in more details as follows.

- Considering the maximum memory size of M available to our program, we calculate the maximum cardinality of each subset of Q that can be processed within M. We divide Q in subsets that do not exceed this maximum cardinality.
- For each of these subsets, we begin at the root.
  - For a subset of query points, we call a procedure that visits a tree node and partitions this subset in groups such that each group uniquely falls within one subregion of this node.
  - If this node points to internal nodes, we calculate and allocate the memory (part of M) that is required for reading the node entries that contain query points and massively read the nodes pointed by these entries.
    * For each of the nodes read and the group of points that fall within the region of this node, we recursively apply this procedure.
  - If a node read points to leaf nodes, we calculate and allocate the memory (part of M) that required for reading the leaves that contain query points and massively read the leaves pointed by the node entries.
    * For each of the leaves read and the group of points that fall within this leaf, we sort this group of points according to the axis along which the leaf points have been sorted and determine the query points that exist in the leaf (using a plane-sweep based technique to minimize comparisons).

4.2   Algorithm for Processing of Batch Window Queries

Here, we present our processing method for Batch Window Queries (BWQ) using xBR$^+$-trees in SSDs. The definition of this query is as follows: Given an index $\mathcal{I}_P$ of a dataset P and a set of rectangular query windows W, the **BWQ** returns the largest set R that contains pairs of objects (p, w) such that $R = \{(p, w) : p \in P \land p \text{ falls inside } w \in W\}$. The basic idea (an extension of the method in Subsect. 4.1) is as follows. We use a main memory area M and we divide W in subsets such that processing of each subset can be done within M. Hierarchically, we visit the tree nodes and for each node we process the regions of the entries contained within, to create a list of the query windows corresponding to each entry, since each region intersected with a query window may be a candidate for containing points of the pairs of the result (R). For the entries of the current node that contain a non-empty list of query windows, we massively read the nodes corresponding to these entries into M. This process continues down to the leaf level, where we read the leaves corresponding to these entries into M. For each leaf, we determine all the points of P that exist into the leaf and fall inside the regions of the query windows of the list. The algorithm is described in more details as follows.

- Considering the maximum memory size of M available to our program, we calculate the maximum cardinality of each subset of W that can be processed within M. We divide W in subsets that do not exceed this maximum cardinality.

- For each of these subsets of query windows, we begin at the root.
  - For a subset of query windows, we call a procedure that visits a tree node and in each entry of the node we append a list of query windows whose region is intersected with the region of the entry (in Subsect. 4.1, we didn't need such lists, since a query point falls in at most one region).
  - If this node points to internal nodes, we calculate and allocate the memory (part of M) that is required for reading the node entries that contain non-empty lists of query windows and massively read the nodes pointed by these entries.
    * For each of the nodes read and the list of query windows that has intersection with the region of this node, we recursively apply this procedure.
  - If a node read points to leaf nodes, we calculate and allocate the memory (part of M) that is required for reading the leaves that contain non-empty lists of query windows and massively read the leaves pointed by the node entries.
    * For each of the leaves read and the list of query windows that have intersection with the region of this leaf we apply the refinement step as follows. We sort this list of windows using as key the maximum coordinate of the axis along which the leaf points have been sorted and determine the leaf points that fall inside the regions of the query windows (using a plane-sweep based technique, to minimize comparisons).

4.3   Algorithm for Processing of Batch Distance-Range Queries

In this subsection, we present our processing method for Batch Distance-Range Queries ($BDRQ$) using xBR$^+$-trees in SSDs. The definition of this query is as follows: Given an index $\mathcal{I}_P$ of a dataset P and a set of query pairs of form (query point, distance threshold) Q, the **BDRQ** returns the largest set R that contains objects $(p, (q, \varepsilon))$ such that $R = \{(p, (q, \varepsilon)) : p \in P, (q, \varepsilon) \in Q \wedge distance(p, q) \leq \varepsilon\}$. The basic idea is as follows. We utilize a main memory area M. We divide Q in subsets such that processing of each subset can be done within M.

- One method of processing is the following. Every query pair could be seen as a query window with circular schema. Therefore, we can follow the filtering step of the BWQ method (presented in Subsect. 4.2) down to the leaf level for the *Minimum Bounding Square* (MBS) of each query pair. At the leaf level, we apply a refinement step for the leaves and the actual query pairs (which are circles). Hierarchically, we visit the tree nodes and for each node we process the regions of the entries contained within, to create a list of the corresponding query pairs for each entry, since each region intersected with the minimum bounding square of a query pair may be a candidate for containing points of the objects of the result (R). For the entries of the current node that contain a non-empty list of query pairs we massively read the nodes corresponding to these entries into M. This process continues down to the leaf level, where we read the leaves corresponding to these entries into M. For each leaf, we determine all the points of P that exist into the leaf and fall inside the regions of the query pairs of the list. Since, in this method we utilize MBSs, we call it *BDRQ-MBS*.

- According to an alternative processing method, every query pair could be seen as the actual circle it represents. Therefore, we can apply the filtering step as follows. Hierarchically, we visit the tree nodes and for each node we process the regions of the entries contained within, to create a list of the corresponding query pairs for each entry. For each entry e of a tree node, we calculate the minimum distance between the region of the entry and the point of the query pair q ($minDist(e, q)$). Every point q with $minDist(e, q) \leq \varepsilon$ is added into the query list of e. It is expected that each region entry having intersection with a query pair may be a candidate to contain points of the objects of the resulting set (R). For the entries of the current node that contain a non-empty list of query pairs, we massively read the nodes corresponding to these entries into M. To simplify the calculations (reduce the execution time) we calculate the square of $minDist$ between a point and the region of an entry and we compare this metric with the square of the given ε. This process continues down to the leaf level, where we read the leaves corresponding to these entries into M. For each leaf, we determine all the points of P that exist into the leaf and fall inside the regions of the query pairs of the list. Since, in this method we utilize $minDist$, we call it *BDRQ-mD*.

5   Experimental Results

We run a large set of experiments to compare the repetitive application of the existing algorithms for processing batch queries to the new algorithms, designed especially for batch queries, in SSDs. We used real spatial datasets of North America representing roads (NArdN with 569082 line-segments) and rail-roads (NArrN with 191558 line-segments). To create sets of 2d points, we transformed the MBRs of line-segments from NArdN and NArrN into points by taking the center of each MBR (i.e. |NArdN| = 569082 points, |NArrN| = 191558 points). Moreover, to get the double amount of points from NArdN, we chose the two points with min and max coordinates of the MBR of each line-segment (i.e. we created a new dataset, |NArdND| = 1138164 points. The data of these three files were normalized in the range $[0, 1]^2$. We have also created synthetic clustered datasets of 250000, 500000 and 1000000 points, with 125 clusters in each dataset (uniformly distributed in the range $[0, 1]^2$), where for a set having N points, $N/125$ points were gathered around the center of each cluster, according to Gaussian distribution. We also used three big real datasets (retrieved from http:// spatialhadoop.cs.umn.edu/datasets.html), which represent water resources of North America (Water) consisting of 5836360 line-segments and world parks or green areas (Park) consisting of 11503925 polygons and world buildings (Build) consisting of 114736539 polygons. To create sets of points, we used the centers of the line-segment MBRs from Water and the centroids of polygons from Park

and Build. All experiments were performed on a Dell Precision T3500 worksta-
tion, running CentOS Linux 7 with Kernel 4.15.4 and equipped with a quad-core
Intel Xeon W3550 CPU, 8 GB of main memory, an 1TB 7.2K SATA-3 Seagate
HDD used for the operating system and a 512 GB SM951A Samsung SSD hosted
on PCI-e 2.0 interface, storing our executables and data. Since our algorithms
are especially designed for maximizing performance when applied on SSDs, the
xBR$^+$-tree was stored on the SSD of our system. However, we tested storing our
structure on the HDD, too and obtained execution times 2 orders of magnitude
larger than the ones on the SSD. Therefore, we present results of execution on
the SSD only.

We run experiments for studying the performance of existing and new algorithms for processing batches of PLQs, WQs and DRQs. We tested batches
consisting of $2^{10}, 2^{12}, 2^{14}$ and 2^{16} queries. We also tested tree node sizes equal to
4 KB, 8 KB and 16 KB. In each experiment, we counted actual disk accesses and
total execution time. Since the existing algorithms answer batch queries by repetitive application for each query of the batch (One-by-One, or ObO, execution),
we experimented with and without the use of LRU buffer equal to 256 internal
nodes and 256 leaf nodes. This discrimination of the two parts of LRU buffer is
necessary, since internal nodes are significantly fewer and a common LRU buffer
would get frequently emptied from internal nodes, although the same internal
nodes are more likely to be needed for separate queries of the batch. Our experiments showed that this buffer size is adequate for maximizing performance, even
for the largest trees tested. The maximum size of M was comparable to LRU size
(although, in many cases this maximum size was not utilized by the algorithms
studied). Therefore, for each query (PLQ, WQ and DRQ), we tested no-LRU
ObO, LRU ObO and the respective new algorithm. The total number of experiments performed equals 972 (combinations of 9 datasets, 3 node sizes, 4 batch
sizes, 3 queries and 3 algorithms for each query). Due to space limitations, in the
following we present indicative (or, a limited part of the) experimental results,
expressing the general trends found.

5.1 PLQ Experiments

To study PLQs, we created batches consisting of 50% existing and 50% non-
existing points in each dataset. Both existing and non-existing points cover the
whole indexed space. In Fig. 3 right, in the upper bar chart, we depict the (%)
gain of LRU ObO vs no-LRU ObO, regarding actual disk accesses and total execution time, for the NArdN dataset, the 3 node sizes (4 KB, 8KB and 16 KB) and
2^{12} batch size. Note that the gain is defined (for both metrics) as the fraction of
the difference of performance of the second and the first algorithms over the performance of the second algorithm ($gain = \frac{noLRU\ ObO - LRU\ ObO}{noLRU\ ObO}$, in this chart).
The LRU version is a clear winner (gain more than 90%, for disk accesses and
more than 88%, for execution time). In Fig. 3 left, in the upper table, we depict
the exact (%) gain figures of LRU ObO vs no-LRU ObO, regarding actual disk
accesses and total execution time for all batch sizes (the first column denotes

number of queries, #Q) and the same values for the rest experimental parameters. Note that the line in bold font corresponds to the diagram next to the table. It is clear that the LRU version maximizes performance for all batch sizes. Among the execution of PLQs using these two algorithms for all datasets, the min/max gain for disk accesses was 80.7%/99.4%, while the min/max gain for execution time was 74.4%/98.2%. In all datasets, as batch size increases, gain is also increased.

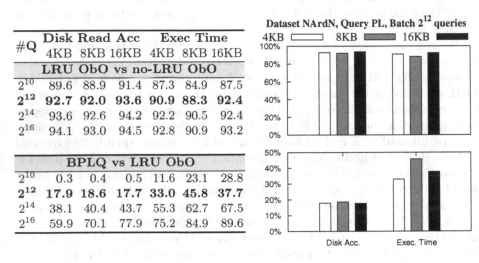

#Q	Disk Read Acc			Exec Time		
	4KB	8KB	16KB	4KB	8KB	16KB
LRU ObO vs no-LRU ObO						
2^{10}	89.6	88.9	91.4	87.3	84.9	87.5
2^{12}	**92.7**	**92.0**	**93.6**	**90.9**	**88.3**	**92.4**
2^{14}	93.6	92.6	94.2	92.2	90.5	92.4
2^{16}	94.1	93.0	94.5	92.8	90.9	93.2
BPLQ vs LRU ObO						
2^{10}	0.3	0.4	0.5	11.6	23.1	28.8
2^{12}	**17.9**	**18.6**	**17.7**	**33.0**	**45.8**	**37.7**
2^{14}	38.1	40.4	43.7	55.3	62.7	67.5
2^{16}	59.9	70.1	77.9	75.2	84.9	89.6

Fig. 3. PLQ: % performance gain (regarding Disk Accesses and Exec. Time) of LRU ObO vs no-LRU ObO and BPLQ vs LRU ObO, for the NArdN dataset.

In Fig. 3 right, in the lower bar chart, we depict the (%) gain of BPLQ vs LRU ObO, regarding actual disk accesses and total execution time, for the same experimental settings as in the upper bar chart. BPLQ is approximately 18% more efficient than LRU ObO regarding disk accesses and more than 33% more efficient than LRU ObO regarding execution time. Note that gain increases in the case of execution time, meaning that BPLQ minimizes computations even more than minimizing disk accesses, in relation to LRU ObO. In Fig. 3 left, in the lower table, we depict the exact (%) gain figures of BPLQ vs LRU ObO, regarding actual disk accesses and total execution time for all batch sizes and the same values for the rest experimental parameters. Note that again the line in bold font corresponds to the diagram next to the table. It is clear that BPLQ maximizes performance for all batch sizes. Among the execution of PLQs using these two algorithms for all datasets, the min/max gain for disk accesses was 0.2%/95.3%, while the min/max gain for execution time was 2.8%/95.8%. Again, in all datasets, as batch size increases, gain is also increased (in the case of BLPQ vs LRU ObO, the relative gain improvement is larger than the one between no-LRU ObO vs LRU ObO).

5.2 WQ Experiments

To study WQs, we created batches with query windows that cover the whole indexed space. Figure 4 (which is analogous to Fig. 3) depicts indicative results for the WQ and the 1000KCN dataset. As it is evident from the upper chart of this figure, the LRU version is a clear winner (gain more than 68% for disk accesses and more than 66% for execution time). It is also clear from the upper table of this figure that the LRU version maximizes performance for all batch sizes. Among the execution of WQs using these two algorithms for all datasets, the min/max gain for disk accesses was 1.4%/95.7%, whereas the min/max gain for execution time was −2.7%/93.8%. In all datasets, gain increases with increasing batch size. Note that the minimum values of gain with respect to actual disk accesses are observed in the cases of smaller batch sizes consisting of query windows with large dispersion. This way, the use of LRU buffering becomes ineffective because it causes an increase in the execution time of the queries (the overhead of buffer management overcomes the benefit of saving accesses). It is evident from the lower chart of Fig. 4 that BWQ is more than 31% more efficient than LRU ObO, regarding disk accesses and more than 75% more efficient than LRU ObO, regarding execution time. Note that gain increases in the case of execution time, meaning that BWQ minimizes computations even more than minimizing disk accesses, in relation to LRU ObO. The dominance of BWQ is verified for all batch sizes, in the lower table of Fig. 4. Among the execution of WQs using these two algorithms for all datasets, the min/max gain for disk accesses was 0%/97.6%, while the min/max gain for execution time was 42.1%/97.1%. Again, in all datasets, as batch size increases, gain is also increased.

#Q	Disk Read Acc			Exec Time		
	4KB	8KB	16KB	4KB	8KB	16KB
LRU ObO vs no-LRU ObO						
2^{10}	36.6	39.4	50.8	34.2	38.4	50.8
2^{12}	58.7	59.8	67.1	55.6	58.6	66.6
2^{14}	**72.5**	**68.3**	**70.9**	**69.9**	**66.9**	**70.4**
2^{16}	74.7	69.4	71.5	73.3	67.7	70

BWQ vs LRU ObO						
2^{10}	0.6	1	2.3	43.9	45.4	48.9
2^{12}	5.7	8.1	24.7	51.6	63.3	77.2
2^{14}	**31.7**	**56.1**	**75.1**	**79.3**	**88.8**	**92.7**
2^{16}	78.2	87.7	93.4	93.5	95.7	96.7

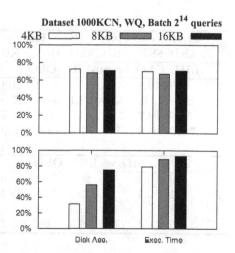

Fig. 4. WQ: % performance gain (regarding Disk Accesses and Exec. Time) of LRU ObO vs no-LRU ObO and BWQ vs LRU ObO, for the 1000KCN dataset.

5.3 DRQ Experiments

To study DRQs, we created batches with query windows that cover the whole indexed space. In the experimental results, the new algorithm used was BDRQ-mD, since, BDRQ-MBS showed worse execution time performance, especially for big datasets. Although, BDRQ-MBS is faster regarding CPU processing, this is overcome by the smaller number of disk accesses needed by BDRQ-mD. Figure 5 (which is analogous to Figs. 3 and 4) depicts indicative results for the DRQ and the Park dataset. As it is evident from the upper chart of this figure, the LRU version is a clear winner (gain more than 78% for disk accesses and more than 77% for execution time).   It is also clear from the upper table of this figure that the LRU version maximizes performance for all batch sizes. Among the execution of DRQs using these two algorithms for all datasets, the min/max gain for disk accesses was 1.2%/95.6%, while the min/max gain for execution time was −0.7%/93.7%. In all datasets, as batch size increases, gain is also increased. Note that the minimum values of gain for the metric of actual disk accesses are observed in the cases of smaller batch sizes consisting of query distance ranges with large dispersion. This way, the use of LRU buffering becomes ineffective as the query execution time is increased. It is evident from the lower chart of Fig. 5 that BDRQ is from 18% more efficient than LRU ObO regarding disk accesses and more than 64% more efficient than LRU ObO regarding execution time. Note that gain increases in the case of execution time, meaning that BDRQ minimizes computations even more than minimizing disk accesses, in relation to LRU ObO. The dominance of BDRQ is verified for all batch sizes, in the lower table of Fig. 5. Among the execution of DRQs using these two algorithms for all datasets, the min/max gain for disk accesses was 0%/97.6%, while the min/max

#Q	Disk Read Acc			Exec Time		
	4KB	8KB	16KB	4KB	8KB	16KB
LRU ObO vs no-LRU ObO						
2^{10}	9.9	19.4	25.8	9	16.2	21.3
2^{12}	28.4	45	53.5	28.1	41.3	47.9
2^{14}	53.6	69.7	75.3	54.1	66.2	68.7
2^{16}	**78.6**	**86.9**	**88.7**	**77.6**	**83.9**	**82.9**

#Q	Disk Read Acc			Exec Time		
BDRQ-mD vs LRU ObO						
2^{10}	0.6	0.4	1	80.5	76.2	69
2^{12}	2	2.4	3.4	75.6	70.1	62.3
2^{14}	5.8	7	9.3	71.4	64	63.1
2^{16}	**18.5**	**21.4**	**27.1**	**66.3**	**64**	**64.7**

Fig. 5. DRQ: % performance gain (regarding Disk Accesses and Exec. Time) of LRU ObO vs no-LRU ObO and BDRQ vs LRU ObO, for the Park dataset.

gain for execution time was 31.4%/97.1%. Again, in all datasets, gain increases with batch size increasing.

6   Conclusions and Future Work

In this paper, for the first time in the literature, we present algorithms for common spatial batch queries on single datasets, using xBR$^+$-trees in SSDs. Processing of spatial queries in SSDs has not received considerable attention in the literature, so far. The new algorithms proposed outperform the repetitive application of existing algorithms by exploiting the massive I/O advantages of SSDs, both regarding actual disk access and execution time, even if the I/O of existing algorithms are assisted by LRU buffering.

For all three queries studied, all batch sizes and all datasets, the new algorithms always exhibit better performance than the existing algorithms, for both metrics (actual disk accesses and execution time). For all three queries studied, the new algorithms exhibit maximum gain of execution time that exceeds 95% for large batches and big datasets. Therefore, the processing proposed is best suited to heavily queried big data. Nevertheless, in the case of WQs and DRQs, maximum gain of execution time is significant (more than 41% and 32%, respectively) even for small batches and small datasets.

Future work plans include:

- Developing and studying the performance of algorithms for other common spatial queries (e.g. K Nearest Neighbors, queries involving two datasets, like K Closest Pairs, Distance-Range Joins, All K Nearest Neighbors, etc.) in SSDs.
- Developing algorithms for spatial queries in SSDs that utilize other structures (e.g. of the R-tree family, or Grid files).
- Developing parallel algorithms, utilizing multiple CPUs/GPU cores, for spatial queries in SSDs.

Acknowledgments. Work of Antonio Corral, Michael Vassilakopoulos and Yannis Manolopoulos funded by the MINECO research project [TIN2017-83964-R].

References

1. Carniel, A.C., Ciferri, R.R., de Aguiar Ciferri, C.D.: A generic and efficient framework for spatial indexing on flash-based solid state drives. In: Kirikova, M., Nørvåg, K., Papadopoulos, G.A. (eds.) ADBIS 2017. LNCS, vol. 10509, pp. 229–243. Springer, Cham (2017). https://doi.org/10.1007/978-3-319-66917-5_16
2. Cho, S., Chang, S., Jo, I.: The solid-state drive technology, today and tomorrow. In: ICDE Conference, pp. 1520–1522 (2015)
3. Cornwell, M.: Anatomy of a solid-state drive. Commun. ACM **55**(12), 59–63 (2012)
4. Fevgas, A., Bozanis, P.: Grid-file: towards to a flash efficient multi-dimensional index. In: Chen, Q., Hameurlain, A., Toumani, F., Wagner, R., Decker, H. (eds.) DEXA 2015. LNCS, vol. 9262, pp. 285–294. Springer, Cham (2015). https://doi. org/10.1007/978-3-319-22852-5_24

5. Gaede, V., Günther, O.: Multidimensional access methods. ACM Comput. Surv. **30**(2), 170–231 (1998)
6. Hady, F.T., Foong, A.P., Veal, B., Williams, D.: Platform storage performance with 3d XPoint technology. Proc. IEEE **105**(9), 1822–1833 (2017)
7. Jin, P., Xie, X., Wang, N., Yue, L.: Optimizing R-tree for flash memory. Expert Syst. Appl. **42**(10), 4676–4686 (2015)
8. Li, G., Zhao, P., Yuan, L., Gao, S.: Efficient implementation of a multi-dimensional index structure over flash memory storage systems. J. Supercomput. **64**(3), 1055–1074 (2013)
9. Lin, S., Zeinalipour-Yazti, D., Kalogeraki, V., Gunopulos, D., Najjar, W.A.: Efficient indexing data structures for flash-based sensor devices. TOS **2**(4), 468–503 (2006)
10. Lv, Y., Li, J., Cui, B., Chen, X.: Log-compact R-tree: an efficient spatial index for SSD. In: Xu, J., Yu, G., Zhou, S., Unland, R. (eds.) DASFAA 2011. LNCS, vol. 6637, pp. 202–213. Springer, Heidelberg (2011). https://doi.org/10.1007/978-3-642-20244-5_20
11. Pawlik, M., Macyna, W.: Implementation of the aggregated R-tree over flash memory. In: Yu, H., Yu, G., Hsu, W., Moon, Y.-S., Unland, R., Yoo, J. (eds.) DASFAA 2012. LNCS, vol. 7240, pp. 65–72. Springer, Heidelberg (2012). https://doi.org/10.1007/978-3-642-29023-7_7
12. Roh, H., Kim, S., Lee, D., Park, S.: As B-tree: a study of an efficient B+-tree for SSDs. J. Inf. Sci. Eng. **30**(1), 85–106 (2014)
13. Roh, H., Park, S., Kim, S., Shin, M., Lee, S.: B^+-tree index optimization by exploiting internal parallelism of flash-based solid state drives. PVLDB **5**(4), 286–297 (2011)
14. Roh, H., Park, S., Shin, M., Lee, S.: Mpsearch: multi-path search for tree-based indexes to exploit internal parallelism of flash SSDs. IEEE Data Eng. Bull. **37**(2), 3–11 (2014)
15. Roumelis, G., Vassilakopoulos, M., Corral, A.: Performance comparison of xBR-trees and R*-trees for single dataset spatial queries. In: Eder, J., Bielikova, M., Tjoa, A.M. (eds.) ADBIS 2011. LNCS, vol. 6909, pp. 228–242. Springer, Heidelberg (2011). https://doi.org/10.1007/978-3-642-23737-9_17
16. Roumelis, G., Vassilakopoulos, M., Corral, A., Manolopoulos, Y.: Bulk-loading xBR+-trees. In: Bellatreche, L., Pastor, Ó., Almendros Jiménez, J.M., Aït-Ameur, Y. (eds.) MEDI 2016. LNCS, vol. 9893, pp. 57–71. Springer, Cham (2016). https://doi.org/10.1007/978-3-319-45547-1_5
17. Roumelis, G., Vassilakopoulos, M., Corral, A., Manolopoulos, Y.: Bulk insertions into xBR+-trees. In: Ouhammou, Y., Ivanovic, M., Abelló, A., Bellatreche, L. (eds.) MEDI 2017. LNCS, vol. 10563, pp. 185–199. Springer, Cham (2017). https://doi.org/10.1007/978-3-319-66854-3_14
18. Roumelis, G., Vassilakopoulos, M., Corral, A., Manolopoulos, Y.: Efficient query processing on large spatial databases: a performance study. J. Syst. Softw. **132**, 165–185 (2017)
19. Roumelis, G., Vassilakopoulos, M., Loukopoulos, T., Corral, A., Manolopoulos, Y.: The xBR+-tree: an efficient access method for points. In: Chen, Q., Hameurlain, A., Toumani, F., Wagner, R., Decker, H. (eds.) DEXA 2015. LNCS, vol. 9261, pp. 43–58. Springer, Cham (2015). https://doi.org/10.1007/978-3-319-22849-5_4
20. Samet, H.: The quadtree and related hierarchical data structures. ACM Comput. Surv. **16**(2), 187–260 (1984)
21. Samet, H.: The Design and Analysis of Spatial Data Structures. Addison-Wesley, Reading (1990)

22. Sarwat, M., Mokbel, M.F., Zhou, X., Nath, S.: FAST: a generic framework for flash-aware spatial trees. In: Pfoser, D. (ed.) SSTD 2011. LNCS, vol. 6849, pp. 149–167. Springer, Heidelberg (2011). https://doi.org/10.1007/978-3-642-22922-0_10

23. Vassilakopoulos, M., Manolopoulos, Y.: External balanced regular (x-BR) trees: new structures for very large spatial databases. In: Advances in Informatics: Selected papers of the 7th Panhellenic Conference on Informatics, pp. 324–333. World Scientific (2000)

24. Wu, C., Chang, L., Kuo, T.: An efficient R-tree implementation over flash-memory storage systems. In: ACM-GIS Conference, pp. 17–24 (2003)

Specification, Verification and Validation

Formalizing Railway Signaling System ERTMS/ETCS Using UML/Event-B

Abderrahim Ait Wakrime[1]([⊠]), Rahma Ben Ayed[1], Simon Collart-Dutilleul[1,2],
Yves Ledru[1,3], and Akram Idani[1,3]

[1] Institut de Recherche Technologique Railenium, 59300 Famars, France
{abderrahim.ait-wakrime,rahma.ben-ayed}@railenium.eu
[2] IFSTTAR-Lille, 20 Rue Elisée Reclus,
BP 70317, 59666 Villeneuve d'Ascq Cedex, France
simon.collart-dutilleul@ifsttar.fr
[3] Univ. Grenoble Alpes, CNRS, Grenoble INP, LIG, 38000 Grenoble, France
{yves.ledru,akram.idani}@imag.fr

Abstract. Critical systems like railway signaling systems need to guarantee important properties such as safety. Formal methods have achieved considerable success in designing critical systems with verified desirable properties. In this paper, we propose a formal model of ERTMS/ETCS (European Rail Traffic Management System/European Train Control System) which is an innovative railway signaling system. This work focuses on Hybrid ERTMS/ETCS Level 3 which is currently under design, by studying and modeling the functionalities and relations of its different sub-systems. The proposed model is based on model transformation from UML (Unified Modeling Language) class diagrams to the Event-B formal language. UML is used as the primary modeling notation to describe the structure and the main characteristics of the studied system. The generated Event-B model is enriched by the formalization of safety properties. We verify and validate the correctness of the proposed formalization using the ProB model-checker and animator.

Keywords: Formal methods · Verification · Event-B · UML
Model checking · Railway Signaling System · ERTMS/ETCS

1 Introduction

In order to harmonize the variety of railway signaling in Europe, European countries launched a major industrial project, ERTMS/ETCS, to streamline international rail traffic. This is achieved by improving border crossings of the signaling systems of each country and by eliminating the need for locomotive changes due to poor interoperability at border points between two countries. ERTMS/ETCS provides benefits regarding lower investment costs and improved safety.

Three levels of ERTMS/ETCS are defined in [1], which differ in the operated equipment and the operation mode. The first two levels are already operational.

© Springer Nature Switzerland AG 2018
E. H. Abdelwahed et al. (Eds.): MEDI 2018, LNCS 11163, pp. 321–330, 2018.
https://doi.org/10.1007/978-3-030-00856-7_21

Level 3 is in design and experimentation phases. Among the main objectives of installing this level is the reduction of operating costs. The ERTMS/ETCS Level 3 implementation requires a prior study which analyses requirements in order to satisfy railway signaling system needs. In this paper, we are interested in Hybrid ERTMS/ETCS Level 3 specified in [2]. We focus on the management of train movements by fixed virtual blocks.

The goal of the research is the formalization of Hybrid ERTMS/ETCS Level 3 in the Event-B formal language. The latter is an evolution of the (classical) B method [3]. Historically, the B method was chosen to develop and validate the automatic train control system in the scope of Meteor project [4]. It has been also used for the development of several safety critical railway systems [5].

In this paper, the starting point of our approach is the modeling of Hybrid ERTMS/ETCS Level 3 system as a UML class diagram. Thereafter, the B4MSecure tool [6] is used to transform the class diagram into B formal specification. The generated model is then adapted to Event-B and enriched with safety properties. Finally, the Event-B model is verified and validated, using model checking and animation. In brief, we adopt the following two phases: (i) we first propose a formal model based on Event-B whose data structures are produced from a UML class diagram, (ii) then we validate the correctness of this formal model using a model-checking and animation technique starting from a given initial state.

This paper is organized as follows. In Sect. 2, some principles of ERTMS/ETCS signaling system and UML modeling of Hybrid ERTMS/ETCS Level 3 are presented. In Sect. 3, we detail our proposed Event-B formalization and our verification process of Hybrid ERTMS/ETCS Level 3. Finally, in Sect. 4, we conclude and provide insights for future work.

2   UML Modeling of Hybrid ERTMS/ETCS Level 3

Figure 1 gives an overview of the basic ERTMS/ETCS components: trackside equipment, on-board sub-system and GSM-R (Global System for Mobile Communications-Railway). RBC (Radio Block Center) and Eurobalise belong to trackside equipment. RBC uses train reports and interlocking status to generate MA (Movement Authority), an authorization given to a train to move to a given point as a supervised movement. Eurobalise is a spot transmission device mainly for location referencing. As on-board sub-system, EVC (European Vital Computer) is connected with trackside equipment to ensure speed regulation of the train. GSM-R is a radio system used to provide communication, i.e. exchange information (voice and data), between trackside equipment and on-board sub-system. Three levels of ERTMS/ETCS are defined. The ERTMS/ETCS Level 3 is in design and experimentation phases. Among the main objectives of installing this level is the reduction of operating costs, because it reduces the need for trackside equipment. The ERTMS/ETCS Level 2 and ERTMS/ETCS Level 3 have similar ERTMS equipment and functionalities, but in the Level 3, shown in Fig. 1, the train detection and the train integrity check are performed by the

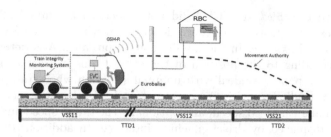

Fig. 1. Hybrid ERTMS/ETCS Level 3

on-board sub-system. The movement authority, in the Level 3, is used without visual signals or marker boards. It is sent by RBC to the train via GSM-R. This movement authority is based on train position and integrity reported by the train. In Fig. 1, the TTD (Trackside Train Detection) corresponds to conventional trackside train location equipment (e.g. track circuits and axle counters). This TTD can be divided into several VSSs (Virtual Sub-Sections). These subdivision principles represent the Hybrid ERTMS/ETCS Level 3, a variant of ERTMS/ETCS Level 3 system. Figure 2 represents an extract of class diagram that is a static view of our proposed Hybrid ERTMS/ETCS Level 3 model. This model provides an overview of the management of train movements depending on the occupancy state of the VSSs. This diagram shows the following system's classes: Train, MA, VSS and TTD.

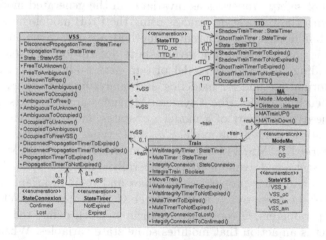

Fig. 2. Class diagram of a part of Hybrid ERTMS/ETCS Level 3.

VSSs are used by RBC and interlocking to ensure the safety of the system since it allows the spacing between trains going in the same direction on the same track. The presence of a train detected by a TTD in a given VSS, makes the VSS state *Occupied*. If a TTD did not detect a train in a VSS, the VSS state becomes *Free*. In this paper, we do not deal with others VSS states like *Ambiguous* and *Unknown*. In the nominal situation, an MA is determined, by the RBC, according to the position of the other trains in front of it in terms of VSSs. In this paper, we deal with nominal situation when train movements are under FS (Full Supervision) operating mode. Under this mode, the real speed, maximal authorized speed, and optionally the target speed and the target distance are displayed by driver machine interface. In addition, the on-board system supervises train speed and movements.

3   Formalizing Hybrid ERTMS/ETCS Level 3

3.1   Proposed Approach

Our approach follows two steps. First, we use the B4MSecure tool [6] to translate the class diagram of Hybrid ERTMS/ETCS Level 3 into B specifications. B4MSecure produces data structures and basic operations for model instantiation (object constructor/destructor, setters for attributes and associations). Some of these basic operations are not useful in our work. However, the data structure is relevant since it reproduces correctly the structure of the class diagram. Then, we adapt the generated B model to Event-B model manually by keeping the data structure of the model, suppressing B operations and introducing events. This is accomplished by introducing user defined events describing the behavioral semantics of Hybrid ERTMS/ETCS Level 3. We also introduce the formalization of safety properties as invariants in the generated model. Finally, we proceed with the verification process using the ProB model-checker and animator. The full details of the Event-B method are not given in this paper, references [3,7] can be useful. We give a short description of Event-B method for understanding the Event-B model of our case study below. Event-B is a state-based formal method for modeling and analyzing systems. A model uses two types of entities to describe a system: Machines and Contexts. A Machine represents the dynamic part of a model *i.e.* states and transitions. A Context contains the static part of the model *i.e.* static types (constants and sets). In our case, Hybrid ERTMS/ETCS Level 3 is modeled by a single Machine, that includes both static and dynamic parts. Generally, a model is defined by a name, sets, constants and their properties, variables and their invariants and events. An event takes the form: **evt** $\triangleq$ **any** x **where** G **then** Act **end**. Where x is the list of event parameters, G represents predicates which define the guard of the event and Act is an action that modifies some state variables. When the guard is satisfied, the event can be fired.

In summary, the main steps of our approach are depicted in Fig. 3: (1) Formalization of Hybrid ERTMS/ETCS Level 3, that is motivated by the management of VSSs. (2) Validation of obtained Event-B formalization using a model-checker and an animator.

3.2   Hybrid ERTMS/ETCS Level 3 Event-B Model

In the initial step, the B4MSecure tool is used to automatically generate the
B data structure of the class diagram. Thereafter, this model is enriched by
some safety properties as invariants and by the definition of events. The guard
and action of each event must be specified in such a way that it establishes
invariant preservation. To illustrate our approach, we generate the B Machine
from the UML class diagram shown in Fig. 2. Listing 1 represents an extract of
the generated machine called *ERTMSETCS3*.

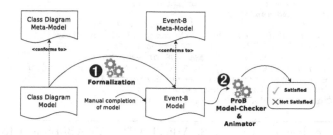

Fig. 3. Overview of the transformation approach.

In Listing 1, the *TRAIN, VSS_AS, TTD_AS, MA_AS* are specified as sets in
the Event-B Machine corresponding respectively to *Train, VSS, TTD* and *MA*
classes. In this paper, we introduced only the useful invariants for the presented
events. The model is more complicated than that, because it covers other mechanisms like propagation timers, waiting timers, mute timers and state of integrity
connection. These latter are used to constrain changes in the state of a VSS, for
example going from *Ambiguous* to *Occupied* states [2]. This work does not show
these mechanisms in the Event-B formalization. We focus only on the VSS state
changes from *Free* to *Occupied* and from *Occupied* to *Free*.

Added Variables. We manually enrich the formalization of the generated
Machine with some variables to expand the state space of the Machine with
additional information. These variables are represented in the *abstract variables
added manually* part of Listing 1.

Added Invariants. We define the typing invariant properties of each added
variable to complete the model construction. Listing 1. includes the invariants
generated by B4MSecure tool and the added invariants (see comments in the
invariant clause). These added invariants ease the formalization of the safety
properties and the specification of events.

```
MACHINE ERTMSETCS3
SETS VSS_AS; TTD_AS; MA_AS; TRAIN; ModeMA = {OS, FS};
      StateVSS = {VSS_fr, VSS_oc, VSS_un, VSS_um};
      StateTTD = {TTD_fr, TTD_oc}
ABSTRACT_VARIABLES
  \\The generated abstract variables by B4MSecure tool
  VSS, TTD, MA, MA_Mode, Train, VSS_State, TTD_State, Train_MA,
  MA_VSS, TTD_VSS, IntegerTrain, MA_Distance
  VSS_next, TTD_next
```

```
\\The abstract variables added manually
  train_VSS_current, train_TTD_current, last_VSS_MA, VSS_with_TTD
INVARIANT
\\The generated invariants by B4MSecure tool
  VSS ⊆ VSS_AS ∧ TTD ⊆ TTD_AS ∧
  MA ⊆ MA_AS ∧ MA_Mode ∈ MA → ModeMA ∧
  Train ⊆ TRAIN ∧
  VSS_State : VSS ↠ StateVSS ∧
  TTD_State : TTD ↠ StateTTD ∧ MA_Distance : MA → Integer
  MA_VSS ∈ MA ↔ P(VSS) ∧    \\ Set of VSS of each MA
  TTD_VSS ∈ TTD ↔ P(VSS) ∧    \\ Set of VSS of each TTD
  Train_MA ∈ Train → MA ∧    \\ MA of each train
  TTD_next ∈ TTD ↣ TTD ∧    \\ Next TTD of each TTD
  VSS_next ∈ VSS ↣ VSS ∧    \\ Next VSS of each VSS
  IntegerTrain ∈ Train → BOOL \\ Train integrity
\\The invariants added manually
  train_VSS_current ∈ Train → VSS ∧    \\ Occupied VSS by train
  train_TTD_current ∈ Train → TTD ∧    \\ Occupied TTD by train
  VSS_with_TTD ∈ VSS ↠ TTD ∧    \\ TTD of each VSS
  last_VSS_MA ∈ MA ↣ VSS ∧    \\ Last VSS of each MA
  ∀(vss, vssSet, tr, ma).(vss ∈ VSS ∧ vssSet ∈ P(VSS) ∧ tr ∈ Train ∧ ma ∈ MA ∧
    (tr ↦ vss ∈ train_VSS_current) ∧ (tr ↦ ma ∈ Train_MA) ∧
      (ma ↦ vssSet ∈ MA_VSS) ⇒ ¬(vss : vssSet))
        \\ Current VSS does not belong to MA ...
END
```

Listing 1. The description of SETS, ABSTRACT_VARIABLES and INVARIANT clauses.

Safety Invariants. In nominal situations, a movement authority of a train moving under FS mode is composed of free VSSs so that the train can run at the maximum authorized speed. However, in some exceptional situations, such as the coupling of two trains (e.g. in OS mode), there are degraded modes which allow the train to be moved to an occupied VSS. We specify the safety properties avoiding trains accidents under FS mode as invariants, in Listing 2. The first invariant allows to verify that, in FS mode, all VSSs affected to an MA are free. The second one checks that each VSS will never contain two trains, hence accidents can not happen. However, the last one ensures that two MA of two different trains do not share any VSS.

```
MACHINE ERTMSETCS3
INVARIANT
\\Invariant 1
  ∀ma.(ma ∈ MA ∧ MA_Mode(ma) = FS ⇒
    ∀vss.(vss ∈ VSS ∧ vss ∈ MA_VSS(ma) ⇒ VSS_State(vss) = VSS_fr)) ∧
\\Invariant 2
  ∀(t1, t2).(t1 ∈ Train ∧ t2 ∈ Train ∧ t1 ≠ t2 ∧
  MA_Mode(Train_MA(t1)) = FS ∧ MA_Mode(Train_MA(t2)) = FS ⇒
    train_VSS_current(t1) ≠ train_VSS_current(t2)) ∧
\\Invariant 3
  ∀(t1, t2).(t1 ∈ Train ∧ t2 ∈ Train ∧ t1 ≠ t2 ∧
  MA_Mode(Train_MA(t1)) = FS ∧ MA_Mode(Train_MA(t2)) = FS ⇒
    MA_VSS(Train_MA(t1)) ∩ MA_VSS(Train_MA(t2)) = ∅)
END
```

Listing 2. Safety properties invariants under FS mode.

Events Specification. In this stage, we specify events in order to model the system behavior. In Listing 3, the event *MoveTrain* allows to move the train from a VSS to another one. However, it does not release the VSS just left by the train. This release is insured by the *OccupiedToFreeVSS* event in Listing 4. Here, we do not take into account the intermediate state in which the train is located on two VSSs. The train moves to the next VSS if it is free and if it belongs to the allocated MA of this train. We note that trains circulate in the same direction. Once the train moves from the current VSS to the next one, the next VSS becomes occupied. The MA is updated by removing the new current VSS. In fact, the current VSS does not belong to the MA (the last invariant in Listing 1). If the train leaves a TTD to go to the next one, the state of this new current TTD changes to occupied. To update MA in parallel with movement of train, we define *MATrainUP* event which is not described here for lack of space. It allows to extend the MA of a train with a free VSS. This event updates an authority for a train to proceed up to an end point of a VSS where it has to stop. It exhibits the safe path of a train in terms of free VSSs.

```
MACHINE ERTMSETCS3
EVENTS
         MoveTrain = ANY  train, vss_crnt, vss_nxt, ma
WHERE    train ∈ Train  ∧  vss_crnt ∈ VSS  ∧  vss_nxt ∈ VSS  ∧  ma ∈ MA  ∧
         vss_crnt ↦ vss_nxt ∈ VSS_next  ∧
         train_VSS_current(train) = vss_crnt  ∧
         train ↦ ma ∈ Train_MA  ∧  vss_nxt ∈ MA_VSS(ma)  ∧
         VSS_State(vss_nxt) = VSS_fr
THEN     train_VSS_current := train_VSS_current  ⩤ {train ↦ vss_nxt}  ||
         train_TTD_current := train_TTD_current  ⩤
                     {train ↦ VSS_with_TTD(vss_nxt)}  ||
         TTD_State(VSS_with_TTD(vss_nxt)) := TTD_oc  ||
         MA_VSS := MA_VSS ⩤ {ma ↦ MA_VSS(ma)
                 − {VSS_next(train_VSS_current(train))}}  ||
         VSS_State(vss_nxt) := VSS_oc
    END; ...
END
```

Listing 3. *Moving train* event.

The event *OccupiedToFreeVSS*, as shown in Listing 4, represents the transition from occupied state to free state of a VSS. When a train with checked integrity (specified by *IntegerTrain* function whose state changes in a specific event) has reported to have left the VSS, the VSS that the train leaves will become free (using a total function *VSS_State(vss_crnt) := VSS_fr*). It is the same case for each TTD: when all its VSSs are free, the TTD becomes free.

```
MACHINE ERTMSETCS3
EVENTS
         OccupiedToFreeVSS = ANY  vss_crnt, vss_nxt, ttd_crnt, ttd_nxt, train
WHERE    ttd_crnt ∈ TTD  ∧  ttd_nxt ∈ TTD  ∧
         vss_crnt ∈ VSS  ∧  vss_nxt ∈ VSS  ∧
         train ∈ Train  ∧
         VSS_State(vss_crnt) = VSS_oc  ∧
         vss_crnt ↦ vss_nxt ∈ VSS_next  ∧
         ttd_crnt ↦ ttd_nxt ∈ TTD_next  ∧
         IntegerTrain(train) = TRUE  ∧
         train_VSS_current(train) = vss_nxt  ∧
         vss_crnt ∉ ran(train_VSS_current)
THEN     VSS_State(vss_crnt) := VSS_fr
    END; ...
END
```

Listing 4. *OccupiedToFreeVSS* event.

3.3   Verification and Validation

We aim to validate Event-B models and to verify that the invariants (typing and safety properties invariants) are preserved by all events. These models have finite state spaces, *i.e.* the objects set remains constant, because, the events do not add Train, TTD, VSS or MA instances. Figure 4 represents our motivating example derived from [2]. It is a running of two single trains (train1 and train2) with integrity confirmed by external device. This example includes three TTDs: TTD10, TTD20 and TTD30. Each TTD contains a set of VSSs like: TTD10 is composed of VSS11 and VSS12, TTD20 consists of VSS21, VSS22 and VSS23, TTD30 is composed of VSS31, VSS32 and VSS33. We give values to the constants, carrier sets and the variables of the model through INITIALISATION clause. This clause specifies the Hybrid ERTMS/ETCS Level 3 model elements values in the initial state. This initialisation and events must preserve typing and safety invariants showing the absence of rear-end accidents. In this model, the face to face accidents are not treated since we do not take into consideration trains moving in opposite directions. We use the ProB model-checker [8]. In this work, theorem proving is not used, because, it requires more training and effort than model checking. On the other side, since the system has a finite state space, the model checking is sufficient to check safety properties for a given initial state. Step 1 of Fig. 4. represents an initial state of our case study.

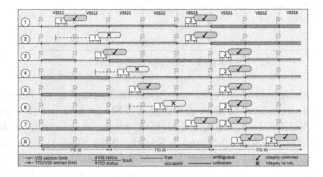

Fig. 4. An example of running of two single trains with integrity confirmed.

Verification Using Model Checking. Model checking is an automatic formal verification technique that is widely applied for the verification of a desired behavioral property of a given system [9]. It allows to verify that a system satisfies a given property using efficient algorithms. These algorithms are based on exhaustive enumeration (explicit or implicit) of all the reachable states from initial state. All experiments were conducted on a 64-bit PC, Ubuntu 16.04 operating system, an Intel Core i5, 2.3 GHz Processor with 4 cores and 8 GB RAM. Using the ProB model-checker and based on mixed breadth and depth search strategy, we have explored all states: 100% of checked states with 1347 distinct states and 3431 transitions during 2566 ms. No invariant violation was found, and all the operations were covered. This verification ensures that invariants are preserved by each event. Otherwise, a counter-example would have been generated.

Validation by Animation. ProB can be used as an animator. It allows automatic animations of Event-B model and to play several scenarios. Indeed, ProB animator displays the values of each variable, the enabled events and the history of chosen events. We have successfully applied the animation of ProB on the operational scenario of Fig. 4. ProB checks our model step by step from initial step to the final one and it shows the behaviour of model in clear terms.

4 Conclusion and Future Works

In this paper, we have presented a formalization and verification of Hybrid ERTMS/ETCS Level 3, using the Event-B modeling language. This approach is based on model transformation of a UML class diagram to Event-B. To do so, we used the B4MSecure tool to transform the structure of the class diagram to Event-B. Then, we enriched the generated model with the specifications of Hybrid ERTMS/ETCS Level 3 and with safety properties to prevent train collisions. We used the ProB model-checker to verify invariant preservation for a given initial state. In addition, we used ProB animator to validate that it supports the simulation of operational scenarios.

In our future work, we are interested in enriching our model by adding agents (*e.g.* train driver, traffic agent) to the model of Hybrid ERTMS/ETCS Level 3. This model will complement the current model, presented in this paper, to express which human and software agents have permission to access the objects and operations of the current model. This adopts a separation of concerns approach similar to the one used in information systems.

Acknowledgments. This work is funded by the NExTRegio project of IRT Railenium. The authors would like to thank SNCF Réseau for its support.

References

1. Schön, W., Larraufie, G., Moëns, G., Poré, J.: Railway Signalling and Automation. Work in Three Volumes. La Vie du Rail, Paris (2013)
2. European Economic Interest Group: Hybrid ERTMS/ETCS Level 3: Principles, Brussels, Belgium, July 2017
3. Abrial, J.R., Abrial, J.R.: The B-book: Assigning Programs to Meanings. Cambridge University Press, New York (2005)
4. Dehm, P., Benoit, P., Faivre, A., Meynadier, J.-M.: Météor: a successful application of B in a large project. In: Wing, J.M., Woodcock, J., Davies, J. (eds.) FM 1999. LNCS, vol. 1708, pp. 369–387. Springer, Heidelberg (1999). https://doi.org/10.1007/3-540-48119-2_22
5. Lecomte, T., Servat, T., Pouzancre, G., et al.: Formal methods in safety-critical railway systems. In: 10th Brasilian Symposium on Formal Methods, pp. 29–31 (2007)

6. Idani, A., Ledru, Y.: B for modeling secure information systems. In: Butler, M., Conchon, S., Zaïdi, F. (eds.) ICFEM 2015. LNCS, vol. 9407, pp. 312–318. Springer, Cham (2015). https://doi.org/10.1007/978-3-319-25423-4_20
7. Abrial, J.R.: Modeling in Event-B: System and Software Engineering. Cambridge University Press, New York (2010)
8. Leuschel, M., Butler, M.: ProB: an automated analysis toolset for the B method. Int. J. Softw. Tools Technol. Transf. **10**(2), 185–203 (2008)
9. Clarke, E.M., Grumberg, O., Peled, D.: Model Checking. MIT press, Cambridge (1999)

A Dynamic Analysis for Reverse Engineering of Sequence Diagram Using CPN

Chafik Baidada$^{(\boxtimes)}$, El Mahi Bouziane, and Abdeslam Jakimi

Software Engineering and Information Systems Engineering Team,
Faculty of Sciences and Technics, Errachidia, Morocco
chafik29@gmail.com, bouzianeelmahi@gmail.com,
ajakimi@yahoo.fr

Abstract. Reverse engineering is a very efficient way to extract automatically behavioral models from legacy systems. This paper proposes a new approach to detect and decipher dynamic information from these systems in order to recover the corresponding sequence diagram. The approach is composed of three steps: trace generation and collection, trace merging using Colored Petri Nets and sequence diagram extraction. Our results show that this approach can produce a more accurate high-level sequence diagram with main operators: "seq", "alt", "opt" and "par".

Keywords: Reverse engineering · UML · Sequence diagram · CPN
Dynamic analysis

1 Introduction

Software engineering activities like maintenance, testing, and integration deals with legacy systems. The most important aspect of all these processes is the comprehension of the components of existing systems and the relationships existing between them. According to some studies, up to 60% of the maintenance time is devoted to understanding these systems [1]. Therefore, it is important to develop tools and techniques that facilitate the task of understanding such systems. An effective comprehension technique to understand these systems is reverse engineering. Reverse engineering can help to understand existing systems by retrieving models from the available software artifacts. The IEEE-1219 [2] standard recommends reverse engineering as a technological solution to deal with legacy systems without updated documentation. In the object-oriented world, the target modeling language most used for reverse engineering is UML (Unified Modeling Language) [3] due to its significant presence in the industry. To better understand systems behavior, dynamic models are needed, such as Sequence Diagrams (SD). UML SD takes an important place in software engineering. They help software engineers to understand existing systems through the visualization of interactions between its objects [4]. To extract SD from an oriented-object program, we concentrate on reverse engineering relying on dynamic analysis. As mentioned in [5], dynamic analysis is more adapted to the reverse engineering of SD due to inheritance, polymorphism and dynamic binding.

© Springer Nature Switzerland AG 2018
E. H. Abdelwahed et al. (Eds.): MEDI 2018, LNCS 11163, pp. 331–345, 2018.
https://doi.org/10.1007/978-3-030-00856-7_22

The paper is organized as follows: Sect. 2 presents some related work. Section 3 introduces a background in reverse engineering of UML SD using Colored Petri Nets (CPN). Section 4 introduces our approach. Section 5 presents our case study. Finally, Sect. 6 concludes this paper.

2 Related Work

Reverse engineering as opposite of forward engineering is the process for identifying and analysis of software's system components, their interrelationships and the representation of their entities at a higher level of abstraction [6, 7].

In reverse engineering, program analysis usually takes place either through two kind of analysis: static analysis and dynamic analysis. Static analysis concerns analyzing the source code of a program by building an abstracted model of it. Various approaches have been developed to capture a system's behavior through static analysis [8–11]. One of the main of these works is that of Rountev et al. [11]. They proposed an approach for the extraction of UML Sequence Diagram from the source code of a system through building control flow graphs. In this study, the nodes represent the basic blocks of a program and the links represent all kinds of interactions between these blocks. The dynamic analysis, on the other hand, is to analyze a software system under execution. As such, runtime objects can be detected, thus making it possible to expose occurrences of polymorphism and late binding in contrast to static analysis. The produced execution traces contain very detailed information on how a system operates. Several studies try to generate SD by analyzing the execution traces. Taniguchi et al. [12] propose an automatic approach for the reverse engineering of SD from the execution traces of an object-oriented program. They present these traces in the form of a tree where each node represents a method call. They present four compaction rules, including compaction of repetitions and compaction of recursive calls, in order for the traces to be reduced in size, thereby producing compact sequence diagrams. In [13], they try to build a High Level Sequence Diagram (HLSD) from combined fragments using the state vector describing the system. The approach presented consists of two phases. During the first phase, a simple SD is generated containing just the method calls. The second phase makes it possible to draw HLSD by combining the diagrams generated in the first step. This is done by analyzing the different states of the system. In [14], it is proposed an approach based on dynamic analysis. They use LTS (Labeled Transition System) for modeling execution traces. Then they generate a HLSD from this LTS.

These approaches have succeeded in generating representative SD. However, they recognize some limitations. These limitations include information filtering problems. As mentioned in [15] Cornelissen et al. defined a catalog of abstractions and filtering in the context of reverse engineering of sequence diagrams. The approaches mentioned above do not use this filtering technics. Its alsow

In addition, these approaches do not lead to the UML operator "par" that is very important in the context of multi-threading applications.

3   UML Sequence Diagram and CPN

In this section, we discuss the dynamic analysis of the reverse engineering of SD diagrams from multiple execution traces and we give some definitions, which helps to explain clearly the proposed approach. First, we explain what a sequence diagram in UML 2.x is. Second, we present the execution trace and how it is obtained. Finally, we introduce CPN and how we used it to represent a HLSD.

3.1   UML2 Sequence Diagrams

Sequence Diagram is the more commonly used diagram for capturing inter-object behavior. Graphically, a SD has two dimensions: a horizontal dimension representing the instances participating in the scenario, and a vertical dimension representing time. SD is typically associated with use case realizations in the logical view of the system under development. It is been significantly changed in UML 2.0 [3].

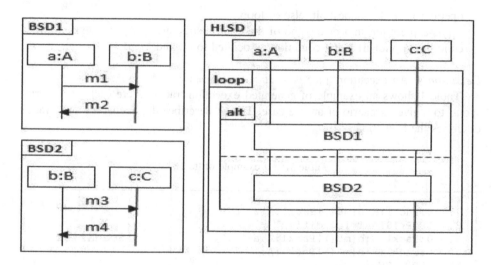

Fig. 1. Example of a HLSD

Notable improvements include the ability to define HLSD. A HLSD is a Sequence Diagram that refers to a set of Basic Sequence Diagrams (BSD) and composes them using a set of interaction operators. The main operators are: seq for sequence, alt for alternatives, loop for iterative actions, and par for parallelism.

Figure 1 shows an example of a HLSD composed of two BSDs using the operators loop and alt. For example, the basic SD BSD1 describes the interactions between two instances a1 (instance of the A class) and b1 (instance of the B class). The behavior specified in the HLSD is then equivalent to the expression loop (BSD1 alt BSD2).

3.2 Execution Traces

To build HLSD using dynamic analyses we have to generate traces of program executions describing the behavior of each thread of a program. Each trace corresponds to a scenario of a given use case. In what follows, we introduce a set of definitions relatives to execution traces, which are necessary to understand the approach.

Definition 1. A trace line is a method invocation or control structure.

Definition 2. A method invocation is a triplet T1=<Sender, Message, Receiver>where:

- Sender is the caller object, expressed in the form threadNumber:package:class: object.
- Message is the invoked method of the receiver object, expressed in the form methodName (par1, par2, …).
- Receiver is the called object, expressed in the form package:class:object.

Definition 3. A control structure is a triplet T2=<operator, status, condition>where:

- operator have the values: alt, else or loop.
- status express the start or the end of the control structure
- condition (optional) is the condition associated to alt and loop.

Definition 4. An execution trace is a set of trace lines.

Table 1 shows an example of generated execution traces where each trace correspond to a given scenario of an use case. Trace1 describes the Scenario1 and Trace2 describes the Scenario2.

Table 1. An example of traces

Trace1 L7.　0:Pack1:B:b|m4()|Pack1:A:a L8.　LOOP |START |condition1 L9.　0:Pack1:B:b|m5()|Pack1:A:a L10. 0:Pack1:B:b|m6()|Pack1:A:a L11. LOOP| END L7.　1:Pack1:B:b|m4()|Pack1:A:a	**Scenario1**
Trace2 *L0.*　*ALT | START | condition2* L1.　0:Pack1:A:a |m1()|Pack1:B:b L2.　ELSE | START L3.　0:Pack2:C:c |m2()|Pack2:D:d L4.　ELSE| END L5.　ALT | END L6.　0:Pack2:D:d |m3()|Pack2:D:c L1.　0:Pack1:A:a |m1()|Pack1:B:b	**Scenario2**

These traces are composed of several lines. L0 to L11 correspond to the name number of each line. Pack1 to Pack2 represents the packages to which classes A, B, C and D belong. m1() to m6() correspond to the methods calls of objects a, b, c and d. the numbers 0 and 1 correspond to the IDs of the threads.

3.3 Colored Petri Nets (CPN)

Petri nets [16] are a well-known and developed formalism with a rich theory, practical applications ranging from communication networks to healthcare systems and are supported by a wide range of commercial and noncommercial tools. CPN are a backward compatible extension of Petri nets. CPN preserve useful properties of Petri nets and at the same time extend initial formalism to allow the distinction between tokens. CPN allow tokens to have a data value attached to them. This attached data value is called token color.

Petri Net blocks are blocks of Petri Nets that have unique input and output places, which are referred to as precondition and post condition respectively. From the many existing variants of Petri nets, CPN are used in composing and integrating scenarios that are represented in the form of SD [17]. Four operators for composing scenarios have been implemented: sequential, conditional, iterative and concurrent. CPNs suit our approach as they can map a HLSD efficiently (Figs. 2 and 3). Transitions can represent BSD or operators such as alt, loop, and par. Colors are used to distinguish between places. All places from the same trace have the same color. That is very helpful to distinguish between scenarios in a HLSD.

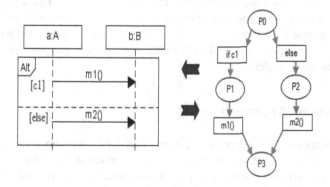

Fig. 2. A HLSD mapped onto CPN with operators loop and alt.

Figure 2 shows how a HLSD can be mapped easily into a CPN. P0 represents the initial precondition when P3 represents the final post condition of the Petri Net block. Transition "if c1" represent the operator alt with the condition C1 that lead to the place P1. Transition "m1 ( ) " refers to the BSD which describes that the object a of the class A sends the message m1 to the object b of the class B. Transition "else" describes when the condition c1 is not verified. This transition leads to the place P2. The transition "m2 ( ) " refers to the BSD which describes that the object a sends the message m2 to the object b. The operators par and seq can be mapped also as it is shown in Fig. 3.

In Fig. 3 transition "m1()" represents the BSD1 which describes that the object a sends the message m1 to the object b. Transition "m2()" represents BSD2 which describes that the object a sends the message m2 to the object b. Transition "m3()" represents BSD3 which describes that the object a sends the message m3 to the object b. The transition par represents that the BSD2 and BSD3 are executed in parallel.

From what precedes, we can conclude that, for a HLSD, we can generate a CPN that can represent all major UML SD operators such as seq, alt, par and loop. We can also do the reverse transformation by mapping a CPN into a HLSD.

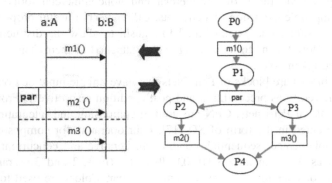

Fig. 3. A HLSD mapped onto CPN with operators par and seq.

In this section, we discussed the reverse engineering of SD and gave definitions that are necessary for the good comprehension of our approach. The problem that arises is how we can reverse this process. I.e.: how, from execution traces, can we generate a CPN that can be mapped onto a HLSD? In the next section, we propose an approach that deals with this problem.

4   Overview of Approach

The proposed approach for reverse engineering of UML Sequence Diagram is illustrated in Fig. 4. The approach is defined in three main steps: trace generation and collection, trace merging using CPN and HLSD extraction. In the following subsections, each step is detailed.

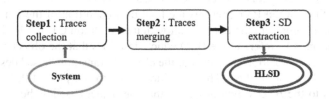

Fig. 4. Overview of our approach.

4.1 Trace Generation and Collection

To extract HLSD from an object- oriented program, we concentrate on reverse engineering relying on dynamic analysis. As mentioned in [4], dynamic analysis is more suited to the reverse engineering of SD of object-oriented systems. This dynamic analysis is usually performed using execution traces. There are multiple ways to generate execution traces [1]. This can include instrumentation of the source code, the byte code, virtual machines (for java programs for instance) or the use of a customized debugger. From these technics, we choose to use byte code instrumentation. In some legacy systems the source code does not have to be available and is therefore not manipulated.

Among several trace collection tools for Java software systems, we chose AspectJ [18]. This one is a Java intermediate code instrumentation tool. It provides a flexible way to instrument an application while the functionality is centrally managed in the aspect.

The system behavior is related to the environment entry data, in particular, values introduced by the user to initialize specific system variables. Thus, one execution session is not enough to identify all system behaviors. Therefore, we chose to run the system several times to generate different executions traces. Each execution trace corresponds to a particular scenario of a given use case of the system. Using AspectJ, a filtering process is applied for the system when it is running. This process is based on two filtering rules: distinction between business classes and architecture classes or the exclusion of certain packages. No lines that contain a package that is not interesting will appear on traces. This process enables us to concentrate on the main behavior of the system. The form of collected traces can differ from one tool to another, which has forced us to develop an adapter that reorganizes the traces into a new adapted form as described in Definition 1, Definition 2 and Definition 3. The role of the adapter is to restructure the trace into a form appropriate to the processing of merging traces.

4.2 Trace Merging Using CPN

This is the main step of our approach. It deals with the known problem of analyzing traces. Indeed, one of the major challenges to reverse engineering HLSD is to analyzing the multiple execution traces to identify operators and method invocations throughout the input traces. Independently from the reverse engineering of SD, the challenge of merging traces is well identified in the grammar inference domain where several well-defined techniques were proposed [19].

In this subsection, we chose to use CPNs in order to merge these execution trace. This is done in two steps: CPN Initialization and Merging.

CPN Initialization
In this step, one CPN for each execution trace is generated. The challenge in this step is identifying the operator "par". As shown in the Subsect. 3.2 every line trace has a thread number. We have developed an algorithm that compares between threads numbers in order to create for each line trace the correspondent CPN. The algorithm focuses on the threads number to detect the "par" operator. After that the first line in trace with child thread number is found, a transition labeled with "par" is added to the

CPN. After that, the algorithm create a CPN path for all trace lines that have the same thread number. These paths are attached to the transition "par". All places that represent trace lines have the same color. These colors allow us to distinguish between the scenarios. This gives the possibility of subdividing an HLSD into several HLSDs to facilitate the task of understanding the system.

CPN Merging

In the previous step, every trace has a correspondent CPN. This CPN includes as transition only method invocation or operator "par". In this second step, the CPNs of the different traces are merged to obtain a single CPN that merges the initial traces. This is done by using the Kbehavior [20]. The Kbehavior is inspired by the Ktail algorithm [21]. Both are used to build an automaton from execution traces. These techniques allow learning a target regular grammar from a set of sequences. For this, a generalization procedure of the automaton is applied iteratively by successive fusion of compatible states. Ktail has a major limitation: The Ktail algorithm is not able to reuse already learned knowledge to adapt to new generated traces, which is not the case for Kbehavior. In our case, we took the main idea of this algorithm. We adapt it to deal with CPNs. When a new trace is given to the algorithm, adapted Kbehavior first identifies sub-traces of the input trace that are accepted by sub-CPN in the current CPN (the sub-traces must have a minimal length k, otherwise they are considered too short to be relevant). Then adapted Kbehavior extends the CPN with the addition of new branches that suitably connect the identified sub-CPN, producing a new version of the CPN that accepts the entire input trace (Fig. 5).

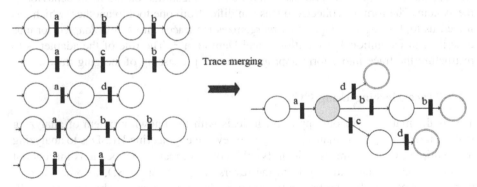

Fig. 5. Example of merging traces using adapted Kbehavior (k = 2)

4.3 HLSD Extraction

In this step, we can easily build HLSD by mapping the resulting CPN using transformation rules as is it shown in Figs. 3 and 2.

5 Case Study

To show the feasibility of our approach, we choose the example of Sales application. The application code provide different types of behavioral interactions (parallel, iterative, optional and alternative) that are the subject of our study. The application developed in Java with six classes: Vendor, Sale, Calcul, Invoice, Payslip and Delivery. The application allows sellers to create sales of articles. To achieve this, the seller sends an order to create a new sale and he can subsequently add articles and calculate the sum. Then the routine addition of items and calculation of the sum is repeated as the number of items ordered (repetitive behavior). After that, either a delivery slip or an invoice must be established in order to be signed by the seller (alternative behavior). If the vendor choose to sign an invoice, a waiting message is displaying while the invoice is established (parallel behavior).

Finally, the creation of a pay slip is the object of choice for the customer (optional behavior). Listing1 shows the source code of some classes of the application.

Listing 1

```
1   public class Vendor {
2   public static void main(String[] args){
3       int nbr_article=4;
4       boolean isInvoice=true;
5       boolean isPayslip=true;
6       Sales sale=new Sales();
7       sale.newSales(nbr_article, isInvoice,isPayslip);
8   }
9   public static void signInvoice(){
10      System.out.println("Invoice signed");
11  }
12  public static void signDelivery(){
13      System.out.println("Delivery signed");
14  }
15  public static void signPayslip(){
16      System.out.println("Payslip signed");
17  }
18  }
19
20  class Sales {
21    public void newSales(int nbr_article,
22    boolean isInvoice, Boolean isPayslip){
23      float oldValue=0;
24      System.out.println("New sale created");
25      for(int i=1;i<=nbr_article;i++){
26       float newValue=addArticle();
27       Calcul calcul= new Calcul();
28       oldValue=calcul.calculAmount(newValue, oldValue);
29      }
30    if(isInvoice){
31      Invoice invoice= new Invoice();
32      invoice.waitMessage();
33      invoice.start();
34    } else {
35      Delivery delivery= new Delivery();
36        delivery.getDelivery();
37    }
38    if(isPayslip)
39      {
```

```
40    Payslip paySlip=new Payslip();
41    payslip.getPayslip();}}
42    public static float addArticle(){
43    System.out.println("New article added");
44    return 1000;
45    }
46 }
47
48 class Invoice extends Thread {
49  public void preparingInvoice(){
50    System.out.println("Preparing Invoice ");
51    }
52    public void waitMessage(){
53    System.out.println("waiting for Invoice ");
54    }
55    public void getInvoice(){
56    System.out.println("Invoice printed");
57    Vendor.signInvoice();
58    }
59 @Override
60 public void run() {
61   try {
62       preparingInvoice();
63       Thread.sleep(1000);
64       getInvoice();
65    } catch (InterruptedException ex) { }
66   }
67 }
68
69 class Payslip {
70  public void getPayslip(){
71    System.out.println("Payslip printed");
72    Vendor.signPayslip();
73   }
74 }
75
76 class Delivery  {
77 public void getDelivery(){
78    System.out.println("Delivery printed");
79    Vendor.signDelivery();
80   }
81 }
```

5.1   Trace Collection

After the instrumentation of bytecode by AspectJ, and the execution of the instru-
mented program, a trace file is generated. The AspectJ tool provides a very interesting
option. The user can choose among the methods of classes of the program those he
wants to follow and instrument. This process enables us to ignore some methods and
concentrate on the main behavior of the system.

To organize the execution log files according to the form proposed by our
approach, we use the adapter that we developed for this purpose. The final execution
traces generated as illustrated in Table 2 can provide different types of behavioral
interactions.

Table 2. Generated traces

_Trace1(nbr_article = 3, isInvoice = false, isPayslip = false):_ L0. 1:Pck:Vendor:vendor | newSales (nbr_article, isInvoice, isPayslip) | Pck:Sale:sale L1. LOOP | START | i<=nbr_article L2. 1: Pck:Sale:sale | addArticle ( ) | Pck:Sale:sale L3. 1: Pck:Sale:sale | calculAmount(newValue, oldValue) | Pck:Calcul:calcul L2. 1: Pck:Sale:sale | addArticle ( ) | Pck:Sale:sale L3. 1: Pck:Sale:sale | calculAmount(newValue, oldValue) | Pck:Calcul:calcul L2. 1: Pck:Sale:sale | addArticle ( ) | Pck:Sale:sale L3. 1: Pck:Sale:sale | calculAmount(newValue, oldValue) | Pck:Calcul:calcul L4. LOOP | END L5. ALT | START | isInvoice L6. ELSE | BEGIN L7. 1: Pck:Sale:sale | getDelivery ( ) | Pck:Delivery:delivery L8. 1: Pck:Delivery:delivery | signDelivery ( ) | Pck:Vendor:vendor L9. ALT | END	Scenario1
_Trace2(nbr_article = 1, isInvoice = true, isPayslip = true):_ L0. 1:Pck:Vendor:vendor | newSales (nbr_article, isInvoice, isPayslip) | Pck:Sale:sale L1. LOOP | START | i<=nbr_article L2. 1: Pck:Sale:sale | addArticle ( ) | Pck:Sale:sale L3. 1: Pck:Sale:sale | calculAmount(newValue, oldValue) | Pck:Calcul:calcul L4. LOOP | END L5. ALT | START | isInvoice L10. 1: Pck:Sale:sale | getInvoice() | Pck:Invoice:invoice L11. 1: Pck:Sale:sale | waitMessage () | Pck:Vendor:vendor L12. 10: Pck:Invoice:invoice | preparingInvoice () | Pck:Invoice:invoice L13. 10: Pck:Invoice:invoice | signInvoice () | Pck:Vendor:vendor L6. ELSE | BEGIN L9. ALT | END L14. 1: Pck:Sale:sale | getPayslip ( ) | Pck: Payslip: paySlip L15. 1: Pck: Payslip: paySlip | signPayslip ( ) | Pck:Vendor:vendor	Scenario 2
_Trace1(nbr_article = 4, isInvoice = false, isPayslip = true):_ L0. 1:Pck:Vendor:vendor | newSales (nbr_article, isInvoice, isPayslip) | Pck:Sale:sale L1. LOOP | START | i<=nbr_article L2. 1: Pck:Sale:sale | addArticle ( ) | Pck:Sale:sale L3. 1: Pck:Sale:sale | calculAmount(newValue, oldValue) | Pck:Calcul:calcul L2. 1: Pck:Sale:sale | addArticle ( ) | Pck:Sale:sale L3. 1: Pck:Sale:sale | calculAmount(newValue, oldValue) | Pck:Calcul:calcul L2. 1: Pck:Sale:sale | addArticle ( ) | Pck:Sale:sale L3. 1: Pck:Sale:sale | calculAmount(newValue, oldValue) | Pck:Calcul:calcul L2. 1: Pck:Sale:sale | addArticle ( ) | Pck:Sale:sale L3. 1: Pck:Sale:sale | calculAmount(newValue, oldValue) | Pck:Calcul:calcul L4. LOOP | END L5. ALT | START | isInvoice L6. ELSE | BEGIN L7. 1: Pck:Sale:sale | getDelivery ( ) | Pck:Delivery:delivery L8. 1: Pck:Delivery:delivery | signDelivery ( ) | Pck:Vendor:vendor L9. ALT | END L14. 1: Pck:Sale:sale | getPayslip ( ) | Pck: Payslip: paySlip L15. 1: Pck: Payslip: paySlip | signPayslip ( ) | Pck:Vendor:vendor	Scenario 3

5.2 Trace Merging

In the previous step, for each scenario an execution trace is generated. At this step every trace has a correspondent CPN. These CPNs include as transition only method invocation or operator "par". The next step is to merge the CPNs of the different traces to obtain a single CPN that represent all the system behaviors. We use for that the adapted kbehavior algorithme. we initialize the variable K of the algorithme with the number 2. Figure 6 shows the obtained CPN from merging traces corresponding to scenario1, scenario2 and scenario3. In this CPN scenario1 has the red color, scenario2 has the bleu color while scenario3 has the green color.

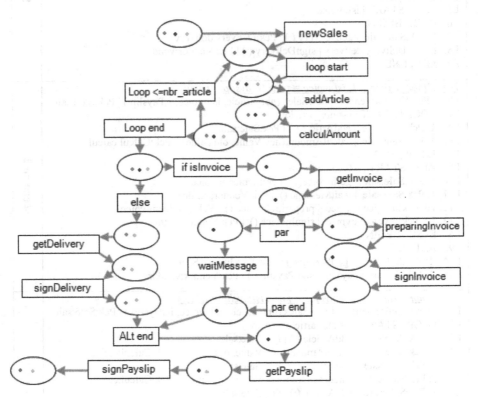

Fig. 6. The merged CPN (Color figure online)

5.3 HLSD Extraction

In this step, the HLSD is completely constructed. This is done by mapping the resulting CPN using transformation rules as is it shown in Figs. 2 and 3. It represents all the system behaviors.

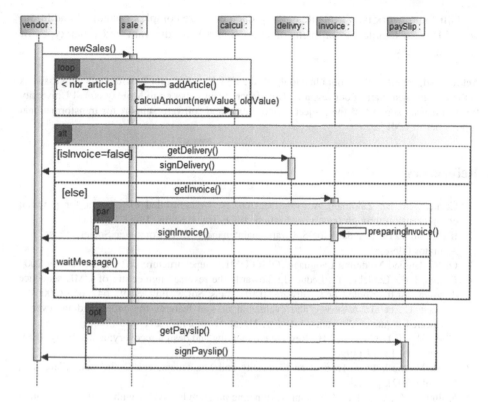

Fig. 7. Extracted HLSD

Our approach, as shown in Fig. 7, is able to generate a comprehensive HLSD with the main UML2 operators (seq, alt, par, and loop). The conditions relating to the combined fragments operators "loop" and "alt" are also extracted. most approaches based on dynamic analysis do not provide these conditions. The operator *par* is also detected. It is an important operator because it helps to describe the behavior of threads running in multi-threaded systems. In addition, the approach is also independent from programing languages. The tracer tool can be changed to support the new language.

6   Conclusion

In this paper, we presented an overview on our approach for the reverse engineering of Sequence Diagram of an object-oriented software system. The approach is based on dynamic analysis. It use an adapted version of the Kbehavior algorithm to merge CPNs that represent execution traces. The colors of petri nets are used to distinguish between scenarios. This enables subdividing an HLSD into several HLSDs to facilitate the task of understanding the system. The approach detects UML interaction operators such as alt, seq, opt and loop. It also enables the detection of the interaction operator par that help to describe parallel behavior of a system.

Our future work is to evaluate our approach on more complex systems. In addition, we will try to handle the problem of extracting a state diagram and other types of diagrams of UML.

Acknowledgements. We would like to thank the FST Errachidia for providing us with assist us in the development part of our research. Our sincere thanks also go to Moulay Ismail University for its financial support of the project "Algorithmic and software support for transformational approaches to UML".

References

1. Cornelissen, B., Zaidman, A., van Deursen, A.: A controlled experiment for program comprehension through trace visualization. IEEE Trans. Softw. Eng., 2 (2011)
2. IEEE. std 1219: Standard for Software maintenance. IEEE Computer Society Press, Los Alamitos (1998)
3. OMG: Unified Modeling Language (OMG UML), Superstructure. V2.1.2, November 2007
4. Briand, L.C., Labiche, Y., Leduc, J.: Towards the reverse engineering of UML sequence diagrams for distributed Java software. IEEE Trans. Softw. Eng. **32**(9), 642–663 (2006)
5. Bennett, C., et al.: A survey and evaluation of tool features for understanding reverse-engineered sequence diagrams. J. Softw. Maint. Evol. **20**(4), 291–315 (2008)
6. Chikofsky, E.J., Cross II, J.H.: Reverse engineering and design recovery: a taxonomy. IEEE Softw. **7**(1), 13–17 (1990)
7. Clerk Maxwell, J.: A Treatise on Electricity and Magnetism, vol. 2, 3rd edn. Clarendon, Oxford (1892). pp. 68–73
8. Kollmann, R., Gogolla, M.: Capturing dynamic program behaviour with UML collaboration diagrams. In: Proceedings of the 5th Conference on Software Maintenance and Reengineering (CSMR 2001), pp. 58–67. IEEE Computer Society (2001)
9. Kollmann, R., Selonen, P., Stroulia, E., Systä, T., Zundorf, A.: A study on the current state of the art in tool-supported UML-based static reverse engineering. In: Proceedings of the 9th Working Conference on Reverse Engineering (WCRE 2002), pp. 22–32. IEEE Computer Society (2002)
10. Rountev, A., Volgin, O., Reddoch, M.: Static control-flow analysis for reverse engineering of UML sequence diagrams. In: ACM SIGSOFT Software Engineering Notes, vol. 31, no. 1, pp. 96–102. ACM (2005)
11. Rountev, A., Connell, B.H.: Object naming analysis for reverse-engineered sequence diagrams. In: Proceedings of the 27th International Conference on Software Engineering (ICSE 2005), pp. 254–263. ACM (2005)
12. Taniguchi, K., Ishio, T., Kamiya, T., Kusumoto, S., Inoue, K.: Extracting sequence diagram from execution trace of Java program. In: International Workshop on Principles of Software Evolution (IWPSE 2005), pp. 148–151 (2005)
13. Delamare, R., Baudry, B., Le Traon, Y.: Reverse-engineering of UML 2.0 sequence diagrams from execution traces. In: Proceedings of the Workshop on Object-Oriented Reengineering at ECOOP 06 (2006)
14. Ziadi, T., da Silva, M.A.A., Hillah, L.M., Ziane, M.: A fully dynamic approach to the reverse engineering of UML sequence diagrams. In: 16th IEEE International Conference on Engineering of Complex Computer Systems, ICECCS, Las Vegas, United States, April 2011

15. Cornelissen, B., van Deursen, A., Moonen, L., Zaidman, A.: Visualizing test suites to aid in software understanding. In: Proceedings of the 11th European Conference on Software Maintenance and Reengineering (CSMR 2007), pp. 213–222. IEEE Computer Society (2007)
16. Jensen, K.: A brief introduction to coloured Petri Nets. In: Brinksma, E. (ed.) TACAS 1997. LNCS, vol. 1217, pp. 203–208. Springer, Heidelberg (1997). https://doi.org/10.1007/BFb0035389
17. Jakimi, A., Sabraoui, A., Badidi, E., Salah, A., El Koutbi, M.: Using UML Scenarios in B2B Systems. IIUM Eng. J. (2010)
18. AspectJ: The AspectJ project at Eclipse.org. http://www.eclipse.org/aspectj/
19. Brzozowski, J.A.: Derivatives of regular expressions. J. ACM **11**(4), 481–494 (1964)
20. Mariani, L., Pezze, M.: Dynamic detection of cots component incompatibility. IEEE Softw. **24**(5), 76–85 (2007)
21. Biermann, A., Feldmann, J.: On the synthesis of finite state machines from samples of their behavior. IEEE Trans. Comput. **21**, 592–597 (1972)

A Formalized Procedure for Database Horizontal Fragmentation in Isabelle/HOL Proof Assistant

Cheikh Salmi$^{(\boxtimes)}$, Mohamed Chaabani$^{(\boxtimes)}$, and Mohamed Mezghiche$^{(\boxtimes)}$

LIMOSE, University of M'Hamed Bougarra, Boumerdes, Algeria
Salmi.cheikh@univ-boumerdes.dz, medchaabani@gmail.com,
mohamed.mezghiche@gmail.com

Abstract. We propose a logical procedure for the horizontal fragmentation problem based on predicate abstraction over the entire domain of database relations. The set of minterm predicates is constructed using rewriting rules similar to the well-known semantic tableau algorithm. The procedure start from an initial set of simple predicates, build the set of minterm predicates until rules are no longer required. To ensure this proposition, we give a formal proof of its correctness namely, it's soundness, completeness and termination with Isabelle proof assistant. The main contribution of this work are: refining the minterm approach by adding a semantic layer to predicates, minimizing the set of minterm predicates by automatically eliminating contradictory ones, detecting and handling subsumptions between them. This leads to the best construction time of the final partitioning schema. Finally, a source code of the procedure is generated automatically by the Isabelle proof assistant.

Keywords: Horizontal fragmentation · Database optimization
Minterm · Tableau calculus · Proof assistant · Formal methods

1 Introduction

Fragmentation is a database optimization process that splits large relations into smaller ones so that the query executor retrieve only a reduced data set when running a user application. It is an important technique in database design since it aims to improve the database system performance. There are two types of fragmentation, vertical and horizontal. Vertical fragmentation creates a set of vertical disjoint fragments each contains a subset of one or more relations columns while horizontal fragmentation (HF) generates disjoint sets of tuples. The usage of query predicates to perform (HF) was studied first in [1–4]. However, the approach has not been formalized and the algorithms (eg. commin) using it are not practical especially when dealing with properties such as minimality, completeness, relevance and implications set definition [4]. To our knowledge, the only research addressing the question of (HF) using predicate abstraction is [5] which is also based on commin. However, our approach brings several benefits.

© Springer Nature Switzerland AG 2018
E. H. Abdelwahed et al. (Eds.): MEDI 2018, LNCS 11163, pp. 346–353, 2018.
https://doi.org/10.1007/978-3-030-00856-7_23

- We formally define a procedure for (HF) of a relation by integrating minimality and completeness rules at the semantic level of predicates.
- Our procedure reduce the number of predicates that are used to perform HF.
- Our approach can be used to resolve other database optimization such as materialized view selection.
- It can be combined with other algorithms, for instance, the solution given by our procedure can be used as a starting point for a genetic algorithm instead of starting with a random solution.

The code of the (HF) procedure can be automatically extracted form our proof assistant formalization as a Scala program, which is a type-safe Java Virtual Machine language that incorporates both object oriented and functional programming. The remainder of this paper is organized as follows. We begin in Sect. 1 by formally defining the horizontal fragmentation and it's related work. In Sect. 2 the formalization of abstract horizontal fragmentation. In Sect. 3 we present the tableau calculus for the HF. Finally, in Sect. 4, we conclude and discuss future work.

2   Abstract Horizontal Fragmentation

Let $R = \{A_1 : D_1, A_2 : D_2, ...A_n : D_n\}$ be a relation schema where each A_i is an attribute defined over a domain D_i. A simple predicate is a condition in the form of $p_k : A_i \; \theta \; Value$ where $\theta \in \{=, \neq, <, \leq, >, \geq\}$ and $Value \in D_i$. A set of all simple predicates is denoted by $Pr = \{P_1, P_2, ...P_m\}$. The set of minterm predicate, $M = \{m_1, m_2, ...m_m\}$, over Pr is defined as the conjunctive normal form of simple predicates or their negations:

$$M = \{m_j | m_j = \bigwedge_{p^k \in Pr} p_k^*\}, k = 1, ..., m, j = 1, ...m$$

where $p_k^* = p^k$ or $p_k^* = \neg \, p^k$. Each minterm defines a horizontal fragment.

Example 1. Let $R = (Age : int; Name : varchar(30); DateofBirth : date)$ be a relation. It can be fragmented by using one of the following minterm. (1) $\{Gender = m\}$ generates two fragments, one contains tuples those values for Gender which are masculine and a second fragment those values for gender which are feminine. (2) $\{DateOfBirth >' March - 11 - 1973' \land DateOfBirth \leq' April - 13 - 1979'\}$ generates two fragments: one with values for DateofBirth between 'March-11-1973' and 'April-13-1979', and the second with values greater than 'April-13-1979' or less than 'March-11-1973'

Isabelle is a proof assistant [6] or an interactive theorem prover. It includes powerful specification tools, e.g. for (co)datatypes, (co)inductive definitions and recursive functions with complex pattern matching. To be able to formalize the (HF) in Isabelle, it is necessary to map relations concrete domains, simple and minterm predicates to abstract ones at the syntactic and semantic level.

2.1 Syntax

Given a relation R, and a set of attributes $\{A_1, ..., A_n\}$ where each attribute A_i belongs to a definition domain D_i. A simple predicate is a boolean expression over attributes of the relation R and constants from its attributes domains. A minterm is a logical combination of simple predicates. The list L of all minterm predicates over a relation R is defined by following BNF grammar:

$$< L > ::= < SP > \;|\; < \neg MT > \;|\; < MT > \wedge < MT > \;|\; < MT > \vee < MT >$$
$$< SP > ::= < A > \theta < v >$$

where SP is a simple predicate, MT is a minterm, A is a database attribute and θ is a binary operation tha belongs to the set $\{=, \neq, <, \leq, >, \geq\}$.

To implement the minterm set in Isabelle proof assistant, we need to define the following abstract data types and functions:

datatype $op\text{-}ord = Eq\;|Lt|Le$
Which defines the basic operators $=$, $<$ and $\leq$. A simple predicate is then abstracted by:
datatype $(\,'nv,\,'na)\;predicate =$
$sp\;'na\;bool\;op\text{-}ord\;'nv$
Where $'nv$ is a set of values and $'na$ is an attribute name. Note that the $\neq$, $>$ and $\geq$ operators are derived using the $bool$ constructor. For example the abstract simple predicate $att \neq val$ is matched by the rule `"sp att False Eq val"`. For the rest of this paper the abstract simple predicates `sp att True Eq val` and `pr att False Eq val` are simply denoted respectively by "$[=]\,att\,val$" and "$[\neq]\,att\,val$". The same notation is used to simplify simple predicates that uses other operators $(<, >, >=, <=)$.

The negative form of a predicate sp ($\neg sp$) can then be easily defined by:

fun $nf\text{-}predicate ::(\,'nv,\,'na)\;predicate \Rightarrow (\,'nv,\,'na) predicate$ **where**
$nf\text{-}predicate\;(sp\;att\;bool\;op\text{-}ord\;val) = (sp\;att\;(\neg\;bool)\;\;op\text{-}ord\;val)$

For instance, the negative form of "$[=]\,att\,val$" is "$[\neq]\,att\,val$".

Finally, the abstraction of a minterm is defined over simple predicates by applying a set of logical operators: negation, conjunction and disjunction, as follows:

datatype $(\,'nv,\,'na)\;form =$
$Atom\;(\,'nv,\,'na)\;predicate$
$|Neg\;(\,'nv,\,'na)\;form$
$|Conj\;(\,'nv,\,'na)\;form\;(\,'nv,\,'na)\;form$
$|Disj\;(\,'nv,\,'na)\;form\;(\,'nv,\,'na)\;form$

2.2 Semantics

The semantic of predicates allows us to detect relations between predicates, which allows to keep only the most relevant to the fragmentation process.

It checks for each of the predicates whether it is satisfiable, eliminated or not. For instance, if the current predicate is already treated by the procedure, it will be eliminated if it appears a second time in its positive or negative form. Another important aspect of the semantic of the predicate is their subsumption. For example, suppose two queries that include two conditions predicates $p_1 : \sigma_{A=20}$ and $p_2 : \sigma_{A<30}$. The commin algorithm generates and tests at least four minterm. This number might increase if these two simple predicates are combined with others. Our procedure only considers two minterm. Two cases are eliminated by subsumption rule ($p < 30 \wedge p = 20$) and contradiction ($p \geq 30 \wedge p = 20$) rules. Therefore, unlike commin, the total number of cases will be significantly improved in case of combination with other simple predicates. Note that our semantic formalization, supports all kind of relations between minterm. This set-theoretic semantics is provided by an interpretation function $\mathcal{I}$. This interpretation function $\mathcal{I}$ is a pair ($att^{\mathcal{I}}, val^{\mathcal{I}}$) mapping an attribute att to a set of individuals (subsets of domain) and a value name val to an individual element of a domain.

record ($'nv, 'na$) $Interp\text{-}g =$
  $interp\text{-}a :: \ 'na \Rightarrow 'nv \ set$
  $interp\text{-}v :: \ 'nv \Rightarrow 'nv$

In the case of databases, the values assigned to attributes are interpreted by themselves, hence, $val^{\mathcal{I}} = val$. The simple predicates interpretation is implemented by the following function:

fun $interp\text{-}predicate::('nv, 'na)predicate \Rightarrow ('nv::linorder, 'na)Interp \Rightarrow 'nv \ set$ **where**
  $interp\text{-}predicate \ ([=]att \ val) \ i= (if \ val \in interp\text{-}a \ i \ att$
                            $then\{ \ val\} \ else \ \{\})$
  $|interp\text{-}predicate \ ([\neq]att \ val) \ i= (interp\text{-}a \ i \ att)-\{val\}$
  $|interp\text{-}predicate \ ([<]att \ val) \ i= \{x \in interp\text{-}a \ i \ att. \ x < val\}$
  $|interp\text{-}predicate \ ([\geq]att \ val) \ i= \{x \in interp\text{-}a \ i \ att. \ x \geq val\}$
  $|interp\text{-}predicate \ ([\leq]att \ val) \ i= \{x \in interp\text{-}a \ i \ att. \ x \leq val\}$
  $|interp\text{-}predicate \ ([>]att \ val) \ i= \{x \in interp\text{-}a \ i \ att. \ x > val\}$

The first step to prove the correction of this interpretation function is to demonstrate that the interpretation of a simple predicate is a subset of its related attribute domain. This proof is implemented via this lemma

lemma $interp\text{-}pr\text{-}att:interp\text{-}predicate \ (sp \ att \ bool \ op\text{-}ord \ val) \ i \subseteq interp\text{-}a \ i \ att$

The interpretation of the disjunction of a simple predicate SP and its negation that are defined on an attribute a is the union of their interpretations which is the hole domain of the attribute a.

lemma $union\text{-}pr\text{-}opposite:SP = sp \ att \ bool \ op\text{-}ord \ val \Longrightarrow$
$interp\text{-}predicate \ SP \ i \ \cup \ interp\text{-}predicate \ (nf\text{-}predicate \ SP) \ i = interp\text{-}a \ i \ att$

As described by the following lemma, the conjunction of a predicate SP and its opposite is interpreted as the empty set.

lemma $inter\text{-}pr\text{-}opposite:$
  $interp\text{-}predicate \ sp1 \ i \ \cap \ interp\text{-}predicate \ (nf\text{-}predicate \ sp1) \ i = \{\}$

Predicates subsumption is an important issue in optimizing the horizontal fragmentation process. It can allow us to reduce the number of simple predicates by taking into account their subsumption relations. The pattern matching function *subsume* is a simple predicate subsumption expression in which pattern matching is performed immediately on the argument.

This function checks if a predicate SP is subsumed by SP' ($SP \sqsubseteq SP'$) such that both SP and SP' are defined on the same attribute *att*. This function will be used to simplify a set of predicates by eliminating the subsumed ones.

fun *subsume*::$('nv::linorder,'na)$ *predicate* $\Rightarrow$ $('nv,'na)$ *predicate* $\Rightarrow$ *bool* **where**
subsume $([=]$ *att val*$)$ $(sp$ *att2 bool op-ord val2*$)$ =
$\qquad$ $(if$ *att= att2* *then*
$\qquad\qquad$ $(case$ $(sp$ *att2 bool op-ord val2*$)$ *of*
$\qquad\qquad\qquad$ $([=]$ *att val2*$)$ $\Rightarrow$ *val=val2*
$\qquad\qquad$ $|$ $([\neq]$ *att val2*$)$ $\Rightarrow$ *val* $\neq$*val2*
$\qquad\qquad$ $|$ $([<]$ *att val2*$)$ $\Rightarrow$ *val* $<$ *val2*
$\qquad\qquad$ $|$ $([\leq]$ *att val2*$)$ $\Rightarrow$ *val* $\leq$ *val2*
$\qquad\qquad$ $|$ $([>]$ *att val2*$)$ $\Rightarrow$ *val* $>$ *val2*
$\qquad\qquad$ $|$ $([\geq]$ *att val2*$)$ $\Rightarrow$ *val* $\geq$ *val2*$)$
$\qquad$ *else False*$)$

To show that this function is semantically correct, we need to demonstrate the implication: if $SP \sqsubseteq SP'$ then $SP^{\mathcal{I}} \subseteq SP^{\mathcal{I}}$. In Isabelle this can be formulated by the following lemma:

lemma *subsume-proof*:
$\quad$ *subsume SP SP'* $\Longrightarrow$ *interp-predicate SP i* $\subseteq$ *interp-predicate SP' i*

Another important property used in reasoning on predicates, is their contradiction called her "Clash". This property means that predicates are disjoint and can not be allowed to be together in the same minterm. It is implemented via the pattern matching function *Clash_predicate*.

This function decides if a boolean combination of the two minterm SP and SP' defined on the same attribute leads to a Clash. This function is formalized in Isabelle by the function *clash_predicate* as follows:

fun *predicate-clash*::$('nv::linorder,'na)$ *predicate* $\Rightarrow$ $('nv,'na)$ *predicate* $\Rightarrow$ *bool* **where**
predicate-clash $([=]$ *att val*$)$ $(sp$ *att2 bool op-ord val2*$)$ = $(if$ *att= att2* *then*
$\qquad\qquad$ $(case$ $(sp$ *att2 bool op-ord val2*$)$ *of*
$\qquad\qquad$ $([=]$ *att val2*$)$ $\Rightarrow$ *val* $\neq$*val2*
$\qquad\qquad$ $|$ $([\neq]$ *att val2*$)$ $\Rightarrow$ *val* $=$ *val2*
$\qquad\qquad$ $|$ $([<]$ *att val2*$)$ $\Rightarrow$ *val* $\geq$ *val2*
$\qquad\qquad$ $|$ $([\leq]$ *att val2*$)$ $\Rightarrow$ *val* $>$ *val2*
$\qquad\qquad$ $|$ $([>]$ *att val2*$)$ $\Rightarrow$ *val* $\leq$ *val2*
$\qquad\qquad$ $|$ $([\geq]$ *att val2*$)$ $\Rightarrow$ *val* $<$ *val2*$)$
$\qquad\qquad\qquad$ *else False*$)$

This function is symmetric, if SP is the opposite predicate of SP' then SP' is also the opposite predicate of SP'. From a semantic point of view the interpretation of each predicate is disjoint from the other.

lemma *sem-contraduction*:
$\quad$ *predicate-clash SP SP'* $\Longrightarrow$ *interp-predicate SP i* $\cap$ *interp-predicate SP' i* $=\{\}$

3 Abstract Tableau Calculus for HF

We now describe our logical procedure for obtaining horizontal fragmentation. We first describe the tableau rules on an abstract level, as a transition system transforming a set of simple predicate (*i.e.* , set of terms) into an optimized one. We then describe in details the procedure of construction of minterm and discuss its main properties in (Sect. 3.1).

$$\text{ELIM} \quad \frac{f = (att\,\theta\,value) \quad \theta \in \{\neq, \geq, >\} \quad (f, True) \in \mathcal{S}}{\mathcal{S}' = (\mathcal{S} - \{(f, True)\}) \cup \{(\neg f, True)\}}{\mathcal{S} \overset{f}{\hookrightarrow} \mathcal{S}'}$$

$$\text{EQ} \quad \frac{f = (att = value) \quad app = True \quad (f, app) \in \mathcal{S}}{\mathcal{S}' = (\mathcal{S} - \{(f, app)\}) \cup \{(f, False)\} \ \lor \ \mathcal{S}' = (\mathcal{S} - \{(f, app)\}) \cup \{(\neg f, False)\}}{\mathcal{S} \overset{f}{\hookrightarrow} \mathcal{S}'}$$

$$\text{LEQ} \quad \frac{f = (att \leq value) \quad app = True \quad (f, app) \in \mathcal{S}}{\mathcal{S}' = (\mathcal{S} - \{(f, app)\}) \cup \{(f, False)\} \ \lor \ \mathcal{S}' = (\mathcal{S} - \{(f, app)\}) \cup \{(\neg f, False)\}}{\mathcal{S} \overset{f}{\hookrightarrow} \mathcal{S}'}$$

$$\text{LT} \quad \frac{f = (att < value) \quad app = True \quad (f, app) \in \mathcal{S}}{\mathcal{S}' = (\mathcal{S} - \{(f, app)\}) \cup \{(f, False)\} \ \lor \ \mathcal{S}' = (\mathcal{S} - \{(f, app)\}) \cup \{(\neg f, False)\}}{\mathcal{S} \overset{f}{\hookrightarrow} \mathcal{S}'}$$

$$\text{SUBSUME} \quad \frac{(f, False) \in \mathcal{S} \quad (f', False) \in \mathcal{S} \quad f \sqsubseteq f' \quad \mathcal{S}' = \mathcal{S} - \{(f, False)\}}{\mathcal{S} \overset{f}{\hookrightarrow} \mathcal{S}'}$$

Fig. 1. Tableau rules

In Fig. 1 we depict what we call transformation rules. These rules typically have the form $\mathcal{A} \overset{sp}{\hookrightarrow} \mathcal{A}'$, where $\mathcal{A}$ is the original set of predicate, $\mathcal{A}'$ is its tableau transformation and sp is the predicate in $\mathcal{A}$ on which the transformation rule is applied. The procedure start with an initial set S of simple predicates, we associate to each predicate a boolean flag called *applicable* (initially True) to indicate that the predicate is already transformed or not.

As each predicate or its negative form produce the same set of minterm, the procedure transforms all negative forms to positive ones using the rule $\overset{Elim}{\longrightarrow}$, hence, predicates will be written only using $=,<$ and $\leq$ operators. Note that all rules are subject to preconditions, which are of two kinds: preconditions ensuring the correctness of the rule, see Sect. 3.1, and those ensuring the termination of the whole calculus (typically the flag "applicable").

As shown in Fig. 2, the execution of our procedure creates a tree whose root is the initial set of predicates and leaves represents the final horizontal

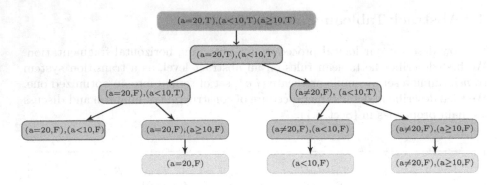

Fig. 2. Horizontal fragments generation tree example

fragments. Interpretation of interior nodes depends on the flag "applicable". The procedure continues until no more rule ($\xrightarrow{=}$, $\xrightarrow{<}$, $\xrightarrow{\leq}$ or $\xrightarrow{Subsume}$) is applicable. Formally, we say that a *set of predicate* is saturated for a rule, *saturated A rl*, iff $\forall A'.\neg rl\ A\ A'$.

3.1   Properties of Tableau Rules

The main properties of the calculus are soundness, completeness, minmality and termination.

Satisfiability: A simple predicate SP defined on attribute att, (denoted by SP_{att}) is interpreted by $(SP_{att}, True)^{\mathcal{I}} = att^{\mathcal{I}}$ otherwise, $(SP_{att}, false)^{\mathcal{I}} = SP_{att}^{\mathcal{I}}$, (see Sect. 2.2). The interpretation of a minterm M_{att} based on a set of simple predicates defined on the same attribute att is the intersection of interpretations of all its simple predicates, i.e., $M_{att}^{\mathcal{I}} = \bigcap SP_{att}^{\mathcal{I}}$, M_{att} is satisfiable iff $M_{att}^{\mathcal{I}} \neq \emptyset$. Finally, a *set of minterm* is said to be *satisfiable* iff all its M_{att} are satisfiable.

Soundness: A rule rl is said to be *sound* iff its application does not introduce a new instance (new model).

$$\forall S\ S'.rl\ S\ S' \longrightarrow satisfiable\ S' \longrightarrow satisfiable\ S$$

Completenss: A rule is complete if the satisfiability of a set of predicates S implies that there exists at least one satisfiable set of predicates S' obtained from S by this rule application.

Minmality: A rule rl preserves a *minimality* if after its application, each value belongs to the left or the right node but not to both.

Termination: The calculus terminates after a finite number of rules application. Its easy to prove this property since the number of applicable predicates (applicable = true) decreases after each rule application.

4   Conclusion

In this paper we presented a formal procedure for the minterm horizontal partitioning approach. Then, we showed how to use this procedure to generate horizontal fragments for a relational database or a data warehouse using only qualitative data access informations. We show it's correctness by proving completeness and termination properties with the Isabelle proof assistant.

The procedure can be easily enhanced by quantitative informations such as the physical properties of attributes, storage devices and buffers. A cost model can then be used to improve the quality of the obtained fragments. Our procedure can be used directly to deal with many other database optimization problems such as vertical partitioning and materialized views selection. A possible direction for a short-term extension of this work is to combine it with a heuristic algorithm to do partitioning with a cost model. Another important theoretical research direction is to use a different formal framework to interpret minterm. One can use description logic as a formal framework. In this case, abstract predicates can be viewed as concepts and their mapping to concrete domains can be done using roles. Finally, we plan to apply our approach on a real case study and validate the results on real database management system such as *Oracle* or *SQL server*.

References

1. Ceri, S., Negri, M., Pelagatti, G.: Horizontal data partitioning in database design. In: Proceedings of the 1982 ACM SIGMOD International Conference on Management of Data, SIGMOD 1982, pp. 128–136. ACM, New York (1982)
2. Bellatreche, L., Karlapalem, K., Simonet, A.: Algorithms and support for horizontal class partitioning in object-oriented databases. Distrib. Parallel Databases **8**(2), 155–179 (2000)
3. Ceri, S., Pelagatti, G.: Distributed Databases: Principles and Systems. McGraw-Hill Computer Science Series. McGraw-Hill, New York (1984)
4. Ozsu, M.T.: Principles of Distributed Database Systems, 3rd edn. Prentice Hall Press, Upper Saddle River (2007)
5. Dimovski, A., Velinov, G., Sahpaski, D.: Horizontal partitioning by predicate abstraction and its application to data warehouse design. In: Catania, B., Ivanović, M., Thalheim, B. (eds.) ADBIS 2010. LNCS, vol. 6295, pp. 164–175. Springer, Heidelberg (2010). https://doi.org/10.1007/978-3-642-15576-5_14
6. Nipkow, T., Wenze, M., Paulson, L.C.: Isabelle/HOL: A Proof Assistant for Higher-Order Logic, vol. 2283. Springer, Heidelberg (2002). https://doi.org/10.1007/3-540-45949-9

Domain-Oriented Verification Management

Vincent Leildé[2]([✉]), Vincent Ribaud[1], Ciprian Teodorov[2],
and Philippe Dhaussy[2]

[1] Lab-STICC, Team MOCS, Université de Bretagne Occidentale, Avenue le Gorgeu,
Brest, France
Vincent.Ribaud@univ-brest.fr
[2] Lab-STICC, Team MOCS, ENSTA-Bretagne, rue François Verny, Brest, France
{vincent.leilde,ciprian.teodorov,philippe.dhaussy}@ensta-bretagne.fr

Abstract. V. Basili stated twenty years ago that a software organization that manages quality should have a corporate infrastructure that links together and transcends the single projects by capitalizing on successes and learning from failures. For critical systems design, the verification tasks play a crucial role; when an unexpected situation is detected, the engineer analyzes the cause, performing a diagnosis activity. To improve the quality of the design, diagnosis information have to be managed through a well-defined method and with a suitable system. In this paper we present how a Verification Organizing System together with a problem-oriented method could achieve these issues. The key aspect of the approach is to follow a step-wise building of the solution, reusing known problems that are relevant for the system under study.

Keywords: Organizing system · Diagnosis · Problem oriented method

1 Introduction

D. Bjorner defines software engineering as a triptych: from descriptions of the *application domain* we construct prescriptions of the *requirements*; and from prescriptions of the requirements we *design* the software, i.e. construct specifications of software [7]. Our area of interest is software formal verification, especially with a model-checking approach. We start the model-checking process with a model of the system under consideration and a formal characterization of the property to be checked, i.e. two legs of the triptych: design and requirements. Then we run the model-checker to check the validity of the property in the system model. When property is violated, the model checker provides us with a counterexample (a witness trace) that triggers a diagnosis activity to analyze the trace and to outline the error causes. Consequently, the system model is corrected and a new process cycle - verification, diagnosis, and correction - is repeated. The third leg is a domain-oriented verification, defined as a process by which information used in verifying software systems is identified, captured, and organized regarding the

© Springer Nature Switzerland AG 2018
E. H. Abdelwahed et al. (Eds.): MEDI 2018, LNCS 11163, pp. 354–370, 2018.
https://doi.org/10.1007/978-3-030-00856-7_24

domain knowledge, with the purpose of making it reusable when modeling and verifying new systems. The process can be applied to various domains, including critical system design.

Our research work is focused on methods and tools intended to ease the verification process, especially diagnosis activities. Generally speaking, research addressing model-checking and diagnosis issues [2,4,6,15,20] are faced with the same difficulties.

First, diagnosing the cause of abnormalities suffers from too detailed observations. It is hard, for instance, to localize relevant parts in a detailed source-level trace when we look for the reasons a verification run failed [14]. Some techniques focus on linking low level information with more abstract information, like model-based diagnosis [30], or case-based reasoning [1].

Second, the techniques require a set of data that is not always available. In addition to the verification steps, the entire verification should be planned, administered, and organized. This is called verification organization by Baier and Katoen [3]. During the engineering process, heterogeneous artifacts are produced, including requirements, system models, properties, runs, or diagnoses. As stated by Ruys [31], they are poorly managed and controlled. As a result, expertise is poorly shared by the verification engineers, and cannot be used for the above techniques.

Third, verification at early stages of the engineering process prevents the presence of expensive defects in the final product. A software organization that manages quality should have a corporate infrastructure that links together and transcends the single projects by capitalizing on successes and learning from failures [5]. These tasks require to manage past diagnosis experiences (gathering a set of heterogeneous artifacts) and to correlate discovered abnormalities with experiences. This can be achieved with a knowledge based system together with a well-defined method. We propose to structure the knowledge base around *problem cases*. A *problem case* packages a problem description with related solutions.

Briefly stated, our approach aims to answer the issues above with a general diagnosis ontology [26], a Verification Organizing System [25], and a domain-oriented method, the latter being the subject of this paper. Some relevant parts of the ontology will be presented in Sect. 3.1. The organizing system - an intentionally arranged collection of resources and the interactions they support [13] - makes easier the management of verification objects and supports reasoning interactions that facilitates diagnosis decisions; some features related to the method are drafted in Sect. 5.1. The method we propose in this paper relies on the idea of performing round trips between problem and solution spaces for improving the verification process. It should help the engineer to bring closer high-level information and abnormalities observations. It focuses on a progressive constitution of a *problem cases* knowledge base, containing both problems and solutions, that can be reused. Solutions are packaging formal designs and verification runs, and *problem cases* are formalized with a set of properties together with a structure of various solutions.

Section 2 overviews background and related work. In Sect. 3, we present the proposed method, its steps and a straightforward example. Section 4 shows the application of the method on the mutual exclusion problem. Section 5 discusses the knowledge base and its services, and Sect. 6 concludes the study.

2   Background and Related Work

Newell and Simon introduced in [28] the problem-space hypothesis: *the fundamental organization unit of all human goal-oriented activity is the problem space*. M. Jackson introduced the concept of *problem frame* [21] for presenting, classifying and understanding software development problems. Problem frames structure the analysis of the world in which the problem is located - the problem domain - and describe what is there and what effects one would like a system located therein to achieve [17]. A problem frame is defined in terms of its context and the characteristics of its domains, interfaces and requirements [21]. The problem frame approach allows engineers to build domain expertise and let practitioners gain experience from this knowledge base. POSE (Problem Oriented Software Engineering) [18] is an extension and generalization of problem frames. It is a representation and step-wise transformation of software problems to progress towards the solution. Software architecture [8], as well as development framework and design patterns [12] have same goals of knowledge construction, share and reuse. This kind of knowledge is generally attributed to the solution space. Compelling arguments justify an early understanding of stakeholders' requirements (focus on the problem). Equally compelling arguments justify an early construction of a suitable software-system architecture (focus on the solution).

Life-cycle model evolved from waterfall models to spiral models. Fine-grained spiral models are used by agile methods. The cornerstone of these processes is that developers craft a system's requirements and its architecture concurrently, and interleave their development [32]. Researchers from the Open University proposed an adaptation of the spiral life-cycle model, called the Twin Peaks Model to emphasize the equal status given to requirements and architecture [17]. The proposed model of software development is an iterative process during which problem structures and solution structures are detailed and enriched. In this context, the Open University team sees the use of architectural support as aiding the focus on the essential design requirements of the problem by allowing design concerns to be treated more abstractly and to be combined with behavioural requirements [17]. They extended problem frames towards this end.

To some extent, the method we propose in this paper borrows the Twin Peaks idea of performing round trips between problem and solution spaces for leveraging diagnoses.

3   Method

The method focuses on a progressive understanding of the problem. First, this should help the designer to find rapidly a solution to his/her problem, by decomposing the problem in smaller subproblems, and reusing existing solutions. Second, it should help the verifier to understand the root causes of abnormalities for a selected solution, by feeding diagnosis task with relevant information. This section describes formalization of problems, and the different steps of the flow.

3.1   Problem Formalization

According to Venkatasubramanian [33], Abnormal Event Management, a key component of supervisory control, involves the timely detection of an abnormal event, diagnosing its causal origins and then taking appropriate supervisory control decisions and actions to bring the process back to a normal, safe, operating state. Generally speaking, we have three main tasks; fault detection, diagnosis, and correction.

Let see the tasks in a model-checking approach. Fault detection establishes that a system run raises an abnormal event: the exhaustive exploration encounters a state that violates the property under consideration, the model checker provides a counterexample, an execution path that leads from the initial system state to the violating state. Many researchers [4,9,10,14] divide the diagnosis in two main tasks: isolation (localization) and causal analysis. Isolation extracts the subset of model parts that needs to be corrected. Causal analysis associates causes to the observed abnormalities.

These are generally burden tasks, particularly due to a huge amount of unrelated information the engineer needs to understand and correlate. One example, known as the semantic gap, is the discrepancy between formalisms used during design and low-level traces obtained during verification. Reasoning on *problem cases* affords the advantage of raising the level of abstraction to a less technology-dependent level.

A conceptual model of the domain is given in Fig. 1. The knowledge about a problem is structured in a *problem case*. *Problem cases* aim to understand and capture both problems and solutions during the design of a software system. Engineers thus constitute a reusable base of expertise related to their engineering domain. *Problem cases* provide models to reason about the chosen solution and facilitates the diagnosis activity. A *problem case* is composed of other *problem cases*, that are made of *propositional objects*. *Propositional objects* comprise immaterial items that are, or represent in some sense, sets of propositions about real or imaginary things [11], essentially about the system objects. For instance, a mutual exclusion algorithm or a counter-example related to a design error are both *propositional objects*. Three classes of *propositional objects* play a key role during the verification process: *design, verification* and *requirement* objects. Systems under verification are modeled with automata and *design* objects are *processes, events, transitions* and *states*. *Requirement* objects are mainly *formal properties* expressed with LTL and more *informal requirements*. *Verification* objects are *runs* and resulting *traces* when the *run* failed. *Problem cases* are connected together with *combination mechanisms*, through *hooks* exposing connection points. A set of *combinations* between *problem cases* may causes abnormalities, for instance when a *problem case* property is violated, and thus

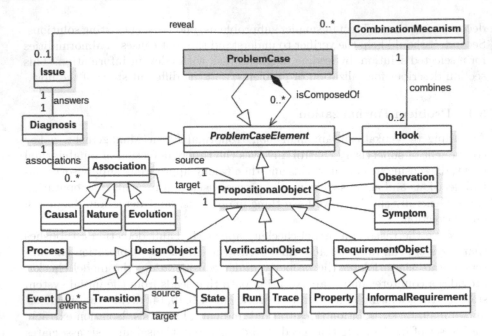

Fig. 1. Problem conceptual model

reveals an *issue*. The *issue* organizes results in a *diagnosis*. As a result of previous work [26], we defined a *diagnosis* as a structured set of *propositional objects* by means of *associations* of different kinds: *causal, nature, evolution*.

3.2 Illustration

To illustrate how the conceptual model is used, let us consider the following example. Suppose a board game with one board and two players. The board asks an infinite number of questions to each player, in a non deterministic manner. A player gives either a right answer, that increases its score by one point, or a wrong answer, and no point is awarded. The match ends when a player reaches 3 points. The behavior of the solution is presented in Fig. 2.

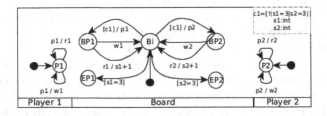

Fig. 2. Initial problem, first design

Transitions between states conforms to the Event-Condition-Action scheme represented as $Si \xrightarrow{\{Event\}[Condition]Action} Sj$. Si and Sj are *states*, arrows stand for *transitions*, labeled with *events* that cause *transitions* to be triggered. A *condition* is a boolean expression, and an *action* represents a statement such as a variable assignment or event sending. When an *event* occurs, the guard *condition* is evaluated and the *transition* is fired only if the *condition* is true, and the *action* is performed.

The model is made of three *processes*, the player one, the player two and a board, and two variables, score one (s1) and score two (s2). Players share the same behavior. They wait for a question from the board (event p1 is a question from the board to the player one, and event p2 is a question from the board to the player two). Each player replies to the board. The response can be right (event r1 or r2) or wrong (event w1 or w2). When the board is in the idle state (Bi), it asks a question, either to the player one or the player two (respectively by sending events p1 or p2), if and only if none of the players have a score equals to 3 (c1 condition is false). If a question is asked to the player one, the board goes in state BP1, and if a question is asked to the player two, the board goes in state BP2. In these states, the board waits for a response, either a right response (event r1 or r2) and in that case the score is incremented, or a wrong response (event w1 or w2). When one of the players reaches a score of 3, the board goes in state EP1 or EP2, and the game is finished.

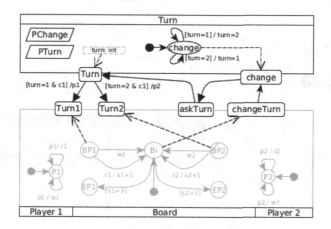

Fig. 3. Simple problem, second design

This model is not fair because in some cases, the board may ask more questions to one player rather the other one. To enable fairness, one can modify the design intuitively, or reuse a shared experience, represented as a *problem case*. A turn mechanism consists in memorizing the current entity that is authorized to do something. The authorized entity changes alternatively, thus, turn is a possible mechanism for fairness. As depicted in Fig. 3, a turn *problem case* has two sides. From the problem side, two properties, *PTurn* and *PChange*, ensure that each entity takes its turn. The solution provides a variable *turn*, representing the current turn, and a mechanism to change the turn.

Reusing the turn *problem case* with the current design can be achieved at the expense of updating the design and defining suited *combinations* links. One relies on connection points called *hooks*. The turn *problem case* provides two *hooks*, one for changing the turn, and one for retrieving the turn variable.

The combination is a causal set of actions invoked from the *Bi* state. The turn change is invoked, then, a new turn value is retrieved, indicating the recipient for the next question. Since each question causes the change of the turn, fairness property is held.

The example presented how a *problem case* is defined, and how it can be used to produce a new solution. In certain cases combination as a COTS is not possible, and other mechanisms may be used. In the following section, we present method steps and various combinations mechanisms.

3.3   Method Steps

The step-wise method is presented by the activity diagram in Fig. 4. The method is reiterated until a satisfactory solution is achieved.

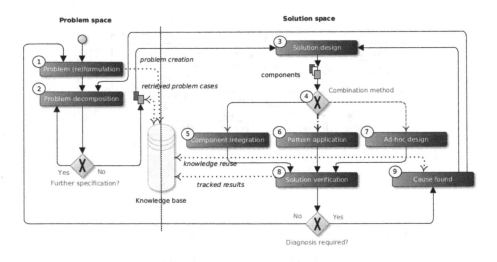

Fig. 4. Method steps

(1) The problem is formulated as a set of properties and constraints (architectural or technical choices), according to the conceptual model of Fig. 1, and captured in a knowledge base. For instance, "at the end of the game, each player has played the same number of times". (2) The problem is decomposed into subproblems, either known problems - called *problem cases* - selected from the knowledge

base, or unknown situations. For instance, "a turn mechanism is used". (3) When the need for a concrete view occurs, we move towards the solution space. The solution elements are organized. For instance, "the turn *problem case* is introduced into the current solution". (4) We consider how to combine the selected *problem case* with the solution[1]. The *problem case* may be either (5) composed with other parts of the solution, (6) applied as a pattern, or acts only as specifications and (7) an ad-hoc design is left to the engineer. (8) At this point, we built a part of the expected solution; hence we are able to start a verification cycle. When abnormalities are observed, it triggers a diagnosis process. Verification results are stored in the knowledge base. (9) When the diagnosis process is performed, knowledge about *problem cases* can be used to ease the process. The design is corrected, and the verification endeavor repeated. In some cases, the selected *problem case* does not suit, hence we have to backtrack and rework the *problem cases* combination, and it might be useful to keep track of the failed attempt.

This step-wide method is repeated several times while useful components can be combined. The engineer is left with a reduced problem for which no known solution exist and where a classical design and verification activity has to be done. The method performs roundtrips between two parts, the problem space, that consists in the problem elaboration, and the solution space, that consists in design and verifying the solution. While the problem elaboration produces specification to the solution design, the resulting solution produces expanded specifications (from design choices) to the problem space. This is similar to the Twin Peak proposal [17], a software iterative development process that focuses on the combination of problem structures and solutions structures.

The method applicability is illustrated in the next section onto a mutual exclusion problem design.

4 Application: Alice and Bob Share a Yard

We borrow our example from an invited talk given by Lamport [22] about two neighbors, Alice and Bob. Alice and Bob share a yard, but also have dogs, and naturally they want to let the dogs use the yard. The problem is that these dogs don't like each other, and they fight, so only one dog at a time can be in the yard. To demonstrate how our method can be applied, we build this example from some initial requirements, and from a minimal set of domain knowledge.

4.1 Domain Description

We suppose that a knowledge base as been defined from previous experiences. In particular, it contains *problem cases* related to the mutual exclusion domain [23,24]. For improving the readability, the i-th property is named Pi and each state (named Si) in a process (named PRi) is noted $PRi@Si$.

---

[1] Each kind of combination is represented with a particular arrow shape.

A concurrent system *problem case* is composed of asynchronous processes, noted PRi. A basic property is that there be no deadlock; the set of processes must ensure the property noted $PDeadlock$.

In the mutual exclusion *problem case*, each process of the collection alternately executes a critical section noted $PRi@CS$ and a noncritical section noted $PRi@NCS$. Two processes cannot execute their critical sections concurrently. A process structure is composed of the following states: - noncritical ($PRi@NCS$); - trying ($PRi@T$); - critical ($PRi@CS$); - exit ($PRi@E$). Both processes in Fig. 5 conform to the structure.

Mutual exclusion *problem case* must ensure the following properties: (1) $PMutex$: "For any pair of distinct processes PRi and PRj, no pair of operation executions $PRi@CS$ and $PRj@CS$ are concurrent". An equivalent LTL formula is $\Box\neg PRi@CS \wedge PRj@CS$. (2) $PNolockout$ (starvation free): "In every execution, if a process PRi is in the trying state $PRi@T$, then there is a later state in which that same process is in the critical section $PRi@CS$". An equivalent LTL formula is $\Box(PRi@T \rightarrow \Diamond PRi@CS)$.

Because the mutual exclusion *problem case* is a concurrent system *problem case*, it must ensure $PDeadlock$. If there is a deadlock, it means that "one or more processes are trying to enter $PRi@CS$, but no process ever does". There is also the possibility that a deadlock occurs because all the processes are stuck in their $PRi@T$ state.

4.2   First Solution

Problem Formalization. The initial requirements are *P1* (and *P2*), when Alice (or Bob) tries to reach the yard, she(he) must finaly access it, and *P3*, Alice and Bob must not be together in the yard. The requirements are formalized in LTL as $P1 : \Box(Alice@Trying \rightarrow \Diamond Alice@Yard)$,
$P2 : \Box(Bob@Trying \rightarrow \Diamond Bob@Yard)$, $P3 : \Box\neg(Alice@Yard \wedge Bob@Yard)$.

Problem Decomposition. Following the method, we decompose our problem and we look for known subproblems. The P3 formula structure is similar to the abstract formula of mutual exclusion, $PMutex : \Box\neg(PRi@CS \wedge PRj@CS)$, considering that PRi is *Alice*, PRj is *Bob* and CS is the *Yard*. We make the assumption that they address the same *problem case*, and thus new properties emerge from this assumption, $PDeadlock$ and $PNoLockout$.

Design and Pattern Application. The design is illustrated in Fig. 5. There are two processes *Alice* and *Bob*, and a shared variable *Yard*. The design applies the mutual exclusion *problem case*. It gathers a problem side (properties $PMutex$, $PDeadlock$ and $PNoLockout$), and a solution side, that provides a structure representing one partial solution (NCS, T, CS, E).

Each process (Alice and Bob) conforms to the structure presented in Sect. 4.1. The behavior is the following: *Alice* tries to access the yard ($Alice@Trying$); then Alice goes into the yard ($Alice@Yard$), the *Yard* corresponds to the CS; and finally exit the yard($Alice@Exit$). The same goes for Bob.

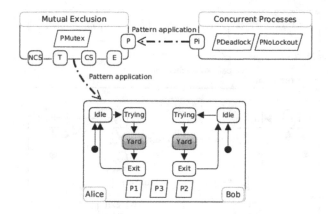

Fig. 5. Automata for Alice and Bob 1

Verification and Diagnosis. Verification can be done using several techniques such as static analysis, theorem proving, or model checking. The later is a formal technique that, given a formal model of the system and a set of properties, explores all possible system states in a brute-force manner [3]. If abnormalities are detected in the design, counter examples are produced, i.e. a trace from the initial state to an unexpected situation. Then diagnosis is triggered based on the observations of such traces. We use a model checker to check exhaustively the properties for this model.

PMutex is violated, indicating that Alice and Bob can be together in the yard at the same time. Since the structure of mutual exclusion *problem case* is applied to Alice and Bob, each element of Alice and Bob can be understood from the point of view of mutual exclusion *problem case*.

4.3   Second Solution - Turn

Problem Decomposition. At this point, we need a mechanism to ensure the access to the critical section. Browsing the knowledge base, we can choose to pick the *turn problem case*. From the specification point of view, the *turn problem case* is defined by a *turn* variable, and two properties, *PChange*: after a process has finished its execution *turn* must be changed; *PTurn*: a process cannot be in execution if it is not its *turn*.

Ad Hoc Design. The *turn problem case* is used to alternate the yard access. The design is presented with the automata in Fig. 6. The turn mechanism has to be combined with *Alice* and *Bob* structure ($NCS \rightarrow Tr \rightarrow CS \rightarrow Ex$). We suppose that the combination is complex enough to require an ad hoc design. The process that had the last access is stored, using the *turn* integer variable. A process checks the value of the *turn* variable in *PRi@Trying* statement. If the value is equal to its personal turn, it is authorized to access the yard. Then, *PRi@Exit* statement sets the *turn* variable to the other process.

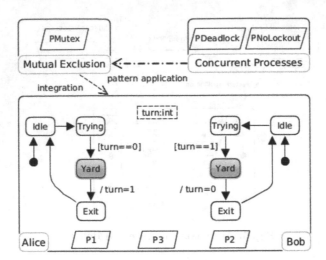

Fig. 6. Automata for Alice and Bob using Turn

Verification and Diagnosis. A new run is performed, the requirement *PMutex* is verified, but *PNoLockout* is violated.

Ad hoc design implies that the concepts of an integrated problem are widespread into the solution. Thus, parts of the problem are difficult to observe. According to the description of *PNoLockout*, *Bob* is continuously trying to access the yard (*Bob@Trying*), but cannot pursue in *Bob@CS*. Indeed, *Bob* has not the *turn* until *Alice* does not take it. If *Alice* does not take the *turn* anymore (*Alice* never goes in *Alice@Trying* state), and if *Bob* requires the *turn*, starvation occurs for *Bob*.

4.4 Turn Problem Formalization

Turn approach is formalized and stored in the knowledge base as follows. Turn is defined by a *turn* variable, followed by the properties: *PChange*: after *PRi@Exit*, *turn* must be equals to 1 and After *PRj@Exit*, *turn* must be equals to 0; *PTurn*: *PRi* cannot be in the *PRi@CS* if *turn* is not equals to 0 and *PRj* cannot be in the *PRj@CS* if *turn* is not equals to 1.

4.5 Using Flags

Problem Decomposition. The *turn problem case* is interesting if we not consider the *PNoLockout* property. Another idea consists in sharing the intention of Alice and Bob to access the yard. This intention can be captured using two flags, one for *Alice* and one for *Bob*. A raised flag means that the person wants to go in the yard, and reciprocally, a lowered flag means the person does not need to.

Design of a New Solution. The new solution is based on an array named *flag* of two booleans. The first boolean indicates if *Alice* want to access to the *Alice@Yard* or not. The second boolean indicates if *Bob* want to access to the *Bob@Yard* or not. *Alice* can access to the *Yard* if and only if *Bob* hasn't raised his *flag*. The same goes for *Bob*. When *Alice* or *Bob* are in the yard, she/he raises the *flag*. Finally the *flag* is lowered in the *Exit* state. The design is illustrated in Fig. 7.

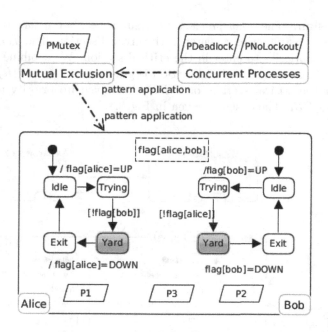

Fig. 7. Automata for Alice and Bob using Flag

Verification and Diagnosis. A new run is performed, and as a result, a deadlock occurs.

Suppose that *Alice* and *Bob* are interrupted in their *Trying* section. At this point each has claimed for entering in the yard but is not sure if the *Yard* is in use. Then each of them sees the *flag* of the other one and wait. Each is waiting indefinitely for the other, a deadlock has occurred.

4.6   Flag Problem Formulation

Flag approach is formalized and stored in the knowledge base as follows. It contains an array of two boolean called *flags*, and a set of following properties: (1) *PRaise*, *PRi* raises its *flag* in *PRi@Trying* state, and *PRj* raises its *flag* in *PRj@Trying* state; (2) *PLower*, *PRi* lower its *flag* in *PRi@Exit* state and *PRj* lower its *flag* in *PRj@Exit* state; (3) *PWait*, *PRi* cannot access *PRi@CS* if *flag* of *PRj* is raised, and *PRj* cannot access *PRj@CS* if *flag* of *PRi* is true.

4.7   Taking Turn and Raising Flags

Problem Formulation. Now, we decide to design a solution that solves all the problems mentioned above. We know that the property *PMutex* is fulfilled either with a turn or a flag. But the first solution violates *PNolockout* property, and the second violates *PDeadlock* property. We try to combine the *problem cases* together to fulfill all properties.

Ad Hoc Design. The *Flag problem case* supposes that a flag raised by a process indicates its intention to enter in the critical section. The *Turn problem case* supposes a priority to enter in the critical section. We combine these two mechanisms; entering to the critical section is granted for *PRi* if *PRj* does not want to enter the critical section, or if *PRj* has given up priority to *PRi* by setting turn to *PRi*. The design is given in Fig. 8.

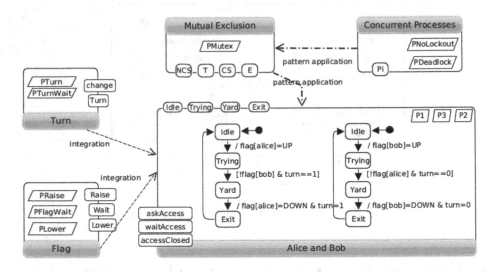

Fig. 8. Automata for Alice and Bob using Flags and Turns

Verification and Problem Reformulation. It turns out that the whole set of properties are verified, thus the solution is acceptable. Finally, we formulate our problem of Alice and Bob sharing a yard, as a combination of *Concurrent Process, Mutual Exclusion, Turn* and *Flag problem cases*.

5   Tool Support

The approach is effective when a significant amount of experiences is available. For capturing experiences, our method must be combined with tools for creating, storing, querying and retrieving *problem cases*.

5.1   A Verification Organizing System

In a previous article [25], we presented the Verification Organizing System (VOS) "an Organizing System is an intentionally arranged collection of resources and the interactions they support [13]." The VOS is a three-layered infrastructure made of a storage tier, a knowledge tier, and an access tier.

The storage tier is characterized by a variety of sources, heterogeneous with respect to several dimensions concerning form and content properties. It is based on a Software Configuration Management (SCM) system that controls versioned artifacts produced. It includes *problem cases*, gathering no exhaustively verification endeavors (run, traces), properties or models.

The knowledge tier, a logic-based, knowledge-rich level, plays the central role of a shared language to connect people to people, people to information, and information to information, represented as an ontology. It allows for knowledge creation, query and inference.

The access tier is used for diagnosis tools interoperability. Heterogeneous tools can interoperate by the underlying mechanism of model federation [16].

These tools can be classified in three categories, model-based, process-history-based and interaction-based. Model-based tools assumes that a model of the system is available [30] allowing to localize the subset of system's constituents generating abnormalities. Process history-based tools relies on the availability of large amount of historical process data, and thus, can be used for extracting knowledge [27], or reasoning [1]. Interaction-based tools allow for observing, controlling, understanding and altering the system execution. Examples includes omniscient debuggers [29], or visualization tools [19].

5.2   Knowledge and Inference

Figure 9 illustrates the various artifacts produced at each step of the method. *Problem cases* (1) are progressively decomposed into other *problem cases* (2). Given the *problem case* structure, the organizing system can be used for querying and retrieving *problems cases* that are the most relevant. This may be achieved, for instance, according to three tasks, search, initially match, and select [1]. Combining *problem cases* (4) is achieved with a certain level of automation. Component integration (5) is the most automated way. *Problem cases* are on the shelf solutions connected through well defined connection points. For pattern application (6), the degree of freedom lies in the rules of application between the problem pattern and the given solution. Ad hoc design (7) means that the design is left to the engineer. (8) It shows how the previous combination techniques may affect the diagnosis task. Possible error locations are represented with black stars. Component integration mainly results in connections errors, pattern application mainly generates errors in the rules of pattern application, and ad hoc design may produce widespread errors. Finally, a solution is kept in the organizing system. It involves the selection of relevant information from the new *problem case* to keep.

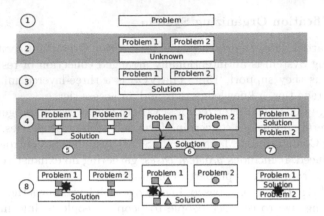

Fig. 9. Artifacts produced

6   Conclusion

Designing a solution for a given problem and diagnosing possible faults in the proposed solution, are tedious tasks. It is mainly due to poorly understood problem and poorly managed information, that results in a lack of diagnosis support and solution reuse. Our hypothesis is that a method is required for analyzing the current problem, storing relevant information, and reusing known solutions as much as possible. When a new solution is designed, for which abnormalities are observed, *problem cases* provide a model for reasoning on the solution problem. In this paper, we have shown the possibility of applying our approach to a typical case. Future works will aim to evaluate the approach scalability by applying it on a real application in a cyber-security context.

References

1. Agnar, A., Enric, P.: Case-based reasoning: foundational issues, methodological variations, and system approaches. AI Commun. **1**, 39–59 (1994)
2. Alrajeh, D., Kramer, J., Russo, A., Uchitel, S.: Automated support for diagnosis and repair. Commun. ACM **58**(2), 65–72 (2015)
3. Baier, C., Katoen, J.P.: Principles of Model Checking. The MIT Press, Cambridge (2008)
4. Ball, T., Naik, M., Rajamani, S.K.: From symptom to cause: localizing errors in counterexample traces. ACM SIGPLAN Not. **38**, 97–105 (2003)
5. Basili, V.R., Caldiera, G.: Improve software quality by reusing knowledge and experience. MIT Sloan Manage. Rev. **37**(1), 55 (1995)
6. Bertoli, P., Bozzano, M., Cimatti, A.: A symbolic model checking framework for safety analysis, diagnosis, and synthesis. In: Edelkamp, S., Lomuscio, A. (eds.) MoChArt 2006. LNCS (LNAI), vol. 4428, pp. 1–18. Springer, Heidelberg (2007). https://doi.org/10.1007/978-3-540-74128-2_1

7. Bjørner, D.: Software Engineering 3. Texts in Theoretical Computer Science. An EATCS Series. Springer, Heidelberg (2006). https://doi.org/10.1007/3-540-33653-2

8. Buschmann, F. (ed.): Pattern-Oriented Software Architecture: A System of Patterns. Wiley, Chichester, New York (1996)

9. Clarke, E.M., Kurshan, R.P., Veith, H.: The localization reduction and counterexample-guided abstraction refinement. In: Manna, Z., Peled, D.A. (eds.) Time for Verification. LNCS, vol. 6200, pp. 61–71. Springer, Heidelberg (2010). https://doi.org/10.1007/978-3-642-13754-9_4

10. Cleve, H., Zeller, A.: Locating causes of program failures, p. 342. ACM Press (2005)

11. Doerr, M.: The CIDOC conceptual reference module: an ontological approach to semantic interoperability of metadata. AI Mag. **24**(3), 75–92 (2003)

12. Gamma, E. (ed.): Design Patterns: Elements of Reusable Object-Oriented Software. Addison-Wesley Professional Computing Series. Addison-Wesley, Reading (1995)

13. Glushko, R.J.: Foundations for "organizing systems". In: Glushko, R.J. (ed.) The Discipline of Organizing (2012)

14. Groce, A., Visser, W.: What went wrong: explaining counterexamples. In: Ball, T., Rajamani, S.K. (eds.) SPIN 2003. LNCS, vol. 2648, pp. 121–136. Springer, Heidelberg (2003). https://doi.org/10.1007/3-540-44829-2_8

15. Gromov, M., Willemse, T.A.C.: Testing and model-checking techniques for diagnosis. In: Petrenko, A., Veanes, M., Tretmans, J., Grieskamp, W. (eds.) FATES/TestCom -2007. LNCS, vol. 4581, pp. 138–154. Springer, Heidelberg (2007). https://doi.org/10.1007/978-3-540-73066-8_10

16. Guychard, C., Guerin, S., Koudri, A., Beugnard, A., Dagnat, F.: Conceptual interoperability through models federation. In: Semantic Information Federation Community Workshop (2013)

17. Hall, J., Jackson, M., Laney, R., Nuseibeh, B., Rapanotti, L.: Relating software requirements and architectures using problem frames, pp. 137–144. IEEE Computer Society (2002)

18. Hall, J.G., Rapanotti, L., Jackson, M.: Problem oriented software engineering: a design-theoretic framework for software engineering, pp. 15–24. IEEE, September 2007

19. Hamou-Lhadj, A., Lethbridge, T.C.: A survey of trace exploration tools and techniques. In: Proceedings of the 2004 Conference of the Centre for Advanced Studies on Collaborative research, pp. 42–55. IBM Press (2004)

20. Holzmann, G.J.: The theory and practice of a formal method: NewCoRe. In: IFIP Congress, vol. 1, pp. 35–44 (1994)

21. Jackson, M.: Problem Frames: Analysing and Structuring Software Development Problems. Addison-Wesley, Harlow (2001). oCLC: 247895444

22. Lamport, L.: Solved problems, unsolved problems and non-problems in concurrency. ACM SIGOPS Oper. Syst. Rev. **19**(4), 34–44 (1985)

23. Lamport, L.: The mutual exclusion problem: part I–a theory of interprocess communication. J. ACM (JACM) **33**(2), 313–326 (1986)

24. Lamport, L.: The mutual exclusion problem: part II–statement and solutions. J. ACM (JACM) **33**(2), 327–348 (1986)

25. Leilde, V., Ribaud, V., Dhaussy, P.: An organizing system to perform and enable verification and diagnosis activities. In: Yin, H., et al. (eds.) IDEAL 2016. LNCS, vol. 9937, pp. 576–587. Springer, Cham (2016). https://doi.org/10.1007/978-3-319-46257-8_62

26. Leildé, V., Ribaud, V., Teodorov, C., Dhaussy, P.: A diagnosis framework for critical systems verification (Short Paper). In: Cimatti, A., Sirjani, M. (eds.) SEFM 2017. LNCS, vol. 10469, pp. 394–400. Springer, Cham (2017). https://doi.org/10.1007/978-3-319-66197-1_27
27. Liu, Y., Xu, C., Cheung, S.: AFChecker: effective model checking for context-aware adaptive applications. J. Syst. Softw. **86**(3), 854–867 (2013)
28. Newell, A., Simon, H.A., et al.: Human Problem Solving, vol. 104. Prentice-Hall, Englewood Cliffs (1972)
29. Pothier, G., Tanter, É., Piquer, J.: Scalable omniscient debugging. ACM SIGPLAN Not. **42**(10), 535–552 (2007)
30. Reiter, R.: A theory of diagnosis from first principles. Artif. Intell. **32**(1), 57–95 (1987)
31. Ruys, T.C., Brinksma, E.: Managing the verification trajectory. Int. J. Softw. Tools Technol. Transf. (STTT) **4**(2), 246–259 (2003)
32. Swartout, W., Balzer, R.: On the inevitable intertwining of specification and implementation. Commun. ACM **25**(7), 438–440 (1982)
33. Venkatasubramanian, V., Rengaswamy, R., Kavuri, S.N.: A review of process fault detection and diagnosis. Comput. Chem. Eng. **27**(3), 313–326 (2003)

A Formal Model for Interaction Specification and Analysis in IoT Applications

Souad Marir[1,2](✉), Faiza Belala[1], and Nabil Hameurlain[2]

[1] LIRE Laboratory, University of Constantine 2 -Abdelhamid Mehri,
Constantine, Algeria
{souad.marir,faiza.belala}@univ-constantine2.dz
[2] University of PAU, LIUPAA, Pau, France
nabil.hameurlain@univ-pau.fr

Abstract. The Internet of Things (IoT) is a concept where connected entities can work and interact with each other in order to facilitate daily life. Although, many research efforts in the IoT realm have been to date devoted to device, networking and application service perspectives, formalization and analysis of IoT systems are still in their infancy. This paper introduces a new BRS-based approach aiming to support specification and verification of interaction and interoperability aspects in IoT systems. The proposed approach is based on a bigraphical-agent model that investigates the spatial structure of the IoT system and its logical structure defining the behaviour and interactions of its different entities. The Tree Query Logic (TQL) is used to formally express and verify some properties inherent to IoT systems.

Keywords: IoT · BRS · Formal specification · Interaction model
TQL

1 Introduction

The Internet of Things (IoT) is the connection of heterogeneous objects, geographically separated, consuming and producing data, in order to offer services. Generally considered as intelligent, IoT systems facilitate considerably every day life of human beings, with a minimum of intervention, working on interoperable networks and reacting to their environment. Developing IoT systems become more and more challenging; due to the ever growth of technologies, IoT systems are wider, distributed, heterogeneous, and involve different types of systems communication. Thus, the interaction between elements of the same system as well as the interaction between different systems is primordial. Modelling and developing IoT systems can be particularly very challenging for many reasons. For instance, the architecture of IoT systems relies on many overlapping factors that should be considered earlier in the design phase. The hardware

© Springer Nature Switzerland AG 2018
E. H. Abdelwahed et al. (Eds.): MEDI 2018, LNCS 11163, pp. 371–384, 2018.
https://doi.org/10.1007/978-3-030-00856-7_25

and software components dependencies along with the complexity of the IoT systems architectures, increase significantly the difficulty of modelling these systems. The aim of this paper is twofold: in one hand, we propose a comprehensive and a generic formal model for IoT applications, reducing their complexity and design, using a judicious combination of BRS model and software agents. Our BCAM4IoT model (Bigraphical Communicating Agent Model for the Internet of Things) gives precise semantics to possible interactions that govern the complex behaviour of these systems. On the other hand, we show how the spatial logic TQL is used to express and analyse more conveniently some relevant properties such as: communication, context awareness and interoperability, which represents a huge interest in the scientific community, we can cite the INTER-IoT project [1] that aims to allow the interoperability among different IoT platforms, the VICINITY project [2], that proposes to define the "interoperability as a service" for IoT by guaranteeing it in the communication part of an IoT system.

Bigraphical Reactive Systems (BRS) via the bigraph model, defined by Milner in [3], emphasize on both locality and connectivity in IoT systems. They propose two types of graphs: a place graph expressing physical/logical location of IoT components, and a link graph describing their interconnections. Additionally, BRS are expressive enough to be adopted for representing IoT system dynamics; in terms of reaction rules. Besides, software agents describe the possible reasoning of each entity and how it self-adapts to context changes. The spatial logic TQL [4] has emerging as an interesting tool to describe properties of several structures. Models for this logic include computational structures such as heaps, trees, graphs [4], concurrent objects [4] as well as process calculi and the Ambient Calculus [4].

The remainder of the paper is structured as follows: in the Sect. 3, we present a multi-levels architecture for IoT, separating physical components (hardware of software) of IoT systems from logical ones. In this section we also explain the most important properties of IoT systems, namely interoperability and context-awareness. In Sect. 4, we introduce the BRS formalism together with the TQL logic. In Sect. 5, we propose BCAM4IoT (Bigraphical Communicating Agent Model for the Internet of Things), a formal model extending the bigraphical agent one for the IoT in order to deal with interaction aspects in IoT systems. In Sect. 6, we explain how the two most challenging properties, interoperability and context-awareness could be expressed and checked in terms of TQL. Section 7 summarises the paper and discusses ongoing work.

2   Related Work

Recently, some approaches in the literature try to apply existing formalisms to model IoT systems while favouring certain aspects to the detriment of others. In this section, we cite some distinctive approaches that deal with formal specification of IoT systems.

Authors of [5] used a model inspired from the nature to specify the behaviour of distributed and dynamic systems while considering the interaction unities as a basic concept. IoT applications has been shown just as a case of study.

In [6], authors propose a runtime model-driven approach focusing on sensor device models description, while our approach focuses on modelling the behaviour of an IoT system with its physical, logical and interaction parts supporting the modelling of IoT systems and thus they proposed a generic architecture for IoT systems.

On the other hand, the research work in [7] focused only on the physical part of an IoT system. Their model supports the heterogeneity of objects and may be applied to all types of IoT systems. Their contribution lies in the definition of an ontology that captures the basic considered concepts and models the dynamical process in a static way.

On another side, there is a few number of works that attempt to check formally models destined to IoT Systems, we can cite authors of [8] that use the SPIN tool (based on the Linear Temporal Logic LTL), to check whether a smart house system modelled in petri nets is working properly. In this work, they focused more on the model checking than on the IoT aspects, it is not specified how their model supports the IoT systems characteristics, in the opposite of our proposition, where we try to model IoT systems aspects.

Contrary to the above cited work, our approach consists in modelling the behaviour of an IoT system, combining the software agents and the bigraphs, which are formal tools, while emphasizing the aspect of interaction between their elements. Moreover, we use appropriate spatial logic in order to check some of their properties.

3 A Multi-levels Architecture for IoT

At a high level of abstraction, IoT applications may be considered as a set of physical and logical components connected via interaction elements. To master their complexity, we propose a generic architecture (Fig. 1) dealing with the separation of the physical part from the logical one, and even the physical part can be structured hierarchically. Thus, entities of the system will be distributed between the layers, and charges of each layer are divided through the components of these layers.

Through this section, we will give, in an incremental manner, the three essential parts of the proposed architecture: Physical part, Logical part and Interaction part.

3.1 Physical Part

Elements belonging to this part may be classified in four different layers:

1. **Hardware:** contains input hardware identifying the objects that capture data from the environment; output hardware for the objects that actuate on the environment and input/output hardware for the components used to interact in an eventual network;
2. **Abstraction:** constitutes an interface, containing all the protocols needed by the top layers to interact with the hardware components;

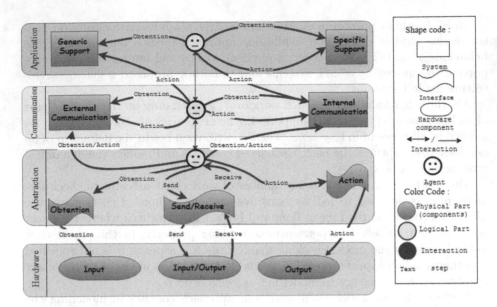

Fig. 1. Multi-layered architecture for an IoT application

3. **Communication:** contains protocols of rooting information from the hardware to the software components (and *vice-versa*), or from one system to another;
4. **Application:** divided into two sub layers: the former recognizes the type of information received, extracts data and gives it an analysable format; the second sub layer is needed to process the desired IoT application.

3.2 Logical Part

The logical part of this architecture is supported by a set of reactive agents which behave according to a control loop (observation, analysis, control), each layer of the physical part (except the hardware one) is managed by one agent type.

- In the abstraction layer, the agent controls each solicitation of the hardware entities by elements of the layers above and *vice-versa*. It also decides if the interaction can occur or not, according to the result of its observation's analysis.
- The agent that manages the communication layer is responsible of making the decisions to send or not information for internal or another system.
- Finally, in the application layer, the agent makes the decisions to make a perceptible action after analysing the data received and the data produced by the specific support.

These agents are responsible of the various communications that may exist between the systems or their components.

3.3   Interaction Part

In an IoT system, the interactions between objects are the most important concept requiring a particular attention. In this architecture, unidirectional arrows are used to illustrate these interactions, that may be of two types:

- **Agent/Component:** In the three high levelled layers of the architecture, the only interaction defined is between agents and physical components. At each time, agents obtain some information from a component, analyse it, and decide to obtain other information from the same component, or to actuate on another one. Modelling a system with a set of agents involve specifying the communications between them using interaction protocols. Specifying the way they interact is interesting and challenging because of their heterogeneity and autonomy [9]. In [10], we modelled the architecture proposed with its different aspects, using the formalism of bi-agents, but, we didn't take care of the communication between the agents which was the weak point of this model.
- **Component/Component:** This kind of interaction exists only between the abstraction layer entities and the hardware ones. It represents the hardware's solicitations of the system's application side and *vice versa*. It is shown that the abstraction agent doesn't interact directly with the hardware components, but through interfaces (this allows the heterogeneity of objects needed in real IoT systems).

The separation of IoT system components using a layered architecture facilitates its modelling. The interaction between the elements of the system becomes the most important part to define in order to reduce more this complexity. In the present paper, by extending an existing architecture [10], we are interested in modelling and checking the two following properties:

- Interoperability: The definition of interoperability in IoT is currently being developed, so a standard definition is not yet established. In the following sections, we consider that interoperability [11] is to deal with the fact that devices must support interoperable communication protocols and can interact with other devices and also with the infrastructure;

- Context awareness [11]: It is the ability of the sensor nodes to gain knowledge about the surrounding context, based on the sensed information about the physical and environmental parameters. The decisions that the sensor nodes take thereafter are context-aware.

In order to model this architecture formally, according to its hierarchical aspects, the different types of connections between its entities, and the management aspect made by agents, the formalism of bigraphical agents seems to be the most adequate. Hence, we choose the Tree Query Logic to check the considered properties using this resulted model. We are motivated by its adaptability to tree structured models as bigraphical ones. Being a spacial logic, it can be used for the analyses of a model's structure as it is given by the properties of interoperability and context awareness, that are independent of the execution scenarios. Some aspects related to the formalism of biagent and the TQL are presented in the next section.

4 Basic Concepts

In this section, we briefly recall the formal concepts used to model and check an IoT system.

4.1 Bigraphical Reactive Systems

A Bigraphical Reactive System (BRS) [3] is the set of bigraphs representing the states of the system obtained from an initial bigraph, and the reaction rules applied successively on it. A bigraph, as shown in the Fig. 2 is composed of two graphs, the place graph used to model the location of physical and logical components, and the link graph can express the connectivity between the components:

– The place graph with a set of nodes $\{v_0, v_1\}$ and a parent function $prnt{:}sites \uplus nodes \rightarrow nodes \uplus regions$, the roots are called regions (as 0 and 1 in Fig. 2), and some special nodes are called sites (dashed boxes 0, 1 and 2 in Fig. 2).

– The link graph is defined also with a set of nodes $\{v_0, v_1\}$, hyperedges e_0 and the link function $X \uplus ports \rightarrow hyperedges \uplus Y$, where X are the internal names (oriented to the bottom) and Y the external ones (oriented to the top).

In addition to that, dynamics of an specified system is defined in terms of reaction rules as explained in [3].

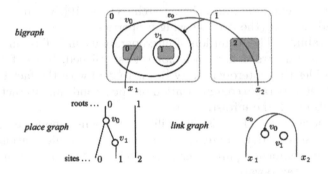

Fig. 2. Example of a bigraph [3] $\langle 3, \{x, y\} \rangle \rightarrow \langle 2, \emptyset \rangle$

4.2 The Tree Query Logic

The Tree Query Logic (TQL) [4] is a spatial logic used in order to reason about eventual updates of tree structures and also permits the model checking of some relevant properties. The TQL is inspired by the Ambient logic, that describes a finite unordered labelled trees called *information trees*, noted, i.t.'s. This logic

Table 1. Some TQL logical formula [4]

0	The empty information tree
n[A]	Single-edge i.t.'s labelled n and leading to a subtree satisfying A
A|B	i.t.'s splittable into two i.t.'s satisfying A and B respectively
T	All information trees
¬A	All i.t.'s not satisfying A
A∧B	i.t.'s satisfying A and B
A∨B	i.t.'s satisfying A or B

permits the use of the quantifiers ∀ and ∃. To understand well a TQL statement, The Table 1 contains some notations:

The empty information tree **0** represents the concept of nothing, having an edge leading to nothing means that there is nothing after. n[A] means that there is an edge of label n leading to something that is between [ ]. The | is the most important operator in a spatial logic, it makes the separation between the elements of the model, if the representation of the model contains at least one |, that means that the model can be separated into at least two parts. **T** helps avoiding repetition. ∧, ∨ and negativity as in all logics are needed for the expression of most properties.

We can express a formula F and checking it by deciding if a tree T satisfies this formula, we note $F(T \vDash F)$. For validating some property, its formula F is valid, if and only if, non F is not satisfiable, we note $\neg(\exists T.T \vDash \neg F)$.

The formalism of bigraphs is used to **model** the behaviour and the structure of a system. In order to **verify** structural and dynamical properties, spatial and temporal logics are used respectively. We notice that the structure of bigraphs can be represented as trees which permits us to use the TQL as a logic of verification of some structural properties. We see in the Sect. 6 how this can be done.

5   BCAM4IoT Model

In this model, we focus on the importance of defining the interaction that exists between the different elements of an IoT system. Agents in Fig. 1 are responsible of the communication in an IoT system, our proposed model should deal with these communication types. This model is formally defined as: $BCAM4IoT = a_{IoT*}^{(i)} \bullet \mathcal{B}_{IoT}$ (BCAM for Bigraphical Communicating Agent Model), where $\mathcal{B}_{IoT}$ its structural part is given by the Definition 1, and $a_{IoT*}^{(i)}$ its virtual part, by the Definition 2.

Definition 1 (The physical structure)

$$\mathcal{B}_{IoT} = (\mathbb{B}, \mathcal{R}, \mathbb{U}, B_0, F)$$

- $\mathbb{B}$ *is the set of bigraphs.*
- $\mathcal{R}$ *is the set of reaction rules.*
- $\mathbb{U} \subset V_{\mathbb{B}} \times \mathcal{R}$ *is the set of controls, which is the application of a reaction rule to a specific node in the bigraph with $V_{\mathbb{B}}$ the set of nodes of every bigraph $B \in \mathbb{B}$.*
- $B_0 \in \mathbb{B}$ *is the first bigraph of $\mathbb{B}$.*
- *F is the control function defining the transition between a bigraph and another according to a control $u_i \in \mathbb{U}$.*

In the Definition 1, the chosen IoT application is modelled by the set of bigraphs $\mathbb{B}$. Each bigraph represents a state of the system, and the transition from a state to another is defined by a control. In order to avoid the non-determinism of a particular reaction rule, there are controls $\mathbb{U}$ that are the application of a reaction rule to a specific node, in other words, they represent an action that changes the system's state according to a specific condition. $B_0 \in \mathbb{B}$ represents the initial state of the IoT system.

Definition 2 (Virtual structure of BCAM4IoT)

$$a_{IoT*}^{(i)} = (\mathcal{O}, obs, an, ctr, mgrt, int, \mathcal{U}, \mathcal{D}, host_0)$$

- $\mathcal{O} \subset \mathbb{B}$ *is the observation space.*
- *the function of observation obs which provides an observation $o \in \mathcal{O}$ using a bigraph and the host of the observant agent: $obs(b, h) = o$.*
- *the analysis function that, with an observation or a set of observations and a host, analyses this host or its sons and returns a decision: $an(o, h) = \alpha \in \mathcal{D}$.*
- *The control function which gives the next succession of rules to be executed, according to a node, using the result of an analysis: $ctr(\alpha) = u \in \mathcal{U}$.*
- *The migration function that provides the next host of the agent according to the current host and an observation: $mgrt(o, h) = h'$.*
- *the interaction function int, using the decision made $\alpha \in \mathcal{D}$ and the host of the agent with whom it interacts, the agent interacts with another one using this function: $int(h, \alpha)$*

$$int : V_{\mathbb{B}} \times \mathcal{D}$$
$$(h, \alpha)$$

- $\mathcal{U}, \mathcal{D}$ *and $host_0$ are respectively the space of controls, of decisions and the initial host of the agent.*

The Definition 2 shows how the semantic of an agent in BCAM4IoT is defined, each one has:

- A set of observations,
- A set of controls,
- A set of decisions,
- An initial host,
- It observes bigraphs,
- It analyses its observation,

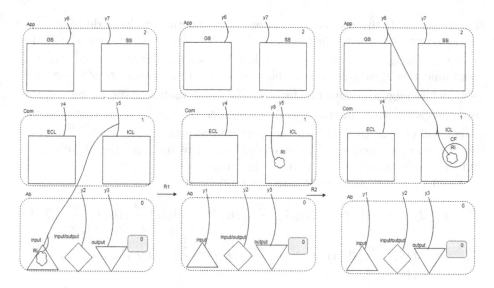

Fig. 3. Example of a trace

– It interacts with other agents giving them its decision.

The regions App, Com and Ab represent respectively the application, the communication and the abstraction layers. The nodes GS, SS, ECL and ICL represent the generic support, the specific support, the external communication layer and the internal communication layer In BCAM4IoT, we emphasis that an agent makes actions according to its context, it analyses its observations and launches a trace of actions after interacting with agents likely to be influenced by its decision.

5.1   Example

We consider a case of a collision avoidance system as example, provided with a radar, a vibrator and a wifi card. We present a simple scenario showing the contribution of BCAM4IoT to support the definition of the interaction semantics between agents. For instance, we present the sequence of executions materialized by the trace: $T = B_0 \overset{R1}{\prec} B_1 \overset{R2}{\prec}$ in Fig. 3. Each state of the system is represented by a bigraph (containing the layers Ab, Com and App), Each layer is represented as a region (dotted boxes) of the bigraph and sub systems, as ECL (External Communication Layer) and ICL (Internal Communication Layer) are represented by simple squares. (In the Fig. 3, the agent is not visible). The radar (input) captures a suspect sound, the abstraction agent captures the sound through the interface of the radar $\overset{R1}{\longrightarrow}$. After its observation $\overset{obs}{\longrightarrow}$, it migrates in the information node representing the sound (RI) $\overset{mgrt}{\longrightarrow}$ in order to analyse its content $\overset{\alpha}{\longrightarrow}$.

It interacts with the communication agent giving the resulting decision $\xrightarrow{int}$: the sound will be sent to the ICL in order to be formatted, and returns to the abstraction layer $\xrightarrow{mgrt}$. After that, the ICL formats the information $\xrightarrow{R2}$ and the communication agent observes the bigraph representing this state of the system $\xrightarrow{obs}$. Before migrating into this format $\xrightarrow{mgrt}$ and analysing the packet $\xrightarrow{\alpha}$, the communication agent interacts with the application agent $\xrightarrow{int}$ saying that the packet will be sent to the general support and returns to its layer $\xrightarrow{mgrt}$. After this sequence of executions T, the application agent manages the highest layer and the instructions cascade down to the hardware.

From T, two projection of traces can be defined:

$$t^{Ab_{Ag}} = (B_0, 0) \overset{R1}{\prec} (B_1, 0) \overset{obs}{\prec} (B_1, 0) \overset{mgrt}{\prec} (B_1, I) \overset{\alpha}{\prec} (B_1, I) \overset{int}{\prec} (B_1, I) \overset{mgrt}{\prec} (B_1, 0)$$

$$t^{Com_{Ag}} = (B_1, 1) \overset{R2}{\prec} (B_1, 1) \overset{obs}{\prec} (B_1, 0) \overset{mgrt}{\prec} (B_1, CF) \overset{\alpha}{\prec} (B_1, CF) \overset{int}{\prec} (B_1, CF) \overset{mgrt}{\prec}$$
$$(B_1, 1)$$

The trace rules defined in this section may serve to model various evolution scenarios of IoT systems. Each scenario consists of a sequence of trace rules applications. In the following section, we proceed to the checking of BCAM4IoT, expressing the considered properties of interoperability and context-awareness, using the TQL logic, and move on to execute the checking process.

6   Formal Analysis

The hierarchical aspect of BCAM4IoT allows us to use the TQL in order to express structural properties of some models. These expressions are made in the purpose of checking our model in terms of a query and its verification. Here, we are interested by two properties: (i) Interoperability guaranteed by the verification of three atomic ones PICP, FRI and AI. (ii) Context-awareness.

Presence of Interoperable Communication Protocols (PICP).
This is defined in BCAM4IoT by the existence of the node ICP (interoperable communication protocols) in the node ICL (internal communication layer) in the region 1 (communication layer) of the bigraph representing a state of the system. This property is represented in the TQL by an information tree (see Fig. 4) and it is noted:

$$B[\, region\,[\,1\,[\,subsystemNode\,[\,ICL\,[\,ICP\,[\,\mathbf{0}\,]\,]\,]\,|\,\mathbf{T}\,]\,]\,|\,\mathbf{T}\,]$$

Formatting Raw Information into Packets (FRI).
This is defined in BCAM4IoT by the ability of the node ICL (internal communication layer) to format (CF) raw information (RI) into packets. This property is represented in the TQL by an information tree (Fig. 5) and it is noted:

$$B[\, region\,[\,1\,[\,subsystemNode\,[\,ICL\,[\,ICP\,[\,\mathbf{0}\,]\,]\,]\,|\,[\,CF\,[\,RI\,]\,]\,]\,|\,\mathbf{T}\,]\,]\,|\,\mathbf{T}\,]$$

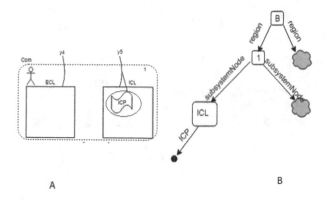

Fig. 4. Formal notation of PICP property

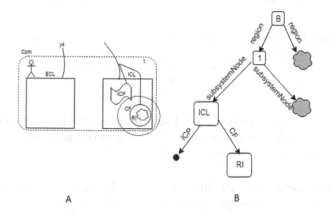

Fig. 5. Formal notation of FRI property

Ability of Interacting (AI).

This is defined in BCAM4IoT by the fact that all the elements of the physical layer interact with each other, by the capacity of the abstraction agent to communicate its decision to the communication agent; from the abstraction layer (0), to the communication layer (1); and by its influence on the interfaces (input, input\output and output) of these elements. This property is represented in the TQL by an information tree as in Fig. 6 and it is noted:

$$B[\,region\,[\,0\,[\,Agents\,[\,Ag^{Ab}\,[\,Operations\,[\,int\,[\,decision\,[\,content]]\,|\,[\,0\,[\,1\,]]]\,|$$
$$[\,ctr\,[\,interfaceNode\,[\,methodes\,]]]]\,|\,\mathbf{T}]]]]]\,|\,\mathbf{T}]$$

In the bigraphical representation of AI property, the operations of the agents are not visible; the following definition of the abstraction agent, especially the functions *int* and *ctrl*, complete the structural definition of BCAM4IoT with

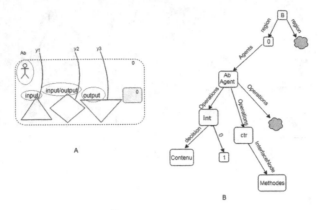

Fig. 6. Formal notation of AI property

the details used to express this property.

$$a_{IoT}^{Ab} = (\mathcal{O}, obs, an, ctr, mgrt, int, \mathcal{U}, \mathcal{D}, host_0)$$

Note 1. We notice that the interoperability between the hardware components of the system is established by making the software components, and their representation in the model, interoperable.

The Context Awareness Property: in BCAM4IoT, this property is defined as: every Action is triggered in the application layer according to an extracted information EI made in the general support sub system GG from the raw information RI formatted with the communication format CF received from the communication layer and captured previously. So the system must have these three states to own this property. In the TQL, it is interpreted as follows:

$$B[\,region\,[\,2\,[\,subsystemNode\,[\,GS\,[\,CF\,[\,RI\,]\,]\,]\,]\,]\,|\,\mathbf{T}\,]\,|\,\mathbf{T}\,]$$
$$\wedge\,B[\,region\,[\,2\,[\,subsystemNode\,[\,GS\,[\,EI\,[\,\mathbf{0}\,]\,]\,]\,]\,]\,|\,\mathbf{T}\,]\,|\,\mathbf{T}\,]$$
$$\wedge\,B[\,region\,[\,2\,[\,subsystemNode\,[\,A\,[\,EI\,[\,\mathbf{0}\,]\,]\,]\,]\,]\,|\,\mathbf{T}\,]\,|\,\mathbf{T}\,]$$

We propose a representation of the initial state in the TQL noted as follows

$$B[region[0[input]\,||\,[in\backslash out]\,||\,[output]\,||\,[site]\,||\,[Agent[Ab[...]]]]]]\,||\,[1[subsystemNode[ICL$$
$$[ICP[\mathbf{0}]]]\,||\,[ECL[ECP|PVS]]]]\,||\,[Agent[com[...]]]]]\,||\,[2[GS[...]]]\,||\,[SS[...]]]\,||\,[Agent[app[...]]]]$$

For example, if we proceed to the validation of the property PICP in the initial state, we find that it is true; but if we try to check for FRI in the same state, it is not valid, because in the initial state of the system, there are no raw information captured yet.

7 Conclusion

Development of IoT applications becomes each year more complex and challenging, this is due to, the highly dynamic cooperation among heterogeneous things, the need of ensuring interconnectivity of software and hardware (physical) entities, and the support of a huge scale of interconnected devices. This paper focused on the use of formal methods to design and specify such applications by supporting the characteristics of complex, distributed and heterogeneous systems. We have proposed an extended Biagent model (called BCAM4IoT), that inherits the benefits of each of the implied concepts (BRS and software agents). The BRS have been adopted to specify the physical part of an IoT application dealing with the spatial distribution, the mobility and the heterogeneity of its constituents. The Agents allowed to describe the logical reasoning of IoT elements, a behavioural semantics of an agent in BCAM4IoT considers various action types, including observation (of the context), analysis (of possible situations), control and communication (with each other).

A nice consequence of using a formal model is that trace rules have been exploited to formally specify IoT systems behaviour, dealing with context-aware feature and interoperability one. We also showed the adequacy of the TQL logic to express and validate these important properties. As a future work, we plan to investigate the formal verification of other IoT inherent properties and also, implementing a tool that permits the edition of our model BCAM4IoT, provided with a model checker which checks the structural and dynamical properties of an IoT system using the bigraphical logic and the TQL.

References

1. INTER-IoT Project: Inter-IoT - Interoperability Internet of Things (2016). http://www.inter-iot-project.eu
2. European Platforms Initiative: Vicinity — Open Virtual Neighbourhood Network to Connect IoT Infrastructures and Smart Objects (2016). https://vicinity2020.eu/vicinity
3. Milner, R.: The Space and Motion of Communicating Agents. Cambridge University Press, New York (2009)
4. Conforti, G., Ghelli, G., Flesca, S., Greco, S., Saccà, D., Zumpano, E.: Spatial tree logics to reason about semistructured data. Language 17, 16 (2003)
5. Ikram, A., Anjum, A., Hill, R., Antonopoulos, N., Liu, L., Sotiriadis, S.: Approaching the Internet of Things (IoT): a modelling, analysis and abstraction framework. Concurr. Comput. Pract. Exp. 27(8), 1966–1984 (2015)
6. Chen, X., Li, A., Zeng, X., Guo, W., Huang, G.: Runtime model based approach to IoT application development. Front. Comput. Sci. 9(4), 540–553 (2015)
7. Bermudez-Edo, M., Elsaleh, T., Barnaghi, P., Taylor, K.: IoT-Lite: a lightweight semantic model for the Internet of Things. In: Ubiquitous Intelligence & Computing, Advanced and Trusted Computing, Scalable Computing and Communications, Cloud and Big Data Computing, Internet of People, and Smart World Congress (UIC/ATC/ScalCom/CBDCom/IoP/SmartWorld), 2016 International IEEE Conferences, pp. 90–97. IEEE (2016)

8. Yamaguchi, S., Tsugawa, S., Nakahori, K.: An analysis system of IoT services based on agent-oriented Petri net PN2. In: 2016 IEEE International Conference on Consumer Electronics-Taiwan (ICCE-TW), pp. 1–2. IEEE (2016)
9. Chopra, A.K., Singh, M.P.: Multiagent systems (2011)
10. Marir, S., Kitouni, R., Benzadri, Z., Belala, F.: BiAgent-based model for IoT applications. In: Braubach, L., Murillo, J.M., Kaviani, N., Lama, M., Burgueño, L., Moha, N., Oriol, M. (eds.) ICSOC 2017. LNCS, vol. 10797, pp. 111–123. Springer, Cham (2018). https://doi.org/10.1007/978-3-319-91764-1_9
11. Ray, P.P.: A survey on Internet of Things architectures. J. King Saud Univ. Comput. Inf. Sci. **30**(3), 291–319 (2016)

Mechanizing the Denotational Semantics of the Clock Constraint Specification Language

Mathieu Montin[1,2] and Marc Pantel[1,2(✉)]

[1] Université de Toulouse, Toulouse INP, IRIT, Toulouse, France
{mathieu.montin,marc.pantel}@enseeiht.fr
[2] CNRS, Institut de Recherche en Informatique de Toulouse (IRIT), Toulouse, France
http://montin.perso.enseeiht.fr, http://pantel.perso.enseeiht.fr

Abstract. Domain Specific Modelling Languages provide the designers with appropriate languages for the task they must conduct. These dedicated languages play a key role in popular Model Driven Engineering (MDE) approaches. Their semantics are usually written in a semi-formal manner mixing natural language and mathematical notations. The mechanization of these semantics rely on formal specification languages. They are usually conducted in order to assess the correctness of verification and transformation tools for such languages. This contribution illustrates such a mechanization for the Clock Constraint Specification Language (CCSL). This language allows to model the timed concurrency concern in the MARTE UML profile and was designed to be easier to master than temporal logics for the system engineers. Its semantics has been defined in the usual semi-formal manner and implemented in the TimeSquare simulation tool. We discuss the interest of this mechanization and show how it allowed to prove properties about this language and ease the definition of a refinement relation for such models. This work relies on the Agda proof assistant and is presented accordingly.

Keywords: DSML · Semantics mechanization · Proof assistants
CCSL

1 Introduction

As systems are getting more and more complex, a strong separation between the various concerns in a system has become a major requirement. Specialists of each engineering domain define their views of the system in their own language, called a Domain Specific Modelling Language (DSML) and these views are then integrated. There are two main drawbacks of this approach: first, these languages, and especially their semantics, are usually defined in a semi-formal way, thus complicating their common understanding; and second, many properties are not preserved during the integration of the various parts as the same concerns are

© Springer Nature Switzerland AG 2018
E. H. Abdelwahed et al. (Eds.): MEDI 2018, LNCS 11163, pp. 385–400, 2018.
https://doi.org/10.1007/978-3-030-00856-7_26

expressed in different DSMLs. Thus, if each concern in different views satisfies some requirements, there is no guarantee the concern of the whole system combining these views will satisfy the same requirements.

A promising approach to tackle this problem is to abstract the common concerns from the various parts expressed in different DSMLs in a common DSML. It allows to reason over this single DSML instead of the different DSMLs of the various views. Then, the whole semantics of this common DSML should be defined in a formal manner to provide a formal semantics for the concern in each DSML. The Clock Constraint Specification Language (CCSL) from the UML MARTE standard, developed by the AOSTE team from INRIA, provides such a user dedicated language for the concurrency concern. Its operational semantics is defined as an interpreter in the TimeSquare tool-set, but it lacks a mechanized denotational semantics to formalize its underlying concepts and conduct proofs both on models and associated tools, which is the core purpose of this work. An added value of this mechanization is that it allowed to detect several issues in the semi-formal CCSL denotational semantics.

This papers starts by defining core aspects of CCSL: The instants which represent the event occurrences, the strict partial orders binding these instants together, the clocks which are entities linking the instants to the actual modelled concerns and finally more advanced concepts such as relations and expressions around clocks to reach constraints definitions.

This work has been done using the Agda proof assistant (a language and tool-set developed by Ulf Norell). Since a semi-formal denotational semantics of CCSL already exists, the accent will be made throughout this paper on the choices made to fit Agda. Pieces of Agda code will be given to point out different aspects in our mechanization. They depict either data structures, definitions or properties. Their representation in this paper is partial and some details have been omitted to make them more understandable. These omissions include some levels of universe, the explicit substitution for some implicit parameters as well as some operators used to adapt the types of some terms. This last family of hidden details is useful in the actual development because the relations and functions are defined on instants where clocks tick, which are represented as pairs of values (the witness instant and the proof that the clock ticks on that instant, encoded as ∃ types). The whole development is available on the first author's web page.

2 Representation of Time

2.1 Instants

The main underlying concept of CCSL is the instants. Informally, an instant is a point in a time-line where events can occur (dually a time-line is a sequence of strictly ordered instants). It fits the common understanding of events that occur at a specific time and can be preceded or followed by occurrences of other events. This vision of time is usually modelled using numbers (real numbers or integers) to represent such instants because they are totally ordered. In distributed systems however, this vision is usually unsuitable because these total orders, however existent, cannot be observed. Only a partial representation of time can be specified and leads to the use of partial order to model time, which will be briefly described later on. This means that the use of numbers to represent time is not any more relevant than any other abstract set. In operational semantics, they will be used again because a specific linearisation of time is chosen but this is not the case in our work. For this reason, instants in our work is an unspecified Agda type - named *Support*, while *Instant* is the name of the algebraic structure it forms when coupled with a partial order.

2.2 Strict Partial Orders

The common vision of a unique time-line on which events occur implies that two instants are always comparable precedence-wise (like numbers with their common order relation). However, in distributed systems, there is no global clock, and only some events can be compared to each other. Partial orders are thus used to represent the possible relations between the instants. In CCSL, each pair of instants is either *strictly comparable*, through a precedence relation $\prec$, *equivalent*, through a coincidence relation $\approx$ or neither of them.

2.3 CCSL Specification

In this work, instants are represented as a classic set with an unspecified strict partial order relation. Every CCSL construct specified in Agda is expressed using this set, which is passed as a parameter to the different modules. This view is different from the CCSL creators' one, who see the instants of a system (the Time Structure [15]) as the union of all the instants on which the different clocks tick. This vision, synthesizing the *Support* set from the clocks, is not suitable for both denotational semantics and tools like Agda. Indeed, sets are not axiomatic in Agda and are emulated by predicates which are not usual sets as seen in the ZFC theory. Thus, we had to change the status of the instants and the associated Time Structure. This vision is more abstract and more suitable to building generic proofs. It is then possible to assess if a given operational semantics behaves as an instance of this more formal semantics.

3   Clocks

3.1   Intuitive Definition

A clock is an entity that tracks the occurrences of a specific event in a given system. A clock ticks whenever (i.e. at every instant) the event it represents occurs. Such a system is represented by a set of clocks representing any possible event that can occur during its execution. Each clock usually ticks an infinite number of times – can be both $\aleph_0$ (countable clocks representing discrete or dense time) or $\aleph_1$ (uncountable clocks representing only dense time)– and is partially represented in a time-line such as Fig. 1. Discrete time means that, between two ordered instants, there exists only a finite number of other instants. Dense time means that, between two ordered instants, there exists always an infinite number of other instants. In this example, the clock called c ticks three times during the portion of time depicted in the diagram. The ticks are separated by a certain amount of time, unspecified – there is no scale on the diagram – because such a system is usually asynchronous. Thus, the only relevant information depicted in this diagram is that the event tracked by c occurred at least three times throughout the lifetime of the system. This is however a very poor information which must be completed with the addition of other clocks and constraints between them.

c

Fig. 1. An example of a clock c

3.2   Formal Definition

Formally, a clock is an Agda record which contains a subset of instants (the ones on which it ticks) and the proof that these instants are totally ordered:

```
record Clock : Set where
  constructor
    [_o_]
  field
    Ticks  : Pred Support
    TicTot : IsStrictTotalOrder {A = ∃ Ticks} (_≡_ on proj₁) (_≺_ on proj₁)
```

This clock record provides a constructor – [_o_] – to build a clock and two fields – `Ticks` and `TicTot`. The first field is a predicate (`Pred`) on the instants to encode the subset on which the clock ticks, and the second is the proof that the ticks of the clock are totally ordered (`IsStrictTotalOrder`). The constructor has two underscores where its parameters will be placed – Assuming `t` is a subset of instants and `tot` is the proof that the underlying partial order form a strict total order on this subset of instants, then [t o tot] is a Clock. Note that the underlying set of this strict partial order is $\exists$ which can be seen as the subset of instants on which the clock ticks. More technically, $\exists$ is the type of elements of the form (x, Tx) where x is an instant and Tx the proof that the clock ticks on x. The underlying relations of the strict partial order are the projections of the coincidence and precedence relations – of the partial order binding the instants – on the first element of these couples. For instance, $\equiv$ on proj₁ is defined this way: (x, Px) $\equiv$ (y, Py) on proj₁ $\Leftrightarrow$ x $\equiv$ y.

4   Relations

4.1   Definition

In a complex and possibly heterogeneous system, many events – hence many clocks – can be identified. An important aspect of CCSL is that it does not handle differently complex and heterogeneous systems (in a way, in CCSL, each system is heterogeneous compared to the atomistic description of each event it provides). Each clock taken separately does not offer many interesting information about the whole system, but bound together, they provide useful specification about its global behaviour. This binding can be given as relations that constrain the execution of the system and, in our framework, are described as predicates over two clocks (mathematical relations). They enforce an order between some instants by requiring some of them to be bound by precedence – red arrows – or by coincidence – dashed blue lines – as depicted in Fig. 2. A relation holds, by default, for the lifetime of the system. The global Agda type for relations is:

```
Relation : Set
Relation = Clock → Clock → Set
```

Any predicate over two clocks (any set of couples of clocks) is a clock relation.

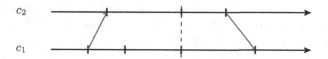

Fig. 2. Some instants are bond

4.2   Main Relations

CCSL provides several relations. Some are defined on generic clocks (both dense and discrete). Others are restricted to discrete clocks. This paper only handles the first kind presented in this section. The other kind is the object of a future work.

Strict Precedence. A clock c_1 is said to strictly precede another clock c_2 when each consecutive ticks of c_2 is strictly preceded by a distinct and consecutive ticks of c_1. Note that the "consecutive" word can only refer to discrete clocks. In dense clocks, the equivalent is that every ticks of c_1 placed between two mapped ticks must be mapped as well. This mapping refers to the precedence function that binds the instants of the two clocks together. This function will be described more formally later on. Before getting to the formal definition of this relation, let us consider some examples in Figs. 3, 4 and 5.

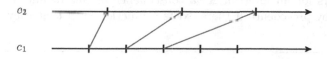

Fig. 3. A standard precedence example

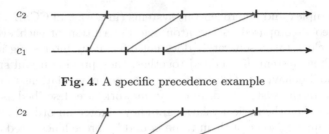

Fig. 4. A specific precedence example

Fig. 5. An incorrect precedence example

In Fig. 3, each instant of c_2 is mapped to an instant of c_1 in a way that the precedence relation looks obvious. However, this definition does not require this mapping to be bijective, which means c_1 could have additional ticks that are not mapped to ticks of c_2. If these ticks occur after the ones mapped to c_2, like on Fig. 4, the precedence is still well-formed, as opposed to Fig. 5 where they are placed in between mapped ticks, thus compromising the relation. One can observe that this problem could be avoided by changing the mapped instant such that the additional ticks are always positioned as on Fig. 3. This seems obvious when the number of ticks is finite, yet not so much when it is not. The current paper version of CCSL denotational semantics does make that last distinction between a well-formed and ill-formed precedence. This was an issue that our mechanization work has revealed. This will be tackled in future versions of CCSL and TimeSquare.

The precedence relation requires the existence of a function h which maps the instants of c_2 with the corresponding instants of c_1. It is defined as follows:

```
1    [_]_≪_ : (_ → _) → Relation
2    [ h ] [ Tc₁ ∘ _ ] ≪ [ Tc₂ ∘ _ ] = ∀ (i j : ∃ Tc₂) p →
3        (h i ∈ Tc₁ × h i ≺ i) ×
4        (i ≺ j → h i ≺ h j) ×
5        (p ∈ᵢ [ h i - h j ] → ∃ λ (k : ∃ Tc₂) → h k ≈ p)
```

This definition is composed of three predicates, at lines 3, 4 and 5. The first one – line 3 – ensures that all ticks of c_2 are mapped with ticks that respect the required precedence; the second one – line 4 – ensures that the binding function preserves the precedence order; the third one – line 5 – ensures that there is no unmapped instants between two mapped instants. The ∀ is a syntactic sugar to introduce quantities while × can be seen as the logical "and" and the brackets are delimiters for an interval. As a consequence of this definition, two clocks are related by precedence if there exists a function such that they are related through it:

```
_≪_ : Relation
c₁ ≪ c₂ = ∃ λ h → [ h ] c₁ ≪ c₂
```

The λ here is a syntactic element used to introduce a new variable h in the context from an existence proof ($\exists$). This definition is transitive, and such a transitivity has been proven in the framework, but is not presented here.

Non-strict Precedence. The non-strict precedence allows two mapped instants to be coincident, thus the underlying relation is $\_\preccurlyeq\_$ instead of $\_\prec\_$. This relation is mostly similar to the strict precedence and will not be detailed thoroughly. A simple example is given in Fig. 6.

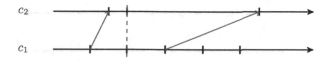

Fig. 6. An example of non-strict precedence

The Agda definition is the same as the strict precedence, except for the substitution of the strict relation by the non-strict one. This relation has been proven transitive as well. The two proofs are factorized through the abstraction of the underlying relation (as well as are the definitions).

Subclocking. A clock c_1 is said to be a subclock of a clock c_2 when every ticks of c_1 is coincident to a tick of c_2. It means that whenever c_1 ticks, c_2 ticks as well. Figure 7 shows an example of subclocking.

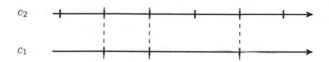

Fig. 7. c_1 is a subclock of c_2

The Agda definition of this relation is as follows:

```
_⊑_ : Relation
[ Tc₁ ∘ _ ] ⊑ [ Tc₂ ∘ _ ] = ∀ (x : ∃ Tc₁) → ∃ λ (y : ∃ Tc₂) → x ≈ y
```

It states that whenever c_1 ticks on an instant $x_1 - \forall$ (x : $\exists$ Tc₁) – there exist an instant x_2 on which c_2 ticks – $\exists$ λ (y : $\exists$ Tc₂) – which coincides with x_1. This relation is transitive:

```
trans⊑ : ∀ {c₁ c₂ c₃} → c₁ ⊑ c₂ → c₂ ⊑ c₃ → c₁ ⊑ c₃
trans⊑ c₁c₂ _     x with c₁c₂ x
trans⊑ _     c₂c₃ _ | y , _  with c₂c₃ y
trans⊑ _     _    _ | _ , x≈y | z , y≈z = z , trans≈ x≈y y≈z
```

This proof uses a `with` construct which allows to add new quantities to the context – and usually case split on them. It relies on the transitivity of the underlying coincidence relation and combines it with the two inputs representing the subclocking proofs.

Alternation. There are some cases where precedence is not enough to fully express the semantics or their relation. In Fig. 8, the clock c_1 ticks a third time before the clock c_2 ticks a second time.

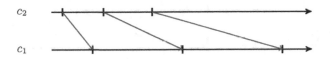

Fig. 8. The precedence is insufficient

There are some cases where this kind of behaviour might be unwanted and must be forbidden accordingly, forcing the clocks to be further constrained. This additional constraint coupled with the original precedence is called alternation. Two clocks are said to be alternated when one precedes the other in such a way that two ticks of a clock cannot occur in between two ticks of the other one. Note that the underlying precedence has to be strict for the relation to be consistent. A non-strict precedence would lead to ill formed cases of alternation. In this case, the trace of our system is actually the one presented on Fig. 9.

Fig. 9. c_1 alternates with c_2

In our framework, this relation is defined as follow:

```
_≪≫_ : Relation
c₁ ≪≫ c₂ = ∃ λ h → [ h ] c₁ ≪ c₂ × (∀ (x y : ∃ (Ticks c₂)) → x ≺ y → x ≺ h y)
```

c_1 alternates with c_2 when the two following predicates hold: there exists a function h such that c_1 strictly precedes c_2 through h; and h satisfies a certain predicate through the precedence relation, hence enabling the alternation instead of the simple precedence. It is thus trivial that alternation implies precedence.

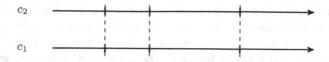

Fig. 10. c_1 is equal to c_2

Equality. Two clocks c_1 and c_2 are equal when they only tick on coincident instant. It means that if c_1 ticks on i then there exists an instant j which coincides with i and where c_2 ticks. An example is represented in Fig. 10.

This definition is exactly equivalent to a double subclocking:

```
_⌣_ : GlobalRelation
c₁ ⌣ c₂ = c₁ ⊑ c₂ × c₂ ⊑ c₁
```

This relation has been proven to be an equivalence.

Exclusion. Two clocks are in exclusion when they have no coincident ticks. An example of exclusion is given on Fig. 11.

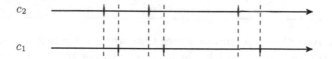

Fig. 11. c_1 is in exclusion with c_2

The Agda definition is the following:

```
_#_ : Relation
[ Tc₁ ∘ _ ] # [ Tc₂ ∘ _ ] = ∀ (x : ∃ Tc₁) (y : ∃ Tc₂) → ¬ x ≈ y
```

This definition consists of a predicate that for any x and y, if c_1 ticks on x and c_2 ticks on y, then x and y are not coincident.

5   Expressions

5.1   Definition

CCSL allows the definition of new clocks from existing clocks, which is acceptable from an operational point of view. Creating new clocks usually sets an arbitrary order between the instants on which the underlying clocks are ticking, which means that instants apparently independent are getting related because a new clock is created out of them. The common example is the union. The union of two clocks ticks whenever one of the two clocks ticks. Since a clock has a total order on its ticks, the ticks of the union must be totally ordered, which leads to a total order on the ticks of the two other clocks. In our denotational framework, everything is already existing, thus we cannot create such new clocks. We assume they already exist and propose to relate them using predicates to state that a clock could be the result of such operation. To better comprehend this notion, let us take the example of the addition between natural numbers. One can say that 3 is the result of the operation $1 + 2$ while another point of view could be that the triplet $(3,2,1)$ is a member of the addition. We take the second point of view to better match the denotational aspect of our work. The type of expressions is thus defined as a relation between three clocks:

```
Expression : Set
Expression = Clock → Clock → Clock → Set
```

5.2   Examples of Expressions

Intersection. A common expression on clocks is the intersection. The clocks which results from the intersection of two clocks only ticks on each instant where they simultaneously tick:

```
_≡_∩_ : Expression
[ Tc o _ ] ≡ [ Tc₁ o _ ] ∩ [ Tc₂ o _ ] =
  (∀ (x : ∃ Tc) → ∃ λ (y : ∃ Tc₁) → ∃ λ (z : ∃ Tc₂) → x ≈ y × x ≈ z) ×
  (∀ (y : ∃ Tc₁) (z : ∃ Tc₂) → y ≈ z → ∃ λ (x : ∃ Tc) → x ≈ y)
```

This first part of this predicate states that whenever c ticks on an instant i, there exists two instants j and k which are coincident to i and on which both c_1 and c_2 ticks respectively. The second part states that if c_1 ticks on i, c_2 ticks on j, and if these instants are coincident, then c ticks on an instant coincident to them. Figure 12 shows an example of intersection.

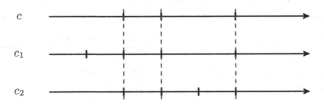

Fig. 12. An example of intersection

Union. The following predicate explains what it means for a clock to be the union of two other clocks.

```
_≡_∪_ : Expression
[ Tc o _ ] ≡ [ Tc₁ o _ ] ∪ [ Tc₂ o _ ] =
  (∀ (x : ∃ (Tc₁ ∪ Tc₂)) → ∃ λ (y : ∃ Tc) → x ≈ y) ×
  (∀ (y : ∃ Tc) → ∃ λ (x : ∃ (Tc₁ ∪ Tc₂)) → x ≈ y)
```

The first part of this predicate states that if either c_1 or c_2 ticks on an instant x then there exists an instant y coincident to x on which c ticks. The second part states that if c ticks on an instant y then there exists an instant x coincident to y and on which either c_1 or c_2 ticks. Figure 13 is an example of union.

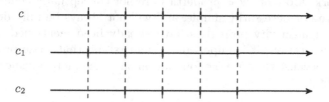

Fig. 13. An example of union

Note that in our framework and example, the clock c happens to be consistent with the idea of the union of c_1 and c_2, but it is not the result of any operation.

Other Expressions. There exists a lot of other expressions (either fundamental or derivative), some of them depending on the death instant, some other being induced by a natural number. None of them will be detailed in this paper, whose goal is not to present all CCSL constructs, but to explain the ideas behind their mechanization.

6 Properties

One advantage of mechanizing a semi-formal semantics is that this one can be validated by proving algebraic properties of the various operators, thus improving confidence in the language definition.

6.1 Goal

A CCSL specification is a set of constraints applied to a set of clocks. These constraints can be either relations or expressions, since both of these can influence the underlying ordering of the instants. The goal of this work is not to solve a set of constraints (this is done by the INRIA TimeSquare tool) but to provide a mechanized semantics for CCSL. It can be used to define and validate additions to the language that may remain unclear or unspecified in a paper version. One of these additions is the instant refinement, which is available at [11]. Regarding a CCSL specification, one of the goals of our work is to reduce the set of constraints it contains. For instance, if one of the constraints in the set can be deduced from the other one, it should be removed. Another example is if one of the clocks needs to be hidden from the specification, all constraints linked to it must disappear without any loss of information regarding the other clocks.

In both cases, we need properties relating the different constraints in order to achieve some unifications between them.

Moreover, we also need these properties to assess the correctness of our denotational semantics regarding the common behaviour one expect about clocks, relations and expressions. This section presents some of the ones we proved in our framework. Most of these properties are not conceptually challenging, but the proofs are not necessarily simple, and will not always be fully detailed. For instance, the transitivity properties have already been mentioned and will be left out of this section. It is important to understand that these properties are fundamental because they are the foundation on which more advanced use cases could be built.

6.2   Examples of Properties

Subclock and Exclusion. If c_1 is in exclusion with c_3 and if c_2 is a subclock of c_3 then c_1 is in exclusion with c_2 as well. This is intuitive since c_2 ticks at most each time c_3 ticks. This can be expressed and proven in Agda:

```
excluSub : ∀ {c₁ c₂ c₃} → c₁ ♯ c₃ → c₂ ⊑ c₃ → c₁ ♯ c₂
excluSub _        c₂⊑c₃ _ y _   with c₂⊑c₃ y
excluSub c₁♯c₃ _        x _ x≈y | z , y≈z = c₁♯c₃ x z (trans≈ x≈y y≈z)
```

The Union Is Commutative. If c can be viewed as the union of c_1 and c_2 then it can also be viewed as the union of c_2 and c_1. To prove this property, we need to be able to swap a sum of types, which is done by the following function:

```
flipSum : ∀ {a b} {A : Set a} {B : Set b} → A ⊎ B → B ⊎ A
flipSum (inj₁ x) = inj₂ x
flipSum (inj₂ y) = inj₁ y
```

Here inj_1 and inj_2 are the two constructors allowing to build an element of a sum of types (either from an element of the first or second type). This leads to the commutativity proof:

```
comUnion : ∀ {c} → Symmetric (c ≡_∪_)
comUnion (prop₁ , prop₂) = (λ {(x , Tx) → prop₁ (x , flipSum Tx)}) ,
   (λ y → case prop₂ y of λ {((x , Tx) , x≈'y) → (x , flipSum Tx) , x≈'y})
```

Union and Subclocking. We can prove that each component of a union is a subclock of the union. This can be proved in both ways (for both clocks) using the symmetry of the union.

```
subUnionₗ : ∀ {c c₁ c₂} → c ≡ c₁ ∪ c₂ → c₁ ⊑ c
subUnionₗ (prop₁ , _) (x , Tc₁x) = prop₁ (x , inj₁ Tc₁x)

subUnionᵣ : ∀ {c c₁ c₂} → c ≡ c₁ ∪ c₂ → c₂ ⊑ c
subUnionᵣ p = subUnionₗ (symUnion p)
```

Unicity of Union. We can prove the union is unique relatively to the clock equality defined earlier. We start by proving that if two clocks correspond to the same union, one is a subclock of the other.

```
uu : ∀ {c₀ c c₁ c₂} → c₀ ≡ c₁ ∪ c₂ → c ≡ c₁ ∪ c₂ → c ⊑ c₀
uu (_      , _) (_ , prop₄) x with prop₄ x
uu (prop₁ , _) (_ , _      ) _ | y , _ with prop₁ y
uu (_      , _) (_ , _      ) _ | _ , x≈y | z , y≈z = z , trans≈ (sym≈ x≈y) y≈z
```

We conclude by applying the previous property both ways.

```
unicityUnion : ∀ {c₀ c c₁ c₂} → c₀ ≡ c₁ ∪ c₂ → c ≡ c₁ ∪ c₂ → c ∾ c₀
unicityUnion p q = uu p q , uu q p
```

Commutativity of Intersection. The intersection is also commutative:

```
comInter : ∀ {c} → Symmetric (c ≡_∩_)
comInter (prop₁ , prop₂) =
   (λ x → case prop₁ x of λ {(y , z , x≈y , y≈z) → z , y , y≈z , x≈y}) ,
   (λ y z x → case (prop₂ z y) (sym≈ x) of λ {(t , t≈z) → t , trans≈ t≈z (sym≈ x)})
```

Intersection and Subclocking. If c is enforced to be the intersection of c_1 and c_2, then c is a subclock of both of them, which can be proven.

```
subInter_l : ∀ {c c₁ c₂} → c ≡ c₁ ∩ c₂ → c ⊑ c₁
subInter_l (prop₁ , _) x with prop₁ x
subInter_l (_      , _) _ | y , _ , x≈y , _ = y , x≈y

subInter_r : ∀ {c c₁ c₂} → c ≡ c₁ ∩ c₂ → c ⊑ c₂
subInter_r c≡c₁∩c₂ = subInter_l (symInter c≡c₁∩c₂)
```

Unicity of Intersection. As for the union, we can prove that the intersection is unique.

```
ui : ∀ {c₀ c c₁ c₂} → c₀ ≡ c₁ ∩ c₂ → c ≡ c₁ ∩ c₂ → c ⊑ c₀
ui (_ , _      ) (prop₃ , _) x with prop₃ x
ui (_ , prop₂) (_      , _) _ | y , z , x≈y , x≈z with prop₂ y z (trans≈ (sym≈ x≈y) x≈z)
ui (_ , _      ) (_      , _) _ | _ , _ , x≈y , _ | t , t≈y = t , trans≈ x≈y (sym≈ t≈y)

unicityInter : ∀ {c₀ c c₁ c₂} → c₀ ≡ c₁ ∩ c₂ → c ≡ c₁ ∩ c₂ → c ∾ c₀
unicityInter p q = ui p q , ui q p
```

Intersection and Union. As a consequence, we can prove that the intersection is a subclock of the union, using the transitivity of the subclocking.

```
subInterUnion : ∀ {c₀ c c₁ c₂} → c₀ ≡ c₁ ∩ c₂ → c ≡ c₁ ∪ c₂ → c₀ ⊑ c
subInterUnion c₀≡c₁∩c₂ c≡c₁∪c₂ = trans⊑' (subInter_l c₀≡c₁∩c₂) (subUnion_l c≡c₁∪c₂)
```

7 Related Work

We provide a mechanization of the semantics of CCSL in a proof assistant. As such, this approach could be reused for other concurrent languages. Such a work has already been done using different kind of formal methods, for example [7] using Higher Order Logic in Isabelle/HOL; [6,13] using the Calculus of Inductive Constructions in Coq, whose description can be found in [2]. The use of Agda in this development is motivated by the expressiveness of the language coupled with its underlying unification mechanism - in other words, Agda allows, for instance, to pattern-match on the equality proof, thus unifying its operands. This provides an interactive proof experience that other tools that do not provide unification lacks: Agda, as opposed to Coq, does not rely on the application of tactics to inhabit types, but gives a well-designed framework to build them in interaction with the type checker and unifier. More on Agda can be found in [3,8,12]. Although they differ from these two aspects, both of these tools rely on the same underlying intuitionist type theory, first described in [9] and clarified in [10].

The denotational semantics of CCSL on which this work is based can be found in [4]. TimeSquare, the tool developed to describe CCSL systems as well as solve constraint sets has been presented in [5]. As for CCSL itself, it was first presented in [1]. Although our semantics aims at being the same as the paper version, it differs through the way it has been expressed, to best suit the constraints and the possibilities offered by Agda. An example of differences is the handling of the notion of TimeStructure - see [15] - which was translated from a constructive mathematical set theory to a generic type to better match the use of a type theory. Other attempts at giving semantics to languages like CCSL have been developed, such as a promising approach to give an operational semantics to TESL that can be found in [14].

8 Conclusion

8.1 Summary

In this work, we have proposed a mechanization of CCSL in Agda. We have clarified some notions inherent to this language (and even detected and corrected an issues in the paper version of the denotational semantics), and have proposed ways of encoding it in a proof assistant. Details about the lifetime of a clock, encoded as a birth instant and a death instant have been omitted. Their presentation would not have been suitable to this article. However, they have been encoded in the framework and will be presented in another paper. This work stands as an example of mechanization in Agda for a concurrent language, as well as an attempt to provide the CCSL developers with a complete mechanized semantics from which different features could eventually be extracted, as explained in the next section.

We advocate that mechanizing such semantics is mandatory when studying complex languages and systems, as standard paper semantics suffer from a lack of precise and complete formal and assisted verification.

8.2   Future Work

This work brings different perspectives that would complete and extend both CCSL and our semantics:

- We will define and prove as many properties as possible over the relations and the expressions defined in CCSL, in order to provide a correct way to reduce the set of constraints related to a certain specification. This will be done by computing derived constraints and comparing them to those that have been provided in the set.
- We are currently extending the language through the definition of instant refinement [11] in order to ultimately encode the notions of simulation, bisimulation and weak bisimulation in the framework to get a better hold over them. It requires to consider sets of clocks and the relations that bind them.
- We will go deeper into the definition of the birth and death instants to handle some difficulties that emerge with these notions. For instance, they induce the loss of some algebraic properties which we would like to handle properly.
- We will handle relations and expressions specific to discrete clocks. This requires to properly model these clocks which can be defined on infinite sets of instants while necessarily having a finite set of ticks. This is currently being investigated through the use of extensional equalities.

Acknowledgement. The authors would like to thank the CCSL team at INRIA for providing them with their time and valuable expertise regarding this language.

References

1. André, C., Mallet, F.: Clock Constraints in UML/MARTE CCSL. Research Report RR-6540, INRIA (2008)
2. Bertot, Y., Castéran, P.: Interactive Theorem Proving and Program Development - Coq'Art: The Calculus of Inductive Constructions. Texts in Theoretical Computer Science. An EATCS Series. Springer, Heidelberg (2004)
3. Bove, A., Dybjer, P.: Dependent types at work. In: Language Engineering and Rigorous Software Development, International LerNetALFA Summer School 2008, Piriapolis, Uruguay, February 24–March 1 2008, Revised Tutorial Lectures, pp. 57–99 (2008)
4. Deantoni, J., André, C., Gascon, R.: CCSL denotational semantics. Research Report RR-8628, INRIA (2014)
5. Deantoni, J., Mallet, F.: TimeSquare: treat your models with logical time. In: TOOLS - 50th International Conference on Objects, Models, Components, Patterns - 2012 (2012)
6. Garnacho, M., Bodeveix, J., Filali-Amine, M.: A mechanized semantic framework for real-time systems. In: Proceedings of Formal Modeling and Analysis of Timed Systems - 11th International Conference, FORMATS 2013, Buenos Aires, Argentina, 29–31 August 2013 (2013)
7. Hale, R., Cardell-Oliver, R., Herbert, J.: An embedding of timed transition systems in HOL. Formal Methods Syst. Des. **3**(1/2) (1993)
8. Malakhovski, J.: Brutal [meta]introduction to dependent types in agda

9. Martin-Löf, P.: Intuitionistic type theory
10. Martin-Löf, P.: Intuitionistic type theory. Notes by Giovanni Sambin
11. Montin, M., Pantel, M.: Ordering strict partial orders to model behavioural refinement. In: Proceedings of 18th Refinement Workshop 2018, affiliated with FM 2018 and part of FLoC 2018 (2018)
12. Norell, U.: Dependently typed programming in agda. In: Proceedings of TLDI 2009: 2009 ACM SIGPLAN International Workshop on Types in Languages Design and Implementation, Savannah, GA, USA, 24 January 2009 (2009)
13. Paulin-Mohring, C.: Modelisation of timed automata in Coq. In: Kobayashi, N., Pierce, B.C. (eds.) TACS 2001. LNCS, vol. 2215, pp. 298–315. Springer, Heidelberg (2001). https://doi.org/10.1007/3-540-45500-0_15
14. Nguyen Van, H., Balabonski, T., Boulanger, F., Keller, C., Valiron, B., Wolff, B.: A symbolic operational semantics for TESL. In: Abate, A., Geeraerts, G. (eds.) FORMATS 2017. LNCS, vol. 10419, pp. 318–334. Springer, Cham (2017). https://doi.org/10.1007/978-3-319-65765-3_18
15. Winskel, G.: Event structures. In: Petri Nets: Central Models and Their Properties, Advances in Petri Nets 1986, Part II, Proceedings of an Advanced Course, Bad Honnef, 8–19 September 1986 (1986)

Ensuring the Functional Correctness of IoT through Formal Modeling and Verification

Samir Ouchani[✉]

LINEACT, Laboratoire d'Innovation Numérique,
École d'Ingénieur en Informatique, CESI eXia, Aix-en-Provence, France
souchani@cesi.fr

Abstract. Recent research initiatives dedicated to formal modeling, functional correctness and security analysis of IoT systems, are generally limited to, model abstract behavioral patterns and look forward possible attacks beneath gauging and providing feasible attacks. This research considers the complementary problem by looking for more accurate attacks in IoT by capturing richer behaviors -technical, physical, and social- including their quantitative features. We propose IoT-SEC framework that establishes an adequate semantics to the IoT's components and their interactions including social actors that behave differently than automated processes. For security analysis, we develop a general approach based on a library of attack trees from where we generate automatically the monitor, the security policies and requirements to harden the IoT model and to check how well the model is secure. We use PRISM model checker to analyze the functionality and to check security of the IoT model. Precisely this contribution ensures the functionality of IoT systems by analyzing their functional correctness.

Keywords: IoT · Security assessment · Attack tree
Security policies · Formal verification · Formal modeling
Model checking · Functional correctness

1 Introduction

Internet of Things (IoT) is the network of physical objects -devices, vehicles, buildings and other items embedded with electronics, software, sensors, and network connectivity- that enables to collect and exchange massively data. This technology of intelligent device-to-device communication provides the much-needed leverage to IoT which make it growing extensively. It promises immense potential for improving the quality of life, health-care, manufacturing, transportation, etc.From a technology perspective, the rise of IoT is not changing widely while using the same technology, connectivity, and trimmed mobile applications. In this context, the challenging issue is checking and ensuring functionality, security and privacy of IoT from the existing and hidden vulnerabilities

© Springer Nature Switzerland AG 2018
E. H. Abdelwahed et al. (Eds.): MEDI 2018, LNCS 11163, pp. 401–417, 2018.
https://doi.org/10.1007/978-3-030-00856-7_27

of the linked objects and the expanded inefficient cyber-security. Behinds, many attack vectors are difficult to manage and to get protected from in IoT especially against computational, memory, and energy limitations due to the large amount of data and messages; e.g. insecure web, cloud, mobile interfaces, network services, and the lack of transport encryption, etc.

For example in IoT health-care system, objects are engaged to monitor remotely patients and in case of a substantial change in the critical data, a notification is sent to alert emergencies. Objects such as fit-bits and pacemakers enclosing different sensors like EEG, BP, ECG, and EMG are deployed to control blood pressure, hearing, etc.For communication, IoT uses a wide range of protocols to transport real-time data which make it critical to ensure the integrity of data and its inaccessibility for unauthorized users. Further, in crisis situations, patients are generally weak which make them an easy target against social engineering attacks [10]. At this level of complexity, security analysis of IoT is tricky while the components of the game are of different nature: people, physical and digital objects, software, cloud services, and infrastructures of multiple forms. We strengthen our analysis methodology by relying to security protocols and formal methods [12,13] to handle different type of IoT assets, and their communications that may happen via conventional and non-conventional protocols (e.g. visual, auditory, kinesthetic). Despite the raising interest in this subject, we target to develop sound techniques that help to automate the security analysis of IoT and to scrutinize *whether, how, at what cost*, and *with which probability*, IoT is secure.

Contributions. This research, firstly, develops IoT-SEC framework that initiates a modeling formalism by capturing the underlying semantics of IoT which is flexible to be extended for more elaborated features. It is rich by covering social behaviors, physical and digital objects, communication protocols, internal and external servers, and computation and storing cloud services. The formalism proposes assigning a cost e.g. time, to the execution of atomic actions, and the IoT components may behave non-deterministically, probabilistically, or deterministically where actions can be guarded by contextual conditions. The formalism also models a library of intruders, as particular process proper to each IoT components, able to act maliciously according to realistic abilities and specific conditions.

Further, this research develops a security analysis methodology for IoT. It is a statistical analysis and model-checking based approach built-up over PRISM tool [9]. To automate their use, we define a mapping from IoT models, expressed in the proposed formalism, to PRISM. Further, to overcome the downside of the expressiveness of monitors and security properties used in PRISM, we propose a library of pre-configured attack trees and we develop instantiation mechanism that help to generate automatically relevant monitors and security properties. Unfortunately due to the limited space, we focus only on the modeling mechanism and the correctness validation approach.

Outline. In summary, we review the related work in Sect. 2 and we describe the main components and goals of the global framework in Sect. 3. Then in Sect. 4, we develop a theory to model for IoT and we detail our approach focusing mainly on the functional correctness. In Sect. 5, we develop a tool that shows the obtained experimental results. Finally, Sect. 6 concludes the paper and sketches the future directions.

2 Related Work

To position our contribution in literature, we compare it within the works that deal with modeling, functional analysis, and security specification, and protocols in IoT. Since IoT research is young, the recent initiatives survey the IoT issues and challenges.

A. Habtamu [1] discusses guidelines to how adapt security standards, practices, and technologies in IoT. Fink et al. [3] classify the vulnerabilities that might arise high impact in IoT. In fact, they discuss a specific class of threats without precising its applicability on which configurations. To trustworthy a model they propose to exploit the physical randomness in IoT to generate keys for authentication and access control that ensure anonymity, likability, and observability. Xu et al. [17] survey design and security challenges in IoT. They propose the digital physical un-clonable function as solution to enable the direct use of hardware security primitives inside an arbitrary digital logic to create secure information flow and public key protocols that require only one clock cycle. Zhang et al. [18] highlight the ongoing challenges in IoT,especially identification, authentication and authorization, privacy, protocols, the related systems and software vulnerabilities. We believe that our framework contributes very well to the discussed challenges and it is a strong starting point to develop and extend easily the discussed research directions.

Hu et al. [5] proposed a face identification and resolution based technique for fog computing to improve processing capacity and save the bandwidth in IoT. To check security and preserve privacy, they propose an authentication and session key agreement protocol using data encryption and integrity checking by expressing CIA attributes in BAN logic. Islam et al. [6] analyzes security requirements in the presence of threat models for a health care scenario by minimizing security risk. They rely on the existing e-health policies and regulations to determine how much a requirement is violated. Ould-Yahia et al. [15] apply Ant colony optimization to care-off between random and uncertain behavior of sensors deployed during medical diagnosis towards e-health measures for IoT and intelligent social insects. The differences between intensities of measures result on the affected or safe path of the propagation of medical information show and quantify different e-health security vulnerabilities. Mohsin et al. [11] proposed a security analysis approach based on SMT for IoT entities mainly device configurations, network topologies, user policies and their related attack surfaces. Entities are formulated as a high-order logic formula, and the policies are a set of discrete constraints. To check the existing vulnerabilities, SMT solver outputs the possible solutions satisfying the constraints within an attack formula. Compared to our framework, this one is applicable only to a well guided configuration and scenario. The proposed approach is limited to a strict IoT schemes and the analysis method is not automated.

F. Kammüller *et al.* [7,8] investigate how Isabelle might help to improve detection of attack traces in IoT e-health by combining ethical requirement elicitation with automated reasoning. To provide trustworthy and secure IoT for vulnerable users in health-care scenarios, they employ high level logical modeling using dedicated Isabelle frameworks for: infrastructures, human actors, security policies, attack tree analysis, and security protocol. Torjusen *et al.* [16] present the high level instantiation of the run-time verification in color Petri net and its validation. They integrate runtime verification enablers in the feedback adaptation loop to guarantee the achievement of self-adaptive security and privacy properties for an e-health settings. At run-time, they enable the contextual state model, the requirements specifications, and the dynamic context monitoring and adaptation.

With respect to the commented work, IoT-SEC covers the probability and costs of actions, formalizes IoT, analyzes the correctness and measures their security level. Moreover, IoT-SEC is automatic by relying on the probabilistic model checking and it takes advantage from the algorithms built within.

3   IoT-SEC Framework

Prior deeper details, we explore first the IoT architecture adopted in IoT-SEC framework, then we overview the global analysis approach and the proposed security model.

3.1   Architecture

We describe the IoT architecture by presenting its components and their interactions. Figure 1 illustrates the proposed IoT architecture enclosing five main components, object devices are physical objects embedded with sensors and software, user devices are physical objects that communicate with servers and collect data from objects, computing services provided by internal, external, and cloud servers; social actors are human agents that can hold and manipulate devices, the environment is the infrastructures and spaces that envelops the IoT entities.

These components interact through communication protocols of different ranges (Human-machine, Bluetooth, ZigBee, WiFi, Cellular, SSH, IpSec, etc.).

3.2   Methodology

The IoT methodology depicted in Fig. 2 shows the main involved steps to evaluate and ensure the well functionality in IoT. It takes as input the IoT model M_{IoT}, the intruder model A_{IoT}, and a library of attack-trees T_{IoT}. First, an instantiation of A_{IoT} ($\widehat{A}_{IoT}$) is generated by the function $\mathscr{G}_A$ to contend M_{IoT}

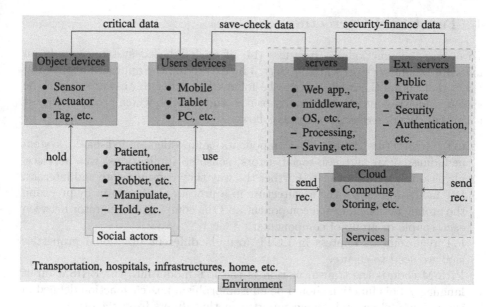

Fig. 1. IoT-SEC components architecture.

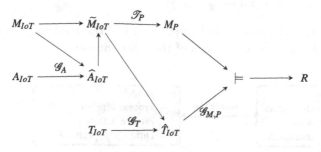

Fig. 2. IoT methodology.

in order to produce a composed model $\widetilde{M}_{IoT}$. For security analysis the composed model $\widetilde{M}_{IoT}$ is abstracted then mapped into a PRISM code (M_P) by the function $\mathscr{T}_P$ [13].

The approach also demonstrates the use of T_{IoT} which produces relevant attack trees $\hat{T}_{IoT}$ to the composed model. To benefit from, the function $\mathscr{G}_{M,P}$ instantiates from $\hat{T}_{IoT}$ a temporal logic formula that expresses the security property and a monitor that control the mal-behaves of the intruder. Finally, the tool ($\vdash$) checks the satisfiability of the security properties in the considered model, and produces the verification result in terms of probability and cost.

In the current work we focus only on ensuring the functional correctness instead of analyzing security.

4   Functional Correctness

To ensure the functional correctness [14] of an IoT-based system, we rely on IoT-SEC framework presented in Sect. 3 by extracting the approach depicted in Fig. 3 that shows the main steps to be followed in order to answer safely if the system under test functions properly or not, and/or with which probability/cost it can fail. We describe the steps as follows.

- IoT architecture defines the components composing an IoT-based system including social and non-social actors, sensors, applications, web services, physical infrastructures, etc.Further the way they communicate and interact.
- IoT model formalizes the architecture in a process algebra form by precizing the atomic actions for each component and the composition operator between each couple or group of components.
- IoT requirements express in PCTL formula different functional properties that we need to ensure.
- PRISM code is the transformation of the IoT model into the PRISM input language. This function should be an isomorphism i.e. each action defined in the IoT model has only one comportment that differs from the others.
- PRISM checks how much a requirement is ensured on the IoT model.
- Results are the output of PRISM, and it can be qualitative (true or false), or quantitative (a probability or a cost).

Following the above described steps we detail the modeling, the generation of PRISM code, and the expression of the requirements.

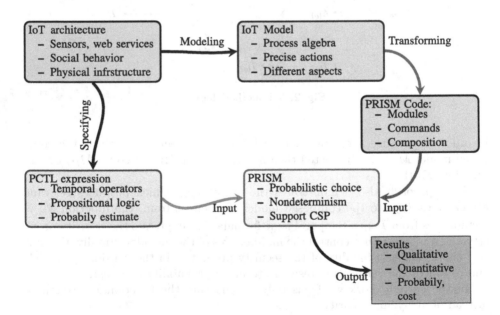

Fig. 3. Functional correctness framework for of IoT.

4.1 IoT Formal Model

Here we develop a formal model by considering the IoT architecture previously showed in Fig. 1 as a composition of interconnected physical objects (devices and controllers, e.g. sensors and buildings), mobiles applications, cloud and computing online services, and people.

We describe an IoT system S by the tuple $\langle Obj, Srv, Act, Env, Prot \rangle$ that defines formally the IoT entities: the connected objects (Obj), the environment (Env), the client-server applications and services (Srv), the social actors (Act), and the communication protocols ($Prot$) that ensure the interaction and the communication between the different types of IoT entities.

Objects. An object can be either physical (e.g. sensor, USB key) or digital (e.g. data, message, information) with different specificities and abilities. An object can be a container, lockable (by digital or physical key), movable or/and destroyable by a program, an intelligent or human being actor. Sensor objects send data to the apps and receive it from the environment. An object Obj is a tuple $\langle O, attr_O, Actuator_O, \Sigma_O, Beh_O \rangle$, where:

- O is a finite set of tags $\epsilon_o, o, o', o_i, \cdots \in O$ identifying the objects, and ϵ_o is the empty object.
- $attr_O : O \to 2^{\mathbb{T}}$ returns the attributes of an object, where $\mathbb{T} = \{p, c, m, d, r\}$, p stands for physical, c for container, m for movable, d for destroyable, and r for reproducible.
- $Actuator_O : O \to L \times 2^O \times O \times \mathbb{B}$ returns the tuple $\langle loc_O, cont_O, key_O, locked_O \rangle$ that specifies the status of an object o by specifying respectively its: location, contained objects, key, and if it is locked or not.
- Σ_O is a finite set of atomic actions that can be executed by an object, where:

$$\Sigma_O = \{\texttt{Start}_O, \texttt{Terminate}_O, \texttt{Send}_O(o, o'), \texttt{Receive}_O(o, o'), \texttt{Update}_O(o, o'),$$
$$\texttt{Lock}_O(o, o'), \texttt{Unlock}_O(o, o'), \texttt{Move}_O(l, l') : o, o' \in O \text{ and } l, l' \in L\}$$

  $\texttt{Start}_O$ and $\texttt{Terminate}_O$ starts and terminates the process of an object, $\texttt{Send}_O(o, o')$ and $\texttt{Receive}_O(o, o')$ sends and receives o to/from o', $\texttt{Update}_O(o, o')$ updates o by o', $\texttt{Lock}_O(o, o')$ and $\texttt{Unlock}_O(o, o')$ lock and unlock o with o', respectively.
- $Beh_O : O \to \mathscr{L}_O$ returns the expression written in the language $\mathscr{L}_O$ that describes the behaviour of an object. The syntax of $\mathscr{L}_O$ is given by: $B_O ::= \texttt{Start}_O \cdot B_O \cdot \texttt{Terminate}_O \mid \alpha_O \cdot B \mid \alpha_O +_{g_o} \alpha'_O \mid \alpha_O$, where $\alpha_O \in \Sigma_O \backslash \{\texttt{Start}_O, \texttt{Terminate}_O\}$ and "$\cdot$" composes sequentially the actions, and $+_{g_o}$ is a guarded choice decision.

Services. Srv ensures a client-server architecture including client applications, computation servers and web services. Srv is presented by the tuple $\langle V, O_V, srv_V, \Sigma_V, Beh_V \rangle$, where:

- V is a finite set of computing and storage services v, v', etc.
- O_V is a finite set of physical objects hosting services from V.
- $srv_V : O_V \rightarrow 2^V$ assigns for a given object a set of services.
- Σ_V is a finite set of actions supported by a service V, where:

$$\Sigma_V = \{\text{Start}_V, \text{Terminate}_V, \text{Send}_V(o, o'), \text{Receive}_V(o, o'), \text{Update}_V(o, o'),$$
$$\text{Lock}_V(o, o'), \text{Unlock}_V(o, o') : o, o' \in O\}$$

Start_O and Terminate_O starts and terminates the process of an object, $\text{Send}_O(o, o')$ and $\text{Receive}_O(o, o')$ sends and receives o to/from o', $\text{Update}_O(o, o')$ updates o by o', $\text{Lock}_O(o, o')$ and $\text{Unlock}_O(o, o')$ lock and unlock o with o', respectively.
- $Beh_V : O_V \rightarrow \mathscr{L}_V$ returns the behaviour of an object hosting a service. The syntax of $\mathscr{L}_V$ is expressed as follows: $B_V ::= \text{Start}_V \cdot B_V \mid \alpha_V +_{g_V} \alpha'_V \mid \alpha_V$, where $\alpha_V \in \Sigma_V \backslash \{\text{Start}_V\}$ and "$\cdot$" composes sequentially the actions and $+_{g_V}$ selects the left action if the guard g_V is true otherwise, the right action is selected.

Actors. Actors are of different categories, they can be, patients hosting sensors, nurses, doctors, or any other types of agents. An actor interacts with others, manipulates objects, and accessing to resources by executing actions depends on his status and context. The execution is constrained by the environment, the possessed objects, the actor's intention and knowledge, and the access policies, etc. Formally, Act is a tuple $\langle A, categ_A, \Sigma_A, Bev_A \rangle$ where:

- A is a finite set of actors.
- $categ_A : A \rightarrow \mathbb{C}$ returns the category of an actor.
- $Actuator_A : A \rightarrow L \times 2^O$ returns the location ($loc_A \in L$) and the possessed objects ($poss_A \subseteq 2^O$) by an actor.
- The finite set of the actors actions Σ_A encloses all actions that can be executed by an agent.

$$\Sigma_A = \{\text{Start}_A, \text{Moving}_A(l, l'), \text{Lock}_A(o, o'), \text{Unlock}_A(o, o'), \text{Send}_A(o, x),$$
$$\text{Receive}_A(o, x), \text{Update}_A(o, o'), \text{Terminate}_A :$$
$$l, l' \in L \text{ and } o, o' \in O \text{ and } a \in A \text{ and } x \in L \cup O \cup A\}$$

As the actions' names mean, they express respectively the moving between locations, locking/unlocking objects, sending/receiving objects from a location, an object, an actor; cloning or updating the content of an object (destroying and cloning objects are a special case of the update).
- $Bev_A : A \rightarrow \mathscr{L}_A$ returns the expression that describes the behaviour of an actor. It expresses the probabilistic decision and the cost (as time) of an execution. The syntax of $\mathscr{L}_A$ is generated by $B ::= Stop \mid \alpha_A.B \mid B + B \mid B +_g B \mid B +_p B$, where α is an atomic action in Σ_A, $+_p$ is a probabilistic decision, and $+_g$ is a deterministic choice.

Environment. *Env* can be any human body or other natural species, or even a physical space that hosts objects to measure the needed metrics in order to be exploited/analyzed by the IoT system. In this model, we consider human body as an actor and the environment as a physical entity hosting all IoT entities. From this perspective we can model the environment as a connected container objects. Formally, *Env* is a tuple $\langle E, L, O_E, Actuator_E \rangle$, where:

- E is a finite set of environments denoted by e, e', etc..
- L is a finite set of locations (l, l', etc.).
- O_E is a finite set of physical objects of type container.
- $Actuator_E \colon O_E \times O_E \to 2^O$ returns the set of objects linking containers by physical objects (e.g. doors connecting two rooms).

Interaction Protocol. *Prot* orchestrates and symphonies the communication and the interaction between the IoT entities. Since these entities differ in their nature, we define different communication protocols. Formally, *Prot* is a tuple $\langle Prot_{h,o}, Prot_{o,o}, Prot_{o,s} \rangle$ where $Prot_{h,o}$ ensures the communications between social actors and the objects, $Prot_{o,o}$ between objects, $Prot_{o,s}$ between objects and services on servers.

Considering an initial configuration of an IoT that defines the evaluation of objects, actors, and services attributes; *Prot* defines the changes of the attributes of each IoT entity regarding the executed actions. The IoT configuration is the association of all states of IoT entities and the changes of a configuration is ruled by transitions. An IoT's state $S = \langle S_O, S_V, S_A, S_E \rangle$ is composed from states of objects, services, actors, and the environment as an instance of $\langle Obj, Srv, Act, Env \rangle$. The transitions between states are labeled and denoted by $S \overset{\ell,c,p}{\hookrightarrow} S'$, l names the action to be executed, c returns its cost and p is its probability value to be run. Due to the space limitation, we selected the following operational rules that synthesize transitions when two physical objects o and o' exchange a digital object o'' (SYN-O-O), an actor a takes an object o' from an object o (REC-A-O), and encrypt an object o' by an object o using o'' (LOC-O-O).

$$\frac{\begin{array}{c} Beh_O(o) = \mathtt{Send}_O(o', \llbracket o'' \rrbracket).Beh'_O(o) \wedge o'' \in cont_O(o) \wedge \llbracket o'' \rrbracket \neq \epsilon_o \\ Beh_O(o') = \mathtt{Receive}_O(o''', \llbracket o'' \rrbracket).Beh'_O(o') \wedge o''' \in cont_O(o) \wedge p \notin attr_O(o'') \end{array}}{\langle\langle o, -, < -, \{o'', \llbracket o'' \rrbracket\} >, - \rangle, \langle o', -, < -, \{o''', \llbracket o''' \rrbracket\} >, -\rangle\rangle \overset{\mathtt{Send}_O(o,o',\llbracket o'' \rrbracket),c,p}{\hookrightarrow} \langle\langle o, Beh'_O(o), < -, \{o'', \llbracket o'' \rrbracket\} >, - \rangle, \langle o', Beh'_O(o'), < -, \{o''', \llbracket o''' \rrbracket\} >, -\rangle\rangle} \; \text{SYN-O-O}$$

$$\frac{\begin{array}{c} Bev_A(a) = \mathtt{Receive}_A(o, o').Bev'_A(a) \wedge loc_A(a) = loc_O(o) \\ \neg locked_U(o) \wedge o' \in cont_O(o) \wedge p \in attr_O(o') \end{array}}{\langle\langle a, -, < -, - >, - \rangle, \langle o, -, < -, \{o'\} >, -\rangle\rangle \overset{\mathtt{Receive}_A(a,o,o'),c,p}{\hookrightarrow} \langle\langle a, Bev'_A(a), < -, \{o'\} >, - \rangle, \langle o, Beh'_O(o), < -, - >, -\rangle\rangle} \; \text{REC A O}$$

$$\frac{Beh_O(o) = \texttt{Lock}_O(o', o'').Beh'_O(o) \land \{o', o''\} \subset cont_O(o) \land [\![o', o'']\!] \neq \epsilon_o}{\langle\langle o, -, < -, \{o', o''\} >, -\rangle, \langle o', -, < -, - >, \neg locked_O(o')\rangle\rangle \xrightarrow{lock_O(o,o',o''),c,p} \langle\langle o, Beh'_O(o), < -, \{o', o''\} >, -\rangle, \langle o', -, < -, - >, locked_O(o')\rangle\rangle} \text{LOC-O-O}$$

We define an IoT's state and how this changes by the effect of actions as a labelled state transition system $\langle \mathbf{S}, S_0, \rightarrow \rangle$ where, $\mathbf{S}$ is the set of the IoT states, $S_0 \in \mathbf{S}$ is the initial state, and $\rightarrow \subseteq (\mathbf{S} \times \mathbf{L} \times \mathbf{S})$ the transition relation between states labeled by $\mathbf{L}$. A transition $\hookrightarrow \in \rightarrow$ denoted by $S \xrightarrow{\ell,c,p} S'$ defines how IoT states change when the IoT entities behave. For example,

4.2 PRISM

PRISM is a probabilistic symbolic model checker that checks probabilistic specifications over probabilistic models. A specification can be expressed either in the probabilistic computation tree logic (PCTL) [2] or in a continuous stochastic logic. A model can be described using PRISM language. A PRISM program is a set of *modules*, each having a countable set of boolean or integer, local, variables. A module's state is fully defined by the evaluation of its local variables, while the program's state is defined by the evaluation of all variables, local and global.

In PRISM, the behavior of a module is defined by a set of probabilistic and/or Dirac commands that specifies textually the effect of an action in a probabilistic transition system. A probabilistic command is expressed by $[\alpha]$ $g \rightarrow p_1 : u_1 + ... + p_m : u_m$, where p_i are probabilities ($p_i \in]0, 1[$ and $\sum_{i=0}^{m} p_i = 1$), α is a label describing the name of an action, g is a propositional logic formula over local and global variables (i.e. a *guard*), and u_i are *updates* for variables. An update, written as $(v'_j = val_j) \& \cdots \& (v'_k = val_k)$, assigns only values val_i to local variables v_i. It means that for a given action α, if the guard g is true, an update u_i is enabled with a probability p_i. The guard is an expression consisting of the evaluation of both local and global variables, and the propositional logic operators. The Dirac case where $p = 1$ is a command written simply by $[a]$ $g \rightarrow u$.

Syntactically, a module named M is delimited by two keywords: the module head "module M", and the module termination "endmodule". Further, we can model costs with reward module R delimited by keywords "rewards R" and "endrewards". It is composed from a *state reward* or a *transition reward*. A state reward associates a cost (reward) of value r to any state satisfying g that is expressed by $g : r$. A transition reward has the form $[a]$ $g : r$ expresses that the transitions labeled a, from states satisfying g, are acquiring the reward of value r.

PRISM supports also composition where modules communicate à la CSP process algebra (e.g. see [4]). For two modules M_1 and M_2, the following composition operators are supported.

- Synchronization: the full synchronization on all shared action is written as $M_1 || M_2$,

- Interfacing: the parallel interface synchronization limited to the set of shared actions $\{a, b, \cdots\}$ is given by $M_1|[a, b, \cdots]|M_2$,
- Interleaving: the interleaving is expressed by $M_1|||M_2$,
- Hiding: $M/\{a, b, \cdots\}$ expresses hiding the actions $a, b, \cdots$ in the module M.
- Renaming: $M\{a \leftarrow b, c \leftarrow d, \ldots\}$ is to rename actions a by b, c by d, $\ldots$.

4.3   Transformation of IoT to PRISM

To generate a PRISM program $\mathscr{P}$ proper to the provided IoT formalism, we define the function $\mathscr{T}_P$ that assigns for each IoT entity behavior its proper PRISM code fragment that is bounded by 'module IoT entity name' and 'endmodule' and the semantic rules of each action is expressed by a PRISM command.

Due to the space limitation, we present the PRISM commands of actions that their semantics rules are already defined in Sect. 4.1. The left side specifies the premises of a rule whereas the right side describes the results of the rules. For example, o_{o_2} is an atomic proposition showing the the object o possess o_2, l_a and l_o present the locations, and p_{o_3} precises the physicality attribute of o_3. Variables and propositions are evaluated first to describe the initial state of the IoT entities by relying on the tuple obtained by the *Actuator* proper to each entity.

$$\mathscr{T}_P(\alpha) = \begin{cases} [Syn_{o_2}]o_{o_2} \wedge o_{1_{o_3}} \wedge \neg p_{o_2} \wedge \neg p_{o_3} \rightarrow (o'_2 = o_2); & \text{iff:} \\ [Syn_{o_2}]o_{o_2} \wedge o_{1_{o_3}} \wedge \neg p_{o_2} \wedge \neg p_{o_3} \rightarrow (o'_3 = o_2); & \text{Send}_O(o_1, o_2) \in \Sigma_O^{o_1}, \\ & \text{Receive}_O(o_3, o_2) \in \Sigma_O^{o_2}. \\ \\ [Tak_{o_1}]l_a = l_o \wedge o_{o_2} \wedge \neg lock_o \wedge p_{o_2} \rightarrow (a'_{o_2} = \top); & \\ [Tak_{o_1}]l_a = l_o \wedge o_{o_2} \wedge \neg lock_o \wedge p_{o_2} \rightarrow (o'_{o_2} = \bot); & \text{Receive}_A(o, o_2) \in \Sigma_A^a. \\ \\ [loc_{o_1}]o_{o_1} \wedge o_{o_2} \wedge \neg k_{o_1} \wedge p_{o_1} = p_{o_2} \rightarrow (k'_{o_1} = \top); & \text{Lock}_O(o_1, o_2) \in \Sigma_O^o. \\ [loc_{o_1}]o_{o_1} \wedge o_{o_2} \wedge \neg k_{o_1} \wedge p_{o_1} = p_{o_2} \rightarrow (o'_{o_1} = \top); & \end{cases}$$

4.4   Functional Requirements

We comment here what properties can be of relevance and how to express them in such a way that they can be checked by running PRISM. A formalism that is able to express all the factors that diagrams describe, paths of actions, propositions on state variables, probabilities of occurrence of one or a sequence of actions.

PCTL formulas ϕ in such a logic are generated by the following BNF grammar:

$$\phi ::= \top \mid ap \mid \phi \wedge \phi \mid \neg \phi \mid P_{\bowtie p}[\psi] \mid R_{\bowtie r}[F\phi]$$
$$\psi ::= X\phi \mid \phi U\phi \mid \phi U^{\leq k}\phi$$

Here, $k \in \mathbb{N}$, $r \in \mathbb{R}^+$, $p \in [0,1]$, and $\bowtie \in \{<, \leq, >, \geq\}$. A state formula can be "ap", an atomic proposition, or any propositional expression built from "ap". $P_{\bowtie p}[\psi]$, called *probabilistic path predicate*, returns true if the probability to satisfy the *path formula* ψ is $\bowtie p$. The *cost predicate* $R_{\bowtie r}[\phi]$ returns true if the cost to satisfy ϕ is $\bowtie r$. Here, F is the temporal logic operator *eventually*. A path formula is built from the typical temporal operators *next* (X), *until* (U), and *bounded until* ($U^{\leq k}$).

As usual, other logic operators can be derived from the basic operators, such as G refers to *Generally*. The semantics of these operators are given as follows.

- $\bot \equiv \neg \top$, $\phi \vee \phi' \equiv \neg(\neg\phi \wedge \neg\phi')$, $\phi \to \phi' \equiv \neg\phi \vee \phi'$, and
- $\phi \leftrightarrow \phi' \equiv \phi \to \phi' \wedge \phi' \to \phi$.
- $F\phi \equiv \top U \phi$, $F^{\leq k}\phi \equiv \top U^{\leq k} \phi$, $G\phi \equiv \neg(F\neg\phi)$, and
- $G^{\leq k}\phi \equiv \neg(F^{\leq k}\neg\phi)$ where $k \in \mathbb{N}$.
- $P_{\geq p}[G\phi] \equiv P_{\leq 1-p}[F\neg\phi]$.

Besides, Pmin, Pmax, Rmin, and Rmax are operators that can be used within path or state formulas to specify the minimum (resp. maximum) probability or cost.

5   Experiments Results

Here we apply the approach presented in Sect. 4, by following the discussed steps above, on a use case presenting a smart health care emergency room.

The IoT Architecture. Figure 4 depicts the main components of a smart emergency composed of: one patient, two rooms, set of sensors, local server, and a station. The goal is to ensure a collection of defined functional requirements.

The IoT Model. In the smart emergency presented in Fig. 4, two rooms l_1 and l_2 are accessible through the object o_1 (unique door) that is initially locked with the physical key o_1^k. The patient a_1 is in l_1 without possessing o_1^k but he has the sensor object o_1^s to measure his vital parameters and communicate it to the local server via the station o_1^d situated in l_2 at the end of medical services: monitoring, analysis, and cloud storage. Herein, we describe briefly the behaviours of the patient a_1, the sensor object o_1^s, the door o_1, the physical key o_1^k, and the station o_1^d, respectively.

- With a probability value of 0.3, a_1 can unlock o_1 before moving to l_2.

$$Bev_A(a_1) = \text{Start}_A.(\text{Unlock}_A(o_1, o_1^k) +_{0.3} \text{Moving}_A(l_1, l_1)).\text{Moving}_A(l_1, l_2).$$

$$\text{Terminate}_A \quad \text{s.t.} \quad Actuator_A(a_1) = \langle l_1, \{o_1^s\} \rangle.$$

- o_1^k moves within its possessor, this possession is described with the guard g_1^k.

$$Beh_O(o_1^k) = \text{Start}_O.(\text{Move}_O(l_1, l_2) +_{g_1^k} \text{Move}_O(l_1, l_1)).\text{Terminate}_O$$

$$\text{s.t.} \quad Actuator_O(o_1^k) = \langle l_1, \epsilon_o, \epsilon_o, \bot \rangle.$$

– o_1^s moves within a_1, and sends the value $[\![o_1^m]\!]$ received from a_1 to the station o_1^d.

$$Beh_O(o_1^s) = \texttt{Start}_O.((\texttt{Receive}_O(a_1, [\![o_1^m]\!]).\texttt{Update}_O(o_1^m, [\![o_1^m]\!]).\texttt{Send}_O(o_1^d, [\![o_1^m]\!]))$$
$$+ (\texttt{Receive}_O(o_1^d, [\![o_2^m]\!]).\texttt{Update}_O(o_2^m, [\![o_2^m]\!])) + (\texttt{Move}_O(l_1, l_2)$$
$$+_{g_1^s} \texttt{Move}_O(l_1, l_1))).\texttt{Terminate}_O \quad \text{s.t.} \quad Actuator_O(o_1^s) = \langle l_1, \epsilon_o, \epsilon_o, \perp \rangle.$$

– o_1^d synchronizes with o_1^s to send $[\![o_2^m]\!]$) and to receive $[\![o_1^m]\!]$).

$$Beh_O(o_1^d) = \texttt{Start}_O.((\texttt{Receive}_O(o_1^s, [\![o_1^m]\!]).\texttt{Update}_O(o_2^m, [\![o_1^m]\!]))$$
$$+ (\texttt{Send}_O(o_1^s, [\![o_2^m]\!]))).\texttt{Terminate}_O \quad \text{s.t.} \quad Actuator_O(o_1^d) = \langle l_2, \epsilon_o, \epsilon_o, \perp \rangle.$$

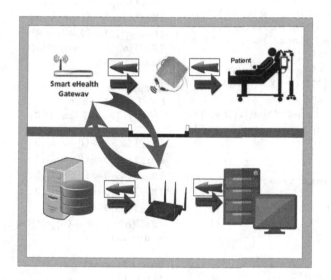

Fig. 4. Smart emergency room

The PRISM Model. For the performance assessment of the smart emergency, its IoT model is encoded into PRISM presented in Listing 1.1. It shows the code fragments of a_1, o_1^s, o_1^k, and o_1^d. Here we sketch a selected commands for each entity. The module a_1 describes the behavior of a_1, its location l_{a_1} is initialized to the first room and its action $\texttt{Moving}_A(l_1, l_1)$ is expressed by the command M_{11}. The action $Ra_1(o_1^m)$ evaluates the body measure o_1^m. The status of o_1 is defined nondeterministically with actions U_{o_1} and L_{o_1} to evaluate equally the predicate $lock_{o_1}$. Actions in the module o_1^k assigns the locations of a_1 when it is possessed by him otherwise its location does not change. Further, o_1^s synchronizes with a_1 in $Ra_1(o_1^m)$ and with o_1^d in So_1^s to receive $a_{o_1^k}$ sent by a_1. The module 'cost' assigns a cost of value 2 to the actions $Ra_1(o_1^m)$ and So_1^s. Furthermore, to add more entities, a user should just instantiates the proper module by renaming only its local variables.

```
mdp

module a1
la1: [1..2] init 1;
ao1s: bool init true;
a1(o1m): [1..5] init 1;
ao1k: bool init true;
aUo1k: bool init false;


[Uo1]  (la1=1)&(locko1)⇒
  0.3:     (a'Uo1k=true)+0.7:(l'a1=1);
[M11](la1=1)&(locko1)⇒(l'a1=1);
[M12](la1=1)&(¬locko1)⇒(l'a1=2);
[M21](la1=2)&(¬locko1)⇒(l'a1=1);
[M22](la1=2)⇒(l'a1=2);
[Uo1](locko1)&(ao1k)⇒(l'a=la);
[Lo1](¬(locko1))&(ao1k)⇒(l'a=la);
[Ra1(o1m)](a1(o1m)<5)⇒
            (a1(o1m)'=a1(o1m)+1);
[Ra1(o1m)](a1(o1m)=5)⇒(a1(o1m)'=1);
endmodule

module o1
locko1:bool init true;

[Uo1](locko1) ⇒ (lock'o1=false);
[Lo1](¬(locko1)) ⇒ lock'o1=true);
endmodule

module o1k
lo1k : [1..2] init 1;

[M11](ao1k)⇒ (l'o1k=la1);
[M12](ao1k)⇒ (l'o1k=la1);
[M21](ao1k)⇒ (l'o1k=la1);
[M22](ao1k)⇒ (l'o1k=la1);
[M22](ao1k)⇒ (l'o1k=la1);
```

```
[](¬(ao1k))⇒(l'o1k=lo1k);
endmodule

module o1s
lo1s:[1..2] init 1;
o1s(o1m):[0..5] init 0;

[M11](ao1s)⇒(l'o1s=la1);
[M12](ao1s)⇒(l'o1s=la1);
[M21](ao1s)⇒(l'o1s=la1);
[M22](ao1s)⇒(l'o1s=la1);
[M22](ao1s)⇒(l'o1s=la1);
[Ra1(o1m)](ao1s)⇒(o1s(o1m)'=a1(o1m));
[So1s](o1m)!=0 ⇒ (o1s(o1m)'=a1(o1m));
endmodule

module o1d
lo1s:[1..2] init 1;
o1d(o1m):[0..5] init 0;

[M11](ao1s)⇒(l'o1s=la1);
[M12](ao1s)⇒(l'o1s=la1);
[M21](ao1s)⇒(l'o1s=la1);
[M22](ao1s)⇒(l'o1s=la1);
[M22](ao1s)⇒(l'o1s=la1);
[So1s](o1m!=0)⇒(o1d(o1m)'=o1s(o1m));
endmodule

rewards cost
true:1;

[Ra1(o1m)] (la=2) : 2;
[So1s] (la=2) : 2;
[](a1(o1m)>3): 3;
[](a1(o1m)<4): 2;
endrewards
```

Listing 1.1. The PRISM Fragment Code of the Smart Emergency.

The Functional Requirements. To ensure the functionality of the smart emergency system, we specify the following functional requirements.

1. *Property 1.* "What is the maximum probability for the patient a_1 to move from l_1 to l_2 when the measure of $a_1(o_1^m)$ is greater then 2?". The PCTL expression of this property is: $Pmax =?[(l_{o_1} = l_1) \land (a_1(o_1^m) < 4) U \leq step \, (l_{o_1} = l_2) \land (a_1(o_1^m) > 3)]$.

   The variable *step* is the number of steps (transitions) to reach the state that satisfies: $(l_{o_1} = l_2) \land (a_1(o_1^m) > 3)$.

2. *Property 2.* "What is the maximum probability to keep both the sensor object o_1^s and the station object o_1^d functioning together?". Its PCTL expression is: $Pmax =?[G(o_1^s(o_1^m) > 0 \land o_1^d(o_1^m) > 0)]$.

3. *Property 3.* it looks to measure the minimum cost to read $a_1(o_1^m)$ and communicate it between o_1^s and o_1^d. It is expressed in PCTL by $Rmin =?[F(a_1(o_1^m) > 0)]$.

4. *Property 4.* It measures the maximum cost for a_1 to move safely and keeping o_1^s functioning. Its PCTL expression is: $Rmax =?[F(o_1^s(o_1^m) > 0)\{l_{a_1} = l_1, l_{a_1} = l_2\}]$.

The Correctness Checking. The verification results of the above properties are depicted in Fig. 5. The results of *Property 1* in Fig. 5(a) show the convergence of the probability evaluation from 0 to 0.001 after 3 steps, then it increases up to 0.00125 after 9 steps. This result shows that the risk is low for a patient to move. Figure 5(b) shows that the probability obtained from the satisfiability of *Property 2* is 1 after step 6 and it converges to 0.9 after 4 steps. It means that the smart emergency model reliable at the most time.

The verification results depicted in Fig. 6(a) show that the minimum reward value obtained from the satisfiability of *Property 3* is 121.59 and Fig. 6(b) presents that the cost to satisfy *Property 4* is at least 14.13. It means that the cost to keep the system always reliable is relatively high for communication and relatively low for the reliability of the smart emergency.

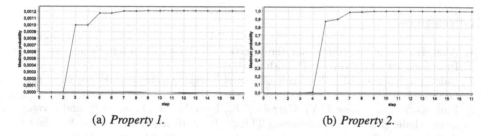

(a) *Property 1.*   (b) *Property 2.*

Fig. 5. The correctness checking results of *Property 1* and *Property 2*.

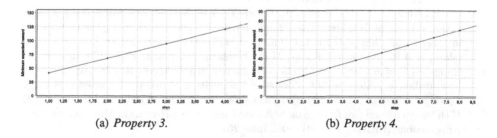

(a) *Property 3.*   (b) *Property 4.*

Fig. 6. The correctness checking results of *Property 3* and *Property 4*.

6   Conclusion

This paper sets the fundamentals of a fully automatic framework for modeling and analysis of IoT. Principally, we detail a part of it by presenting a formalism that captures the main structure and comportment of IoT entities covering physical and information infrastructures, services, assets, social actors, and also their activities and interactions. The execution of an action has a cost and guided by probabilities and/or contextual conditions. Further, the formalism has a rich and flexible semantics, which we use it to capture the IoT functional requirements expressing the possibility, the likelihood, and the cost of actions. Further, it is developed to be easy for other extensions and refinements. To carry our functional correctness analysis automatically, we devised an algorithm that maps an IoT model into the input language of PRISM in order to be checked against the requirements expressed in PCTL. Finally, the effectiveness of the proposed framework is validated on a case study.

This work sets the stage for further development. In the extended version of this work, we provide the complete set of rules, a detailed transformation function, and more experiments. Further, we intend to enrich our model with more assets: refine the contextual conditions, provide the security aspect of the IoT model, complete the other parts of the framework. Also from a solid theoretical point of view, we have to prove the correctness and the soundness of each developed step in a proof assistant (e.g. Coq). Furthermore, we implement the framework as a full standing tool and validated it on different case studies and real systems.

References

1. Abie, H.: Adaptive Security for the Internet of Things: Research, Standards, and Practices. 1st edn. Syngress Publishing (2017)
2. Baier, C., Katoen, J.P.: Principles of Model Checking. The MIT Press, New York (2008)
3. Fink, G.A., Zarzhitsky, D.V., Carroll, T.E., Farquhar, E.D.: Security and privacy grand challenges for the Internet of Things. In: 2015 International Conference on Collaboration Technologies and Systems (CTS), pp. 27–34, June 2015
4. Hoare, C.A.R.: Communicating Sequential Processes. Prentice Hall International Incorporated, Upper Saddle River (1985)
5. Hu, P., Ning, H., Qiu, T., Song, H., Wang, Y., Yao, X.: Security and privacy preservation scheme of face identification and resolution framework using fog computing in Internet of Things. IEEE Int. Things J. 4(5), 1143–1155 (2017)
6. Islam, S.M.R., Kwak, D., Kabir, M.H., Hossain, M., Kwak, K.S.: The internet of things for health care: a comprehensive survey. IEEE Access 3, 678–708 (2015)
7. Kammüller, F., Augusto, J.C., Jones, S.: Security and privacy requirements engineering for human centric IoT systems using eFRIEND and isabelle. In: 2017 IEEE 15th International Conference on Software Engineering Research, Management and Applications (SERA), pp. 401–406, June 2017
8. Kammüller, F.: Formal modeling and analysis with humans in infrastructures for IoT health care systems. In: Tryfonas, T. (ed.) HAS 2017. LNCS, vol. 10292, pp. 339–352. Springer, Cham (2017). https://doi.org/10.1007/978-3-319-58460-7_24

9. Kwiatkowska, M., Norman, G., Parker, D.: PRISM 4.0: verification of probabilistic real-time systems. In: Gopalakrishnan, G., Qadeer, S. (eds.) CAV 2011. LNCS, vol. 6806, pp. 585–591. Springer, Heidelberg (2011). https://doi.org/10.1007/978-3-642-22110-1_47

10. Lenzini, G., Mauw, S., Ouchani, S.: Security analysis of socio-technical physical systems. Comput. Electr. Eng. **47**, 258–274 (2015)

11. Mohsin, M., Anwar, Z., Husari, G., Al-Shaer, E., Rahman, M.A.: IoTSAT: a formal framework for security analysis of the Internet of Things (IoT). In: 2016 IEEE Conference on Communications and Network Security (CNS), pp. 180–188, October 2016

12. Ouchani, S., Mohamed, O.A., Debbabi, M.: A security risk assessment framework for SysML activity diagrams. In: 2013 IEEE 7th International Conference on Software Security and Reliability (2013)

13. Ouchani, S., Ait Mohamed, O., Debbabi, M.: Efficient probabilistic abstraction for SysML activity diagrams. In: Eleftherakis, G., Hinchey, M., Holcombe, M. (eds.) SEFM 2012. LNCS, vol. 7504, pp. 263–277. Springer, Heidelberg (2012). https://doi.org/10.1007/978-3-642-33826-7_18

14. Ouchani, S., Mohamed, O.A., Debbabi, M., Pourzandi, M.: Verification of the correctness in composed UML behavioural diagrams. In: Lee, R., Ormandjieva, O., Abran, A., Constantinides, C. (eds.) Software Engineering Research, Management and Applications 2010. Studies in Computational Intelligence, vol. 296, pp. 163–177. Springer, Heidelberg (2010). https://doi.org/10.1007/978-3-642-13273-5_11

15. Ould-Yahia, Y., Banerjee, S., Bouzefrane, S., Boucheneb, H.: Exploring formal strategy framework for the security in IoT towards e-health context using computational intelligence. In: Bhatt, C., Dey, N., Ashour, A.S. (eds.) Internet of Things and Big Data Technologies for Next Generation Healthcare. SBD, vol. 23, pp. 63–90. Springer, Cham (2017). https://doi.org/10.1007/978-3-319-49736-5_4

16. Torjusen, A.B., Abie, H., Paintsil, E., Trcek, D., Skomedal, Å.: Towards run-time verification of adaptive security for IoT in ehealth. In: Proceedings of the 2014 European Conference on Software Architecture Workshops, ECSAW 2014, pp. 4:1–4:8. ACM (2014)

17. Xu, T., Wendt, J.B., Potkonjak, M.: Security of IoT systems: design challenges and opportunities. In: Proceedings of the 2014 IEEE/ACM International Conference on Computer-Aided Design, ICCAD 2014, pp. 417–423. IEEE Press (2014)

18. Zhang, Z.K., Cho, M.C.Y., Wang, C.W., Hsu, C.W., Chen, C.K., Shieh, S.: IoT security: ongoing challenges and research opportunities. In: 2014 IEEE 7th International Conference on Service-Oriented Computing and Applications, pp. 230–234, November 2014

Extensions to Hybrid Event-B to Support Concurrency in Cyber-Physical Systems

Klaus-Dieter Schewe[✉]

Laboratory for Client-Centric Cloud Computing, Linz, Austria
kdschewe@acm.org

Abstract. Event-B is one of the most commonly used rigorous methods that has proven its value in many applications. To support the development of cyber-physical systems (CPS) continuous extensions to the method have already been proposed and extensions to supporting tools are under development. In this paper further extensions are proposed addressing the need to support asynchronous behaviour of autonomous components in CPS. This can be accomplished by multiple Event-B machines with a semantics defined by concurrent runs, which preserve the semantics of single Event-B machines. This makes only sense, if shared locations are supported as well. A third extension covers partial updates, by means of which conflicting updates to shared locations with bulk data values such as sets or relations that are predominant in Event-B are avoided.

1 Introduction

Event-B [2], B [1], Abstract State Machines (ASM) [10] and TLA$^+$ [19] are the most commonly used rigorous methods that have proven their value in many complex systems applications. These methods are further supported by sophisticated tools such as RODIN [30], Pro-B [22], Atelier-B [20], ASMeta [17], Core-ASM [15] and the TLA tool suite [19].

Cyber-physical systems (CPS)[1] provide a new challenge for rigorous methods, as these systems integrate continuous and discrete behaviour, the former one usually associated with hardware, electronical and mechanical components, the latter one usually associated with software and control components. It is already a common insight that in order to successfully specify and refine CPS it is necessary to deal with real numbers and continuous functions. A continuous extension of Event-B leading to hybrid Event-B has been presented in [5]. Extensions to the RODIN platform are proposed in [28], while a theory plug-in for real numbers has been made available in [3]. These extensions are exploited in research investigating the use of Event-B and RODIN for the development of CPS [14]. A similar extension for ASMs is described in [6].

---

[1] See [24] for a survey on foundations of CPS.

© Springer Nature Switzerland AG 2018
E. H. Abdelwahed et al. (Eds.): MEDI 2018, LNCS 11163, pp. 418–433, 2018.
https://doi.org/10.1007/978-3-030-00856-7_28

These extensions are further connected to research on hybrid systems engineering, for which a meromorphic conceptual model has been developed combining a structural model of components with a behaviour model that exploits ASMs [13] or similarly Event-B [11]. The usefulness of the model has been demontrated on case studies for a landing gear system [7] and a hemodialysis machine [23].

However, this hybrid systems engineering method and the case studies conducted with it also show that the continuous extensions to the rigorous methods alone are insufficient. In particular, there is a need to capture the asynchronous behaviour of multiple components in CPS. Banach's treatment of impulsive physics in Event-B-based hybrid systems specifications in [4] contains many events that have been declared to run asynchronously, but the impact on the semantics of Event-B, which per se does not support asynchronous parallelism has not been addressed. A difference between the ASM-based and the Event-B-based formalisation of the behavioural part of the model is that for ASMs a concurrent extension has been introduced in [8] and grounded in a behavioural theory of concurrency. This has been further extended in [9] to capture communication via messages. A similar extension to Event-B has not yet been undertaken, though the proposal to carry the concurrent semantics from ASMs over to Event-B has been launched in [11]. A detailed description of the Event-B-based conceptual model for hybrid systems engineering together with fragments of the application to the hemodialysis machine case study was given in [12]. It exploits extensions to Event-B that need further investigation.

In this paper we formally investigate such an extension in more detail. At its core we simply foresee multiple Event-B machines, each of which can be understood in the way defined in [2], i.e. the semantics is defined by sequences of states. There is an obvious analogy to concurrent ASMs, which are just families of (sequential) ASMs[2] indexed by agents.

In the light of the Gurevich's behavioural theory of sequential algorithms (aka the sequential ASM thesis) [18] and the proof that sequential ASMs capture sequential algorithms it is not overly difficult to prove also that all sequential algorithms can be step-by-step simulated by a behaviourally equivalent Event-B machine[3]. Extending sequential algorithms by unbounded choice then gives rise to a proof that Event-B captures all algorithms that are essentially sequentially, but support unbounded choice—the corresponding theory for ASMs with only bounded parallelism, but unbounded choice has been developed in [26]. This can be used as the basis for the definition of the semantics of multiple Event-B-machines using concurrent runs.

---

[2] In this paper we disregard extensions concerning unbounded parallelism [16] that is supported by parallel ASMs and can be integrated with concurrency. Unbounded parallelism is not supported by Event-B.

[3] This implies further that parallel assignments are sufficient, and every sequential ASM can be normalised in a way that the bounded parallel constructor only applies to assignments. It further gives a theoretical underpinning for the translations between Event-B machines and sequential ASMs investigated in [21].

However, as machines that do not interact with each other are not overly interesting, it appears as a natural consequence that shared data, at least mailboxes, have to be supported by multiple Event-B machines. There are different ways to introduce sharing, but they all amount to a determination, which state variables can be accessed by which machines.

Besides multiple machines with concurrent runs and shared data we propose partial updates [27] as a third extension. Partial updates are motivated by the fact that the simultaneous update of a bulk value such as a set or a relation by several machines may lead to a conflict, though in many cases (e.g. for insertions) the intended changes can be combined into a single total update.

The remainder of this paper is organised as follows. In Sect. 2 we first give a brief description of the semantics of Event-B, and discuss extensions have already been used in Hybrid Event-B and hybrid systems engineering. In Sect. 3 we introduce a concurrent semantics for multiple Event-B machines as well as the sharing of data. Section 4 is then dedicated to partial updates. The paper concludes with a brief summary and outlook in Sect. 5.

2 Hybrid Extensions to Event-B

Though concurrent extensions to Event-B makes sense in a purely discrete context we like to stress their particular importance for cyber-physical systems. Therefore, we first discuss hybrid extensions to Event-B that have been introduced together with Hybrid Event-B. The most important ones are real number, continuous functions and differentiation operators, which we complement by terms for definite descriptions.

2.1 Event-B in a Nutshell

In a nutshell an Event-B machine[4] comprises a finite set $\mathcal{V}$ of *state variables*, an *invariant* $\mathcal{I}$ and a finite set $\mathcal{E}$ of *events*. One of the events is an *initialisation* event *init*.

We may assume a *universe* $\mathcal{U}$ of values and several pre-defined domains $\mathcal{D}_i \subseteq \mathcal{U}$ such as domains of integers, Booleans, real numbers, character strings, etc. For all these domains we may further assume pre-defined operations such as addition, multiplication, concatenation, etc.

An Event-B machine is bound to a *context*, in which further sets and further operations on them can be defined. For these the usual constructors for sets such as comprehension, products, unions, etc. as well as λ-abstraction to define functions can be exploited.

Using constants, operations and predicates provided by the context, the state variables (treated as constants) plus other variables we may define *terms* and first-order *formulae* in the usual way. The invariant $\mathcal{I}$ must be a closed formula defined in this way.

---

[4] For details and concrete syntax we refer to [2].

A *state* is defined by assigning a value in $\mathcal{U}$ to each state variable $x \in \mathcal{V}$. We write $\text{val}_S(x)$ for the value assigned to x in state S.

We may interpret terms and formulae in a state S and extend the evaluation function val in this way. If t is a term, say $t = f(t_1, \ldots, t_n)$, then $\text{val}_S(f(t_1, \ldots, t_n)) = f(\text{val}_S(t_1), \ldots, \text{val}_S(t_n))$. Note that f on the write-hand-side of this equation denotes the pre-defined operation f. Clearly, the evaluation of a term that is a state variable x is given by its value in the state. If x is an arbitrary variable, not a state variable, then its interpretation requires a *variable assignment*, i.e. a function σ from the set of such variables to $\mathcal{U}$, and we have $\text{val}_S(x) = \sigma(x)$.

Atomic formulae are interpreted in the same way resulting in a truth value **true** or **false**. This is then extended in the usual way for negation, conjunction, disjunction, implication and quantified formulae. In particular, as $\mathcal{I}$ is a closed formulae, $\text{val}_S(\mathcal{I})$ denotes a truth value. As usual, we write $S \models \mathcal{I}$ iff $\text{val}_S(\mathcal{I}) = $ **true** holds, in which case we say that $\mathcal{I}$ *is satisfied* in state S. A state S is a *valid state* iff $\mathcal{I}$ is satisfied in S.

Each event $e \in \mathcal{E}$ comprises a *guard* $\text{grd}(e)$ defined by a closed formula, and a *rule* $\text{rule}(e)$. The rule takes the form

$$\textbf{ANY } y_1, \ldots, y_n \textbf{ WITH } \varphi \textbf{ DO } x_1 := t_1 \| \ldots \| x_m := t_m,$$

i.e. it is an unbounded choice with a parallel assignment. Here $y_1, \ldots, y_n$ are arbitrary variables, φ is a formula that contains at most $y_1, \ldots, y_n$ as free variables, $x_1, \ldots, x_m$ are the state variables, and $t_1, \ldots, t_m$ are terms that may use the variables $y_1, \ldots, y_n$.

An event $e = (\text{grd}(e), \text{rule}(e))$ is *enabled* in state S iff $S \models \text{grd}(e)$ holds. An enabled event may fire, which results in a *successor state* S' of S. Informally, choose a variable assignment σ such that φ is satisfied in S using this variable assignment, then determine $v_i = \text{val}_S(t_i)$ using σ for the interpretation of the free variables $y_1, \ldots, y_n$ and let $\text{val}_{S'}(x_i) = v_i$.

For brevity it is permitted to omit some state variables from the parallel assignment in a rule, in which case the effect of firing the rule becomes $\text{val}_{S'}(x_i) = \text{val}_S(x_i)$. Furthermore, the choice may be omitted, if there is nothing to choose.

For the initialisation event *init* we have $\text{grd}(init) = $ **true**. An *initial state* is a state that results from firing *init* in an arbitrary state[5].

Then a *run* of the machine is a sequence $S_0, S_1, S_2, \ldots$ of valid states such that S_0 is an initial state and for each i the state S_{i+1} is a successor state of S_i resulting from firing an event e_i that is enabled in S_i.

---

[5] Usually, the resulting state should not depend on the chosen state, so we could use a state, in which all state variables are undefined.

Note that this definition of run is highly non-deterministic, as first an event is chosen[6] among those that are enabled in a state S_i and second the unbounded choice allows us to select values for the variables $y_1, \ldots, y_n$, which determine the new values that are assigned to the state variables.

2.2 Reals, Continuous Functions and Definite Descriptions

The notion of run as defined above is standard for the definition of semantics of discrete systems. As a matter of fact time is irrelevant in a discrete system; in particular, it does not matter how long it takes to make a transition from a state to a successor state. Phrased differently, as long as no successor state is produced, the values assigned to the state variables remain unchanged.

This changes in hybrid systems, which integrate discrete and continuous changes, the latter ones being characteristic for physical components such as electronical, mechanical and hydraulic devices. This can be captured by states that change continuously over time[7], and discrete changes are subsumed by piecewise constant functions. This requires the presence of the set $\mathbb{R}$ of real numbers.

Furthermore, instead of continuous sequences of states over time it suffices to permit continuous functions as values, which is accomplished by providing a data type constructor $\to$ such that $A \to B$ denotes the set of continuous functions from A to B. For $\mathbb{R}$ the common Euclidean topology can be assumed, for all other types the discrete topology can be taken. Taking product topologies ensures that the continuous function type constructor can be applied to arbitrary types A and B.

As continuous functions in hybrid system are often given implicitly as solutions to ordinary differential equations, we require a derivation operator $\mathcal{D}_t = \dfrac{\partial}{\partial t}$ that is defined for (partial) functions with domain $REAL$. Naturally, $\mathcal{D}_t(f)$ is also a partial function with domain $REAL$, and $\mathcal{D}_t(f)(x)$ is the derivative of f at the point x, provided this exists. Note that $\mathcal{D}_t$ is actually a functional.

Wenn dealing with differential equations it is common to assume a well=posed initial value problem over a time interval $[t, t')$, i.e. the differential equation takes the form $\mathcal{D}_t f(t) = \phi(f(t), t)$ with a Lipschitz-continuous function ϕ with uniformly bounded Lipschitz constants (see e.g. [5]), and in addition an

---

[6] Note that there is a slight discrepancy between the intended reactive semantics of Event-B and the fact that only a single enabled event is selected for execution. One might argue that by observing the guards of events, an event should always be executed once it becomes enabled. However, this requires to deal with synchronous or asynchronous parallelism, which is deliberately avoided in Event-B. In this paper we do not intend to question fundamental decisions concerning the semantics of Event-B, but we provide extensions that will address some of the issues, while the semantics of single Event-B machines will be preserved.

[7] Mathematically speaking this requires the set of states to carry the structure of a topological space.

initial value $f(\text{now})$. This guarantees that a unique solution exists, which can be determined by common numerical methods.

For such implicit function definitions through differential equations it appears to be convenient to exploit *definite descriptions*, i.e. terms of the form $\mathbf{I}x.\varphi$ with a variable x and a formula φ, in which x is free, to denote *the unique value x satisfying φ*[8]. In particular, φ may formulate the differential equation.

Example 2.1. In the landing gear case study [7] hydraulic cylinders are foreseen for the opening and closing of doors and the extension and retraction of wheels, respectively. These cylinders are duplicated for the front wheel and door and the doors and wheels on the left and right. The operation of all cylinders is in principle identical, and the approach to hybrid systems engineering [13] provides several such cylinder components, which may give rise to a machine CYLINDER. The machine must provide variables such as left_cylinder_pressure_in, right_cylinder_pressure_out, etc. of type $Pressure = \mathbb{R} \to \mathbb{R}$). In addition, there are variables such as front_cylinder_extension of type $Volume = \mathbb{R} \to \mathbb{R}$.

Pressurisation is controlled by an electric value, which gives rise to a variable electric_port of type *Bool*. With this we candefine an event *Pressurize_Extension* using the following deterministic event:

WHEN E_VALVE(i_{ev}).electric_port $=$ **true**
DO   front_cylinder_pressure_in $:= inp\|$
       left_cylinder_pressure_in $:= inp\|$
       right_cylinder_pressure_in $:= inp\|$
       front_cylinder_pressure_out $:= min\|$
       left_cylinder_pressure_out $:= min\|$
       right_cylinder_pressure_out $:= min\|$

$$\text{front\_cylinder\_extension} := \max(\mathbf{I}f.(\frac{\partial f}{\partial x}(x) = \frac{const}{inp(x)^2} \cdot \frac{\partial inp}{\partial x}(x)$$
$$\wedge\ f(\text{now}) = \text{front\_cylinder\_extension}(\text{now})), max_f)\|$$

$$\text{left\_cylinder\_extension} := \max(\mathbf{I}g.(\frac{\partial g}{\partial x}(x) = \frac{const}{inp(x)^2} \cdot \frac{\partial inp}{\partial x}(x)$$
$$\wedge\ g(\text{now}) = \text{left\_cylinder\_extension}(\text{now})), max_\ell)\|$$

$$\text{right\_cylinder\_extension} := \max(\mathbf{I}h.(\frac{\partial h}{\partial x}(x) = \frac{const}{inp(x)^2} \cdot \frac{\partial inp}{\partial x}(x)$$
$$\wedge\ h(\text{now}) = \text{right\_cylinder\_extension}(\text{now})), max_r)$$

Note that the differential equation used for the update of the variables of type *Volume* express nothing more than the dependency between pressure and volume in a closed system (assuming that there is no leakage).

---

[8] Note that terms of the form @$x.\varphi$ denoting an *arbitrary value x satisfying φ* are already present in Event-B. Both kinds of terms were originally introduced by David Hilbert—using j instead of $\mathbf{I}$ and ϵ instead of @. Our change of notation is in accordance with the use of $\mathbf{I}$ in Fourman's formalisation of higher-order intuitionistic logic and the use of **ANY** in Event-B.

The work in [13] contains a more detailed treatment of the landing gear case study. The work in [12] addresses the hemodialysis machine case study in more detail.

Example 2.2. Another example from the landing gear case study concerns a machine HANDLE managing the effects of the movement of the handle by the pilot. Among others the following event *Close_Analogue_Switch* with a deterministic rule is defined for this machine:

> WHEN analogue_switch_ctl_state = open $\wedge$
>   analogue_switch_handle = **true**
> DO   analogue_switch_ctl_state := closing$\|$
>   analogue_switch_timing
>   := max$(0, \mathbf{I}f.(\mathcal{D}_t(f)(t) = -1 \wedge f(\mathrm{now}) = 0.8))\|$
>   analogue_switch_state := open$\|$
>   analogue_switch_out := **false**$\|$
>   analogue_switch_handle := **false**

In this case we use a variable analogue_switch_timing to control the timing requirement that closing the analogue switch should be completed within at most 0.8 s. When the value of the associated continuous function becomes 0, the value of analogue_switch_ctl_state must already be closed, unless a different event has occurred in the meantime.

3   Multiple Event-B Machines with Concurrent Runs

In the previous section we already provided examples of events associated with different Event-B machines. In a hybrid system there are many changes that occur simultaneously, and the control of the corresponding components is done completely asynchronously. For instance, as emphasised in [13] in the landing gear case study the handle operated by the pilot runs asynchronously to the operation of the valves and cylinders, and any alert is activated immediately. Similarly, the hemodialysis case study [11] involves many asynchronous events, and the treatment of the Rugby club problem in [4] explicitly uses a keyword `async` in Event-B machines to indicate asynchronous behaviour[9].

Therefore, we now present an extension of Event-B using multiple machines with shared data and asynchronous events. For this we develop terminology that is inspired by the theory of concurrency in [8].

3.1   Update Sets and Concurrent Runs

If $S_0, S_1, S_2, \ldots$ is a run of an Event-B machine with state variables $\mathcal{V} = \{x_1, \ldots, x_m\}$, then we obtain *differences* between a state S_i and its successor S_{i+1}. For this let $\mathrm{Diff}_i = \{x \in \mathcal{V} \mid \mathrm{val}_{S_i}(x) \neq \mathrm{val}_{S_{i+1}}(x)\}$ be the set of state

---

[9] Actually, in doing so Banach extends Event-B without defining the semantics of the extension.

variables, on which the state S_i and its successor S_{i+1} differ. Then define the *difference set* (or *update set*) $\Delta_i = \{(x, \text{val}_{S_{i+1}}(x)) \mid x \in \text{Diff}_i\}$. This is called update set, because the change from S_i to S_{i+1} updates exactly the state variables in Diff_i to their new value given in Δ_i. Correspondingly, each element of Δ_i, i.e. a pair comprising a state variable and a value, is called an *update*.

If Δ is an arbitrary set of updates on a state S, then $S + \Delta$ denotes the state resulting from S by applying the update set to it. For each state variable x we have

$$\text{val}_{S+\Delta}(x) = \begin{cases} v & \text{if } (x, v) \in \Delta \text{ and } \Delta \text{ is consistent} \\ \text{val}_S(x) & \text{otherwise} \end{cases}$$

An update set is called *consistent* iff for all $x \in V$ and all $v_1, v_2 \in U$ with $(x, v_1) \in \Delta$ and $(x, v_2) \in \Delta$ we have $v_1 = v_2$. Note that the update set defined by the difference of two states in a run is always consistent, and we have $S_{i+1} = S_i + \Delta_i$.

Phrased differently, each run of an Event-B machine can be seen as the result of building update sets and applying them. For a rule of an event e the possible update sets in state S take the form $\{(x_i, \text{val}_S(t_i)\}$. As the values resulting from the interpretation of the terms t_i depend on the variable assignment for the variable y_i and furthermore, the event must be enabled, we define

$$\Delta_i = \{\{(x_j, \text{val}_{S_i}(t_j))\} \mid S_i \models \varphi(y_1, \ldots, y_n) \wedge \text{grd}(e)\}.$$

Δ_i is the set of possible update sets of the Event-B machine in state S_i. Thus in a run $S_0, S_1, S_2, \ldots$ we always have $S_{i+1} = S_i + \Delta$ for some $\Delta \in \Delta_i$.

Let us now proceed from single Event-B machines to multiple machines. For this take a finite family $\{\mathcal{M}_i \mid i \in I\}$ of Event-B machines $\mathcal{M}_i$ (for convenience we use some finite index set I here). For the semantics the key idea is to separate the building of update sets from their application, by means of which we take care of the different pace, with which the autonomous machines $\mathcal{M}_i$ operate. This reflects the essential property of asynchronously collaborating machines of having each its own clock according to which they make steps.

Let $V = \bigcup_{i \in I} V_i$ be the union of the sets of state variables of the machines $\mathcal{M}_i$. A state S defined over V is called *global*, whereas the restricted states $\text{res}_i(S)$ built over V_i are called *local* for $\mathcal{M}_i$. While $\text{res}_i(S)$ is valid iff it satisfies the local invariant $\mathcal{I}_i$ associated with the machine $\mathcal{M}_i$, a global state S is *valid* iff $S \models \bigwedge_{i \in I} \mathcal{I}_i$ holds.

Then a *concurrent run* of $\{\mathcal{M}_i \mid i \in I\}$ is a sequence $S_0, S_1, S_2, \ldots$ of valid global states, in which S_{i+1} is a successor state of S_i.

For this definition it remains to clarify the notion of successor state of a global state. For this consider first finite subsets $I_i \subseteq I$ of indices of those machines that initiate a step in S_i. For each $j \in I_i$ we obtain a set $\Delta_{i,j}$ of possible update sets of $\mathcal{M}_i$ in the local state $\text{res}_j(S_i)$ arising by restriction from the global state S_i.

For the transition from the global state S_i to a successor S_{i+1} we take another finite subset $\hat{I}_i \subseteq I$ of indices of those machines that finish their step in S_{i+1}. Then for each $j \in \hat{I}_i$ there exists an index $k(j) \leq i$ such that the step of $\mathcal{M}_j$

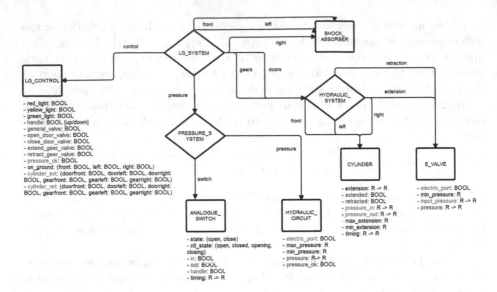

Fig. 1. Components in the landing gear case study

was initiated in state $S_{k(j)}$. So we obtain an update set $\Delta_i = \bigcup_{j\in\hat{I}_i} \Delta_{k(j),j}$ selecting update sets $\Delta_{k(j),j} \in \boldsymbol{\Delta}_{k(j),j}$, with which we can define the successor state $S_{i+1} = S_i + \Delta_i$.

Informally phrased, in a concurrent run the sequence of global states results from simultaneously applying update sets of several individual machines that have been built on previous (not necessarily the last nor the same) states. Note that the definition leaves it completely open, how big the difference between i and $k(j)$ is, which reflects that a machine may operate slowly or fast, but is completely oblivious to the activities of the other machines in the concurrent family. This adds another source of non-determinism; even if the individual machines operate deterministically, the multi-machine family will not[10].

Example 3.1. Let us use the landing gear system of a plane as an example to illustrate how to obtain multiple Event-B machines. The general architecture and detailed description of the system requirements can be found in [7, page 4].

Figure 1 illustrates the structuring of a landing gear system into components using the structural part of the CyPHER conceptual model in [13], which itself is grounded in Thalheim's higher-order entity relationship model (HERM [29]). The landing gear system comprises the landing gear control, the pressure system, two hydraulic systems for gears and doors, respectively, and three shock absorbers associated with the front left and back gears, respectively. This gives rise to labelled components *control*:LG_CONTROL, *pressure*:PRESSURE_SYSTEM,

---

[10] It has been argued that simultaneous access to shared locations by different machines is physically impossible. Consequently, the set $\hat{I}_i \subseteq I$ of indices of those machines that finish their step in S_{i+1} should always contain only one element j.

doors:HYDRAULIC_SYSTEM, *gears*:HYDRAULIC_SYSTEM, *front*:SHOCK_ABSORB-ER, *right*:SHOCK_ABSORBER, *left*:SHOCK_ABSORBER of LG_SYSTEM[11].

The pressure system of the plane comprises the analogue switch and a hydraulic circuit, which gives rise to PRESSURE_SYSTEM with labelled components *switch*:ANALOGUE_SWITCH and *pressure*:HYDRAULIC_CIRCUIT. Each hydraulic system for the doors and gears, respectively, comprises three cylinders and two electric valves. This give rise to the definition of HYDRAULIC_SYSTEM with labelled components *front*:CYLINDER, *left*:CYLINDER, *right*:CYLINDER, *extension*:E_VALVE, *retraction*:E_VALVE.

The remaining components in Fig. 1 are elementary, and comprise attributes. For SHOCK_ABSORBER we have a single attribute on_ground with data type *BOOL*. For LG_CONTROL we have attributes red_light, yellow_light, green_light, general_valve, open_door_valve, close_door_valve, extend_gear_valve, retract_gear_valve, pressure_ok, on_ground, cylinder_ext, cylinder_ret, and handle. We may use a data type $OnOff = (on:\mathbb{1}) \uplus (off:\mathbb{1})$—i.e. a type with exactly two values on and off—associated with attributes red_light, yellow_light and green_light. Analogously, handle has the data type $UpDown = (up:\mathbb{1}) \uplus (down:\mathbb{1})$. The data type associated with each of general_valve, open_door_valve, close_door_valve, extend_gear_valve, retract_gear_valve and pressure_ok is *BOOL*. The data type associated with on_ground is (front:*BOOL*, left:*BOOL*, right:*BOOL*), and type(cylinder_ext) = type(cylinder_ret) = (door-front:*BOOL*, doorleft:*BOOL*, dooright:*BOOL*, gearfront:*BOOL*, gearleft:*BOOL*, gearright:*BOOL*).

ANALOGUE_SWITCH has attributes state, ctl_state, in, out, timing and handle with type(state) = $(open:\mathbb{1}) \uplus (close:\mathbb{1})$, type(ctl_state) = $(open:\mathbb{1}) \uplus (closed:\mathbb{1}) \uplus (opening:\mathbb{1}) \uplus (closing:\mathbb{1})$, type(in) =type(out) = type(handle) = *BOOL*, and type(timing) = $\mathbb{R} \to \mathbb{R}$. HYDRAULIC_CIRCUIT has attributes electric_port, max_pressure, min_pressure, pressure and pressure_ok with type(electric_port) = type(pressure_ok) = *BOOL*, type(max_pressure) = type(min_pressure) = $\mathbb{R}$, and type(pressure) = $\mathbb{R} \to \mathbb{R}$.

CYLINDER has attributes extension, extended, retracted, pressure_in, pressure_out, max_extension, min_extension and timing. The type of each of extension, pressure_in, pressure_out and timing is $\mathbb{R} \to \mathbb{R}$, the type of each extended and retracted is *Bool*, and the type of max_extension and min_extension is $\mathbb{R}$. Finally, E_VALVE has attributes electric_port, min_pressure, input_pressure and pressure with type(electric_port) = *BOOL*, type(min_pressure) = $\mathbb{R}$, and type(input_pressure) = type(pressure) = $\mathbb{R} \to \mathbb{R}$.

Each of the elementary components give rise to a separate Event-B machine, as all these components operate asynchronously. Then all the attributes give rise to the definition of state variables. However, some state variables in one machine directly influence state variables in another machine. For instance, the attribute pressure on E_VALVE in the extension role is linked to the attribute pressure_in on CYLINDER for all three occurrences that are associated with the

---

[11] The whole LG_SYSTEM and all components are formally defined by so-called *block types* in the CyPHER method (see [12,13]).

same HYDRAULIC_SYSTEM, and values of these attributes must be equal. So the corresponding state variables have to be identified and shared among the different machines.

There are many other such dependencies that lead to shared state variables as discussed in detail in [13].

Example 3.2. Another example showing explicitly multiple Event-B machines with concurrent semantics is given by the hemodialysis machine case study, which was sketched in [11] and further elaborated in [12].

Furthermore, building the update set Δ_i as a union of update sets $\Delta_{k(j),j}$ for a finite set of Event-B machines $\mathcal{M}_j$ may lead to *clashes*, i.e. Δ_i is inconsistent containing updates (ℓ, v_1) and (ℓ, v_2) with $v_1 \neq v_2$. Naturally, this gives rise to the obligation that such clashes cannot occur, unless a restriction to a clash-free fragment is used (as discussed for ASMs in [25]).

As we did not change the semantics of single-machine Event-B, the updates in the participating update sets $\Delta_{k(j),j}$ are defined by a single event e. In particular, locations appearing in these updates are exactly the state variables $x_1, \ldots, x_m$ that are used in rule(e). So clashes can only occur for events e and e' in machines $\mathcal{M}_j$ and $\mathcal{M}_{j'}$, respectively, if rule(e) and rule(e') update a shared state variable. Such clashes can only be excluded, if the access to shared state variables is controlled[12].

Further note that the asynchronous parallel behaviour of the machines $\mathcal{M}_i$ in the family as expressed by the definition of concurrent runs does not rely on interleaving, but permits simultaneous updates by several machines. It is not a weakness but a strength of state-based methods that any mimicking of collaboration in parallel[13] by means of interleaving can be dispensed with.

3.2 Sharing Data Among Multiple Machines

The semantics of a family of Event-B machines has been defined by concurrent runs in the previous section, i.e. by sequences of global states. These assign values to all state variables in the union of the sets of state variables of the individual machines. If these sets $\mathcal{V}_i$ are pairwise disjoint, this will not create any conflicts, but otherwise the machines would be completely independent, which is not what we expect in a concurrent system.

In general, we have to expect that the sets of state variables of the individual machines overlap, i.e. that state variables are shared. This can be declared in various ways:

---

[12] However, if concurrent runs are restricted to permit only a single machine $\mathcal{M}_j$ to finalise its latest step in state S_{i+1}, then it is impossible to have clashes.

[13] In fact, interleaving expresses parallelism by sequentialisation, which is not exactly what happens in reality. For systems with a sequential implementation—this includes all those built at the time the notion of interleaving was invented—this may be acceptable, for truly asynchronous systems—this includes all distributed systems with multiple processors spread over a network—this workaround is not needed, but in contrast counter-productive.

1. We can add a *sharing specification* to each Event-B machine $\mathcal{M}_i$, which assigns to each state variable $x \in \mathcal{V}_i$ a set of machines $\{\mathcal{M}_j \mid j \in I_x \subseteq I\}$ with which the variable is shared.
2. We can use *mutual sharing specifications* for pairs of machines by defining subsets $\mathcal{V}_{i,j} \subseteq \mathcal{V}_i$ and $\mathcal{V}_{j,i} \subseteq \mathcal{V}_j$ (for $i, j \in I$, $i \neq j$) together with a bijection $\mathrm{sh}_{i,j} : \mathcal{V}_{i,j} \to \mathcal{V}_{j,i}$.
3. We can simply employ a *unique name assumption*, i.e. a state variable appearing in $\mathcal{V}_i \cap \mathcal{V}_j$ is considered to be shared between $\mathcal{M}_i$ and $\mathcal{M}_j$.

There is no need to modify the definition of concurrent run in case of shared state variables. However, the presence of shared variables may lead to inconsistent update sets, in which case no successor state can be built. This is well in accordance with what may happen in a concurrent system, though the nondeterminism arising from the differing pace of the participating machines mitigates this problem. If conflicts are to be excluded a separate machine for synchronisation will be required.

4   Partial Updates

Event-B is largely set-based, so state variables are often bound to set values or relations. This increases the likeliness of conflicts in update sets. For instance, if two machines both insert a new element into a set, then the simultaneous occurrence of these two updates formally defines a clash as discussed in the previous section, though in principle it is no problem to combine the two insertions into a single update. Partial updates mitigate this problem. If both insertions are declared to be partial, then if possible all partial updates will first be combined into a single total update. Partial updates were discussed in detail in [27] in the context of ASMs, but the theory does not depend on ASMs at all.

4.1   Update Multisets

As indicated above partial updates provide a means to mitigate the problem of possible clashes in concurrent systems. This problem is irrelevant for Event-B with single machines, but it becomes important with the concurrent semantics for multiple machines.

A *partial update* of x takes the form $x \mathrel{\leftleftarrows^\imath} t$ with a term t of type τ and a binary operator $\imath$ over τ. Partial updates can be used in the rule part of an event instead of assignments.

Partial updates give rise to shared updates. A *shared update* is a triple $(x, v, \imath)$ consisting of a state variable x of type τ, a value v of type τ, and a binary operator $\imath : \tau \times \tau \to \tau$, where $\imath$ is given by the partial update and v results from the interpretation of the term t analogously to the way we defined strict updates.

Example 4.1. Let us take a state variable *counter* that is to serve as a counter, i.e. it is bound to a natural number. If the counter is increased by $k \in \mathbb{N}$, the binary addition function $+$ over $\mathbb{N}$ will be associated with the location, i.e. $+$ specifies that k is *added* to the location content. That is, the partial update takes the form *counter* $\leftModels^+ t$, where t is a term that evaluates to k. When several numbers are added to the same location *counter* simultaneously, a multiset of partial updates with the specified numbers is obtained. For instance, if in machines $\mathcal{M}_i$ $(i = 1, \ldots, n)$ we have *counter* $\leftModels^+ t_i$ and the terms t_i are evaluated to values $k_i \in \mathbb{N}$, we obtain the multiset $\langle\!\langle (counter, k_i, +) \mid 1 \leq i \leq n \rangle\!\rangle$ of shared updates.

Example 4.2. Similarly to the previous example, when inserting a string into a set of strings associated with a state variable *strings*, this can be expressed by a partial update *strings* $\leftModels^\cup t$, where t is a term that evaluates to a string. If in different machines $\mathcal{M}_i$ $(i = 1, \ldots, n)$ with shared state variable *strings* we have partial updates *strings* $\leftModels^{cup} \{t_i\}$ and the terms t_i are evaluated to values $\mathrm{str}_i \in STRING$, we obtain the multiset $\langle\!\langle (strings, \{\mathrm{str}_i\}, \cup) \mid 1 \leq i \leq n \rangle\!\rangle$ of shared updates.

Different to strict updates arising from assignments there may be more than one partial update to the same state variable. These may even give rise to the same shared update. Therefore, instead of possible update sets we now obtain possible update multisets. For concurrent runs we then build multiset unions— i.e. the multiplicities add up—of individual update multisets.

4.2 Collapse of Update Multisets

The crucial aspect of partial updates in concurrent systems is that the built update multiset sets are not applied directly to define a successor state. Instead, they are collapsed to an update set, the application of which is standard. For the collapse all shared updates affecting the same state variable are combined into a single strict update, if the involved operators are *compatible*.

Compatibility of shared updates and conditions for consistent collapse of an update multiset into an update set have been investigated intensively in [27] and can be applied to concurrent runs of multiple Event-B machines. Here we only discuss the simpler case of operator-compatibility.

As a convention let $loc(\chi)$ and $opt(\chi)$ denote the set of locations and the set of operators occurring in an update multiset χ, respectively, i.e. $loc(\chi) = \{\ell \mid (\ell, a, \imath) \in \chi\}$ and $opt(\chi) = \{\imath \mid (\ell, a, \imath) \in \chi\}$. Let χ_ℓ denote the submultiset of an update multiset χ containing all shared updates that have the location ℓ, i.e. $\chi_\ell = \langle\!\langle u \mid u \in \chi \wedge u = (\ell, a, \imath) \rangle\!\rangle$.

Example 4.3. Consider the set operations union $\cup$, intersection $\cap$, difference $\ominus$, symmetric difference $\oslash$, etc. Then the partial updates $x \leftModels^\cup \{a_1, a_2\}$ and $x \leftModels^\cup \{a_2, a_3, a_4\}$ produce an operator-compatible update multiset

$$\langle\!\langle (x, \{a_1, a_2\}, \cup), (x, \{a_2, a_3, a_4\}, \cup) \rangle\!\rangle.$$

Let χ_ℓ be a multiset of shared updates on the same location ℓ, say $\chi_\ell = \langle\!\langle (\ell, a_i, \imath_i) \mid i = 1, \ldots, k \rangle\!\rangle$. Then χ_ℓ is *operator-compatible* iff for all two permutations $(p_1, \ldots, p_k)$ and $(q_1, \ldots, q_k)$ we have for all x

$$\imath_{p_k}(\ldots \imath_{p_1}(x, a_{p_1}) \ldots, a_{p_k}) = \imath_{q_k}(\ldots \imath_{q_1}(x, a_{q_1}) \ldots, a_{q_k}).$$

An update multiset χ is *operator-compatible* iff for all locations ℓ the sub-multiset $\chi_\ell = \langle (\ell, v, \iota) \in \chi \rangle$ is operator-compatible.

This definition suggests that χ_ℓ is operator-compatible iff the shared updates in χ_ℓ are independent from the order, in which they are applied. However, this does not apply to the whole update multiset χ_ℓ, as locations may depend on each other.

In the simplest case, if the operators commute and are associative, they may be concatenated in some order. However, it is not always as simple as that. For instances, inserting new branches into a tree can be integrated, but the first insertion affects the location, to which the second one has to be applied.

A binary operator ι_1 (over the domain D) is *compatible* to the binary operator ι_2 (notation: $\iota_1 \preceq \iota_2$) (over D) iff ι_2 is associative and commutative and for all $x \in D$ there is some $\dot{x} \in D$ such that for all $y \in D$ we have $y \, \iota_1 \, x = y \, \iota_2 \, \dot{x}$.

Obviously, each associative and commutative operator ι is compatible to itself. More generally, if ι_1 and ι_2 are two binary operators over domain D such that (D, ι_2) defines a commutative group, and $(x \, \iota_1 \, y) \, \iota_2 \, y = x$ holds for all $x, y \in D$, then $\iota_1 \preceq \iota_2$ holds.

Compatibility $\iota_1 \preceq \iota_2$ permits replacing each shared update (ℓ, v, ι_1) by the shared update $(\ell, \dot{v}, \iota_2)$. Then the associativity and commutativity of ι_2 guarantees order-independence. A non-empty multiset χ_ℓ of shared updates on the same location ℓ is operator-compatible if either $|\chi_\ell| = 1$ holds, or there exists a $\iota \in Op(\chi_\ell)$ such for all $\iota_1 \in Op(\chi_\ell)$ (the set of operators appearing in χ_ℓ) $\iota_1 \preceq \iota$ holds.

Example 4.4. For χ_{ℓ_1} with $Op(\chi_{\ell_1}) = \{+, -\}$, χ_{ℓ_2} with $Op(\chi_{\ell_2}) = \{\times, \div\}$, and χ_{ℓ_3} with $Op(\chi_{\ell_3}) = \{\cap, \ominus\}$ we obtain operator-compatibility. However, χ_{ℓ_4} with $Op(\chi_{\ell_4}) = \{\cap, \cup\}$ is not operator-compatible.

5 Conclusion

In this paper we proposed three straightforward extensions to Event-B: (1) using multiple Event-B machines with a semantics defined by concurrent runs to enable truly asynchronous, concurrent behaviour, (2) to permit variables to be shared between several of these machines, and (3) to enable updates to be declared as partial, in which case simultaneous compatible updates by several machines on the same state variable will be enabled. We argued that in addition to the provision of real numbers and continuous functions these extensions are important to support the rigorous development of cyber-physical systems.

These extensions preserve the semantics of single Event-B machines. In this way Event-B and ASMs remain different approaches. In particular, we do not propose to integrate unbounded parallelism that is characteristic for ASMs into Event-B.

References

1. Abrial, J.-R.: The B-book - Assigning Programs to Meanings. Cambridge University Press, Cambridge (2005)
2. Abrial, J.-R.: Modeling in Event-B - System and Software Engineering. Cambridge University Press, New York (2010)
3. Abrial, J.-R., Butler, M., Hallerstede, S., Leuschel, M., Schmalz, M., Voisin, L.: Proposals for mathematical extensions for Event-B. Technical report (2010). http://deploy-eprints.ecs.soton.ac.uk/216/
4. Banach, R.: Issues in automated urban train control: 'Tackling' the rugby club problem. In: Butler, M., Raschke, A., Hoang, T.S., Reichl, K. (eds.) ABZ 2018. LNCS, vol. 10817, pp. 171–186. Springer, Cham (2018). https://doi.org/10.1007/978-3-319-91271-4_12
5. Banach, R.: Core hybrid event-B I: single hybrid event-B machines. Sci. Comput. Program. **105**, 92–123 (2015)
6. Banach, R., Zhu, H., Su, W., Wu, X.: ASM, controller synthesis, and complete refinement. Sci. Comp. Progr. **94**, 109–129 (2014)
7. Boniol, F., Wiels, V.: The landing gear system case study. In: Boniol, F., Wiels, V., Ait Ameur, Y., Schewe, K.-D. (eds.) ABZ 2014. CCIS, vol. 433, pp. 1–18. Springer, Cham (2014). https://doi.org/10.1007/978-3-319-07512-9_1
8. Börger, E., Schewe, K.-D.: Concurrent abstract state machines. Acta Informatica **53**(5), 469–492 (2016)
9. Börger, E., Schewe, K.-D.: Communication in abstract state machines. J. Univ. Comp. Sci. **23**(2), 129–145 (2017)
10. Börger, E., Stärk, R.: Abstract State Machines. Springer, Heidelberg, New York (2003)
11. Buga, A., Mashkoor, A., Nemeş, S.T., Schewe, K.-D., Songprasop, P.: Conceptual modelling of hybrid systems. In: Ouhammou, Y., Ivanovic, M., Abelló, A., Bellatreche, L. (eds.) MEDI 2017. LNCS, vol. 10563, pp. 277–290. Springer, Cham (2017). https://doi.org/10.1007/978-3-319-66854-3_21
12. Buga, A., Mashkoor, A., Nemeş, S.T., Schewe, K.-D., Songprasop, P.: An Event-B-based approach to hybrid systems engineering and its application to a hemodialysis machine case study. In: Computer Languages - Systems and Structures (2018, to appear)
13. Buga, A., Nemeş, S.T., Schewe, K.-D., Songprasop, P.: A conceptual model for systems engineering and its formal foundation. In: Sornlertlamvanich, V., et al. (eds.) Information Modelling and Knowledge Bases XXIX (EJC 2017). Frontiers in Artificial Intelligence and Applications, vol. 301, pp. 1–20. IOS Press (2017)
14. Dupont, G., Aït-Ameur, Y., Pantel, M., Singh, N.K.: Proof-based approach to hybrid systems development: dynamic logic and event-B. In: Butler, M., Raschke, A., Hoang, T.S., Reichl, K. (eds.) ABZ 2018. LNCS, vol. 10817, pp. 155–170. Springer, Cham (2018). https://doi.org/10.1007/978-3-319-91271-4_11
15. Farahbod, R., Gervasi, V., Glässer, U.: CoreASM: an extensible ASM execution engine. Fundamenta Informaticae **77**(1–2), 71–103 (2007)
16. Ferrarotti, F., Schewe, K.-D., Tec, L., Wang, Q.: A new thesis concerning synchronised parallel computing - simplified parallel ASM thesis. Theor. Comput. Sci. **649**, 25–53 (2016)
17. Gargantini, A., Riccobene, E., Scandurra, P.: A metamodel-based language and a simulation engine for Abstract State Machines. J. Univ. Comp. Sci. **14**(12), 1949–1983 (2008)

18. Gurevich, Y.: Sequential abstract state machines capture sequential algorithms. ACM Trans. Comput. Logic **1**(1), 77–111 (2000)
19. Lamport, L.: Specifying Systems, the TLA$^+$ Language and Tools for Hardware and Software Engineers. Addison-Wesley, Boston (2002)
20. Lecomte, T., Deharbe, D., Prun, E., Mottin, E.: Applying a formal method in industry: a 25-year trajectory. In: Cavalheiro, S., Fiadeiro, J. (eds.) SBMF 2017. LNCS, vol. 10623, pp. 70–87. Springer, Cham (2017). https://doi.org/10.1007/978-3-319-70848-5_6
21. Leuschel, M., Börger, E.: A compact encoding of sequential ASMs in event-B. In: Butler, M., Schewe, K.-D., Mashkoor, A., Biro, M. (eds.) ABZ 2016. LNCS, vol. 9675, pp. 119–134. Springer, Cham (2016). https://doi.org/10.1007/978-3-319-33600-8_7
22. Leuschel, M., Butler, M.J.: ProB: an automated analysis toolset for the B method. STTT **10**(2), 185–203 (2008)
23. Mashkoor, A.: The hemodialysis machine case study. In: Butler, M., Schewe, K.-D., Mashkoor, A., Biro, M. (eds.) ABZ 2016. LNCS, vol. 9675, pp. 329–343. Springer, Cham (2016). https://doi.org/10.1007/978-3-319-33600-8_29
24. Platzer, A.: Analog and hybrid computation: dynamical systems and programming languages. Bull. EATCS **114**, 152–199 (2014)
25. Schellhorn, G., Ernst, G., Pfähler, J., Bodenmüller, S., Reif, W.: Symbolic execution for a clash-free subset of ASMs. Sci. Comput. Program. **158**, 21–40 (2018)
26. Schewe, K.-D., Ferrarotti, F., Tec, L., Wang, Q.: Towards a behavioural theory for random parallel computing. In: Beierle, C., Brewka, G., Thimm, M. (eds.) Computational Models of Rationality - Essays Dedicated to Gabriele Kern-Isberner on the Occasion of her 60th Birthday, Tributes, vol. 29, pp. 365–373. College Publications (2016)
27. Schewe, K.-D., Wang, Q.: Partial updates in complex-value databases. In: Heimbürger, A., et al., (eds.) Information and Knowledge Bases XXII. Frontiers in Artificial Intelligence and Applications, vol. 225, pp. 37–56. IOS Press (2011)
28. Su, W., Abrial, J.-R., Zhu, H.: Formalizing hybrid systems with event-B and the Rodin platform. Sci. Comput. Program. **94**, 164–202 (2014)
29. Thalheim, B.: Entity-Relationship Modeling - Foundations of Database Technology. Springer, Heidelberg (2000)
30. Voisin, L., Abrial, J.R.: The Rodin platform has turned ten. In: Ait Ameur, Y., Schewe, K.D. (eds.) Abstract State Machines, Alloy, B, TLA, VDM, and Z. ABZ 2014. Lecture Notes in Computer Science, vol. 8477, pp. 1–8. Springer, Heidelberg (2014). https://doi.org/10.1007/978-3-662-43652-3_1

Author Index

Printed in the United States
By Bookmasters